The Continuum of Literacy Learning, Grades K–8

The Continuum of Literacy Learning, Grades K–8

Behaviors and Understandings to Notice, Teach, and Support

Gay Su Pinnell & Irene C. Fountas

HEINEMANN
Portsmouth, NH

Heinemann
A division of Reed Elsevier Inc.
361 Hanover Street
Portsmouth, NH 03801–3912
www.heinemann.com

Offices and agents throughout the world

The authors and publisher wish to thank those who have generously given permission to reprint borrowed material:

Little Book spreads from *Fountas & Pinnell Benchmark Assessment System 1* by Irene C. Fountas and Gay Su Pinnell. Copyright © 2008 by Irene C. Fountas and Gay Su Pinnell. Published by Heinemann, Portsmouth, NH. All rights reserved.

Excerpts in the Appendix originally appeared in *Phonics Lessons, Grade 2* by Gay Su Pinnell and Irene C. Fountas and *Word Study Lessons, Grade 3* by Irene C. Fountas and Gay Su Pinnell. Copyright © 2006 by Irene C. Fountas and Gay Su Pinnell. Published by Heinemann, Portsmouth, NH. All rights reserved.

Library of Congress Cataloging-in-Publication Data
Pinnell, Gay Su.
The continuum of literacy learning, grades K–8 : behaviors and understandings to notice, teach, and support / Gay Su Pinnell and Irene C. Fountas.
p. cm.
Includes bibliographical references.
ISBN-13: 978-0-325-01239-1
ISBN-10: 0-325-01239-3
1. Language arts (Elementary)—Curricula. 2. Language arts (Middle school)—Curricula. I. Fountas, Irene C. II. Title.
LB1576.P5786 2007
372.6043—dc22 2007027252

Editor: Tina Miller
Production: Elizabeth Valway
Cover design: Lisa Fowler
Little Book art spreads developed by Brown Publishing Network
Interior design: Lisa Fowler and Jenny Jensen Greenleaf
Composition: Technologies 'N Typography, Inc.
Manufacturing: Steve Bernier

Printed in the United States of America on acid-free paper
11 10 09 08 07 ML 1 2 3 4 5

Contents

Introduction

Teachers who work together can reach the goal of high student achievement if they share a common vision. This learning continuum is designed to help educators teach from the specific body of understandings that students in grades kindergarten through eight must acquire to become highly effective users of oral and written language. With this foundation, you can set clear goals for learning and plan specific lessons across many instructional contexts.

This volume is a companion to two grade-level books: *The Continuum of Literacy Learning, Grades K–2* and *The Continuum of Literacy Learning, Grades 3–8*. The K–2 and 3–8 volumes are organized by grade level (or by text level A–Z) for teacher convenience; each grade or level section contains continua that list characteristics and goals appropriate to the specific grade or level. This K–8 volume contains the same text characteristics and goals as the K–2 and 3–8 books, but here they are organized by continuum; each continuum section contains characteristics and goals lists for each level from kindergarten to grade eight.

As an administrator, lead teacher, literacy coach, or staff developer, you can use this comprehensive continuum to provide an overall guide to the texts used in different arenas of instruction, to grade-level expectations, and to specific behaviors and understandings to notice, teach, and support in daily instruction across the school year, grade by grade. In this introduction we provide a brief overview of the content of the entire continuum and its organization. We then describe ways that teachers can use it to increase the effectiveness of instruction. We end with some suggestions on how administrators and staff developers can use the continuum to support the work of teachers.

Content of the Continuum

Across the seven continua included in this volume, several principles are important to consider:

- ***Students learn by talking.*** We engage students in conversation that is grounded in a variety of texts—those that students read, hear read aloud, or write—and that expands their ability to comprehend and use language.
- ***Students need to process a large amount of written language.*** A dynamic language and literacy curriculum provides many daily opportunities for students to read books of their choice independently, to read more challenging

instructional material with teacher guidance, and to hear teacher-selected and grade-appropriate texts read aloud.

- ***The ability to read and comprehend texts is expanded through talking and writing.*** Students need to acquire a wide range of ways to write about their reading and also to talk about texts with the teacher and other students.

- ***Learning deepens when students engage in reading, talking, and writing about texts across many different instructional contexts.*** Each mode of communication provides a new way to process the ideas learned from oral and written texts and from each other.

This continuum provides a way to look for specific evidence of learning from kindergarten through grade eight, and across seven curricular areas. To create it, we examined a wide range of research on language and literacy learning, and we asked teachers and researchers for feedback. We also examined the curriculum standards of many states. Some guiding principles were:

- Learning does not occur in stages but is a continually evolving process.

- The same concepts are acquired and then elaborated over time.

- Many complex literacy concepts take years to develop.

- Students learn by applying what they know to the reading and writing of increasingly complex texts.

- Learning does not automatically happen; most students need expert teaching to develop high levels of reading and writing expertise.

- Learning is different but interrelated across different kinds of language and literacy activities; one kind of learning enhances and reinforces others.

In this volume, we include seven different learning continua (see Figure I–1). Each of these continua focuses on a different aspect of the language and literacy framework; and each contributes substantially, in different but complementary ways, to students' development of reading, writing, and language processes. Each of the continua is described in more detail in a separate introduction, but we briefly describe them here.

Reading Process

Four of the continua specifically address reading: interactive read-aloud and literature discussion, shared and performance reading, guided reading, and writing about reading. In these four we focus on strategic actions for thinking:

FIG. I–1 *The Continuum of Literacy Learning*

CURRICULUM COMPONENT	DESCRIPTION OF THE CONTINUUM
Interactive Read-Aloud and Literature Discussion	• Year by year • Genres appropriate to grades K–8 • Specific behaviors and understandings that are evidence of thinking within, beyond, and about the text
Shared and Performance Reading	• Year by year, grades K–8 • Genres appropriate to grades K–8 • Specific behaviors and understandings that are evidence of thinking within, beyond, and about the text
Writing About Reading	• Year by year, grades K–8 • Genres/forms for writing about reading appropriate to grades K–8 • Specific evidence in the writing that reflects thinking within, beyond, and about the text
Writing	• Year by year, grades K–8 • Genres/forms for writing appropriate to grades K–8 • Aspects of craft, conventions, and process that are evident in children's writing, K–8
Oral, Visual, and Technological Communication	• Year by year, grades K–8 • Specific behaviors and understandings related to listening and speaking, presentation, and technology
Phonics, Spelling, and Word Study	• Year by year, grades K–8 • Specific behaviors and understandings related to nine areas of understanding related to letters, sounds, and words, and how they work in reading and spelling
Guided Reading	• Level by level, A to Z • Genres appropriate to grades K–8 • Specific behaviors and understandings that are evidence of thinking within, beyond, and about the text • Specific suggestions for word work (drawn from the phonics and word analysis continuum)

- ***Within the text*** (literal understanding achieved through solving words, monitoring and correcting, searching for and using information, summarizing, maintaining fluency, and adjusting for purposes and genre of text)
- ***Beyond the text*** (making predictions; making connections with personal experience, content knowledge and other texts; inferring what is implied but not stated; and synthesizing new information)
- ***About the text*** (analyzing or critiquing the author's craft)

See the inside back cover for a summary chart showing the twelve systems of strategic actions.

In ***interactive read-aloud and literature discussion,*** students have the opportunity to extend their understandings through talk. In interactive read-aloud, teachers have the opportunity to engage students with texts that are usually more complex than they can read for themselves. Teachers can take strategic moments to stop for quick discussion during the reading and continue talking after the end. Student talk provides evidence of their thinking.

Shared and performance reading offer an authentic reason for reading aloud. As they read in unison or read parts in readers' theater, students need to read in phrases, notice punctuation and dialogue, and think about the meaning of the text. All of these actions provide evidence that they understand the text and are processing it effectively. On these familiar texts, teachers have the opportunity to support and extend students' understandings.

Guided reading offers small-group support and explicit teaching to help students take on more challenging texts. As they read texts that are organized along a gradient of difficulty from A–Z, students expand their systems of strategic actions by meeting the demands of increasingly complex texts. They provide evidence of their thinking through oral reading, talk, and extension through writing. The guided reading continuum is related to text reading levels rather than grade levels because we envision continuous progress along these levels. The Text Gradient chart in Figure I–2 indicates a range of levels that approximately correlates with goals for each grade level.

In addition to specific evidence of thinking within, beyond, and about a text, each of these three continua described above lists genres of texts that are appropriate for use at each grade level or text level.

The fourth reading continuum, ***writing about reading,*** often includes drawing and is another way for students to extend their understanding and provide evidence of thinking. Writing about reading may be used in connection with interactive read-aloud and literature discussion or with guided reading.

As you work with the continua related to reading, you will see a gradual increase in the complexity of the kinds of thinking that readers do. Most of the principles of learning cannot be pinpointed at one point in time or even one year. You will usually see the same kind of principle (behavior or understanding) repeated across grades or across levels of text; each time remember that the learner is applying the principle in a more complex way to read harder texts.

Oral and Written Communication

Writing is a way of experimenting with and deepening understanding of genres students have read. Although writing about reading is an excellent approach to help students extend their thinking and support discussion, it does not take

FIG. I–2 *Fountas and Pinnell Text Gradient Chart*

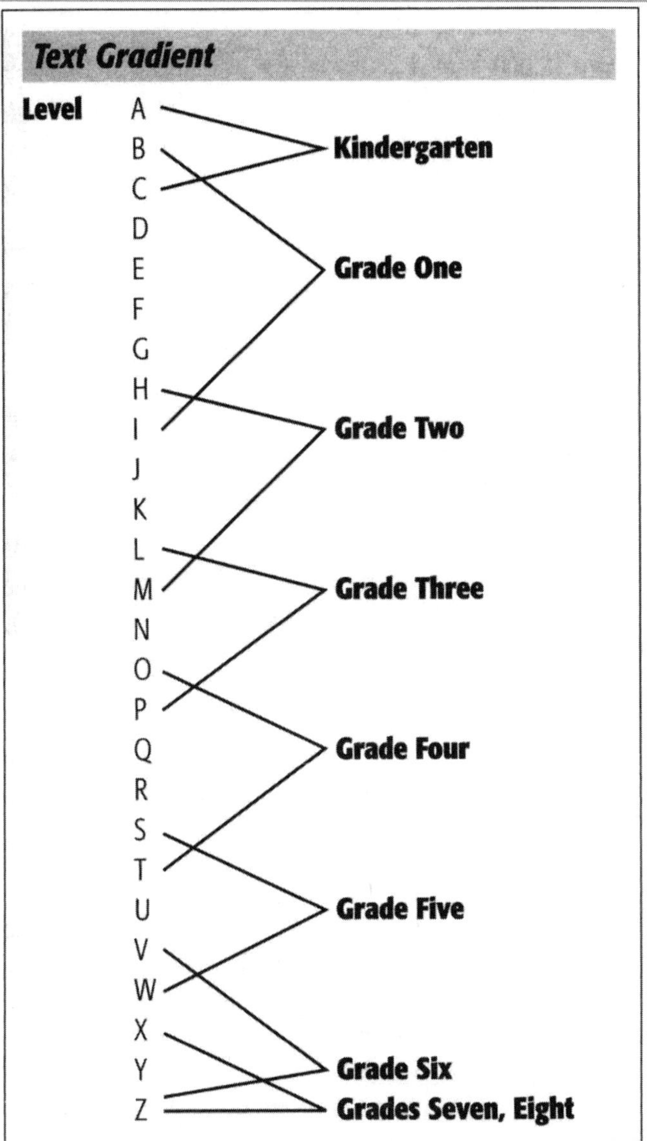

the place of specific instruction devoted to helping students develop as writers. Through the writing workshop, teachers help young writers continually expand their learning of the craft, conventions, and process of writing for the purpose of communicating meaning to an audience. The writing continuum in this book lists specific understandings for each grade level related to craft, conventions, and process. It also suggests genres for students to learn how to write at each grade level.

Oral, visual, and technological communication are integral to all literacy processes; you'll see their presence in all other continua. This continuum singles out particular behaviors and understandings for intentional instruction.

Word Study

Finally, we include a continuum for *phonics, spelling, and word study.* This grade-by-grade continuum is drawn from the longer continuum originally published in *Phonics Lessons* (Pinnell and Fountas 2003) and *Word Study Lessons* (Fountas and Pinnell 2004) which is included in the appendix at the back of this book. For appropriate grades in this continuum section, you will find specific principles related to nine areas of learning: 1) early literacy concepts, 2) phonological awareness, 3) letter knowledge, 4) letter-sound relationships, 5) spelling patterns, 6) high-frequency words, 7) word meaning, 8) word structure, and 9) word-solving actions. Here, too, you will find specific understandings related to spelling, which interface with the section on conventions provided in the writing continuum.

Some Cautions

In preparing these continua we considered the typical range of students that can be found in kindergarten through grade eight classrooms. We also consulted teachers about their expectations and vision as to appropriate instruction at each grade level. We thought about the district and state standards we know. We need to have a vision of expected levels of learning because it helps in making effective instructional decisions; and even more important, it helps us to identify students who need intervention.

At the same time, we would not want to apply these expectations in an inflexible way. We need to recognize that students vary widely in their progress—sometimes moving quickly and sometimes getting bogged down. They may make faster progress in one area than another. The continua should help you intervene in more precise ways to help students. But it is also important to remember that learners may not necessarily meet *every* expectation at all points in time. Nor should any one of the understandings and behaviors included in this document be used as criteria for promotion. Educators can look thoughtfully across the full range of grade-level expectations as they make decisions about individual students.

It is also important to recognize that just because grade-level expectations exist, all teaching may not be pitched at that level. Through assessment, you may learn that your class only partially matches the behaviors and understandings on the continuum. Almost all teachers find that they need to consult the material at lower and higher levels (one reason that the guided reading continuum is not graded).

Organization of the Continuum

Seven continua are included in this document. They are arranged in the following way.

Grade by Grade

Six of the continua are organized by grade level: 1) interactive read-aloud and literature discussion; 2) shared and performance reading; 3) writing about reading; 4) writing; 5) oral, visual, and technological communication; and 6) phonics, spelling, and word study. Within each continuum section you will find a continuum for each grade level, kindergarten through grade eight. You can turn to the tabbed section for any continuum and find all eight grades.

Level by Level

The guided reading continuum is organized according to Fountas and Pinnell text gradient levels A to Z. These levels typically correlate to grades K through 8, but students may vary along them in their instructional levels. It is important for all students to receive guided reading instruction at a level that allows them to process texts successfully with teacher support.

Additional Resources

At the end of the book, we have included the expanded Phonics and Word Study continuum from which the grade-level Phonics, Spelling and Word Study continuum as well as the word work section of Guided Reading were derived. Consult this expanded version if you need greater detail to guide the teaching of phonics.

Finally, you will find a glossary of terms at the end of the book that will assist you in interpreting the continuum. For additional information on instruction, consult the texts in the references section, also found at the end of this book.

Ways Teachers Can Use the Continuum

We see many different uses for this continuum, including the following.

Foundation for Teaching

As you think about individual, small-group, and whole-group instruction, you may consult different areas of the continuum. For example, if you are planning instruction for students in guided reading at level M, use the lists of behaviors and understandings to plan introductions to texts, guide observations and interactions with individuals, and shape teaching points. The word work section will give specific suggestions for principles to explore at the end of the guided reading lessons. You can plan embedded teaching as you examine the section on interactive read-aloud and literature discussion. The interactive read-aloud and literature discussion as well as the writing and word study continua will be useful in planning explicit minilessons.

Guide for Curriculum Planning

The continuum can also be used with a grade-level team or school staff to plan the language and literacy curriculum. It offers a starting point for thinking very specifically about goals and expectations. Your team may adapt the continuum to meet your own goals and district expectations.

Linking Assessment and Instruction

Sometimes assessment is administered and the results recorded, but then the process stops. Teachers are unsure what to do with the data or where to go next in their teaching. This continuum can be used as a bridge between assessment data and the specific teaching that students need. With assessment, you learn what students know; the continuum will help you think about what they almost know and need to know next.

Evaluation and Grading

The continuum can also serve as a guide for evaluating student progress over time. You can evaluate whether students are meeting grade-level standards. Remember that no student would be expected to demonstrate every single competency to be considered on grade level. *Grade level* is always a term that encompasses a range of levels of understanding at any given time.

Reporting to Parents

We would not recommend that you show parents such an overwhelming document as this continuum. It would get in the way of good conversation. However, you can use the continuum as a resource for the kind of information you need to provide to parents, but in easy-to-understand language.

Guide to Intervention

Many students will need extra support in order to achieve the school's goals for learning. Assessment and observation will help you identify the specific areas in which students need help. Use the continuum to find the specific understandings that can guide intervention.

Tool for Learning About Texts

The detailed grade-by-grade and level-by-level descriptions in the continua serve as an excellent tool for learning about the supports and challenges for readers in texts. By understanding how to look at texts, you will be able to provide more effective teaching.

Ways Administrators or Staff Developers Can Use the Continuum

As a staff developer or an administrator, this document will give you a comprehensive view of language and literacy learning and how it changes and develops over time. The continuum is intended to provide teachers with a conceptual tool that they can use to think constructively about their work. We want to support them in crafting instruction that will link their observations and deep knowledge of their own students with learning over time. Administrators and staff developers are the key to teachers' support system as they grow in conceptual understanding of their work.

Foundation for Setting School and/or District Goals

Since this continuum is a detailed description of every aspect of the language arts, you may want to adopt the continuum as your goals for instruction. Alternatively, you may want to review the document to select goals for your school or district. Remember, too, that these grade-level expectations are consistent with national standards. Depending on local priorities, you may want to adjust them lower or higher.

Link to State Standards

This continuum was checked against numerous examples of state standards to assure consistency and comprehensiveness. In general, you will find *The Continuum* to be much more detailed than state standards; so, it offers a way to make your state goals more specific as a basis for instruction.

Helping Administrators and Teachers Achieve a Common Vision

Examining the continuum together, administrators and teachers can discuss their common expectations for students' achievement in each curriculum area, grade by grade. They can compare current expectations with the document and focus on goals that they want their students to achieve. For example, a principal and teachers in an elementary school or middle school can work together over a few weeks or months. In grade-level groups they can examine one instructional area at a time and then share their perspectives with teachers of other grades. Looking across the grades will help them to understand a long continuum of learning, as well as to work more effectively with students who are below or above their own grade levels. Working intensively with the continuum at their own grade levels (and perhaps the level below), they can make specific plans for instruction in the particular area.

A Basis for Instructional Coaching

An instructional coach (often called a literacy coach) can use the continuum as a foundation for coaching conversations. It will be useful for coaches to help teachers become able to access information quickly as part of their reflection on lessons they have taught and on their planning. In other words, the coach can help teachers really get to know the continuum guide so that they can access information easily. Typically, the coach and teacher would use the guide as a reference before, during, and after the observation of a lesson. The guide enables the coach to focus the conversation on critical areas of teaching and learning—behaviors to notice, teach, and support to help students read, write, and talk proficiently. It is also an excellent tool for discussing and analyzing texts in a variety of genres and at a variety of levels. The guide will add specificity to the conversation that will extend teachers' understandings of learning processes and development over time.

Pre-Observation Conference

- The coach and teacher think about and analyze their strengths, as well as their learning needs, referring to the continuum as appropriate.
- They may examine data from student assessment or the teacher's ongoing observation, again, using the continuum expectations as a reference.
- They may look at lesson artifacts—texts they are using or student writing—and consider them in the light of text characteristics for the particular area, thinking about the learning opportunities for students.

Observation of Lessons

- The continuum is not designed to be used as a checklist. Rather it is a foundation for discussing critical areas of development.
- During observation, coaches can keep in mind the evidence of student understanding and shifts in learning. This foundational knowledge will help the coach gather evidence of student learning that can be discussed later with the teacher.

Post-Observation Conference

- The coach and teacher can use the continuum to analyze the teaching and its effectiveness in meeting the goals discussed in the pre-observation conference.
- They can discuss examples of behaviors that provide evidence of student understanding or lack of understanding.
- They can also discuss teaching interactions that supported or extended student understanding, as well as potential interactions for working with the students in the next lesson.
- The continuum will also provide a guide as to the appropriateness of texts or tasks in terms of students' current understandings and what they need to learn next.
- Together the coach and teacher can use the guide to help set new learning goals for the students and to begin to plan for teaching.

The ultimate goals of every coaching interaction are to help the teacher expand knowledge of language and literacy learning and to analyze the effectiveness of the teaching. By talking about the ideas in the continuum guide and observing students intensively, teachers will come to understand more about the process of learning language, reading, writing, and technology. The continuum will serve as a guide that becomes internalized over time through its consistent use.

Interactive Read-Aloud and Literature Discussion

Introduction to Interactive Read-Aloud and Literature Discussion

In creating curriculum goals for an interactive read-aloud, you will want to consider text selection and opportunities for new learning. At all grade levels, students need to listen to texts in a variety of genres and increasingly complex texts within those genres. Story problems, characters, content, and topics should be matched to the particular age group, with consideration of students' background, experience, and interests. You will also want to consider a variety of text formats and types of texts.

Beyond text selection, it is important to think about how to support readers' thinking within, beyond, and about a text. The chart on the inside back cover of this book provides a handy summary of these ways of thinking. Before, during, and after listening to a text read aloud, teachers will want to notice evidence of students' literal understanding. Did readers pick up the most important information? Could they follow the plot? Could they remember important details? In addition, you want students to think beyond the text, making predictions and important connections. Teachers need to look for evidence that students can notice and incorporate new information into their own understandings, as well as make inferences based on the available information. Finally, you want students to form opinions about their reading and develop their own reading preferences. Consider evidence indicating that students can think analytically about texts, noticing the writer's craft and style; it is also important for them to think critically about the quality, content, and accuracy of texts.

When students are actively listening to and discussing a text, all of the strategic actions for comprehending are in operation. In an interactive read-aloud, the listener is freed from decoding and is supported by the oral reader's fluency, phrasing, and stress—all elements of what we sometimes call *expression.* The scene is set for a high level of comprehending or thinking together through a text.

Interactive Read-Aloud and Literature Discussion

From kindergarten through eighth grade, literature discussion is a part of shared reading and interactive read-aloud (see Fountas and Pinnell 2001, 2006). Students may discuss the book as a whole class but they will also need to be engaged in more intimate routines like a "turn and talk" (focused on any aspect of text) for a minute or two a few times within the larger discussion. These types of routines provide opportunities for individuals to engage in more talk than would otherwise be possible in a whole-group discussion. Inserting such routines into your interactive read-aloud session will make whole-group discussions livelier and give all students the opportunity for active participation. After students have spent some time talking in pairs, triads, or small circles, they will become skilled in small-group discussion. After students have had a great deal of experience using the routines, you may decide they are ready for a more extended discussion with their peers—literature discussion or book club. You can find extensive information about these instructional approaches in *Teaching for Comprehending and Fluency: Thinking, Talking, and Writing About Reading, K–8* (Fountas and Pinnell 2006).

Interactive read-aloud and literature discussion abound with *text talk*—shared talk in which students examine ideas and thinking about narrative, expository, or poetic texts. Every engagement gives students opportunities for thinking about texts in new ways. The more they have a chance to do it, the better they get at using talk to explore the meaning of texts. As students work together in groups, they develop a backlog of shared meanings that increasingly deepens their talk.

Interactive read-aloud and literature discussion are placed together in this continuum because in both settings we seek age-appropriate, grade-appropriate reading materials that have the potential to extend students' thinking and their ability to talk about texts. For kindergarten and grade-one students, most literature discussions will take place during interactive read-aloud. But as students gain more experience through turn and talk routines, they can begin to prepare for and engage in small-group discussions. For small-group literature discussion, students usually choose from several texts that you have preselected. If they can read the selection independently, they read at home or during the reading workshop. If they cannot read the text easily on their own, an audio recording or a support system with another student or family member reading the text aloud can provide access to the text. Sometimes, students engage in book clubs based on texts they have heard read aloud to the entire class. Thus, in selecting books for interactive read-aloud and literature discussion, you do not need to consider a specific Fountas and Pinnell text level, but you will want to think about the text characteristics as well as texts that are age and grade appropriate.

Framework for the Continuum of Learning

The continuum that follows is a guide for setting goals and creating instructional plans for interactive read-aloud and literature discussion. This continuum provides grade-by-grade information that includes:

- characteristics of texts (descriptions of text factors to keep in mind when selecting and reading aloud texts)
- curriculum goals (descriptions of behaviors to teach, notice, and support to help readers think within, beyond, and about the text you have selected)

Characteristics of Texts

Ten text factors are important to consider when selecting texts for any kind of reading instruction. When selecting texts for interactive read-aloud, teachers need to consider the high level of support they provide to students to help them process or think about the text. The vocabulary in the text must be understandable to listeners, but you don't need to worry about word-solving difficulty since the adult reader will be doing the decoding. Descriptions of all ten text factors, in terms of interactive read-aloud, follow.

1. *Genre.* We have listed a variety of types of texts that are appropriate at each grade level. For the most part, you will want to use the full range of genres at every grade level, but be selective about the particular examples you choose.

2. *Text Structure.* The structure of a text refers to the way it is organized. Fiction texts are generally organized in a *narrative* structure, with a problem and a sequence of events that leads to the resolution of the problem. Interactive read-aloud is a context in which listeners can internalize plot structure and learn how stories *work.* Nonfiction texts may also be narrative; biographies, for example, usually tell the stories like fiction texts do. But most informational texts are organized categorically by subtopic with underlying structures such as description, temporal sequence, comparison and contrast, cause and effect, and problem and solution. Often these structures are used in combination. Interactive read-aloud and literature discussion provide a setting within which you can teach students to recognize and understand these structures.

3. *Content.* The subject matter of the text should be accessible and interesting to listeners. Over time, the sophistication and complexity of content can be increased. Although direct experiences are always necessary for learning, students can acquire a great deal of content knowledge from hearing written language read aloud. Content is helpful to listeners when they already have some prior knowledge to bring to understanding new information.

4. *Themes and Ideas.* The major ideas of the books chosen for read-aloud should be appropriate for all students' age and background experience. Interactive read-aloud is an ideal way to stretch students' knowledge, but they must be able to make connections to their existing knowledge. They can extend their own understanding of the themes and ideas as they discuss them with others.

5. *Language and Literary Features.* The way the writer uses language creates the literary quality of a text. It is important to select texts that students can understand in terms of language and literary features. Interactive read-aloud and literature discussion provide opportunities to expand students' ability to process literary language, including dialogue and figurative language. Other literary features include the development of elements such as setting, plot, and characters.

6. *Sentence Complexity.* The structure of sentences—their length, word order, and the number of embedded phrases and clauses—is another key factor. Through the primary, elementary, and intermediate grades, students can generally understand sentences that are more complex than those they can read. Interactive read-aloud provides a way to help them gradually internalize more complex sentence structures. Discussion with others will help students unpack complex sentences and understand them better.

7. *Vocabulary.* Vocabulary refers to the words that an individual knows and understands in both oral and written language. The words that the writer has selected may present a challenge to readers. Written text usually includes many words that are not in our everyday oral vocabulary; we constantly expand vocabulary by reading or hearing written language read aloud. Through interactive read-aloud and literature discussion, students can greatly expand their vocabulary.

8. *Words.* When selecting books for students to read for themselves, we always consider the challenges the words present: length, number of syllables, inflectional endings, and general ease of solving. In interactive read-aloud, however, the teacher solves the words, so this will not be a major factor in text selection. Also, remember that for literature discussion, students may use audio recordings of texts that they are not yet ready to read independently. Attention to vocabulary will take into account word complexity.

9. *Illustrations.* Illustrations (or other forms of art) provide a great deal of information to readers and listeners. A high-quality picture book is a coherent form of literary art. Think of a picture book as a short story that has beautiful illustrations. Picture books are appropriate for a wide range of ages and all genres. For students of all ages, illustrations increase engagement and enjoyment. Illustrations for younger children provide a great deal of information; for older students they help create mood and often present symbols that have deep meaning. Informational texts (and increasingly some fiction texts) also include graphics in the form of maps, diagrams, and drawings. These graphics may provide information that is additional to the body of the text. Some graphics may be large enough for students to see and discuss during interactive read-aloud, but students may attend to them during small-group discussion.

10. *Book and Print Features.* When selecting books for interactive read-aloud, the physical aspects of the text, such as length, size, and layout, should be considered. Book and print features include tools like the table of contents, glossary, pronunciation guide, indexes, sidebars, and headings. All of these features may be pointed out and discussed during interactive read-aloud or literature discussion.

Curriculum Goals

We have stated curriculum goals in terms of behaviors and understandings to notice, teach, and support at each level. These are further divided into evidence that the reader is thinking *within, beyond,* and *about* the text.

- ***Within the Text.*** To effectively and efficiently process a text and derive the literal meaning, readers must solve the words and monitor and self-correct their reading. In interactive read-aloud, readers are relieved of the task of decoding and they hear fluent, phrased reading; but they must self-monitor their own understanding, remember information in summary form, and adjust their thinking to the understanding of different fiction and nonfiction genres.

- ***Beyond the Text.*** Readers make predictions and connections to previous knowledge and their own lives. They also make connections between and among texts. They bring background knowledge to the reading of a text, synthesize new information by incorporating it into their own understandings, and think about what the writer has not stated but implied. Readers may infer the feelings and motivations of characters in fiction texts or the implications of the writer's statements in nonfiction. Interactive read-aloud provides many opportunities to support students' thinking beyond the literal meaning. By engaging students in discussion before and after reading, teachers can demonstrate how to think beyond the text and help students expand their own ability to do so. Stopping at selected intervals while reading aloud to discuss text elements can also prompt expanded thinking.

- ***About the Text.*** Readers think analytically about the text as an object, noticing and appreciating elements of the writer's craft, such as use of language, characterization, organization, and structure. Reading like a writer helps students notice aspects of craft and more fully enjoy a text, sometimes revisiting it. Readers also think critically about texts, evaluating the quality and considering the writer's accuracy or objectivity. Interactive read-aloud time is ideal time for demonstrating the kind of sophisticated thinking that effective readers do. It provides the opportunity for students to engage in analytic thinking about texts. In addition, the read-aloud books become a collection of shared texts that can be turned to again and again to notice more about craft.

See the inside back cover for a summary of the systems of strategic action—thinking within, beyond, and about the text.

Using the Continuum

The continuum does not reference specific texts, topics, or content areas. You will apply the continuum's goals in connection with your district or state content requirements. You can use this guide to set overall curriculum goals for grades K–8 or you can refer to it as you plan for interactive read-aloud.

We use the term *intentional conversation* to describe the instructional moves you can make during the conversation surrounding books in interactive read-aloud or in small-group literature discussion. The first goals when reading aloud to students and engaging them in small-group discussions are to engage their interest, to make the occasion enjoyable, and to guide them in active conversation. Interactive read-aloud and literature discussion give students opportunities to share their own ideas, to express their own meanings, and to contribute to deeper understanding of the text. Conversation must be genuine, but the teacher always keeps in mind the curriculum goals, that is, what makes the conversation intentional.

Without being heavy-handed or stifling students' comments, teachers can guide the conversation so that students are constantly expanding their thinking. During the interactive read-aloud and literature discussion, the teacher:

- Keeps in mind the systems of strategic actions (see the inside back cover) that readers must use.
- Knows the text deeply and understands its demands and the opportunities it provides for learning.
- Provides conversational leads to focus students' attention.
- Models and demonstrates behaviors that help students achieve better understanding.
- Asks students to share their thinking in a focused way.
- Prompts students to listen to and respond to one another rather than always being the center of the conversation.
- Keeps the conversation grounded in the text.
- Turns the conversation back to students, asking for deeper thinking.
- Requires students to be accountable for their comments, asking for more than opinion and asking for evidence from the text or personal experience.
- Gives feedback to students on what they are learning and the kinds of thinking they are doing.
- Asks students to self-evaluate their conversation about the text.

You will find that interactive read-aloud and literature discussion provide rich opportunities for students to expand their background knowledge, experience age-appropriate and grade-appropriate texts, and learn a variety of ways to think deeply about any text they read.

Interactive Read-Aloud and Literature Discussion

Selecting Texts Characteristics of Texts for Reading Aloud and Discussion

Genres/Forms

Genres

- Short poems, nursery rhymes, and songs
- Poems
- Traditional folktales
- Simple animal fantasy
- Realistic fiction
- Factual texts (ABC books, label books, concept books, counting books, simple informational books)

Forms

- Oral stories
- Picture books
- Wordless picture books

Text Structure

- Informational texts that present a clear and simple sequence
- Informational texts with simple description on each page–sometimes repeating patterns
- Many traditional tales with particular structures (cumulative tales, circular stories, and use of "three's")
- Simple structure with beginning, series of episodes, and an ending
- Many books with repetition of episodes and refrains
- Stories with repeating patterns

Content

- Language and word play (rhymes, nonsense, alliteration, alphabet)
- Everyday events (eating, playing, shopping)
- Familiar topics (animals, pets, families, food, plants, school, friends, growing, senses, neighborhood, weather and seasons, health)
- A few topics beyond children's immediate experiences (such as the farm)

Themes and Ideas

- Humor that is easy to grasp (silly characters, situations, games)
- Obvious themes (sharing, being friends, belonging, working, growing, responsibility, behavior)

Language and Literary Features

- Simple plots with clear problems and resolutions
- Memorable characters
- Characters that change for reasons that are clear within the text (learn lessons from mistakes)
- Memorable characters, many in folktales, that have predictable characteristics (sly foxes)
- Stories with multiple characters
- Some figurative language that is easy to understand
- Simple dialogue easily attributed to characters

Sentence Complexity

- Sentences that are more complex than children would use in oral conversation
- Sentences that are complex but also easy for children to follow
- A few sentences that are long with many embedded phrases and clauses

Vocabulary

- Some words of high interest that will be memorable to children
- Many words that are in children's speaking vocabulary
- A few new content words related to concepts that are easy to explain

Illustrations

- Large, clear, colorful illustrations in a variety of media
- Very simple graphics (maps, labeled drawings)
- Illustrations that offer high support for comprehension

Book and Print Features

- Some books with large print for children to see during read-aloud
- Some special features in the illustrations and print that engage interest and make texts interactive (pop-up books, lift-the-flap books, see-through holes, sound effects)
- Title, author, and illustrator on cover and title page

Interactive Read-Aloud and Literature Discussion

Selecting Goals

Behaviors and Understandings to Notice, Teach, and Support

Thinking *within* the Text

- Acquire understanding of new words from context
- Acquire new vocabulary from listening and use in discussion
- Follow the events of a plot and remember them after reading
- Talk about interesting information in a text
- Pick up important information and remember it to use in discussion
- Tell a summary of the text after reading
- Understand the meaning of the words during reading
- Talk about characters, problems, and events in a story
- Notice and ask questions when meaning is lost or understanding is interrupted
- Notice and derive information from pictures
- When joining in on refrains or repetitive text, mimic the teacher's intonation and stress
- Notice and respond to stress and tone of voice while listening and afterward

Thinking *beyond* the Text

- Bring background knowledge to understanding characters and their problems
- Bring background knowledge to understanding the content of a text
- Predict what will happen next
- Make connections between texts and their own life experiences
- Make connections between new texts and those heard before
- Make predictions about what a character is likely to do
- Infer characters' intentions or feelings
- Interpret the illustrations
- Use details from illustrations to support points made in discussion
- Recognize interesting new information and add it to their understandings
- Give reasons to support thinking

Thinking *about* the Text

- Notice and understand texts that are based on established sequences such as numbers, days of the week, seasons
- Recognize and identify some aspects of text structure, such as beginning and ending
- Understand that an author wrote the book
- Understand that an artist illustrated the book
- Notice words that the writer has used to make the story or content interesting
- Recognize some authors by the style of their illustrations, their topics, or the characters they use
- Have some favorite writers or illustrators
- Have opinions about texts and state the basis for opinions (tell why)
- Notice how texts are different from each other (such as fiction versus nonfiction)
- Check information in the text against own experiences
- Compare different versions of the same story, rhyme, or traditional tale
- Use specific vocabulary to talk about texts: *author, illustrator, cover, wordless picture book, picture book, character, problem, events*

Interactive Read-Aloud and Literature Discussion

Selecting Texts — Characteristics of Texts for Reading Aloud and Discussion

Genres/Forms

Genres

- Short poems, nursery rhymes, and songs
- Poems
- Traditional folktales
- Simple animal fantasy
- Realistic fiction
- Factual texts (ABC books, label books, concept books, counting books, simple informational books)
- Memoir

Forms

- Oral stories
- Picture books
- Wordless picture books
- Informational picture books

Text Structure

- Informational texts that present a clear and simple sequence
- Informational texts with simple description on each page—sometimes repeating patterns
- Factual texts with clearly defined categories
- Many traditional tales with particular structures (cumulative tales, circular stories, and use of "three's")
- Simple structure with beginning, series of episodes, and an ending
- Many books with repetition of episodes and refrains
- Stories with repeating patterns

Content

- Everyday events (eating, playing, seasons, weather, shopping, games)
- Familiar topics (animals, pets, families, food, plants, school, friends, growing, senses, neighborhood, weather and seasons, health)
- Content beyond most students' immediate experience (historic animals, zoo animals in nature, space, the environment—ocean and desert, nutrition)

Themes and Ideas

- Humor that is easy to grasp (play with words)
- Obvious themes (sharing, friends, belonging, working, growing, family, responsibility, behavior)
- Some themes going beyond everyday events

Language and Literary Features

- Simple plots with clear problems and resolutions
- Memorable characters
- Characters that change for reasons that are clear within the text (learn lessons from mistakes)
- Memorable characters, many in folktales, that have predictable traits (sly foxes)
- Stories with multiple characters
- Some figurative language that is easy to understand
- Simple dialogue easily attributed to characters

Sentence Complexity

- Sentences that are more complex than children would use in oral conversation
- Sentences that are complex but also easy for children to follow—no tricky structures
- A few sentences that are long with embedded phrases and clauses

Vocabulary

- Some words of high interest that will be memorable to children
- Many words that are in children's speaking vocabulary
- A few new content words related to concepts children are learning and that are easy to explain

Illustrations

- Large, clear, colorful illustrations in a variety of media
- Very simple graphics (maps, labeled drawings)
- Illustrations that offer high support for comprehension

Book and Print Features

- Some books with large print for children to see during read-aloud
- Some special features in the illustrations and print that engage interest and make texts interactive (pop-up books, lift-the-flap books, see-through holes, sound effects)
- Title, author, and illustrator on cover and title page

Interactive Read-Aloud and Literature Discussion

Selecting Goals Behaviors and Understandings to Notice, Teach, and Support

Thinking *within* the Text

- Follow the events of a plot with multiple events
- Follow plots that have particular patterns, such as accumulation or a circular structure
- Pick up important information and remember it to use in discussion
- Tell a summary of the text after reading
- Talk about interesting and new information in a text
- Understand the problem in a story
- Understand when and why the problem is solved
- Recognize characters and report important details after reading
- Notice and ask questions when meaning is lost or understanding is interrupted
- Notice and derive information from pictures
- Understand the words while listening to a story or factual text
- Acquire new vocabulary from listening and use in discussion
- Derive meaning of new words from context
- Know what the story is about after hearing the beginning
- Provide specific examples and evidence from the text to support thinking
- Use details from illustrations to support points made in discussion
- When joining in on refrains or repetitive text, mimic the teacher's intonation and stress
- Notice and respond to stress and tone of voice while listening and afterward

Thinking *beyond* the Text

- Bring background knowledge to understanding characters and their problems
- Bring background knowledge to understanding the content of a text
- Make connections between texts and their own life experiences
- Predict what will happen next
- Predict what will happen after the end
- Make predictions about what a character is likely to do
- Use evidence from the text to support predictions (I think . . . because . . .)
- Infer characters' intentions or feelings
- Interpret the illustrations
- Discuss specific examples from the text to support or justify the ideas they are expressing
- Make connections between familiar texts and discuss similarities and differences
- Develop new concepts and ideas from listening to and discussing texts

Thinking *about* the Text

- Notice and understand texts that are based on established sequences such as numbers, days of the week, days of the month, seasons
- Recognize and identify some aspects of text structure, such as beginning, events in sequential order, and ending
- Understand that an author wrote the book
- Understand that an artist illustrated the book
- Recognize the names of some authors and illustrators and have favorites
- Notice similarities and differences among texts that are by the same author or are on the same topic
- Discuss the characteristics of the work of some authors and illustrators
- Notice words that the writer has used to make the story or content interesting
- Name some favorite authors or illustrators and state reasons for liking them
- Have opinions about texts and state the basis for opinions (tell why)
- Notice how texts are different from each other (such as fiction versus nonfiction)
- Understand fiction as stories that are not real and nonfiction as texts that provide real information
- Understand realistic fiction as stories that could be real and fantasy as stories that could not be real
- Compare different versions of the same story, rhyme, or traditional tale
- Use specific vocabulary to talk about texts: *author, illustrator, cover, wordless picture book, picture book, character, problem, events*

Interactive Read-Aloud and Literature Discussion

Selecting Texts — Characteristics of Texts for Reading Aloud and Discussion

Genres/Forms

Genres

- Poems
- Traditional literature (cumulative, *pourquoi,* beasts, cyclical, fables, tall tales)
- Fantasy
- Realistic fiction
- Informational texts
- Simple biographies on well-known subjects
- Memoir
- Special types of genres: mystery
- Hybrid texts (a text in one genre with a simple form of another genre embedded in it)

Forms

- Oral stories
- Informational picture books
- Picture story books
- Beginning chapter books
- Beginning series books

Text Structure

- Informational texts with simple description on each page–sometimes repeating patterns
- Factual texts that incorporate sequence (for example, life cycles and how-to books)
- Factual texts that include description, temporal sequence, and compare and contrast
- Factual texts with clearly defined categories
- Traditional folk- and fairy tales with more repeating patterns
- Simple structure with beginning, series of episodes, and an ending
- A few stories with repeating patterns

Content

- Content that verifies as well as extends students' experiences
- Some scientific and technical topics (human body, wide variety of animals–many not in children's common experiences, how-to books, technology)
- Many texts centering on problems related to family, friends, and school

Themes and Ideas

- Humor that is obvious
- Themes important to second graders (friendship, family, neighborhood)
- Most themes explicitly stated or easy to derive

Language and Literary Features

- Longer plots with more episodes
- Stories with multiple characters
- Characters that develop over time, learning from mistakes and creating relationships
- Literary language, including some use of metaphor and simile, as well as description
- A few literary devices (for example, story within a story)
- A variety of dialogue between more than one or two characters
- Some informational texts with categories and subcategories

Sentence Complexity

- Some long and complex sentences that require attention to follow
- A variety of sentence structures

Vocabulary

- Some words of high interest that will be memorable to children
- Many words that are in children's speaking vocabulary
- New commonly used vocabulary words that are explained in the text or shown in the illustrations
- Increased amount of technical vocabulary in informational text
- Some complex vocabulary words that are understandable given students' background knowledge

Illustrations

- Labeled drawings or photographs
- Pictures with legends
- Simple graphics, clearly labeled
- More complex illustrations that have detail and add more to the meaning of the text
- Chapter books with just a few black-and-white illustrations
- Picture books with illustrations that reflect the theme and writer's tone and make it a coherent work of art
- Illustrations that help the reader understand the mood of the story

Book and Print Features

- Title, author, and illustrator on cover and title page
- Some simple chapter books with titles on each chapter
- A few simple navigational tools (table of contents and index)

Interactive Read-Aloud and Literature Discussion

Selecting Goals Behaviors and Understandings to Notice, Teach, and Support

Thinking *within* the Text

- Notice and remember facts, concepts, or ideas from a text
- Provide an oral summary of a text
- Notice and remember the events of a story in sequence
- Notice and understand the problem of a story and how it is solved
- Self-monitor understanding and ask questions when meaning is lost
- Notice and derive information from pictures
- When joining in on refrains or repetitive text, mimic the teacher's intonation and stress
- Notice and respond to word stress and tone of voice while listening and afterward
- Recognize new meanings for known words by using context
- Recognize and actively work to solve new vocabulary words
- Add new vocabulary words to known words and use them in discussion and in writing
- Follow multiple events in a story to understand the plot

Thinking *beyond* the Text

- Bring background knowledge to understanding characters and their problems
- Make connections to prior knowledge
- Infer characters' intentions or feelings
- Infer characters' feelings and motivations from description, what they do or say, and what others think about them
- Interpret illustrations and discuss how they make readers feel
- Use evidence from the text to support predictions (I think . . . because . . .)
- Support thinking beyond the text with specific evidence based on personal experience or knowledge or evidence from the text
- Make predictions using information from the text
- Predict what will happen after the end
- Make connections to other texts by topic, major ideas, authors' styles, and genres
- Specify the nature of connections in discussion
- Develop new concepts and ideas from listening to and discussing texts
- Think about and interpret the significance of events in a story
- Relate important ideas in the text to each other and to ideas in other texts

Thinking *about* the Text

- Recognize and identify some aspects of text structure, such as beginning, events in sequential order, most exciting point in a story, and ending
- Discuss the characteristics of the work of some authors and illustrators
- Notice the writer's use of language (for example, word choice)
- Notice similarities and differences among texts that are by the same author or are on the same topic
- Talk about the connections between the illustrations and the text
- Recognize how the writer or illustrator has placed ideas in the text and in the graphics
- Form and state the basis for opinions about authors, illustrators, and texts
- State the basis for opinions about a text (tell why)
- Understand fiction as stories that are not real and nonfiction as texts that provide real information
- Understand realistic fiction as stories that could be real and fantasy as stories that could not be real
- Understand biography as the story of a person's life
- Compare different versions of the same story, rhyme, or traditional tale
- Use specific vocabulary to talk about texts: *author, illustrator, cover, wordless picture book, picture book, character, problem, events, series book, dedication, endpapers, book jacket, title page, chapters, resolution, main character, setting, fiction, nonfiction, poetry*

Interactive Read-Aloud and Literature Discussion

Selecting Texts — Characteristics of Texts for Reading Aloud and Discussion

Genres/Forms

Genres

- Poems
- Traditional literature (cumulative, *pourquoi,* beasts, cyclical, fables, tall tales, cultural variants of tales, humorous twists)
- Fantasy
- Realistic fiction
- Historical fiction
- Informational texts
- Simple biographies on well-known subjects
- Memoir
- Autobiography
- Special types of genres: mystery
- Hybrid texts (a text in one genre with a simple form of another genre embedded in it)

Forms

- Short stories
- Informational picture books
- Picture story books
- Chapter books, some with sequels
- Series books
- Simple texts utilizing diaries, logs, and letters

Text Structure

- Factual texts that include description, temporal sequence, and compare and contrast
- Factual texts that include temporal description, sequence, comparison and contrast, problem and solution, cause and effect
- Factual texts with clearly defined categories
- Factual texts with categories and subcategories, defined by sections and headings
- Some traditional literature with complex repeating patterns
- A few texts with complex structures, such as flashback and story within story, that are easily followed
- Texts with multiple episodes

Content

- Many texts on topics that go well beyond students' own experiences
- Content requiring the reader to take on diverse perspectives and learn about other cultures
- Some scientific and technical topics (the environment, technology)
- Many texts centering on problems (friendship, teasing, self-esteem)
- Settings that are accessible given typical background knowledge of mid-elementary students

Themes and Ideas

- Some subtle humor
- Themes important to third graders (friendship, teasing, self-esteem)
- Some mature themes (courage, prejudice, diverse perspectives)
- Most themes explicitly stated or easy to derive
- A few abstract ideas but highly supported by text and illustrations

Language and Literary Features

- Complex plots with some subplots
- Multiple characters revealed by what they say, think, and do and what others say/think about them
- Memorable characters with both good and bad traits that change over time
- Use of literary language (extended description of setting and characters, figurative language)
- Some obvious symbolism
- A few literary devices (for example, story within a story)
- Informational texts with categories and subcategories
- Some narratives that are highly literary
- Some complex fantasy elements
- Settings that are important to the plot and are distant in time and space from students' experience

Sentence Complexity

- Many long sentences with embedded clauses
- Literary uses of language that increase sentence complexity

Vocabulary

- New commonly used vocabulary words that are explained in the text or shown in the illustrations
- Some specialized words in informational texts
- Some complex vocabulary words that have high context support in the text

Illustrations

- Complex graphics requiring study (maps, drawings with labels, diagrams, cutaways)
- Complicated illustrations with many details, some needing description while the teacher is reading
- Chapter books with just a few black-and-white illustrations
- Some chapter books with no illustrations, requiring readers to imagine content
- Illustrations that enhance the writer's tone
- Picture books with illustrations that reflect the theme and writer's tone and make it a coherent work of art
- Illustrations that help the reader understand the mood of the story
- Some illustrations with symbolic elements requiring interpretation

Book and Print Features

- Some simple chapter books usually with titles on each chapter
- Short, illustrated fiction and nonfiction texts
- Long informational texts that may be used by selecting a section only
- Readers' tools (table of contents, headings and subheadings, index, glossary)

Interactive Read-Aloud and Literature Discussion

Selecting Goals

Behaviors and Understandings to Notice, Teach, and Support

Thinking *within* the Text

- Recognize and actively work to solve new vocabulary words
- Add new vocabulary words to known words and use them in discussion and in writing
- Recognize and actively work to learn the meaning of new vocabulary words, including complex, specialized, and technical words
- Follow and remember multiple events in a story, often involving the stories of multiple characters, to understand the plot
- Understand how one event builds on another throughout the text
- Access information and develop new concepts and ideas from reading
- Summarize orally or in writing a text, including appropriate information
- Notice and understand the problem of a story and how it is solved
- Notice and remember attributes and actions that will help in understanding character development
- Self-monitor understanding and ask questions when meaning is lost
- Notice and remember significant information from illustrations or graphics
- Notice and respond to stress and tone of voice while listening and afterward
- Notice and remember story details of time and place

Thinking *beyond* the Text

- Make connections to prior knowledge and use it to identify and incorporate new knowledge
- Make connections between the lives and motivations of characters and their own lives, even if the setting is a fantasy world or in the past
- Make a wide range of predictions based on information
- Hypothesize underlying motivations of characters that are not stated
- Infer characters' feelings and motivations from description, what they do or say, and what others think about them
- Interpret the mood of illustrations
- Interpret graphics and integrate information with the text
- Recognize, understand, and discuss some obvious symbolism
- Hypothesize the significance of the setting in influencing characters' decisions and attitudes
- Hypothesize the significance of events in a story
- Support thinking beyond the text with specific evidence based on personal experience or knowledge or evidence from the text
- Make connections to other texts by topic, major ideas, authors' styles, and genres
- Extend understanding to incorporate new ideas and content
- Notice new information and ideas and revise ideas in response to it
- Relate important ideas in the text to each other and to ideas in other texts

Thinking *about* the Text

- Discuss the characteristics of the work of some authors and illustrators
- Make note of interesting new words and intentionally remember them to use in oral discussion or writing
- Examine the writer's word choice
- Recognize how the writer or illustrator has placed ideas in the text and in the graphics
- Notice how the writer has organized an informational text (categories and subcategories, sequence, and others)
- Notice and understand when the writer uses temporal sequence, comparison and contrast, and description
- Recognize the genre of the text and use it to form expectations of the text
- Critically examine the quality or accuracy of the text, citing evidence for opinions
- Understand biography as the story of a person's life
- Notice ways the writer makes characters seem real
- Recognize and discuss aspects of narrative structure (beginning, series of events, high point of the story, ending)
- Use specific vocabulary to talk about texts: *author, illustrator, cover, wordless picture book, picture book, character, problem, events, series book, dedication, endpapers, book jacket, title page, chapters, resolution, main character, setting, fiction, nonfiction, poetry, author's note, illustrator's note, double-page spread,* names of fiction genres (for example, *historical fiction, legend*)

Interactive Read-Aloud and Literature Discussion

Selecting Texts Characteristics of Texts for Reading Aloud and Discussion

Genres/Forms

Genres

- Poems
- Traditional literature (humorous twists, legends, tall tales, cultural variants of tales)
- Fantasy
- Realistic fiction
- Science fiction
- Historical fiction
- Informational texts
- Simple biographies on well-known subjects
- Memoir
- Autobiography
- Special types of genres (mystery, adventure, survival)
- Hybrid texts (a text in one genre with a simple form of another genre embedded in it)

Forms

- Short stories
- Informational picture books
- Picture story books
- Chapter books, some with sequels
- Series books
- Texts utilizing a variety of forms (letters, diaries, journal entries)
- Photo essays and news articles of human interest

Text Structure

- Informational books that present ideas in chronological sequence (biography, history)
- Factual texts that include temporal description, sequence, comparison and contrast, problem and solution, cause and effect
- Factual texts with clearly defined categories and subcategories, defined by sections and headings
- Traditional literature with underlying characteristic motifs (for example, "three")
- Some texts with complex structures, such as flashback and story within story
- Series of short stories with plots that intertwine
- Narrative structure in illustrated short stories (picture books) and longer texts that include chapters with multiple episodes related to a single plot

Content

- Topics that go well beyond listeners' personal experiences
- Content requiring knowledge of cultural diversity
- Many texts on scientific and technical topics (the environment, ecology, space, technology, animals–current and historic)
- Many texts centering on typical age-related problems (friendship, teasing, self-esteem)
- Historical settings that require content knowledge (history)
- Fiction texts that require knowledge of content (geography, customs)

Themes and Ideas

- Themes important to fourth graders (friendship, teasing, popularity, sports, differences, self-esteem, growing up, family problems)
- Some mature issues that require experience to interpret
- Themes reflecting human problems and reveal social issues (war, hardship, poverty, racism, environment, making a difference)
- Multiple themes and ideas that are not explicitly stated
- Complex themes on which there are different perspectives (no right answers)

Interactive Read-Aloud and Literature Discussion

Selecting Texts — Characteristics of Texts for Reading Aloud and Discussion

Language and Literary Features

- Complex plots with one or more subplots
- Multiple characters revealed by what they say, think, and do and what others say/think about them
- Characters that are complex and change over time
- Long stretches of descriptive language important to understanding setting and characters
- Use of symbolism
- A few literary devices (for example, story within a story)
- Complex narratives that are highly literary
- Some complex fantasy elements
- Settings distant in time and space from students' experience

Sentence Complexity

- Vocabulary and literary uses of language that increase sentence complexity

Vocabulary

- Many new complex words that must be derived from context and may require teacher explanation
- Many new specialized words related to scientific or technical content
- Many words with connotative meanings essential to understanding the text
- Many words used figuratively (metaphor, simile, idiom)
- Some words used in regional or historical dialects
- Some words from languages other than English

Illustrations

- Complex graphics requiring study (legends, maps, drawings with labels, cutaways)
- Complicated illustrations with many details, some needing description while the teacher is reading
- Chapter books with few or no illustrations, requiring readers to imagine content
- Picture books with illustrations that reflect the theme and writer's tone and make it a coherent work of art
- Picture books with illustrations that contribute to mood (feeling derived from text and illustrations)
- Some illustrations with symbolic characteristics requiring interpretation

Book and Print Features

- Short, illustrated fiction and nonfiction texts
- Long informational texts that may be used by selecting a section only
- Long fiction texts requiring several days to complete
- Readers' tools (table of contents, headings and subheadings, index, glossary)

Interactive Read-Aloud and Literature Discussion

Selecting Goals Behaviors and Understandings to Notice, Teach, and Support

Thinking *within* the Text

- Add new vocabulary words to known words and use them in discussion and in writing
- Recognize and actively work to learn the meaning of new vocabulary words, including complex, specialized, and technical words
- Recognize subtle meaning for words used in context
- Recognize new meanings for known words by using context, including words used figuratively
- Follow and remember multiple events in a story, often involving the stories of multiple characters, to understand the plot
- Understand how one event builds on another throughout the text
- Access the important information in a text
- Remember important information from the text over several days of reading
- Access prior information summarized from the text while hearing more
- Summarize orally or in writing a text, including appropriate information
- Notice and understand the problem of a story and how it is solved
- Notice and remember attributes and actions that will help in understanding character development
- Notice and remember details of the setting and discuss the impact of the setting on characters and problem
- Identify and discuss the problem, the events of the story, and the problem resolution
- Self-monitor understanding and ask questions when meaning is lost
- Notice and remember significant information from illustrations or graphics
- Notice and respond to stress and tone of voice while listening and afterward

Thinking *beyond* the Text

- Make connections to prior knowledge and use it to identify and incorporate new knowledge
- Apply background knowledge gained from experience, content study, and wide reading
- Make connections between the lives and motivations of characters and their own lives, even if the setting is a fantasy world or in the past
- Make predictions based on information in the text as to what will happen, what characters are likely to do, and how it will end
- Infer characters' feelings and motivations from description, what they do or say, and what others think about them
- Hypothesize underlying motivations of characters that are not stated
- Interpret the mood of the text, using illustrations in combination with the writer's tone
- Interpret graphics and integrate information with the text
- Hypothesize the significance of the setting in influencing characters decisions' and attitudes (fiction, biography)
- Support thinking beyond the text with specific evidence based on personal experience or knowledge or evidence from the text
- Make connections to other texts by topic, major ideas, authors' styles, and genres
- Ask questions about concepts
- Notice new information and ideas and revise ideas in response to it
- Hypothesize the significance of events in a story
- Maintain memory of many different texts and use them as resources for making connections.
- Notice and discuss the information provided in section titles, headings, and subheadings to predict information provided in a text
- Form implicit questions and search for answers in the text while listening and during discussion
- Identify and discuss cultural and historical perspectives that are in conflict in the text or that are different from their own perspective
- Derive and interpret the writer's underlying messages (themes)

Interactive Read-Aloud and Literature Discussion

Selecting Goals — Behaviors and Understandings to Notice, Teach, and Support

Thinking *about* the Text

- Notice and understand text structure including description, temporal sequence, comparison and contrast, cause and effect, and problem and solution
- Evaluate the quality or authenticity of the text, including the writer's qualifications
- Make note of interesting new words and intentionally remember them to use in oral discussion or writing
- Critically examine the writer's word choice
- Notice the writer's use of graphics and effective ways of placing them in the text
- Recognize, understand, and discuss some obvious symbolism
- Recognize the genre of the text and use it to form expectations
- Analyze an author's characteristic way of writing–characters, plot, style
- Analyze the way an author creates authentic characters
- Recognize and discuss the differences between narrative and other structures
- Understand and discuss how layout contributes to the meaning and effectiveness of both fiction and nonfiction texts
- Recognize and discuss the artistic aspects of a text, including how illustrations and narrative form a cohesive whole
- Notice how the writer has organized an informational text (categories and subcategories, sequence, and others)
- Recognize the narrator of the text and discuss how the choice of first or third person point of view contributes to the effectiveness of the writing
- Provide specific examples and evidence to support statements about the quality, accuracy, or craft of the text
- Recognize the genre of the text and use it to form expectations of the text
- Notice and appreciate the author's use of figurative and literary language to evoke imagery, feeling, and mood
- Think critically about informational texts in terms of quality of writing, accuracy, and the logic of conclusions
- Recognize and discuss aspects of narrative structure (beginning, series of events, high point of the story, ending)
- Notice how the writer reveals the underlying messages or the theme of a text (through a character, through plot and events)
- Use specific vocabulary to talk about texts: *author, illustrator, cover, wordless picture book, picture book, character, problem, events, series book, dedication, endpapers, book jacket, title page, chapters, resolution, main character, setting, fiction, nonfiction, poetry, author's note, illustrator's note, double-page spread,* names of fiction genres (for example, *historical fiction, legend*), *character development, point of view, theme*

Interactive Read-Aloud and Literature Discussion

Selecting Texts **Characteristics of Texts for Reading Aloud and Discussion**

Genres/Forms

Genres

- Poems
- Traditional literature (humorous twists, legends, tall tales, cultural variants of tales)
- Fantasy
- Realistic fiction
- Science fiction
- Historical fiction
- Informational texts
- Biographies, autobiographies, and memoir on a variety of subjects
- Memoir
- Autobiography
- Special types of genres (mystery, adventure, survival)
- Hybrid texts (multiple genres within one text)

Forms

- Short stories
- Informational picture books
- Picture story books
- Chapter books, some with sequels
- Series books
- Texts utilizing forms (letters, diaries, journal entries)
- Photo essays and news articles of human interest

Text Structure

- Informational books that present ideas in chronological sequence (biography, memoir, history)
- Factual texts that include description, temporal sequence, and compare and contrast
- Factual texts that include temporal description, sequence, comparison and contrast, problem and solution, cause and effect–often combined in complex ways
- Factual texts with clearly defined categories and subcategories, defined by sections and headings
- Traditional literature with underlying characteristic motifs
- Unusual text organizations, such as flashbacks
- Series of short stories with plots that intertwine
- Narrative structure in illustrated short stories (picture books) and longer texts that include chapters with multiple episodes related to a single plot
- Complex plots with many multiple story lines

Content

- Content requiring knowledge of cultural diversity
- Content requiring the reader to take on diverse perspectives (race, language, culture)
- Many texts on scientific and technical topics (the environment, technology)
- Fiction texts that require knowledge of content (geography, customs)
- Historical settings that require content knowledge (events, attitudes, circumstances of the times)
- Essential content supported or provided by illustrations in most informational texts, requiring reader attention and interpretation
- Heavy content load in many texts, fiction and nonfiction, requiring extended discussion
- Critical thinking required to judge the authenticity of informational texts, historical fiction, and biography

Themes and Ideas

- Themes that appeal to preadolescents (growing up, responsibility, moving to a new school, social life, individuality, sports, competition)
- Wide range of challenging themes that build social awareness and reveal insights into the human condition (war, poverty, racism, historical injustices)
- Many texts presenting mature societal issues, especially those important to preadolescents and that require background of experience to understand (crime, tragedy, family problems, abuse, drugs)
- Multiple themes and ideas that are not explicitly stated
- Complex themes on which there are different perspectives (no right answers)
- Many texts presenting multiple themes that may be understood in many layers

Interactive Read-Aloud and Literature Discussion

Selecting Texts Characteristics of Texts for Reading Aloud and Discussion

Language and Literary Features

- Complex plots with one or more subplots
- Multiple characters revealed by what they say, think, and do and what others say/think about them
- Characters that are complex (neither good nor bad) and develop over time
- Long stretches of descriptive language important to understanding setting and characters
- Use of symbolism
- Full range of literary devices (for example, flashback, story within a story, change of narrator, present and past tense combination)
- Heroic or larger-than-life characters in fantasy who represent symbolic struggle of good or evil
- Fantasy requiring knowledge of traditional motifs (the quest, the numbers three and seven, the trickster)
- Settings distant in time and space from students' experience

Sentence Complexity

- Vocabulary and literary uses of language that increase sentence complexity

Vocabulary

- Many new complex words that must be derived from context and may require teacher explanation
- Many specialized words requiring background knowledge or teacher explanation
- Many words with connotative meanings essential to understanding the text
- Many words used figuratively (metaphor, simile, idiom)
- Some words used in regional or historical dialects
- Some words from languages other than English
- Some archaic words
- Words with multiple meanings within the same text–often signaling subtle meanings
- Some author-created words to fit a particular setting

Illustrations

- Full range of complex graphics that may require attention or discussion during or after reading (legends, maps, drawings with labels, cutaways)
- Complicated illustrations with many details, some needing description while the teacher is reading
- Chapter books with few or no illustrations, requiring readers to imagine content
- Picture books with illustrations that reflect the theme and writer's tone and make it a coherent work of art
- Picture books with illustrations that contribute to mood (feeling derived from text and illustrations)
- Some illustrations with symbolic characteristics requiring interpretation

Book and Print Features

- Short, illustrated fiction and nonfiction texts
- Long informational texts that may be used by selecting a section only
- Long fiction texts requiring several days to complete
- Readers' tools (table of contents, headings and subheadings, index, glossary)

Interactive Read-Aloud and Literature Discussion

Selecting Goals Behaviors and Understandings to Notice, Teach, and Support

Thinking *within* the Text

- Add new vocabulary words to known words and use them in discussion and in writing
- Recognize and actively work to learn the meaning of new vocabulary words, including complex, specialized, and technical words
- Recognize subtle meaning for words used in context
- Recognize new meanings for known words by using context, including words used figuratively
- Follow complex plots, tracking multiple events and gathering information about many characters and their traits and relationships
- Access information and develop new concepts and ideas from reading
- Gather information from factual texts and use strategies for remembering it
- Remember where to find information in more complex texts so opinions and theories can be checked through revisiting
- Keep mental summaries of text while listening (often over several days)
- Gather and understand details while listening to the text that will help in understanding characters, setting, and problem
- Identify and discuss the problem, the events of the story, and the problem resolution
- Self-monitor understanding and ask questions when meaning is lost
- Notice and remember significant information from illustrations or graphics
- Notice and respond to stress and tone of voice while listening and afterward

Thinking *beyond* the Text

- Make connections between the lives and motivations of characters and their own lives, even if the setting is a fantasy world or in the past
- Infer characters' feelings and motivations from description, what they do or say, and what others think about them
- Make predictions based on information in the text as to what will happen, what characters are likely to do, and how it will end
- Interpret graphics and integrate information with the text
- Recognize, understand, and discuss symbolism
- Hypothesize the influence of setting and events on characters' decisions (fiction, biography or autobiography)
- Support thinking beyond the text with specific evidence based on personal experience or knowledge or evidence from the text
- Make connections to other texts by topic, major ideas, authors' styles, and genres
- Notice new information and ideas and revise ideas in response to it
- Change opinions or understandings based on new information or insights gained from fiction or nonfiction texts
- Hypothesize the significance of events in a story
- Maintain memory of many different texts and use them as resources for making connections.
- Make connections using sensory imagery in fiction and poetry
- Notice and discuss the information provided in section titles, headings, and subheadings to predict information provided in a text
- Form implicit questions and search for answers in the text while listening and during discussion
- Identify and discuss cultural and historical perspectives that are in conflict in the text or that are different from their own perspective
- Compare perspectives with other readers and build on the ideas of others in discussion
- Derive and interpret the writer's underlying messages (themes)

Interactive Read-Aloud and Literature Discussion

Selecting Goals — Behaviors and Understandings to Notice, Teach, and Support

Thinking *about* the Text

- Notice and understand when the writer uses description, temporal sequence, comparison and contrast, cause and effect, and problem and solution
- Evaluate the quality or authenticity of the text, including the writer's qualifications
- Make note of interesting new words and intentionally remember them to use in oral discussion or writing
- Understand the importance of word choice from the writer's point of view; consider alternative word choices
- Notice how the writer has organized an informational text (categories and subcategories, sequence, and others)
- Recognize that a fiction text is told from the perspective of one or more characters and hypothesize the writer's rationale for choosing this perspective
- Recognize the writer's choice of first, second, or third person and discuss and hypothesize the reasons for this decision
- Provide specific examples and evidence to support statements about the quality, accuracy, or craft of the text
- Recognize the genre of the text and use it to form expectations of the text
- Notice the writer's use of language (or the illustrator's use of art) to evoke sensory images, feeling, and mood
- Think critically about informational texts in terms of quality of writing, accuracy, and the logic of conclusions
- Think critically about realistic fiction texts in terms of authenticity of characters, accurate portrayal of current issues, appropriate voice and tone
- Think critically about historical fiction in terms of authentic portrayal of character within the setting and accurate reflection of historical events
- Recognize and discuss aspects of narrative structure (beginning, series of events, high point of the story, ending)
- Notice how the writer reveals the underlying messages or the theme of a text (through a character, through plot and events)
- Understand and discuss how layout contributes to the meaning and effectiveness of both fiction and nonfiction texts
- Recognize and discuss the artistic aspects of a text, including how illustrations and narrative form a cohesive whole
- Use specific vocabulary to talk about texts: *author, illustrator, cover, wordless picture book, picture book, character, problem, events, series book, dedication, endpapers, book jacket, title page, chapters, resolution, main character, setting, fiction, nonfiction, poetry, author's note, illustrator's note, double-page spread,* names of fiction genres (for example, *historical fiction, legend*), *character development, point of view, theme, supporting characters, plot*

Interactive Read-Aloud and Literature Discussion

Selecting Texts Characteristics of Texts for Reading Aloud and Discussion

Genres/Forms

Genres

- Poems
- Traditional literature (legends, myths, cultural variants of tales)
- Fantasy
- Realistic fiction
- Science fiction
- Historical fiction
- Informational texts
- Biographies on well-known and lesser-known or controversial subjects
- Memoir
- Autobiography
- Special types of genres (mystery, adventure, survival, satire)
- Hybrid texts (multiple genres within one text)

Forms

- Short stories
- Informational picture books
- Picture story books
- Chapter books, some with sequels
- Series books
- Texts utilizing forms (letters, diaries, journal entries)
- Photo essays and news articles of human interest

Text Structure

- Informational books that present ideas in chronological sequence (biography, memoir, history)
- Factual texts that include description, temporal sequence, and compare and contrast
- Factual texts that include temporal description, sequence, comparison and contrast, problem and solution, cause and effect–often combined in complex ways
- Factual texts with clearly defined categories and subcategories, defined by sections and headings
- Texts with unusual structures for presenting genre (flashbacks, change of narrator, long gaps in time)
- Many texts with the complex structure of adult-level reading (multiple story lines and subplots)
- Some collections of short stories that have interrelated themes or build a single plot across separate stories
- Texts with organizational structures typical of the content area disciplines

Content

- Content requiring knowledge of cultural diversity
- Content requiring the reader to take on diverse perspectives (race, language, culture)
- Many texts on scientific and technical topics (the environment, technology)
- Fiction texts that require knowledge of content (geography, customs)
- Many fiction and nonfiction texts requiring knowledge of history
- Essential content supported or provided by illustrations in most informational texts, requiring reader attention and interpretation
- Heavy content load in many texts, fiction and nonfiction, requiring extended discussion
- Critical thinking required to judge the authenticity of informational texts, historical fiction, and biography

Themes and Ideas

- Themes that appeal to preadolescents (popularity, dating, growing up, family problems, sports, celebrities, music, competition)
- Wide range of challenging themes that build social awareness and reveal insights into the human condition (war, poverty, racism, historical injustices)
- Many texts presenting mature societal issues, especially those important to preadolescents and that require background of experience to understand (crime, tragedy, family problems, abuse, drugs)
- Multiple themes and ideas that are not explicitly stated
- Complex themes on which there are different perspectives (no right answers)
- Many texts presenting multiple themes that may be understood in many layers

Interactive Read-Aloud and Literature Discussion

Selecting Texts Characteristics of Texts for Reading Aloud and Discussion

Language and Literary Features

- Complex plots with one or more subplots
- Multiple characters revealed by what they say, think, and do and what others say/think about them
- Characters that are complex (neither good nor bad) and develop over time
- Long stretches of descriptive language important to understanding setting and characters
- Language that often violates conventional grammar to provide authentic dialogue or achieve the writer's voice
- Complex and subtle use of symbolism
- Full range of literary devices (for example, flashback, story within a story, change of narrator, present and past tense combination)
- Heroic or larger-than-life characters in fantasy who represent symbolic struggle of good or evil
- Fantasy requiring knowledge of traditional motifs (the quest, the numbers three and seven, the trickster)
- Settings distant in time and space from students' experience

Sentence Complexity

- Vocabulary and literary uses of language that increase sentence complexity

Vocabulary

- Many specialized words requiring background knowledge or teacher explanation
- Many words with connotative meanings essential to understanding the text
- Many words used figuratively (metaphor, simile, idiom)
- Some words used in regional or historical dialects
- Some words from languages other than English
- Some archaic words
- Words with multiple meanings within the same text–often signaling subtle meanings
- Some author-created words to fit a particular setting

Illustrations

- Full range of complex graphics that may require attention or discussion during or after reading (legends, maps, drawings with labels, cutaways)
- Illustrations in picture books that are an integral part of comprehending the text as a work of art
- Picture books with illustrations that reflect the theme and writer's tone and make it a coherent work of art
- Picture books with illustrations that contribute to mood (feeling derived from text and illustrations)
- Some illustrations with symbolic characteristics requiring interpretation
- Some symbolic decoration on margins or at chapter headings that contributes to interpretation

Book and Print Features

- Short, illustrated fiction and nonfiction texts
- Long informational texts that may be used by selecting a section only
- Long fiction texts requiring several days to complete
- Readers' tools (table of contents, headings and subheadings, index, glossary, pronunciation guide, references)
- Texts with unusual print layout that contributes to the meaning and requires discussion and teacher explanation

Interactive Read-Aloud and Literature Discussion

Selecting Goals **Behaviors and Understandings to Notice, Teach, and Support**

Thinking *within* the Text

- Recognize subtle meaning for words used in context
- Keep flexible definitions of complex words in order to derive new meanings for them or understand figurative or connotative use
- Consistently use strategies for noticing new vocabulary words and adding them to speaking, listening, and writing vocabularies
- Follow complex plots, tracking multiple events and gathering information about many characters and their traits and relationships
- Gather information from factual texts and use strategies for remembering it
- Remember where to find information in more complex texts so opinions and theories can be checked through revisiting
- Remember information in summary form so that it can be used in discussion with others and in writing
- Identify and discuss the problem, the events of the story, and the problem resolution
- Notice and remember significant attributes for multiple characters (what characters do, say or think, and what the writer and other characters say about them)
- Self-monitor understanding and ask questions when meaning is lost
- Notice and remember significant information from illustrations or graphics
- Notice and respond to stress and tone of voice while listening and afterward
- Listen and engage in discussion to acquire understanding of the life decisions of subjects of biography

Thinking *beyond* the Text

- Make connections to their own lives and contemporary issues and problems across all genres, including historical fiction and high fantasy
- Hypothesize reasons for character development
- Understand and discuss main and supporting characters and their development using information from description; what characters say, think, and do; and what other characters say and think about them
- Recognize, understand, and discuss symbolism
- Hypothesize and discuss the significance of the setting in character development and plot resolution
- Support thinking beyond the text with specific evidence based on personal experience or knowledge or evidence from the text
- Make connections to other texts by topic, major ideas, authors' styles, and genres
- Change opinions or understandings based on new information or insights gained from fiction or nonfiction texts
- Understand the setting and symbolism in high fantasy and the implications for morality and politics
- Maintain memory of many different texts and use them as resources for making connections
- Make connections using sensory imagery in fiction and poetry
- Make connections among informational texts and historical fiction and content area study, using information from one setting to assist comprehending in the other
- Notice and discuss the information provided in section titles, headings, and subheadings to predict information provided in a text
- Consistently make predictions before, during, and after reading using evidence from the text to support thinking
- Form implicit questions and search for answers in the text while listening and during discussion
- Identify and discuss cultural and historical perspectives that are in conflict in the text or that are different from their own perspective
- Compare perspectives with other readers and build on the ideas of others in discussion
- Think deeply about social issues as revealed in realistic and historical fiction and discuss ideas with others
- Understand subtexts where the author is saying one thing but meaning another

Interactive Read-Aloud and Literature Discussion

Selecting Goals **Behaviors and Understandings to Notice, Teach, and Support**

Thinking *about* the Text

- Notice and understand when the writer uses description, temporal sequence, comparison and contrast, cause and effect, and problem and solution
- Evaluate the quality or authenticity of the text, including the writer's qualifications and background knowledge
- Notice and provide examples of the ways writers select words to convey precise meaning
- Understand and discuss how layout contributes to the meaning and effectiveness of both fiction and nonfiction texts
- Recognize and discuss the artistic aspects of a text, including how illustrations and narrative form a cohesive whole
- Notice how the writer has organized an informational text (categories and subcategories, sequence, and others) and evaluate the quality or coherence of the organization
- Discuss alternative ways of organizing expository text and apply to own writing
- Recognize the writer's choice of first, second, or third person and discuss and hypothesize the reasons for this decision
- Provide specific examples and evidence to support statements about the quality, accuracy, or craft of the text
- Recognize the genre of the text and use it to form expectations of the text
- Recognize bias in fiction and nonfiction texts
- Recognize the writer's use of language to convey irony or to evoke sensory images, feelings, or mood
- Think critically about informational texts in terms of quality of writing, accuracy, and the logic of conclusions
- Think critically about realistic fiction texts in terms of authenticity of characters, accurate portrayal of current issues, appropriate voice and tone
- Think critically about historical fiction in terms of authentic portrayal of character within the setting and accurate reflection of historical events
- Recognize and discuss aspects of narrative structure (beginning, series of events, high point of the story, ending)
- Notice how the writer reveals the underlying messages or the theme of a text (through a character, through plot and events)
- Appreciate poetic and literary texts in terms of language, sentence or phrase construction, and organization of the text
- Use specific vocabulary to talk about texts: *author, illustrator, cover, wordless picture book, picture book, character, problem, events, series book, dedication, endpapers, book jacket, title page, chapters, resolution, main character, setting, fiction, nonfiction, poetry, author's note, illustrator's note, double-page spread,* names of fiction genres (for example, *historical fiction, legend*), *character development, point of view, theme, supporting characters, plot, conflict*

Interactive Read-Aloud and Literature Discussion

Selecting Texts **Characteristics of Texts for Reading Aloud and Discussion**

Genres/Forms

Genres

- Poems
- Traditional literature (legends, myths, cultural variants of tales)
- Fantasy
- Realistic fiction
- Science fiction
- Historical fiction
- Informational texts
- Biographies on well-known and lesser-known or controversial subjects
- Memoir
- Autobiography
- Special types of genres (mystery, adventure, survival, satire)
- Hybrid texts (multiple genres within one text)
- Editorials or opinion pieces (for critique)

Forms

- Short stories
- Informational picture books
- Picture story books
- Chapter books, some with sequels
- Series books
- Texts utilizing forms (letters, diaries, journal entries)
- Photo essays and news articles of human interest

Text Structure

- Informational books that present ideas in chronological sequence (biography, memoir, history)
- Factual texts that include temporal description, sequence, comparison and contrast, problem and solution, cause and effect–often combined in complex ways
- Factual texts with clearly defined categories and subcategories, defined by sections and headings
- Texts with unusual structures for presenting genre (flashbacks, change of narrator, long gaps in time)
- Many texts with the complex structure of adult-level reading (multiple story lines and subplots)
- Some collections of short stories that have interrelated themes or build a single plot across separate stories
- Texts with organizational structures typical of the content area disciplines

Content

- Vicarious experiences of people in settings far distant from today's culture, requiring content knowledge to understand cultures and perspectives
- Many texts on scientific and technical topics (the environment, technology)
- Fiction texts that require knowledge of content (geography, customs)
- Many fiction and nonfiction texts requiring knowledge of history
- Heavy content load in many texts, fiction and nonfiction, requiring extended discussion
- Critical thinking required to judge the authenticity of informational texts, historical fiction, and biography
- Great variety of content areas with writing typical of the discipline

Themes and Ideas

- Themes of significance to adolescents (popularity, dating, growing up, rebellion, cliques and gangs, music, sports, competition)
- Wide range of challenging themes that build social awareness and reveal insights into the human condition (war, poverty, racism, historical injustices)
- Many texts presenting mature societal issues, especially those important to preadolescents and that require background of experience to understand (crime, tragedy, family problems, abuse, drugs)
- Multiple themes and ideas that are not explicitly stated and may be understood in many layers
- Complex themes on which there are different perspectives (no right answers)
- Themes in fantasy involving the quest of the hero and symbolic struggle between good and evil
- Political themes in historical or realistic fiction as well as informational texts that shed light on today's issues

Interactive Read-Aloud and Literature Discussion

Selecting Texts Characteristics of Texts for Reading Aloud and Discussion

Language and Literary Features

- Complex plots with one or more subplots
- Multiple characters revealed by what they say, think, and do and what others say/think about them
- Characters that are complex (neither good nor bad) and develop over time
- Long stretches of descriptive language important to understanding setting and characters
- Language that often violates conventional grammar to provide authentic dialogue or achieve the writer's voice
- Archaic language to create mood or help in understanding characters
- Complex and subtle use of symbolism
- Full range of literary devices (for example, flashback, story within a story, change of narrator, present and past tense combination, satire, irony)
- Heroic or larger-than-life characters in fantasy who represent symbolic struggle of good or evil
- Fantasy requiring knowledge of traditional motifs (the quest, the numbers three and seven, the trickster)
- Settings distant in time and space from students' experience

Sentence Complexity

- Highly complex sentences of a wide variety (related to high-level vocabulary and literary uses of language)

Vocabulary

- Many new words that listeners or readers must derive from context or that the teacher will need to explain (figurative language, unusual connotations)
- Some highly specialized vocabulary words requiring background knowledge or teacher explanation
- Many words with connotative meanings essential to understanding the text
- Many words used figuratively (metaphor, simile, idiom)
- Some words used in regional or historical dialects (archaic words)
- Some words from languages other than English
- Words with multiple meanings within the same text–often signaling subtle meanings
- Some author-created words to fit a particular setting

Illustrations

- Full range of complex graphics that may require attention or discussion during or after reading (legends, maps, drawings with labels, cutaways)
- Illustrations in picture books that are an integral part of comprehending the text as a work of art
- Picture books with illustrations that reflect the theme and writer's tone and make it a coherent work of art
- Picture books with illustrations that contribute to mood (feeling derived from text and illustrations)
- Some illustrations with symbolic characteristics requiring interpretation
- Some symbolic decoration on margins or at chapter headings that contributes to interpretation

Book and Print Features

- Short, illustrated fiction and nonfiction texts
- Long informational texts that may be used by selecting a section only
- Long fiction texts requiring several days to complete
- Readers' tools (table of contents, headings and subheadings, index, glossary, pronunciation guide, references)
- Texts with unusual print layout that contributes to the meaning and requires discussion and teacher explanation

Interactive Read-Aloud and Literature Discussion

Selecting Goals Behaviors and Understandings to Notice, Teach, and Support

Thinking *within* the Text

- Recognize subtle meaning for words used in context
- Keep flexible definitions of complex words in order to derive new meanings for them or understand figurative or connotative use
- Consistently use strategies for noticing new vocabulary words and adding them to speaking, listening, and writing vocabularies
- Question the meaning of words in context, considering alternatives
- Use listening to expand knowledge of words and consciously build specialized vocabulary related to content areas
- Follow complex plots, tracking multiple events and gathering information about many characters and their traits and relationships
- Gather information from factual texts and use strategies for remembering it
- Remember where to find information in more complex texts so opinions and theories can be checked through revisiting
- Remember information in summary form so that it can be used in discussion with others and in writing
- Identify and discuss the problem, the events of the story, and the problem resolution
- Notice and remember significant attributes for multiple characters (what characters do, say or think, and what the writer and other characters say about them)
- Self-monitor understanding and ask questions when meaning is lost
- Notice and remember significant information from illustrations or graphics
- Notice and respond to stress and tone of voice while listening and afterward
- Listen and engage in discussion to acquire understanding of the life decisions of subjects of biography

Thinking *beyond* the Text

- Make predictions on an ongoing basis (progression of the plot, characteristics of the setting, actions of characters)
- Infer characters' motivations and feelings, understanding inner conflict
- Understand the deeper meanings of poetry and prose texts (symbolism, allusion, irony)
- Hypothesize and discuss the significance of the setting in character development and plot resolution
- Support thinking beyond the text with specific evidence based on personal experience or knowledge or evidence from the text
- Change opinions or understandings based on new information or insights gained from fiction or nonfiction texts
- Revise understandings and/or change opinions based on new information acquired through listening, reading, or discussion
- Understand the setting and symbolism in high fantasy and the implications for morality and politics
- Make connections among informational texts and historical fiction and content area study, using information from one setting to assist comprehending in the other
- Consistently make predictions before, during, and after reading using evidence from the text to support thinking
- Form implicit questions and search for answers in the text while listening and during discussion
- Think deeply about social issues as revealed in realistic and historical fiction and discuss ideas with others
- Actively see diverse perspectives and search for understanding of other cultures while listening, writing, and discussing texts
- Understand subtexts where the author is saying one thing but meaning another
- Draw conclusions from dialogue, including language with double meaning (satire)
- Infer the significance of satirical texts (identify what is being satirized and discuss its significance)
- Recognize underlying political messages in fiction and nonfiction texts
- Identify the sources of conflict in fiction texts and draw implications for the issues of today

Interactive Read-Aloud and Literature Discussion

Selecting Goals Behaviors and Understandings to Notice, Teach, and Support

Thinking *about* the Text

- Notice and understand when the writer uses description, temporal sequence, comparison and contrast, cause and effect, and problem and solution
- Evaluate the quality or authenticity of the text, including the writer's qualifications and background knowledge
- Notice and provide examples of the ways writers select words to convey precise meaning
- Understand and discuss how layout contributes to the meaning and effectiveness of both fiction and nonfiction texts
- Recognize and discuss the artistic aspects of a text, including how illustrations and narrative form a cohesive whole
- Notice how the writer has organized an informational text (categories and subcategories, sequence, and others) and evaluate the quality or coherence of the organization
- Discuss alternative ways of organizing expository text and apply to own writing
- Recognize the writer's choice of first, second, or third person and discuss and hypothesize the reasons for this decision
- Provide specific examples and evidence to support statements about the quality, accuracy, or craft of the text
- Recognize the genre of the text and use it to form expectations of the text
- Analyze texts to determine genre and literary devices the writer has used (irony, figurative language, symbolism)
- Recognize bias in fiction or nonfiction texts and hypothesize the writer's point of view
- Think critically about informational texts in terms of quality of writing, accuracy, and the logic of conclusions
- Think critically about realistic fiction texts in terms of authenticity of characters, accurate portrayal of current issues, appropriate voice and tone
- Think critically about historical fiction in terms of authentic portrayal of character within the setting and accurate reflection of historical events
- Notice how the writer reveals the underlying messages or the theme of a text (through a character, through plot and events)
- Appreciate poetic and literary texts in terms of language, sentence or phrase construction, and organization of the text
- Use specific vocabulary to talk about texts: *author, illustrator, cover, wordless picture book, picture book, character, problem, events, series book, dedication, endpapers, book jacket, title page, chapters, resolution, main character, setting, fiction, nonfiction, poetry, author's note, illustrator's note, double-page spread,* names of fiction genres (for example, *historical fiction, legend*), *character development, point of view, theme, supporting characters, plot, conflict*

Shared and Performance Reading

Shared and Performance Reading

Introduction to Shared and Performance Reading

Shared reading and performance reading have many of the same goals as interactive read-aloud, but they go beyond active listening and discussion: Students actually participate in the reading in some way. We define shared reading and performance reading as instructional contexts that involve reading aloud for the pleasure of oneself and others. All forms of performed reading involve:

- Processing print in continuous text.
- Working in a group (usually).
- Using the voice to interpret the meaning of a text.
- Often reading in unison with others, although there may be parts or solos.
- Opportunities to learn more about the reading process.

In *Teaching for Comprehending and Fluency: Thinking, Talking, and Writing About Reading, K–8* (Fountas and Pinnell 2006), we described three contexts for shared and performance reading.

1. ***Shared reading*** usually refers to students' reading from a common enlarged text, either a large-print book, a chart, or a projected text. Individuals may have their own copies. The teacher leads the group, pointing to words or phrases. Reading is usually in unison, although there are adaptations, such as groups alternating lines or individuals reading some lines.

2. ***Choral reading*** usually refers to any group of people reading from a common text, which may be printed on a chart, projected on a screen, or provided as individual copies. The text is usually longer and/or more complex than one used for shared reading. The emphasis is on interpreting the text with the voice. Some reading is in unison by the whole group or subgroups, and there may be solos or duets.

3. ***Readers' theater*** usually refers to the enactment of a text in which readers assume individual or group roles, although there may be a chorus. Readers' theater is similar to traditional play production, but the text is generally not memorized and props are rarely used. The emphasis is on vocal interpretation. Usually individuals read parts although groups may read some roles. Readers' theater scripts are usually constructed from all kinds of texts, not from original plays.

In selecting and using books and other written texts for shared and performance reading, a teacher needs to consider some of the same kinds of factors as for guided and independent reading; after all, students do need to be able to read and understand them. However, since shared and performance reading provides a high level of support and students will be reading texts many times, it is not necessary to use the A–Z levels (see the Guided Reading continuum in this book, pages 234–343). Instead, features like interesting language, rhyme and rhythm, language play, poetic language, appeal to students, and other aspects of texts make them ideal for performance.

Characteristics of Texts

In thinking about texts for shared and performance reading, we again consider the ten text factors. As with interactive read-aloud, the vocabulary in the text must be understandable to listeners, but word solving is a relatively minor consideration. Students can easily pronounce and appreciate words like *fantabulous* or *humongous* in humorous poems or words like *somber* or *ponderous* from readers' theater once they are taught the meaning of the words. Descriptions of all ten text characteristics, in terms of shared and performance reading, follow.

1. *Genre.* We have listed a variety of types of texts that are appropriate at each grade level. We include poetry, songs, and chants. For the most part, you will want to use the full range of genres at every grade level, but be selective about the particular examples you choose. Both fiction and nonfiction texts can be used for shared and performance reading. Often, a narrative text is turned into a play or poetic text to create readers' theater scripts.

2. *Text Structure.* The structure of a text refers to the way it is organized. Fiction texts are generally organized in a *narrative* structure, with a problem and a sequence of events that lead to the resolution of the problem. Younger children generally read short texts that have humor or rhyme. Traditional tales are an excellent resource. When longer texts are turned into plays or readers' theater scripts, they are generally shortened: students present a particular moment in time, perform the essence of the plot, or show the main character's feelings or point of view. Nonfiction texts may also be narrative; biographies, for example, are relatively easy to turn into readers' theater scripts. But most informational texts are organized categorically by subtopic with underlying structures such as description; temporal sequence; comparison and contrast; cause and effect; and problem and solution. Often these structures are used in combination. Through shared or performance reading, your students can highlight some of the underlying structures and they will enjoy turning some content area learning (for example, a text on environmental pollution or a period of history) into readers' theater.

3. *Content.* The subject matter of the text should be accessible and interesting to listeners. Content is helpful to listeners when they already have some prior knowledge to bring to understanding new information. Through shared and performance reading, particularly of biography, students can think deeply about many different topics.

4. *Themes and Ideas.* The major ideas of the material chosen for shared and performance reading should be appropriate for all students' age and experience. Students can extend their understanding of the themes and ideas as they discuss how texts should be read or performed.

5. *Language and Literary Features.* The way the writer uses language creates the literary quality of a text. It is important to select texts that students can understand in terms of language and literary features. Shared reading and performance reading provide an ideal setting in which to "try on" different interpretations of a text through changes in the voice.

6. *Sentence Complexity.* The structure of the sentences—their length and the number of embedded phrases and clauses—is another key factor. Through the primary and elementary grades, students can generally understand sentences that are more complex than those they can read. Practicing sentences for performance helps students internalize various sentence structures.

7. *Vocabulary.* Vocabulary refers to the words that an individual knows and understands in both oral and written language. Working with a text in shared or performance reading, students have the opportunity to meet new words many times and thus expand their vocabularies. It is important that students understand the text used in shared and performance reading; they will not enjoy the activity if they do not understand the words.

8. *Words.* The teacher will be offering high support for word solving, and students will be reading selections several times, so words are not a major factor in text selection. Texts with words that students understand and can pronounce with your help should be chosen. Shared and performance reading offers an excellent context within which students can learn more about how words work. As repeated readings make a text familiar, students will gradually add to the core of high-frequency words they know. They will also begin to notice beginnings, endings, and other parts of words and make connections between words.

9. *Illustrations.* Many texts used as a basis for shared and performance reading are full of illustrations that help students interpret text meaning. Along with the teacher support inherent in shared and performance reading, illustrations enable young children to read higher-level big books together. For older students, too, performance reading may be based on picture books (fiction and nonfiction) that have illustrations contributing to the mood. Sometimes, students may perform their reading in conjunction with a slide show of some important illustrations. For some texts, however, illustrations may not be a factor. For example, it would be unusual for shared and performance reading to include graphics such as those in informational texts.

10. *Book and Print Features.* When younger students are engaged in shared reading of enlarged texts (books and poems), print features such as length, layout, clarity of font, and number of lines on a page affect their ability to participate. In general, students can read more complex texts in shared reading than they can in guided or independent reading, but if a text is too difficult it loses its effectiveness. Even older readers might find it difficult to read a long and complex poem in unison from an overhead transparency. We address book and print features for shared reading in kindergarten through grade two. After that, book and print features are not so important. In addition, readers' tools like the table of contents, glossary, pronunciation guide, indexes, sidebars, and headings may be included in some big books used for shared reading.

Curriculum Goals

We have stated curriculum goals in terms of behaviors and understandings to notice, teach, and support at each level. These are further divided into evidence that the reader is thinking *within, beyond,* or *about* the text, ways of thinking that are summarized on the inside back cover of this book.

- ***Within the Text.*** To effectively and efficiently process a text and derive the literal meaning, readers must solve the words and monitor and self-correct their reading. During shared and performance reading, students need to follow what the text is saying, picking up important information that will help them reflect that meaning in their voices. They must self-monitor their own understanding, remember information in summary form, and sometimes adjust their reading to reflect the genre. One of the major benefits of shared and performance reading is that students are producing a fluent, phrased, and expressive oral reading of a text. This instructional setting provides a great deal of practice and an authentic reason to read aloud (not simply to let the teacher check on you!).
- ***Beyond the Text.*** Readers make predictions and connections based on previous knowledge and their own experiences. They also make connections between and among texts. They bring background knowledge to the reading of a text, synthesize new information by incorporating it into their own understandings, and think about what the writer has not stated but implied. Readers may infer the feelings and motivations of characters in fiction texts or the implications of the writer's statements in nonfiction. To reflect interpretation with their voices, readers must actively seek meaning and even consider alternative meanings for

a text. Shared reading, choral reading, and readers' theater all provide many opportunities for thinking beyond the text. To read with a character's voice, for example, you need to think deeply about how that character feels.

- ***About the Text.*** Readers think analytically about the text as an object, noticing and appreciating elements of the writer's craft, such as use of language, characterization, organization, and structure. Reading like a writer helps students notice aspects of craft and more fully enjoy a text, sometimes prompting them to revisit it. Readers also think critically about texts, evaluating the quality and considering the writer's accuracy or objectivity. Texts are selected and created for shared and performance reading based on the quality of the writing. When students perform parts of a text or a readers' theater script made from a text, they have the opportunity to get to know the language. It is an opportunity to internalize and sometimes even memorize some high-quality language. Shared and performance reading enable you to build a large repertoire of shared texts that can be revisited often to notice more about the writer's craft.

Using the Continuum

The continuum does not reference specific texts, topics, or content areas. You will apply the continuum's goals in connection with your district or state content requirements. You can use this guide to set overall curriculum goals for grades K–8, or you can refer to it as you plan for shared and performance reading.

Shared and Performance Reading

Selecting Texts Characteristics of Texts for Sharing and Performing

Genres

- Simple fantasy, most with talking animals
- Factual texts—ABC books, label books, concept books, counting books, very simple informational books
- Short poems, nursery rhymes, and songs
- Traditional folktales
- Realistic fiction

Forms

- Texts produced through interactive writing—lists, letters, stories, poems, description
- Enlarged poems
- Enlarged picture books

Text Structure

- Stories with simple and predictable repeating patterns
- Many books with repetition of episodes and refrains
- Informational texts with simple description on each page—sometimes repeating patterns
- Informational texts that present a clear and simple sequence
- Simple structure with beginning, series of episodes, and an ending
- Many traditional tales with particular structures (cumulative tales, circular stories, use of "three's")

Content

- Nonsensical situations and characters
- Language and word play—rhymes, alliteration, alphabet
- Familiar topics—animals, pets, families, food, plants, school, friends, growing, senses, neighborhood, weather and seasons, health
- A few topics beyond children's immediate experience; for example, farm, fire station, trains

Themes and Ideas

- Obvious humor—silly situations, and language play
- Familiar themes such as work, solving problems, playing tricks, friends, family

Language and Literary Features

- Some figurative language that is easy to understand
- Simple but complete stories with beginning, middle, end
- Many texts with rhyme and rhythm
- Some memorable characters
- Simple dialogue easily attributed to characters
- Characters' actions that have clear consequences (rewarding good and punishing naughtiness)
- Predictable plots and stories

Sentence Complexity

- Sentences that are more complex than children would use in oral conversation
- Sentences that are easy for children to follow—no tricky sentence structures that children find hard to repeat (consider ELL children in this)

Vocabulary

- A few new content words related to concepts children are learning that are easy to explain
- Many words that are in children's speaking vocabulary
- Some words of high interest that will be memorable to children

Words

- Simple plurals using *-s* or *-es*
- Some words with endings, for example, *-ed, -ing*
- Words that have the same rime (ending part such as *-it, bit, sit*) at the end
- Many high-frequency words that will help children to build a beginning repertoire

Illustrations

- Some poems and pieces from interactive writing that have no pictures
- Illustrations that offer high support for comprehending
- Large, clear, colorful illustrations in a variety of media

Book and Print Features

- All texts on charts or in big books
- Enlarged print that the entire group of children can see
- Some words in bold to assist in stress
- From 1 or 2 lines of print per page at the beginning of the year to about 6 lines at the end of the year
- Simple punctuation (period, comma, question mark, exclamation mark, quotation marks)
- Title, author, and illustrator on cover and title page for books
- Ample space between words and between lines
- Layout that supports phrasing by presenting word groups
- Page numbers

Shared and Performance Reading

Selecting Goals Behaviors and Understandings to Notice, Teach, and Support

Thinking *within* the Text

- Acquire understanding of new words from context
- Understand the meaning of the words during reading
- Recognize a few high-frequency words as signposts in continuous texts
- Remember and use repeating language patterns when rereading
- Notice and use spaces to define word boundaries
- Track print left to right and top to bottom with the assistance of the teacher's pointer
- Notice and ask questions when meaning is lost or understanding is interrupted
- Notice information in pictures
- Talk about characters, problems, and events in a story
- Remember and talk about interesting information in a text
- Follow the events of a story and remember them after reading in summary form
- Read along with others on familiar texts
- Read aloud with fluency
- Reflect meaning with the voice through pause, stress, and phrasing
- Recognize and use simple punctuation (reflecting it in the voice while reading)

Thinking *beyond* the Text

- Make predictions as to what will happen next
- Show interpretation of character's intentions or feelings in the voice while reading
- Show anticipation in the voice when reading
- Express personal connections through discussion
- Make connections between texts that they have read or heard before
- Use background knowledge and experience to contribute to text interpretation
- Use details from illustrations to support points made in discussion

Thinking *about* the Text

- Recognize and identify some aspects of text structure, such as beginning and ending
- Understand that an individual wrote the book
- Understand that an individual illustrated the book
- Have opinions about texts
- Notice how the writer has used language or words to make a text interesting or funny
- Recognize when texts are realistic, fantasy, or true informational texts
- Compare different versions of the same story, rhyme, or traditional tale
- Notice and understand texts that are based on established sequences such as numbers, days of the week, seasons
- Notice how layout of pictures or print affects the way you read it–for example, larger font or bold
- Check information in the text against their own experiences

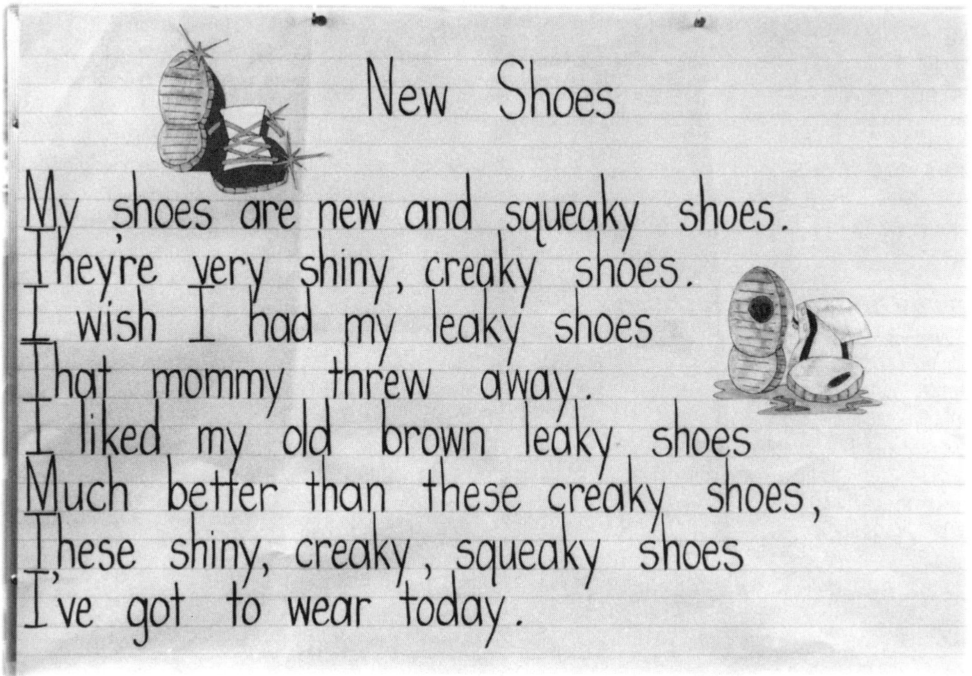

New Shoes
My shoes are new and squeaky shoes.
Theyre very shiny, creaky shoes.
I wish I had my leaky shoes
That mommy threw away.
I liked my old brown leaky shoes
Much better than these creaky shoes,
These shiny, creaky, squeaky shoes
I've got to wear today.

Shared and Performance Reading

Selecting Texts — Characteristics of Texts for Sharing and Performing

Genres
- Simple fantasy–many with talking animals
- Factual texts–ABC books, label books, concept books, counting books, very simple informational books
- Short poems, nursery rhymes, and songs
- Traditional folktales
- Realistic fiction

Forms
- Easy, brief readers' theater scripts (toward the middle and end of the year)
- Texts produced through interactive writing–lists, letters, stories, poems, descriptions, story retellings, directions, informational reports
- Enlarged poems
- Individual poetry anthologies
- Easy, brief plays (toward the middle and end of the year)
- Enlarged picture books

Text Structure
- Many books with repetition of episodes and refrains
- Informational texts with simple description on each page–sometimes repeating patterns
- Informational texts that present a clear and simple sequence
- Simple structure with beginning, series of episodes, and an ending
- Many traditional tales with particular structures (cumulative tales, circular stories, use of "three's")

Content
- Language and word play–rhymes, nonsense, alliteration, alphabet
- Familiar topics–animals, families, food, plants, school, transportation, community, health and nutrition, differences
- Topics and ideas beyond children's immediate experience–exotic or fanciful animals and people, historic animals, zoo animals in nature, space, environment (ocean, desert)
- Content that verifies as well as extends students' experiences
- Stories with repeating patterns that increase in complexity across the year
- Everyday events–eating, playing, seasons, weather, shopping, games

Themes and Ideas
- Obvious humor–silly situations, and language play
- Familiar themes such as sharing, friends, belonging, growing, responsibility, behavior

Language and Literary Features
- Some figurative language that is easy to understand
- Simple but complete stories with beginning, middle, end
- Many texts with rhyme and rhythm
- Some memorable characters
- Simple dialogue easily attributed to characters
- Characters' actions that have clear consequences (rewarding good and punishing naughtiness)
- Predictable plots and stories

Sentence Complexity
- A few sentences that are long with embedded phrases and clauses
- Sentences that are more complex than children would use in oral conversation
- Sentences that are easy for children to follow–no tricky sentence structures that children find hard to repeat (consider ELL children in this)

Vocabulary
- New content words related to concepts children are learning that are easy to explain
- Words that guide readers in interpretation of the text
- Many words that are in children's speaking vocabulary
- Some words of high interest that will be memorable to children

Words
- A full range of plurals in contexts that make them easy to understand and use language syntax
- Many multisyllable words with endings–*ed, -ing*
- Words that have the same rime (ending part such as *–ing, ring, sing; -ight, fight, might*) at the end; full range of complex rimes
- Many high-frequency words that will help children to build a beginning repertoire

Illustrations
- Some poems and pieces from interactive writing that have no pictures
- Large, clear, colorful illustrations in a variety of media
- Illustrations that offer high support for comprehending

Book and Print Features
- Most texts on charts or in big books
- Enlarged print that the entire group of children can see
- Some words in bold to assist in using appropriate word stress
- From 2 to 8 lines of print per page at the beginning of the year to about 10–12 lines at the end of the year
- Simple punctuation (period, comma, question mark, exclamation mark, quotation marks)
- Title, author, and illustrator on cover and title page for books
- Title at the top of poems and other pieces
- Some individual copies of plays or scripts
- Ample space between words and between lines
- Layout that supports phrasing by presenting word groups
- Variation in layout across a text
- Parts of a letter (date, salutation, body, closing, P.S.)

Shared and Performance Reading

Selecting Goals — Behaviors and Understandings to Notice, Teach, and Support

Thinking *within* the Text

- Track print left to right and top to bottom with the assistance of the teacher's pointer either pointing to words, sliding under words, or pointing to the beginning of a line (changing across the year)
- Acquire understanding of new words through repeated reading
- Understand the meaning of the words during reading
- Recognize a core of high-frequency words as signposts in continuous texts
- Participate in more complex reading with alternate parts, recognizing turn by cues from the text
- Read along with others on familiar texts, demonstrating high accuracy
- Read aloud with fluency
- Reflect meaning with the voice through pause, stress, and phrasing
- Recognize and use simple punctuation (reflecting it in the voice while reading)
- Remember and use repeating language patterns when rereading
- Notice and use spaces to define word boundaries
- Mimic the teacher's expression
- Notice and ask questions when meaning is lost or understanding is interrupted
- Notice and use information from pictures
- Talk about characters, problems, and events in a story in a discussion of how to read the text

Thinking *beyond* the Text

- Make predictions as to what will happen next in a story
- Show interpretation of character's intentions or feelings in the voice while reading
- Show anticipation in the voice when reading
- Express personal connections through discussion
- Make connections between texts that they have read or heard read
- Use background knowledge and experience to contribute to text interpretation
- Use details from illustrations to support points made in discussion
- Predict what a character will do in preparation for reading
- Infer a character's feelings or motivations in preparation for reading

Thinking *about* the Text

- Recognize and identify parts of stories, such as beginning, series of events, and endings
- Understand and discuss title, author, and illustrator
- Express opinions about the appropriateness of the ending
- Notice how the writer has used language or words to make a text interesting or funny
- Recognize when texts are realistic, fantasy, or true informational texts
- Compare different versions of the same story, rhyme, or traditional tale
- Notice and understand texts that are based on established sequences such as numbers, days of the week, seasons
- Notice how layout of pictures or print affects the way you read it–for example, larger font or bold
- Check information in the text against their own experiences

Shared and Performance Reading

Selecting Texts Characteristics of Texts for Sharing and Performing

Genres
- Simple fantasy–many with talking animals
- Factual texts–simple informational books, some organized as sophisticated ABC books
- Longer poems of all kinds
- Songs and traditional rhymes from many cultures
- Traditional folktales
- Realistic fiction

Forms
- Readers' theater scripts
- Texts produced through shared writing–stories, poems, descriptions, story retellings, directions, informational reports
- Enlarged poems
- Individual poetry anthologies
- Plays
- Enlarged picture books

Text Structure
- Informational texts with description, compare/contrast, sequence
- Many traditional tales with particular structures (cumulative tales, circular stories, use of "three's")

Content
- Nonsensical characters (animal and human)
- Language and word play–rhymes, nonsense, alliteration
- Many topics centering on problems related to family, friends, school
- Some scientific and technical topics–human body, wide variety of animals (many not in children's common experiences), "how-to" books, space and technology

Themes and Ideas
- Obvious humor–silly situations, and language play
- Themes important to second graders–making friends, playing fair, helping the family, belonging
- Most themes explicitly stated or easy to derive

Language and Literary Features
- Figurative language and play on words
- Stories with multiple episodes offering selection for readers' theater
- Many texts with rhyme and rhythm
- Characters who learn and change
- Dialogue that lends itself to readers' theater
- Predictable plots and stories

Sentence Complexity
- A few sentences that are long with many embedded phrases and clauses
- Sentences that are more complex than children would use in oral conversation

Vocabulary
- New content words related to concepts children are learning that are easy to explain
- Words to assign dialogue that guide readers in interpretation of the text (*cried, shouted, whispered*)
- Many synonyms, antonyms, and homophones
- Many words that are in children's speaking vocabulary
- Some words of high interest that will be memorable to children

Words
- A full range of plurals
- A full range of words with inflectional endings and suffixes
- Many high-frequency words that help the reading of the text to move along
- Many multisyllable words that offer opportunities to notice word structure

Illustrations
- Many poems and other texts that have no pictures
- Illustrations that offer high support for comprehending
- Large, clear, colorful illustrations in a variety of media

Book and Print Features
- Most texts on charts or in big books with enlarged print that the entire group can see
- Some words in bold and italics to assist in using word stress
- Up to about 20 lines on a page
- Full range of punctuation
- Title, author, and illustrator on cover and title page for books
- Title at the top of poems and other pieces
- Some reading from individual copies of plays or scripts
- Ample space between words and between lines for both common and individual texts
- Variation in layout across a text

Shared and Performance Reading

Selecting Goals Behaviors and Understandings to Notice, Teach, and Support

Thinking *within* the Text

- Track print left to right and top to bottom with only line indication from the teacher's pointer
- Acquire understanding of new words through repeated reading
- Understand the meaning of the words during reading
- Use high-frequency words to monitor accuracy of reading and gain momentum
- Read with high accuracy
- Read aloud with fluency
- Reflect meaning with the voice through pause, stress, and phrasing
- Recognize and use simple punctuation (reflecting it in the voice while reading)
- Self-correct intonation, phrasing, and pausing while reading aloud
- Use multiple sources of information to monitor reading accuracy, pronunciation, and understanding of words
- Participate in more complex reading with alternate parts, recognizing turn by cues from the text
- Use a full range of punctuation and reflect it in the voice while reading
- Remember and emphasize important information in a text while reading it aloud
- Talk about characters, problems, and events in a story in a discussion of how to read it

Thinking *beyond* the Text

- Make predictions as to what will happen next or what characters might do as preparation for reading
- Show interpretation of character's intentions or feelings in the voice while reading
- Show anticipation in the voice when reading
- Express personal connections through discussion
- Make connections between texts that they have read or heard before
- Use background knowledge and experience to contribute to text interpretation
- Use details from illustrations to contribute to text interpretation
- Infer a character's feelings or motivations as preparation for reading in the character's voice

Thinking *about* the Text

- Recognize and identify parts of stories, such as beginning, series of events, and endings
- Understand and discuss title, author, and illustrator
- Notice language that has potential for shared and performance reading
- Recognize when texts are realistic, fantasy, or true informational texts and read them differently as appropriate
- Compare different versions of the same story, rhyme, or traditional tale
- Begin to understand the subtle changes in meaning that a writer can convey through word choice
- Notice when the writer has used words with different connotations and reflect understanding in the voice
- Notice characters that have memorable traits and would be good for performance reading
- Notice how layout of pictures or print affects the way you read it—for example, larger font or bold

Shared and Performance Reading

Selecting Texts — Characteristics of Texts for Sharing and Performing

Genres
- Simple fantasy
- Informational texts
- Longer poems of all kinds
- Songs and traditional rhymes from many cultures
- Traditional folktales
- Realistic fiction
- Simple biographies

Forms
- Readers' theater scripts
- Poems and songs on charts and overhead projector
- Individual poetry anthologies
- Plays

Text Structure
- Informational texts with description, compare/contrast, sequence, problem/solution, cause/effect
- Many traditional tales with particular structures (cumulative tales, circular stories, use of "three's"), presented as plays or readers' theater
- Narrative texts, sometimes presented in parts or as plays

Content
- Language and word play–rhymes, nonsense
- Many texts centering on problems such as friendship, teasing, school, chores, family problems
- Many texts on content that goes well beyond students' own experiences
- A few historical settings that are familiar and accessible through typical experiences of third graders
- Some scientific and technical topics–the environment, science, historical and contemporary animals, different regions or geographic areas (beach, desert, mountains, city)

Themes and Ideas
- Some subtle humor, subject to interpretation
- Themes important to third graders–friendship, teasing, self-esteem
- Some subtle themes requiring communication through differences in voice
- Some mature themes such as courage, prejudice, diverse perspectives
- Social issues

Language and Literary Features
- Figurative language and play on words
- Stories with multiple episodes offering selection for readers' theater
- Many texts with rhyme and rhythm
- Poetic texts that do not rhyme
- Characters who learn and change
- Dialogue that lends itself to readers' theater
- Settings distant in time and geography from student's own experience
- Predictable plots and stories

Sentence Complexity
- Sentences that are long with many embedded phrases and clauses
- Poetic texts that are not necessarily expressed in standard sentences
- Sentences that are more complex than students would use in oral conversation
- Literary language not expressed in sentences

Vocabulary
- New content words related to concepts students are learning that are easy to explain
- Words to assign dialogue that guide readers in interpretation of the text (*cried, shouted, whispered*)
- Onomatopoetic words
- Some words of high interest that will be memorable to students

Words
- A full range of plurals
- A full range of words with inflectional endings and suffixes
- Many high-frequency words that help the reading of the text to move along
- Many multisyllable words that offer opportunities to notice word structure
- Many synonyms, antonyms, and homophones

Illustrations
- Many poems and other texts that have no pictures
- Illustrations that offer high support for comprehending
- Large, clear, colorful illustrations in a variety of media

Book and Print Features
- Some words in bold and italics to assist in stress
- Varied number of lines on each page
- Full range of punctuation
- Charts, individual copies of plays or scripts, and texts on overhead transparency
- Ample space between words and between lines for both common and individual texts
- Variation in layout across a text

Shared and Performance Reading

Selecting Goals **Behaviors and Understandings to Notice, Teach, and Support**

Thinking *within* the Text

- Understand the meaning of the words during reading
- Notice that words have multiple meanings and use this knowledge to understand and interpret a text
- Read with accuracy, fluency, and phrasing in unison with others and in solo parts
- Reflect meaning with the voice through pause, stress, and phrasing
- Recognize and use simple punctuation (reflecting it in the voice while reading)
- Self-correct intonation, phrasing, and pausing while reading aloud
- Use multiple sources of information to monitor reading accuracy, pronunciation, and understanding of words
- Automatically recognize and use a full range of punctuation, reflecting it in the voice while reading
- Remember and emphasize important parts of the text
- Participate in readings with alternate parts, recognizing turn by cues from the text

Thinking *beyond* the Text

- Make predictions as to what will happen next or what characters might do and show anticipation in the voice
- Use voice quality and volume to reflect inferences as to characters' attributes, feelings, and underlying motivations
- Express personal connections through discussion and use to inform oral reading
- Make connections between texts that they have read before and use knowledge to inform oral reading
- Use background knowledge and experience to contribute to text interpretation
- Understand the connotative meaning of words and use in interpretation of a text

Thinking *about* the Text

- Recognize and identify parts of stories, such as beginning, series of events, and endings
- Understand and discuss title, author, and illustrator
- Notice language that has potential for shared and performance reading
- Recognize when texts are realistic, fantasy, or true informational texts and read them differently as appropriate to genre
- Begin to understand the subtle changes in meaning that a writer can convey through word choice
- Notice when the writer has used words with different connotations and reflect understanding in the voice
- Use texts processed in shared or performance reading as resources for writing
- Notice characters that have memorable traits and would be good for performance reading
- Notice how layout of pictures or print affects the way you read it—for example, larger font or bold

Shared and Performance Reading

Selecting Texts Characteristics of Texts for Sharing and Performing

Genres
- More complex fantasy
- Informational texts
- Longer poems of all kinds
- Songs and traditional rhymes from many cultures
- Traditional folktales, including myths, legends, and fables
- Realistic fiction
- Simple biographies
- Historical fiction

Forms
- Readers' theater scripts, some designed by students
- Wide range of poetry on many topics, much unrhymed
- Individual poetry anthologies
- Plays

Text Structure
- Informational texts with description, compare/contrast, sequence, problem/solution, cause/effect
- More complex myths and legends, diverse in culture
- Narrative texts, sometimes presented in parts or as plays
- Short stories that can be turned into readers' theater scripts
- Realistic and historical fiction presented as plays or readers' theater
- Biography presented as readers' theater

Content
- Topics important to preadolescents–sibling rivalry, friendship, growing up, family problems, and conflicts
- Serious topics and ideas that go well beyond many students present experience–poverty, death
- Historical settings that require content knowledge
- Fiction texts that require knowledge of content (geography, customs and cultural diversity, history)

Themes and Ideas
- Humor
- More subtle themes requiring communication through differences in voice
- Social issues
- Chants and readers' theater focusing on courage, heroism, memories of unforgettable characters

Language and Literary Features
- Literary language than can be turned into dialogue or used as a narrator's part
- Complex stories with multiple episodes offering selection for readers' theater
- Poetic texts that do not rhyme
- Characters with distinct attributes and voices
- Dialogue that lends itself to readers' theater
- Settings distant in time and geography from students own experience
- Poems that offer subtle meanings and literary devices such as symbolism, to be communicated through the voice

Sentence Complexity
- Sentences that are long with many embedded phrases and clauses
- Poetic texts that are not necessarily expressed in standard sentences

Vocabulary
- New content words related to understanding and effective oral reading of fiction and nonfiction texts
- Words to assign dialogue that guide readers in interpretation of the text (*cried, shouted, whispered*)
- Onomatopoetic words
- Some words of high interest that will be memorable to students

Words
- A full range of plurals
- A full range of words with inflectional endings and suffixes
- Many high-frequency words that help the reading of the text to move along
- Many multisyllable words that offer opportunities to notice word structure
- Many synonyms, antonyms, and homophones

Illustrations
- Many poems and other texts that have no pictures
- Illustrations that offer high support for comprehending
- Large, clear, colorful illustrations in a variety of media

Book and Print Features
- Some words in bold and italics to assist in stress
- Varied number of lines on each page
- Full range of punctuation
- Charts, individual copies of plays or scripts, and texts on overhead transparency
- Ample space between words and between lines for both common and individual texts
- Variation in layout across a text

Shared and Performance Reading

Selecting Goals Behaviors and Understandings to Notice, Teach, and Support

Thinking *within* the Text

- Understand the meaning of new words from context
- Notice that words have multiple meanings and use this knowledge to understand and interpret a text
- Read with accuracy, fluency, and phrasing in unison with others and in solo parts
- Reflect meaning with the voice through pause, stress, and phrasing
- Recognize and use a full range of punctuation (reflecting it in the voice while reading)
- Use multiple sources of information to monitor reading accuracy, pronunciation, and understanding of words
- Remember and select the most important information from a text to use in readers' theater
- Pick up important information and bring it out in discussion prior to performance or afterwards
- Follow the events of a story in realistic or historical fiction and create ways to show these events with the voice

Thinking *beyond* the Text

- Make predictions while reading and decide how to foreshadow using the voice
- Use voice quality and volume to reflect inferences as to characters' attributes, feelings, and underlying motivations
- Bring personal experiences and background knowledge to deciding how to use the voice during choral reading or readers' theater
- Make connections between plays, scripts, and narratives
- Understand the connotative meaning of words and use in interpretation of a text
- Weave the story around a play, thinking what is happening by examining the dialogue
- Notice character attributes and reflect in the voice

Thinking *about* the Text

- Prepare for shared or choral reading by thinking about the language and meaning of a poem
- Begin to understand the subtle changes in meaning that a writer can convey through word choice
- Notice when the writer has used words with different connotations and reflect understanding in the voice
- Work collaboratively with a group to design readers' theater scripts and perform them
- Use plays and other texts as resources for writing
- Analyze characters in preparation for reading their voice aloud
- Use texts processed in choral reading or readers' theater as resources for writing
- Discuss characters in preparation for choral reading or readers' theater performances
- Talk about the writer's tone and style and prepare to represent it through choral reading or readers' theater performances

Shared and Performance Reading

Selecting Texts Characteristics of Texts for Sharing and Performing

Genres
- More complex fantasy
- Informational texts
- Traditional folktales, including myths, legends, and fables
- Realistic fiction
- Historical fiction

Forms
- Readers' theater scripts, some designed by students
- Wide range of poetry on many topics, much unrhymed
- Individual poetry anthologies
- Short stories

Text Structure
- Informational texts with description, compare/contrast, sequence, problem/solution, cause/effect
- More complex myths and legends, diverse in culture
- Narrative texts presented in parts or as plays
- Realistic and historical fiction presented as plays or readers' theater
- Biography presented as readers' theater

Content
- Many texts requiring knowledge of cultural diversity (ways of talking, customs)
- Many texts requiring knowledge of historical or current events
- Many texts on scientific and technical topics–the environment, space, technology
- Heavy content load in many texts, fiction and nonfiction, requiring extended discussion before making into readers' theater scripts
- Critical thinking required to judge the authenticity of informational texts, historical fiction and biography and the selection of facts to include in choral reading, poetic texts, or readers' theater scripts

Themes and Ideas
- Complex language play, often using homophones, metaphor, idioms
- Themes presenting personal and societal issues important to adolescents
- Themes and subthemes that require communication through differences in voice
- Wide range of challenging themes that build social awareness and reveal insights into the human condition–war, poverty racism, historical injustices
- Chants and readers' theater focusing on courage, heroism, memories of unforgettable characters
- Texts presenting multiple themes that may be understood (and communicated) in many layers

Language and Literary Features
- Literary language than can be turned into dialogue or used as a narrator's part
- Complex stories with multiple episodes offering selection for readers' theater
- Poems and prose poems that do not rhyme
- Characters with distinct attributes and voices
- Dialogue that lends itself to readers' theater
- Settings distant in time and geography from students own experience
- Poems that offer subtle meanings and literary devices such as symbolism, to be communicated through the voice

Sentence Complexity
- Sentences that are long with many embedded phrases and clauses
- Poetic texts that are not necessarily expressed in standard sentences

Vocabulary
- New content words related to understanding and effective oral reading of fiction and nonfiction texts
- Words with multiple meanings, requiring interpretation to be shown through the voice

Words
- A full range of plurals
- A full range of words with inflectional endings and suffixes
- Many high-frequency words that help the reading of the text to move along
- Many multisyllable words that offer opportunities to notice word structure
- Many synonyms, antonyms, and homophones

Illustrations
- Many poems and other texts that have no pictures
- Illustrations and symbolic graphics that students have designed to enhance choral reading or readers' theater

Book and Print Features
- Varied number of lines on each page
- Full range of punctuation
- Charts, individual copies of plays or scripts, and texts on overhead transparency

Shared and Performance Reading

Selecting Goals **Behaviors and Understandings to Notice, Teach, and Support**

Thinking *within* the Text

- Understand the meaning of new words from context
- Notice that words have multiple meanings and use this knowledge to understand a text
- Read with accuracy, fluency, and phrasing in unison with others and in solo parts
- Reflect meaning with the voice through pause, stress, and phrasing
- Recognize and use a full range of punctuation (reflecting it in the voice while reading)
- Use multiple sources of information to monitor reading accuracy, pronunciation, and understanding of words
- Remember and select the most important information from a text to use in readers' theater
- Select important information and discuss it in preparation for performance
- Follow the events of a story in realistic or historical fiction and create ways to show these events with the voice

Thinking *beyond* the Text

- Make predictions while reading and decide how to foreshadow using the voice
- Use voice quality and volume to reflect inferences as to characters' attributes, feelings, and underlying motivations
- Bring personal experiences and background knowledge to deciding how to use the voice during choral reading or readers' theater
- Make connections between plays, scripts, and narratives
- Understand the connotative meaning of words and use in interpretation of a text
- Weave the story around a play, thinking what is happening by examining the dialogue
- Discuss characters feelings and motivations in preparation for choral reading or readers' theater performances

Thinking *about* the Text

- Look closely at the written language to discover relationships among words and writing techniques
- Compare different readers' theater scripts based on the same text
- Begin to understand the subtle changes in meaning that a writer can convey through word choice
- Notice when the writer has used words with different connotations and reflect understanding in the voice
- Work collaboratively with a group to design readers' theater scripts and perform them in a way that reflects deep understanding
- Use plays and choral reading texts as resources for writing
- Talk about the writer's tone and style and prepare to represent them through choral reading or readers' theater performances
- Give close attention to an informational text to look for particular features (signal words, comparisons) and use the information gained to produce readers' theater scripts
- Engage in close examination of a text in order to plan a choral reading or readers' theater interpretation of it

Shared and Performance Reading

Selecting Texts Characteristics of Texts for Sharing and Performing

Genres
- More complex fantasy
- Informational texts, used as basis for performances (for example newscasts and documentaries)
- Traditional folktales, including myths, legends, and fables
- Realistic fiction
- Historical fiction

Forms
- Readers' theater scripts, many designed by students
- Wide range of poetry on many topics, much unrhymed
- Individual poetry anthologies
- Longer plays
- Short stories from which readers' theater scripts are prepared
- Sections of longer chapter books that can be adapted to choral reading or readers' theater

Text Structure
- Informational texts with description, compare/contrast, sequence, problem/solution, cause/effect
- More complex myths and legends, diverse in culture
- Narrative texts presented in parts or as plays
- Realistic and historical fiction presented as plays or readers' theater
- Biography presented as readers' theater

Content
- Topics of interest to adolescents; personal and societal issues such as growing up, racism, sexism, oppression
- Many texts requiring sophisticated content knowledge of history, science, geography, and different cultures around the world
- Heavy content load in many texts, fiction and nonfiction, requiring extended discussion before making into readers' theater scripts
- Critical thinking required to judge the authenticity of informational texts, historical fiction and biography and the selection of facts to include in choral reading, poetic texts, or readers' theater scripts

Themes and Ideas
- Complex language play, often using homophones, metaphor, idioms
- Themes important to sixth graders–adolescence, popularity, dating, developing character, family members who are absent or dead
- Themes and subthemes that require communication through differences in voice
- Wide range of challenging themes that build social awareness and reveal insights into the human condition–war, poverty, racism, historical injustices, social justice
- Chants and readers' theater focusing on courage, heroism, memories of unforgettable characters
- Texts that may be understood from different perspectives, sometimes prompting alternative scripts for readers' theater
- Themes and subthemes that require voices to reflect cultural diversity

Language and Literary Features
- Literary language than can be turned into dialogue or used as a narrator's part
- Use of figurative language and idiom
- Complex stories with multiple episodes offering selection for readers' theater
- Poems and prose poems that do not rhyme
- Characters with distinct attributes and unusual voices
- Dialogue that lends itself to readers' theater
- Settings distant in time and geography from students' own experience
- Poems that offer subtle meanings and literary devices such as symbolism, to be communicated through the voice

Sentence Complexity
- Sentences that are long with many embedded phrases and clauses
- Poetic texts that are not necessarily expressed in standard sentences

Vocabulary
- New content words related to understanding and effective oral reading of fiction and nonfiction texts
- Words with multiple meanings, requiring interpretation to be shown through the voice
- Words with different connotations, to be signaled through performances
- Idioms and figurative use of words

Words
- A full range of plurals
- A full range of words with inflectional endings and suffixes
- Many multisyllable words that offer opportunities to notice word structure
- Many synonyms, antonyms, and homophones

Illustrations
- Many poems and other texts that have no pictures
- Illustrations and symbolic graphics that students have designed to enhance choral reading or readers' theater

Book and Print Features
- Clear print that is easy to follow while concentrating on performance
- Individual copies of plays or scripts, and texts on overhead transparency

Shared and Performance Reading

Selecting Goals

Behaviors and Understandings to Notice, Teach, and Support

Thinking *within* the Text

- Learn new words and the meanings for known words from the context of texts
- Notice that words have multiple meanings and use this knowledge to understand a text
- Read with accuracy, fluency, and phrasing in unison with others and in solo parts
- Reflect meaning with the voice through pause, stress, phrasing, and intonation
- Use multiple sources of information to monitor reading accuracy, pronunciation, and understanding of words
- Remember and select the most important information from a text to use in readers' theater
- Follow the events of a story in realistic or historical fiction and create ways to show these events with the voice

Thinking *beyond* the Text

- Use voice quality and volume to reflect inferences as to characters' attributes, feelings, and underlying motivations
- Bring personal experiences and background knowledge to deciding how to use the voice during choral reading or readers' theater
- Make connections between plays, scripts, and narratives
- Understand the connotative meaning of words and use in interpretation of a text
- Interpret texts in preparation for performing scripts based on them
- Consider alternative meanings and try out different interpretations of texts through oral reading
- Work cooperatively with others to reach consensus on the meaning of a text and how to interpret it through performance
- Notice and interpret dialogue and the meanings that are implied by it
- Discuss characters in preparation for choral reading or readers' theater performances
- Weave the story around a play, thinking what is happening by examining the dialogue

Thinking *about* the Text

- Look closely at the written language to discover relationships among words and writing techniques
- Select language from texts that are good examples of the writer's craft
- Compare different readers' theater scripts based on the same text
- Notice when the writer has used words with different connotations and reflect understanding in the voice
- Use texts processed in choral reading or readers' theater as resources for writing
- Talk about the writer's tone and style and prepare to represent them through choral reading or readers' theater performances
- Give close attention to an informational text to look for particular features (signal words, comparisons) and use the information gained to produce readers' theater scripts
- Engage in close examination of a text in order to plan a choral reading or readers' theater interpretation of it
- Notice the characteristics of a group of related texts in order to explore their potential for choral reading or readers' theater presentation

Shared and Performance Reading

Selecting Texts — Characteristics of Texts for Sharing and Performing

Genres
- More complex fantasy
- Informational texts, used as basis for performances (for example newscasts and documentaries)
- Articles from a wide range of sources that offer interesting bases for informational oral presentations and readers' theater
- Traditional folktales, including myths, legends, and fables
- Realistic fiction
- Historical fiction

Forms
- Readers' theater scripts, many designed by students
- Poetry and prose poems, largely unrhymed
- Individual poetry anthologies
- Longer plays
- Short stories from which readers' theater scripts are prepared
- Sections of longer chapter books that can be adapted to choral reading or readers' theater

Text Structure
- Informational texts with description, compare/contrast, sequence, problem/solution, cause/effect
- Factual accounts of history that depict heroes or shed light on current issues
- More complex myths and legends, diverse in culture
- Narrative texts presented in parts or as plays
- Realistic and historical fiction presented as plays or readers' theater
- Biography presented as readers' theater

Content
- Texts requiring understanding of very diverse settings and people
- Great variety of content areas with writing typical of the discipline
- Critical thinking require to select and design readers' theater scripts, considering authenticity, importance, and different perspectives, some in conflict

Themes and Ideas
- Complex language play, often using homophones, metaphor, idioms
- Themes of significance to adolescents–growing up, cliques and gangs, music, sports
- Multiple layers of themes that require communication through differences in voice and may prompt alternative readers' theater scripts
- Wide range of challenging themes that build social awareness and reveal insights into the human condition–war, poverty, racism, historical injustices, social justice
- Chants and readers' theater focusing on courage, heroism, memories of unforgettable characters
- Themes and subthemes that requires voices to reflect cultural diversity
- Themes in fantasy involving heroic questions and the struggle between good and evil

Language and Literary Features
- Literary language than can be turned into dialogue or used as a narrator's part
- Use of figurative language and idiom
- Complex stories with multiple episodes offering selection for readers' theater
- Poems and prose poems that do not rhyme
- Characters with distinct attributes and unusual voices
- Dialogue that lends itself to readers' theater (use dialogue to carry story or message)
- Settings distant in time and geography from students' own experience
- Poems that offer subtle meanings and literary devices such as symbolism, to be communicated through the voice

Sentence Complexity
- Sentences that are long with many embedded phrases and clauses
- Poetic texts that are not necessarily expressed in standard sentences

Vocabulary
- New content words related to understanding and effective oral reading of fiction and nonfiction texts
- Words with multiple meanings, requiring interpretation to be shown through the voice
- Words with different connotations, to be signaled through performances
- Idioms and figurative use of words

Words
- A full range of plurals
- A full range of words with inflectional endings and suffixes
- Many multisyllable words that offer opportunities to notice word structure
- Many synonyms, antonyms, and homophones

Illustrations
- Many poems and other texts that have no pictures
- Illustrations and symbolic graphics that students have designed to enhance choral reading or readers' theater

Book and Print Features
- Clear print that is easy to follow while concentrating on performance
- Individual copies of plays or scripts

Shared and Performance Reading

Selecting Goals Behaviors and Understandings to Notice, Teach, and Support

Thinking *within* the Text

- Learn new words and the meanings for known words from the context of texts
- Notice interesting words and discuss origins or roots
- Notice that words have multiple meanings and use this knowledge to understand a text
- Read with accuracy, fluency, and phrasing in unison with others and in solo parts
- Reflect meaning with the voice through pause, stress, and phrasing
- Use dramatic expression where appropriate to communicate additional meaning for a text
- Use multiple sources of information to monitor reading accuracy, pronunciation, and understanding of words
- Remember and select the most important information from a text to use in readers' theater
- Follow the events of a story in realistic or historical fiction and create ways to show these events with the voice

Thinking *beyond* the Text

- Use voice quality and volume to reflect inferences as to characters' attributes, feelings, and underlying motivations
- Bring personal experiences and background knowledge to deciding how to use the voice during choral reading or readers' theater
- Make connections between plays, scripts, and narratives
- Understand the connotative meaning of words and use in interpretation of a text
- Interpret texts in preparation for performing scripts based on them
- Consider alternative meanings and try out different interpretations of texts through oral reading
- Work cooperatively with others to reach consensus on the meaning of a text and how to interpret it through performance
- Notice and interpret dialogue and the meanings that are implied by it
- Discuss characters in preparation for choral reading or readers' theater performances
- Weave the story around a play, thinking what is happening by examining the dialogue

Thinking *about* the Text

- Look closely at the written language to discover relationships among words and writing techniques
- Notice when the writer has used words with different connotations and reflect understanding in the voice
- Talk about the writer's tone and style and prepare to represent it through choral reading or readers' theater performances
- Give close attention to an informational text to look for particular features (signal words, comparisons) and use the information gained to produce readers' theater scripts
- Engage in close examination of a text in order to plan a choral reading or readers' theater interpretation of it
- Apply genre-specific knowledge to understand the structure of a text and design readers' theater scripts with that in mind
- Change the genre of a text to perform it orally (for example, making a prose poem out of a news article)
- Notice the characteristics of a group of related texts in order to explore their potential for combining them in one choral reading or readers' theater performance

Writing About Reading

Introduction to Writing About Reading

Students' written responses to what they have read provide evidence of their thinking. When we examine writing in response to reading, we can make hypotheses about how well readers have understood a text. But there are more reasons to make writing an integral part of your reading instruction. Through writing—and drawing as well—readers can express and expand their thinking and improve their ability to reflect on a text. They can also communicate their thinking about texts to a variety of audiences for a variety of purposes. Writers can analyze effective examples of writing about reading to learn the characteristics of each form so that they can "try it out" for themselves. The models serve as "mentor texts" that students can refer to as they experiment with different types of writing.

We do not recommend simply "assigning" writing about reading. When working with young children, usually the teacher introduces a genre through demonstration or shared/interactive writing, and students experience many examples. They get a chance to participate in composition and construction (actual act of writing) before they are expected to produce it independently. So as you look at the writing about reading continuum for kindergarten and grade one, consider group writing. Very young children experience the genres mostly through shared and interactive writing, which are defined below:

- In ***shared writing,*** the teacher and students compose a text together. The teacher is the scribe. Often, especially with younger children, the teacher works on a chart displayed on an easel. Children participate in the composition of the text, word by word, and reread it many times. Sometimes the teacher asks children to say the word slowly as they think about how a word is spelled. At other times, the teacher (with student input) writes a word quickly on the chart. The text becomes a model, example, or reference for student writing and discussion. (See McCarrier, Fountas, and Pinnell 2000.)

- ***Interactive writing,*** an approach for use with young children, is identical to and proceeds in the same way as shared writing, with one exception: Occasionally the teacher, while making teaching points that help children attend to various features of letters and words, will invite a student to come up to the easel and contribute a letter, a word, or part of a word. (See McCarrier, Fountas, and Pinnell 2000.)

After students are confident with a form of writing through the analysis of effective examples, whole- or small-group discussion can support their independent writing about reading. Discussion reminds writers of key characteristics of the text and the author's craft.

In this continuum, we describe many different forms of writing about reading in four categories: functional writing, narrative writing, informational writing, and poetic writing. The goal is for students to read many examples in each category, identify the specific characteristics, and have opportunities to apply their understandings in independent writing.

Functional Writing

Functional writing is undertaken for communication or to "get a job done." During a literacy block, a great deal of functional writing takes place around reading. Students make notes to themselves about written texts that they can use as a basis for an oral discussion or presentation or to support writing of more extended pieces. Or they may write notes or letters to others to communicate their thinking.

Second graders can begin with a simple blank notebook. Minilessons help them understand the various kinds of functional writing they can place in the notebook. (See Fountas and Pinnell 2001 and 2006.) Some examples of functional writing about reading are:

- notes and sketches—words, phrases, or sketches on sticky notes or in a notebook
- "short-writes"—a few sentences or paragraphs produced quickly in a notebook or a large sticky note that is then placed in a notebook
- graphic organizers—words, phrases, sketches, or sentences
- letters—letters written to other readers or to the author or illustrator of a book
- diary entries—an entry or series of entries in a journal or diary from the perspective of a biographical subject or character

A key tool for learning in grades two through eight is the reader's notebook, in which students reflect on their reading in various forms, including dialogue letters that are answered by the teacher.

Narrative Writing

Narrative writing tells a story. Students' narrative writing about reading might retell some or all of a plot or recount significant events in the life of a biographical subject. Or students might tell about an experience of their own that is similar to the one in a text or has a similar theme. Some examples of narrative writing about reading are:

- summary—a few sentences that tell the most important information in a text
- cartoon/storyboarding—a succession of graphics or stick figures that present a story or information

Informational Writing

Informational writing organizes facts into a coherent whole. To compose an informational piece, the writer organizes data into categories and may use underlying structures such as description; comparison and contrast; cause and effect; time sequence; and problem and solution. Some examples of informational writing about reading are:

- author study—a piece of writing that provides information about an author and his or her craft
- illustrator study—a piece of writing that provides information on an illustrator
- interview (with an author or expert)—a series of questions and responses designed to provide information about an author or expert on a topic
- "how-to" book—an explanation of how something is made or done
- "all about" book—factual information presented in an organized way

Poetic Writing

Poetic writing entails carefully selecting and arranging words to convey meaning in ways that evoke feelings and sensory images. Poetry condenses meaning into short language groupings. It lends itself to repeated readings and to being read aloud for the pleasure of listening to the language. Poetic writing about reading includes poetry written in response to a prose text or to reflect or respond to a poem.

Using the Writing About Reading Continuum

All the genres and forms for writing about reading will give you evidence of how students are thinking and will help them become more reflective about their reading. The continuum is organized by grade. First, we list the genres and forms that are appropriate for students to be writing at the grade level. Then we specify behaviors and understandings to notice, teach, and support as students think *within, beyond,* and *about* a text. (Note that you can find evidence in both illustrations and writing.) Remember that genres and forms are demonstrated and co-constructed through the use of interactive and shared writing with young writers *before* they are expected to produce them independently as assignments. After experiencing the genres or forms several times with group support, young students will be able to produce them on their own. Older writers are able to analyze "mentor texts" as they learn how to write about reading by examining effective examples. Gradually, students build up a repertoire of ways of writing about reading that they can select from according to their purpose.

Writing About Reading

Selecting Genres and Forms

Genres and forms for writing about reading are demonstrated through interactive, shared, or modeled writing, often with close attention to mentor texts. Children learn how to respond to reading in different forms and for a variety of purposes and audiences. After they learn about the forms in a supported experience, they use them independently as they respond to books they read.

Functional Writing

- Sketches or drawings that reflect content of a text
- Selected interesting words from a text (written or illustrated)
- Short sentences responding to a text (for example, stating a prediction, an opinion, or an interesting aspect of the text)
- Lists to support memory (characters, events in a story)
- Notes to other classes or individuals in the school (about text or based on them)
- Labels for photographs or any kind of drawing
- Directions that show a simple sequence of actions based on a text

Narrative Writing

- Drawings showing the sequence of events in a text (sometimes with speech bubbles to show dialogue)
- Simple statements summarizing a text
- Simple statements telling the sequence of events
- Innovations on known texts (for example, new endings or similar plots with different characters)

Informational Writing

- List of facts from a text
- Short sentences and/or drawings reporting some interesting information from a text
- One or two simple sentences with information about an author or illustrator

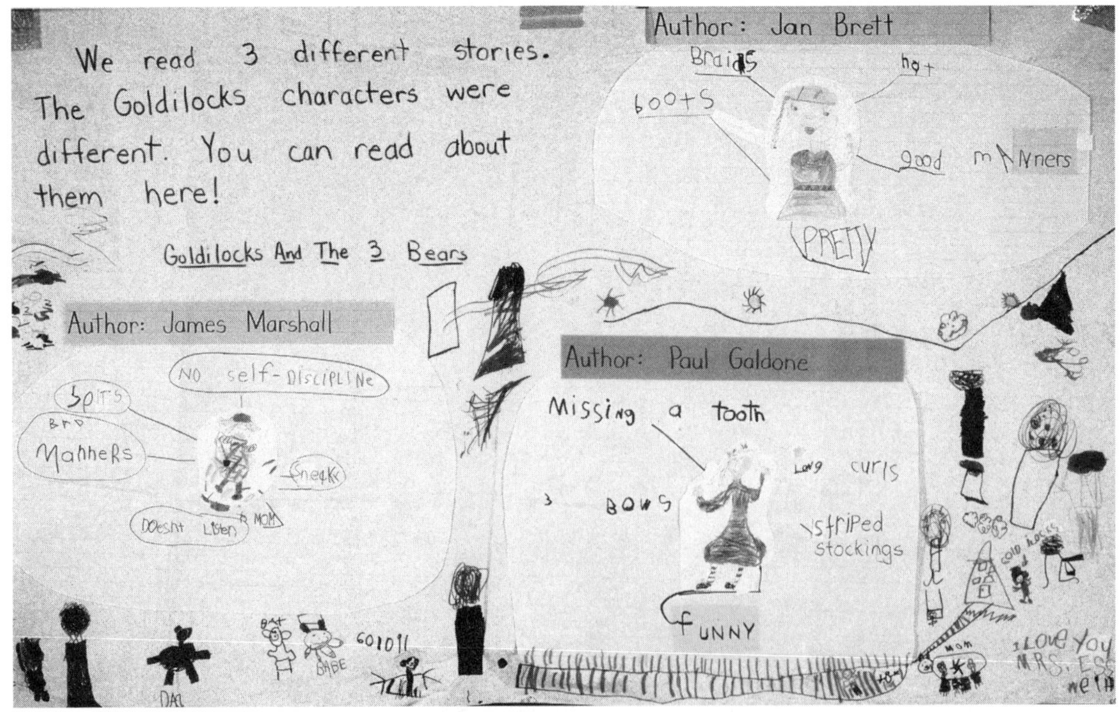

Writing About Reading

Selecting Goals Behaviors and Understandings to Notice, Teach, and Support

Thinking *within* the Text

- Record interesting information about events or characters from a text
- Illustrate a text by drawing (for example, characters or events)
- Write or draw about interesting facts
- Notice and sometimes use new words from a text
- Reread to remember what has been written
- Notice and use some details from texts in group or independent writing
- Compose notes, lists, letters, or statements based on a text in a group or independently
- Tell important information from writing
- Reread to assure meaningfulness, language structure, and appropriate word use
- Use the names of authors and illustrators

Thinking *beyond* the Text

- Predict what will happen next in a text or what a character will do
- Express opinions about stories or poems
- Express opinions about characters or about their feelings or motives
- Infer how a character feels
- Reflect what a character is really like
- Compose innovations on very familiar texts
- Write or draw about something in the reader's own life when prompted by a text

Thinking *about* the Text

- Create texts that have some of the characteristics of published texts (cover, title, author, illustrator, illustrations, beginning, ending, events in a sequence, about the author page)
- Sometimes borrow the style or some words from a writer
- Express opinions about facts or information learned
- Recognize and use some aspects of text structure (for example, beginning and ending or a pattern)
- Differentiate between stories and informational texts
- Notice and sometimes use interesting language from a text

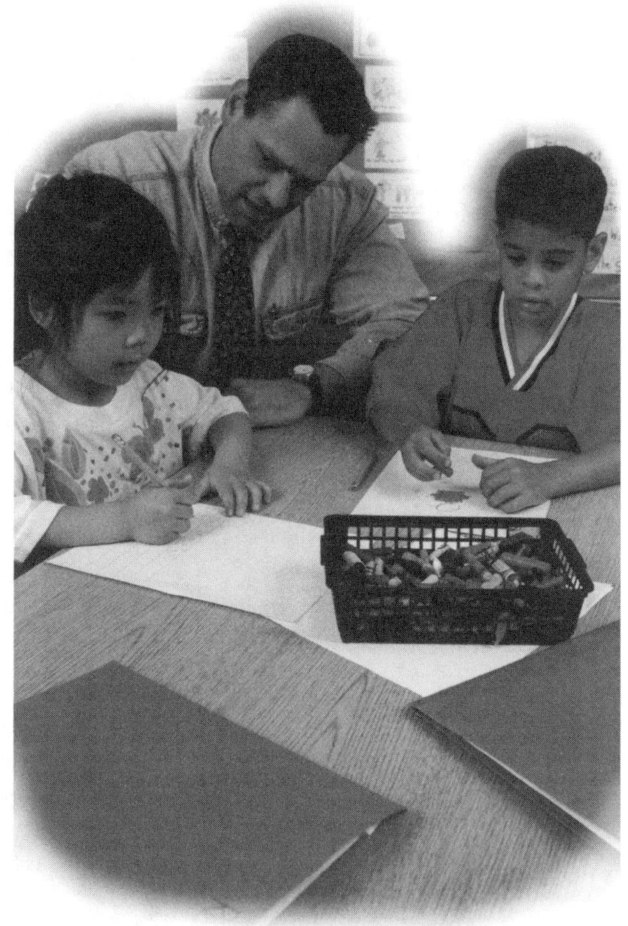

Writing About Reading

Selecting Genres and Forms

Genres and forms for writing about reading are demonstrated through interactive, shared, or modeled writing, often with close attention to mentor texts. Children learn how to respond to reading in different forms and for a variety of purposes and audiences. After they learn about the forms in a supported experience, they use them independently as they respond to books they read.

Functional Writing

- Sketches or drawings that reflect content of a text
- Interesting words or phrases from a text
- Short sentences responding to a text (for example, stating a prediction, an opinion, or an interesting aspect of the text)
- Lists to support memory (characters, events in a story)
- Simple charts (graphic organizers) to show comparison or sequence
- Letters to other readers or to authors and illustrators (including dialogue letters in a reader's notebook)
- Labels for photographs or any kind of drawing
- Written directions (sometimes with drawings) that show a simple sequence of actions based on a text

Narrative Writing

- Simple statements telling the sequence of events
- Drawings showing the sequence of events in a text (sometimes with speech bubbles to show dialogue)
- Simple statements summarizing a text
- Innovations on known texts (for example, new endings or similar plots with different characters)

Informational Writing

- List of facts from a text
- Short sentences and/or drawings reporting some interesting information from a text
- Summaries of information learned with headings to show sections
- One or two simple sentences with information about an author or illustrator
- Representations (through writing and drawing) of a sequence of actions or directions from a text
- Labeling of drawings that represent interesting information from a text

Writing About Reading

Selecting Goals Behaviors and Understandings to Notice, Teach, and Support

Thinking *within* the Text

- Write short sentences to report or summarize important details from a text
- Represent a character through drawing or writing
- Represent a sequence of events through drawing (often with labels or legends)
- Notice and sometimes use new words from a text
- Tell important information from a story
- Reread to assure accuracy of sentence structure and word use as well as meaningfulness
- Use text as a resource for words, phrases, ideas
- Remember information from a text to produce lists, simple sequence of actions, and directions
- Use the names of authors and illustrators

Thinking *beyond* the Text

- Reflect both prior knowledge and new knowledge from the text
- Predict what will happen next in a text or what a character will do
- Infer how a character feels
- Reflect what a character is really like
- Express opinions about stories or poems
- Compose innovations on very familiar texts
- Produce innovations on a text by changing ending, series of events, the characters, or the setting
- List or write sentences and opinions about new information learned from a text
- Write or draw about something in the reader's own life when prompted by a text

Thinking *about* the Text

- Create texts that have some of the characteristics of published texts (cover, title, author, illustrator, illustrations, beginning, ending, events in a sequence, about the author page)
- Sometimes borrow the style or some words from a writer
- Express opinions about a story or poem
- Notice the way a text is organized and sometimes apply organization to writing (for example, sequence of events or established sequence such as numbers or days of the week)
- Recognize and use some aspects of text structure (for example, beginning and ending)
- Differentiate between informational and fiction texts
- Notice and sometimes use interesting language from a text
- Produce some simple graphic representations of a story (for example, story map or timeline)
- Use specific vocabulary to write about texts (*author, illustrator, cover, title character, problem, events*)

Writing About Reading

Selecting Genres and Forms

Students learn different ways to share their thinking about reading in explicit minilessons. Using modeled or shared writing, the teacher may demonstrate the process and engage the students in the construction of the text. Often, the teacher and students read several examples of a form, identify its characteristics, and try out the type of response. Then, students can select from the range of possible forms when responding to reading (usually in a reader's notebook).

Functional Writing

- Sketches or drawings that assist in remembering a text, interpreting a character or event, or representing content of a text
- Short-writes responding to a text in a variety of ways (for example, a prediction, an opinion, or an interesting aspect of the text)
- Lists to support memory (characters, events in a story)
- Notes to remember something about a text or to record interesting information or details, or record interesting language or words
- Simple charts or webs (graphic organizers) to show comparison or sequence
- Grids to show relationships among different kinds of information
- Letters to other readers or to authors and illustrators (including dialogue letters in a reader's notebook)
- Labels for photographs or any kind of drawing
- Written directions (sometimes with drawings) that show a simple sequence of actions based on a text
- Directions or how-to descriptions drawn from a text

Narrative Writing

- Drawings showing the sequence of events in a text (sometimes with speech bubbles to show dialogue)
- Simple statements summarizing a text
- Innovations on known texts (for example, new endings or similar plots with different characters)

Informational Writing

- List of facts from a text supported by illustrations
- Headings that show subtopics or information to follow
- Sentences reporting some interesting information from a text
- A few sentences with information about an author
- A few sentences with information about an illustrator
- Representations (through writing and drawing) of a sequence of actions or directions from a text
- Labeling of drawings that represent interesting information from a text

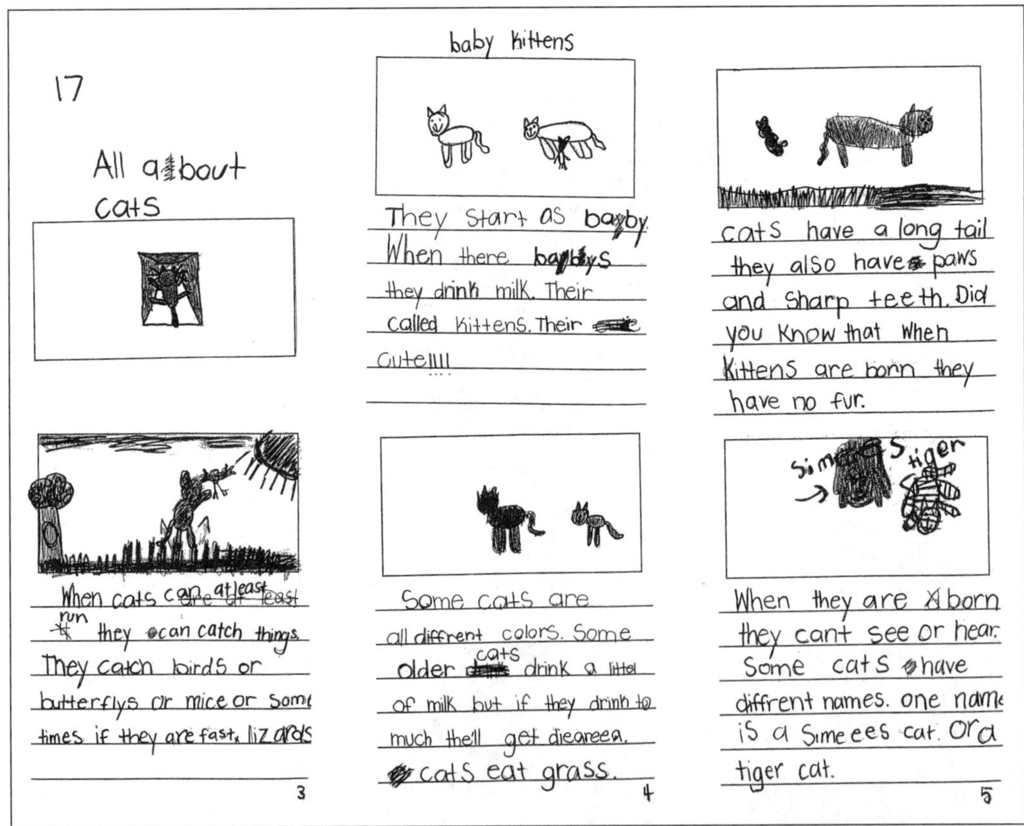

A second grader's writing after listening to and looking at lots of books about cats

Writing About Reading

Selecting Goals Behaviors and Understandings to Notice, Teach, and Support

Thinking *within* the Text

- Accurately reflect information from a text
- Represent information, concepts, setting, events, characters, and story problems through drawing and/or writing
- Notice and sometimes use new words from a text
- Use new vocabulary words appropriately to reflect meaning
- Reread to remember what has been written
- Reread to assure meaningfulness, accuracy of sentence structure, and appropriate word use
- Report information from a text or summarize it in a few sentences
- Write summaries that reflect literal understanding of a text
- Represent important information about a fiction text (characters, events) or informational text
- List significant events in a story or ideas in an informational text
- Write and/or draw about facts

Thinking *beyond* the Text

- Provide specific examples and evidence from personal experience or the text
- Express connections to prior knowledge, to other texts, and to personal background or experience
- Predict what will happen next in a text or what a character will do
- Describe or illustrate characters' feelings and motivations, inferring them from the text
- Produce innovations on a text by changing ending, series of events, the characters, or the setting
- Make notes of new information and understandings
- Write about and illustrate new information
- Express opinions about new learning or interesting facts
- Use drawings to relate important ideas in a text to each other or to other texts
- Write or draw about something in the reader's own life when prompted by a text

Thinking *about* the Text

- Create texts that have some of the characteristics of published texts (cover, title, author, illustrator, illustrations, beginning, ending, events in a sequence, about the author page)
- Sometimes borrow the style of a writer
- Describe the relationships between illustrations and text
- Write opinions about a text and back them up with specific information or reasons
- Notice the way a text is organized and sometimes apply organization to writing (for example, sequence of events or established sequence such as numbers or days of the week)
- Show awareness of temporal sequence, compare and contrast, and cause and effect
- Identify and record whether a text is fiction or nonfiction
- Notice and sometimes use interesting language from a text
- Produce some simple graphic representations of a story (for example, story map or timeline)
- Compare different versions of the same story or traditional tale with graphic organizers, drawings, or in sentences
- Use specific vocabulary to write about texts: *cover, endpapers, title, author, illustrator, table of contents, character, fiction, nonfiction, biography, informational texts, problem and solution*

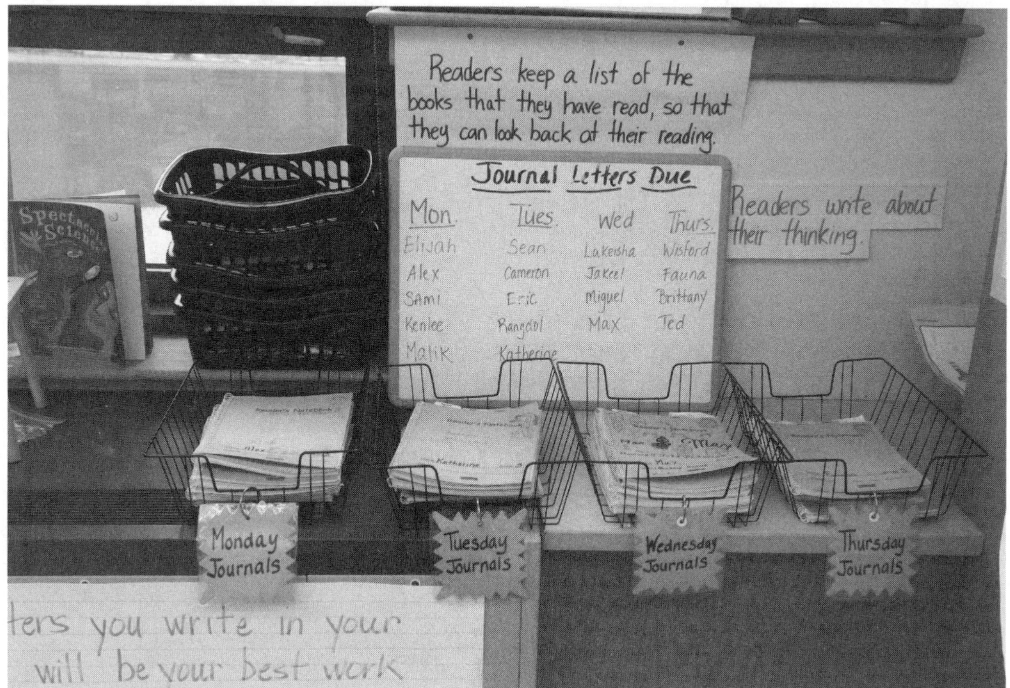

Writing About Reading

Selecting Genres and Forms

Students learn different ways to share their thinking about reading in explicit minilessons. Using modeled or shared writing, the teacher may demonstrate the process and engage the students in the construction of the text. Often, the teacher and students read several examples of a form, identify its characteristics, and try out the type of response. Then, students can select from the range of possible forms when responding to reading (usually in a reader's notebook).

Functional Writing

- Sketches or drawings to represent or interpret a text
- Short-writes responding to a text in a variety of ways (for example, a prediction, an opinion, or an interesting aspect of the text)
- Lists to support memory (characters, events in a story, setting, memorable words or phrases)
- Notes representing interesting language from a text or examples of the writer's craft (quotes from a text)
- Notes to be used in later discussion or writing
- Grids to show comparisons of texts or to organize information about texts
- Graphic organizers that show relationships among different kinds of information or that connect more than one text (for example, comparisons, timelines, webs)
- Letters to other readers or to authors and illustrators (including dialogue letters in a reader's notebook)
- Labels and legends for illustrations (drawings, photographs, maps)
- Directions or how-to descriptions drawn from a text

Narrative Writing

- Cartoons, comics, or storyboards to present a story or information
- Plot summaries

Informational Writing

- Lists of facts from a text
- Short reports utilizing information from one or more texts
- Book recommendations
- A few sentences with information about an author
- A few sentences with information about an illustrator
- Author studies, reflecting knowledge of biographical information or response to one or more books by an author
- Illustrator studies, reflecting knowledge of biographical information or response to one or more books by an artist
- Directions or how-to pieces, sometimes illustrated with drawings showing a sequence of actions
- Drawings or photographs with labels or legends illustrating information from a text
- Lists of headings that reflect the overall organization of a text

Poetic Writing

- Poetic texts written in response to a prose text

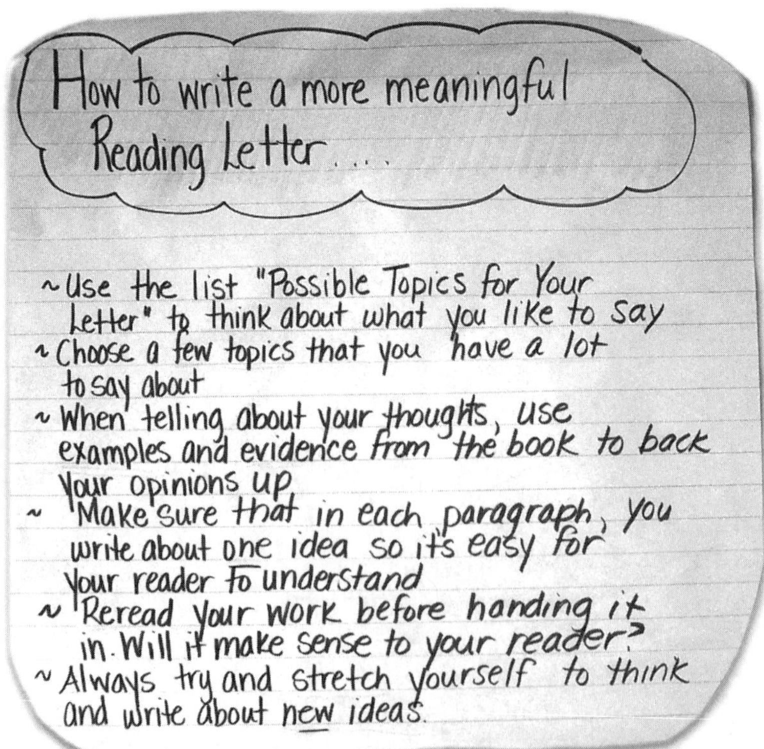

Writing About Reading

Selecting Goals Behaviors and Understandings to Notice, Teach, and Support

Thinking *within* the Text

- Accurately reflect information from a text
- Include appropriate and important details when summarizing texts
- Notice and sometimes use new words from a text
- Use new vocabulary words appropriately to reflect meaning
- Reread to remember what has been written
- Reread to assure accuracy of sentence structure and word use
- Report information from a text or summarize it in a few sentences
- Use notes as a basis for discussion or later writing
- Write summaries that reflect literal understanding of a text
- Represent the important information about a fiction text (characters, events)
- Include important details from the content of an informational text
- Include details that show a character's traits
- Revisit texts for ideas or to check details when writing or drawing
- Reflect both prior knowledge and evidence from the text in responses to texts
- List significant events in a story or ideas in an informational text

Thinking *beyond* the Text

- Provide evidence from the text or from personal experience to support written statements about a text
- Express connections to prior knowledge, to other texts, and to personal background or experience
- Write or draw about something in the reader's own life when prompted by a text
- Predict logically, supported by evidence, what will happen next in a text or what a character will do
- Describe or illustrate characters' feelings and motivations, inferring them from the text
- Infer characters' feelings and motivations and include evidence from the text to support thinking
- Identify and record in notes new information and understandings gained from reading a text
- Relate important ideas in a text to each other or to other texts
- Interpret or respond to illustrations and relate ideas in graphics and print
- Tell why some events in a story are important
- Reflect awareness of the author's underlying messages (themes)
- Describe implications of factual information

Thinking *about* the Text

- Describe the relationships between illustrations and text
- Write opinions about a text and back them up with specific information or reasons
- Show how a text is organized (narrative and expository)
- Show awareness of temporal sequence, compare and contrast, and cause and effect
- Identify and record the genre of a text (realistic and historical fiction, fantasy, traditional literature, biography, informational)
- Select examples of the writer's use of language and write opinions about or responses to that language
- Make note of interesting new words and intentionally remember them to use in oral discussion or writing
- Compare different works by a writer
- Compare two or more writers with graphic organizers or drawings
- Compare different versions of the same story or traditional tale with graphic organizers or drawings
- Describe (or interpret through drawing) the characteristics of a writer's work or an illustrator's work
- Use specific vocabulary to write about texts: *title, author, illustrator, cover, dedication, endpapers, author's note, illustrator's note, character, main character, setting, problem, events, resolution, theme, fiction/nonfiction, poetry, table of contents, topics*

Writing About Reading

Selecting Genres and Forms

Students learn different ways to share their thinking about reading in explicit minilessons. Using modeled or shared writing, the teacher may demonstrate the process and engage the students in the construction of the text. Often, the teacher and students read several examples of a form, identify its characteristics, and try out the type of response. Then, students can select from the range of possible forms when responding to reading (usually in a reader's notebook).

Functional Writing

- Sketches or drawings to represent a text and provide a basis for discussion or writing
- Short-writes responding to a text in a variety of ways (for example, a prediction, an opinion, or an interesting aspect of the text)
- Lists to support memory (characters, events in a story, setting, memorable words or phrases)
- Notes representing interesting language from a text or examples of the writer's craft (quotes from a text)
- Notes to be used in later discussion or writing
- Grids that show analysis of a text (a form of graphic organizer)
- Graphic organizers that show relationships among different kinds of information or that connect more than one text (for example, comparisons, timelines, webs)
- Letters to other readers or to authors and illustrators (including dialogue letters in a reader's notebook)
- Labels and legends for illustrations (drawings, photographs, maps)
- Directions or how-to descriptions drawn from a text
- Poster or advertisement that tells about a text in an attention-getting way

Narrative Writing

- Cartoons, comics, or storyboards to present a story or information
- Plot summaries
- Scripts for readers' theater

Informational Writing

- Short report utilizing information from one or more texts
- Book recommendations
- Book reviews
- Author study, reflecting knowledge of biographical information or response to one or more books by an author
- Biographical sketch on an author or the subject of a biography
- Illustrator study, reflecting knowledge of biographical information or response to one or more books by an artist
- Directions or how-to pieces, sometimes illustrated with drawings showing a sequence of actions
- How-to articles that require the writer to be an expert who explains to readers how something is made or done
- Drawings or photographs with labels or legends illustrating information from a text
- Lists of headings and subheadings that reflect the overall organization of a text

Poetic Writing

- Poetic texts written in response to a prose text
- Poetic texts written in response to poems (same style, topic, mood)

Dear Cynthia Rylant,

I've read many of your books, and lots of people read your books to me. I loved them. My teacher reads alot of your books to us and your autobiography too. I loved learning about you. Sometimes when I'm doing a piece of writing I get ideas from you. I like when you put your words together with and, just like you did in The Relatives Came. I wrote: "The roller coaster was long and windy and scary!" I just finished that piece not to long ago.

Before I start a piece of writing I go back to my Writer's Notebook and see if I want to use any of my stories. I wonder if you do that too, do you? I do most of my writing at school in class, but I like to write in my Writer's Notebook at home in my bedroom. I get ideas from you. When I'm stuck I think of stories that you wrote.

I said lots of stuff about me. Let's talk more about you. I read the book Dog Heaven. I felt real sad that your friend's dog died. I think it was nice to write that book for your friend. It reminded me of when my cat died. I felt the same way. I thought it was cool that you did your own pictures in Dog Heaven. I always do a sketch to go with my writing too.

We had fun with your book Night in the Country. We read it a lot and then we turned it into a poem and acted it out. We all had favorite lines.

I hope you keep writing because I like reading your books.

Sincerely,
Tomas

Tomas' letter to the author, Cynthia Rylant, in response to several books

Writing About Reading

Selecting Goals

Behaviors and Understandings to Notice, Teach, and Support

Thinking *within* the Text

- Include appropriate and important details when summarizing texts
- Provide evidence from the text or from personal experience to support written statements about a text
- Use new vocabulary in appropriate ways in writing
- Purposefully acquire vocabulary from text and use new words in talk and writing (including technical words)
- Reread what has been written to check on accuracy, clarity of expression, and meaning
- Use notes as a basis for discussion or later writing
- Make notes and write longer responses to indicate acquisition of new information and ideas
- Make note of important or new information while reading nonfiction
- Access information from both print and graphics
- Write summaries that reflect literal understanding of a text
- Represent important information about a fiction text (characters, problems, sequence of events, problem resolution)
- Provide details that are important to understanding the relationship among plot, setting, and character traits
- Include details that show a character's traits
- Include important details from the content of an informational text
- Revisit texts for ideas or to check details when writing or drawing
- Reflect both prior knowledge and evidence from the text in responses to texts

Thinking *beyond* the Text

- Provide specific examples and evidence from personal experience or the text
- Describe connections between background knowledge and new information in a text
- Express a wide range of predictions using (and including) information as evidence from the text
- Describe or illustrate characters' feelings and motivations, inferring them from the text
- Infer characters' feelings and motivations and include evidence from the text to support thinking
- Formulate expectations and questions as preparation for reading
- Express changes in understanding in response to new ideas in a text
- Relate important ideas in the text to each other and to ideas in other texts
- Make connections to other texts by topic, major ideas, authors' styles, and genres
- Show connections between the setting, characters, and events of a text and reader's own personal experiences
- Identify, discuss, or write (sometimes with illustration) about some obvious use of symbolism
- Identify the significance or impact of setting in fiction or biography (influence on characters' or subjects' feelings, motivations, life decisions)
- Interpret or respond to illustrations
- Derive and record information from graphics
- Interpret the mood of illustrations and language in a text
- Reflect awareness of the author's underlying messages (themes)

BOOK RECOMMENDATIONS
- Write the title of the book (underlined) and the author's name at the top.
- Tell a little summary without giving the whole story away.
- Tell what genre the book is.
- Explain why you liked it and why you think someone else would like it.
- Be as specific as you can.
- Write at least 5 sentences.

Thinking *about* the Text

- Describe how the illustrations add to the meaning, mood, and quality of a text
- Provide specific examples and evidence (either orally or in writing) to support written statements about the quality, accuracy, or craft of a text
- Note specific examples of the writer's craft (leads, dialogue, definition of terms within the text, divisions of text, use of descriptive language, interesting verbs, ending)
- Show how a text is organized (narrative and expository)
- Show awareness of temporal sequence, compare and contrast, cause and effect, and problem and solution
- Identify and record the genre of a text (realistic and historical fiction, fantasy, traditional literature, biography, informational)
- Use knowledge of genre to write about the quality or characteristics of a text
- Use genre to interpret a text or make predictions about it
- Select examples of the writer's use of language and write opinions about or responses to it
- Make note of interesting new words and intentionally remember them to use in oral discussion or writing
- Comment on the writer's use of words precisely to convey meaning or mood (subtle shades of meaning)
- Write statements of the underlying message or theme of the story and include examples from the text or rationales
- Comment on aspects of the writer's craft noticed in a particular text or more than one text by an author
- Comment on how layout contributes to the meaning and effectiveness of both fiction and nonfiction texts
- Critique the quality or accuracy of a text, citing evidence for opinions
- State opinions about texts including specific rationales for thinking
- Comment on the writer's use of graphic tools and effective ways of placing them in the text
- Use specific vocabulary to write about texts: *title, author, illustrator, cover, dedication, endpapers, author's note, illustrator's note, character, main character, setting, problem, events, resolution, theme, fiction/nonfiction, genre, events, timeline, caption, legend, accuracy and authenticity, names of genres, poetry, table of contents, topics*

Writing About Reading

Selecting Genres and Forms

Students learn different ways to share their thinking about reading in explicit minilessons. Using modeled or shared writing, the teacher may demonstrate the process and engage the students in the construction of the text. Often, the teacher and students read several examples of a form, identify its characteristics, and try out the type of response. Then, students can select from the range of possible forms when responding to reading (usually in a reader's notebook).

Functional Writing

- Sketches or drawings to represent a text and provide a basis for discussion or writing
- Short-writes responding to a text in a variety of ways (for example, personal response, interpretation, character analysis, description, or critique)
- Notes representing interesting language from a text or examples of the writer's craft (quotes from a text)
- Notes to be used in later discussion or writing
- Grids that show analysis of a text (a form of graphic organizer)
- Graphic organizers that show relationships among different kinds of information or that connect more than one text (for example, comparisons, timelines, webs)
- Letters to other readers or to authors and illustrators (including dialogue letters in a reader's notebook)
- Labels and legends for illustrations (drawings, photographs, maps)
- Poster or advertisement that tells about a text in an attention-getting way

Narrative Writing

- Cartoons, comics, or storyboards to present a story or information
- Plot summaries
- Scripts for readers' theater
- Storyboards to represent significant events in a text

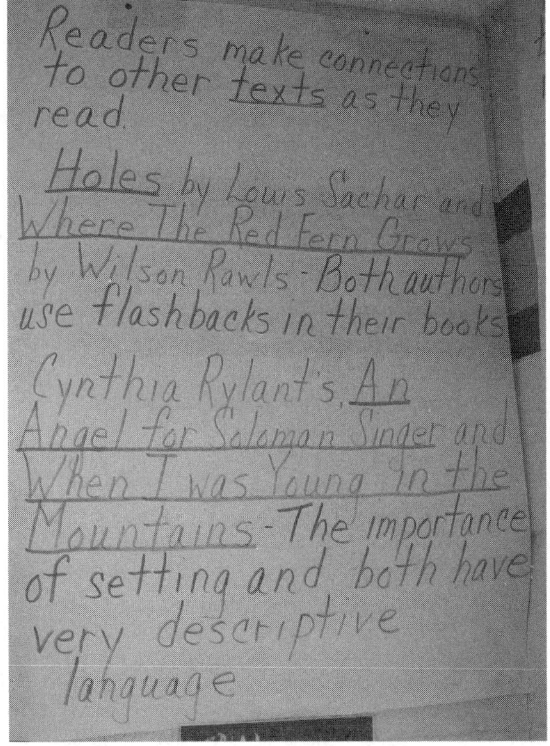

How to Write a Book Review

- Include the title of the book and its author at the beginning. Talk about the genre and/or format.
- Start with a good lead.
- Tell the reader enough information about the story so he/she understands what the book is about.
- Don't give away all the surprises!
- Give your opinion on the book.
- Use details and rich words (examples from text).
- Sell the book to your reader!
- Include publication information: title, author, illustrator, publisher, number of pages and price
- Revise, revise, revise!

Writing About Reading

Selecting Genres and Forms

Informational Writing

- Book recommendations
- Projects that present ideas and opinions about texts or topics in an organized way (using text and visual images)
- Reports that include text and graphic organizers to present information drawn from texts
- Book reviews
- Author study, reflecting knowledge of biographical information or response to one or more books by an author
- Biographical sketch on an author or the subject of a biography
- Illustrator study, reflecting knowledge of biographical information or response to one or more books by an artist
- How-to articles that require the writer to be an expert who explains to readers how something is made or done
- Drawings or photographs with labels or legends illustrating information from a text
- Outlines that include headings, subheadings, and sub-subheadings to reflect the organization of the text
- Interviews with an author or expert (questions and responses designed to provide information)

Poetic Writing

- Poetic texts written in response to a prose text
- Poetic texts written in response to poems (same style, topic, mood)

Dear Mrs. C.

The book, Wishes, Kisses, and Pigs, by Betsy Hearne tells about a girl named Louise who wishes accidently on a star that her brother was a pig. He dissapears, but her mother finds a stray pig with extraordinary blue eyes outside their pigpen. I have only gotten that far.

I think that Louise will soon notice that that stray pig is her brother. I will tell you in my next letter if I'm right. If I were Louise, I would tell my mom about the wish, and probably try talking to the pig. I might rather have a talking pet pig than an annoying brother! I think that her brother turning into a pig will help Louise get closer to him.

In Wishes, Kisses, and Pigs, I noticed that problem started out very close to the beginning. Does that make it better or worse? Does it depend? Please try to help me.

Your student,
Tara

One of Tara's dialogue journal entries for *Wishes, Kisses, and Pigs*

Writing About Reading

Selecting Goals Behaviors and Understandings to Notice, Teach, and Support

Thinking *within* the Text

- Include appropriate and important details when summarizing texts
- Provide evidence from the text or from personal experience to support written statements about a text
- Purposefully acquire vocabulary from text and use new words in talk and writing (including technical words)
- Notice, comment on, and actively work to acquire new vocabulary and intentionally use it (including complex and specialized words)
- Record information to support the memory of a text over several days of reading (notes, chapter summary statements)
- Make note of important or new information while reading nonfiction
- Access information from both print and graphics
- Write summaries that reflect literal understanding of a text
- Represent important information about a fiction text (characters, problems, sequence of events, problem resolution)
- Provide details that are important to understanding the relationship among plot, setting, and character traits
- Provide evidence of understanding complex plots with multiple events and characters in responses to reading and in-text summaries
- Continuously check with the evidence in a text to ensure that writing reflects understanding

Things You Can Write About in Your Reading Journal

- how the book reminds you of something from your own life
- how the author describes things
- how you feel about the book
- how the book makes you feel
- whether you like the book or not and WHY
- why you chose a book
- whether or not you would recommend the book to someone
- why you abandoned a book
- what you would change about the book and WHY
- explain what you found interesting
- whether the book is easy, just right, or too hard for now and WHY
- genre
- a little background information about what's going on in your book

Thinking *beyond* the Text

- Make connections between historical and cultural knowledge and a text
- Support thinking beyond the text with specific evidence from the text or personal knowledge
- Make a wide range of predictions using (and including) information as evidence from the text
- Predict what will happen in a text or after a text ends
- Predict what a character might do in other circumstances
- Infer characters' feelings and motivations and include evidence from the text to support thinking
- Record background information and formulate expectations and questions prior to reading a text; record new information learned from a text
- Make connections among the ideas in a text and among other texts on the same topic or by the same writers
- Specify the nature of connections in discussion and in writing
- Show connections between the setting, characters, and events of a text and reader's own personal experiences
- Infer the meaning of the writer's use of symbolism
- Make hypotheses about the significance of aspects of setting in the characters' or subjects' feelings, attitudes, and decisions
- Reflect diverse perspectives, especially when a text reveals insights into other cultures and parts of the world
- Interpret the mood of a text using language, illustrations, or the integration of both
- Reflect awareness of the author's underlying messages (themes)

Writing About Reading

Selecting Goals Behaviors and Understandings to Notice, Teach, and Support

Thinking *about* the Text

- Describe how the illustrations add to the meaning, mood, and quality of a text
- Analyze the picture book as an artistic whole, including how the illustrations and text work together to create meaning and mood
- Provide specific examples and evidence (either orally or in writing) to support written statements about the quality, accuracy, or craft of a text
- Comment on how layout contributes to the meaning and effectiveness of both fiction and nonfiction texts
- Critique the quality or authenticity of a text, including author's qualifications
- Note specific examples of the writer's craft (leads, dialogue, definition of terms within the text, divisions of text, use of descriptive language, interesting verbs, ending)
- Comment critically on the authenticity of the text, including the writer's qualifications
- Show how a text is organized (narrative and expository)
- Recognize and comment on aspects of narrative structure (beginning, series of events, high point of the story, ending)
- Show awareness of temporal sequence, compare and contrast, cause and effect, and problem and solution
- Note the different ways the nonfiction writer organized and provided information
- Represent in writing, graphic organizer, diagram, outline, or drawing the organizational structure of a nonfiction text (categories, subcategories, headings, subheadings)
- Identify and record the genre of a text (realistic and historical fiction, fantasy, traditional literature, biography, informational)
- Use knowledge of genre to write about the quality or characteristics of a text
- Use genre to interpret a text or make predictions about it
- Comment on the writer's use of words precisely to convey meaning or mood (subtle shades of meaning)
- Comment on the author's word choice and use of language to create subtle shades of meaning and to create the mood
- Show awareness of a writer's use of figurative language and sensory imagery
- Recognize the narrator and discuss how the choice of first or third person point of view affects the reader
- Write statements of the underlying message or theme of the story and include examples from the text or rationales
- Comment on how the author has revealed the underlying messages or the theme of a story (through character, plot, events)
- Use specific vocabulary to write about text: *title, author, illustrator, cover, dedication, endpapers, author's note, illustrator's note, character, main character, supporting characters, character development, setting, problem, events, resolution, theme, fiction/nonfiction, genre, events, timeline, caption, legend, accuracy and authenticity, names of genres, poetry, table of contents, topics, subject* (of biography), *sections, subheadings, categories, index, glossary*

Writing About Reading

Selecting Genres and Forms

Students learn different ways to share their thinking about reading in explicit minilessons. Using modeled or shared writing, the teacher may demonstrate the process and engage the students in the construction of the text. Often, the teacher and students read several examples of a form, identify its characteristics, and try out the type of response. Then, students can select from the range of possible forms when responding to reading (usually in a reader's notebook).

Functional Writing

- Sketches or drawings to represent a text and provide a basis for discussion or writing
- Short-writes responding to a text in a variety of ways (for example, personal response, interpretation, character analysis, description, or critique)
- Notes representing interesting language from a text or examples of the writer's craft (quotes from a text)
- Notes to be used in later discussion or writing
- Grids that show analysis of a text (a form of graphic organizer)
- Graphic organizers that show how the ideas in a text are related to each other or show comparisons, timelines, and so on
- Letters to other readers or to authors and illustrators (including dialogue letters in a reader's notebook)
- Letters to newspaper or magazine editors in response to articles
- Poster or advertisement that tells about a text in an attention-getting way

Narrative Writing

- Cartoons, comics, or storyboards to present a story or information
- Plot summaries
- Scripts for readers' theater
- Storyboards to represent significant events in a text

Dear Ms. O.

I think it is half/half true that all stories need happy endings. Sometimes, books like Snowbound just end. Epics tend to have a good ending, although it feels there is always some-thing else to be told. And realistic fictions seem to end super-happy. Personally, I prefer the "epic" ending (that I described). And what I said about "extreme" fantastical ele-ments' is that the things like the Ringwraith pursuit, and dangers of orcs, etc.

Well, for a ~~the~~ breif update of the book. The Fellowship has "met up" with Haldir and his two brothers, with the same quote "You breath so loud we could have shot you in the dark," (pretty much the same quote) but under different circumstances. A thing I've noticed is that in each realm of the book (i.e. elves, hobbits, men, and dwarves the species in the realm of which they "belong" to, the person(s) that is with that race temporarily takes lead of the group. And I've made a connection between Gimli and I. We both can be stubborn people, and overly cautious of our, "belongings." I think that J.R.R. Tolkien makes each place seem new, and mysterious too. And here's a question, if you were a species of Middle-Earth, which one would you like to be. I'd choose to be an elf or man.

Sincerely,
Ethan

A reader's notebook entry from Ethan as he reads J.R.R. Tolkien

Writing About Reading

Selecting Genres and Forms

Informational Writing

- Projects that present ideas and opinions about texts or topics in an organized way (using text and visual images)
- Reports that include text and graphic organizers to present information drawn from texts
- Book reviews
- News or feature article based on reading one or more texts
- Author study, reflecting knowledge of biographical information or response to one or more books by an author
- Biographical sketch on an author or the subject of a biography
- Illustrator study, reflecting knowledge of biographical information or response to one or more books by an artist
- How-to articles that explain how something is made or done (based on one or more texts)
- Drawings or photographs with labels or legends illustrating information from a text
- Outlines that include headings, subheadings, and sub-subheadings to reflect the organization of the text
- Photo essay or picture essay explaining a topic or representing a setting or plot
- Interviews with an author or expert (questions and responses designed to provide information)

Poetic Writing

- Poetic texts written in response to a prose text
- Poetic texts written in response to poems (same style, topic, mood)

Reading Response Letters
A response might include:
• What you felt when you read the book
• what you noticed about the author's style (opinion)
• why you think he/she wrote this way
• what you liked and didn't like and why
• predictions that you have
• anything that this book reminds you of
• questions that you have
• use of underlining and some important words
• how your life does or doesn't relate to book
• talk about characters

Writing About Reading

Selecting Goals Behaviors and Understandings to Notice, Teach, and Support

Thinking *within* the Text

- Include appropriate and important details when summarizing texts
- Provide evidence from the text or from personal experience to support written statements about a text
- Purposefully acquire vocabulary from text and use new words in talk and writing (including technical words)
- Notice, comment on, and actively work to acquire new vocabulary and intentionally use it (including complex and specialized words)
- Record information to support the memory of a text over several days of reading (notes, chapter summary statements)
- Make note of important or new information while reading nonfiction
- Make notes to help in remembering where to find information in long and complex texts so that opinions and theories can be checked through revisiting and as preparation for writing longer pieces
- Write statements that reflect understanding of both the text body and graphics and the integration of the two
- Represent important information about a fictional text (characters, setting, plot)
- Provide details that are important to understanding the relationship among plot, setting, and character traits
- Provide evidence of understanding complex plots with multiple events and characters in responses to reading and in-text summaries
- Continuously check with the evidence in a text to ensure that writing reflects understanding

Thinking *beyond* the Text

- Make connections between historical and cultural knowledge and a text
- Support thinking beyond the text with specific evidence from the text or personal knowledge
- Make a wide range of predictions using (and including) information as evidence from the text
- Predict what will happen in a text or after a text ends
- Predict what a character might do in other circumstances
- Write inferences as to characters' traits, motivations, attitudes, and decisions based on evidence from the text
- Express changes in opinions or understandings as a result of reading
- Show connections using graphic organizers, drawings, or writing to other texts by topic, major ideas, authors' styles, and genres
- Show evidence of connections to other texts (theme, plot, characters, structure, writing style)
- Show connections between the setting, characters, and events of a text and reader's own personal experiences
- Make connections between texts and reader's own personal life (including historical fiction and high fantasy)
- Recognize and discuss the author's use of symbols and their meaning
- Show the setting's importance to the plot and to characters' decisions (and the subjects of biography)
- Recognize and discuss different cultural and historical perspectives
- Interpret the mood of a text using language, illustrations, or the integration of both
- State an interpretation of the writer's underlying messages (themes)

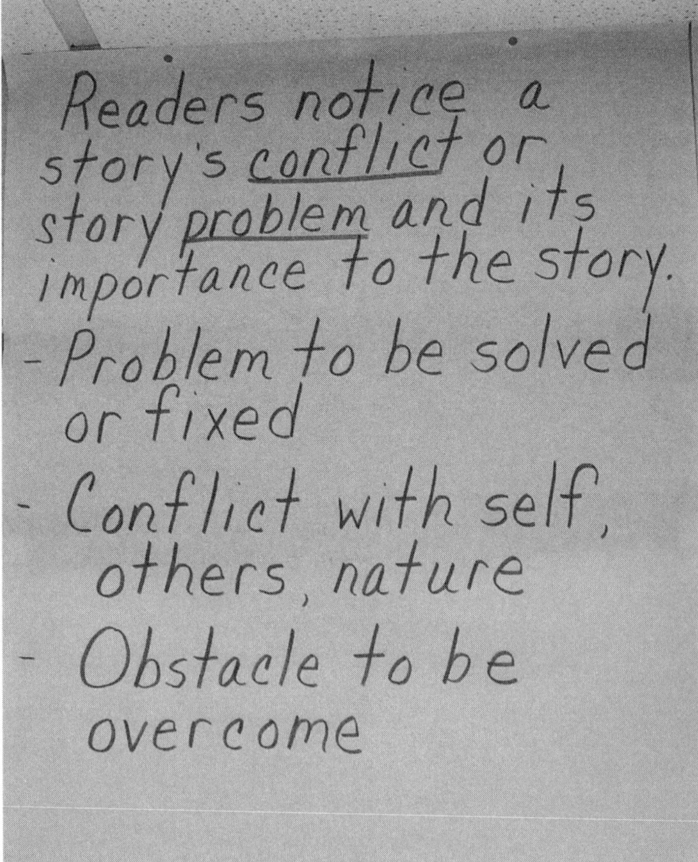

Readers notice a story's conflict or story problem and its importance to the story.
- Problem to be solved or fixed
- Conflict with self, others, nature
- Obstacle to be overcome

Writing About Reading

Selecting Goals Behaviors and Understandings to Notice, Teach, and Support

Thinking *about* the Text

- Analyze the picture book as an artistic whole, including how the illustrations and text work together to create meaning and mood
- Provide specific examples and evidence (either orally or in writing) to support written statements about the quality, accuracy, or craft of a text
- Note specific examples of the writer's craft (leads, dialogue, definition of terms within the text, divisions of text, use of descriptive language, interesting verbs, ending)
- Comment critically on the authenticity of the text, including the writer's qualifications
- Analyze a text or group of texts to reveal insights into the writer's craft (the way the writer reveals characters or uses symbolism, humor, irony, suspense)
- Critically analyze the quality of a poem or work of fiction or nonfiction, offering rationales for points
- Describe, analyze, and write critically about a text as an integrated whole, including how text, illustrations, and other features work together to convey meaning
- Recognize and comment on aspects of narrative structure (beginning, series of events, high point of the story, ending)
- Note the different ways the nonfiction writer organized and provided information
- Represent in writing, graphic organizer, diagram, outline, or drawing the organizational structure of a nonfiction text (categories, subcategories, headings, subheadings)
- Use knowledge of genre to interpret and write about the quality or characteristics of a text
- Specify the genre (full range) and demonstrate use of genre characteristics to understand the text
- Comment on the author's word choice and use of language to create subtle shades of meaning and to create the mood
- Recognize and comment on how a writer uses language to evoke sensory images
- Recognize and comment on how a writer uses language to create symbolic meaning
- Recognize the narrator and discuss how the choice of first or third person point of view affects the reader
- Recognize the narrator and discuss how the choice of first, second, or third person point of view contributes to the reader's enjoyment and understanding
- Comment on how the author has revealed the underlying messages or the theme of a story (through character, plot, events)
- State an interpretation of the writer's underlying messages (themes)
- Comment on how layout and the format of a text contribute to the meaning, effectiveness, and artistic quality of both fiction and nonfiction
- Use specific vocabulary to write about text: *title, author, illustrator, cover, dedication, endpapers, author's note, illustrator's note, character, main character, supporting characters, character development, "round" and "flat" characters, setting, problem, events, resolution, theme, fiction/nonfiction, genre, events, timeline, caption, legend, accuracy and authenticity, names of genres, poetry, table of contents, topics, subject* (of biography), *sections, subheadings, categories, index, glossary*

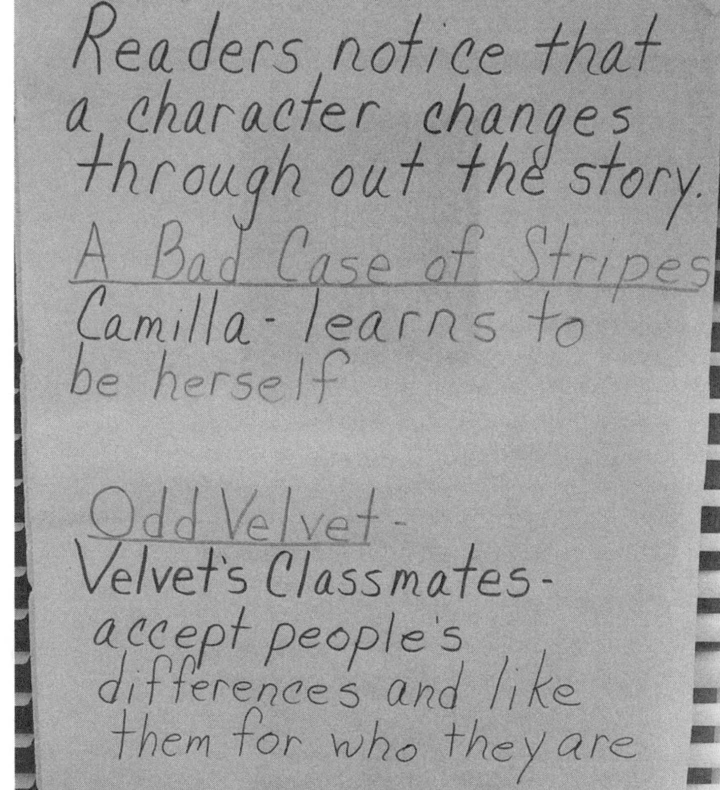

Readers notice that a character changes through out the story.
A Bad Case of Stripes
Camilla - learns to be herself
Odd Velvet -
Velvet's Classmates - accept people's differences and like them for who they are

Writing About Reading

Selecting Genres and Forms

Students learn different ways to share their thinking about reading in explicit minilessons. Using modeled or shared writing, the teacher may demonstrate the process and engage the students in the construction of the text. Often, the teacher and students read several examples of a form, identify its characteristics, and try out the type of response. Then, students can select from the range of possible forms when responding to reading (usually in a reader's notebook).

Functional Writing

- Sketches or drawings to represent a text and provide a basis for discussion or writing
- Short-writes responding to a text in a variety of ways (for example, personal response, interpretation, character analysis, description, or critique)
- Notes representing interesting language from a text or examples of the writer's craft (quotes from a text)
- Notes to be used in later discussion or writing
- Grids that show analysis of a text (a form of graphic organizer)
- Letters to other readers or to authors and illustrators (including dialogue letters in a reader's notebook)
- Letters to newspaper or magazine editors in response to articles
- Poster or advertisement that tells about a text in an attention-getting way

Narrative Writing

- Cartoons, comics, or storyboards to present a story or information
- Plot summaries
- Scripts for readers' theater
- Storyboards to represent significant events in a text

THE KITE RUNNER
By Khaled Hosseini.
324 pp. New York:
Riverhead Books

In his debut novel, Khaled Hosseini offers a gripping, unique look into modern Afghanistan. The essence of the book is the build-up of a friendship between Amir, an upper class boy, and Hassan, his servant, age-mate and friend, and the subsequent feelings that Amir experiences when he abandons Hassan as he is brutally attacked and raped.

The first third of the book takes place in Afghanistan thirty years ago, before the Russian invasion. Things have a warm and safe feeling, as Amir and Hassan play and grow up together. There is an underlying tension as plot elements foretell the conflict ahead. As Amir and his father escape the Russians, Hosseini's depiction of the trip, under cramped and hot conditions and with terrifying anxiety, is reminiscent of Elie Wiesel's account of his train ride to Auschwitz in Night. In the dramatic conclusion, Amir returns to Afghanistan to look for Hassan.

In The Kite Runner, Hosseini brilliantly weaves fiction and current events. These interlace so well that one forgets this is fiction and not autobiographical. Unlike most writers today, he does not candy-coat reality, accurately portraying the horrors of modern-day Afghanistan.

This first attempt is a real page turner. It provides a heart-wrenching window into the struggles of the Afghan people.

First page of Adrian's book review of *The Kite Runner*

Writing About Reading

Selecting Genres and Forms

Informational Writing

- Projects that present ideas and opinions about texts or topics in an organized way (using text and visual images)
- Reports that include text and graphic organizers to present information drawn from texts
- Book reviews
- News or feature article based on reading one or more texts
- Critiques or analyses of informational articles
- Literary essays that present ideas about a text and may include examples and a short retelling of the text
- Author study, reflecting knowledge of biographical information or response to one or more books by an author
- Biographical sketch on an author or the subject of a biography
- Illustrator study, reflecting knowledge of biographical information or response to one or more books by an artist
- How-to articles that explain how something is made or done (based on one or more texts)
- Drawings or photographs with labels or legends illustrating information from a text
- Outlines that include headings, subheadings, and sub-subheadings to reflect the organization of the text
- Photo essay or picture essay explaining a topic or representing a setting or plot
- Interviews with an author or expert (questions and responses designed to provide information)

Poetic Writing

- Poetic texts written in response to a prose text
- Poetic texts written in response to poems (same style, topic, mood)

Dear Ms D

Now I'm also finished, Behind the Bedroom Wall by Laura E. Williams. This is an breathtaking book that is based in the time of the Nazis.

Before, Korrina shunned Jews and loved Hitler, the man who would make their Fatherland stronger. But now Korrina realizes that Jews are nothing to despise, and the Fuhrer is the man to hate.

This book is historical fiction. It takes place during and around World War 2, and many of these sort of events did take place during history. But this book is fictional because the names and story were fake, even though similar things happened to other families.

I think that Korrina made the right choice by not turning her parents in, and opening her eyes to see what's really going on. She shouldn't have trusted Rita, even though she was her best friend. During that time period, you should never tell anyone who is involved in being a "loyal German" that you like Jews, or feel sorry for them, unless you are completely certain they have the same feelings about it (like Korrina's parents.)

Happy Reading,
Kirstie

Kirstie's reader's notebook entry for *Behind the Bedroom Wall*

Writing About Reading

Selecting Goals Behaviors and Understandings to Notice, Teach, and Support

Thinking *within* the Text

- Provide evidence from the text or from personal experience to support written statements about a text
- Purposefully acquire vocabulary from text and use new words in talk and writing (including technical words)
- Consistently and automatically notice new vocabulary words and use them appropriately
- Explore and comment on complex definitions for new words, including figurative and connotative uses
- Make notes to help in remembering where to find information in long and complex texts so that opinions and theories can be checked through revisiting and as preparation for writing longer pieces
- Notice and make notes or write descriptions to help in remembering significant attributes for multiple characters
- Notice and make note of or summarize significant information from illustrations or graphics; include information from graphics in writing summaries of texts
- Write statements that reflect understanding of both the text body and graphics and the integration of the two
- Provide evidence of understanding complex plots with multiple events and characters in responses to reading and in-text summaries
- Continuously check with the evidence in a text to ensure that writing reflects understanding

Thinking *beyond* the Text

- Make connections between historical and cultural knowledge and a text
- Support thinking beyond the text with specific evidence from the text or personal knowledge
- Predict what will happen in a text or after a text ends
- Predict what a character might do in other circumstances
- Reflect inferences about the main and supporting characters' feelings, motivations, attitudes, and decisions based on information from the text (also for subjects of biography)
- Express changes in opinions, attitudes, or understandings based on insights gained from fiction or nonfiction texts
- Use graphic organizers, drawings, or writing to other texts by topic, major ideas, authors' styles, and genres to show connections
- Show evidence of connections to other texts (theme, plot, characters, structure, writing style)
- Describe connections between fiction and nonfiction texts, historical fiction and content area study, fantasy and realism
- Show connections between the setting, characters, and events of a text and reader's own personal experiences
- Make connections between texts and reader's own personal life (including historical fiction and high fantasy)
- Recognize and discuss the author's use of symbols and their meaning
- Note the significance of setting and its relationship to the plot and characters' actions
- Compare perspectives on a given text or writer
- Express understanding of the diversity of our society gained from reading a text
- State an interpretation of the writer's underlying messages (themes)
- Infer and describe a writer's attitudes toward social issues as revealed in texts
- Recognize parts of a text in which a writer is saying one thing but meaning another
- Use organized notes or outlines as a support for writing about a variety of texts

Writing About Reading

Selecting Goals Behaviors and Understandings to Notice, Teach, and Support

Thinking *about* the Text

- Provide specific examples and evidence (either orally or in writing) to support written statements about the quality, accuracy, or craft of a text
- Critically analyze the quality of a poem or work of fiction or nonfiction, offering rationales for points
- Describe, analyze, and write critically about a text as an integrated whole, including how text, illustrations, and other features work together to convey meaning
- Critique realistic fiction texts in terms of authenticity of characters, accurate portrayal of current or historical issues, and appropriate voice and tone
- Critique informational texts in terms of the quality of writing, accuracy, the logic of conclusions, and the coherence of the organization
- Recognize bias in fiction or nonfiction texts and identify appropriate examples and rationales
- Recognize and comment on aspects of narrative structure (beginning, series of events, high point of the story, ending)
- Represent in writing, graphic organizer, diagram, outline, or drawing the organizational structure of a nonfiction text (categories, subcategories, headings, subheadings)
- Specify the genre (full range) and demonstrate use of genre characteristics to understand the text
- Comment on the author's word choice and use of language to create subtle shades of meaning and to create the mood
- Recognize and comment on the writer's use of language in a satirical way or to convey irony
- Recognize and comment on how a writer uses language to evoke sensory images
- Recognize and comment on how a writer uses language to create symbolic meaning
- Recognize the narrator and discuss how the choice of first, second, or third person point of view contributes to the reader's enjoyment and understanding
- Note aspects of the writer's craft, including word selection, choice of narrator (first, second, or third person), use of symbolism, leads, dialogue, definition of terms within the text, divisions of text, and use of description
- State an interpretation of the writer's underlying messages (themes)
- Analyze a text or group of texts to reveal insights into the writer's craft (the way the writer reveals characters or uses symbolism, humor, irony, suspense)
- Comment on how layout and the format of a text contribute to the meaning, effectiveness, and artistic quality of both fiction and nonfiction
- Use specific vocabulary to write about text: *title, author, illustrator, cover, dedication, endpapers, author's note, illustrator's note, character, main character, supporting characters, character development, "round" and "flat" characters, setting, problem, events, resolution, theme, fiction/nonfiction, genre, events, timeline, caption, legend, accuracy and authenticity, names of genres, poetry, table of contents, topics, subject* (of biography), *sections, subheadings, categories, index, glossary*

Writing

Introduction to Writing

The classroom, from kindergarten through middle school, is a place where writers grow. They learn by engaging in the writing process with the expert help of the teacher and with the support of their peers. Writing is multifaceted in that it orchestrates thinking, language, and mechanics. The writing process includes several subprocesses (getting an idea, drafting, revising, editing, and publishing), many of which are recursive and may happen simultaneously.

Writing is a basic tool for learning as well as for communicating with others. In our schools, students are expected to write in every subject area. We want them to become individuals who can use many types of writing for a wide range of purposes and audiences throughout their lives. Elsewhere we have written that "the writing terrain spreads out in many directions, real and imaginary, and encompasses in-depth intellectual investigations of biology, geology, history, anthropology, and other fields" (Fountas and Pinnell 2001b, 423).

We want to help students develop a basic knowledge of the writing process and to know how to vary the process for different genres and purposes. Even young children can produce simple publications; as they write year after year, they engage in the same basic process but at more sophisticated levels. Their range becomes broader and their publications more complex.

Almost every genre listed in the continuum is first demonstrated in a read-aloud or with examples of *shared, interactive,* or *modeled writing.* Young children will have a shared or group experience in all genres they are eventually expected to produce independently.

- In *shared writing,* the teacher and students compose a text together. The teacher is the scribe. Often, especially with very young children, the teacher works on a chart displayed on an easel. Children contribute each word of the composition and reread it many times. Sometimes the teacher asks the children to say the word slowly as they think how a word is spelled. At other times the teacher (with student input) writes the composition on the chart more quickly. The text becomes a model, example, or reference for student writing and discussion.

- *Interactive writing* is identical to and proceeds in the same way as shared writing, with one exception: occasionally the teacher, while making teaching points that help children attend to various features of letters and words, will invite a student to come up to the easel and contribute a letter, word, or part of a word.

- *Modeled writing* may be used at every grade level. Here, the teacher demonstrates the process of writing in a particular genre, sometimes thinking aloud to reveal what is going on in his mind. The teacher may have prepared the piece of writing prior to class but talks through the process with the students.

We believe that a major component in learning to write in a particular genre is to study mentor texts—works of children's literature, fiction, and nonfiction that you have read and discussed—and we have built the study of mentor texts into every appropriate Understanding the Genre section. Writers learn from other writers. If students experience several books by an author and illustrator, they soon learn what is special about that writer's craft. They start to notice topics, characteristics of illustrations, types of stories, and language. They may record or remember words and language in order to borrow it. As they grow more sophisticated, they understand that writers use other writers as examples and learn from them. They notice what writers do to make their writing effective and begin to use mentor texts as models when planning, revising, and publishing writing. They notice purpose, topic, and genre choice and begin to make those choices for themselves. Students may even participate in formal study of authors to learn about their craft—how they portray characters, use dialogue, and organize information. Graphics and illustrations offer many examples to young writers relative to illustrating their work clearly. Very sophisticated readers and writers are still learning from mentor texts as they seek examples of the treatment of themes or ideas, create dialogue and show character development, and prepare persuasive or critical pieces. Through the process of taking on all of the understandings listed in this continuum, the students realize that other writers can be their mentors.

Additional complexity is introduced into the process of becoming a writer if the learner is an English language learner. The expectations for each grade level of the continuum are the same for students whose first language is and for speakers whose second language is English. The expectations for instruction, however, are different. English language learners will need a greater level of support as they expand their control of oral English and, alongside it, written English. Start where students are, but give them rich opportunities to hear written language read aloud and to talk about concepts and ideas before they are expected to write about them.

Interactive writing is an effective tool for helping English language learners begin to compose and construct written text. By composing text collaboratively, with the teacher as scribe to guide the structure and control conventions, students can create their own exemplar texts. Interactive writing offers group support and strong models. As students reread the interactive writing, they internalize conventional English syntactic patterns, relevant vocabulary, and the features of the genre. In individual conferences, teachers can help English language learners rehearse what they want to write and help them expand their ideas. Also include frequent experiences with shared and performance reading, which involves students in rereading and thinking about the meaning of familiar texts.

Looking across the writing continuum grade by grade, we can see a gradual building of expertise but only a few actual changes in goals. Since learning to write is akin to a spiral, many of the same goals are repeated across the grades. However, students will be working toward these goals in increasingly sophisticated ways.

In this continuum, we describe writing in four major areas: purpose and genre; craft; conventions; and process. These four areas of learning apply to all students, kindergarten through grade eight.

Purpose and Genre

The writer has a purpose in mind and selects the genre accordingly. You may want to tell a story that will communicate a larger meaning; you may want to inform or entertain; you may want to persuade people to take action on an issue that is important to you. It is important to recognize that effective writers do not write in a genre just to practice it. They choose the genre that will best convey the meaning they intend. Of course, teachers introduce new genres to students so that they can learn to write in those genres, but the ultimate goal is to establish a repertoire of genres from which they can choose. It is important to establish the desire to write in a genre by making it interesting and enjoyable. For instructional purposes, we have described traditional genres within each purpose category, even as we recognize that virtually any genre might be used to support a given purpose—an informational friendly letter, for example, or a functional poem.

In the overall continuum, we categorize writing genres under four purposes: narrative; informational; poetic; and functional. For grades six through eight, we have added a fifth category, hybrids. Hybrid texts combine genres to support any chosen purpose. For each genre within these categories, we have two important sets of information: Understanding the Genre, which reflects key understandings particular to the genre (what students need to *know* about the genre); and Writing in the Genre, which refers to the way the student demonstrates understanding by taking on the various kinds of writing within the genre (what students *do* with the genre). Also for each genre, we list sample forms of writing that can, among others, be part of the writing curriculum.

Narrative Genres

A narrative is a story with a beginning, a series of events, and an ending. Narratives may be fiction or nonfiction, and they usually tell about important or exciting events from a character's (or subject's) life. A narrative can be very simple or highly complex. This continuum encompasses three kinds of narratives: memoir, short fiction, and biography. For each type of text, we describe important understandings and identify specific goals related to writing in that genre.

Memoir. Memoir includes personal narrative. We want students to learn the craft and conventions of memoir by writing about their own lives. Very young students begin by sketching, telling, and writing simple stories about their families, friends, and pets. It is important for students to understand from the beginning that they are writing about what they know. In doing so, they will learn to observe their worlds closely, looking for examples that will be true to life. Students develop the ability to write fiction by telling these stories from experience.

Throughout the grades, students continue to write memoir. They learn to write about "small moments" that capture strong feelings or significant experiences. They begin to understand the more formal notion of memoir as a brief, often intense memory of an event or person. A memoir has an element of reflection and communicates a larger meaning to the reader.

Short fiction. Students can think of fiction as a short story about an event in the life of a main character that gets across a point. We want them to learn that good fiction reveals something about life, connects with readers, and communicates the deeper meanings of a theme. Short fiction can be realistic fiction or fantasy, contemporary or historical. Younger children may write very simple stories about people or animals; they may retell their own version of an animal fantasy. As they grow more sophisticated, students will undertake such aspects of fiction as characterization and plot development.

Biography. Biography is nonfiction but it is usually presented as a narrative. We want students to learn that biography is a true story about a person. Younger writers can tell simple stories about family members or friends; older writers can produce fully documented biographical sketches or profiles of role models or public figures, contemporary or historical. In all cases, the biographer selects a subject for stated reasons and selects events and tells the story in a way that shows readers the writer's perspective. Writers use craft to make the biography interesting. It may be fictionalized for interest and readability, but the writer must disclose anything that is not documented.

Informational Genres

Informational texts include literary nonfiction, expository nonfiction, and essays.

Literary nonfiction. Not all nonfiction writing takes the form of reports or textbooks! Especially in recent years, we have seen the publication of highly engaging and literary short and longer nonfiction. We want students to learn from these mentor texts how to produce interesting, literary nonfiction that focuses on a topic or one aspect of a topic. They learn how to use resources to be sure they have accurate information and how to sustain focus. They also learn that they need to make the writing interesting to readers and help readers learn about the topic in new ways.

Expository nonfiction. Throughout our schooling and beyond, the ability to write a feature article or a report is useful and necessary. Students learn that a feature article focuses on one aspect of a topic and that a report includes several aspects of a topic. In both kinds of text, the writer makes statements and backs them up with facts, examples, and other evidence. The writer may seek to persuade readers to take a particular view or take action. (We do not suggest teaching this genre to younger writers because of the sophistication it requires.)

Essay. An essay is a highly sophisticated, short literary composition in which the author clearly states a point of view. The essay may be analytical, critical, or persuasive. The ability to compose an essay is based on many years not only of writing but also of engaging in critical thinking. Essays are appropriate in the upper elementary grades and middle school.

Poetic Genres

Young writers need to learn to understand poetry as a special genre for communicating meaning and describing feelings and sensory images. There are many different forms of poetry: traditional rhymes, songs, and verses; free verse; lyric poetry; narrative poetry; limericks; cinquains; concrete poetry; haiku; "found" poetry; list poems; and formula poems. Once students have a well-established understanding of free verse, you can introduce them to a variety of other forms through mentor texts. Before writing poetry, students need to hear poems read aloud and read poems aloud themselves. This exposure gives students the feel of poetry and lets them gradually internalize the forms it can take. They learn to observe the world closely and to experiment with words and phrases so that they begin to produce poetic language.

Functional Genres

As adults, we use a large range of functional texts every day, ranging from very simple communications to sophisticated letters. The genres that follow are categorized as functional.

Friendly letters. Notes, cards, invitations, email, and friendly letters are written communications that require the writer to provide particular kinds of information and to write in a tone and form that is appropriate.

Formal letters. Business letters and editorials are formal documents written with a particular purpose. They get right to the point, exclude extraneous details, and have required parts.

Lists and procedures. Lists are planning tools that help people accomplish daily tasks; they are also the building blocks of more complicated texts, such as poems and informational pieces. Procedures, like how-to texts and directions, require student writers to think through and clearly explain the steps in a process.

Test writing. Test writing is required in academia. Students must learn that some writing is for the expressed purpose of showing someone else how much you know. They need to analyze a test for the expectations and write to the point.

Writing about reading. Writing about reading, too, is required in school to reflect students' thinking within, beyond, and about a text they have read. Almost any genre or form can be used to respond to a text. We have provided a complete separate continuum for this important area of literacy.

Hybrids

Hybrid texts, those that combine more than one genre into a coherent whole, serve any purpose the writer chooses. They may engage, inform, persuade, or serve a functional purpose. We have included these at the upper levels only. At their simplest—embedding a friendly letter into an ongoing narrative, for example—they may be manageable for the fluent intermediate grade writer. More complex forms—parallel explanation and narrative, for example—require deft perspective and style changes that can only be managed by advanced writers.

Craft

The previous section describes the product of writing—what young writers are expected to produce as an outcome. Getting to that product is an educational process and requires attention to skills and strategies in the next three sections: craft, conventions, and the process of writing.

All the previous genres involve crafting an effective piece of writing that is clearly organized and contains well-developed ideas. The writer must use language appropriate for the genre, to include the specific words selected. We want younger students to consider word choice carefully so that the piece conveys precise meaning. Older students will have larger vocabularies, but they can also use tools like a thesaurus. Above all, the writing must have *voice*—it must reveal the person behind the writing. That means the writing takes on characteristics that reveal the writer's unique style and personality. Younger children can write with voice if they are expressing feelings or telling about events that are important to them. Voice develops throughout a writer's career and it is revealed in the way the writer uses every aspect of craft—sentence structure, word choice, language, and punctuation.

The craft section of the continuum states goals for each area. These goals apply in general to all genres, though some are more relevant to some than others. We include the following:

Organization. This section addresses the way the writer arranges the information or structures the narrative. It includes the structure of the whole text—beginnings and endings, and the arrangement of ideas.

Idea development. Idea development focuses on the way the writer presents and supports the main ideas and themes of the text.

Language use. This section describes goals for the way the writer uses sentences, phrases, and expressions to describe events, actions, or information.

Word choice. Word choice attends to the particular words the writer selects to convey meaning.

Voice. Voice is the individual's unique style as a writer.

Conventions

Knowing and observing the conventions of writing makes it possible to communicate ideas clearly. Substance must be there and so must craft, but without correct spelling, conventional grammar, and punctuation, it will be difficult to get people to value the writing. Of course, great writers often violate some of these conventions, especially in fiction, but they do so for an artistic purpose. The first eight years of the elementary school is the place to establish a firm grasp of the conventions of writing, including:

Text layout. Young children must learn the basics of writing words left to right across the page with spaces between them. But even sophisticated writers must develop the ability to use layout in a way that contributes to and enhances meaning.

Grammar. The grammar of written language is more formal than spoken language. There are rules for how sentences are put together, how parts of speech are used, how verb tense is made consistent, and how paragraphs are formed.

Capitalization. The appropriate use of capital letters makes texts more readable and signals proper nouns and specialized functions (titles, for example).

Punctuation. Punctuation adds meaning to the text, makes it more readable, and signals to the reader the writer's intentions in terms of using meaningful phrases.

Spelling. Conventional spelling is critical to the presentation of a piece of writing, both in appearance and meaning.

Handwriting and word processing. The writer's handwriting must be legible. Effective handwriting also increases writing fluency and ease, so the writer can give more attention to the message. For the same reasons, it is important for students to develop rapid, efficient keyboarding skills.

Learning these conventions is a challenging and complex task, one accomplished over many years. We do not want students to devote so much time and energy to conventions that they become fearful writers or do not develop voice. We do want conventions to be an important part of the editing process.

Writing Process

Students learn to write by writing—by engaging in all of the component processes many times. The writing process is recursive; the components take place roughly in order, but at any point in the process the writer can and will use any or all of the components. In this continuum, we describe four key phases in the process: rehearsing and planning, drafting and revising, editing and proofreading, and publishing. In addition, we've included two overarching categories that pervade the entire process: sketching and drawing and viewing self as a writer.

Rehearsing and Planning

Rehearsing and planning involves gathering information, trying out ideas, and thinking about some critical aspects of the text, such as purpose and audience, before beginning to write. Of course, a writer will often stop during drafting and gather more information or rethink the purpose after discussing it with others. This area includes curriculum goals for:

Purpose. The writer has a clear purpose for writing the text and this purpose influences genre selection and organization.

Audience. The writer thinks of the audience, which may be known or unknown. It is important even for younger students to think of the audience as all readers of the text—not just the teacher.

Oral language. Writers can generate ideas and try out their ideas through conversation with others.

Gathering seeds. An important tool of the writer is a notebook in which he or she can collect ideas, experiment, sketch, diagram, and freewrite. The writer uses this notebook as a resource for ideas, formats, and techniques.

Content, topic, theme. The content or topic of the piece is selected carefully with interest, purpose, and theme in mind.

Inquiry and research. In preparation for writing informational texts and biography, the writer will often spend an extended time gathering information. This is also true when an individual is writing historical fiction or developing a plot in an unfamiliar setting.

Genre/form. With audience in mind, as well as content or purpose, the writer selects the genre for the piece and the particular form of the genre.

Drafting and Revising

The writer may produce an initial draft and then revise it to make it more effective, but most writers revise while drafting and sometimes also draft more material after revising. There are a limited number of ways to draft and revise a text, and students use them throughout the grades, including:

Producing a draft. The writer writes an initial draft, getting ideas down quickly.

Rereading. The writer rereads to remember what has been written, to assess clarity, and to revise.

Adding information. The writer adds ideas, details, words, phrases, sentences, paragraphs, or dialogue to a piece of writing to make it more effective.

Deleting information. The writer deletes redundancy, unimportant information, and extraneous details to make the piece clearer.

Reorganizing information. The writer moves information around to make the piece more logical or more interesting.

Changing text. The writer identifies vague parts and provides specificity; works on transitions; or changes words, phrases, and sentences.

Using tools and techniques. The writer acquires a repertoire of tools and techniques for drafting and revising a text.

Understanding the process. The writer actively works on drafting and revising and uses other writers as mentors and peer reviewers.

Editing and Proofreading

Once the content and organization are in place, students may wish to polish selected drafts to prepare them for publication. The editing and proofreading phase focuses on the form of the composition.

Editing for conventions. Over the years, as students acquire knowledge of the conventions, we can expect them to use that knowledge in editing their writing.

Using tools. Students also need to learn the tools that will help them in editing—for example, the dictionary, a thesaurus, and computer technology.

Understanding the process. Students learn when, how, and why to elicit editing help.

Publishing

Writers will produce many final drafts that are shared with their peers, but sometimes they will publish pieces. That means that the piece will have received a final edit and will include all the elements of a published work, including a cover with all the necessary information, typed and laid-out text, and graphics as appropriate. For some students, publishing means reading a piece to peers to celebrate the writing. Taking this final step is important for young writers because it gives them a sense of accomplishment and gives them an opportunity to share their talent with a wider audience. Over time, as they build up many published pieces, they can reflect on their own development as writers.

Sketching and Drawing

Whether used to capture ideas, store quick images to aid recall, visually arrange ideas to clarify structure or information in a draft, or to enhance the effectiveness of a published work, sketching and drawing support the entire writing process. Goals in this section apply to all phases of the writing process.

Viewing Self as Writer

Finally, we need to think of our students as lifelong writers. Developing as a writer means more than producing piece after piece and gradually improving. We want our students to make writing a part of their lives—to see themselves as writers who are constantly observing the world and gathering ideas and information for their writing. They need to become independent, self-motivated writers, consciously entering into their own learning and development. Most of all, they need to be able to seek out mentors so that they can continue to expand their understandings of the possibilities of this craft. In the last section of the continuum, we list goals in this area.

Writing

Selecting Purpose and Genre

Narrative: To tell a story

***Memoir** (personal narrative, autobiography)*

Understanding the Genre

- Understand how to craft personal narratives and memoirs from mentor texts
- Understand that a story from your life is usually written in first person (using *I*)
- Understand that writers tell stories from their own lives
- Understand that the writer can look back or think about the memory or experience and share thoughts and feelings about it
- Understand that a story should be one that is important to the writer

Writing in the Genre

- Think of topics, events, or experiences from own life that are interesting to write about
- Write an engaging beginning and a satisfying ending to stories
- Understand that a story can be a "small moment" (description of a brief but memorable experience)
- Provide some descriptive details to make the story more interesting
- Use dialogue as appropriate to add to the meaning of the story
- Use simple words that show the passage of time (*then, after*)
- Explain one's thoughts and feelings about an experience or event
- Develop voice as a writer through telling own stories or memories from own life
- Usually write in first person to achieve a strong voice
- Tell a story across several pages in order to develop the story or idea
- Tell events in order that they occurred in personal narratives

Informational: To explain or give facts about a topic

Literary Nonfiction

Understanding the Genre

- Understand how to write literary nonfiction from mentor texts
- Understand literary nonfiction as writing that engages and entertains readers but teaches them about a topic

Writing in the Genre

- Write books or short pieces that are enjoyable to read and at the same time give information to readers about a topic
- Use features (for example, page numbers, title, labeled pictures, table of contents, or others) to guide the reader
- Think about the audience when writing on a topic
- Select interesting information to include

Poetic: To express feelings, sensory images, ideas, or stories

***Poetry** (free verse, rhyme)*

Understanding the Genre

- Understand that a writer can use familiar poems as mentor texts
- Understand poetry as a way to communicate in sensory images about everyday life
- Understand poetry as a unique way to communicate about and describe thoughts and feelings
- Understand the way print and space work in poems and use this knowledge when writing poems
- Understand that poems can be created from other kinds of texts
- Notice specific words when reading poetry
- Understand that there are different kinds of poems
- Understand that poems do not have to rhyme
- Notice language that "sounds like" a poem (rhythmic, descriptive, or sensory language)

Writing in the Genre

- Closely observe the world (animals, objects, people) to get ideas for poems
- Use line breaks and white space when writing poems
- Shape words on the page to look like a poem
- Write poems that convey feelings or images
- Use language to describe how something looks, smells, tastes, feels, or sounds

Writing

Selecting Purpose and Genre

Functional: To perform a practical task

Labels

Understanding the Genre

- Understand that a writer or illustrator can add labels to help readers
- Understand that labels can add important information

Writing in the Genre

- Write labels for objects in the classroom
- Add words to pictures
- Create labels for illustrations that accompany written pieces
- Make label books as one type of book

Friendly Letters (notes, cards, invitations, email)

Understanding the Genre

- Understand how to learn about writing notes, cards, and invitations by noticing the characteristics of examples
- Understand that the receiver and sender must be clearly shown
- Understand notes, cards, invitations, and email as written communication among people
- Understand that invitations must include specific information
- Understand that the form of written communication is related to the purpose

Writing in the Genre

- Write notes, cards, invitations, and emails to others
- Write to a known audience or a specific reader
- Write with the specific purpose in mind
- Include important information in the communication
- Write with a friendly tone (conversational language)

Lists and Procedures (how-to)

Understanding the Genre

- Understand that the form of a list is usually one item under another and it may be numbered
- Understand that captions can be written under pictures to give readers more information
- Understand procedural writing (how-to) as a list of sequential directions for how to do something with lists of what is needed
- Understand that pictures can accompany the writing to help readers understand the information
- Understand lists are a functional way to organize information

Writing in the Genre

- Use lists to plan activities or support memory
- Place items in the list that are appropriate for its purpose or category
- Make lists in the appropriate form with one item under another
- Use drawing in the process of drafting, revising, or publishing procedural writing
- Write captions under pictures

Writing About Reading (all genres)

(See the Writing About Reading continuum.)

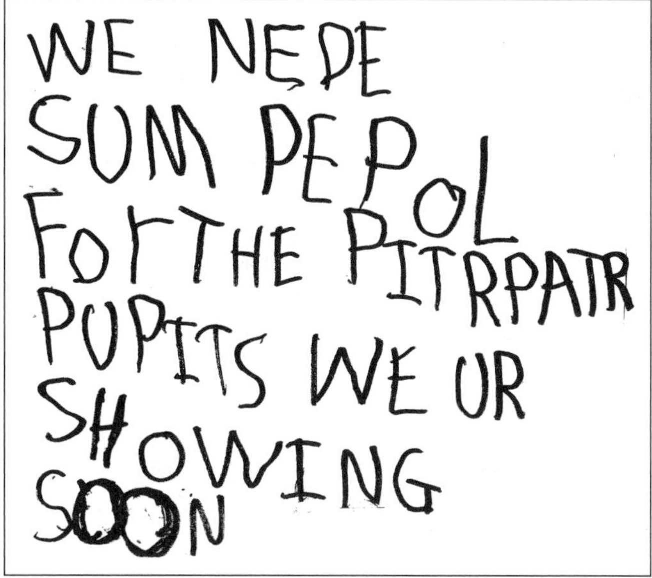

An invitation to a puppet show

Writing

Selecting Goals: Behaviors and Understandings to Notice, Teach, and Support

Craft

Organization

Text Structure

- Include facts and details in informational writing
- Put together the related details on a topic in a text
- Put the facts or information in order
- Write stories that have a beginning, a series of things happening, and an ending
- Write a title and the author's name on the cover of a story or book
- Write an author page at the beginning or end of a book that gives information about the author (picture, writing)
- Dedicate a story to someone and write *dedication* on the cover, on the title page or copyright page, or on a page of its own
- Create a picture book as one form of writing

Beginnings, Endings, Titles

- Use a variety of beginnings to engage the reader
- Use endings that are interesting, leave the reader satisfied, or get the reader to think more about a story or topic
- Select an appropriate title for a poem, story, or informational book

Presentation of Ideas

- Tell about experiences or topics the way one would talk about them to others
- Present ideas in logical sequence
- Introduce ideas followed by supportive details and examples
- Use time appropriately as an organizing tool
- Tell one part, idea, or group of ideas on each page of a book

Idea Development

- Communicate clearly the main points intended for readers to understand
- Provide supportive description or details to explain the important ideas

Language Use

- Understand that the writer is using language to communicate meaning
- Show evidence of using language from books that have been read aloud

Word Choice

- Learn new words or phrases from reading and try them out in writing
- Use vocabulary appropriate for the topic

Voice

- Write with a unique perspective
- Write in the way one would speak about an experience, event, or topic
- State information in a unique or surprising way
- Share one's thoughts and feelings about a topic
- Write about what is known and remembered

Conventions

Text Layout

- Use spaces between words to help readers understand the writing
- Place titles and headings in the appropriate place on a page
- Use underlining and bold print to convey meaning
- Understand that layout of print and illustrations are important in conveying the meaning of a text
- Place words in lines, starting left to right, top to bottom
- Understand that the print and pictures can be placed in a variety of places on the page within a book

Grammar

Sentence Structure

- Use conventional sentence structure (noun + verb)

Parts of Speech

- Use noun and verb agreement (*I can*)
- Use prepositional phrases (*to the bus, on the bus*)
- Use modifiers (*red* dress; ran *fast*)

Tense

- Write in past tense (*I went home yesterday.*)
- Write in present tense (*I like . . .*)
- Write in future tense (*I'm going to go . . .*)

Writing

Selecting Goals: Behaviors and Understandings to Notice, Teach, and Support

Capitalization

- Demonstrate knowledge of the use of upper- and lowercase letters of the alphabet
- Use capital letters in the beginning position in a few familiar, known proper nouns
- Show awareness of the first place position of capital letters in words
- Use a capital letter for the first word of a sentence
- Capitalize *I*
- Use uppercase letters in titles

Punctuation

- Notice the use of punctuation marks in books and try them out in own writing
- Use periods, exclamation points, and question marks as ending marks
- Read one's writing aloud and think where punctuation would go

Spelling

- Spell twenty-five or more high-frequency words conventionally
- Use a few simple phonogram patterns to generate words (*cat, fat*)
- Attempt unknown words through sound analysis
- Say words slowly to hear a sound and write a letter that represents it
- Write some words with consonant letters appropriate for sounds in words (beginning and ending)
- Write a letter for easy-to-hear vocal sounds
- Understand that letters represent sounds
- Construct phonetic spellings that are readable
- Use conventional symbols to write words
- Use simple resources to check spelling (word walls)

Handwriting/Word-Processing

- Write letters in groups to form words
- Leave appropriate space between words
- Hold pencil or pen with satisfactory grip
- Write left to right in lines
- Return to the left margin to start a new line
- Use a preferred hand consistently for writing
- Write letters and words that can be easily read
- Form upper- and lowercase letters efficiently in manuscript print
- Form upper- and lowercase letters proportionately in manuscript print
- Access and use simple programs on the computer (easy word-processing, games)
- Locate letter keys on a computer keyboard to type simple messages

Writing Process

Rehearsing/Planning

Purpose

- Write for a specific purpose
- Think about the purpose for writing each text
- Think about how the purpose affects the kind of writing
- Choose type of text to fit the purpose (for example, poem, factual book, alphabet book, photo book, label book, story with pictures)
- Choose paper to match desired organization and the genre
- Write to inform or entertain readers
- Write name and date on writing
- Tell whether a piece of writing is a story or an informational text

Audience

- Think about the people who will read the writing and what they will want to know
- Include information that the readers will need to understand the text

Oral Language

- Generate and expand ideas through talk with peers and teacher
- Look for ideas and topics in personal experiences, shared through talk
- Use storytelling to generate and rehearse language (that may be written later)
- Tell stories in chronological order
- Retell stories in chronological order

Gathering Seeds/Resources/Experimenting with Writing

- Make lists or ideas for writing
- Understand that writers gather information for their writing
- Record information in words or drawings
- Use drawings to share or remember thinking

Writing

Selecting Goals: Behaviors and Understandings to Notice, Teach, and Support

Rehearsing/Planning (con't)

Content, Topic, Theme

- Observe carefully (objects, animals, people, places, actions) before writing about them
- Select own topics for informational writing
- Select information or facts that will support the topic
- Select topics for story or poem writing

Inquiry/Research

- Use drawings to tell about a topic or tell a story
- Ask questions and gather information on a topic
- Remember important information about a topic in order to write about it
- Participate actively in experiences and remember details that contribute to writing and drawing
- Remember important labels for drawings

Drafting/Revising

Understanding the Process

- Understand the role of the writing conference in helping writers
- Understand that writers can get help from other writers
- Understand that writers can change writing in response to peer or teacher feedback
- Understand that writers can learn how to write from other writers

Producing a Draft

- Uses words and drawings to compose and revise writing
- Write a continuous message on a simple topic

Rereading

- Reread writing each day before continuing to write
- Reread stories to be sure the meaning is clear
- Reread the text to be sure there are no missing words or information
- Review drawings to revise by adding (or deleting) information

Adding Information

- Add words, phrases, or sentences to make the writing more interesting or exciting for readers
- Add words, phrases, or sentences to provide more information
- Add dialogue to provide information or provide narration (in quotes or speech balloons)
- Add details to drawings to give more information

Deleting Information

- Delete words or sentences that do not make sense

Reorganizing Information

- Move sentences from one part to another to make the sequence better
- Reorder writing by cutting apart or laying out pages
- Reorder drawings by cutting apart or laying out pages

Changing Text

- Add information to make writing or drawings clear

Using Tools and Techniques

- Add letters, words, phrases, or sentences using a caret or sticky note
- Add words, phrases, or sentences using spider legs or an extra piece of paper glued, taped, or stapled to the piece
- Add pages to a book or booklet
- Cross out words or sentences with pencil or marker

Writing

Selecting Goals: Behaviors and Understandings to Notice, Teach, and Support

Editing and Proofreading

Understanding the Process

- Understand that the writer shows respect to the reader by applying what is known to correct errors
- Understand that the better the spelling and space between words, the easier it is for the reader to read it

Editing for Conventions

- Check and correct letter formation or orientation
- Edit for spelling errors by making another attempt
- Edit for spelling errors by circling words that do not look right and trying to spell them another way
- Recognize that the teacher may be the final editor who will make the edits the writer has not yet learned how to do prior to publishing

Using Tools

- Use beginning reference tools (for example, word walls)

Publishing

- Create illustrations for pieces of writing
- Share writing by reading it to the class
- Put several stories or poems together
- Select a poem, story, or informational book to publish
- Use labels and captions on drawings that are displayed

Sketching and Drawing

- Use sketches and drawing to plan, draft, revise, and publish writing
- Create drawings that are related to the written text and increase readers' understanding and enjoyment
- Use drawings to represent people, places, things, and ideas
- Add or remove details to drawings to revise

Viewing Self as a Writer

- Take on writing independently
- Take risks as a writer
- View self as writer
- Have a list of topics in mind to write about
- Think about what to work on next as a writer
- Select best pieces of writing from own collection
- Self-evaluate own writing and talk about what is good about it and what techniques were used
- Produce a quantity of writing within the time available (for example, one or two pages per day)
- Keep working independently rather than waiting for teacher instructions
- Make attempts to solve own problems
- Try out techniques other writers used

Writing

Selecting Purpose and Genre

Narrative: **To tell a story**

Memoir *(personal narrative, autobiography)*

Understanding the Genre

- Understand how to craft personal narratives and memoirs from mentor texts
- Understand that a story from your life is usually written in first person (using *I*)
- Understand that writers tell stories from their own lives
- Understand that the writer can look back or think about the memory or experience and share thoughts and feelings about it
- Understand that a story should be one that is important to the writer

Writing in the Genre

- Think of topics, events, or experiences from own life that are interesting to write about
- Write an engaging beginning and a satisfying ending to stories
- Understand that a story can be a "small moment" (description of a brief, memorable experience)
- Provide some descriptive details to make the story interesting
- Use dialogue as appropriate to add to the meaning of the story
- Use simple words that show the passage of time (*then, after*)
- Explain one's own thoughts and feelings about a topic
- Develop voice as a writer through telling own stories or memories from own life
- Usually write in first person to achieve a strong voice
- Tell a story across several pages in order to develop the story or idea
- Tell events in order that they occurred in personal narratives

Informational: **To explain or give facts about a topic**

Literary Nonfiction

Understanding the Genre

- Understand how to write literary nonfiction from mentor texts
- Understand literary nonfiction as writing that engages and entertains readers but teaches them about a topic
- Understand that the writer works to get readers interested in a topic

Writing in the Genre

- Write books and short pieces of writing that are enjoyable to read and at the same time give information to readers about a topic
- Use features (for example, headings, page numbers, labeled pictures, table of contents, or others) to guide the reader
- Think about the readers (audience) and what they need to know
- Select interesting information to include

Poetic: **To express feelings, sensory images, ideas, or stories**

Poetry *(free verse, rhyme)*

Understanding the Genre

- Understand that a writer can use familiar poems as mentor texts
- Understand poetry as a way to communicate in sensory images about everyday life
- Understand poetry as a unique way to communicate about and describe thoughts and feelings
- Understand the way print and space work in poems and use this knowledge when writing poems
- Understand that poems can be created from other kinds of texts
- Understand the importance of specific word choice in poetry
- Understand that there are different kinds of poems
- Understand that poems do not have to rhyme
- Recognize poetic language (rhythm, descriptive words that evoke senses, some rhyme)

Writing in the Genre

- Closely observe the world (animals, objects, people) to get ideas for poems
- Use line breaks and white space when writing poems
- Shape words on the page to look like a poem
- Write poems that convey feelings or images
- Use language to describe how something looks, smells, tastes, feels, or sounds
- Write poems from other kinds of texts (story, informational text)
- Sometimes borrow specific words or phrases from writing and make them into a poem

Selecting Purpose and Genre

Functional: To perform a practical task

Labels

Understanding the Genre

- Understand that labels can add important information
- Understand that a writer or illustrator can add labels to help readers

Writing in the Genre

- Write labels for objects in the classroom
- Add words to pictures
- Create labels for illustrations that accompany written pieces
- Make label books as one type of book

Friendly Letters *(notes, cards, invitations, email)*

Understanding the Genre

- Understand how to write notes, cards, and invitations from looking at examples
- Understand that the receiver and sender must be clearly shown
- Understand notes, cards, invitations, and email as written communication among people
- Understand that invitations must include specific information
- Understand that the form of written communication is related to the purpose

Writing in the Genre

- Write notes, cards, invitations, and emails to others
- Write to a known audience or a specific reader
- Write with the specific purpose in mind
- Include important information in the communication
- Write with a friendly tone (conversational language)

Lists and Procedures *(how-to)*

Understanding the Genre

- Understand lists as a functional way to organize information
- Understand that the form of a list is usually one item under another and it may be numbered
- Understand procedural writing (how-to) as a list of sequential directions for how to do something and lists of what is needed
- Understand that pictures can accompany the writing to help readers understand the information
- Understand that captions can be written under pictures to give readers more information

Writing in the Genre

- Place items in the list that are appropriate for its purpose or category
- Make lists in the appropriate form with one item under another
- Use drawings in the process of drafting, revising, or publishing procedural writing
- Write captions under pictures
- Use lists to plan activities or support memory
- Write sequential directions in procedural or how-to books

Writing About Reading *(all genres)*

(See the Writing About Reading continuum.)

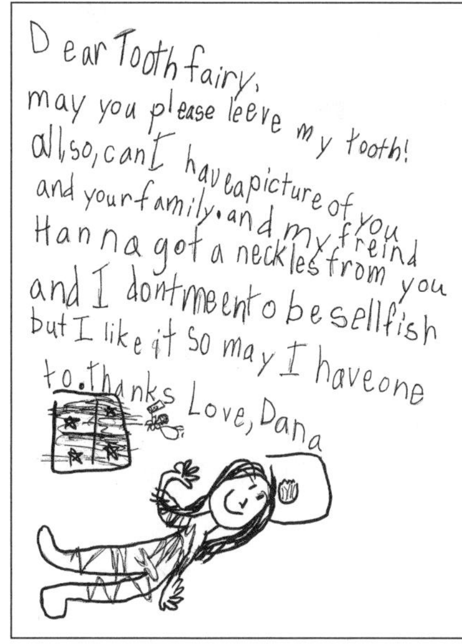

Dear Tooth fairy,
may you please leeve my tooth!
allso, can I have a picture of you
and your family. and my freind
Hanna got a neckles from you
and I dont meent to be sellfish
but I like it so may I have one
to. thanks Love, Dana

A friendly letter to the Tooth Fairy

Writing

Selecting Goals: Behaviors and Understandings to Notice, Teach, and Support

Craft

Organization

Text Structure
- Include facts and details in informational writing
- Put together the related details on a topic in a text
- Put the facts or information in order
- Write stories that have a beginning, a series of things happening, and an ending
- Write a title and the author's name on the cover of a story or book
- Write an author page at the beginning or end of a book that tells details about the author (picture, writing)
- Dedicate a story to someone and write the dedication on the inside of the cover, on the title page or copyright page, or on a page of its own
- Create a picture book as one form of writing

Beginnings, Endings, Titles
- Use a variety of beginnings to engage the reader
- Use endings that are interesting, leave the reader satisfied, or get the reader to think more about a story or topic
- Select an appropriate title for a poem, story, or informational book

Presentation of Ideas
- Tell about experiences or topics the way one would talk about them to others
- Present ideas in logical sequence
- Introduce ideas followed by supportive details and examples
- Show steps in enough detail that a reader can follow a sequence
- Tell one part, idea, or group of ideas on each page of a book
- Use time appropriately as an organizing tool

Idea Development
- Communicate clearly the main points intended for the reader to understand
- Provide supportive description, details, or examples to explain the important ideas

Language Use
- Understand that the writer is using language to communicate meaning
- Show evidence of using book language or language from other texts

Word Choice
- Learn new words or phrases from reading and try them out in writing
- Use vocabulary appropriate for the topic
- Vary word choice to create interesting description and dialogue

Voice
- Write with a unique perspective
- Write in the way one would speak about the experience, event, or topic
- State information in a unique or surprising way
- Share one's thoughts and feelings about a topic
- Write about what is known and remembered

Conventions

Text Layout
- Understand that the print and pictures can be placed in a variety of places on the page within a book
- Place words in lines, starting left to right, top to bottom
- Place titles and headings in the appropriate place on a page
- Use underlining and bold print to convey meaning
- Understand that layout of print and illustrations are important in conveying the meaning of a text
- Use spaces between words

Grammar

Sentence Structure
- Use conventional sentence structure (noun + verb)

Parts of Speech
- Use noun and verb agreement (*I can*)
- Use prepositional phrases (*to the bus, on the bus*)
- Use modifiers (*red* dress; ran *fast*)

Tense
- Write in past tense (*I went home yesterday.*)
- Write in future tense (*I'm going to go . . .*)

Writing

Selecting Goals: Behaviors and Understandings to Notice, Teach, and Support

Capitalization
- Demonstrate knowledge of the use of upper- and lowercase letters of the alphabet
- Capitalize *I*
- Show awareness of the first place position of capital letters in words
- Use uppercase letters in titles
- Use a capital letter for the first word of a sentence
- Use capital letters in the beginning position in a few familiar, known proper nouns

Punctuation
- Use periods, exclamation points, and question marks as ending marks
- Notice the use of punctuation marks in books and try them out in own writing
- Read one's writing aloud and think where punctuation would go

Spelling
- Use conventional symbols to write words
- Spell one hundred or more high-frequency words conventionally
- Say words to break them into syllables to spell them
- Use some phonogram patterns to generate words
- Attempt unknown words through sound analysis
- Say words slowly to hear a sound and write a letter that represents it
- Write some words with consonant letters appropriate for sounds in words (beginning and ending)
- Write a letter for easy-to-hear vowel sounds
- Represent several sounds, including beginning and ending

Spelling (con't)
- Represent many short and long vowel sounds in words
- Spell words with regular consonant-sound relationships and with regular short vowel patterns correctly
- Represent many consonant sounds or vowel sounds with letters
- Attempt unknown words using known word parts
- Construct phonetic spellings that are readable
- Include a vowel in each word
- Represent consonant blends and digraphs with letter clusters in words
- Use simple resources to check spelling (word walls, personal word lists)

Handwriting/Word-Processing
- Leave appropriate space between words
- Hold pencil or pen with satisfactory grip
- Return to the left margin to start a new line
- Use a preferred hand consistently for writing
- Write left to right in lines
- Write letters and words that can be easily read
- Write letters in groups to form words
- Form upper- and lowercase letters efficiently in manuscript print
- Form upper- and lowercase letters proportionately in manuscript print
- Access and use simple programs on the computer (easy word-processing, games)
- Locate letter keys on a computer keyboard to type simple messages

Writing Process

Rehearsing/Planning

Purpose
- Think about the purpose for writing each text
- Write for a specific purpose
- Consider how the purpose affects the kind of writing
- Choose type of text to fit the purpose (for example, poem, factual book, alphabet book, photo book, label book, story with pictures)
- Choose paper to match genre and organization
- Write name and date on writing
- Tell whether a piece of writing is a story or an informational text

Audience
- Write with an understanding that it is meant to be read by others
- Think about the people who will read the writing and what they will want to know
- Include information that the readers will need to understand the text

Oral Language
- Generate and expand ideas through talk with peers and teacher
- Look for ideas and topics in personal experiences, shared through talk
- Use storytelling to generate and rehearse language (that may be written later)
- Tell stories in chronological order
- Retell stories in chronological order

Gathering Seeds/Resources/Experimenting with Writing
- Make a list of ideas on topics for writing
- Gather information for writing
- Record information in words or drawings
- Make lists to plan for writing
- Use drawings to share or remember thinking

Content, Topic, Theme
- Choose topics that one knows about or cares about
- Choose topics that are interesting
- Select information that will support the topic
- Observe carefully (objects, animals, people, places, actions) before writing about them
- Select topics for story or poem writing
- Select own topics for informational writing and state what is important about the topic
- Stay focused on a topic

Selecting Goals: Behaviors and Understandings to Notice, Teach, and Support

Rehearsing/Planning (con't)

Inquiry/Research

- Ask questions and gather information on a topic
- Take notes or make sketches to help in remembering information
- Remember important information about a topic in order to write about it
- Participate actively in experiences and remember details that contribute to writing and drawing
- Remember important labels for drawings

Genre/Form

- Select from a variety of forms the kind of text that will fit the purpose (books with illustrations and words; books with illustrations only; alphabet books; label books; poetry books; question and answer books; illustration-only books)

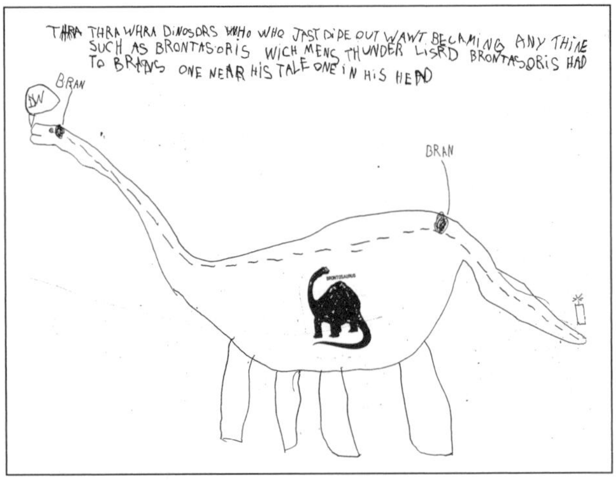

An Expository Text

Drafting/Revising

Understanding the Process

- Understand the role of the writing conference in helping writers
- Understand that writers can get help from other writers
- Understand that writers can change writing in response to peer or teacher feedback

Producing a Draft

- Use drawings to tell about a topic or tell a story
- Uses words and drawings to compose a story
- Write a continuous message on a simple topic

Rereading

- Reread writing each day before continuing to write
- Reread stories to be sure the meaning is clear
- Reread the text to be sure there are no missing words or information
- Review drawings to revise by adding (or deleting) information

Adding Information

- Add words, phrases, or sentences to make the writing more interesting or exciting
- Add words, phrases, or sentences to provide more information to readers
- Add dialogue to provide information or provide narration (in quotes or speech balloons)

Deleting Information

- Delete words or sentences that do not make sense
- Delete extra words or sentences

Reorganizing Information

- Move sentences from one part to another to make the sequence better
- Reorder writing by cutting apart or laying out pages
- Reorder drawings by cutting apart or laying out pages

Changing Text

- Mark parts that are not clear and provide more information

Using Tools and Techniques

- Add letters, words, phrases, or sentences using a caret or sticky note
- Add words, phrases, or sentences using spider legs or an extra piece of paper glued, taped, or stapled to the piece
- Add pages to a book or booklet
- Cross out words or sentences with pencil or marker

Selecting Goals: Behaviors and Understandings to Notice, Teach, and Support

Editing and Proofreading

Understanding the Process

- Understand that the writer shows respect to the reader by applying what is known to correct errors
- Understand that the better the spelling and space between words, the easier it is for the reader to read it

Editing for Conventions

- Check and correct letter formation or orientation
- Edit for spelling errors by making another attempt
- Edit for spelling errors by circling words that do not look right and trying to spell them another way
- Edit for the spelling of known words (should be spelled conventionally)
- Recognize that the teacher is the final editor who will make the edits the writer has not yet learned how to do prior to publishing

Using Tools

- Use beginning reference tools (for example, word walls or personal word lists to assist in word choice or checking spelling)

Publishing

- Create drawings for pieces of writing
- Share writing by reading it to the class
- Put several stories or poems together
- Select a poem, story, or informational book to publish
- Use labels and captions on drawings that are displayed

Sketching and Drawing

- Use drawing to plan, draft, revise, or publish writing
- Create drawings that are related to the written text and increase readers' understanding and enjoyment
- Use drawings to represent people, places, things, and ideas
- Add or remove details to drawings to revise information

Viewing Self as a Writer

- Take risks as a writer
- View self as writer
- Have a list of topics in mind to write about
- Think about what to work on next in writing
- Select best pieces of writing from own collection
- Self-evaluate own writing and talk about what is good about it and what techniques were used
- Produce a quantity of writing within the time available (for example, one or two pages per day)
- Keep working independently rather than waiting for teacher instructions
- Make attempts to solve own problems
- Take on writing independently
- Try out techniques other writers used

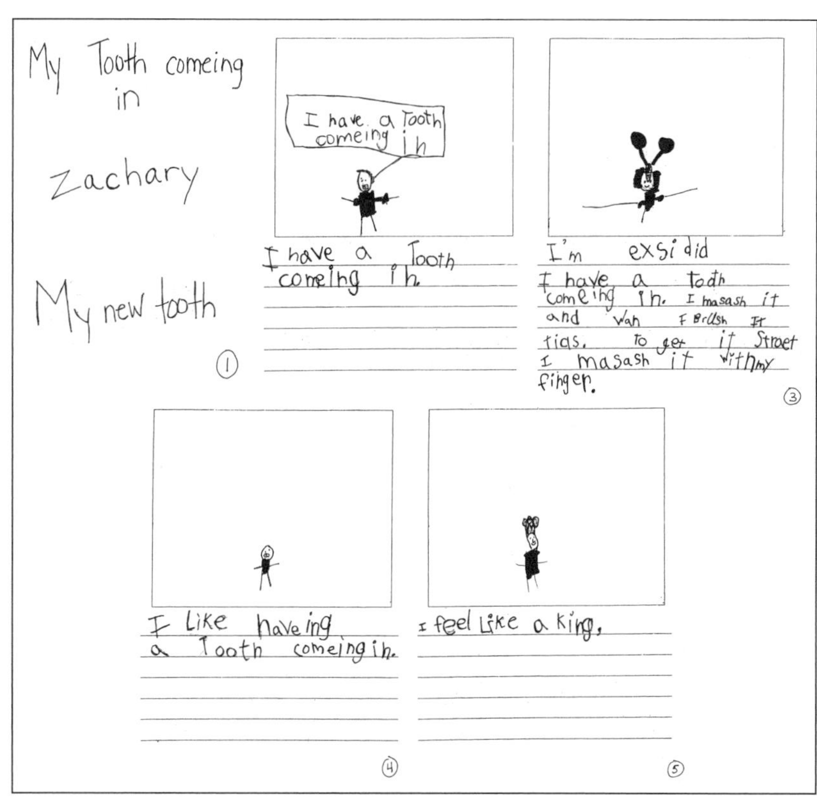

Writing

Selecting Purpose and Genre

Narrative: To tell a story

Memoir *(personal narrative, autobiography)*

Understanding the Genre

- Understand how to craft personal narratives and memoirs from mentor texts
- Understand personal narrative as a story from the author's life, usually told in first person
- Understand memoir as a reflection of a memorable experience or a person

Writing in the Genre

- Write an engaging beginning and a satisfying ending to stories
- Select "small moments" or experiences and share thinking and feeling about them
- Describe a setting and how it is related to the writer's experiences
- Use dialogue as appropriate to add to the meaning of the story
- Use words that show the passage of time
- Tell details about the most important moments in a story or experience while eliminating unimportant details
- Describe characters by what they do, say, and think and what others say about them
- Use some literary language that is different from oral language
- Show the significance of the story
- Usually write in first person to achieve a strong voice
- Select meaningful topics
- Reveal something important about self or about life

Short Fiction *(short story, short realistic fiction, or historical fiction)*

Understanding the Genre

- Understand how to craft fiction by using mentor texts as models
- Understand fiction as a short story about an event in the life of the main character
- Understand that fiction may be realism or fantasy (tall tales, fable)
- Understand the elements of fiction, including setting, problem, characters, and problem resolution

Writing in the Genre

- Describe characters by how they look and what they do
- Describe the setting with appropriate detail
- Write simple fictional stories (realism or fantasy)

Informational: To explain or give facts about a topic

Literary Nonfiction

Understanding the Genre

- Understand how to write literary nonfiction from studying mentor texts
- Understand literary nonfiction as a text that helps people learn something and is interesting to read
- Understand that writers write informational texts for readers to learn about a topic
- Understand that the writer of literary nonfiction works to help readers become interested in a topic
- Understand that nonfiction can tell a story and give information
- Understand that to write literary nonfiction, the writer needs to become very knowledgeable about the topic
- Understand that a report usually has several subtopics related to the main topic

Writing in the Genre

- Write pieces that are enjoyable to read
- Use headings, labeled drawings and diagrams, table of contents, or other features of informational text to guide the reader
- Write about a topic keeping the audience and their interests and knowledge in mind
- Provide interesting details around a topic
- Introduce information in categories
- Provide supporting details in each category
- Use some vocabulary specific to the topic
- Provide information that teaches readers about a topic
- Use a narrative structure to help readers understand information and interest them in a topic

Writing

Selecting Purpose and Genre

Poetic: To express feelings, sensory images, ideas, or stories

Poetry *(free verse, rhyme)*

Understanding the Genre

- Understand poetry as a unique way to communicate about and describe feelings, sensory images, ideas, or stories
- Understand the way print works in poems
- Understand that poems can take a variety of shapes
- Understand that poems can be created from other kinds of texts
- Understand the importance of specific word choice in poetry
- Understand that there are different kinds of poems
- Understand that poems do not have to rhyme

Writing in the Genre

- Write a variety of poems
- Notice and use line breaks and white space as they are used in poetry
- Observe closely to select topics or content and write with detail
- Shape words on the page to look like a poem
- Remove extra words to clarify the meaning and make the writing more powerful
- Use poetic language to communicate meaning

Functional: To perform a practical task

Friendly Letters *(notes, cards, invitations, email)*

Understanding the Genre

- Understand that the form of written communication is related to the purpose
- Understand notes, cards, invitations, friendly letters, and email as written communication among people
- Understand how to write effective notes, invitations, emails, cards, and friendly letters by studying examples
- Understand that invitations need to include specific information about the time and place of the event
- Understand a friendly letter as a more formal kind of communication between people
- Understand that a friendly letter has parts (date, salutation, closing, signature, and sometimes P.S.)
- Understand notes and cards need to include short greetings and relevant information

Writing in the Genre

- Write to a known audience or a specific reader
- Address the audience appropriately
- Write a card, note, invitation, or friendly letter with the purpose in mind
- Write notes, cards, invitations, and email for a variety of purposes
- Include important information in the communication
- Write a friendly letter with all parts

Lists and Procedures *(how-to)*

Understanding the Genre

- Understand lists are a functional way to organize information
- Understand that the form of a list or procedure is usually one item under another and it may be numbered
- Understand procedural writing (how-to) as a list of directions for how to do something and a list of what is needed
- Understand how to craft procedural writing from mentor texts
- Understand how drawings can help the reader understand information

Writing in the Genre

- Make lists in the appropriate form with one item under another
- Use lists to plan activities or support memory
- Use a list to inform writing (poems or informational)
- Use number words or transition words
- Make lists with items that are appropriate to the purpose of the list
- Write procedural or how-to books
- Write steps of a procedure with appropriate sequence and explicitness
- Include pictures to illustrate the steps in a procedure

Test Writing *(extended response, short answer)*

Understanding the Genre

- Understand that test writing often requires writing about an assigned topic
- Understand that test writing is a particular kind of writing used when taking tests
- Understand that some writing serves the purpose of demonstrating what a person knows or can do as a writer
- Understand that test writing often requires writing about something real

Writing in the Genre

- Analyze the prompt to understand the purpose, genre, and audience for the writing
- Read and internalize the criteria for an acceptable response
- Write focused responses to questions and to prompts
- Write concisely and to the direction of the question or prompt
- Elaborate on important points
- Exclude extraneous details
- Incorporate one's knowledge of craft in shaping response

Writing About Reading *(all genres)*

(See the Writing About Reading continuum.)

Writing

Selecting Goals: Behaviors and Understandings to Notice, Teach, and Support

Craft

Organization

Text Structure

- Organize texts in different ways
- Write a text that is narrative ordered by time
- Understand that an informational text is ordered by logic (categories, sequences, ideas related to each other)
- Write an author page at the beginning or end of a book to give information about the author
- Dedicate a story to someone and write the dedication inside the cover, on the title page or copyright page, or on a page of its own
- Create a picture book as one kind of writing

Beginnings, Endings, Titles

- Use a variety of beginnings to engage the reader
- Use a variety of endings to engage and satisfy the reader (for example, surprise, circular story)
- Use a variety of beginning, middle, and ending structures appropriate to the genre
- Select an appropriate title for a poem, story, or informational book

Presentation of Ideas

- Tell one part, idea, or group of ideas on each page of a book
- Present ideas clearly
- Organize information into categories for presentation
- Show major topics by using headings
- Use headings, a table of contents, and other features to help the reader find information and understand how facts are related
- Use time appropriately as an organizing tool
- Show steps in enough detail that a reader can follow a sequence
- Bring a piece to closure through an ending or summary statement
- Order the writing in ways that are characteristic to the genre (narrative or informational)
- Use graphics (diagrams, illustrations, photos) to provide information
- Use some vocabulary specific to the topic or content

Idea Development

- Communicate main points clearly to readers
- Provide supporting information or examples that are accurate, relevant, and helpful
- Gather and internalize information and then write it in own words

Language Use

- Borrow a word, phrase, or a sentence from another writer
- Use memorable words or phrases
- Show through language instead of telling
- Use examples to make meaning clear to readers

Word Choice

- Show ability to vary the text by choosing alternative words (for example, alternatives for *said*)
- Learn new words from reading and try them out in writing
- Use transitional words for time flow (*after, then*)
- Use vocabulary appropriate for the topic

Voice

- Write with a unique perspective
- Write in a way that speaks directly to the reader
- State information in a unique or surprising way
- Use punctuation to make the text interesting and effective

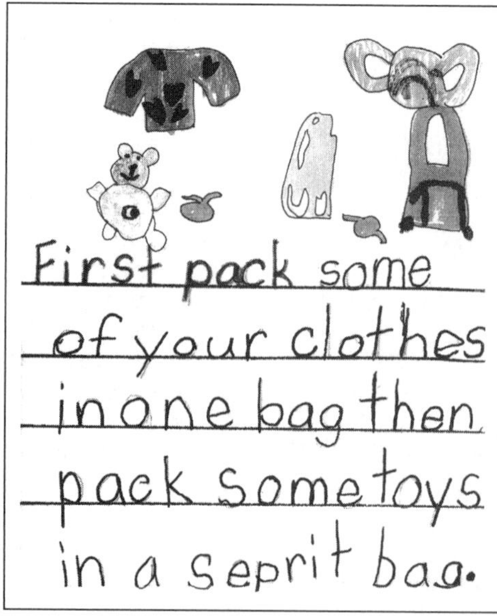

Writing

Selecting Goals: Behaviors and Understandings to Notice, Teach, and Support

Conventions

Text Layout

- Arrange print on the page to support the text's meaning and to help the reader notice important information
- Understand that layout of print and illustrations are important in conveying the meaning of a text
- Understand how to use layout, spacing, and size of print to create titles, headings, and subheadings

Grammar

SENTENCE STRUCTURE

- Write complete sentences
- Use a range of complete sentences (declarative, interrogative, exclamatory)

PARTS OF SPEECH

- Use subject and verb agreement in simple sentences (*we were*)
- Use nouns and pronouns that are in agreement (*Mike/he*)
- Use prepositional phrases, adjectives, and adverbs correctly

TENSE

- Write in past tense (*I went home yesterday.*)
- Write in present tense (*Owls love to . . .*)
- Write in future tense (*I'm going to go . . .*)

Capitalization

- Use a capital letter for the first word of a sentence
- Use capital letters appropriately to capitalize days, months, cities, states
- Use capitals for names of people and places
- Use all capital letters for a head or for emphasis
- Use capitals to start the first letter in the first word, last word, and most other words in titles

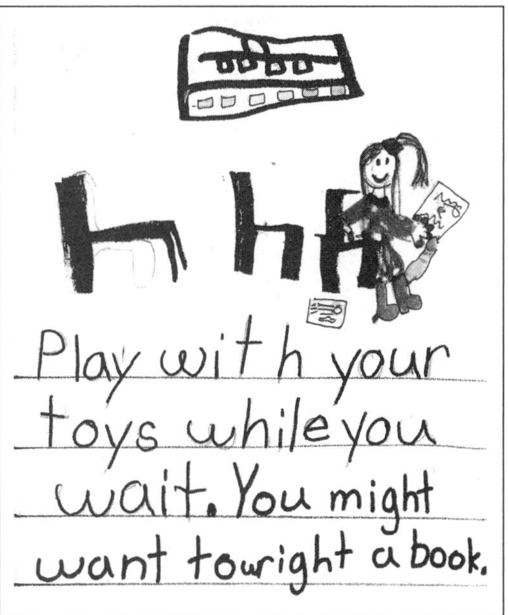
Play with your
toys while you
wait. You might
want towright a book.

Punctuation

- Understand and use ellipses to show pause or anticipation, usually before something surprising
- Use dashes and ellipses for emphasis or to slow down the text for readers
- Use periods, exclamation points, and question marks as ending marks
- Use quotation marks around the speaker's exact words
- Use periods after abbreviations
- Notice the use of punctuation marks in books and try them out in own writing
- Use apostrophes in contractions and possessives
- Use commas to identify a series

Spelling

- Correctly spell familiar high-frequency words (200+), words with regular letter-sound relationships (including consonant blends and digraphs and some vowel patterns), and commonly used endings
- Take apart multisyllable words to spell the parts accurately or close to accurately
- Use knowledge of phonogram patterns to generate multisyllable words
- Spell simple and some complex plurals
- Use simple rules for adding inflectional endings to words (drop *e*, double letter)
- Spell simple possessives
- Spell most contractions
- Spell words that have been studied (spelling words)
- Write easy compound words accurately
- Spell many one-syllable words that have vowel and *r* correctly

Handwriting/Word-Processing

- Begin to develop efficient keyboarding skills
- Form upper- and lowercase letters efficiently and proportionately in manuscript print
- Use word processor to plan, draft, revise, edit, and publish
- Make changes on the screen to revise and edit, and publish documents

Writing

Selecting Goals: Behaviors and Understandings to Notice, Teach, and Support

Writing Process

Rehearsing/Planning

Purpose
- Write for a specific purpose: to inform, entertain, persuade, reflect, instruct, retell, maintain relationships, plan
- Understand how the purpose of the writing influences the selection of genre
- Select the genre for the writing based on the purpose
- Tell whether a piece of writing is a story or an informational text

Audience
- Write with a specific reader or audience in mind
- Understand how the writing meets the needs of a specific reader or audience
- Plan and organize information for the intended reader(s)
- Understand audience as all readers rather than just the teacher

Oral Language
- Generate and expand ideas through talk with peers and teacher
- Look for ideas and topics in personal experiences, shared through talk
- Expolre relevant questions in talking about a topic
- Identify the meaning to convey a message
- Use talk and storytelling to generate and rehearse language (that may be written later)
- Use language in stories that is specific to a topic
- Tell stories in chronological order
- Retell stories in chronological order

Gathering Seeds/Resources/Experimenting with Writing
- Use a writer's notebook or booklet as a tool for collecting ideas, experimenting, planning, sketching, or drafting
- Reread a writer's notebook to select topics
- Use sketching, webs, lists, and freewriting to think about, plan for, and try out writing
- Try out beginnings

Content, Topic, Theme
- Observe carefully events, people, settings, and other aspects of the world to gather information on a topic
- Get ideas from other books and writers about how to approach a topic
- Choose a topic that is significant
- Decide what is most important about the topic or story
- Use resources, including the Internet, to get information on a topic
- Select own topics for informational writing and state what is important about the topic
- Stay focused on a topic
- Select details that will support the topic

Rehearsing/Planning (con't)

Inquiry/Research/Exploration
- Form questions to answer about a topic
- Take notes or make sketches to help in remembering or generating information
- Participate actively in experiences and remember details that contribute to writing and drawing
- Select the most important information about a topic or story
- Gather information (with teacher assistance) about a topic from books or other print and media resources while preparing to write about it

Genre/Form
- Select from a variety of forms the kind of text that will fit the purpose (book with illustrations and words; alphabet book; label book; poetry book; question and answer book; illustration-only book)
- Understand that illustrations play different roles in a text (increase reader's enjoyment, add information, show sequence)

Drafting/Revising

Understanding the Process
- Understand the role of the writer, teacher, or peer writer in conference
- Understand that other writers can be helpful in the process
- Change writing in response to peer or teacher feedback

Producing a Draft
- Write a draft or discovery draft (write fast and as much as possible on a topic)
- Engage the reader with a strong lead
- Bring the piece to closure with an ending or final statement
- Establish an initiating event and follow with a series of events in a narrative
- Maintain control of a central idea across the piece
- Present ideas in logical order across the piece

Rereading
- Mark the most important part of a piece of writing
- Reread and revise the draft or rewrite a section to clarify meaning
- Reread each day before writing more

Adding Information
- Add information to the middle to clarify meaning
- Expand information through adding details or examples
- Add dialogue to provide information, provide narration, or show thoughts and feelings (in quotes or speech balloons)

Deleting Information
- Take out repetitive words, phrases, or sentences, or add to meaning
- Delete words or sentences that do not make sense
- Take out unnecessary words, phrases, or sentences

Reorganizing Information
- Move sentences around for better sequence
- Move information from one part of the text to another to make a text clearer

Writing

Selecting Goals: Behaviors and Understandings to Notice, Teach, and Support

Drafting/Revising (con't)

Changing Text

- Identify vague parts and provide specificity
- Change words to make the writing more interesting

Using Tools and Techniques

- Add letters, words, phrases, or sentences using a caret or sticky note with an asterisk
- Use a spider leg or piece of paper taped on to insert text
- Use a number to identify place to add information and an additional paper with numbers to write the information to insert
- Reorder a piece by cutting it apart or laying out the pages

Editing and Proofreading

Understanding the Process

- Understand that the writer shows respect to the reader by applying what is known to correct errors
- Understand that the better the spelling and space between words, the easier it is for the reader to read it
- Know how to use an editing and proofreading checklist

Editing for Conventions

- Check and correct letter formation
- Edit for conventional spelling of important words (for publication)
- Edit for the spelling of known words (should be spelled conventionally)
- Edit for spelling errors by circling or underlining words that do not look right and making another attempt
- Understand that the teacher will be final spelling editor for the published piece (after the student has used everything known)
- Edit for capitalization and end punctuation
- Edit for sentence sense

Using Tools

- Use simple spell check programs on the computer
- Use beginning reference tools (for example, word walls, personal word lists, or word cards to assist in word choice or checking spelling)

Publishing

- Select a poem, story, or informational book to publish
- Include graphics or illustrations as appropriate to the text
- Generate multiple titles to arrive at the most suitable and interesting
- Select a title that fits the content of the piece to publish (or complete as final draft)
- Share a text with peers by reading it aloud
- Add to the text during the publishing process (for example, illustrations and other graphics, cover spread, title, dedication, table of contents, about the author piece)
- Attend to layout of text in final publication
- Use labels and captions on drawings that are displayed
- Understand publishing as the sharing of a piece of writing with an audience

Sketching and Drawing

- Create drawings that are related to the written text and increase readers' understanding and enjoyment
- Use sketching to support memory and help in planning
- Use drawing to capture detail that is important to a topic
- Provide important information in illustrations
- Use drawings and sketches to represent people, places, things, and ideas in the composing, revising, and publishing process
- Add labels or sentences to drawings as needed to explain them
- Add details to drawings to add information or increase interest
- Create drawings that employ careful attention to color or detail

Viewing Self as a Writer

- Write in a variety of genres across the year
- Understand writing as a vehicle to communicate meaning
- Take risks as a writer
- View self as writer
- Write with independence
- Write with initiative and investment
- Produce a reasonable quantity of writing within the time available
- Attend to the language and craft of other writers in order to learn more as a writer
- Show ability to discuss what is being worked on as a writer in a conference
- Seek feedback on writing
- Be willing to work at the craft of writing, incorporating new learning from instruction
- Select best pieces of writing from own collection and give reasons for the selections
- Self-evaluate own writing and talk about what is good about it and what techniques were used
- Compare previous to revised writing and notice and talk about the differences
- State what was learned from each piece of writing

Writing

Selecting Purpose and Genre

Narrative: **To tell a story**

Memoir *(personal narrative, autobiography)*

Understanding the Genre

- Understand how to craft personal narratives and memoirs from mentor texts
- Understand personal narrative as a story from the author's life, usually told in first person
- Understand memoir as a reflection of a memorable experience or a person

Writing in the Genre

- Write an engaging beginning and a satisfying ending to stories
- Select "small moments" or experiences and share thinking and feelings about them
- Use small experiences to communicate a bigger message
- Describe a setting and how it is related to the writer's experiences
- Use dialogue as appropriate to add to the meaning of the story
- Use words that show the passage of time
- Tell details about the most important moments in a story or experience while eliminating unimportant details
- Describe characters by what they do, say, and think and what others say about them
- Use some literary language that is different from oral language
- Show the significance of the story
- Usually write in first person to achieve a strong voice
- Select meaningful topics
- Reveal something important about self or about life

Short Fiction *(short story, short realistic fiction, or historical fiction)*

Understanding the Genre

- Understand that writers can learn to craft fiction by using mentor texts as models
- Understand fiction as a short story about an event in the life of the main character
- Understand that fiction may be realism or fantasy
- Understand that the purpose of a short story is to explore a theme or teach a lesson
- Understand the elements of fiction, including setting, problem, characters, and problem resolution

Writing in the Genre

- Describe characters by how they look, what they do, say, and think, and what others say about them
- Show rather than tell how characters feel
- Develop an interesting story with believable characters and a realistic plot
- Expose the problem of the story
- Describe the setting with appropriate detail

Informational: **To explain or give facts about a topic**

Literary Nonfiction

Understanding the Genre

- Understand that writers write informational texts for readers to learn about a topic
- Understand that writers can learn how to write literary nonfiction from mentor texts
- Understand literary nonfiction as a text that helps people learn something and is interesting to read
- Understand that the writer of literary nonfiction works to help readers become interested in a topic
- Understand that literary nonfiction can tell a story and give information
- Understand that to write literary nonfiction, the writer needs to become very knowledgeable about the topic

Writing in the Genre

- Write books that are enjoyable to read
- Use headings, labeled diagrams, drawings, table of contents, or other features of informational text to guide the reader
- Write about a topic keeping the audience and their interests and knowledge in mind
- Provide interesting details around a topic
- Introduce information in categories
- Use some vocabulary specific to the topic
- Write books that give information or teach readers about a topic in an engaging way
- Use a narrative structure to help readers understand information and interest them in a topic

Writing

Selecting Purpose and Genre

Poetic: To express feelings, sensory images, ideas, or stories

***Poetry** (free verse, rhyme)*

UNDERSTANDING THE GENRE

- Understand poetry as a unique way to communicate about and describe feelings, sensory images, events, or ideas
- Understand the way print works in poems
- Understand the purpose of white space and line breaks
- Understand that poems can take a variety of shapes
- Understand that poems can be created from other kinds of texts
- Understand the importance of specific word choice in poetry
- Understand that there are different kinds of poems
- Understand that poems do not have to rhyme
- Understand the difference between poetic language and ordinary language

WRITING IN THE GENRE

- Write a variety of types of poems
- Notice and use line breaks and white space as they are used in poetry
- Observe closely to select topics or content and write with detail
- Shape words on the page to look like a poem
- Use comparisons (simile and metaphor)
- Remove extra words to clarify the meaning and make the writing more powerful
- Use repetition, refrain, rhythm, and other poetic techniques
- Use poetic language to communicate meaning

Functional: To perform a practical task

***Friendly Letters** (notes, cards, invitations, email)*

UNDERSTANDING THE GENRE

- Understand that the form of written communication is related to the purpose
- Understand notes, cards, invitations, friendly letters, and email as written communication among people
- Understand that writers can learn how to write effective notes, invitations, emails, cards, and friendly letters by studying examples
- Understand that invitations need to include specific information about the time and place of the event
- Understand a friendly letter as a more formal kind of communication between people
- Understand that a friendly letter has parts (date, salutation, closing, signature, and sometimes P.S.)
- Understand notes and cards need to include short greetings and relevant information

WRITING IN THE GENRE

- Write to a known audience or a specific reader
- Address the audience appropriately
- Write a card, note, invitation, or friendly letter with the purpose in mind
- Write notes, cards, invitations, and email for a variety of purposes
- Include important information in the communication
- Write a friendly letter with all parts
- Write with the purpose in mind
- Write to a known audience or a specific reader

***Lists and Procedures** (how-to)*

UNDERSTANDING THE GENRE

- Understand lists are a functional way to organize information
- Understand that the form of a list or procedure is usually one item under another and it may be numbered
- Understand procedural writing (how-to) as a list of directions for how to do something and a list of what is needed
- Learn how to craft procedural writing from mentor texts

WRITING IN THE GENRE

- Make lists in the appropriate form with one item under another
- Use lists to plan activities or support memory
- Use a list to inform writing (poems or informational)
- Use number words or transition words
- Make lists with items that are appropriate to the purpose of the list
- Write procedural or how-to books
- Write steps of a procedure with appropriate sequence and explicitness
- Include pictures to illustrate the steps in a procedure

***Test Writing** (extended response, essay test, short answer)*

UNDERSTANDING THE GENRE

- Understand that test writing is a particular kind of writing used when taking tests
- Use the term *test writing* to describe the genre
- Understand that some writing serves the purpose of demonstrating what a person knows or can do as a writer
- Understand that test writing involves analyzing what is expected of the writer
- Understand that test writing often requires the student to write about something real
- Understand test writing as a response carefully tailored to meet precise instructions
- Understand that test writing often requires writing about an assigned topic

WRITING IN THE GENRE

- Analyze the prompt to understand the purpose, genre, and audience for the writing
- Read and internalize the criteria for an acceptable response
- Write focused responses to questions and to prompts
- Write concisely and to the direction of the question or prompt
- Elaborate on important points
- Exclude extraneous details
- Incorporate one's knowledge of craft in shaping the response

***Writing About Reading** (all genres)*

(See the Writing About Reading continuum.)

Writing

Selecting Goals: Behaviors and Understandings to Notice, Teach, and Support

Craft

Organization

Text Structure

- Write texts that are organized in different ways
- Use organization in writing that is related to purpose and genre
- Write an informational text that is ordered by logic (categories, sequences, ideas related to each other)
- Write a narrative text that is ordered by time

Beginnings, Endings, Titles

- Use a variety of beginnings to engage the reader
- Use a variety of endings to engage and satisfy readers (for example, surprise, circular story)
- Use a variety of beginning, middle, and ending structures appropriate to the genre
- Select an appropriate title for a poem, story, or informational book

Presentation of Ideas

- Tell one part, idea, or group of ideas on each page of a book
- Present ideas clearly and in logical sequence
- Organize information into categories
- Show topics and subtopics by using headings
- Classify information under headings
- Use headings and subheadings, a table of contents, and other features to help the reader find information and understand how facts are related
- Introduce ideas followed by supportive details and examples
- Use time appropriately as an organizing tool
- Show steps in enough detail that a reader can follow a sequence
- Order the writing in ways that are characteristic to the genre (narrative or informational)
- Use graphics (diagrams, illustrations, photos, charts) to provide information
- Use vocabulary specific to the topic or content
- Bring a piece to closure through an ending or summary statement

Idea Development

- Communicate main points clearly
- Provide supporting details that are accurate, relevant, and helpful
- Gather and internalize information and then write it in own words
- Introduce, develop, and conclude the topic

Language Use

- Use variety in sentence structure
- Borrow a word, phrase, or sentence from another writer
- Use memorable words or phrases
- Use language to create sensory images
- Show through language instead of telling
- Use examples to make meaning clear
- Use figurative language to make comparisons (simile)

Word Choice

- Show ability to vary the text by choosing alternative words (for example, alternatives for *said*)
- Use a range of descriptive words to enhance the meaning
- Learn new words from reading and try them out in writing
- Use transitional words for time flow (*after, then*)
- Use vocabulary appropriate for the topic
- Vary word choice to create interesting description and dialogue

Voice

- Write with a unique perspective
- Write in a way that speaks directly to the reader
- Express the writer's commitment to the topic or involvement with the piece
- State information in a unique or surprising way
- Use engaging titles and language

Table of Contents

Introduction 1
Family 2
Education 3
Important Events 4
Conclusion 5
Fun Facts 6

Introduction

James A. Garfeild is important because he help the north. He is the 20th president. James A. Garfeild is Special because he was the first left hand president.

Page 1

Writing

Selecting Goals: Behaviors and Understandings to Notice, Teach, and Support

Conventions

Text Layout

- Arrange print on the page to support the text's meaning and to help the reader notice important information
- Use layout of print and illustrations to convey the meaning of a text
- Use the size of print to convey meaning in printed text
- Use layout, spacing, and size of print to create titles, headings, and subheadings
- Use underlining, italics, and bold print to convey a specific meaning
- Use underlining for first and most words in titles

Grammar

Sentence Structure

- Write some sentences with embedded clauses (complex) and dialogue
- Use conventional structure for both simple and compound sentences
- Use a range of complete sentences (declarative, interrogative, exclamatory)
- Write uninterrupted dialogue in conventional structure

Parts of Speech

- Use subject and verb agreement (*we were*)
- Use nouns and pronouns that are in agreement (*Mike/he*)
- Use prepositional phrases, adjectives, and adverbs appropriately
- Use nouns and adjectives correctly

Tense

- Write in past tense (*I went home yesterday.*)
- Write in present tense (*Alligators eat . . .*)
- Write in future tense (*I'm going to go . . .*)

Capitalization

- Use a capital letter for the first word of a sentence
- Use capital letters appropriately to capitalize days, months, city and state names, and specific places
- Use capitals to start the first, last, and most other words in a title
- Use capitals for names of people and places
- Use all capital letters for a head or for emphasis
- Use capitals for the first word in a greeting in a letter
- Use capital letters correctly in uninterrupted dialogue

Punctuation

- Use periods, exclamation points, and question marks as ending marks
- Understand and use quotation marks to indicate simple dialogue
- Notice the use of punctuation marks in books and try them out in own writing
- Use apostrophes in contractions and possessives
- Use commas to identify a series
- Understand and use ellipses to show pause or anticipation, usually before something surprising
- Break words at the syllables at the end of a line using a hyphen
- Use correct punctuation uninterrupted in dialogue

Spelling

- Correctly spell a large core of high-frequency words (300+), words with regular letter-sound relationships (including consonant blends and digraphs and some vowel patterns), and commonly used endings
- Take apart multisyllable words to spell the parts accurately or close to accurate
- Use knowledge of syllables and phonogram patterns to generate multisyllable words
- Spell simple and some complex plurals
- Use simple rules for adding inflectional endings to words (drop *e*, double letter)
- Spell most possessives (singular and plural)
- Spell most contractions
- Spell words that have been studied (spelling words)
- Write many compound words accurately
- Spell many one and two syllable words, that have vowel and *r*, correctly
- Write common abbreviations correctly

Handwriting/Word-Processing

- Use word processor to plan, draft, revise, edit, and publish
- Make changes on the screen to revise and edit, and publish documents
- Use efficient keyboarding skills
- Write fluently in both manuscript and cursive handwriting with appropriate spacing

Writing

Selecting Goals: Behaviors and Understandings to Notice, Teach, and Support

Writing Process

Rehearsing/Planning

Purpose
- Understand how the purpose of the writing influences the selection of genre
- Select the genre for the writing based on the purpose
- Have clear goals and understand how the goals will affect the writing
- Write for a specific purpose: to inform, entertain, persuade, reflect, instruct, retell, maintain relationships, plan

Audience
- Write with a specific reader or audience in mind
- Write to meet the needs of a specific reader or audience
- Plan and organize information for the intended reader(s)
- Understand audience as all readers rather than just the teacher

Oral Language
- Generate and expand ideas through talk with peers and teacher
- Look for ideas and topics in personal experiences, shared through talk
- Explore relevant questions in talking about a topic
- Identify the meaning or message to convey
- Use talk and storytelling to share the writing and to generate and rehearse language (that may be written later)
- Use language in stories that is specific to a topic

Gathering Seeds, Resources, and Experimenting with Writing
- Use a writer's notebook or booklet as a tool for collecting ideas, experimenting, planning, sketching, or drafting
- Reread a writer's notebook to select topics
- Use sketching, webs, lists, and freewriting to think about, plan for, and try out writing
- Make diagrams to assist in planning
- Try out new writing techniques
- Make notes about crafting ideas

Content, Topic, Theme
- Observe carefully events, people, settings, and other aspects of the world to gather information on a topic
- Get ideas from other books and writers about how to approach a topic
- Choose a topic that is significant
- Decide what is most important about a topic
- Use resources, including the Internet, to get information on a topic
- Select own topics for informational writing and state what is important about the topic
- Stay focused on a topic
- Select details that will support the topic
- Generate multiple titles to arrive at the most suitable and interesting
- Select a title that fits the content to publish or complete as final draft

Rehearsing/Planning (con't)

Inquiry/Research/Exploration
- Form questions to answer about a topic
- Take notes or make sketches to help in remembering information
- Participate actively in experiences and remember details that contribute to writing and drawing
- Remember important labels for drawings
- Select the most important information
- Gather information (with teacher assistance) about a topic from books or other print and media resources while preparing to write about it

Genre/Form
- Select from a variety of forms the kind of text that will fit the purpose (books with illustrations and words; alphabet books; label books; poetry books; question and answer books; illustration-only books)
- Understand that illustrations play different roles in a text (increase reader's enjoyment, add information, show sequence)

Drafting/Revising

Understanding the Process
- Understand the role of the writer, teacher, or peer writer in conference
- Understand that other writers can be helpful in the process
- Change writing in response to peer or teacher feedback
- Know how to use an editing and proofreading checklist

Producing a Draft
- Write a draft or discovery draft (write fast and as much as possible on a topic)
- Engage the reader with a strong lead
- Bring the piece to closure with an ending or final statement
- Establish an initiating event and follow with a series of events in a narrative
- Maintain control of a central idea across the piece
- Present ideas in logical order across the piece

Rereading
- Reread each day before writing more
- Reread a piece asking oneself–Have I made clear what I want readers to understand?
- Mark the most important part of a piece of writing
- Reread and revise the draft or rewrite sections to clarify meaning

Adding Information
- Add information to the middle to clarify meaning
- Expand information through adding details or examples
- Add dialogue to provide information, communicate thoughts/feelings, or provide narration (in quotes or speech balloons)

Deleting Information
- Take out repetitive words, phrases, or sentences that don't add to meaning
- Delete words or sentences that do not make sense
- Take out unnecessary words, phrases, or sentences
- Eliminate extraneous information

Writing

Selecting Goals: Behaviors and Understandings to Notice, Teach, and Support

Drafting/Revising (con't)

Reorganizing Information

- Move sentences around for better sequence
- Move information from one part of the text to another to make a text clearer

Changing Text

- Identify vague parts and provide specificity
- Change words to make the writing more interesting

Using Tools and Techniques

- Add letters, words, phrases, or sentences using a caret or sticky note with an asterisk
- Use a spider leg or piece of paper taped on to insert text
- Use a number in the writing to identify a place to add information and an additional numbered paper to write the information to insert
- Reorder a piece by cutting it apart or laying out the pages

Editing and Proofreading

Understanding the Process

- Understand that the writer shows respect to the reader by applying what is known to correct errors
- Understand that the better the spelling and space between words, the easier it is for the reader to read it
- Know how to use an editing and proofreading checklist

Editing for Conventions

- Check and correct letter formation
- Edit for conventional spelling of important words (for publication)
- Edit for the spelling of known words (should be spelled conventionally)
- Edit for spelling errors by circling or underlining words that do not look right and making another attempt
- Understand that the teacher will be final spelling editor for the published piece (after the student has used everything known)
- Edit for capitalization
- Edit for end punctuation
- Edit for sentence sense

Using Tools

- Use simple spell check programs on the computer
- Use beginning reference tools (for example, dictionaries or personal word lists, to assist in word choice or checking spelling)

Publishing

- Include graphics or illustrations as appropriate to the text
- Add information about the author
- Add dedication
- Add cover spread with title and author information
- Share a text with peers by reading it aloud
- Add to the text during the publishing process (for example, illustrations and other graphics, cover spread, title, dedication, table of contents, about the author piece)
- Attend to layout of text in final publication
- Select a poem, story, or informational book from own collection of writing to publish
- Use labels and captions on drawings that are displayed
- Begin to understand the importance of citing sources of information

Sketching and Drawing

- Understand the difference between drawing and sketching and use them to support planning, revising, and publishing the writing process
- Use sketching to create quick representations of images, usually an outline in pencil or pen
- Use sketching to support memory and help in planning
- Use drawings to capture detail that is important to a topic
- Create drawings that are related to the written text and increase readers' understanding and enjoyment
- Provide important information in the illustrations
- Use drawings and sketches to represent people, places, things, and ideas in the composing, revising, and publishing process
- Add labels or sentences to drawings as needed to explain them
- Add detail to drawings to add information or increase interest
- Create drawings that employ careful attention to color or detail

Viewing Self as a Writer

- Write in a variety of genres across the year
- Understand writing as a vehicle to communicate meaning
- Take risks as a writer
- View self as writer
- Write with initiative, investment, and independence
- Select best pieces of writing from own collection and give reasons for the selections
- Self-evaluate own writing and talk about what is good about it and what techniques were used
- Compare previous to revised writing and notice and talk about the differences
- Show ability to discuss what one is currently working on in a writer's conference
- State what was learned from each piece of writing
- Produce a reasonable quantity of writing within the time available
- Be willing to work at the craft of writing incorporating new learning from instruction
- Attend to the language and craft of other writers in order to learn more as a writer
- Seek feedback on writing

Writing

Selecting Purpose and Genre

Narrative: To tell a story

Memoir (personal narrative, autobiography)

Understanding the Genre

- Learn how to craft memoir by studying mentor texts
- Understand a personal narrative as a type of memoir that tells a story from the writer's life
- Understand that memoir can be comprised of a series of vignettes
- Understand memoir as a brief, often intense, memory of an event or a person with reflection
- Understand that memoirs have significance in the writer's life and usually show something significant to others
- Understand that personal narratives and memoirs have many characteristics of fiction, including setting, problem or tension, characters, dialogue, and problem resolution
- Use the term *memoir* to describe the type of writing
- Understand that autobiography is a biography written by the subject

Writing in the Genre

- Write an ending that fits the piece
- Select "small moments" or experiences and share thinking and feelings about them
- Use small experiences to communicate a bigger message
- Write a personal narrative as a "small moment"–show a character trying to do something, add details and setting as significant, show how character develops (character learns or changes)
- Describe and develop a setting and explain how it is related to the writer's experiences
- Use dialogue as appropriate to add to the meaning of the story
- Use words that show the passage of time
- Experiment with different time structures (for example, single-day flashback)
- Use only the important parts of the narrative, eliminating unnecessary information
- Describe characters by how they look, what they do, say, and think, and what others say about them
- Develop characters and show how the main character (author) changes
- Experiment with literary language (powerful nouns and verbs, figurative language)
- Imply or state the importance of the story
- Select meaningful topics
- Reveal something important about self or about life
- Create a series of vignettes that together communicate a bigger message

Short Fiction

Understanding the Genre

- Write various kinds of fiction by studying mentor texts
- Understand fiction as a short story about an event in the life of the main character
- Understand that fiction may be realism or fantasy
- Understand that the purpose of a short story is to explore a theme or teach a lesson
- Understand that the setting of fiction may be current or historical
- Understand the elements of fiction, including setting, problem, characters, and problem resolution
- Understand the structure of narrative, including lead or beginning, introduction of characters, setting, problem, series of events, and ending
- Use the term *fable, fairy tale,* or *tall tale* to describe the genre
- Use the terms *fantasy, short story, short fiction,* or *historical fiction* to describe the genre

Writing in the Genre

- Describe characters by how they look, what they do, say, and think, and what others say about them
- Take the point of view of one character by seeing the situation through his or her eyes
- Show rather than tell how characters feel
- Develop a plot that includes tension and one or more scenes
- Develop an interesting story with believable characters and a realistic or fantastic plot
- Expose the problem of the story
- Describe the setting with appropriate detail
- Take points of view by writing in first or third person
- Begin with a compelling lead to capture reader's attention
- Write a believable and satisfying ending to the story
- With fantasy, include imaginative character, setting, and plot elements

Writing

Selecting Purpose and Genre

Biography (biographical sketch)

Understanding the Genre

- Write various kinds of biographical pieces by studying mentor texts
- Understand biography as a true account of a person's life
- Understand that a biography can be about the person's whole life or a part of it
- Understand that to write a biography you need to select the most important events in a person's life
- Understand that a biography can be fictionalized (for example, adding dialogue to the events) or that it can be completely factual
- Understand the difference between true biography and fictionalized biography
- Use the terms *biographical sketch* or *biography* to describe the genre of the writing
- Establish the significance of events and personal decisions made by the subject of a biography
- Establish the significance of events and personal decisions made by the subject of a biography

Writing in the Genre

- Select important events to include and exclude extraneous events and details
- Describe subject's important decisions and turning point
- Choose a subject and state a reason for the selection
- Describe the subject by what she did or said as well as others' opinions
- Show the significance of the subject
- Include dialogue as appropriate
- Tell events in chronological order or in some other logical order (for example, categories)

Informational: To explain, persuade, or give facts about a topic

Literary Nonfiction

Understanding the Genre

- Understand that writers can learn how to write literary nonfiction by studying mentor texts
- Understand that literary nonfiction informs the reader about a topic in an entertaining or interesting way
- Understand that the writer of literary nonfiction works to help readers become interested in a topic
- Understand that to write literary nonfiction and reports, the writer needs to become very knowledgeable about the topic
- Understand that a report is a formal presentation of a topic
- Understand that literary nonfiction may be written in narrative form
- Understand that literary language, including figurative language, can be used
- Understand that literary nonfiction may include both fiction and nonfiction (hybrid)
- Use the term *literary nonfiction* to describe the genre

Writing in the Genre

- Use headings and subheadings to organize different parts
- Include features (for example, table of contents, boxes of facts set off from the text, diagrams, charts) and other tools (for example, glossary) to provide information to the reader
- Use headings and subheadings to guide the reader
- Keep the audience and their interests and likely background knowledge in mind
- Present information in categories or some other logical order
- Provide interesting details around a topic
- Include facts, figures, and graphics
- Use a narrative structure to help readers understand information and interest them in a topic
- Use organizational structures (for example, compare and contrast, cause and effect, temporal sequence, problem and solution, and description)
- Use literary language to make topic interesting to readers
- Add information to a narrative text to make it informational

Expository Nonfiction (feature article, report)

Understanding the Genre

- Understand that writers can learn how to write feature articles or reports by analyzing and using mentor texts
- Understand that a feature article begins with a lead paragraph, with more detailed information in subsequent paragraphs, and a conclusion
- Understand that a feature article usually focuses on one aspect of a topic
- Understand that a feature article reveals the writer's point of view
- Understand that feature articles and reports require research and organization
- Use the terms *feature article* or *report* to describe the genre
- Understand that people write informational texts to help readers learn about a topic
- Understand that a report may include several aspects of the same topic
- Understand that a report has an introductory section, followed by more information in categories or sections

Writing in the Genre

- Select topics of interest
- Write an effective lead paragraph and conclusion
- Present information in categories
- Write with a focus on a topic, including several aspects (report)
- Write with a focus on one aspect of a topic (feature article)
- Use italics for stress or emphasis as appropriate
- Use quotes from experts (written texts, speeches, or interviews)
- Include facts, statistics, examples, and anecdotes
- Use descriptive and specific vocabulary
- Use new vocabulary specific to the topic
- Use parentheses to explain further

Writing

Selecting Purpose and Genre

Essay *(opinion editorial)*

Understanding the Genre

- Learn to write essays through studying examples and published mentor texts
- Understand an essay as a short literary composition used to clearly state the author's point of view
- Understand that the purpose of an essay can be to persuade readers to think like the author
- Understand that the purpose of an essay can be to persuade readers to improve their world
- Understand the basic structure of an essay (introduction, body, conclusion)
- Use the term *essay* to describe the genre

Writing in the Genre

- Begin with a title or opening that tells the reader what is being argued or explained and end with a conclusion
- Provide a series of clear arguments or reasons to support the argument
- Take topics from stories or everyday observations
- Include illustrations, charts, or diagrams to inform or persuade the reader
- Use opinions supported by facts
- Provide "expert testimony" or quotes to support argument

Poetic: **To express feelings, sensory images, ideas, or stories**

Poetry *(free verse, rhyme)*

Understanding the Genre

- Understand that writers can learn to write a variety of poems from studying mentor texts
- Understand poetry as a unique way to communicate about and describe feelings, sensory images, ideas, or stories
- Understand the way print works in poems and demonstrate the use in reading and writing haiku, cinquain
- Understand that poems can take a variety of shapes
- Notice the beat or rhythm of a poem and its relation to line breaks
- Understand the importance of specific word choice in poetry
- Understand that there are different kinds of poems including informatonal
- Understand that poems do not have to rhyme
- Understand the difference between poetic language and ordinary language
- Use the term *poem* to describe the writing or use the specific term for the kind of poetry

Writing in the Genre

- Write a variety of types of poems
- Use white space and line breaks to communicate the meaning and tone of the poem
- Understand the role of line breaks, white space for pause, breath, or emphasis
- Observe closely to select topics or content and write with detail
- Shape words on the page to look like a poem
- Use words to convey images
- Use words to convey strong feelings
- Write with detail and create images
- Select topics that are significant and help readers see in a new way
- Select topics that have strong meaning
- Write a poetic text in response to another poem, reflecting the same style, topic, mood, or voice
- Write a poetic text in response to prose texts, either narrative or informational
- Remove extra words to clarify the meaning and make the writing more powerful
- Use repetition, refrain, rhythm, and other poetic techniques
- Use words to show not tell
- Choose a title that communicates the meaning of a poem

Functional: **To perform a practical task**

Friendly Letters *(notes, cards, invitations, email)*

Understanding the Genre

- Understand that a friendly letter has parts (date, salutation, closing, signature, and sometimes P.S.)
- Understand that the form of written communication is related to the purpose
- Understand notes, cards, invitations, email, and letters are written communication among people
- Understand that while email is a quick form of communication, it is a written document and care should be taken in tone and quality
- Understand that invitations require specific information to be communicated
- Understand that a friendly letter has parts (date, salutation, closing, signature, and sometimes P.S.)
- Use the terms *notes, invitations, email,* and *letter* to describe the forms

Writing in the Genre

- Write notes, cards, invitations, and email for a variety of purposes
- Write with the specific purpose in mind
- Write to a known audience or a specific reader
- Include important information in the communication
- Address the audience appropriately
- Vary level of formality appropriate to purpose and audience
- Write letters with all required parts
- Write letters to an author that demonstrate appreciation for and thinking about texts that the individual has written
- Write letters to an illustrator that demonstrate noticing details and style and appreciation for the art
- Write persuasive letters

Writing

Selecting Purpose and Genre

Formal Letters *(business letter, letter to the editor)*

Understanding the Genre

- Understand that writers can learn to write effective business letters by studying examples
- Understand that a business letter is a formal document and has a particular purpose
- Understand that a business letter has parts (date, inside address, formal salutation followed by a colon, body—organized into paragraphs, closing, signature and title of sender, and sometimes notification of a copy or enclosure)
- Use the term *business letter* or *letter the editor* to describe the form or genre

Writing in the Genre

- Write to a specified audience that may be an individual or an organization or group
- Include important information
- Exclude unnecessary details
- Address the audience appropriately
- Organize the body into paragraphs
- Understand the component parts of a business letter and how to lay them out on a page (date, return address, address and salutation, body, closing, information about copies or enclosures)
- Write persuasive and informative letters

Lists and Procedures *(how-to)*

Understanding the Genre

- Understand a list as a collection of items, one below another, that may be used as a planning tool
- Understand procedural writing (how-to) as a list of directions for how to do something and a list of what is needed

Writing in the Genre

- Use lists to plan activities or support memory
- Write clear directions, guides, and "how-to" texts

Test Writing *(extended response, essay test, short answer)*

Understanding the Genre

- Learn how to write on tests by studying examples of short answers and extended responses
- Understand that test writing is a particular kind of writing used when taking tests (short answer, extended response)
- Understand that in test writing the topic is usually assigned
- Understand that some writing serves the purpose of demonstrating what a person knows or can do as a writer
- Understand that test writing often requires the student to write about something real
- Understand test writing as a response carefully tailored to meet precise instructions
- Understand that test writing involves analyzing what is expected of the writer
- Understand that test writing often requires inferring the motives of an individual
- Understand that test writing often requires taking a position, developing a clear argument, and providing evidence for points
- Use the term *test writing* to describe the genre

Writing in the Genre

- Analyze prompts to determine purpose, audience, and genre (story, essay, persuasive letter)
- Read and internalize the criteria for acceptable response
- Write focused answers to questions and to prompts
- Write concisely and to the direction of the question or prompt
- Elaborate on important points
- Exclude extraneous details
- Reflect on bigger ideas and make or defend a claim that is substantiated
- Respond to a text in a way that reflects analytic or aesthetic thinking
- Restate a claim with further evidence
- State a point of view and provide evidence
- Proofread carefully for spelling and conventions

Writing About Reading *(all genres)*

(See the Writing About Reading continuum.)

Sean

Staying Healthy

People should Stay healthier. There are a bunch of ways to protect your body from fractures, breaks, heart attacks, Strokes etc. Here are Some Ways.

Take at least 10 minutes a day to run around, Stretch, Play sports, or even just take a walk. Choose at least one of these things. If you do, you're getting healthier each Second. It might not be fun, but your bones get Stronger your muscles get Stronger and your heart get's healthier. This will also happen if you go to the gym, lift weights, or use machines like a treadmill.

Eat your vegtables. That is a really good way of Staying healthy and So is fruit. Some vegtables are: Carrots, Celery, broccoli, Apples, Pears, Etc.

It doesn't hurt to try any of this stuff. If one routine doesn't work for you just try a different one. Take my advice it helps.

Writing

Selecting Goals: Behaviors and Understandings to Notice, Teach, and Support

Craft

Organization

Text Structure

- Write using the structure of exposition—a nonnarrative, with facts and information ordered in a logical way
- Write using the structure of narrative—characters involved in a plot, with events ordered by time
- Choose a narrative or informational genre and organize the text appropriately

Beginning and Ending

- Use a variety of beginnings and endings to engage the reader (for example, surprise, circular story)
- Begin with a purposeful and engaging lead
- Bring a piece to closure with a concluding statement
- End an informational piece with a thoughtful or enlightening conclusion
- End a narrative with a problem solution and a satisfying conclusion
- Understand that narratives can begin at the beginning, middle, or end

Presentation of Ideas

- Present ideas clearly and in logical sequence or categories
- Clearly show topics and subtopics and indicate them with headings and subheadings in expository writing
- Introduce ideas followed by supportive details and examples
- Support ideas with facts, details, examples, and explanations from multiple authorities
- Use paragraphs to organize ideas
- Use well-crafted transitions to support the pace and flow of the writing
- Use a variety of underlying structures to present different kinds of information (established sequence, temporal sequence, compare and contrast, problem and solution, cause and effect)
- Show steps in enough detail that a reader can follow a sequence
- Use time appropriately as an organizing tool
- Organize information according to purpose

Idea Development

- Clearly communicate main points
- Provide supporting details that are accurate, relevant, and helpful
- Provide details that are accurate, relevant, interesting, and vivid
- Hold the reader's attention with clear, focused content
- Engage the reader with ideas that show strong knowledge of the topic

Language Use

- Use a variety of sentence structures and lengths
- Vary sentence length to create feeling or mood
- Use language typical of written texts, sometimes imitating writers of books
- Use memorable words or phrases
- Use concrete sensory details and descriptive language to develop plot (tension and problem resolution) and setting in memoir, biography, and fiction
- Show through language instead of telling
- Use descriptive language and dialogue to present characters/subjects who appear and develop in memoir, biography, and fiction
- Use language to show feelings of characters
- Use a variety of transitions and connections (words, phrases, sentences, and paragraphs)
- Arrange simple and complex sentences for an easy flow and sentence transition
- Use examples to make meaning clear
- Use language to elicit feelings
- Use words in figurative ways to make comparisons (simile, metaphor)
- Use language to establish a point of view
- Vary language and style as appropriate to audience and purpose
- Write in both first and third person and understand the differences in effect so as to choose appropriately
- Understand the differences between first and third person
- Select a point of view with which to tell a story
- Use dialogue and action to draw readers into the story

Writing

Selecting Goals: Behaviors and Understandings to Notice, Teach, and Support

Word Choice

- Select precise words to reflect the intended message or meaning
- Use a range of descriptive words to enhance the meaning
- Use strong verbs (active rather than passive, and more descriptive or interesting than words typically used; for example, *hurled* instead of *threw*)
- Use strong nouns (more descriptive or interesting than words typically used; for example, *matriarch* instead of *mother*)
- Learn new words from reading and try them out in writing
- Use transitional words for time flow (*finally, after some time*)
- Use memorable or vivid words (*gigantic, desperate*)
- Use vocabulary appropriate for the topic
- Vary word choice to create interesting description and dialogue
- Use figurative language to make comparisons (simile, metaphor)
- Use colorful modifiers and style as appropriate to audience and purpose
- Choose words with the audience's background knowledge in mind
- Use words that convey an intended mood or effect

Voice

- Write with a unique perspective
- Write in a way that speaks directly to the reader
- Write in a way that shows care and commitment to the topic
- Share thoughts through inner dialogue
- Use punctuation to support voice or tell the reader how to read the text (commas, ellipses, dashes, colons)
- Show enthusiasm and energy for the topic
- State information in a unique or unusual way
- Produce expository writing that is persuasive and well constructed, and reveals the stance of the writer toward the topic
- Produce narratives that are engaging, honest, and reveal the person behind the writing
- Include details that add to the voice
- Use dialogue selectively to communicate voice

Conventions

Text Layout

- Understand that layout of print and illustrations are important in conveying the meaning of a text
- Understand that size of print conveys meaning in printed text
- Use layout, spacing, and size of print to create titles, headings, and subheadings
- Use underlining, italics, and bold print to convey meaning
- Arrange print on the page to support the text's meaning and to help the reader notice important information
- Use indentation or spacing to set off paragraphs

Grammar

Sentence Structure

- Write complete sentences with noun and verb
- Place clauses in sentences
- Place phrases in sentences
- Use conventional sentence structure for complex sentences with embedded clauses
- Write simple and compound sentences
- Sometimes vary sentence structure and length for reasons of craft
- Use a range of sentence types (declarative, interrogative, imperative, exclamatory)
- Write dialogue in conventional structures
- Write sentences in past, present, future, present perfect, and past perfect tenses

Parts of Speech

- Use nouns and pronouns that are in agreement (*Mike/he*)
- Use objective and nominative case pronouns correctly (*me, him, her; I, he, she*)
- Use indefinite and relative pronouns correctly (*everyone, both; who, whom*)
- Use prepositions and prepositional phrases correctly
- Use verbs that are often misused (*lie, lay; rise, raise*)
- Use verb and objects that are often misused ([verb] *to her and me; she and I* [verb])
- Use adjectives and adverbs correctly
- Use nouns
- Use adjectives
- Use adverbs

Tense

- Maintain consistency of tense
- Write sentences in past, present, future, present perfect, and past perfect tenses

Paragraphing

- Use paragraph structure (indented or block) to organize sentences that focus on one idea
- Create transitions between paragraphs to show the progression of ideas
- Use paragraphing to show speaker change in dialogues

Writing

Selecting Goals: Behaviors and Understandings to Notice, Teach, and Support

Capitalization

- Use a capital letter for the first word of a sentence
- Use capital letters appropriately for the first letter in days, months, holidays, city and state names, and titles of books
- Use capital letters correctly in dialogue
- Use capitalization for specialized functions (emphasis, key information, voice)
- Use more complex capitalization with increasing accuracy, such as abbreviations and quotation marks in split dialogue

Punctuation

- Learn about the possibility of using punctuation and its effect on readers by studying mentor texts
- Notice effective or unusual use of punctuation marks by authors
- Try out new ways of using punctuation
- Understand and use ellipses to show pause or anticipation, usually before something surprising
- Use dashes to indicate a longer pause or slow down the reading to emphasize particular information
- Consistently use periods, exclamation points, and question marks as ending marks
- Use commas and quotation marks correctly in writing interrupted and uninterrupted dialogue
- Use apostrophes in contractions and possessives
- Use commas to identify a series and to introduce clauses
- Break words apart at the syllable break and at the end of a line using a hyphen
- Use brackets to set aside a different idea or kind of information
- Use colons to indicate something is explained or described
- Use commas and parentheses to set off parenthetical information
- Use hyphens to divide words
- Use indentation to identify paragraphs

Spelling

- Spell a large number of high-frequency words (500+), a wide range of plurals, and base words with inflectional endings
- Use a range of spelling strategies to take apart and spell multisyllable words (word parts, connections to known words, complex sound-to-letter cluster relationships)
- Spell complex plurals correctly (*knife, knives; woman, women; sheep, sheep*)
- Be aware of the spelling of common suffixes (for example, *-ion, -ment, -ly*)
- Spell a full range of contractions, plurals, and possessives, and compound words
- Correctly spell words that have been studied (spelling words)
- Spell two or three syllable words, that have vowel and *r,* correctly
- Use difficult homophones (*their, there*) correctly

Handwriting/Word-Processing

- Write fluently and legibly in cursive handwriting with appropriate spacing
- Use word-processing with understanding of how to produce and vary text (layout, font, special techniques)
- Use word processor to get ideas down, revise, edit, and publish
- Use efficient keyboarding skills to create drafts, revise, edit, and publish
- Show familiarity with computer and word-processing terminology
- Create website entries and articles with appropriate text layout, graphics, and access to information through searching
- Make wide use of computer skills in presenting text

Writing Process

Rehearsing/Planning

Purpose

- Write for a specific purpose: to inform, entertain, persuade, reflect, instruct, retell, maintain relationships, plan
- Understand how the purpose of the writing influences the selection of genre
- Select the genre for the writing based on content and purpose
- Select form to reflect content and purpose
- Have clear goals and understand how the goals will affect the writing

Audience

- Write with a specific reader or audience in mind
- Understand how the writing meets the needs of a specific reader or audience
- Plan and organize information for the intended reader(s)
- Understand audience as all readers rather than just the teacher

Oral Language

- Generate and expand ideas through talk with peers and teacher
- Look for ideas and topics in personal experiences, shared through talk
- Explain relevant questions in talking about a topic
- Use talk and storytelling to shape the writing and to generate and rehearse language (that may be written later)
- Use language in stories that is specific to a topic

Writing

Selecting Goals: Behaviors and Understandings to Notice, Teach, and Support

Rehearsing/Planning (con't)

Gathering Seeds/Resources and Experimenting with Words

- Use a writer's notebook or booklet as a tool for collecting ideas, experimenting, planning, sketching, or drafting
- Gather a variety of entries (character map, timeline, sketches, observations, freewrites, drafts, lists) in a writer's notebook
- Reread a writer's notebook to select topics
- Use sketches, webs, lists, diagrams, and freewriting to think about, plan for, and try out writing
- Think through a topic, focus, organization, and audience
- Try out different heads and endings in a writer's notebook
- Try out titles, develop characters and setting in a writer's notebook
- Explore knowledge about a topic using a list or web
- Note observations about craft from mentor texts
- Take notes on new writing techniques
- Take notes from interviews or observations
- Make a plan for an essay that makes a claim and contains supporting evidence
- Choose helpful tools (for example, webs, T-charts, sketches, charts, diagrams, lists, outlines, flow charts)
- Select small moments, full of emotion, that can be expanded

Content, Topic, Theme

- Observe carefully events, people, settings, and other aspects of the world to gather information on a topic
- Develop a clear main idea around which a piece of writing will be planned
- Choose a topic that is significant
- Get ideas from other books and writers about how to approach a topic
- Use texts, including those found on the Internet, to get ideas on a topic
- Use the organizing features of electronic text (bulletin boards, databases, keyword searchers, email addresses) to locate information
- State what is important about the topic
- Select details that will support the topic
- Stay focused on a topic to produce a longer, well-organized piece of writing
- Take audience and purpose into account when choosing a topic
- Understand a range for genres and forms and select from them according to topic and purpose

Inquiry/Research

- Form questions to explore and locate sources for information about a topic, characters, or setting
- Understand the concept of plagiarism
- Create categories of information
- Determine when research is necessary to cover a topic adequately
- Use notes to record and organize information
- Select and include only the information that is appropriate to the topic and to the category
- Identify and select important information from the total available
- Conduct research to gather information in planning a writing project (for example, live interviews, Internet, artifacts, articles, books)
- Search for appropriate information from multiple sources (books and other print materials, websites, interviews)
- Record sources of information for citation

Rehearsing/Planning (con't)

Genre/Form

- Select from a variety of forms the kind of text that will fit the purpose (books with illustrations and words; alphabet books; label books; poetry books; question and answer books; illustration-only books)
- Understand that illustrations play different roles in a text (increase reader's enjoyment, add information, etc.)

Drafting/Revising

Understanding the Process

- Understand the role of the writer, teacher, or peer writer in conference
- Understand revision as a means for making written messages stronger and clearer to readers
- Change writing in response to peer or teacher feedback
- Use writers as mentors in making revisions and publishing
- Name, understand the purpose of, try out, and internalize crafting techniques
- Understand that a writer rereads and revises while drafting (recursive process)
- Know how to use an editing/proofreading checklist

Producing a Draft

- Write a discovery draft (write fast and as much as possible on a topic)
- Draft multiple leads or endings to select the most effective
- Arouse reader interest with a strong lead
- Establish an initiating event in a narrative with a series of events flowing from it
- Produce multiple-paragraph pieces
- Create paragraphs that group related ideas
- Maintain central idea or focus across paragraphs
- Show steps in an informational text in enough detail to follow a sequence
- Establish the situation, plot or problem, and point of view
- Provide insight as to why an incident or event is memorable
- Bring the piece to closure with an ending or final statement
- Bring the piece to closure with effective summary, parting idea, or satisfying ending
- Establish the significance of events and personal decisions made by the subject of a biography
- Generate multiple titles to help think about the focus of the piece
- Select a title that fits the content

Writing

Selecting Goals: Behaviors and Understandings to Notice, Teach, and Support

Drafting/Revising (con't)

Rereading
- Mark the most important part of a piece of writing
- Reread and revise the discovery draft or rewrite sections to clarify meaning
- Reread writing to think about what to write next
- Reread writing to check for clarity and purpose

Adding Information
- Add details or examples to make the piece clearer or more interesting
- Add information to the middle to clarify meaning
- Add transitional words and phrases to clarify meaning and make the writing smoother
- Reread and change or add words to ensure that meaning is clear
- Add descriptive words and details to writing or drawings
- Add dialogue to provide information, communicate thoughts/feelings, or provide narration (in quotes or speech balloons)
- Use footnotes to add information

Deleting Information
- Delete redundant or unnecessary information to make a piece clearer or more interesting
- Reread and cross out words to ensure that meaning is clear
- Eliminate extraneous details
- Delete information that is unnecessary

Reorganizing Information
- Reorganize paragraphs for better sequence or logical progression of ideas
- Move information from one part of the text to another to make a text clearer

Changing Text
- Identify vague parts and provide specificity
- Vary word choice to make the piece more interesting
- Work on transitions to achieve better flow
- Reread writing to rethink and make changes
- Reshape writing to make the text into a different genre (for example, personal narrative to poem)

Using Tools and Techniques
- Use a caret or sticky note with an asterisk to insert text
- Use a number in the writing to identify a place to add information and an additional numbered paper to write the information to insert
- Use a spider leg or piece of paper taped on to insert text
- Reorder a piece by cutting it apart or laying out the pages
- Cut, paste, and staple pieces of a text
- Use word-processing to add or delete text
- Use word-processing to change text
- Use word-processing to move text by cutting and pasting

Editing and Proofreading

Understanding the Process
- Understand that the writer shows respect for the reader by applying what is known about conventions
- Know how to use an editing and proofreading checklist
- Understand that a writer can ask another person to do a final edit (after using what is known)
- Understand the limitations of grammar check on the computer
- Understand the limitations of spell check on the computer
- Understand how to use tools to self-evaluate writing and assist self-edit

Editing for Conventions
- Edit for spelling errors
- Prepare final draft with self-edit and submit to teacher–edit prior to publishing
- Edit for capitalization
- Edit for punctuation
- Edit for grammar
- Check and correct spacing and layout
- Determine where new paragraphs should begin
- Edit for word suitability and precise meaning

Using Tools
- Use spell check on the computer, monitoring changes carefully
- Use a dictionary to check on spelling and meaning
- Use a thesaurus to search for more interesting words
- Use grammar check on the computer, monitoring changes carefully

Writing

Selecting Goals: Behaviors and Understandings to Notice, Teach, and Support

Publishing

- Create illustrations or other art for pieces that are in final form
- Often include graphics as appropriate to the text
- Add information about the author
- Add dedication
- Add cover spread with title and author information
- Attend to layout of text in final publication
- Use a variety of print characteristics to make the text more accessible to the reader (titles, headings, and subheadings)
- Use a variety of print characteristics to present information in an interesting way (insets, call-outs)
- Add table of contents and glossary where needed
- Understand the purposes of publication

Sketching and Drawing

- Use sketches or drawings to represent people, places, and things, and also to communicate mood and abstract ideas
- Understand the difference between drawing and sketching and use them to support the writing process
- Use sketching to create quick representations of images, usually an outline in pencil or pen
- Use sketching to support memory and help in planning
- Use sketching to capture detail that is important to a topic
- Create drawings that are related to the written text and increase readers' understanding and enjoyment
- Provide important information in the illustrations
- Add detail to drawings to add information or increase interest
- Create drawings that employ careful attention to color or detail
- Sketch and draw with a sense of relative size and perspective
- Use the terms *sketching* and *drawing* to refer to these processes and forms

Viewing Self as a Writer

- Write in a variety of genres across the year
- Understand writing as a vehicle to communicate meaning
- Take risks as a writer
- View self as writer
- Write with initiative, investment, and independence
- Experiment with and approximate writing
- Articulate goals as a writer
- Notice what makes writing effective and name the craft or technique
- Mark the most important part of a piece of writing (one's own and others')
- Produce a reasonable quantity of writing within the time available
- Show ability to discuss what one is working on as a writer in a conference
- Show interest in and work at crafting good writing, incorporating new learning from instruction
- Seek feedback on writing
- Suggest possible revisions to peers
- Select examples of best writing in all genres attempted
- Self-evaluate own writing and talk about what is good about it and what techniques were used
- Compare previous to revised writing and notice and talk about the differences
- State what was learned from each piece of writing
- Self-evaluate pieces of writing in light of what is known about a genre

Norway

There are animals all around you. Sports are being played. Farms are all about. Fjords and glaciers are sitting there gracefully. Kids running all over in the grass. The smell of fresh air. Beautiful scenery everywhere. If you would like some place like this, then Norway is the place for you! And you can find out more from this book.

Writing

Selecting Purpose and Genre

Narrative: To tell a story

Memoir *(personal narrative, autobiography)*

Understanding the Genre

- Learn how to craft memoir by studying mentor texts
- Understand a personal narrative as a type of memoir that tells a story from the writer's life
- Understand that memoir can be comprised of a series of vignettes
- Understand memoir as a brief, often intense, memory of an event or a person with reflection
- Understand that memoirs have significance in the writer's life and usually show something significant to others
- Understand that memoir can be fictionalized or be fiction
- Understand that personal narratives and memoirs have many characteristics of fiction, including setting, problem or tension, characters, dialogue, and problem resolution
- Use the term *memoir* to describe the type of writing
- Understand that autobiography is a biography written by the subject
- Use the term *autobiography* to describe this type of writing

Writing in the Genre

- Write an engaging lead that captures interest and foreshadows the content
- Use small experiences to communicate a bigger message
- Describe and develop a setting and explain how it is related to the writer's experiences
- Use dialogue in a way that reflects setting and attributes of self and others
- Use words that show the passage of time
- Experiment with different time structures (for example, single-day flashback)
- Use only the important parts of the narrative, eliminating unnecessary information
- Describe characters by what they do, say, and think and what others say about them
- Develop characters and show how the main character (usually author) changes
- Experiment with literary language (powerful nouns and verbs, figurative language)
- Imply or state the importance of the story
- Select meaningful topics
- Reveal something important about self or about life
- Create a series of vignettes that together communicate a message
- Write an ending that fits the piece

Short Fiction *(short story, short fiction, or historical fiction)*

Understanding the Genre

- Write various kinds of fiction by studying mentor texts
- Understand fiction as a short story about an event in the life of the main character
- Understand that fiction may be realism or fantasy
- Understand that the purpose of a short story is to explore a theme or teach a lesson
- Understand that the setting of fiction may be current or historical
- Understand the elements of fiction, including setting, problem, characters, and problem resolution
- Understand the structure of narrative, including lead or beginning, introduction of characters, setting, problem, series of events, and ending
- Use the terms *tall tale, fairy tale, myth, fable,* or *legend* to describe the genre
- Use the terms *fantasy, short story, short fiction,* or *historical fiction* to describe the genre

Writing in the Genre

- Describe characters by how they look, what they do, say, and think, and what others say about them
- Take the point of view of one character by seeing the situation through his or her eyes
- Show rather than tell how characters feel
- Develop a plot that includes tension and one or more scenes
- Develop an interesting story with believable characters and a realistic plot (realistic fiction) or a fantastic plot (fantasy)
- Expose the problem of the story
- Describe the setting with appropriate detail
- Take points of view by writing in first or third person
- Assure that the events and setting for historical fiction are accurate
- Begin with a compelling lead to capture reader's attention
- Write a believable and satisfying ending to the story
- With fantasy, include imaginative character, setting, and plot elements

Writing

Selecting Purpose and Genre

Biography (biographical sketch)

UNDERSTANDING THE GENRE

- Understand biography as a true account of a person's life
- Understand that a biography can be about the person's whole life or a part of it
- Understand that to write a biography you need to select the most important events in a person's life
- Understand that a biography can be fictionalized (for example, adding dialogue) even though the events are true or that it can be completely factual
- Understand the difference between true biography and fictionalized biography
- Use the terms *biographical sketch* or *biography* to describe the genre of the writing

WRITING IN THE GENRE

- Write various kinds of biographical pieces by studying mentor texts
- Choose a subject and sometimes state a reason for the selection
- Establish the significance of events and personal decisions made by the subject of a biography
- Select important events to include and exclude extraneous events and details
- Describe subject's important decisions and turning points
- Describe the subject by what he did or said as well as others' opinions
- Show the significance of the subject
- Include dialogue as appropriate
- Tell events in chronological order or in some other logical order (for example, categories or with flashbacks or flashforward)
- Use interviews and documents (books, Internet, letters, news articles) to inform the writing of a biography

Informational: To explain, persuade, or give facts about a topic

Literary Nonfiction

UNDERSTANDING THE GENRE

- Understand that writers can learn how to write literary nonfiction by studying mentor texts
- Understand that literary nonfiction informs the reader about a topic in an entertaining or interesting way
- Understand that the writer of literary nonfiction works to help his or her readers become interested in a topic
- Understand that to write literary nonfiction, the writer needs to become very knowledgeable about the topic
- Understand that literary ninfiction is a common type of hybrid text
- Understand that literary nonfiction may be written in narrative form
- Understand that literary language, including figurative language, can be used
- Understand that nonfiction may include both fiction and nonfiction (hybrid)
- Use the term *literary nonfiction* to describe the genre

WRITING IN THE GENRE

- Use headings and subheadings to organize different parts and guide the reader
- Include features (for example, table of contents, boxes of facts set off from the text, diagrams, charts) and other tools (for example, glossary) to provide information to the reader
- Use headings and subheadings to guide the reader
- Keep the audience and their interests and background knowledge in mind
- Present information in categories or some other logical order
- Provide interesting details around a topic
- Provide details and interesting examples that develop the topic
- Include facts, figures, and graphics
- Use a narrative structure to help readers understand information and interest them in a topic
- Use organizational structures (for example, compare and contrast, cause and effect, temporal sequence, problem and solution, and description)
- Use literary language to make topic interesting to readers
- Add information to a narrative text to inform readers; sometimes create hybrid texts
- Include argument and persuasion where appropriate
- Reveal the writer's convictions about the topic through the writer's unique voice
- Write an engaging lead and first section that orient the reader and provide an introduction to the topic

Writing

Selecting Purpose and Genre

Expository Nonfiction *(feature article, report)*

Understanding the Genre

- Reveal the writer's convictions about the topic through a unique voice
- Learn how to write feature articles or reports using mentor texts
- Understand that a report has an introductory section, followed by more information in categories or sections
- Understand that a feature article begins with a lead paragraph, with more detailed information in subsequent paragraphs, and a conclusion
- Understand that a report may include several aspects of the same topic
- Understand that a feature article usually focuses on one aspect of a topic
- Understand that informational texts help readers learn about a topic
- Understand that feature articles and reports require research and organization
- Understand writers of feature articles show fascination with a subject
- Use the terms *feature article* or *report* to describe the genre

Writing in the Genre

- Select topics that are interesting and substantive
- Credit sources of information as appropriate
- Write an effective lead paragraph and conclusion
- Present information in categories, organized locally
- Write multiple paragraphs with smooth transitions
- Write with a focus on a topic, including several aspects (report)
- Write with a focus on one aspect of a topic (feature article)
- Use italics for stress or emphasis as appropriate
- Use quotes from experts (written texts, speeches, or interviews)
- Include facts, statistics, examples, and anecdotes
- Use descriptive and specific vocabulary
- Use new vocabulary specific to the topic
- Select topics to which the writer is committed
- Use parentheses to explain further

Essay *(opinion editorial)*

Understanding the Genre

- Learn to write essays by studying examples and published mentor texts
- Understand an essay as a short literary composition used to clearly state the author's point of view
- Understand the structure of an essay (introduction, body, conclusion)
- Understand that the purpose of an essay can be to persuade readers to think like the author on an issue
- Understand that the purpose of an essay can be to persuade readers to improve their world or critique society
- Understand the structure of an essay
- Use the term *essay* to describe the genre

Writing in the Genre

- Begin with a title or opening that tells the reader what is being argued or explained and conclude with a summary
- Provide a series of clear arguments or reasons to support the argument
- Take topics from stories or everyday observations
- Include illustrations, charts, or diagrams to inform or persuade the reader
- Use opinions supported by facts
- Write a logical, thoughtful ending
- Write well-crafted sentences that express the writer's convictions
- Use "expert testimony" or quotes to support point of view

Poetic: **To express feelings, sensory images, ideas, or stories**

Poetry *(free verse, rhyme)*

Understanding the Genre

- Understand that there are different kinds of poems such as informational and ballads
- Understand that writers can learn to write poems from studying mentor texts
- Understand poetry as a unique way to communicate about and describe feelings, sensory images, ideas, or stories
- Understand the way print works in poems and demonstrate knowledge by reading and writing them on a page using white space and line breaks
- Understand that poems can take a variety of shapes
- Notice the beat or rhythm of a poem and its relation to line breaks
- Understand the importance of specific word choice in poetry
- Understand that poems do not have to rhyme
- Understand the difference between poetic and ordinary language
- Recognize different forms of poetry such as free verses, haiku, cinquain, limerick
- Use the term *poem* to describe the writing or use the specific term for the kind of poetry

Writing in the Genre

- Write a variety of types of poems
- Use white space and line breaks to communicate meaning and tone
- Understand the role of line breaks and white space for pause or emphasis
- Observe closely to select topics or content and write with detail
- Shape words on the page to look like a poem
- Use words to convey images
- Use words to convey strong feelings
- Write with detail and create images
- Select topics that are significant and help readers see in a new way
- Select topics that have strong meaning
- Write a poetic text in response to another poem, reflecting the same style, topic, mood, or voice
- Write a poetic text in response to prose texts (narrative or informational)
- Remove extra words to clarify meaning and make writing more powerful
- Use figurative language and other literary devices such as alliteration, personification, simile, metaphor, onomatopeia
- Use repetition, refrain, rhythm, and other poetic techniques
- Use words to show not tell
- Choose a title that communicates the meaning of a poem

Writing

Selecting Purpose and Genre

Functional: To perform a practical task

Friendly Letters (notes, cards, invitations, email)

Understanding the Genre

- Understand that form and purpose of written communication are related
- Understand notes, cards, invitations, email, and letters are written communication among people
- Understand that while email is a quick form of communication, it is a written document and care should be taken in tone and quality
- Understand that invitations require specific information
- Understand that a friendly letter has parts (date, salutation, closing, signature, and sometimes P.S.)
- Use the terms *notes, invitations, email,* and *letter* to describe the forms

Writing in the Genre

- Write notes, cards, invitations, and email for a variety of purposes
- Write with the purpose in mind
- Write to a known audience or a specific reader and address appropriately
- Include important information in the communication
- Vary level of formality appropriate to purpose and audience
- Write letters with all required parts
- Write letters to an author that demonstrate appreciation for and thinking about texts that the individual has written
- Write letters to an illustrator that demonstrate noticing details and style and appreciation for the art
- Write persuasive letters

Formal Letters (business letter, letter to the editor)

Understanding the Genre

- Learn to write effective business letters by studying examples
- Understand that a business letter is formal and has a particular purpose
- Understand that a business letter has parts (date, inside address, formal salutation followed by a colon, body, closing, signature and title of sender, and sometimes notification of a copy or enclosure)
- Use the term *business letter* or *letter to the editor* to describe the genre

Writing in the Genre

- Write to a specified audience (e.g., individual, organization, or group)
- Include important information and exclude unnecessary details
- Address the audience appropriately
- Organize the body into paragraphs
- Write persuasive and informative letters
- Understand the component parts of a business letter and how to lay them out on a page (date, return address, address and salutation, body, closing, information about copies or enclosures)

Test Writing (extended response, essay test, short answer)

Understanding the Genre

- Learn how to write on tests by studying examples of short answers and extended responses
- Understand that test writing is a particular kind of writing used when taking tests (short answer, extended response)
- Understand that test writing involves responding to an assigned topic
- Understand that some writing serves the purpose of demonstrating what a person knows or can do as a writer
- Understand that test writing often requires writing about something real
- Understand test writing is a response tailored to meet instructions
- Understand test writing involves analyzing what is expected of the writer
- Understand test writing often requires inferring motives of an individual
- Understand that test writing often requires taking a position, developing a clear argument, and providing evidence for points
- Understand that test writing sometimes requires taking a perspective that may come from a different time or setting than the reader
- Use the term *test writing* to describe the genre

Writing in the Genre

- Analyze prompts to determine purpose, audience, and genre (story, essay, persuasive letter)
- Read and internalize the criteria for acceptable response
- Write focused answers to questions and to prompts
- Write concisely and to the direction of the question or prompt
- Elaborate on important points
- Exclude extraneous details
- Reflect on bigger ideas and make or defend a claim that is substantiated
- Respond to a text in a way that reflects analytic or aesthetic thinking
- Restate a claim with further evidence
- State a point of view and provide evidence
- State the point of view of another individual

Writing About Reading (all genres)

(See the Writing About Reading continuum.)

Hybrid: To engage, inform, or persuade

Hybrid Texts (mixed genres)

Understanding the Genre

- Understand writers can learn to write hybrid texts by studying mentor texts
- Understand that literary nonfiction is a common type of hybrid text
- Understand that a hybrid/multigenre text mixes two or more genres in order to communicate information in different ways
- Understand that writers use more than one genre to increase engagement or make the text come alive (letters, poem in a narrative)
- Understand that the genres in the text must be integrated into a harmonious whole that communicates a message
- Use the term *hybrid text* to describe the genre

Writing in the Genre

- Select different genres with a clear purpose in mind
- Write pieces of the text in different genres according to purpose
- Integrate the genres to create a coherent text
- Transition smoothly from one tense to another
- Transition smoothly from writing in one person to writing in another (for example, from first person to third person)
- Guide the reader so that the transitions between genres are accessible

Selecting Goals: Behaviors and Understandings to Notice, Teach, and Support

Craft

Organization

Understanding Text Structure

- Use the structure of exposition to write a nonnarrative, with facts and information ordered in a logical way
- Use the structure of narrative–characters involved in a plot, with events ordered by time
- Choose a narrative or informational genre and organize the text appropriately
- Use underlying structures to present different kinds of information (established sequence, temporal sequence, compare and contrast, problem and solution, cause and effect)

Beginning and Ending

- Use a variety of beginnings and endings to engage the reader (for example, surprise, circular story)
- Begin with a purposeful and engaging lead
- Bring a piece to closure with a concluding statement
- End an informational text with a thoughtful or enlightening conclusion
- Begin a narrative at the beginning, middle, or end
- End a narrative text with problem resolution and a satisfying conclusion

Presentation of Ideas

- Present ideas clearly and in logical sequence or categories
- Clearly show topics and subtopics and indicate them with headings and subheadings in expository writing
- Introduce ideas followed by supportive details and examples
- Support ideas with facts, details, examples, and explanations from multiple authorities
- Use paragraphs to organize ideas
- Use well-crafted transitions to support the pace and flow of the writing
- Use a variety of underlying structures to present different kinds of information (established sequence, temporal sequence, compare and contrast, problem and solution, cause and effect)
- Show steps in enough detail that a reader can follow a sequence
- Use time appropriately as an organizing tool
- Organize information according to purpose

Idea Development

- Clearly communicate main points
- Provide supporting details that are accurate, relevant, and helpful
- Provide details that are accurate, relevant, interesting, and vivid
- Hold the reader's attention with clear, focused content
- Engage the reader with ideas that show strong knowledge of the topic

Language Use

- Use a variety of sentence structures and lengths
- Vary sentence length to create feeling or mood and communicate meaning
- Use language typical of written texts, sometimes imitating writers of books
- Use memorable words or phrases
- Use concrete sensory details and descriptive language to develop plot (tension and problem resolution) and setting in memoir, biography, and fiction
- Show through language instead of telling
- Use descriptive language and dialogue to present characters who appear and develop in memoir, biography, and fiction
- Use language to show feelings of characters or elicit feelings from readers
- Use a variety of transitions and connections (words, phrases, sentences, and paragraphs)
- Arrange simple and complex sentences for an easy flow and sentence transition
- Use examples to make meaning clear
- Use words in figurative ways to make comparisons (simile, metaphor)
- Use language to establish a point of view
- Vary language and style as appropriate to audience and purpose
- Write in both first and third person
- Use dialogue and action to draw readers into the story
- Use repeated language for particular purposes
- Use a range of figurative language such as alliteration, hyperbole, personification, or onomatopeia

Writing

Selecting Goals: Behaviors and Understandings to Notice, Teach, and Support

Word Choice
- Select precise words to reflect what the writer is trying to say
- Use a range of descriptive words that enhance the meaning
- Use strong verbs (active rather than passive, and more descriptive or interesting than words typically used; for example, *hurled* instead of *threw*)
- Use strong nouns (more descriptive or interesting than words typically used; for example, *matriarch* instead of *mother*)
- Learn new words from reading and try them out in writing
- Use transitional words for time flow (*eventually, suddenly*)
- Use memorable or vivid words (*gigantic, savage*)
- Select and write appropriate words to convey intended meaning
- Use vocabulary appropriate for the topic
- Vary word choice to create interesting description and dialogue
- Use figurative language to make comparisons (simile, metaphor)
- Use colorful modifiers and style as appropriate to audience and purpose
- Choose words with the audience's background knowledge in mind
- Use words that convey an intended mood or effect
- Use repeated words to create a particular effect

Voice
- Write with a unique perspective
- Write in a way that speaks directly to the reader
- Write in a way that shows care and commitment to the topic
- Share thoughts through inner dialogue
- Use punctuation to support voice or tell the reader how to read the text (commas, ellipses, dashes, colons)
- Show enthusiasm and energy for the topic
- State information in a unique or unusual way
- Produce expository writing that is persuasive and well constructed, and reveals the stance of the writer toward the topic
- Produce narratives that are engaging, honest, and reveal the person behind the writing
- Include details that add to the voice
- Use dialogue to add voice to writing

Conventions

Text Layout
- Use layout of print and illustrations to convey the meaning in a text
- Use the size of print to convey meaning in printed text
- Use layout, spacing, and size of print to create titles, headings, and subheadings
- Use underlining, italics, and bold print to convey meaning
- Arrange print on the page to support the text's meaning and to help the reader notice important information
- Use indentation or spacing to set off paragraphs

Grammar

Sentence Structure
- Write complete sentences with noun and verb agreement
- Use conventional sentence structure for complex sentences with embedded clauses and phrases
- Write simple and compound sentences
- Vary sentence structure and length for reasons of craft
- Use a range of sentence types (declarative, interrogative, imperative, exclamatory)
- Write uninterrupted and interrupted dialogue with correct punctuation
- Use split dialogue correctly
- Write sentences in past, present, future, present perfect, and past perfect tenses

Parts of Speech
- Use nouns and pronouns that are in agreement (*Mike/he*)
- Use objective and nominative case pronouns (*me, him, her; I, he, she*)
- Use indefinite and relative pronouns (*everyone, both; who, whom*)
- Use verbs that are often misused (*lie, lay; rise, raise*) correctly
- Use verb and objects that are often misused ([verb] *to her and me; she and I* [verb]) correctly
- Use prepositions and prepositional phrases correctly
- Use nouns, adjectives, and adverbs correctly

Tense
- Write sentences in past, present, future, present perfect, and past perfect tenses
- Maintain consistency of tense

Paragraphing
- Use paragraph structure (indented or block) to organize sentences that focus on one idea
- Create transitions between paragraphs to show the progression of ideas
- Use paragraphs to show speaker change in dialogue

Writing

Selecting Goals: Behaviors and Understandings to Notice, Teach, and Support

Capitalization

- Use a capital letter for the first word of a sentence
- Use capital letters appropriately for the first letter in days, months, city and state names
- Use capital letters for first letter in first and last word and most other words in titles
- Identify and use special uses of capitalization (headings, titles, emphasis)
- Use capitalization for specialized functions (emphasis, key information, voice)
- Use more complex capitalization with increasing accuracy, such as abbreviations and within quotation marks

Punctuation

- Learn about the possibility of using punctuation and its effect on readers by studying mentor texts
- Notice effective or unusual use of punctuation marks by authors
- Try out new ways of using punctuation
- Consistently use periods, exclamation points, and question marks as ending marks
- Understand and use ellipses to show pause or anticipation, usually before something surprising
- Use dashes to indicate a longer pause or slow down the reading to emphasize particular information
- Use commas and quotation marks in writing uninterrupted and interrupted dialogue
- Use apostrophes in contractions and possessives
- Use commas to identify a series, to introduce clauses, and in the direct address of a person
- Use brackets to set aside a different idea or kind of information
- Use colons to indicate something is explained or described
- Use commas and parentheses to set off parenthetical information
- Use hyphens to divide words at the end of a line at a syllable break
- Use indentation to identify paragraphs
- Use semicolons to divide related parts of a compound sentence

Spelling

- Spell a large number of high-frequency words (500+), a wide range of plurals, and base words with inflectional endings
- Use a range of spelling strategies to take apart and spell multisyllable words (word parts, connections to known words, complex sound-to-letter cluster relationships)
- Spell complex plurals correctly (*knife, knives; woman, women; sheep, sheep*)
- Be aware of the spelling of common suffixes (for example, *-ion, -ment, -ly*)
- Spell a full range of contractions, plurals, and possessives, and compound words
- Correctly spell words that have been studied (spelling words)
- Spell multisyllable words that have vowel and *r*
- Use difficult homophones (*their, there*) correctly

Handwriting/Word-Processing

- Write fluently and legibly in cursive handwriting with appropriate spacing
- Use word-processing with understanding of how to produce and vary text (layout, font, special techniques)
- Use word processor to get ideas down, revise, edit, and publish
- Use efficient keyboarding skills to create drafts, revise, edit, and publish
- Show familiarity with computer and word-processing terminology
- Create website entries and articles with appropriate text layout, graphics, and access to information through searching
- Make wide use of computer skills in presenting text (text, tables, graphics, multimedia)

Writing

Selecting Goals: Behaviors and Understandings to Notice, Teach, and Support

Writing Process

Rehearsing/Planning

Purpose

- Understand how the purpose of the writing influences the selection of genre
- Select genre or form to reflect content and purpose
- Write for a specific purpose: to inform, entertain, persuade, reflect, instruct, retell, maintain relationships, plan
- Have clear goals and understand how the goals will affect the writing

Audience

- Write with a specific reader or audience in mind
- Understand how the writing meets the needs of a specific reader or audience
- Plan and organize information for the intended reader(s)
- Understand audience as all readers rather than just the teacher

Oral Language

- Generate and expand ideas through talk with peers and teacher
- Look for ideas and topics in personal experiences, shared through talk
- Ask relevant questions in talking about a topic
- Use talk and storytelling to generate and rehearse language (that may be written later)
- Use language in stories that is specific to a topic
- Vary the intended audience for which the piece is written

Gathering Seeds/Resources and Experimenting with Writing

- Use a writer's notebook or booklet as a tool for collecting ideas, experimenting, planning, sketching, or drafting
- Gather a variety of entries (character map, timeline, sketches, observations, freewrites, drafts, lists) in a writer's notebook
- Reread a writer's notebook to select topics
- Use sketches, webs, lists, diagrams, and freewriting to think about, plan for, and try out writing
- Think through a topic, focus, organization, and audience
- Try out different heads and endings in a writer's notebook
- Try out titles, develop characters and setting in a writer's notebook
- Explore knowledge about a topic using a list or web
- Note observations about craft from mentor texts
- Take notes on new writing techniques
- Take notes from interviews or observations
- Make a plan for an essay that makes a claim and contains supporting evidence
- Plan for a story by living *inside the story,* gaining insight into characters so that the story can be written as it happens
- Choose helpful tools (for example, webs, T-charts, sketches, charts, diagrams, lists, outlines, flow charts)
- Select small moments, full of emotion, that can be expanded

Content, Topic, Theme

- Observe carefully events, people, settings, and other aspects of the world to gather information on a topic
- Develop a clear main idea around which a piece of writing will be planned
- Get ideas from other books and writers about how to approach a topic
- Choose a topic that is significant
- Use texts, including those found on the Internet, to get ideas on a topic
- Use the organizing features of electronic text (bulletin boards, databases, keyword searchers, email addresses) to locate information
- Generate multiple titles to help think about the focus of the piece
- Select a title that fits the content
- State what is important about the topic
- Stay focused on a topic to produce a longer, well-organized piece of writing
- Take audience and purpose into account when choosing a topic
- Understand a range for genres and forms and select from them according to topic and purpose
- Select details that will support the topic

Inquiry/Research/Exploration

- Form questions and locate sources for information about a topic
- Understand the concept of plagiarism
- Create categories of information
- Determine when research is necessary to cover a topic adequately
- Use notes to record and organize information
- Select and include only the information that is appropriate to the topic and to the category
- Identify and select important information from the total available
- Conduct research to gather information in planning a writing project (for example, live interviews, Internet, artifacts, articles, books)
- Search for appropriate information from multiple sources (books and other print materials, websites, interviews)
- Record sources of information for citation

Genre/Form

- Select from a variety of forms the kind of text that will fit the purpose (books with illustrations and words; alphabet books; label books; poetry books; question and answer books; illustration-only books)
- Understand that illustrations play different roles in a text (increase reader's enjoyment, add information, etc.)

Writing

Selecting Goals: Behaviors and Understandings to Notice, Teach, and Support

Drafting/Revising

Understanding the Process

- Understand the role of the writer, teacher, or peer writer in a conference
- Understand revision as a means for making written messages stronger and clearer to readers
- Change writing in response to peer or teacher feedback
- Use mentor texts in making revisions and publishing
- Name, understand the purpose of, try out, and internalize crafting techniques
- Understand that a writer rereads and revises while drafting (recursive process)

Producing a Draft

- Bring the piece to closure with an ending or final statement
- Bring the piece to closure with effective summary, parting idea, or satisfying ending
- Arouse reader interest with a strong lead
- Establish an initiating event in a narrative with a series of events flowing from it
- Draft multiple leads or endings to select the most effective
- Write a discovery draft (write fast and as much as possible on a topic)
- Produce multiple-paragraph pieces
- Establish the significance of events and personal decisions made by the subject of a biography
- Create paragraphs that group related ideas
- Maintain central idea or focus across paragraphs
- Show steps in an informational text in enough detail to follow a sequence
- Establish the situation, plot or problem, and point of view
- Provide insight as to why an incident or event is memorable

Rereading

- Mark the most important part of a piece of writing to clarify what is important for the reader to understand
- Reread and revise the discovery draft or rewrite sections to clarify meaning
- Reread writing to think about what to write next
- Reread writing to check for clarity and purpose

Adding Information

- Add details to make the piece clearer or more interesting
- Add information to the middle to clarify meaning
- Add transitional words and phrases to clarify meaning and make the writing smoother
- Reread and change or add words to ensure that meaning is clear
- Add descriptive words and details to writing or drawings to enhance meaning, not simply to add information
- Add dialogue to provide information or provide narration (in quotes or speech balloons)
- Add information in footnotes or endnotes

Deleting Information

- Delete redundant or unnecessary information to make a piece clearer or more interesting
- Reread and cross out words to ensure that meaning is clear
- Eliminate extraneous details
- Delete information that is unnecessary

Reorganizing Information

- Reorganize paragraphs for better sequence or logical progression of ideas
- Move information from one part of the text to another to make a text clearer

Changing Text

- Identify vague parts and provide specificity
- Vary word choice to make the piece more interesting
- Work on transitions to achieve better flow
- Reread writing to rethink and make changes
- Reshape writing to make the text into a different genre (for example, personal narrative to poem)

Using Tools and Techniques

- Use a number in the writing to identify a place to add information and an additional numbered paper to write information to insert
- Use a caret or sticky note with an asterisk to insert text
- Use a spider leg or piece of paper taped on to insert text
- Use word-processing to add or delete text
- Use word-processing to change text
- Use word-processing to move text by cutting and pasting
- Reorder a piece by cutting it apart or laying out the pages
- Cut, paste, and staple pieces of a text

Writing

Selecting Goals: Behaviors and Understandings to Notice, Teach, and Support

Editing and Proofreading

Understanding the Process

- Understand that the writer shows respect for the reader by applying what is known about conventions
- Know how to use an editing and proofreading checklist
- Understand that a writer can ask another person to do a final edit (after using what is known)
- Understand the limitations of grammar check on the computer
- Understand the limitations of spell check on the computer
- Use tools to self-evaluate writing and assist self-edit

Editing for Conventions

- Edit for spelling errors
- Prepare final draft with self-edit and submit to teacher–edit prior to publishing
- Edit for capitalization, punctuation, and grammar
- Check and correct spacing and layout
- Determine where new paragraphs should begin
- Edit for word suitability and precise meaning
- Integrate quotations and citations into written text in a way that maintains the coherence and flow of the writing

Using Tools

- Use a dictionary to check on spelling and meaning
- Use a thesaurus to search for more interesting words
- Use grammar check on the computer, monitoring changes carefully
- Use spell check on the computer, monitoring changes carefully

Publishing

- Create illustrations for pieces that are in final form
- Often include graphics as appropriate to the text
- Add information about the author
- Add dedication
- Add cover spread with title and author information
- Attend to layout of text in final publication
- Use a variety of print characteristics to make the text more accessible to the reader (titles, headings, and subheadings)
- Use a variety of print characteristics to present information in an interesting way (insets, call-outs)
- Add table of contents and glossary where needed
- Understand the purposes of publication
- Add bibliography of sources where needed

Sketching and Drawing

- Understand the difference between drawing and sketching and use them to support the writing process
- Use sketching to create quick representations of images, usually an outline in pencil or pen
- Use sketching to support memory and help in planning
- Use sketching to capture detail that is important to a topic
- Create sketches and drawings that are related to the written text and increase readers' understanding and enjoyment
- Use sketches or drawings to represent people, places, and things, and also to communicate mood and abstract ideas
- Add detail to sketches or drawings to add information or increase interest
- Create drawings or sketches that employ careful attention to color or detail
- Sketch and draw with a sense of relative size and perspective
- Use sketches to create drawings in published pieces
- Provide important information in the illustrations
- Use the terms *sketching* and *drawing* to refer to these processes and forms

Viewing Self as a Writer

- Write in a variety of genres across the year
- Take risks as a writer
- View self as writer
- Write with initiative, investment, and independence
- Experiment with and approximate writing
- Articulate goals as a writer
- Notice what makes writing effective and name the craft or technique
- Select examples of best writing in all genres attempted
- Discuss what one is working on as a writer in the writing conference
- Self-evaluate own writing and talk about what is good about it and what techniques were used
- Compare previous to revised writing and notice and talk about the differences
- State what was learned from each piece of writing
- Self-evaluate pieces of writing in light of what is known about a genre
- Produce a reasonable quantity of writing within the time available
- Show interest in and work at crafting good writing, applying what has been learned about crafting in each piece
- Seek feedback on writing
- Suggest possible revisions to peers
- Understand that all revision is governed by the writer's decision making of what will communicate meaning to the reader

Writing

Selecting Purpose and Genre

Narrative: To tell a story

Memoir (personal narrative, autobiography)

Understanding the Genre

- Understand that writers can learn how to craft memoir by studying mentor texts
- Understand that a memoir can be written in first, second, or third person, although it is usually in first person
- Understand personal narrative as a story from the writer's life
- Understand that memoir can be comprised of a series of vignettes
- Understand memoir as a brief, often intense, memory of an event or a person with reflection
- Understand that memoirs have significance in the writer's life and usually show something significant to others
- Understand that memoir can be fictionalized or be fiction
- Understand that personal narratives and memoirs have many characteristics of fiction, including setting, problem or tension, characters, dialogue, and problem resolution
- Understand that a memoir can take different forms (story, poem, series of vignettes, "slice of life," vivid description)
- Use the term *memoir* to describe the type of writing
- Understand that autobiography is a biography written by the subject
- Use the term *autobiography* to describe this type of writing

Writing in the Genre

- Select "small moments" or experiences and share thinking about them in a way that communicates a larger meaning
- Describe and develop a setting and explain how it is related to the writer's experiences
- Use dialogue in a way that reflects setting and attributes of self and others
- Experiment with different time structures (for example, single-day flashback)
- Use only the important details and parts of the narrative, eliminating unnecessary information
- Describe self and others by how they look, what they do, say, and think, and what others say about them
- Develop characters (self and others) and show how and why they change
- Use literary language (powerful nouns and verbs, figurative language)
- Reveal something important about self or about life
- Create an internal structure that begins with a purposeful lead
- Write with imagery so that the reader understands the feelings of the writer or others
- Create a series of vignettes that together communicate a message
- Write an ending that communicates the larger meaning of the memoir

Short Fiction (short story)

Understanding the Genre

- Understand how to write various kinds of fiction by studying mentor texts (e.g., myth, legends, fable, fairytale, historical fiction, fantasy)
- Understand fiction as a short story about an event in the life of the main character
- Understand that fiction may be realism or fantasy
- Understand that the purpose of a short story is to explore a theme or teach a lesson
- Understand that the setting of fiction may be current, historical, or imagined
- Understand the elements of fiction, including setting, problem, characters, and problem resolution
- Understand the structure of narrative, including lead or beginning, introduction of characters, setting, problem, series of events, and ending
- Use the terms *fantasy, short story, short realistic fiction, historical fiction, myth, legend, fable, fairytale,* or *modern fantasy* to describe the genre
- Understand that a work of fiction may use time flexibly to begin after the end, at the end, in the middle, or at the beginning

Writing in the Genre

- Take the point of view of one character by seeing the situation through her eyes
- Write in the third person to show another point of view
- Describe and develop believable characters
- Show characters' motivations and feelings by how they look, what they do, say, and think, and what others say about them
- Show rather than tell how characters feel
- Use dialogue skillfully in ways that show character traits and feelings
- Develop a plot that includes tension and one or more scenes
- Compose a narrative with setting, dialogue, plot or conflict, main characters, specific details, and a satisfying ending
- Develop a plot that is believable and engaging to readers
- Move the plot along with action
- Show readers how the setting is important to the problem of the story
- Take points of view by writing in first or third person
- Assure that the events and setting for historical fiction are accurate
- Begin with a compelling lead to capture reader's attention
- Write a believable (or fantastic) and satisfying ending to the story
- With fantasy, develop a consistent imaginary world

Writing

Selecting Purpose and Genre

Biography *(biographical sketch)*

Understanding the Genre

- Write various kinds of biographical pieces by studying mentor texts
- Understand biography as a true account of a person's life
- Understand that a biography may begin at any point in the story of a person's life
- Understand the need for a biographer to report *all* important information in an effort to take an unbiased view
- Understand that a biography can be fictionalized (for example, adding dialogue) even though the events are true or that it can be completely factual
- Understand the difference between true biography and fictionalized biography
- Recognize that writers use elements of craft for creating fictional characters or characteristics in order to bring historical characters to life
- Understand the significance of events and personal decisions made by the subject of a biography
- Understand that biographers select their subjects to show their importance and impact
- Understand that the biographer reveals his own stance toward the subject by selection of information and by the way it is described
- Understand the need to document evidence and cite sources
- Use the term *subject* to refer to the person the biography is about
- Use the terms *biographical sketch* or *biography* to describe the genre of the writing

Writing in the Genre

- Exclude extraneous events and details
- Describe subject's important decisions and turning points, and show how those decisions influenced his or her life or the lives of others
- Reveal the reasons for omitting significant parts of the subject's life (for example, focusing only on childhood or the presidential years)
- Choose a subject and sometimes state a reason for the selection
- Describe the subject by what he or she did or said as well as others' opinions
- Create interest in the subject by selecting and reporting of information in an engaging way
- Reveal the subject's feelings by describing actions or using quotes
- Include dialogue as appropriate
- Tell events in chronological order or in some other logical order (for example, categories or flashbacks or flashforwards)
- Use interviews and documents (books, Internet, letters, news articles) to inform the writing of a biography
- Reveal the writer's own point of view by selection and reporting of information

Informational: To explain, persuade, or give facts about a topic

Literary Nonfiction

Understanding the Genre

- Understand that writers can learn how to write literary nonfiction by studying mentor texts
- Understand that literary nonfiction informs the reader about a topic in an entertaining or interesting way
- Understand that the writer of literary nonfiction works to help his or her readers become interested in a topic
- Understand that nonfiction may be written in narrative or other form
- Understand that nonfiction may include both fiction and nonfiction (hybrid)
- Understand that literary language, including figurative language, can be used when writing nonfiction
- Use the term *literary nonfiction* to describe the genre

Writing in the Genre

- Include features (for example, table of contents, boxes of facts set off from the text, diagrams, charts) and other tools (for example, glossary) to provide information to the reader
- Use headings and subheadings to guide the reader
- Write with the audience and their interests and background knowledge in mind
- Include facts, figures, and graphics as appropriate
- Present details and information in categories or some other logical order
- Provide details and interesting examples that develop the topic
- Help readers think in new ways about a subject or topic
- Use a narrative structure to help readers understand information and interest them in a topic
- Use organizational structures (for example, compare and contrast, cause and effect, temporal sequence, problem and solution, and description)
- Use literary language to make topic interesting to readers
- Add information to a narrative text to make it informational, sometimes creating hybrid texts
- Include argument and persuasion where appropriate
- Provide details and interesting examples that develop the topic
- Reveal the writer's convictions about the topic through the writer's unique voice
- Write an engaging lead and first section that orient the reader and provide an introduction to the topic

Writing

Selecting Purpose and Genre

Expository Nonfiction (feature article, report)

Understanding the Genre

- Understand that writers can learn how to write feature articles or reports by analyzing and using mentor texts
- Understand that a feature article begins with a lead paragraph, with more detailed information in subsequent paragraphs, and a conclusion
- Understand that a feature article usually focuses on one aspect of a topic
- Understand that feature articles and reports require research and organization
- Understand that a report has an introductory section, followed by more information in categories or sections
- Understand that a report may include several aspects of the same topic
- Use the terms *feature article* or *report* to describe the genre

Writing in the Genre

- Use italics for stress or emphasis as appropriate
- Use quotes from experts (written texts, speeches, or interviews)
- Include facts, statistics, examples, and anecdotes
- Accurately document reports and articles with references, footnotes, and citations
- Include a bibliography of references, in appropriate style, to support a report or article
- Use new vocabulary specific to the topic
- Select topics that are interesting to the writer
- Select topics to which the writer is committed
- Use parentheses to explain further
- Write with a wider audience in mind

Essay (opinion editorial)

Understanding the Genre

- Understand that writers can learn to write essays through studying examples and published mentor texts
- Understand an essay as a short literary composition used to clearly state the author's point of view
- Understand that the purpose of an essay can be to persuade readers to think like the author on an issue
- Understand that the purpose of an essay can be to persuade readers to improve their world or critique society
- Understand the structure of an essay
- Understand that a literary essay is an essay that analyzes a piece or pieces of literature (see Writing About Reading continuum)
- Use the term *essay* to describe the genre

Writing in the Genre

- Begin with a title or opening that tells the reader what is being argued or explained—a clearly stated thesis
- Provide a series of clear arguments or reasons to support the argument
- Provide details, examples, and images that develop and support the thesis
- Include illustrations, charts, or diagrams to inform or persuade the reader
- Use "expert testimony" or quotes to support a point of view
- Use opinions supported by facts
- Write a logical, thoughtful ending
- Write well-crafted sentences that express the writer's convictions

Poetic: To express feelings, sensory images, ideas, or stories

Poetry (free verse, rhyme)

Understanding the Genre

- Understand that writers can learn to write a variety of types of poems from studying mentor texts
- Understand poetry as a unique way to communicate about and describe feelings, sensory images, ideas, or stories
- Understand that different forms of poetry communicate different moods
- Understand the difference between poetic language and ordinary language
- Understand that poetry is a spare way of communicating deeper meanings
- Understand that poetry often includes symbolism and sensory images
- Understand that different forms of poetry appeal to readers in different ways
- Recognize different forms of poetry such as ballad and informational
- Use the term *poem* to describe the writing or use the specific term for the kind of poetry

Writing in the Genre

- Understand and use line breaks, white space for pause, breath, or emphasis
- Observe closely to capture sensory images in poetry
- Use words to evoke imagery and feelings
- Select the form appropriate to the meaning and purpose of the poem
- Select subjects that have strong meaning for the writer
- Write a poetic text in response to another poem, reflecting the same style, topic, mood, or voice
- Write a poetic text in response to prose texts, either narrative or informational
- Remove extra words to clarify the meaning and make the writing more powerful
- Use repetition, refrain, rhythm, and other poetic techniques
- Use words to show not tell
- Choose a title that communicates the meaning of a poem
- Write a strong ending to a poem
- Collect language and images as a basis for writing poetry
- Help readers see the world in a new way
- Use poetry for persuasion
- Use symbolism
- Use figurative language such as alliteration, personification, onomatopeia, or metaphor

Writing

Selecting Purpose and Genre

Functional: To perform a practical task

Formal Letters *(business letter, letter to the editor)*

Understanding the Genre

- Understand that writers can learn to write effective business letters by studying examples
- Understand that a business letter is a formal document and has a particular purpose
- Understand that a business letter has parts (date, inside address, formal salutation followed by a colon, body–organized into paragraphs, closing, signature and title of sender, and sometimes notification of a copy or enclosure)
- Use the term *business letter* or *letter the editor* to describe the form or genre

Writing in the Genre

- Write to a specified audience that may be an individual or an organization or group
- Include important information
- Exclude unnecessary details
- Address the audience appropriately
- Organize the body into paragraphs
- Understand the component parts of a business letter and how to lay them out on a page (date, return address, address and salutation, body, closing, information about copies or enclosures)
- Write persuasive and informative letters

Test Writing *(extended response, essay test, short answer)*

Understanding the Genre

- Understand that writers can learn how to write on tests by studying examples of short answers and extended responses
- Understand that test writing is a particular kind of writing used when taking tests (short answer, extended response)
- Understand that some writing serves the purpose of demonstrating what a person knows or can do as a writer
- Understand test writing as a response carefully tailored to meet precise instructions
- Understand that test writing involves analyzing what is expected of the writer
- Understand that test writing often requires inferring the motives of an individual
- Understand that test writing often requires taking a position, developing a clear argument, and providing evidence for points
- Understand that test writing sometimes requires taking the perspective of an individual other than the reader
- Use the term *test writing* to describe the genre

Writing in the Genre

- Analyze prompts to determine purpose, audience, and genre (story, essay, persuasive letter)
- Read and internalize the qualities of responses that will score high on a test
- Write a clear and focused response that will be easy for the evaluator to understand
- Write concisely and to the direction of the question or prompt
- Elaborate on important points
- Reflect on bigger ideas and make or defend a claim that is substantiated
- Respond to a text in a way that reflects analytic or aesthetic thinking
- Restate a claim with further evidence
- State a point of view and provide evidence
- State alternate points of view and critically analyze the evidence for each

Writing About Reading *(all genres)*

(See the Writing About Reading continuum.)

Hybrid: To engage, inform, or persuade

Hybrid Texts *(mixed genres)*

Understanding the Genre

- Learn to write hybrid texts from studying mentor texts
- Understand that a hybrid or multigenre text is one that mixes two or more genres
- Understand that literary nonfiction is a common type of hybrid text
- Understand that a hybrid text has mixed genres in order to communicate information in different ways to readers
- Understand that the writer uses more than one genre to increase reader engagement or make the text come alive
- Understand that the genres in the text must be integrated into a harmonious whole that communicates a message
- Use the term *hybrid text* to describe the genre

Writing in the Genre

- Select different genres with a clear purpose in mind
- Write pieces of the text in different genres according to purpose
- Integrate the genres to create a coherent text
- Transition smoothly from one tense to another
- Transition smoothly from writing in one person to writing in another (for example, from first person to third person)
- Guide the reader so that the transitions between genres will be accessible

Writing

Selecting Goals: Behaviors and Understandings to Notice, Teach, and Support

Craft

Organization

Text Structure

- Use the structure of exposition–a nonnarrative, with facts and information ordered in a logical way
- Use the structure of narrative–characters involved in a plot, with events ordered by time
- Organize the text appropriately as a narrative or informational piece
- Organize the information to fit the purpose of the piece (persuasive, entertaining, informative)
- Use underlying structures to present different kinds of information (established sequence, temporal sequence, compare and contrast, problem and solution, cause and effect)
- Vary organizational structures to add interest to the piece (temporal sequence, story within story, flashback, flashforward, mixture of narrative and expository text)

Beginning and Ending

- Begin with a purposeful and engaging lead that sets the tone for the piece
- Bring the piece to closure, to a logical conclusion, through an ending or summary statement
- Decide whether a piece is unbiased or persuasive and use the decision to influence the lead and the development of ideas
- Engage readers' interest by presenting a problem, conflict, interesting person, or surprising information
- Bring a narrative text to a satisfying problem resolution and concluding scene
- End an informational text with a thoughtful or enlightening conclusion

Presentation of Ideas

- Put important ideas together to communicate about a topic (categories)
- Clearly show topics and subtopics and indicate them with headings and subheadings in expository writing
- Support ideas with facts, details, examples, and explanations from multiple authorities
- Use well-crafted paragraphs to organize ideas
- Use well-crafted transitions to support the pace and flow of the writing
- Show steps in enough detail that a reader can follow a sequence
- Use time appropriately as an organizing tool
- Establish a main or controlling idea that provides perspective on the topic
- Build tension by slowing down or speeding up scenes
- Present reports that are clearly organized with introduction, facts and details to illustrate the important ideas, logical conclusions, and common expository structures (compare and contrast, temporal sequence, established sequence, cause and effect, problem and solution, description)
- Use language to foreshadow the ending

Idea Development

- Clearly communicate main points
- Provide details that are accurate, relevant, interesting, and vivid
- Hold the reader's attention with clear, focused content
- Engage the reader with ideas that show strong knowledge of the topic
- Use a variety of ways to focus a subject (time and thematic)

Language Use

- Use a variety of sentence structures and lengths
- Vary sentence length to create feeling or mood and communicate meaning
- Vary sentence length and take risks in grammar to achieve an intended effect
- Use language typical of written texts, sometimes imitating writers of books
- Write phrases and sentences that are striking and memorable
- Use concrete sensory details and descriptive language to develop plot (tension and problem resolution) and setting in memoir, biography, and fiction
- Show through language instead of telling or commentary
- Use descriptive language and dialogue to present characters who appear and develop in memoir, biography, and fiction
- Use language to show feelings of characters or elicit feelings from readers
- Use a variety of transitions and connections (words, phrases, sentences, and paragraphs)
- Arrange simple and complex sentences for an easy flow and sentence transition
- Use repetition of a word, phrase, or sentence to create effect
- Use examples to make meaning clear
- Use language to elicit feelings
- Use words in figurative ways to make comparisons (simile, metaphor)
- Use a variety of forms of figurative language such as alliteration, hyperbole, personification, or onomatopeia
- Use language to establish a point of view
- Vary language and style as appropriate to audience and purpose
- Write in first, second, and third person to create different effects
- Write in second person when talking directly to the reader to inform or persuade
- Use dialogue and action to draw readers into the story

Writing

Selecting Goals: Behaviors and Understandings to Notice, Teach, and Support

Word Choice

- Select precise words to reflect the intended message or meaning
- Use a range of descriptive words that enhance the meaning
- Use strong verbs (active rather than passive, and more descriptive or interesting than words typically used; for example, *hurled* instead of *threw*)
- Use strong nouns (more descriptive or interesting than words typically used; for example, *matriarch* instead of *mother*)
- Learn new words from reading and try them out in writing
- Use transitional words for time flow (*next, while*)
- Use memorable or vivid words (*transcend, luminous*)
- Select and write appropriate words to convey intended meaning
- Use vocabulary appropriate for the topic
- Vary word choice to create interesting description and dialogue
- Use figurative language to make comparisons (simile, metaphor)
- Use colorful modifiers and style as appropriate to audience and purpose
- Choose words with the audience's background knowledge in mind
- Use words that convey an intended mood or effect
- Use repetition to create a particular effect

Voice

- Write in a way that shows care and commitment to the topic
- Share thoughts, feelings, inner conflict, and convictions through inner dialogue
- Use punctuation to support voice or tell the reader how to read the text (commas, ellipses, dashes, colons)
- Write texts that have energy
- State information in a unique or unusual way
- Produce expository writing that is persuasive and well constructed, and reveals the stance of the writer toward the topic
- Produce narratives that are engaging, honest, and reveal the person behind the writing
- Write with a cadence that demonstrates the individualistic style of the writer

Conventions

Text Layout

- Understand that layout of print and illustrations are important in conveying the meaning of a text
- Indicate the structure of the text through variety in layout and print characteristics, including titles, headings, and subheadings
- Use a full range of print characteristics to communicate meaning (white space, layout, italics, bold, font size and style, icons)
- Indicate the importance of information through layout and print characteristics
- Use indentation or spacing to set off paragraphs

Grammar

Sentence Structure

- Write a variety of complex sentences using conventions of word order and punctuation
- Vary sentence structure and length for reasons of craft
- Use a range of sentence types (declarative, interrogative, imperative, exclamatory)

Parts of Speech

- Use correct verb agreement (tense, plurality, verb to object)
- Use objective and nominative case pronouns (*me, him, her; I, he, she*)
- Use indefinite and relative pronouns (*everyone, both; who, whom*)
- Correctly use verbs that are often misused (*lie, lay; rise, raise*)
- Identify all parts of speech
- Use dependent and independent clauses correctly to communicate meaning
- Correctly use verb and objects that are often misused ([verb] *to her and me; she and I* [verb])
- Use nouns, verbs, pronouns, adjectives, adverbs, and prepositions in agreement and in conventional order within sentences

Tense

- Write sentences in past, present, future, present perfect, past perfect, and future perfect tenses
- Maintain consistency of tense

Paragraphing

- Use paragraph structure (indented or block) to organize sentences that focus on one idea
- Create transitions between paragraphs to show the progression of ideas

Writing

Selecting Goals: Behaviors and Understandings to Notice, Teach, and Support

Capitalization

- Use a capital letter for the first word of a sentence
- Use capital letters for all proper nouns
- Identify and use special uses of capitalization (headings, titles, emphasis)
- Use capitalization correctly within titles and headings
- Use capitalization for specialized functions (emphasis, key information, voice)
- Use more complex capitalization with increasing accuracy, such as abbreviations and within quotation marks

Punctuation

- Notice effective or unusual use of punctuation marks by authors
- Try out new ways of using punctuation
- Understand and use ellipses to show pause or anticipation, usually before something surprising
- Use dashes to indicate a longer pause or slow down the reading to emphasize particular information
- Consistently use periods, exclamation points, and question marks as ending marks
- Use commas and quotation marks in writing dialogue
- Use apostrophes in contractions and possessives
- Use commas to identify a series
- Appropriately punctuate heading, sidebars, and titles
- Use brackets to set aside a different idea or kind of information
- Use colons to indicate something is explained or described
- Use commas and parentheses to set off parenthetical information
- Use hyphens to divide words
- Use indentation to identify paragraphs
- Use semicolons to divide related parts of a compound sentence

Spelling

- Spell a large number (500+) of high-frequency words, a wide range of plurals, and base words with inflectional endings
- Use a range of spelling strategies to take apart and spell multisyllable words (word parts, connections to known words, complex sound-to-letter cluster relationships)
- Be aware of the spelling of common suffixes (for example, *-ion, -ment, -ly*)
- Spell a full range of contractions, plurals, and possessives correctly
- Spell words that have been studied (spelling words) correctly
- Spell multisyllable words that have vowel and *r*
- Use difficult homophones (*principal, principle–counsel, council*) correctly
- Understand that many English words come from other languages and have Greek or Latin roots
- Use word origin to assist in spelling and expanding writing vocabulary

Handwriting/Word-Processing

- Use word-processing with understanding of how to produce and vary text (layout, font, special techniques)
- Use word processor to get ideas down, revise, edit, and publish
- Use efficient keyboarding skills to create drafts, revise, edit, and publish
- Write fluently and legibly in cursive handwriting with appropriate spacing
- Create website entries and articles with appropriate text layout, graphics, and access to information through searching
- Make wide use of computer skills in presenting text (tables, graphics, multimedia)

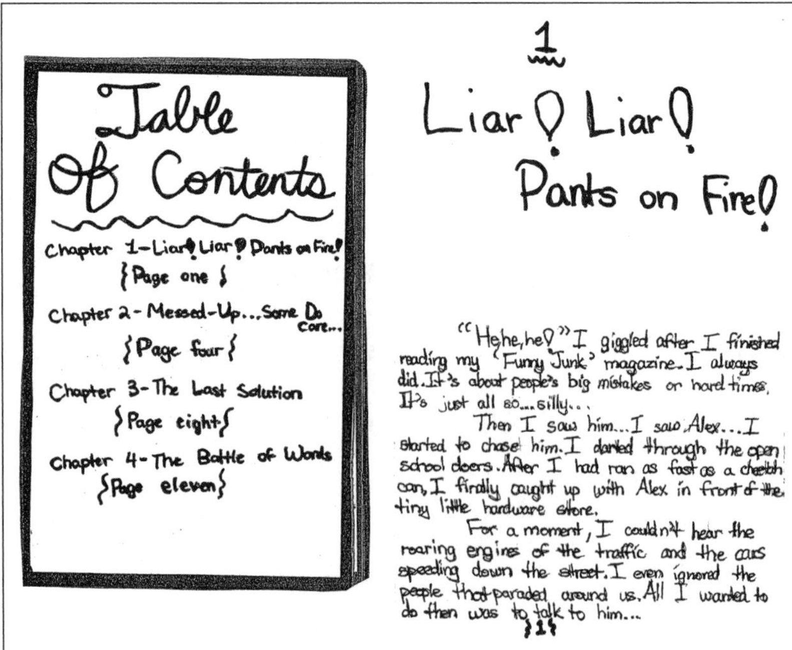

Writing

Selecting Goals: Behaviors and Understandings to Notice, Teach, and Support

Writing Process

Rehearsing/Planning

Purpose

- Understand how the purpose of the writing influences the selection of genre
- Select the genre for the writing based on the purpose
- Select genre or form to reflect content and purpose
- Have clear goals and understand how the goals will affect the writing
- Write for a specific purpose: to inform, entertain, persuade, reflect, instruct, retell, maintain relationships, plan

Audience

- Write with a specific reader or audience in mind
- Understand how the writing meets the needs of a specific reader or audience
- Plan and organize information for the intended reader(s)
- Understand audience as all readers rather than just the teacher
- Vary the audience for which a piece is written
- Write for a broader, unknown audience

Oral Language

- Generate and expand ideas through talk with peers and teacher
- Look for ideas and topics in personal experiences, shared through talk
- Ask relevant questions in talking about a topic
- Use talk and storytelling to generate and rehearse language (that may be written later)
- Use language in stories that is specific to a topic
- Experiment with language that is particular to a setting (archaic, accents, words or language structure other than English)

Gathering Seeds/Resources and Experimenting with Writing

- Use a writer's notebook or booklet as a tool for collecting ideas, experimenting, planning, sketching, or drafting
- Gather a variety of entries (character map, timeline, sketches, observations, freewrites, drafts, lists) in a writer's notebook
- Reread a writer's notebook to select topics for expansion
- Use sketches, webs, lists, diagrams, and freewriting to think about, plan for, and try out writing
- Plan for a story by living *inside the story,* gaining insight into characters so that the story can be written as it happens
- Think through an informational topic to plan organization and treatment of the topic
- Try out different heads and endings in a writer's notebook
- Try out titles, develop characters and setting in a writer's notebook
- Explore knowledge about a topic using a list or web
- Note observations about craft from mentor texts
- Take notes on new writing techniques
- Take notes from interviews or observations
- Choose helpful tools (for example, webs, T-charts, sketches, charts, diagrams, lists, outlines, flow charts)
- Select small moments, full of emotion, that can be expanded

Content, Topic, Theme

- Observe carefully events, people, settings, and other aspects of the world to gather information on a topic or to make a story and characters true to life
- Develop a clear main idea or thesis around which a piece of writing will be planned
- Get ideas from other books and writers about how to approach a topic or theme
- Choose a topic or theme that is significant
- Use the organizing features of electronic text (bulletin boards, databases, keyword searchers, email addresses) to locate information
- Generate multiple titles to help think about the focus of the piece
- Select a significant title that fits the content or the main theme of the story
- Show through writing what is important about the topic
- Select details that will support the topic
- Stay focused on a topic to produce a longer, well-organized piece of writing
- Take audience and purpose into account when choosing a topic or addressing a theme
- Understand a range for genres and forms and select from them according to topic, purpose, or theme

Inquiry/Research

- Form questions and locate sources for information about a topic
- Understand the concept of plagiarism and avoid it (for example, using quotes and citing sources)
- Create categories of information and organize categories into larger sections
- Determine when research is necessary to enable the writer to cover a topic adequately
- Use notes to record and organize information
- Identify and select important information from the total available
- Conduct research to gather information in planning a writing project (for example, live interviews, Internet, artifacts, articles, books)
- Search for appropriate information from multiple sources (books and other print materials, websites, interviews)
- Record sources of information for citation
- Document sources while gathering information so that it will be easy to provide references

Genre/Form

- Select from a variety of forms the kind of text that will fit the purpose (poems; books with illustrations and words; alphabet books; label books; poetry books; question and answer books; illustration-only books; letters; newspaper accounts; broadcasts)
- Understand that illustrations play different roles in a text (increase reader's enjoyment, add information, etc.)

Writing

Selecting Goals: Behaviors and Understandings to Notice, Teach, and Support

Drafting/Revising

Understanding the Process

- Understand the role of the writer, teacher, or peer writer in conference
- Understand revision as a means for making written messages stronger and clearer to readers
- Change writing in response to peer or teacher feedback
- Write successive drafts to show substantive revisions
- Emulate the writing of other good writers by thinking of or examining mentor texts during the drafting and revision processes
- Name, understand the purpose of, try out, and internalize crafting techniques
- Understand that a writer rereads and revises while drafting (recursive process)
- Understand that all revision is governed by the writer's decision of what will communicate meaning to the reader

Producing a Draft

- Bring the piece to closure with effective summary, parting idea, or satisfying ending
- Arouse reader interest with a strong lead
- Draft multiple leads or endings to select the most effective
- Write a discovery draft (write fast and as much as possible on a topic)
- Establish an initiating event in a narrative with a series of events flowing from it
- Produce multiple-paragraph pieces and longer texts when appropriate
- Establish the significance of events and personal decisions made by the subject of a biography
- Create paragraphs that group related ideas
- Maintain central idea or focus across paragraphs
- Establish the situation, plot or problem, point of view, and setting
- Describe memorable events from the inside to help the reader gain insight into the emotions of the writer or the characters

Rereading

- Reread and revise the discovery draft or rewrite sections to clarify meaning
- Clarify what is important for the reader to understand
- Reread writing to think about what to write next
- Reread writing to check for clarity and purpose

Adding Information

- Add details and examples to make the topic more interesting
- Add words, phrases, sentences, and paragraphs to add excitement to a narrative
- Add transitional words and phrases to clarify meaning and make the writing smoother
- Add words, phrases, sentences, and paragraphs to clarify meaning
- Add descriptive words and details to increase imagery or enhance meaning, not simply to add information

Deleting Information

- Delete redundancy to tighten the writing and make it more interesting
- Reread and cross out words to ensure that meaning is clear
- Delete information (details, description, examples) that clutters up the writing and obscures the central meaning
- Eliminate extraneous details

Reorganizing Information

- Reorganize paragraphs or sections for better sequence or logical progression of ideas
- Move information from one part of the text to another to group ideas logically
- Move information to increase suspense or move the action
- Move information to the front or end of the text for greater impact on the reader

Changing Text

- Identify vague parts and change the language or content to be more precise, to the point, or specific
- Vary word choice to make the piece more interesting
- Work on transitions to achieve better flow
- Reshape writing to make the text into a different genre (for example, personal narrative to poem)
- Embed genres within the text to create a hybrid text

Using Tools and Techniques

- Use a number in the writing to identify a place to add information and an additional numbered paper to write the information to insert
- Use a caret or sticky note with an asterisk to insert text
- Use a spider leg or piece of paper taped on to insert text
- Use a full range of word-processing skills to draft and revise a draft
- Use standard symbols for revising and editing
- Reorder a piece by cutting it apart or laying out the pages
- Cut, paste, and staple pieces of a text

Writing

Selecting Goals: Behaviors and Understandings to Notice, Teach, and Support

Editing and Proofreading

Understanding the Process

- Understand that the writer shows respect for the reader by applying what is known about conventions
- Know how to use an editing and proofreading checklist
- Understand that a writer can ask another person to do a final edit (after using what is known)
- Understand the limitations of grammar check on the computer
- Understand the limitations of spell check on the computer
- Use tools to self-evaluate writing and assist self-edit
- Know the function of an editor and respond to suggestions without defensiveness

Editing for Conventions

- Prepare final draft with self-edit and submit to teacher–edit prior to publishing
- Edit for spelling errors
- Edit for capitalization
- Edit for punctuation
- Edit for grammar
- Check and correct spacing and layout
- Determine where new paragraphs should begin
- Edit for word suitability and precise meaning
- Integrate quotations and citations into written text in a way that maintains the coherence and flow of the writing
- Edit for cadence of sentences

Using Tools

- Use spell check on the computer, monitoring changes carefully
- Use a dictionary to check on spelling and meaning
- Use a thesaurus to search for more interesting words
- Use grammar check on the computer, monitoring changes carefully
- Make corrections in response to editing marks by the teacher or other writers

Publishing

- Create illustrations and graphics for pieces that are in final form
- Add cover spread with title and author, dedication, and information about the author
- Use a variety of print characteristics to make the text more accessible to the reader (titles, headings, and subheadings)
- Use a variety of print characteristics to present information in an interesting way (insets, call-outs)
- Understand the purposes of publication
- Add abstract or short summary where needed
- Add bibliography of sources where needed

Sketching and Drawing

- Understand the difference between drawing and sketching and use them to support the writing process
- Use sketching to create quick representations of images, usually an outline in pencil or pen
- Use sketching to support memory and help in planning
- Use sketching to capture detail that is important to a topic
- Create sketches and drawings that are related to the written text and increase readers' understanding and enjoyment
- Use sketches or drawings to represent people, places, and things, and also to communicate mood and abstract ideas
- Add detail to sketches or drawings to add information or increase interest
- Create drawings or sketches that employ careful attention to color or detail
- Sketch and draw with a sense of relative size and perspective
- Use sketches to create drawings in published pieces
- Provide important information in the illustrations
- Use the terms *sketching* and *drawing* to refer to these processes and forms

Viewing Self as a Writer

- Write in a variety of genres across the year
- Take risks as a writer
- View self as writer
- Write with initiative, investment, and independence
- Experiment with and approximate writing
- Write with fluency and ease
- Articulate goals and a plan for improving writing
- Select examples of best writing in all genres attempted
- Self-evaluate own writing and talk about what is good about it and what techniques were used
- Compare previous to revised writing and notice and talk about the differences
- Discuss what one is working on as a writer
- State what was learned from each piece of writing
- Self-evaluate pieces of writing in light of what is known about a genre
- Be productive as a writer; write a specified quantity within a designated time period (for example, one piece each week)
- Write with independence
- Name the qualities or techniques of good writing, and work to acquire them
- Seek feedback on writing
- Provide editing help to peers

Writing

Selecting Purpose and Genre

Narrative: To tell a story

***Memoir** (personal narrative, autobiography)*

Understanding the Genre

- Understand that writers can learn how to craft memoir by studying mentor texts
- Understand that a memoir can be written in first, second, or third person, although it is usually in first person
- Understand personal narrative as an important story from the writer's life
- Understand that memoir can be comprised of a series of vignettes
- Understand memoir as a brief, often intense, memory of an event or a person with reflection
- Understand that memoirs have significance in the writer's life and usually show something significant to others
- Understand that memoir can be fictionalized or be fiction
- Understand that personal narratives and memoirs have many characteristics of fiction, including setting, problem or tension, characters, dialogue, and problem resolution
- Understand that a memoir can take different forms (story, poem, series of vignettes, slice of life, vivid description)
- Use the term *memoir* to describe the type of writing
- Understand that autobiography is a biography written by the subject
- Use the term *autobiography* to describe this type of writing

Writing in the Genre

- Select small moments or experiences and share thinking about them in a way that communicates a larger meaning
- Describe and develop a setting and explain how it is related to the writer's experiences
- Experiment with different time structures (for example, single-day flashback)
- Use only the important details and parts of the narrative, eliminating unnecessary information
- Describe self and others by how they look, what they do, say, and think and what others say about them
- Develop characters (self and others) and show how and why they change
- Use literary language (powerful nouns and verbs, figurative language)
- Reveal something important about self or about life
- Create an internal structure that begins with a purposeful lead
- Write an ending that communicates the larger meaning of the memoir
- Write with imagery so that the reader understands the feelings of the writer or others
- Create a series of vignettes that together communicate a message

***Short Fiction** (short story, short realistic fiction, or historical fiction)*

Understanding the Genre

- Write various kinds of fiction by studying mentor texts
- Understand fiction as a short story about an event in the life of the main character
- Understand that fiction may be realism or fantasy
- Understand that the purpose of a short story is to explore a theme or teach a lesson
- Understand that the setting of fiction may be current, historical, or imagined
- Understand the elements of fiction, including setting, problem, characters, and problem resolution
- Understand the structure of narrative, including lead or beginning, introduction of characters, setting, problem, series of events, and ending
- Understand that a work of fiction may use time flexibly to begin after the end, at the end, in the middle, or at the beginning
- Use the terms *fantasy, short story, short realistic fiction, historical fiction, myth, legend,* or *modern fantasy* to describe the genre

Writing in the Genre

- Take the point of view of one character by seeing the situation through his or her eyes
- Describe and develop believable and appealing characters
- Show characters' motivations and feelings by how they look, what they do, say, and think and what others say about them
- Show rather than tell how characters feel
- Use dialogue skillfully in ways that show character traits and feelings
- Develop a plot that includes tension and one or more scenes
- Compose a narrative with setting, dialogue, plot or conflict, main characters, specific details, and a satisfying ending
- Develop a plot that is believable and engaging to readers
- Move the plot along with action
- Show readers how the setting is important to the problem of the story
- Take points of view by writing in first or third person
- Assure that the events and setting for historical fiction are accurate
- Begin with a compelling lead to capture reader's attention
- Write a believable and satisfying ending to the story
- With fantasy, develop a consistent imaginary world
- Use elements of fantasy and/or science to write a story

Writing

Selecting Purpose and Genre

Biography (biographical sketch)

Understanding the Genre

- Understand that writers can learn how to write various kinds of biographical pieces by studying mentor texts
- Understand biography as a true account of a person's life
- Understand that a biography may begin at any point in the story of a person's life
- Understand the need for a biographer to report *all* important information in an effort to take an unbiased view
- Understand that a biography can be fictionalized (for example, adding dialogue) even though the events are true or that it can be completely factual
- Understand the difference between true biography and fictionalized biography
- Recognize that writers use elements of craft for creating fictional characters or characteristics in order to bring historical characters to life
- Establish the significance of events and personal decisions made by the subject of a biography
- Understand that biographers select their subjects to show their importance and impact
- Understand that the biographer reveals his own stance toward the subject by selection of information and by the way it is described
- Understand the need to document evidence and cite sources
- Use the term *subject* to refer to the person the biography is about
- Establish the significance of events and personal decisions made by the subject of a biography
- Use the terms *biographical sketch* or *biography* to describe the genre of the writing

Writing in the Genre

- Select important events to include and exclude extraneous events and details
- Describe subject's important decisions, and show how those decisions influenced his or her life or the lives of others
- Reveal the reasons for omitting significant parts of the subject's life (for example, focusing only on childhood or the presidential years)
- Choose a subject and sometimes state a reason for the selection
- Describe the subject by what he or she did or said as well as others' opinions
- Create interest in the subject by selecting and reporting of information in an engaging way
- Reveal the subject's feelings by describing actions or using quotes
- Include dialogue as appropriate
- Tell events in chronological order or in some other logical order (for example, categories)
- Use interviews and documents (books, Internet, letters, news articles) to inform the writing of a biography
- Reveal the writer's own point of view by selection and reporting of information or by writing an afterword or foreword

Informational: **To explain, persuade, or give facts about a topic**

Literary Nonfiction

Understanding the Genre

- Understand that writers can learn how to write literary nonfiction by studying mentor texts
- Understand that literary nonfiction informs the reader about a topic in an entertaining or interesting way
- Understand that the writer of literary nonfiction works to help his or her readers become interested in a topic
- Understand that nonfiction may be written in narrative or other form
- Understand that literary language, including figurative language, can be used
- Understand that nonfiction may include both fiction and nonfiction (hybrid)
- Use the term *literary nonfiction* to describe the genre
- Understand that literary language, including figurative language, can be used when writing nonfiction

Writing in the Genre

- Write an engaging lead and first section that orient the reader and provide an introduction to the topic
- Include features (for example, table of contents, boxes of facts set off from the text, diagrams, charts) and other tools (for example, glossary) to provide information to the reader
- Use headings and subheadings to guide the reader
- Write literary nonfiction with the audience and their background knowledge in mind
- Present details and information in categories or some other logical order
- Provide details and interesting examples that develop the topic
- Help readers think in new ways about a subject or topic
- Include facts, figures, and graphics
- Use a narrative structure to help readers understand information and interest them in a topic
- Use organizational structures (for example, compare and contrast, cause and effect, temporal sequence, problem and solution, and description)
- Use literary language to make topic interesting to readers
- Add information to a narrative text to make it informational
- Include argument and persuasion where appropriate
- Provide details and interesting examples that develop the topic
- Reveal the writer's convictions about the topic through the writer's unique voice

Writing

Selecting Purpose and Genre

Expository Nonfiction *(feature article, report)*

Understanding the Genre

- Understand that writers can learn how to write feature articles or reports by analyzing and using mentor texts
- Understand that a report has an introductory section, followed by more information in categories or sections
- Understand that a report may include several aspects of the same topic
- Understand that a feature article begins with a lead paragraph, with more detailed information in subsequent paragraphs, and a conclusion
- Understand that a feature article usually focuses on one aspect of a topic
- Understand that a feature article demonstrates passion for the topic
- Understand that feature articles and reports require research and organization
- Use the terms *feature article* or *report* to describe the genre

Writing in the Genre

- Select topics that are interesting and substantive
- Use quotes from experts (written texts, speeches, or interviews)
- Include facts, statistics, examples, and anecdotes
- Accurately document reports and articles with references, footnotes, and citations
- Write an effective lead paragraph and conclusion
- Present information in categories, organized logically
- Write multiple paragraphs with smooth transitions
- Write with a focus on a topic, including several aspects (report)
- Write with a focus on one aspect of a topic (feature article)
- Use italics for stress or emphasis as appropriate
- Use new vocabulary specific to the topic
- Use parentheses to explain further
- Include a bibliography of references, in appropriate style, to support a report or article
- Select topics to which the writer is committed
- Avoid bias and/or present perspectives and counterperspectives on a topic
- Write with a wide audience in mind

Essay *(opinion editorial)*

Understanding the Genre

- Learn to write essays through studying examples and published mentor texts
- Understand an essay as a short literary composition used to clearly state the author's point of view
- Understand that the purpose of an essay can be to persuade readers to think like the author on an issue
- Understand that the purpose of an essay can be to persuade readers to improve their world or critique society
- Use the term *essay* to describe the genre
- Understand that a literary essay is writing that analyzes a piece or pieces of literature (see Writing About Reading continuum)
- Understand the structure of an essay

Writing in the Genre

- Begin with a title or opening that tells the reader what is being argued or explained—a clearly stated thesis
- Provide a series of clear arguments or reasons to support the argument
- Provide details, examples, and images that develop and support the thesis
- Include illustrations, charts, or diagrams to inform or persuade the reader
- Use opinions supported by facts
- Write well-crafted sentences that express the writer's convictions
- Write a logical, thoughtful ending that sometimes repeats the point

Poetic: To express feelings, sensory images, ideas, or stories

Poetry *(free verse, rhyme)*

Understanding the Genre

- Understand that writers can learn to write a variety of types of poems from studying mentor texts
- Understand poetry as a unique way to communicate about and describe feelings, sensory images, ideas, or stories
- Understand that different forms of poetry communicate different moods
- Understand the difference between poetic language and ordinary language
- Understand that there are different kinds of poems (e.g., epic, ballad, ode)
- Use the term *poem* to describe the writing or use the specific term for the kind of poetry
- Understand that poetry is a spare way of communicating deeper meanings
- Understand that poetry often includes symbolism and sensory images
- Understand that different forms of poetry appeal to readers in different ways

Writing in the Genre

- Understand and use line breaks and white space for pause or emphasis
- Observe closely to capture sensory images in poetry
- Use words to evoke imagery and feelings
- Select the form appropriate to the meaning and purpose of the poem
- Select subjects that have strong meaning for the writer
- Write a poetic text in response to another poem, reflecting the same style, topic, mood, or voice
- Write a poetic text in response to prose texts (narrative or informational)
- Remove extra words to clarify meaning and make writing more powerful
- Use repetition, refrain, rhythm, and other poetic techniques
- Use words to show not tell
- Choose a title that communicates the meaning of a poem
- Write a strong ending to a poem
- Collect language and images as a basis for writing poetry
- Help readers see the world in a new way
- Use poetry for persuasion
- Use symbolism
- Write a variety of poetic texts (e.g., ballad, ode, parody)

Writing

Selecting Purpose and Genre

Functional: To perform a practical task

Formal Letters *(business letter, letter to the editor)*

Understanding the Genre

- Learn to write effective business letters by studying examples
- Understand that a business letter is a formal document and has a particular purpose
- Understand that a business letter has parts (date, inside address, formal salutation followed by a colon, body–organized into paragraphs, closing, signature and title of sender, and sometimes notification of a copy or enclosure)
- Use the term *business letter* or *letter the editor* to describe the form or genre

Writing in the Genre

- Understand the component parts of a business letter and how to lay them out on a page (date, return address, address and salutation, body, closing, information about copies or enclosures)
- Write to a specified audience that may be an individual or an organization or group
- Include important information
- Exclude unnecessary details
- Address the audience appropriately
- Organize the body into paragraphs
- Write persuasive and informative letters

Test Writing *(extended response, essay test, short answer)*

Understanding the Genre

- Understand how to write on tests by studying examples of short answers and extended responses
- Understand that test writing is a particular kind of writing used when taking tests (short answer, extended response)
- Understand that test writing involves responding to as assigned topic
- Understand that some writing serves the purpose of demonstrating what a person knows or can do as a writer
- Understand test writing as a response tailored to meet precise instructions
- Understand that test writing involves analyzing expectations
- Understand that test writing often requires inferring motives
- Understand that test writing often requires taking a position, developing a clear argument, and providing evidence for points
- Understand that test writing sometimes requires taking the perspective of a particular individual (historical figure, fictional character)
- Use the term *test writing* to describe the genre

Writing in the Genre

- Analyze prompts to determine purpose, audience, and genre (story, essay, persuasive letter)
- Read and internalize the qualities of responses that will score high on a test
- Write a clear and focused response that will be easy for the evaluator to understand
- Write concisely and to the direction of the question or prompt
- Elaborate on important points
- Reflect on bigger ideas and make or defend a claim that is substantiated
- Respond to a text in a way that reflects analytic or aesthetic thinking
- Restate a claim with further evidence
- State a point of view and provide evidence
- State alternate points of view and analyze and critique the audience for each

Writing About Reading *(all genres)*

(See the Writing About Reading continuum.)

Hybrid: To engage, inform, or persuade

Hybrid Texts *(multigenre texts)*

Understanding the Genre

- Understand how to write hybrid texts from studying mentor texts
- Understand that a hybrid or multigenre text mixes two or more genres
- Understand that a hybrid text has mixed genres in order to communicate information in different ways to readers (e.g., narrative, poem, and list)
- Understand that the writer uses more than one genre to increase reader engagement or make the text come alive
- Understand that the genres in the text must be integrated into a harmonious whole that communicates a message
- Use the term *hybrid text* to describe the genre

Writing in the Genre

- Select different genres with a clear purpose in mind
- Write pieces of the text in different genres according to purpose
- Integrate the genres to create a coherent text
- Transition smoothly from one tense to another
- Transition smoothly from writing in one person to writing in another (for example, from first person to third person)
- Guide the reader so that the transitions between genres will be accessible

Writing

Selecting Goals: Behaviors and Understandings to Notice, Teach, and Support

Craft

Organization

Understanding Text Structure

- Use the structure of exposition–nonnarrative, with facts and information ordered in a logical way
- Use the structure of narrative–characters involved in a plot, with events ordered by time
- Organize the text to fit the choice of narrative or informational genre
- Organize information to fit the purpose of the piece (persuasive, entertaining, informative)
- Use underlying structures to present different kinds of information (established sequence, temporal sequence, compare and contrast, problem and solution, cause and effect)
- Vary organizational structures to add interest to the piece (temporal sequence, story within story, flashback, mixture of narrative and expository text)

Beginning and Ending

- Begin with a purposeful and engaging lead that sets the tone for the piece
- Bring the piece to closure, to a logical conclusion, through an ending or summary statement
- End a narrative with believable problem resolution and satisfying conclusion
- Decide whether a piece is unbiased or persuasive and use the decision to influence the lead and the development of ideas
- Engage readers' interest by presenting a problem, conflict, interesting person, or surprising information

Presentation of Ideas

- Put important ideas together to communicate about a topic (categories)
- Clearly show topics and subtopics and indicate them with headings and subheadings in expository writing
- Support ideas with facts, details, examples, and explanations from multiple authorities
- Use well-crafted paragraphs to organize ideas
- Use well-crafted transitions to support the pace and flow of the writing
- Show steps in enough detail that a reader can follow a sequence
- Use time appropriately as an organizing tool
- Establish a main or controlling idea that provides perspective on the topic
- Present reports that are clearly organized with introduction, facts, and details to illustrate the important ideas, logical conclusions, and common expository structures (compare and contrast, temporal sequence, established sequence, cause and effect, problem and solution description)
- Use language to foreshadow the ending
- Build tension by slowing down or speeding up scenes

Idea Development

- Clearly communicate main points
- Provide details that are accurate, relevant, interesting, and vivid
- Hold the reader's attention with clear, focused content
- Engage the reader with ideas that show strong knowledge of the topic
- Use a variety of ways to focus a subject (time and thematic)

Language Use

- Use a variety of sentence structures and lengths
- Vary sentence length to create feeling or mood and communicate meaning
- Vary sentence length and take risks in grammar to achieve an intended artistic or literary effect
- Use language typical of written texts, sometimes borrowing language or technique from writers selected as mentors
- Write phrases and sentences that are striking and memorable
- Use concrete sensory details and descriptive language to develop plot (tension and problem resolution) and setting in memoir, biography, and fiction
- Show through language instead of telling or commentary
- Use descriptive language and dialogue to present characters who appear and develop in memoir, biography, and fiction
- Use language to show feelings of characters, or elicit feelings from readers
- Use a variety of transitions and connections (words, phrases, sentences, and paragraphs)
- Arrange simple and complex sentences for an easy flow and sentence transition
- Use examples to make meaning clear
- Use repetition of a word, phrase, or sentence to create effect
- Use language to elicit feelings
- Use words in figurative ways to make comparisons (simile, metaphor)
- Use language to establish a point of view
- Vary language and style as appropriate to audience and purpose
- Write in both first and third person
- Write in second person to talk directly to the reader or for literary effect
- Use dialogue and action to draw readers into the story
- Use a variety of figurative language such as onomatopeia, alliteration, metaphor, or personification

Word Choice

- Select precise words to reflect what the writer is trying to say
- Use a range of descriptive words that enhance the meaning
- Use strong verbs (active rather than passive, and more descriptive or interesting than words typically used; for example, *hurled* instead of *threw*)
- Use strong nouns (more descriptive or interesting than words typically used; for example, *matriarch* instead of *mother*)
- Learn new words from reading and try them out in writing

Writing

Selecting Goals: Behaviors and Understandings to Notice, Teach, and Support

Word Choice (con't)

- Use transitional words for time flow (*meanwhile, next*)
- Use memorable or vivid words (*transcend, luminous*)
- Select and write appropriate words to convey intended meaning
- Use vocabulary appropriate for the topic
- Vary word choice to create interesting description and dialogue
- Use figurative language to make comparisons (simile, metaphor)
- Use colorful modifiers and style as appropriate to audience and purpose
- Choose words with the audience's background knowledge in mind
- Use words that convey an intended mood or effect

Voice

- Write in a way that shows care and commitment to the topic
- Share thoughts, feelings, inner conflict, and convictions through inner dialogue
- Use punctuation to support voice or tell the reader how to read the text (commas, ellipses, dashes, colons)
- Write texts that have energy
- State information in a unique or unusual way
- Produce expository writing that is persuasive and well constructed, and reveals the stance of the writer toward the topic
- Produce narratives that are engaging, honest, and reveal the person behind the writing
- Engage in self-reflection to reveal the writer's unique perspective
- Write with a cadence that demonstrates the individualistic style of the writer
- Communicate informational text with voice

Conventions

Text Layout

- Understand that layout of print and illustrations are important in conveying the meaning of a text
- Indicate the structure of the text through variety in layout and print characteristics, including titles, headings, and subheadings
- Use a full range of print characteristics to communicate meaning (white space, layout, italics, bold, font size and style, icons)
- Indicate the importance of information through layout and print characteristics
- Use indentation or spacing to set off paragraphs

Grammar

SENTENCE STRUCTURE

- Write a variety of complex sentences using conventions of word order and punctuation
- Sometimes vary sentence structure and length for reasons of craft
- Use a range of sentence types (declarative, interrogative, imperative, exclamatory)
- Write sentences in past, present, future, present perfect, and past perfect tenses

PARTS OF SPEECH

- Use correct verb agreement (tense, plurality, verb to object)
- Use objective and nominative case pronouns (*me, him, her; I, he, she*)
- Use indefinite and relative pronouns (*everyone, both; who, whom*)
- Correctly use verbs that are often misused (*lie, lay; rise, raise*)
- Correctly use verb and objects that are often misused ([verb] *to her and me; she and I* [verb])
- Use nouns, verbs, pronouns, adjectives, adverbs, and prepositions in agreement and in conventional order within sentences

TENSE

- Maintain consistency of tense
- Write sentences in past, present, future, present perfect, past perfect, and future perfect tenses

PARAGRAPHING

- Use paragraph structure (indented or block) to organize sentences that focus on one idea
- Create transitions between paragraphs to show progression of ideas

Book Review of *The Diary of Anne Frank*

Anne Frank,
The Diary of a Young Girl

During the Holocaust over 11,000,000 people died. Six million of those killed were Jews. Others who were victims of Adolph Hitler's horrid wrath included Catholics, Gypsies, homosexuals, and people of African Origin. Anne Frank, the Diary of Young Girl is a sad, yet true, account of one Jewish girl's life in hiding from the Nazis and their power.

In the year 1942 Anne's family, which consisted of her, her sister, Margot, her mother, Edith, and her father, Otto, moved into 263 Prisengracht Road, in Amsterdam, Holland, in the hopes that they could stay alive and together during the war. With them was the Van Dann family and a man named Albert Dussel. The eight of them lived in fear of the fact that one day the SS men could push aside the bookshelf that separated their home from the outside world, and send them off to a concentration camp. Sadly, on August 4, 1944 their worst nightmares became a reality. SS Sgt. Karl Silberbauer entered the Annex, and took them to one of the SS headquarters, where they sent the different family members to Auschwitz where all of them besides Otto Frank lost their lives. This book tells the story of their time in hiding from Anne's very own eyes and ears. Anne talks about a side of the war that you hardly ever hear of. It shows a true account of what one girl thought while she was in hiding, and how with each passing day her hope could strengthen, weaken, or possibly die.

In my opinion this book is an extremely sad, but touching story. The feeling that Anne is able to convey through her journal is unbelievable. Anne was a humble girl who was always optimistic, and that alone seemed to be more inspiration than anything else in this book. To me the book showed a side of the Holocaust that could not have been expressed in 1,000,000 museums. The book was real, it was not a vision of what most probably was true, it was the hard core truth. It taught me about what someone would have to give up to try to stay alive, and how in most situations that person's attempts would fail. It also taught me about the bravery of those who risked their lives to save those in danger. I would recommend this book to anybody who wants to learn about the holocaust, and is not afraid of the terror that went on during the six years between the beginning of the war in 1939, and the liberation of the work and concentration camps in 1945. This book has touched many people in this world, and today one of those people is me. We can never take back the millions who were lost during the Holocaust, but we can help prevent such terrors from happening again. It could be as simple as not letting people talk cruelly about others behind their backs, or not assuming that just because you dislike one person you will not like everybody else around them. This book has opened my eyes to a new side of this world's history and I will never forget what I have learned from it.

Writing

Selecting Goals: Behaviors and Understandings to Notice, Teach, and Support

Capitalization

- Use a capital letter for the first word of a sentence
- Use capital letters for all proper nouns
- Use capitalization correctly within titles and headings
- Use capitalization for specialized functions (emphasis, key information, voice)
- Use more complex capitalization with increasing accuracy, such as abbreviations and within quotation marks
- Use capitalization correctly in interrupted dialogue

Punctuation

- Notice effective or unusual use of punctuation marks by authors
- Try out new ways of using punctuation
- Understand and use ellipses to show pause or anticipation, usually before something surprising
- Use dashes to indicate a longer pause or slow down the reading to emphasize particular information
- Consistently use periods, exclamation points, and question marks as ending marks
- Use commas and quotation marks correctly in writing dialogue
- Make purposeful choices for punctuation to reveal the intended meaning
- Use apostrophes in contractions and possessives
- Use commas to identify a series, introduce a speaker, or introduce a clause
- Appropriately punctuate heading, sidebars, and titles
- Use brackets to set aside a different idea or kind of information
- Use colons to indicate something is explained or described
- Use commas and parentheses to set off parenthetical information
- Use hyphens to divide words
- Use indentation to identify paragraphs
- Use semicolons to divide related parts of a compound sentence

Spelling

- Spell a large number of high-frequency words, a wide range of plurals, and base words with inflectional endings
- Use a range of spelling strategies to take apart and spell multisyllable words (word parts, connections to known words, complex sound-to-letter cluster relationships)
- Be aware of the spelling of common suffixes (for example, *-ion, -ment, -ly*)
- Spell a full range of contractions, plurals, and possessives, and compound words
- Correctly spell words that have been studied (spelling words)
- Spell words that have vowel and *r*
- Use difficult homophones (*their, there*)
- Understand that many English words come from other languages and have Greek or Latin roots
- Use word origin to assist in spelling and expanding written vocabulary

Handwriting/Word-Processing

- Write fluently and legibly in cursive handwriting with appropriate spacing
- Use word-processing with understanding of how to produce and vary text (layout, font, special techniques)
- Use word processor to get ideas down, revise, edit, and publish
- Use efficient keyboarding skills to create drafts, revise, edit, and publish
- Create website entries and articles with appropriate text layout, graphics, and access to information through searching
- Make wide use of computer skills, including PowerPoint, in presenting text (tables, layouts, graphics, and multimedia)

You Call Yourself
My Friend?

When you encourage me to disrespect another, instead of treating him like a brother. You call yourself my friend?

When you say to me "Be cool and smoke," you make us both look like a joke. You call yourself my friend?

And when we hang it's cool to curse, but that just makes us both seem worse. You call yourself my friend?

When you say, "Let's do drugs, it's really fun", but my parents say it should never be done. You call yourself my friend?

We'll steal to get them, no one will know, until it's off to jail we go. You call yourself my friend?

I'm wiser now and take better care, because of what I learned in D.A.R.E.. Of friends like you, I should beware.

By: Tom

Writing

Selecting Goals: Behaviors and Understandings to Notice, Teach, and Support

Writing Process

Rehearsing/Planning

Purpose

- Understand how the purpose of the writing influences the selection of genre
- Select genre or form to reflect content and purpose
- Have clear goals and understand how the goals will affect the writing
- Write for a specific purpose: to inform, entertain, persuade, reflect, instruct, retell, maintain relationships, plan

Audience

- Write with a specific reader or audience in mind
- Understand how the writing meets the needs of a specific reader or audience
- Plan and organize information for the intended reader(s)
- Understand audience as all readers rather than just the teacher
- Write for a broader, unknown audience

Oral Language

- Generate and expand ideas through talk with peers and teacher
- Look for ideas and topics in personal experiences, shared through talk
- Ask relevant questions in talking about a topic
- Use talk and storytelling to generate and rehearse language (that may be written later)
- Experiment with diverse forms of language (archaic uses, dialect, slang, language other than English–vocabulary and syntactic patterns)
- Use language in stories that is specific to a topic

Gathering Seeds/Resources and Experimenting with Writing

- Use a writer's notebook or booklet as a tool for collecting ideas, experimenting, planning, sketching, or drafting
- Gather a variety of entries (character map, timeline, sketches, observations, freewrites, drafts, lists) in a writer's notebook
- Reread a writer's notebook to select topics for expansion
- Use sketches, webs, lists, diagrams, and freewriting to think about, plan for, and try out writing
- Plan for a story by *"living inside the story,"* gaining insight into characters so that the story can be written as it happens
- Think through an informational topic to plan organization and treatment of the topic
- Try out different heads and endings in a writer's notebook
- Try out titles, develop characters and setting in a writer's notebook
- Explore knowledge about a topic using a list or web
- Note observations about craft from mentor texts
- Take notes on new writing technique
- Take notes from interviews or observations
- Choose helpful tools (for example, webs, T-charts, sketches, charts, diagrams, lists, outlines, flow charts)
- Select "small moments," full of emotion, that can be expanded

Content, Topic, Theme

- Choose a topic or theme that is significant
- Observe carefully events, people, settings, and other aspects of the world to gather information on a topic or to make a story and characters true to life
- Develop a clear main idea or thesis around which a piece of writing will be planned
- Get ideas from other books and writers about how to approach a topic or theme
- Use the organizing features of electronic text (bulletin boards, databases, keyword searchers, email addresses) to locate information
- Generate multiple titles to help think about the focus of the piece
- Select a significant title that fits the content or the main theme of the story
- Select own topics for informational writing and show through writing what is important about the topic
- Stay focused on a topic to produce a longer, well-organized piece of writing
- Take audience and purpose into account when choosing a topic or addressing a theme
- Understand a range for genres and forms and select from them according to topic, purpose, or theme
- Select details that will support the topic

Writing

Selecting Goals: Behaviors and Understandings to Notice, Teach, and Support

Rehearsing/Planning *(con't)*

Inquiry/Research

- Form questions and locate sources for information about a topic
- Create categories of information and organize into larger sections
- Determine when research is necessary to enable the writer to cover a topic adequately
- Use notes to record and organize information
- Identify and select important information from the total available
- Conduct research to gather information in planning a writing project (for example, live interviews, Internet, artifacts, articles, books)
- Search for appropriate information from multiple sources (books and other print materials, websites, interviews)
- Record sources of information for citation
- Document sources while gathering information so that it will be easy to provide references
- Understand the concept of plagiarism and avoid it (for example, using quotes and citing sources)
- Evaluate sources for validity and point of view

Genre/Form

- Select from a variety of forms the kind of text that will fit the purpose (poems; books with illustrations and words; alphabet books; label books; poetry books; question and answer books; illustration-only books; letters; newspaper accounts; broadcasts)
- Understand that illustrations play different roles in a text (increase reader's enjoyment, add information, etc.)

Drafting/Revising

Understanding the Process

- Understand the role of the writer, teacher, or peer writer in conference
- Understand revision as a means for making written messages stronger and clearer to readers
- Change writing in response to peer or teacher feedback
- Write successive drafts to show substantive revisions
- Emulate the writing of other good writers by thinking of or examining mentor texts during the drafting and revision processes
- Name, understand the purpose of, try out, and internalize crafting techniques
- Understand that a writer rereads and revises while drafting (recursive process)

Producing a Draft

- Write a discovery draft (write fast and as much as possible on a topic)
- Bring the piece to closure with effective summary, parting idea, or satisfying ending
- Arouse reader interest with a strong lead
- Draft multiple leads or endings to select the most effective
- Establish an initiating event in a narrative with a series of events flowing from it
- Produce multiple-paragraph pieces and longer texts when appropriate
- Establish the significance of events and personal decisions made by the subject of a biography
- Create paragraphs that group related ideas
- Maintain central idea or focus across paragraphs
- Establish the situation, plot or problem, point of view, and setting
- Describe memorable events from the inside to help the reader gain insight into the emotions of the writer or the characters

Drafting/Revising *(con't)*

Rereading

- Reread and revise the discovery draft or rewrite sections to clarify meaning
- Reread writing to check for clarity and purpose

Adding Information

- Add details and examples to make the topic more interesting
- Add words, phrases, sentences, and paragraphs to add excitement to a narrative
- Add transitional words and phrases to clarify meaning and make the writing smoother
- Add words, phrases, sentences, and paragraphs to clarify meaning
- Add descriptive words and details to increase imagery
- Use footnotes or endnotes to add information

Deleting Information

- Delete redundancy to tighten the writing and make it more interesting
- Reread and cross out words to ensure that meaning is clear
- Delete information (details, description, examples) that clutters up the writing and obscures the central meaning
- Eliminate extraneous details

Reorganizing Information

- Reorganize paragraphs or sections for better sequence or logical progression of ideas
- Move information from one part of the text to another to group ideas logically
- Move information to increase suspense or move the action
- Move information to the front or end of the text for greater impact on the reader

Changing Text

- Identify vague parts and change the language or content to be more precise, to the point, or specific
- Vary word choice to make the piece more interesting
- Work on transitions to achieve better flow
- Reshape writing to make the text into a different genre (for example, personal narrative to poem)
- Embed genres within the text to create a hybrid text

Using Tools and Techniques

- Use a caret or sticky note with an asterisk to insert text
- Use a spider leg or piece of paper taped on to insert text
- Use standard symbols for revising and editing
- Reorder a piece by cutting it apart or laying out the pages
- Cut, paste, and staple pieces of a text
- Use a full range of word-processing skills to draft and revise a draft

Writing

Selecting Goals: Behaviors and Understandings to Notice, Teach, and Support

Editing and Proofreading

Understanding the Process

- Understand that the writer shows respect for the reader by applying what is known about conventions
- Know how to use an editing and proofreading checklist
- Understand that a writer can ask another person to do a final edit (after using what is known)
- Understand the limitations of grammar check on the computer
- Understand the limitations of spell check on the computer
- Use tools to self-evaluate writing and assist self-edit
- Know the function of an editor and respond to suggestions without defensiveness

Editing for Conventions

- Edit for spelling errors
- Prepare final draft with self-edit and submit to teacher–edit prior to publishing
- Edit for capitalization, punctuation, and grammar
- Check and correct spacing and layout
- Determine where new paragraphs should begin
- Edit for word suitability and precise meaning
- Integrate quotations and citations into written text in a way that maintains the coherence and flow of the writing
- Edit for cadence of sentences

Using Tools

- Use a dictionary to check on spelling and meaning
- Use a thesaurus to search for more interesting words
- Make corrections in response to editing marks by the teacher or other writers
- Use grammar check on the computer, monitoring changes carefully
- Use spell check on the computer, monitoring changes carefully

Publishing

- Create illustrations and graphics for pieces that are in final form
- Add cover spread with title and author, dedication, and information about the author
- Use a variety of print characteristics to make the text more accessible to the reader (titles, headings, and subheadings)
- Use a variety of print characteristics to present information in an interesting way (insets, call-outs)
- Understand the purposes of publication
- Add abstract or short summary where needed
- Add bibliography of sources where needed

Sketching and Drawing

- Understand the difference between drawing and sketching and use them to support the writing process
- Use sketching to create quick representations of images, usually an outline in pencil or pen
- Use sketching to support memory and help in planning
- Use sketching to capture detail that is important to a topic
- Create sketches and drawings that are related to the written text and increase readers' understanding and enjoyment
- Provide important information in the illustrations
- Use sketches or drawings to represent people, places, and things, and also to communicate mood and abstract ideas
- Add detail to sketches or drawings to add information or increase interest
- Create drawings or sketches that employ careful attention to color or detail
- Sketch and draw with a sense of relative size and perspective
- Use sketches to create drawings in published pieces
- Use the terms *sketching* and *drawing* to refer to these processes and forms

Viewing Self as a Writer

- Write in a variety of genres across the year
- Take risks as a writer
- View self as writer
- Write with initiative, investment, and independence
- Experiment with and approximate writing
- Write with fluency and ease
- Articulate goals and a plan for improving writing
- Select examples of best writing in all genres attempted
- Self-evaluate own writing and talk about what is good about it and what techniques were used
- Compare previous to revised writing and notice and talk about the differences
- State what was learned from each piece of writing
- Self-evaluate pieces of writing in light of what is known about a genre
- Be productive as a writer; write a specified quantity within a designated time period (for example, one piece each week)
- Name the qualities or techniques of good writing, and work to acquire them
- Seek feedback on writing
- Provide editing help to peers

Oral, Visual, and Technological Communication

Introduction to Oral, Visual, and Technological Communication

Language is a child's first and most powerful learning tool. Within all of the instructional contexts that are part of a comprehensive language and literacy curriculum, learning is mediated by oral language. There are numerous references to oral language in every continuum presented in this book. Students reveal their thinking about texts through discussion with others. Their talk is a prelude to writing. They learn how words work through listening to, talking about, and working with them. By listening to texts read aloud, they internalize language that they will use as they talk and write. They learn language by using it for a variety of purposes. So, in a sense, oral communication is not only an integral part of every component of the curriculum but a building block toward future communication. We need to intentionally develop the kind of oral language skills that students need to take them into the future.

We have created this continuum to focus on the broader area of *communication* beyond the printed word. We cannot now know exactly the kinds of communication skills that will be important in 2020 and beyond, but we can equip our students with the foundational competencies in listening, speaking, and technology that will allow them to take advantage of new opportunities for communication. In this continuum, we examine critical curriculum goals in three areas: listening and speaking, presentation, and technology.

Listening and Speaking

Students learn by listening and responding to others. Interaction is key to gaining a deeper understanding of texts. Students need the kind of interactive skills that make good conversation possible; they also need to develop the ability to sustain a deeper and more extended discussion of academic content. This area includes:

- ***Listening and Understanding.*** Students spend a good deal of time in school listening to explanations and directions. They learn by active listening, so it is important that they develop a habit of listening with attention and remembering details. Also, it is important that they listen actively to texts read aloud. Through listening during daily interactive read-aloud sessions, students have the opportunity to internalize the syntactic patterns of written language, to learn how texts work, and to expand vocabulary. You will find specific information related to vocabulary development in the Phonics, Spelling, and Word

Study continuum (see Word Meaning); however, listening is an important part of the process.

- ***Social Interaction.*** Social interaction is basic to success on the job as well as a happy personal life. Through conversation, people bond with each other and get things done. In the elementary and middle school, students develop their ability to interact with others in positive ways. They learn the social conventions that make conversation work.

- ***Extended Discussion.*** In content areas, social interaction extends to deeper discussion. Discussion is central to learning in all areas, but it is critical to the development of reading comprehension. Through extended discussion, students expand their understanding of texts they have read or heard read aloud. They develop the ability to remember the necessary details of texts and to think beyond and about them. Extended discussion requires knowledge and skill. Students need to be able to sustain a thread of discussion and to listen and respond to others. They need to learn such conventions as getting a turn in the discussion or taking the role of leader. Even young children can begin to learn how to sustain a text discussion and their ability only grows across the years.

- ***Content.*** It also matters what students talk about. Their ideas must be substantive. They need to be able to explain and describe their thinking, make predictions and inferences, and back up their talk with evidence from texts or personal experience. Through daily discussion over the years, they learn the art of argument. Growing competence in listening, social interaction, extended discussion, and content will help students use language as a tool for learning across the curriculum.

Presentation

The ability to speak effectively to a group—small or large—is an enormous advantage. Many students are afraid of speaking to a group, largely because of inexperience or even a bad experience. We see performance as a basic skill that needs to be developed across the years. Even young children can talk to the class about their own lives or their writing; they can even prepare illustrations to help them. As students move into the upper elementary grades, they have many tools to help them such as PowerPoint and other presentation tools that enable them to combine media, for example. We describe a continuum of learning in six areas related to presentation: voice, conventions, organization, word choice, ideas and content, and media.

- ***Voice.*** Here, *voice* refers to the speaker's personal style. We have all watched gifted speakers who captivate their audience. While we are not expecting every student to become a public speaker, we do hope that each individual can develop ways of speaking that capture the interest and attention of those listening. Speakers learn how to begin in a way that engages the audience and to use voice modulation and gesture in interesting ways.

- ***Conventions.*** Certain conventions are basic to making effective presentations. For example, the speaker needs to enunciate words clearly, talk at an appropriate volume, and use an effective pace—not too slow and not too fast. Looking directly at the audience and making eye contact is also helpful. With practice, these conventions can become automatic, freeing the speaker to concentrate on the ideas he or she is expressing.

- ***Organization.*** An effective presentation is well planned and organized. The speaker can organize information in various ways—comparison and contrast or cause and effect, for example. Effective presentations are concise and clear rather than unfocused and random. The speaker needs to keep the audience in mind when planning the organizational structure of a particular presentation.

- ***Word Choice.*** Effective speakers choose their words carefully both to make an impact on the audience and to communicate meaning clearly. Speakers often need to use specific words related to the content area they are covering, and they may need to define these words for the audience. Speakers can also use more literary language to increase listeners' interest. Speakers choose their words with the audience in mind; more formal language may be needed in a professional presentation than in an everyday conversation or a discussion.

- ***Ideas and Content.*** The substance of a presentation is important. Technique is wasted if the ideas and content are not substantive. Effective speakers demonstrate their understanding through the information they have chosen to present. They know how to establish an argument, use persuasive strategies, provide examples, and cite relevant evidence.

- ***Media.*** Media can be overused, but in general presentations are enhanced by the use of visual displays. For young children, this may mean pictures, drawings, or posters. As their presentations grow more sophisticated, students can make use of a wide array of electronic resources to create multimedia presentations. Speakers may even need to think of presentation in new ways; for example, the creation of interactive nonlinear websites that members of the audience can explore individually is a kind of extended presentation.

Technology

Learning to use technology for communication is an absolute necessity in today's society. Often, students are much more sophisticated than their teachers are in this area! We need to give careful attention to helping students use their technological skills in the interest of learning and demonstrating what they know. We want them to be comfortable with electronic conversations and learning groups, to use rapid and efficient keyboarding for word processing, to create websites and multimedia presentations, and to use the Internet as a tool for gathering information. At the same time, it is important that even younger students begin to understand that using the Internet requires caution as well as ethical and responsible behavior.

- ***Gathering Information/Research.*** Nonprint media from radio and television to the Internet have become primary sources for learning about the world. Providing opportunities to explore and use these media is a critical part of a literacy curriculum. From initial computer awareness at the early grades to sophisticated Web research and data management at the upper grades, technology can play an important role in literacy development.

- ***Publishing.*** The computer has changed the process of writing in significant ways and has added new ways for students to communicate their messages. Spelling and grammar checkers, cutting and pasting, and access to digital images have made the creation of polished final drafts easier than ever.

Today people rely increasingly on media beyond print-on-paper. We need our students to be as effective with oral, visual, and technological media as they are with books and newspapers. The world is changing, and global communication is more important than ever.

Oral, Visual, and Technological Communication

Selecting Goals **Behaviors and Understandings to Notice, Teach, and Support**

Listening and Speaking

Listening and Understanding

- Listen with attention and understanding to directions
- Demonstrate the ability to remember and follow simple directions
- Listen actively to others read or talk about their writing and give feedback
- Show interest in listening to and talking about stories, poems, or informational texts
- Listen with attention and understanding to oral reading of stories, poems, and informational texts
- Compare personal knowledge with what is heard

Social Interaction

- Engage in imaginary play
- Enter into dramatic dialogue in play or role play contexts
- Use polite conversational conventions (*please, thank you,* greetings)
- Speak at an appropriate volume—not too loud but loud enough to be heard and understood by others
- Adjust volume as appropriate for different contexts
- Speak clearly enough to be understood by others in conversation
- Enter a conversation appropriately
- Engage in the turn-taking of conversation
- Sustain a conversation with a variety of audiences, including peers, teacher, and family

Extended Discussion

- Follow the topic and add to the discussion
- Build on the statements of others
- Engage actively in routines (for example, turn and talk)
- Form clear questions to gain information
- Participate actively in whole-class discussion or with peers as partners, or in a small group
- Use grade level-appropriate specific vocabulary when talking about texts (*title, author*)

Content

- Begin to verbalize reasons for problems, events, and actions
- Explain cause-and-effect relationships
- Express opinions and explain reasoning (*because . . .*)
- Predict future events in a story
- Offer solutions and explanations for story problems
- Explain and describe people, events, places, and objects
- Describe similarities and differences among people, places, events, and objects
- Report interesting information from background experience or reading
- Ask many questions, demonstrating curiosity
- Initiate and join in on songs, rhymes, and chants
- Share knowledge of story structure by describing setting, characters, events, or ending
- Show interest in the meaning of words
- Express and reflect on feelings of self and others

Oral, Visual, and Technological Communication

Selecting Goals Behaviors and Understandings to Notice, Teach, and Support

Presentation

Voice

- Speak about a topic with enthusiasm
- Talk with confidence
- Tell stories in an interesting way

Conventions

- Speak at appropriate volume to be heard
- Look at the audience while talking
- Speak at an appropriate rate to be understood by the audience
- Enunciate words clearly

Organization

- Have the topic or story in mind before starting to speak
- Show knowledge of story structure
- Tell personal experiences in a logical sequence
- Have an audience in mind before starting to speak
- Have a clear purpose
- Present ideas and information in a logical sequence

Word Choice

- Use language from stories when retelling them
- Use words that describe (adjectives and adverbs)

Ideas and Content

- Recite short poems and songs
- Tell stories and retell familiar stories
- Tell personal experiences
- Make brief oral reports that demonstrate understanding of a simple, familiar topic

Media

- Use props or illustrations to extend the meaning of a presentation
- Perform plays and puppet shows that involve speaking as a character
- Read aloud and discuss own writing with others

Technology

General Communication

- Find buttons and icons on the computer screen to make simple programs work
- Use simple computerized desktop, lap, and handheld toys that require interaction (math, ABC, literacy, and other)
- Use the computer to play simple games
- Use mouse or keys effectively
- Use email for conversation

Gathering Information/Research

- Know some favorite websites and use them to get information (approved sites)

Oral, Visual, and Technological Communication

Selecting Goals Behaviors and Understandings to Notice, Teach, and Support

Listening and Speaking

Listening and Understanding

- Listen with attention and understanding to directions
- Demonstrate the ability to remember and follow simple directions
- Listen actively to others read or talk about their writing and give feedback
- Show interest in listening to and talking about stories, poems, or informational texts
- Listen with attention and understanding to oral reading of stories, poems, and informational texts
- Compare personal knowledge with what is heard

Social Interaction

- Engage in imaginary play
- Enter into dramatic dialogue in play or role play contexts
- Use polite conversational conventions (*please, thank you,* greetings)
- Speak at an appropriate volume–not too loud but loud enough to be heard and understood by others
- Adjust volume as appropriate for different contexts
- Speak clearly enough to be understood by others in conversation
- Enter a conversation appropriately
- Engage in the turn-taking of conversation
- Sustain a conversation with a variety of audiences, including peers, teacher, and family

Extended Discussion

- Follow the topic and add to the discussion
- Build on the statements of others
- Engage actively in routines (for example, turn and talk)
- Form clear questions to gain information
- Participate actively in whole-class discussion or with peers, as partners, or in a small group
- Use grade level-appropriate specific vocabulary when talking about texts (*title, author*)

Content

- Begin to verbalize reasons for problems, events, and actions
- Explain cause-and-effect relationships
- Express opinions and explain reasoning (*because* . . .)
- Predict future events in a story
- Offer solutions and explanations for story problems
- Explain and describe people, events, places, and objects
- Describe similarities and differences among people, places, events, and objects
- Report interesting information from background experience or reading
- Ask many questions, demonstrating curiosity
- Initiate and join in on songs, rhymes, and chants
- Share knowledge of story structure by describing setting, characters, events, or ending
- Show interest in the meaning of words
- Express and reflect on feelings of self and others

Oral, Visual, and Technological Communication

Selecting Goals **Behaviors and Understandings to Notice, Teach, and Support**

Presentation

Voice

- Speak about a topic with enthusiasm
- Talk with confidence
- Tell stories in an interesting way

Conventions

- Speak at appropriate volume to be heard
- Look at the audience while talking
- Speak at an appropriate rate to be understood by the audience
- Enunciate words clearly

Organization

- Have the topic or story in mind before starting to speak
- Show knowledge of story structure
- Tell personal experiences in a logical sequence
- Have an audience in mind before starting to speak
- Have a clear purpose
- Present ideas and information in a logical sequence

Word Choice

- Use language from stories when retelling them
- Use words that describe (adjectives and adverbs)

Ideas and Content

- Recite short poems and songs
- Tell stories and retell familiar stories
- Tell personal experiences
- Make brief oral reports that demonstrate understanding of a topic

Media

- Use props or illustrations to extend the meaning of a presentation
- Perform plays and puppet shows that involve speaking as a character
- Read aloud and discuss own writing with others

Technology

General Communication

- Find buttons and icons on the computer screen to make simple programs work
- Use simple computerized desktop, lap, and handheld toys that require interaction (math, ABC, literacy, and other)
- Use the computer to play simple games
- Use mouse or keys effectively
- Use email for conversation

Gathering Information/Research

- Know some favorite websites and use them to get information (approved sites)
- Bookmark favorite sites

Oral, Visual, and Technological Communication

Selecting Goals **Behaviors and Understandings to Notice, Teach, and Support**

Listening and Speaking

Listening and Understanding

- Listen to remember, and follow two- and three-step directions
- Listen actively to others read or talk about their writing and give feedback
- Listen with attention during lessons and respond with statements and questions
- Listen with attention and understanding to oral reading of stories, poems, and informational texts
- Listen attentively to presentations by the teacher and fellow students and be able to identify the main idea
- Understand and interpret information presented in visual media

Social Interaction

- Use conventions of respectful speaking
- Speak at an appropriate volume—not too loud but loud enough to be heard and understood by others
- Speak at appropriate volume in different contexts
- Speak clearly enough to be understood by others in conversation
- Engage in the turn-taking of conversation
- Actively participate in conversation; listening and looking at the person who is speaking

Extended Discussion

- Listen to and build on the talk of others
- Engage actively in routines (for example, turn and talk)
- Ask clear questions during small-group and whole-class discussion
- Ask questions for clarification to gain information
- Participate actively in small-group and whole-class discussion
- Use grade level-appropriate specific vocabulary when talking about texts (*title, author*)
- Relate or compare one's own knowledge and experience with information from other speakers

Content

- Describe cause-and-effect relationships
- Provide reasons and argue for a point, using evidence
- Predict and recall stories or events
- Offer solutions and explanations for story problems
- Explain and describe people, events, places, and objects
- Describe similarities and differences among people, places, events, and objects
- Categorize objects, people, places, and events
- Report interesting information from background experience or reading

Presentation

Voice

- Show enthusiasm while speaking about a topic
- Show confidence when presenting
- Vary the voice to emphasize important aspects of events or people
- Tell stories in an interesting way
- Present facts in an interesting way

Conventions

- Speak at appropriate volume to be heard when addressing large and small groups
- Look at the audience while talking
- Speak at an appropriate rate to be understood by the audience
- Enunciate words clearly
- Correctly pronounce all words except for a few sophisticated new content words
- Use intonation and word stress to emphasize important ideas
- Vary language according to purpose

Organization

- Have the topic or story in mind before starting to speak
- Have an audience in mind before starting to speak
- Maintain a clear focus on the important or main ideas
- Present ideas and information in a logical sequence
- Have a clear beginning and conclusion
- Have a plan or notes to support the presentation

Word Choice

- Use language from stories and informational texts when retelling stories or making a report
- Use words that describe (adjectives and adverbs)
- Use language appropriate to oral presentation words (rather than literary language or slang)
- Use content-specific words when needed to explain a topic

Ideas and Content

- Recite some poems from memory
- Recite poems or tell stories with effective use of intonation and word stress to emphasize important ideas, engage listeners' interest, and show character traits
- Engage in role play of characters or events encountered in stories
- Make brief oral reports that demonstrate understanding of a topic
- Demonstrate understanding of a topic by providing relevant facts and details

Media

- Read aloud and discuss own writing with others
- Use visual displays as appropriate (diagrams, charts, illustrations)
- Use illustrations as appropriate to communicate meaning
- Identify and acknowledge sources of the information included in oral presentations

Oral, Visual, and Technological Communication

Selecting Goals **Behaviors and Understandings to Notice, Teach, and Support**

Technology

General Communication

- Use mouse or keyboard effectively to move around the computer screen and search for information
- Use effective keyboarding movements for efficient use of the computer
- Send and respond to email messages

Gathering Information/Research

- Bookmark favorite sites
- Use a simple search engine to find information (from approved and accessible sites)
- Locate information (text, pictures, animation) within approved and accessible websites
- Open and close approved websites (for example, children's authors' websites)
- Open approved websites and search for information within nonlinear presentations (topics and categories)
- Download selected information

Publishing

- Use word-processing programs to produce drafts
- Use simple word-processing programs to prepare some pieces for publication
- Use spell check

Oral, Visual, and Technological Communication

Selecting Goals **Behaviors and Understandings to Notice, Teach, and Support**

Listening and Speaking

Listening and Understanding

- Listen to remember, and follow directions with two or more steps
- Listen actively to others read or talk about their writing and give feedback
- Listen with attention during lessons and respond with statements and questions
- Listen with attention and understanding to oral reading of stories, poems, and informational texts
- Listen attentively to presentations by the teacher and fellow students and be able to identify the main idea
- Understand and interpret information presented in visual media

Social Interaction

- Use conventions of respectful speaking
- Speak at an appropriate volume—not too loud but loud enough to be heard and understood by others
- Speak at appropriate volume in different contexts
- Speak clearly enough to be understood by others in conversation
- Engage in the turn-taking of conversation
- Actively participate in conversation; listening and looking at the person who is speaking

Extended Discussion

- Listen to and build on the talk of others
- Engage actively in routines (for example, turn and talk or getting a turn)
- Ask clear questions during small-group and whole-class discussion
- Ask questions for clarification to gain information
- Participate actively in small-group and whole-class discussion
- Use grade level-appropriate specific vocabulary when talking about texts (*title, author, character, etc.*)
- Relate or compare one's own knowledge and experience with information from other speakers

Content

- Predict and recall stories or events
- Offer solutions and explanations for story problems
- Explain and describe people, events, places, and objects
- Describe similarities and differences among people, places, events, and objects
- Categorize objects, people, places, and events
- Report interesting information from background experience or reading
- Describe cause-and-effect relationships
- Provide reasons and argue for a point, using evidence

Presentation

Voice

- Show enthusiasm while speaking about a topic
- Show confidence when presenting
- Vary the voice to emphasize important aspects of events or people
- Tell stories in an interesting way
- Report information in an interesting way

Conventions

- Speak at appropriate volume to be heard when addressing large and small groups
- Look at the audience while talking
- Speak at an appropriate rate to be understood by the audience
- Enunciate words clearly
- Correctly pronounce all words except for a few sophisticated new content words
- Use mostly conventional grammar and word usage
- Use intonation and word stress to emphasize important ideas
- Vary language according to purpose
- Stand with good posture

Organization

- Have the topic or story in mind before starting to speak
- Have an audience in mind before starting to speak
- Maintain a clear focus on the important or main ideas
- Present ideas and information in a logical sequence
- Have a clear beginning and conclusion
- Have a plan or notes to support the presentation

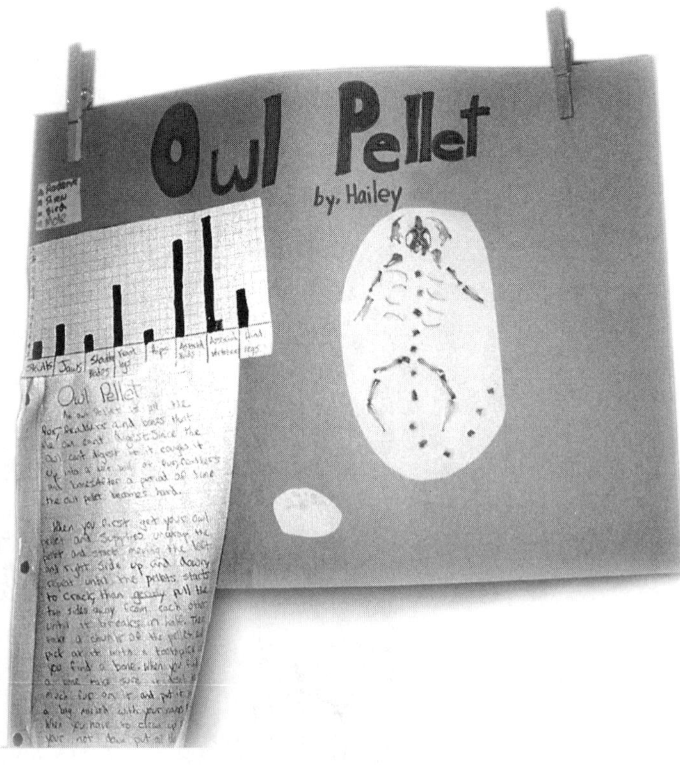

Oral, Visual, and Technological Communication

Selecting Goals **Behaviors and Understandings to Notice, Teach, and Support**

Word Choice

- Use language from stories and informational texts when retelling stories or making a report
- Use words that describe (adjectives and adverbs)
- Use language appropriate to oral presentation words (rather than literary language or slang)
- Use content-specific words when needed to explain a topic

Ideas and Content

- Recite some poems from memory
- Recite poems or tell stories with effective use of intonation and word stress to emphasize important ideas, engage listeners' interest, and show character traits
- Engage in role play of characters or events encountered in stories
- Make brief oral reports that demonstrate understanding of a topic
- Demonstrate understanding of a topic by providing relevant facts and details

Media

- Read aloud and discuss own writing with others
- Use visual displays as appropriate (diagrams, charts, illustrations)
- Use illustrations as appropriate to communicate meaning
- Identify and acknowledge sources of the information included in oral presentations

Technology

General Communication

- Use mouse or keyboard effectively to move around the computer screen and search for information
- Use effective keyboarding movements for efficient use of the computer
- Send and respond to email messages

Gathering Information/Research

- Bookmark favorite sites
- Use a simple search engine to find information (from approved and accessible sites)
- Locate information (text, pictures, animation) within approved and accessible websites
- Open and close approved websites (for example, students' authors' websites)
- Open approved websites and search for information within nonlinear presentations (topics and categories)
- Download selected information

Publishing

- Use word-processing programs to produce drafts
- Use simple word-processing programs to prepare some pieces for publication
- Use spell check

Oral, Visual, and Technological Communication

Selecting Goals **Behaviors and Understandings to Notice, Teach, and Support**

Listening and Speaking

Listening and Understanding

- Listen actively to others read or talk about their writing and give feedback
- Listen with attention and understanding to oral reading of stories, poems, and informational texts
- Listen attentively to oral presentations and identify a speaker's purpose
- Analyze how a speaker uses evidence and examples effectively
- Summarize ideas from oral presentations or reading

Social Interaction

- Use conventions of respectful speaking
- Demonstrate awareness of balance and participation in conversation
- Actively participate in conversation, listening and looking at the person who is speaking
- Use conversational techniques that encourage others to talk
- Show knowledge of the way words work within sentences (conjunctions to express relationships between ideas, clauses, parenthetical information)
- Understand and use language for the purpose of humor (jokes, riddles, puns)
- Actively work to use nonsexist and nonracist language
- Understand the role of nonverbal language
- Work to use tone and gesture in a collaborative and meaningful way

Extended Discussion

- Build on the talk of others, making statements related to the speaker's topic, and responding to cues
- Play the role of group leader when needed
- Evaluate one's own part as a discussant as well as the effectiveness of the group
- Facilitate the entire group's discussion by ensuring that no one dominates and everyone has a chance to speak
- Use turn-taking conventions skillfully
- Ask clear questions and follow-up questions
- Actively engage in conversation during whole- and small-group discussion
- Suggest new lines of discussion
- Restate points that have been made and extend or elaborate them
- Demonstrate awareness of the subtle differences in the meaning of words (*bright, glowing*)
- Identify and understand new meanings of words when they are used as similes and metaphors
- Identify the connotation and denotation of words
- Relate new information to what is already known
- Recall information, big ideas, or points made by others in conversation or from presentations by students or teacher
- Use language to make hypotheses

Content

- Explain cause and effect
- Express opinions and support with evidence
- Make predictions based on evidence
- State problems and solutions
- Compare and contrast people, places, events, and objects
- Use descriptive language when talking about people and places
- Report interesting information from background experience or reading
- Express and reflect on feelings of self and others

Presentation

Voice

- Communicate interest in and enthusiasm about a topic
- Speak with confidence when presenting
- Use expression, tone, and pitch, where appropriate to emphasize aspects of events or people
- Have an effective beginning to capture attention
- Plan modulation of the voice to create an interesting presentation
- Pause effectively to enhance interest and emphasize points
- Demonstrate interpretation and personal style when reading aloud
- Present informational pieces, recite poems or tell stories with effective use of intonation and word stress to emphasize important ideas
- Present information in ways that engage the listeners' attention

Conventions

- Speak with appropriate volume for the size of audience and place of presentation
- Speak directly to the audience, making eye contact with individuals
- Speak at an appropriate rate to be understood by the audience
- Enunciate words clearly
- Study word pronunciation for a presentation so that all words are pronounced correctly
- Use intonation and word stress to emphasize important ideas
- Demonstrate the use of specific language for different kinds of presentation (dramatic, narrative, reports, news programs)
- Stand with good posture
- Use conventions of respectful speaking

Oral, Visual, and Technological Communication

Selecting Goals **Behaviors and Understandings to Notice, Teach, and Support**

Organization

- Have an audience in mind before starting to speak
- Make points in logical order, keeping audience in mind
- Sequence ideas, examples, and evidence in a way that shows their relationship
- Use examples that are clearly related to the topic
- Make presentations that are well organized (clear introduction, body, and conclusion)
- Demonstrate organizational structures common to expository texts (compare and contrast, description, cause and effect, problem and solution, chronological sequence)
- Have a plan or notes to support the presentation

Word Choice

- Vary word choice to be specific and precise about communicating information
- Vary word choice to create images
- Use figurative language to create visual images where appropriate
- Use language appropriate to oral presentation words (rather than literary language or slang)
- Use specific content words in informational presentations
- Define words within a presentation in a way that helps the audience to understand
- Vary word choice keeping the audience in mind

Ideas and Content

- Recite poems or tell stories with effective use of intonation and word stress to emphasize important ideas, engage listeners' interest, and show character traits
- Engage in role play of characters or events encountered in stories
- Demonstrate understanding of an informational topic through formal presentation
- Add evaluative comments, making clear that opinion is being stated (*I think . . .*)
- Make persuasive presentations that establish a clear argument and support it with documented evidence

Media

- Read aloud and discuss own writing with others
- Use technology (PowerPoint, video, etc.) as an integral part of presentations
- Use visual displays (diagrams, charts, illustrations, technology, multimedia) in ways that are clearly related to and extend the topic of a presentation
- Identify and acknowledge sources of the information included in oral presentations
- Create nonlinear presentations using video, photos, voice-over, and other elements

Technology

General Communication

- Send and respond to email messages
- Participate in online learning groups
- Understand ethical issues related to electronic communication
- Understand how to protect personal identification on the Internet

Gathering Information/Research

- Bookmark favorite sites
- Open approved websites and search for information within nonlinear presentations (topics and categories)
- Download selected information
- Draw information from both text (print) and nontext (photos, sound effects, animation, illustrations, variation in font and color) elements
- Locate and validate information on the Internet (from approved sites)
- Use technology tools for research and problem solving across curriculum areas
- Understand the importance of multiple sites and sources for research
- Recognize that information is framed by the source's point of view and use this information to detect bias on websites

Publishing

- Scan materials, such as photos, to incorporate into reports and nonlinear presentations
- Select appropriate forms of graphics to represent particular types of data (for example, bar or line graphs)
- Use digital photos or illustrations from the Internet
- Rapidly and efficiently use keyboarding while working with word-processing programs
- Compose drafts using the keyboard
- Use a variety of technology tools (dictionary, thesaurus, grammar checker, calculator, spell checker) to maximize the accuracy of technology-produced products
- Use knowledge of print and nonprint media to create persuasive productions
- Use spreadsheet software to organize data and create charts, graphs, and tables
- Cite and credit material downloaded from interactive media
- Create nonlinear presentations (Web pages) that convey information
- Create slides (for example, PowerPoint) to accompany a report
- Understand the connection between presentation (text and nontext elements) on a website and its intended audience

Oral, Visual, and Technological Communication

Selecting Goals **Behaviors and Understandings to Notice, Teach, and Support**

Listening and Speaking

Listening and Understanding

- Listen actively to others read or talk about their writing and give feedback
- Listen with attention and understanding to oral reading of stories, poems, and informational texts
- Listen attentively to oral presentations and identify a speaker's purpose in presentations
- Analyze how a speaker uses evidence and examples effectively
- Summarize ideas from oral presentations or reading

Social Interaction

- Use conventions of respectful speaking
- Demonstrate awareness of balance and participation in conversation
- Actively participate in conversation; listening and looking at the person who is speaking
- Take responsibility for assuring that others have a chance to talk and use conversational techniques that encourage others to talk
- Show knowledge of the way words work within sentences (conjunctions to express relationships between ideas, clauses, parenthetical information)
- Understand and use language for the purpose of humor (jokes, riddles, puns)
- Actively work to use nonpejorative and inclusive (nonsexist, nonracist, unbiased language)
- Understand the role of nonverbal language
- Work to use tone and gesture in a collaborative and meaningful way

Extended Discussion

- Build on the talk of others, making statements related to the speaker's topic, and responding to cues
- Demonstrate effectiveness as a group leader
- Evaluate one's own part as a discussant as well as the effectiveness of the group
- Facilitate the entire group's discussion by ensuring that no one dominates and everyone has a chance to speak
- Use turn-taking conventions skillfully in small and large groups
- Ask clear questions and follow-up questions
- Suggest new lines of discussion
- Restate points that have been made and extend or elaborate them
- Demonstrate awareness of the subtle differences in the meaning of words (*bright, glowing*)
- Identify and understand new meanings of words when they are used as similes and metaphors
- Identify the connotation and denotation of words
- Relate new information to what is already known
- Recall information, big ideas, or points made by others in conversation or from presentations by students or teacher
- Negotiate issues without conflict or anger
- Deal with mature themes and difficult issues in a thoughtful and serious way
- Use language to make hypotheses
- Use language to express independent, critical thinking
- Vary language to help listeners better understand points

Content

- Explain cause and effect
- Express opinions and support with evidence
- Make predictions based on evidence
- State problems and solutions
- Demonstrate understanding of underlying themes and deeper ideas
- Compare and contrast people, places, events, and objects
- Use descriptive language when talking about people and places
- Demonstrate depth of knowledge in content areas by reporting information from areas studied in school or from reading
- Express and reflect on feelings of self and others

Presentation

Voice

- Communicate interest in and enthusiasm about a topic
- Speak with confidence and in a relaxed manner
- Use expression, tone, and pitch, where appropriate to emphasize aspects of events or people
- Have an effective beginning to capture attention and an effective closing to summarize information, persuade, or stimulate action or thinking
- Plan modulation of the voice to create an interesting presentation
- Pause effectively to enhance interest and emphasize points
- Demonstrate interpretation and personal style when reading aloud
- Present informational pieces, recite poems, or tell stories with effective use of intonation and word stress to emphasize important ideas
- Present information in ways that engage the listeners' attention

Conventions

- Speak with appropriate volume for the size of audience and place of presentation
- Speak directly to the audience, making eye contact with individuals
- Speak at an appropriate rate to be understood by the audience
- Enunciate words clearly
- Study word pronunciation for a presentation so that all words are pronounced correctly
- Use intonation and word stress to emphasize important ideas
- Demonstrate the use of specific language for different kinds of presentation (dramatic, narrative, reports, news programs)
- Stand with good posture
- Use hand gestures appropriately
- Use conventions of respectful speaking

Oral, Visual, and Technological Communication

Selecting Goals **Behaviors and Understandings to Notice, Teach, and Support**

Organization

- Have an audience in mind before starting to speak
- Make points in logical order, keeping audience in mind
- Sequence ideas, examples, and evidence in a way that shows their relationship
- Use examples that are clearly related to the topic
- Make presentations that are well organized (clear introduction, body, and conclusion)
- Demonstrate organizational structures common to expository texts (compare and contrast, description, cause and effect, problem and solution, chronological sequence)
- Have a plan or notes to support the presentation

Word Choice

- Use figurative language to create visual images where appropriate
- Vary word choice to create images
- Use language appropriate to oral presentation words (rather than literary language or slang)
- Demonstrate awareness of and sensitivity to the use of words that impute stereotypes (race, gender, age) in general as well as to a particular audience
- Demonstrate awareness of words that have connotative meaning relative to social values
- Use specific content words in informational presentations
- Vary word choice to be specific and precise about communicating information
- Define words within a presentation in a way that helps the audience to understand
- Vary word choice keeping the audience in mind

Ideas and Content

- Recite poems or tell stories with effective use of intonation and word stress to emphasize important ideas, engage listeners' interest, and show character traits
- Engage in role play of characters or events encountered in stories
- Demonstrate understanding of an informational topic through formal presentation
- Add evaluative comments, making clear that opinion is being stated (*I think . . .*)
- Make persuasive presentations that establish a clear argument and support it with documented evidence

Media

- Read aloud and discuss own writing with others
- Use technology (PowerPoint, video, etc.) as an integral part of presentations
- Use visual displays (diagrams, charts, illustrations, technology, multimedia) in ways that are clearly related to and extend the topic of a presentation
- Identify and acknowledge sources of the information included in oral presentations
- Create nonlinear presentations using video, photos, voice-over, and other elements

Technology

General Communication

- Send and respond to email messages, varying level of formality appropriate to audience
- Participate in online learning groups
- Understand ethical issues and act in an ethical manner related to electronic communication
- Understand how to protect personal identification on the Internet

Gathering Information/Research

- Bookmark favorite sites
- Open approved websites and search for information within nonlinear presentations (topics and categories)
- Download selected information
- Draw information from both text (print) and nontext (photos, sound effects, animation, illustrations, variation in font and color) elements
- Locate and validate information on the Internet (from approved sites)
- Use technology tools for research, problem solving across curriculum areas
- Understand the importance of multiple sites and resources for research
- Recognize that information is framed by the source's point of view and use this information to detect bias on websites
- Verify the authenticity of sources
- Demonstrate knowledge of strategies used by media games, video, radio/TV broadcasts, websites to entertain and influence people
- Read material published on Internet critically and compare points of view

Publishing

- Scan materials, such as photos, to incorporate into reports and nonlinear presentations
- Select appropriate forms of graphics to represent particular types of data (for example, bar or line graphs)
- Use digital photos or illustrations from the Internet
- Rapidly and efficiently use keyboarding while working with word-processing programs
- Compose drafts using the keyboard
- Use a variety of technology tools (dictionary, thesaurus, grammar checker, calculator, spell checker) to maximize the accuracy of technology-produced products
- Use knowledge of print and nonprint media to create persuasive productions
- Use spreadsheet software to organize data and create charts, graphs, and tables
- Cite and credit material downloaded from interactive media
- Create nonlinear presentations (Web pages) that convey information
- Create slides (for example, PowerPoint) to accompany a report
- Understand the connection between presentation (text and nontext elements) on a website and its intended audience

Oral, Visual, and Technological Communication

Selecting Goals — Behaviors and Understandings to Notice, Teach, and Support

Listening and Speaking

Listening and Understanding

- Monitor understanding and ask questions to clarify
- Critique presentations for subtexts–significant inclusions or exclusions
- Critique presentations with regard to logic or presentation of evidence for arguments
- Examine information regarding the credibility of the speaker (or media messages)
- Recognize faulty reasoning and bias in presentations and media messages
- Identify, analyze, and critique persuasive techniques
- Understand dialect and its relationship to meaning
- Understand the meaning of idioms

Social Interaction

- Use conventions of respectful speaking
- Demonstrate awareness of balance and participation in conversation
- Use conversational techniques that encourage others to talk
- Respond to others' ideas before changing the subject
- Actively work to use unbiased and nonpejorative (nonsexist, nonracist, and inclusive language)
- Understand the role of nonverbal language
- Work to use tone and gesture in a collaborative and meaningful way

Extended Discussion

- Evaluate one's own part as a discussant as well as the effectiveness of the group
- Facilitate the entire group's discussion by ensuring that no one dominates and everyone has a chance to speak
- Use turn-taking conventions skillfully
- Monitor own understanding of others' comments and ask for clarification and elaboration
- Restate points that have been made and extend or elaborate them
- Listen and respond, taking an alternative perspective
- Sustain a line of discussion, staying on the main topic and requesting or signaling a change of topic
- Identify and understand new meanings of words when they are used as similes and metaphors
- Identify the connotation and denotation of words
- Restate or paraphrase the statements of others
- Remember others' comments and consider one's own thinking in relation to them
- Anticipate disagreement and use language to prevent conflict and engender collaborative discussion
- Recognize potential disagreement and use language to help the group reach agreement or maintain equanimity
- Negotiate issues without conflict or anger
- Deal with mature themes and difficult issues in a thoughtful and serious way
- Use language to make hypotheses
- Use language to express independent, critical thinking
- Vary language to help listeners better understand points

Content

- Explain cause and effect
- Express opinions and support with evidence
- Make predictions based on evidence
- State problems and solutions
- Compare and contrast people, places, events, and objects
- Use descriptive language when talking about people and places
- Demonstrate depth of knowledge in content areas by reporting information from areas studied in school or from reading

Presentation

Voice

- Use expression, tone, and pitch, where appropriate to emphasize aspects of events or people
- Begin with an introduction that captures listeners' attention and stimulates interest
- Plan modulation of the voice to create an interesting presentation
- Pause effectively to enhance interest and emphasize points
- Where appropriate, use dramatic devices such as volume increase or decrease and pausing, to keep listeners interested
- Demonstrate interpretation and personal style when reading aloud
- Develop and demonstrate a personal style as a speaker
- Deliver both formal and informal presentations in a dynamic way

Conventions

- Speak with appropriate volume for the size of audience and place of presentation
- Speak directly to the audience, making eye contact with individuals
- Speak at an appropriate rate to be understood by the audience
- Enunciate words clearly
- Study word pronunciation for a presentation so that all words are pronounced correctly
- Recite poems or tell stories with effective use of intonation and word stress to emphasize important ideas, engage listeners' interest, and show character trait
- Demonstrate the use of specific language for different kinds of presentation (dramatic, narrative, reports, news programs)
- Stand with good posture
- Use hand gestures appropriately
- Demonstrate effective body language while speaking

Oral, Visual, and Technological Communication

Selecting Goals **Behaviors and Understandings to Notice, Teach, and Support**

Organization
- Have an audience in mind before planning the presentation
- Demonstrate awareness of the knowledge base and interests of the audience
- Select genre of oral presentation with audience in mind
- Demonstrate a well-organized presentation with a clear introduction, body, and well-drawn conclusions
- Use organizational structures common to expository text (cause and effect, description, temporal sequence, problem and solution, compare and contrast)
- Have a plan or notes to support the presentation
- Demonstrate the ability to select important information for a concise presentation

Word Choice
- Use figurative language to create visual images where appropriate
- Vary word choice to create images
- Identify and understand new meanings of words when they are used as similes and metaphors and apply these understandings to analyzing the whole text in terms of deeper meanings
- Use language appropriate to oral presentation (rather than slang or dense lifeless text)
- Demonstrate awareness of and sensitivity to the use of words that impute stereotypes (race, gender, age) in general as well as to a particular audience
- Demonstrate awareness of words that have connotative meaning relative to social values
- Demonstrate awareness of the underlying connotation of words
- Identify the connotation and denotation of words
- Use specific vocabulary to argue, draw contrasts, indicate agreement and disagreement

Ideas and Content
- Demonstrate understanding through full development of a topic using facts, statistics, examples, anecdotes, and quotations
- Make expository presentations that report research or explore a topic thoroughly
- Differentiate between evidence and opinion
- Make persuasive presentations that present a clear and logical argument
- Use persuasive strategies (compelling examples, appeal to emotion)
- Address counterarguments and listener bias
- Deliver both formal and informal presentations and vary content, language, and style appropriately
- Establish the argument at the beginning of the presentation
- Support the argument with relevant evidence
- Use effective presentation devices (examples, case studies, analogy)

Media
- Use technology (PowerPoint, video, etc.) as an integral part of presentations
- Use visual displays (diagrams, charts, illustrations, video, multimedia and all available technology) in ways that illustrate and extend the major points of the presentation
- Document multiple sources (primary and secondary) to support points
- Create nonlinear presentations using video, photos, voice-over, and other elements

Technology

General Communication
- Send and respond to email messages, adjusting style to audience
- Participate in online learning groups
- Understand ethical issues related to electronic communication
- Understand how to protect personal identification on the Internet
- Understand the concept of networking and be able to identify various components of a computer system

Gathering Information/Research
- Draw information from both text (print) and nontext (photos, sound effects, animation, illustrations, variation in font and color) elements
- Locate and validate information on the Internet (from approved sites)
- Search for and download information on a wide range of topics
- Understand the importance of multiple sites and resources for research
- Use technology tools for research across curriculum areas
- Recognize that information is framed by the source's point of view and use this information to detect bias on websites
- Demonstrate knowledge of strategies used by media games, video, radio/TV broadcasts, websites to entertain and influence people
- Critically read material published on Internet and compare points of view
- Search to authenticate sources of information
- Understand that material downloaded from interactive media should be credited and cited
- Use spreadsheet software to organize data and create charts, graphs, and tables
- Use the Internet to examine current events, gathering several points of view

Publishing
- Scan materials, such as photos, to incorporate into reports and nonlinear presentations
- Select appropriate forms of graphics to represent particular types of data (for example, bar or line graphs)
- Use digital photos or illustrations from the Internet
- Rapidly and efficiently use keyboarding while working with word-processing programs
- Compose drafts using the keyboard
- Use a variety of technology tools (dictionary, thesaurus, grammar checker, calculator, spell checker) to maximize the accuracy of technology-produced products
- Cite and credit material downloaded from interactive media
- Create nonlinear presentations (Web pages) that convey information
- Create slides (for example, PowerPoint) to accompany a report
- Understand the connection between presentation (text and nontext elements) on a website and its intended audience
- Communicate knowledge through multimedia presentations, desktop published reports, and other electronic media
- Frame points and issues to create persuasive productions

Oral, Visual, and Technological Communication

Selecting Goals Behaviors and Understandings to Notice, Teach, and Support

Listening and Speaking

Listening and Understanding

- Monitor understanding and ask questions to clarify
- Critique presentations for subtexts–significant inclusions or exclusions
- Critique presentations with regard to logic or presentation of evidence for arguments
- Examine information regarding the credibility of the speaker (or media messages)
- Recognize faulty reasoning and bias in presentations and media messages
- Identify, analyze, and critique persuasive techniques
- Understand dialect and its relationship to meaning
- Understand idioms

Social Interaction

- Use conventions of respectful speaking
- Demonstrate awareness of balance and participation in conversation
- Use conversational techniques that encourage others to talk
- Respond to others' ideas before changing the subject
- Actively work to use unbiased and nonpejorative (nonsexist nonracist, and inclusive language)
- Understand the role of nonverbal language
- Work to use tone and gesture in a collaborative and meaningful way

Extended Discussion

- Evaluate one's own part as a discussant as well as the effectiveness of the group
- Facilitate the entire group's discussion by ensuring that no one dominates and everyone has a chance to speak
- Use turn-taking conventions skillfully
- Monitor own understanding of others' comments and ask for clarification and elaboration
- Restate points that have been made and extend or elaborate them
- Listen and respond, taking an alternative perspective
- Sustain a line of discussion, staying on the main topic and requesting or signaling a change of topic
- Identify and understand new meanings of words when they are used as similes and metaphors
- Identify the connotation and denotation of words
- Restate or paraphrase the statements of others
- Remember others' comments and consider one's own thinking in relation to them
- Anticipate disagreement and use language to prevent conflict and engender collaborative discussion
- Recognize potential disagreement and use language to help the group reach agreement or maintain equanimity
- Negotiate issues without conflict or anger
- Deal with mature themes and difficult issues in a thoughtful and serious way
- Use language to make hypotheses
- Use language to express independent, critical thinking
- Vary language to help listeners better understand points

Content

- Explain cause and effect
- Express opinions and support with evidence
- Make predictions based on evidence
- State problems and solutions
- Compare and contrast people, places, events, and objects
- Use descriptive language when talking about people and places
- Demonstrate depth of knowledge in content areas by reporting information from areas studied in school or from reading

Presentation

Voice

- Use expression, tone, and pitch, where appropriate to emphasize aspects of events or people
- Begin with an introduction that captures listeners' attention and stimulates interest and end in a way that brings closure and stimulates action or thinking
- Plan modulation of the voice to create an interesting presentation
- Pause effectively to enhance interest and emphasize points
- Where appropriate, use dramatic devices such as volume increase or decrease and pausing, to keep listeners interested
- Demonstrate interpretation and personal style when reading aloud
- Demonstrate a personal style as a speaker
- Deliver both formal and informal presentations in a dynamic way

Conventions

- Speak with appropriate volume for the size of audience and place of presentation
- Speak directly to the audience, making eye contact with individuals
- Speak at an appropriate rate to be understood by the audience
- Enunciate words clearly
- Study word pronunciation for a presentation so that all words are pronounced correctly, including words from languages other than English and all names
- Recite poems or tell stories with effective use of intonation and word stress to emphasize important ideas, engage listeners' interest, and show character trait
- Demonstrate the use of specific language for different kinds of presentation (dramatic, narrative, reports, news programs)
- Stand with good posture
- Use hand gestures appropriately
- Demonstrate effective body language while speaking

Oral, Visual, and Technological Communication

Selecting Goals **Behaviors and Understandings to Notice, Teach, and Support**

Organization
- Have an audience in mind before planning a presentation
- Demonstrate awareness of the knowledge base and interests of the audience
- Select genre of oral presentation with audience in mind
- Demonstrate a well-organized presentation with a clear introduction, body, and well-drawn conclusions
- Use organizational structures common to expository text (cause and effect, description, temporal sequence, problem and solution, compare and contrast)
- Have a plan or notes to support the presentation
- Demonstrate the ability to select important information for a concise presentation

Word Choice
- Use figurative language to create visual images where appropriate
- Vary word choice to create images
- Identify and understand new meanings of words when they are used as similes and metaphors and apply these understandings to analyzing the whole text in terms of deeper meanings
- Use language appropriate to oral presentation words (rather than slang or overly formal dense prose)
- Demonstrate awareness of and sensitivity to the use of words that impute stereotypes (race, gender, age) in general as well as to a particular audience
- Demonstrate awareness of words that have connotative meaning relative to social values
- Demonstrate awareness of the underlying connotation of words
- Identify the connotation and denotation of words
- Use specific vocabulary to argue, draw contrasts, indicate agreement and disagreement

Ideas and Content
- Demonstrate understanding through full development of a topic using facts, statistics, examples, anecdotes, and quotations
- Make expository presentations that report research or explore a topic thoroughly
- Differentiate between evidence and opinion
- Make persuasive presentations that present a clear and logical argument
- Use persuasive strategies (compelling examples, appeal to emotion)
- Address counterarguments and listener bias
- Deliver both formal and informal presentations and vary content, language, and style appropriately
- Establish the argument at the beginning of the presentation
- Support the argument with relevant evidence
- Use effective presentation devices (examples, case studies, analogy)
- Recognize and address opposing points of view on an issue or topic

Media
- Use technology (PowerPoint, video, etc.) as an integral part of presentations
- Use visual displays (diagrams, charts, illustrations, video, multimedia, and all available technology) in ways that illustrate and extend the major points of the presentation
- Document multiple sources (primary and secondary) to support points
- Create nonlinear presentations using video, photos, voice-over, and other elements

Technology

General Communication
- Send and respond to email messages
- Participate in online learning groups
- Understand ethical issues related to electronic communication
- Understand how to protect personal identification on the Internet
- Understand the concept of networking and be able to identify various components of a computer system

Gathering Information/Research
- Draw information from both text (print) and nontext (photos, sound effects, animation, illustrations, variation in font and color) elements
- Locate and validate information on the Internet (from approved sites)
- Search for and download information on a wide range of topics
- Understand the importance of multiple sites and sources for research
- Use technology tools for research across curriculum areas
- Recognize that information is framed by the source's point of view and use this information to detect bias on websites
- Demonstrate knowledge of strategies used by media games, video, radio/TV broadcasts, websites to entertain and influence people
- Read material published on Internet critically and compare points of view
- Understand that material downloaded from interactive media should be credited and cited
- Use spreadsheet software to organize data and create charts, graphs, and tables
- Use the Internet to examine current events including several points of view or sources on issues

Publishing
- Scan materials, such as photos, to incorporate into reports and nonlinear presentations
- Select appropriate forms of graphics to represent particular types of data (for example, bar or line graphs)
- Use digital photos or illustrations from the Internet
- Rapidly and efficiently use keyboarding while working with word-processing programs
- Compose drafts using the keyboard
- Use a variety of technology tools (dictionary, thesaurus, grammar checker, calculator, spell checker) to maximize the accuracy of technology-produced products
- Cite and credit material downloaded from interactive media
- Create nonlinear presentations (Web pages) that convey information
- Create slides (for example, PowerPoint or video) to accompany a report
- Understand the connection between presentation (text and nontext elements) on a website and its intended audience
- Communicate knowledge through multimedia presentations, desktop published reports, and other electronic media
- Frame points and issues to create persuasive productions

Phonics, Spelling, and Word Study

Introduction to Phonics, Spelling, and Word Study

This continuum of learning for phonics, spelling, and word study is derived from lessons we have previously published (Pinnell and Fountas 2003, Fountas and Pinnell 2004). These lessons are based on a detailed continuum specifying principles that learners develop over time. We have included this continuum in the appendix at the end of this book. Here, we present these understandings as a grade-by-grade continuum; in the Guided Reading continuum, they appear again as Word Work. All of the principles are based on the nine areas of learning that we have previously described and are summarized below.

Grade-by-Grade Continuum

This grade-by-grade Phonics, Spelling, and Word Study continuum presents a general guide to the kinds of understandings students will need to acquire by the end of each grade. These understandings are related to the texts that they are expected to read at the appropriate levels. In presenting this grade-by-grade continuum, *we are not* suggesting that students should be held back because they do not know specific details about letters, sounds, and words. Instead, we are suggesting that specific teaching will be needed to support learners. The continuum can support instruction and extra services.

Word Work for Guided Reading (Included in the Guided Reading Continuum)

Grade-by-grade general expectations may be found here; but some information (consistent with this continuum) may also be found in the Guided Reading continuum (pages 221-343). For the Guided Reading continuum we have selected principles that have good potential for the word work teachers might include within guided reading at a particular text level, depending on the needs of the students. At the end of a guided reading lesson, teachers should consider including a few minutes of work with letters or words to help readers develop fluency and flexibility in taking words apart. Teachers may demonstrate a principle on chart paper or a white board. Students may write on individual white boards or use magnetic letters to make words and take them apart. The principles in the Guided Reading continuum are stated in terms of the actions teachers may take, but remember they are selected from a larger set. Teachers will evaluate them against assessment of their own students and visit the grade-by-grade learning continuum for more goals.

Nine Areas of Learning

Each grade level lists principles over which students will have developed control by the end of the school year. Across grades K through eight, the principles, organized into nine broad categories of learning, are related to the levels of text that students are expected to read upon completing that grade. (They are also related to writing in that students use letter-sound relationships, spelling patterns, and word structure as they spell words while writing meaningful messages. You will find much evidence of learning about phonics as you examine their writing.) The nine areas of learning follow.

Early Literacy Concepts

Even before they can read, children begin to develop some awareness of how written language works. For example, early understandings about literacy include knowing that:

- You read the print, not the pictures.
- You turn pages to read and look at the left page first.
- You read left to right and then go back to the left to start a new line.
- Words are groups of letters with a space on either side.
- There is a difference between a word and a letter.
- There are uppercase (or capital) and lowercase letters.
- A letter is always the same and you look at the parts to identify it.
- The first word in a sentence is on the left and the last word is before the ending punctuation mark.
- The first letter in a word is on the left and the last letter is right before the space (or ending punctuation).

More of the understandings listed above are stated in the continuum.

Many children enter kindergarten with good knowledge of early literacy concepts. If they do not, explicit and systematic instruction can help them become oriented quickly. While most of these early literacy concepts are not considered phonics, they are basic to the child's understanding of print and should be mastered early.

Phonological Awareness

A key to becoming literate is the ability to hear the sounds in words. Hearing individual sounds allows the learner to connect sounds to letters. Children respond to the sounds of language in a very natural way. They love rhyme, repetition, and rhythm. Young children naturally enjoy and remember nursery rhymes and songs because of the way they sound. This general response to the sounds of language is called *phonological awareness.* As students become more aware of language, they notice sounds in a more detailed way. *Phonemic awareness* involves recognizing the *individual* sounds in words and, eventually, being able to identify, isolate, and manipulate them. Students with phonemic awareness have an advantage in that being able to hear the sounds allows them to connect sounds with letters.

Letter Knowledge

Letter knowledge refers to what students need to know about the graphic characters in our alphabet—how the letters look, how to distinguish one from another, how to detect them within continuous text, and how to use them in words. A finite set of twenty-six letters, a capital and a lowercase form of each, is used to indicate all the sounds of the English language (approximately forty-four phonemes). The sounds in the language change as dialect, articulation, and other speech factors vary but all must be connected to letters. Children will also encounter alternative forms of some letters (*a* and ɑ for example) and will eventually learn to recognize letters in cursive writing. Children need to learn the names and purposes of letters, as well as their distinguishing features (the small differences that help you separate a *d* from an *a,* for example). When children can identify letters, they can associate them with sounds, and the alphabetic principle is mastered.

Letter-Sound Relationships

The sounds of oral language are related in both simple and complex ways to the twenty-six letters of the alphabet. Learning the connections between letters and sounds is basic to understanding written language. Students tend to learn the regular connections between letters and sounds (*b* for the first sound in *bat*) first. But they must also learn that often letters appear together—for example, it is efficient to think of the two sounds at the beginning of *black* together. Sometimes a single sound like */ch/* is represented by two letters; sometimes a group of letters represents one sound, as in *eigh* for */a/.* Students learn to look for and recognize these letter combinations as units, which makes their word solving more efficient.

Spelling Patterns

Efficient word solvers look for and find patterns in the way words are constructed. Knowing spelling patterns helps students notice and use larger parts of words, thus making word solving faster and easier. Patterns are also helpful to students in writing words because they can quickly produce the patterns rather than work laboriously with individual sounds and letters. One way to look at word patterns is to examine the way simple words and syllables are put together. In the consonant-vowel-consonant (CVC) pattern, the vowel is usually a short (terse) sound, as in *tap.* In the consonant-vowel-consonant-silent *e* (CVC*e*) pattern, the vowel usually has a long (lax) sound. Students do not need to use this technical language, but they can learn to compare words with these patterns.

Phonograms are spelling patterns that represent the sounds of *rimes* (the last parts of words or syllables within words). They are sometimes called *word families.* Some examples of rimes are *-at, -am,* and *-ot.* When you add the *onset* (first part of the word or syllable) to a phonogram like *-ot,* you can make *pot, plot,* or *slot.* A word like *ransom* has two onsets (*r-* and *s-*) and two rimes (*-an* and *-om*). Not every phonogram must be taught as a separate item. Once students understand that there are patterns and learn how to look for them, they will quickly discover more for themselves.

High-Frequency Words

Knowing a core of high-frequency words is a valuable resource for students as they build their reading and writing processing systems. We can also call these *high-utility* words because they appear often and can sometimes be used to help in solving other words. Automatically recognizing high-frequency words allows students to concentrate on understanding and on solving new words. In general, children first learn simple words and in the process develop efficient systems for learning more words; the process accelerates. Students continuously add to the core of high-frequency words they know. Lessons devoted to high-frequency words can develop automaticity and help students look more carefully at the features of words.

Word Meaning and Vocabulary

The term *vocabulary* refers to the words one knows in oral or written language. For comprehension and coherence, students need to know the meaning of the words in the texts they read and write. It is important for them to expand their listening, speaking, reading, and writing vocabularies constantly and to develop a more complex understanding of words they already know (for example, words may have multiple meanings or be used figuratively). Expanding vocabulary means developing categories of words: labels, concept words, synonyms, antonyms, and homonyms. The meaning of a word often varies with the context; accuracy in spelling frequently requires knowing the meaning if you want to write the word. Comprehending words and pronouncing them accurately are also related to knowing word meanings. Knowing many synonyms and antonyms will help students build more powerful systems for connecting and categorizing words.

Word Structure

Words are built according to rules. Looking at the structure of words will help students learn how words are related to one another and how they can be changed by adding letters, letter clusters, and larger word parts. Readers who can break down words into syllables and notice categories of word parts can also apply word-solving strategies efficiently.

Words are built by adding parts that signal meaning. For example, a word part may signal relationships (*tall, taller, tallest*) or time (*work, worked; carry, carried*). An *affix* is a letter or letters added before a word (in which case it's called a *prefix*) or after a word (in which case it's called a *suffix*) to change its function and meaning. A *base word* is a complete word; a *root word* is the part that may have Greek or Latin origins (such as *phon* in *telephone*). It will not be necessary for young children to make these distinctions when they are beginning to learn about simple affixes, but noticing these word parts will help students read and understand words as well as spell them correctly. Principles related to word structure include understanding the meaning and structure of compound words, contractions, plurals, and possessives.

Word-Solving Actions

Word solving is related to all of the categories of learning previously described, but we have created an additional category, "word-solving actions," that is devoted specifically to word solving that focuses on the strategic moves readers and writers make when they use their knowledge of the language system while reading and writing continuous text. These strategies are "in-the-head" actions that are invisible, although we can often infer them from overt behaviors. The principles listed in this section represent readers' and writers' ability to use all the information in the continuum.

The Phonics, Spelling, and Word Study Continuum and Reading

Word solving is basic to the complex act of reading. When readers can employ a flexible range of strategies for solving words rapidly and efficiently, attention is freed for comprehension. Words solving is fundamental to fluent, phrased reading.

We place the behaviors and understandings included in the Phonics, Spelling, and Word Study continuum mainly in the "thinking within the text" category in the twelve systems for strategic actions. At the bottom line, readers must read the words at a high level of accuracy in order to do the kind of thinking necessary to understand the literal meaning of the text. In addition, this continuum focuses on word meanings, or vocabulary. Vocabulary development is an important factor in understanding the meaning of a text and has long been recognized as playing an important role in reading comprehension.

Teachers can use the grade-by-grade phonics continuum as an overall map when planning the school year. It is useful for planning phonics and vocabulary minilessons, which will support students' word solving in reading, as well as for planning spelling lessons, which will support students' writing. In addition, this continuum will serve as a good resource in teaching word study strategies during shared and guided reading lessons. Finally, this continuum will be helpful in connecting daily phonics lessons (see Pinnell and Fountas 2003) with other areas of the curriculum.

Phonics, Spelling, and Word Study

Selecting Goals **Behaviors and Understandings to Notice, Teach, and Support**

Early Literacy Concepts

- Distinguish between print and pictures
- Understand the purpose of print in reading and writing
- Locate the first and last letters of words in continuous text
- Recognize one's name
- Understand that one says one word for one group of letters when you read
- Understand the concept of *sentence* (as a group of words with ending punctuation)
- Understand the concepts of *letter* and *word* (as a single character or group of characters)
- Understand the concepts of *first* and *last* in written language
- Use left-to-right directionality of print in reading and writing
- Use one's name to learn about words and make connections to words
- Use spaces between words when writing
- Match one spoken to one written word while reading and pointing

Phonological Awareness

- Segment sentences into words
- Blend two or three phonemes in words (*d-o-g, dog*)
- Segment words into phonemes (*b-a-t*)
- Manipulate phonemes (*mat-at, and-hand*)
- Connect words by the sounds (*sat, sun*)
- Hear and recognize word boundaries
- Hear and say beginning phonemes (sounds) in words (*run/race, mom/make*) and ending (*win/fun, get/sit*)
- Hear and say syllables (*to-ma-to, can-dy, um-brel-la*)
- Hear, say, connect, and generate rhyming words (*fly, high, buy, sky*)

Letter Knowledge

- Categorize letters by features–by slant lines (*v, w, x*) and straight lines (*p, l, b, d*); by circles (*o, b, g, p*) and no circles (*k, x, w, r*); by tunnels (*n, h*); by tails (*y, p, g*); by no tails (*r, s*); by dots/no dots; by tall/short; by consonants/vowels
- Distinguish letter forms
- Make connections between words by recognizing letters (*bat, big, ball*), letter clusters (*feat, meat, heat*), and letter sequences
- Recognize and produce the names of most upper- and lowercase letters
- Identify a word that begins with the sound of each letter
- Recognize consonants and vowels
- Recognize letters that are embedded in words and in continuous text
- Recognize uppercase and lowercase letters
- Understand alphabetical order
- Understand special uses of letters (capital letters, intials)
- Use efficient and consistent motions to form letters when writing

Phonics, Spelling, and Word Study

Selecting Goals Behaviors and Understandings to Notice, Teach, and Support

Letter/Sound Relationships

- Recognize and use beginning consonant sounds and the letters that represent them to read and write words
- Understand that there is a relationship between sounds and letters
- Recognize simple CVC words (*cat, sun*)
- Attempt to write words by writing one letter for each sound heard

Spelling Patterns

- Recognize and use a few simple phonograms with a VC pattern (easiest): (*-ad, -ag, -an, -am, -at, -ed, -en, -et, -ig, -in, -it, -og, -op, -ot, -ut*)
- Recognize that words have letter patterns that are connected to sounds (phonograms and other letter patterns)
- Recognize and use the consonant-vowel-consonant (CVC) pattern (*cab, fad, map*)

High-Frequency Words

- Write a core of twenty to twenty-five high-frequency words (*a, am, an, and, at, can, come, do, go, he, I, in, is, it, like, me, my, no, see, so, the, to, up, we, you*)
- Read a core of twenty to twenty-five high-frequency words (*a, am, an, and, at, can, come, do, go, he, I, in, is, it, like, me, my, no, see, so, the, to, up, we, you*)

Word Meaning

CONCEPT WORDS

- Recognize and use concept words (color names, number words, days of the week, months of the year)

COMPOUND WORDS

- Recognize and use simple compound words (*into, myself, itself, cannot, inside, maybe, nobody*)

Word Structure

SYLLABLES

- Understand that words can have one, two, or more syllables
- Understand that you can hear syllables and demonstrate by clapping (*horse, a-way, farm-er, morn-ing, bi-cy-cle, to-geth-er, ev-er-y*)

Word-Solving Actions

- Recognize and locate words (names)
- Make connections between names and other words
- Use own first and last names (and same names of others) to read and write words
- Use known words to help in spelling new words
- Recognize and spell known words quickly
- Use known words to monitor reading and spelling
- Use letters and relationships to sounds to read and write words

Phonics, Spelling, and Word Study

Selecting Goals **Behaviors and Understandings to Notice, Teach, and Support**

Early Literacy Concepts

- Locate the first and last letters of words in continuous text
- Recognize one's name in isolation and in continuous text
- Understand that one says one word for one group of letters when you read
- Understand the concept of *sentence* (as a group of words with ending punctuation)
- Understand the concepts of *letter* and *word* (as a single character or a group of letters)
- Understand the concepts of *first* and *last* in written language
- Use left-to-right directionality of print in reading and writing
- Use one's name to learn about words and make connections to words
- Use spaces between words when writing
- Match one spoken to one written word while reading and writing

Phonological Awareness

- Segment sentences into words
- Hear and recognize word boundaries
- Hear, say, connect, and generate rhyming words (*fly, high, buy, sky*)
- Blend two to four phonemes in words (*d-o-g, dog, t-e-n-t*)
- Segment words into phonemes (*b-a-t, t-e-n-t*)
- Connect words by the sounds (*Mom, my*)
- Manipulate phonemes (*cat-at, and, sand*)
- Hear and say beginning phonemes (sounds) in words (*run/race, mom/make*) and ending (*win/fun, get/sit*)
- Hear and say syllables (*to-ma-to, can-dy, um-brel-la*)

Letter Knowledge

- Categorize letters by features–by slant lines (*v, w, x*) and straight lines (*p, l, b, d*); by circles (*o, b, g, p*) and no circles (*k, x, w, r*); by tunnels (*n, h*); by tails (*y, p, g*); by no tails (*r, s*); by dots/no dots; by tall/short; by consonants/vowels
- Distinguish letter forms
- Make connections between words by recognizing letters (*bat, big, ball*), letter clusters (*feat, meat, heat*), and letter sequences
- Recognize and produce the names of most of the upper- and lowercase letters
- Identify a word that begins with the sound of each letter
- Recognize consonants and vowels
- Recognize letters that are embedded in words and in continuous text
- Recognize uppercase and lowercase letters
- Understand alphabetical order
- Understand special uses of letters (capital letters, intials)
- Use efficient and consistent motions to form letters when writing

Letter/Sound Relationships

- Recognize and use beginning consonant sounds and the letters that represent them to read and write words
- Recognize that letter clusters (blends and digraphs: *st, pl sh, ch, th*) represent consonant sounds
- Hear and identify long (*make, pail, day*) and short (*can, egg, up*) vowel sounds in words and the letters that represent them
- Recognize and use other vowel sounds (*oo* as in *moon, look; oi* as in *oil; oy* as in *boy; ou* as in *house; ow* as in *cow; aw* as in *paw*)

Spelling Patterns

- Recognize and use a large number of phonograms (VC, CVC, CVCe, VCC)
- Recognize that words have letter patterns that are connected to sounds (phonograms and other letter patterns)
- Recognize and use the consonant-vowel-consonant (CVC) pattern (*cab, fad, map*)

Phonics, Spelling, and Word Study

Selecting Goals Behaviors and Understandings to Notice, Teach, and Support

High-Frequency Words

- Write a core of at least fifty high-frequency words (*a, all, am, an, and, are, at, be, but, came, come, can, do, for, from, get, got, had, have, he, her, him, his, I, if, in, is, it, like, me, my, no, of, on, one, out, said, saw, see, she, so, that, the, their, then, there, they, this, to, up, was, we, went, were, with, you, your*)
- Read a core of at least fifty high-frequency words (*a, all, am, an, and, are, at, be, but, came, come, can, do, for, from, get, got, had, have, he, her, him, his, I, if, in, is, it, like, me, my, no, of, on, one, out, said, saw, see, she, so, that, the, their, then, there, they, this, to, up, was, we, went, were, with, you, your*)

Word Meaning

Concept Words

- Recognize and use concept words (color names, number words, days of the week, months of the year)

Compound Words

- Recognize and use simple compound words (*into, myself, itself, cannot, inside, maybe, nobody*)

Synonyms and Antonyms

- Recognize and use synonyms (words that mean about the same: *begin/start, close/shut, fix/mend, earth/world, happy/glad, high/tall, jump/leap*)
- Recognize and use antonyms (words that mean the opposite: *hot/cold, all/none, break/fix, little/big, long/short, sad/glad, stop/start*)

Homographs and Homophones

- Recognize and use simple homophones (sound the same, different spelling and meaning: *to/too/two, here/hear, blue/blew, there/their/they're*)

Word Structure

Syllables

- Understand the concept of syllables and demonstrate by clapping (*horse, a-way, farm-er, morn-ing, bi-cy-cle, to-geth-er, ev-er-y*)
- Understand how vowels appear in syllables (every syllable has a vowel)

Plurals

- Understand the concept of plurals and plural forms: adding *-s* (*dogs, cats, apples, cans, desks, faces, trees, monkeys*); adding *-es* (when words end in *x, ch, sh, s, ss, tch, zz*)

Verb Endings

- Recognize and use endings that add *-s* to a verb to make it agree with the subject (*skate/skates, run/runs*)
- Recognize and use endings that add *-ing* to a verb to denote the present participle (*play/playing, send/sending*)
- Recognize and use endings that add *-ed* to a verb to make it past tense (*walk/walked, play/played, want/wanted*)

Contractions

- Recognize and understand contractions with *am* (*I'm*), *is* (*he's*), *will* (*I'll*), *not* (*can't*)

Possessives

- Recognize and use possessives that add an apostrophe and an *s* to a singular noun (*dog/dog's, woman/woman's, girl/girl's, boy/boy's*)

Base Words

- Remove the ending from a base word to make a new word (*running, run*)

Word-Solving Actions

- Use known words to help in spelling new words
- Make connections between names and other words
- Recognize and locate words (names)
- Recognize and spell known words quickly
- Use the letters in names to read and write words (*Chuck/chair, Mark/make*)
- Use known words to monitor reading and spelling
- Use letters and relationships to sounds to read and write words
- Use known words and word parts to help in reading and spelling new words (*can, candy*)
- Change beginning, middle, and ending letters to make new words (*sit/hit, day/play, hit/hot, sheet/shirt, car/can/cat*)
- Change the onset or rime to make a new word (*bring/thing, bring/brown*)
- Break words into syllables to read or write them

Phonics, Spelling, and Word Study

Selecting Goals **Behaviors and Understandings to Notice, Teach, and Support**

Letter/Sound Relationships

- Recognize and use the full range of consonant letters and letter clusters (*st, ch*) in beginning, middle, and ending position in words
- Recognize and use long and short vowel sounds in words
- Recognize and use letter combinations that represent long vowel sounds (*ai, ay, ee, ea, oa, ow*)
- Recognize and use vowel sounds in open syllables (CV: *ho-tel*)
- Recognize and use vowel sounds in closed syllables (CVC: *lem-on*)
- Recognize and use vowel sounds with *r* (*car, first, hurt, her, corn, floor, world, near*)
- Recognize and use letters that represent no sound in words (*lamb, light*)

Spelling Patterns

- Recognize and use a large number of phonogram patterns (VC, CVC, CVCe, VCC, VVC, VVCC, VVCe, VCCC, VVCCC)

High-Frequency Words

- Write and read 150 to 200 high-frequency words automatically
- Employ self-monitoring strategies for continually accumulating ability to read and write accurately a large core of high-frequency words (working toward automatic knowledge of the five hundred most frequent)

Word Meaning

Compound Words

- Recognize and use a variety of compound words (*into, myself, itself, cannot, inside, maybe, nobody, outside, sunshine, today, together, upset, yourself, without, sometimes, something*)

Synonyms and Antonyms

- Recognize and use synonyms (words that mean about the same: *begin/start, close/shut, fix/mend, earth/world, happy/glad, high/tall, jump/leap*)
- Recognize and use antonyms (words that mean the opposite: *hot/cold, all/none, break/fix, little/big, long/short, sad/glad, stop/start*)

Homographs and Homophones

- Recognize and use homophones (sound the same, different spelling and meaning: *to/too/two, here/hear, blue/blew, there/their/they're*)
- Recognize and use homographs (same spelling and different meaning: *bat/bat, well/well, wind/wind*)
- Recognize and use words with multiple meanings (*play/play*)

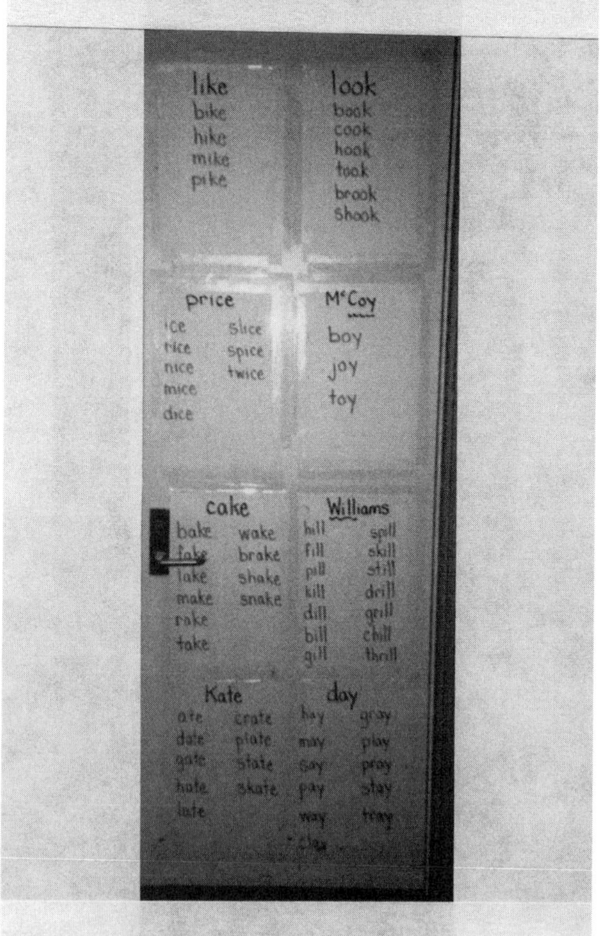

Phonics, Spelling, and Word Study

Selecting Goals **Behaviors and Understandings to Notice, Teach, and Support**

Word Structure

Syllables

- Understand how vowels appear in syllables (every syllable has a vowel)
- Recognize and use syllables in words with double consonants (*lad-der*) and in words with the VV pattern (*ri-ot*)

Plurals

- Understand the concept of plurals and plural forms: adding *-s* (*dogs, cats, apples, cans, desks, faces, trees, monkeys*); adding *-es* (when words end in *x, ch, sh, s, ss, tch, zz*); changing spelling (*foot/feet, goose/geese, man/men, mouse/mice, woman/women*)

Verb Endings

- Recognize and form present and past tense by using endings (*-es, -ed: like, likes, liked*); form present participle by adding *-ing* (*liking*); make a verb past tense (*-ed, d: played, liked*)
- Recognize and use endings: *-er* to a verb to make a noun (*read/reader, play/player, jump/jumper*), *-er* to a verb that ends with a short vowel and a consonant (*dig/digger, run/runner*), *-r* to a verb that ends in silent *r* (*bake/baker, hike/hiker*), *-er* to a verb ending in *y* (*carry/carrier*)

Endings for Adjectives

- Recognize and use endings that show comparisons (*-er, -est*)

Contractions

- Recognize and understand contractions with *am* (*I'm*), *is* (*he's*), *will* (*I'll*), *not* (*can't*)

Possessives

- Recognize and use possessives that add an apostrophe and an *s* to a singular noun (*dog/dog's, woman/woman's, girl/girl's, boy/boy's*)

Base Words

- Remove the ending from a base word to make a new word (*running, run*)

Prefixes

- Recognize and use common prefixes (*re-, un-*)

Word-Solving Actions

- Use known words to monitor reading and spelling
- Use letters and relationships to sounds to read and write words
- Break words into syllables to read or write them
- Add, delete, and change letters (*in/win, bat/bats*), letter clusters (*an/plan, cat/catch*), and word parts to make new words
- Take apart compound words or join words make compound words (*into/in-to, side-walk/sidewalk*)
- Use letter-sound knowledge to monitor reading and spelling accuracy
- Use the parts of compound words to solve a word and derive the meaning
- Use known words and word parts (onsets and rimes) to help in reading and spelling new words (*br-ing, cl-ap*)
- Notice patterns and categorize high-frequency words to assist in learning them quickly
- Recognize base words and remove prefixes and suffixes to break them down and solve them

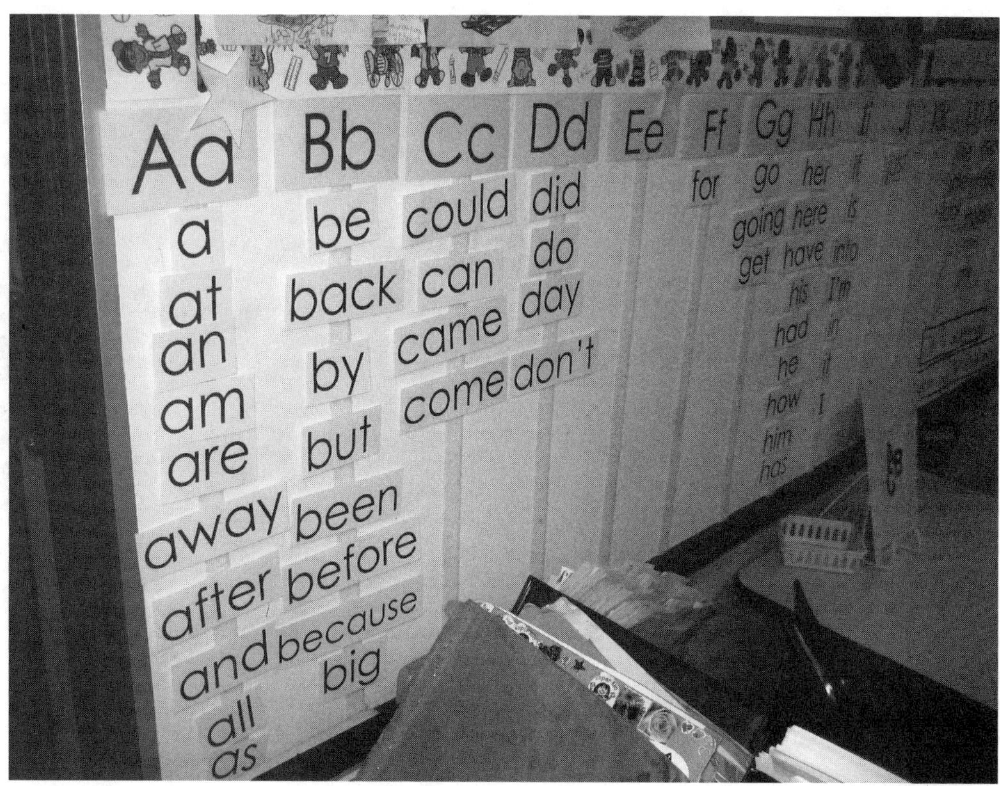

Phonics, Spelling, and Word Study

Selecting Goals — Behaviors and Understandings to Notice, Teach, and Support

Letter/Sound Relationships

- Recognize and use letters that represent no sound in words (*lamb, light*)
- Understand and use all sounds related to the various consonants and consonant clusters
- Understand that some consonant letters represent several different sounds (*ch-: cheese, school, machine, choir, yacht*)
- Understand that some consonant sounds can be represented by several different letters or letter clusters (final *k* by *c, k, ck*)
- Recognize and use vowel sounds in open syllables (CV: *ho-tel*)
- Recognize and use vowel sounds in closed syllables (CVC: *lem-on*)
- Recognize and use vowel sounds with *r* (*car, first, hurt, her, corn, floor, world, near*)
- Recognize and use letters that represent the wide variety of vowel sounds (long, short)

Spelling Patterns

- Recognize and use a large number of phonograms (VC, CVC, CVC*e*, VCC, VVC, VVCC, VVC*e*, VCCC, and VVCCC; vowels plus *r;* and *-oy* and *-ow*)
- Notice and use frequently appearing short vowel patterns that appear in multisyllable words (other than most frequent) (*-a, -ab, -ad, -ag, -age, -ang, -am, -an, -ant, -ap, -ent, -el(l), -ep, -es, -ev, -id, -ig, -il(l), -ob, -oc(k), -od, -ol, -om, -on, -op, -ot, -ub, -uc(k), -ud, -uf, -ug, -up, -um, -us, -ut, -uz*)

High-Frequency Words

- Employ self-monitoring strategies for continually accumulating ability to read and write accurately a large core of high-frequency words (intentially work toward automatic knowledge of the five hundred most frequent)

Word Meaning

Compound Words

- Recognize and use a variety of complex compound words (*airplane, airport, another, anyone, anybody, anything, everyone, homesick, indoor, jellyfish, skyscraper, toothbrush, underground, whenever*)

Synonyms and Antonyms

- Recognize and use synonyms (words that mean about the same: *begin/start, close/shut, fix/mend, earth/world, happy/glad, high/tall, jump/leap*)
- Recognize and use antonyms (words that mean the opposite: *hot/cold, all/none, break/fix, little/big, long/short, sad/glad, stop/start*)

Homographs and Homophones

- Recognize and use homographs (same spelling and different meaning: *bat/bat, well/well, wind/wind*)
- Recognize and use homophones (sound the same and are spelled differently: *to/too/two, here/hear, blue/blew, there/their/they're*)
- Recognize and use words with multiple meanings (*beat, run, play*)

Nouns

- Recognize and use words that represent a person, place, or thing

Verbs

- Recognize and use action words

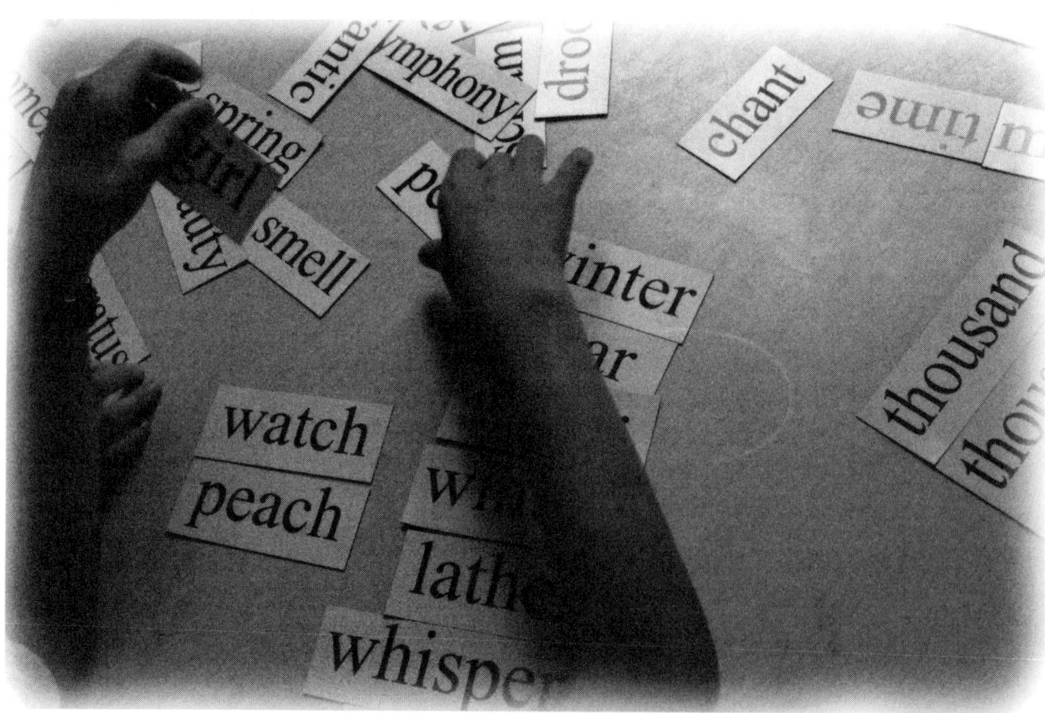

Phonics, Spelling, and Word Study

Selecting Goals Behaviors and Understandings to Notice, Teach, and Support

Adjectives

- Recognize and use words that describe

Figurative Language

- Recognize and use words to make comparisons
- Recognize and use words that represent sounds (onomatopoetic)
- Recognize and use action words

Word Structure

Syllables

- Recognize and use syllables in words with double consonants (*lad-der*) and in words with the VV pattern (*ri-ot*)
- Recognize and use syllables: open syllable (*ho-tel*), closed syllable (*lem-on*), syllables with a vowel and silent e (*hope-ful*), syllables with vowel combinations (*poi-son, cray-on*), syllables with a vowel and *r* (*corn-er, cir-cus*), syllables in words with VV pattern (*ri-ot*), syllables with double consonants (*lad-der*)

Plurals

- Understand the concept of plurals and plural forms: adding *-s* (*dogs, cats, apples, cans, desks, faces, trees, monkeys*); adding *-es* (when words end in *x, ch, sh, s, ss, tch, zz*); changing *-y* to *-i* and adding *-es*; changing spelling (*foot/feet, goose/geese, man/men, mouse/mice, woman/women*)

Verb Endings

- Recognize and form various tenses by adding endings (*-es, -ed, -ing, -d*) to verbs

Endings for Adjectives

- Recognize and use endings that show comparisons (*-er, -est*)

Adverbs

- Recognize and use endings that form adverbs (*-ly*)

Suffixes

- Recognize and use suffixes that change verbs and nouns for different functions (*-er, -es, -r, -ing*)

Contractions

- Recognize and understand contractions with *am* (*I'm*), *is* (*he's*), *will* (*I'll*), *not* (*can't*), *have* (*could've*), *would* or *had* (*I'd, you'd*)

Possessives

- Recognize and use possessives that add an apostrophe and an *s* to a singular noun (*dog/dog's, woman/woman's, girl/girl's, boy/boy's*)

Prefixes

- Recognize and use common prefixes (*re-, un-*)

Word-Solving Actions

- Break words into syllables to read or write them
- Use known words and word parts (onsets and rimes) to help in reading and spelling new words (*br-ing, cl-ap*)
- Notice patterns and categorize high-frequency words to assist in learning them quickly
- Recognize base words and remove prefixes and suffixes to break them down and solve them
- Add, delete, and change letters, letter clusters, and word parts to base words to help in reading or spelling words
- Use word parts to derive the meaning of a word
- Use the context of the sentence, paragraph, or whole text to help determine the precise meaning of a word

Phonics, Spelling, and Word Study

Selecting Goals **Behaviors and Understandings to Notice, Teach, and Support**

Letter/Sound Relationships

- Recognize and use letters that represent no sound in words (*lamb, light*)
- Understand that some consonant letters represent several different sounds (*ch-: cheese, school, machine, choir, yacht*)
- Understand that some consonant sounds can be represented by several different letters or letter clusters (final *k* by *c, que, ke, k, ck;* final *f* by *ff, gh*)
- Recognize and use vowel sounds in open syllables (CV: *ho-tel*)
- Recognize and use vowel sounds in closed syllables (CVC: *cab-in*)
- Recognize and use vowel sounds with *r* (*car, first, hurt, her, corn, floor, world, near*)
- Recognize and use letters that represent the wide variety of vowel sounds (long, short)

Spelling Patterns

- Recognize and use a large number of phonograms (VC, CVC, CVCe, VCC, VVC, VVCC, VVCe, VCCC, and VVCCC; vowels plus *r;* and *-oy* and *-ow*)
- Notice and use frequently appearing short vowel patterns that appear in multisyllable words (other than most frequent) (*-a, -ab, -ad, -ag, -age, -ang, -am, -an, -ant, -ap, -ent, -el(l), -ep, -es, -ev, -id, -ig, -il(l), -ob, -oc(k), -od, -ol, -om, -on, -op, -ot, -ub, -uc(k), -ud, -uf, -ug, -up, -um, -us, -ut, -uz*)
- Notice and use frequently appearing syllable patterns in multisyllable words (*-en, -ago, -ar, -at, -it, -in, -is, -un, -be, -re, -or, -a, -y, -ey, -ble, -l, –ur, -um, -ic(k), -et, -im*)
- Understand that some words have double consonants in the pattern (*coffee, address, success, accident, mattress, occasion*)

High-Frequency Words

- Employ self-monitoring strategies for continually accumulating ability to read and write accurately a large core of high-frequency words (working toward automatic knowledge of the five hundred most frequent)

Word Meaning

Compound Words

- Recognize and use a variety of complex compound words and hyphenated compound words (*airplane, airport, another, anyone, anybody, anything, everyone, homesick, indoor, jellyfish, skyscraper, toothbrush, underground, whenever, empty-handed, well-being, re-elect, father-in-law*)

Synonyms and Antonyms

- Recognize and use synonyms (words that mean about the same: *begin/start, close/shut, fix/mend, earth/world, happy/glad, high/tall, jump/leap*) and antonyms (words that mean the opposite: *hot/cold, all/none, break/fix, little/big, long/short, sad/glad, stop/start*)

Homographs and Homophones

- Recognize and use homographs (same spelling and different meaning: *bat/bat, well/well, wind/wind*), homophones (sound the same and are spelling differently: *to/too/two, here/hear, blue/blew, there/their/they're*), and words with multiple meanings (*beat, run, play*)

Nouns

- Recognize and use words that represent a person, place, or thing

Verbs

- Recognize and use action words

Adjectives

- Recognize and use words that describe

Figurative Language

- Recognize and use words as metaphors and similes to make comparisons

Portmanteau Words

- Recognize and use words that are blended together (*brunch*)

Idioms

- Recognize and use metaphors that have become traditional sayings and in which the comparisons are not evident (*raining cats and dogs*)

Phonics, Spelling, and Word Study

Selecting Goals Behaviors and Understandings to Notice, Teach, and Support

Word Structure

Syllables

- Recognize and use syllables: open syllable (*ho-tel*), closed syllable (*lem-on*), syllables with a vowel and silent *e* (*hope-ful*), syllables with vowel combinations (*poi-son, cray-on*), syllables with a vowel and *r* (*corn-er, cir-cus*), syllables in words with VV pattern (*ri-ot*), syllables with double consonants (*lad-der*)

Plurals

- Understand the concept of plurals and plural forms: adding -*s* (*dogs, cats, apples, cans, desks, faces, trees, monkeys*); adding -*es* (when words end in *x, ch, sh, s, ss, tch, zz*); changing -*y* to -*i* and adding -*es*; changing spelling (*foot/feet, goose/geese, man/men, mouse/mice, woman/women*); adding an unusual suffix (*ox/oxen, child/students*), keep the same spelling in singular and plural form (*deer, lamb, sheep, mouse*), add either -*s* or -*es* in words that end in a vowel and *o* or a consonant and *o* (*radios, rodeos, kangaroos, zeroes, heroes, potatoes, volcanoes*)

Verb Endings

- Recognize and form various tenses by adding endings (-*es*, -*e*, -*ing*, -*d*, -*ful*) to verbs

Endings for Adjectives

- Recognize and use endings for adjectives that add meaning or change the adjective to an adverb (-*ly*, -*ally*)
- Recognize and use endings for adjectives that add meaning or change the adjective to a noun (-*tion*, -*ible* for partial words; -*able* for whole words) and some exceptions

Adverbs

- Recognize and use endings that form adverbs (-*ly*, -*ally*)

Suffixes

- Recognize and use suffixes that change verbs and nouns for different functions, such as adjectives and adverbs (-*er*, -*es*, -*r*, -*ing*, -*ily*, -*able*, -*ible*, -*ar*, -*less*)

Contractions

- Recognize and understand contractions with *am* (*I'm*), *is* (*he's*), *will* (*I'll*), *not* (*can't*), *have* (*could've*), *would* or *had* (*I'd, you'd*)

Possessives

- Recognize and use possessives that add an apostrophe and an *s* to a singular noun (*dog/dog's, woman/woman's, girl/girl's, boy/boy's*), that *its* does not use an apostrophe, and that a plural possessive like *women* uses an apostrophe and an *s* (*students/children's; men/men's*)

Prefixes

- Recognize and use common prefixes (*re-, un-, im-, in-, il-, dis-, non-, mis-*) as well as prefixes that refer to numbers (*uni-, bi-, tri-, cent-, dec-, mon-, multi-, cot-, pent-, poly-, quad-, semi-*)

Abbreviations

- Recognize and use abbreviations (state names; weights; *Sr., Jr.*)

Word-Solving Actions

- Break words into syllables to read or write them
- Use known words and word parts (onsets and rimes) to help in reading and spelling new words (*br-ing, cl-ap*)
- Notice patterns and categorize high-frequency words to assist in learning them quickly
- Recognize base words and remove prefixes and suffixes to break them down and solve them
- Add, delete, and change letters, letter clusters, and word parts to base words to help in reading or spelling words
- Use word parts to derive the meaning of a word
- Use the context of the sentence, paragraph, or whole text to help determine the precise meaning of a word
- Use the pronunciation guide in a dictionary
- Connect words that are related to each other because they have the same base or root word (*direct, direction, directional*)

Phonics, Spelling, and Word Study

Selecting Goals **Behaviors and Understandings to Notice, Teach, and Support**

Spelling Patterns

- Notice and use frequently appearing long vowel patterns that appear in multisyllable words (*-e, beginning; -ee, agree; -ea, reason; -ide, decide; -ire, entirely; ise, revise; -ive, survive; -ize, realize; -ade, lemonade; -aid, braided; -ail, railroad; -ale, female; -ain, painter; -ate, crater; -ope, antelope; -one, telephone; -oke, spoken; -u, tutor; -ture, furniture*)
- Notice and use other vowel patterns that appear in multisyllable words (*-al, always; -au, author; -aw, awfully; -ea, weather; -i, sillier; i-e, police; -tion, attention; -sion, tension; -y, reply; -oi, noisy; -oy, enjoy; -ou, about; -ow, power; -oo, booster; -ove, remove; -u, tuna; -ook, looking; -oot, football; -ood, woodpile; -ul(l), grateful*)
- Understand that some words have double consonants in the pattern (*coffee, address, success, accident, mattress, occasion*)

High-Frequency Words

- Read and write the five hundred words that occur with highest frequency in English rapidly and automatically

Word Meaning

Compound Words

- Recognize and use a variety of complex compound words and hyphenated compound words (*airplane, airport, another, anyone, anybody, anything, everyone, homesick, indoor, jellyfish, skyscraper, toothbrush, underground, whenever, empty-handed, well-being, re-elect, father-in-law*)

Figurative Language

- Recognize and use words as metaphors and similes to make comparisons

Idioms

- Recognize and use metaphors that have become traditional sayings and in which the comparisons are not evident (*raining cats and dogs*)

Acronyms

- Recognize and use words that are made by combining initials (*NATO, UNICEF*)

Word Origins

- Understand English words come from many different sources (other languages, technology, place names)

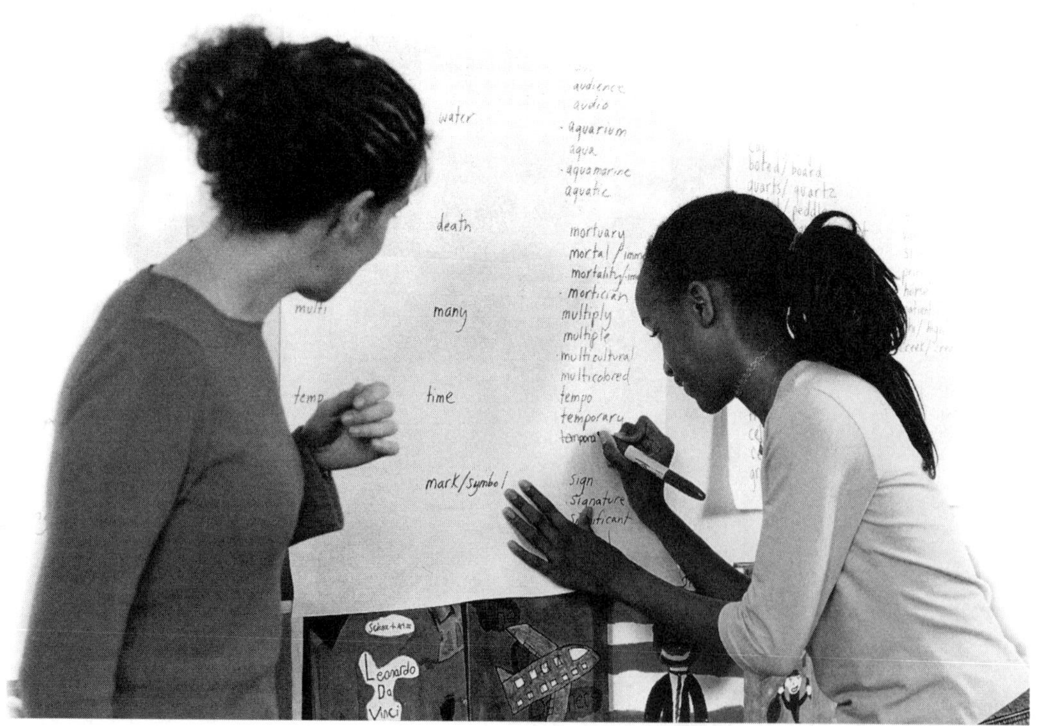

Phonics, Spelling, and Word Study

Selecting Goals **Behaviors and Understandings to Notice, Teach, and Support**

Word Structure

Syllables

- Recognize and use syllables: open syllable (*ho-tel*), closed syllable (*lem-on*), syllables with a vowel and silent e (*hope-ful*), syllables with vowel combinations (*poi-son, cray-on*), syllables with a vowel and *r* (*corn-er, cir-cus*), syllables in words with VV pattern (*ri-ot*), syllables with double consonants (*lad-der*), syllables with consonant and *le* (*ta-ble*)

Plurals

- Understand the concept of plurals and plural forms: adding *-s* (*dogs, cats, apples, cans, desks, faces, trees, monkeys*); adding *-es* (when words end in *x, ch, sh, s, ss, tch, zz*); changing *-y* to *-i* and adding *-es;* changing spelling (*foot/feet, goose/geese, man/men, mouse/mice, woman/women*); adding an unusual suffix (*ox/oxen, child/students*), keep the same spelling in singular and plural form (*deer, lamb, sheep, mouse*), add either *-s* or *-es* in words that end in a vowel and *o* or a consonant and *o* (*radios, rodeos, kangaroos, zeroes, heroes, potatoes, volcanoes*)

Verb Endings

- Recognize and form various tenses by adding endings (*-es, -e, -ing, -d, -ful*) to verbs

Endings for Adjectives

- Recognize and use endings for adjectives that add meaning or change the adjective to an adverb (*-ly, -ally*)
- Recognize and use endings for adjectives that add meaning or change the adjective to a noun (*-tion, -ible* for partial words; *-able* for whole words) and some exceptions

Nouns

- Recognize and use nouns that are formed by adding *-ic, -al, -ian, -ial, -cial;* add *-er* or *-ar* to a verb; *-ment*

Adverbs

- Recognize and use adverbs that end in e (keep or drop the *e: truly, merely*), that end in *-ic* (*tragically, frantically*)

Suffixes

- Recognize and use suffixes that change verbs and nouns for different functions, such as adjectives and adverbs (*-er, -es, -r, -ing, -ily, -able, -ible, -ar, -less, -ness, -ous, -cious, -tious*)

Contractions

- Recognize and understand contractions with *am* (*I'm*), *is* (*he's*), *will* (*I'll*), *not* (*can't*), *have* (*could've*), *would* or *had* (*I'd, you'd*)

Possessives

- Recognize and use possessives that add an apostrophe and an *s* to a singular noun (*dog/dog's, woman/woman's, girl/girl's, boy/boy's*), that *its* does not use an apostrophe, and that a plural possessive like *women* uses an apostrophe and an *s* (*students/children's; men/men's*)

Prefixes

- Recognize and use common prefixes (*re-, un-, im-, in-, il-, dis-, non-, mis-*) as well as prefixes that refer to numbers (*uni-, bi-, tri-, cent-, dec-, mon-, multi-, cot-, pent-, poly-, quad-, semi-*)

Abbreviations

- Recognize and use abbreviations (state names; weights; *Sr., Jr., Ph.D.*)

Word-Solving Actions

- Break words into syllables to read or write them
- Recognize base words and remove prefixes and suffixes to break them down and solve them
- Use word parts to derive the meaning of a word
- Use the context of the sentence, paragraph, or whole text to help determine the precise meaning of a word
- Use the pronunciation guide in a dictionary
- Connect words that are related to each other because they have the same base or root word (*direct, direction, directional*)
- Use the dictionary to discover word history
- Distinguish between multiple meanings of words when reading texts

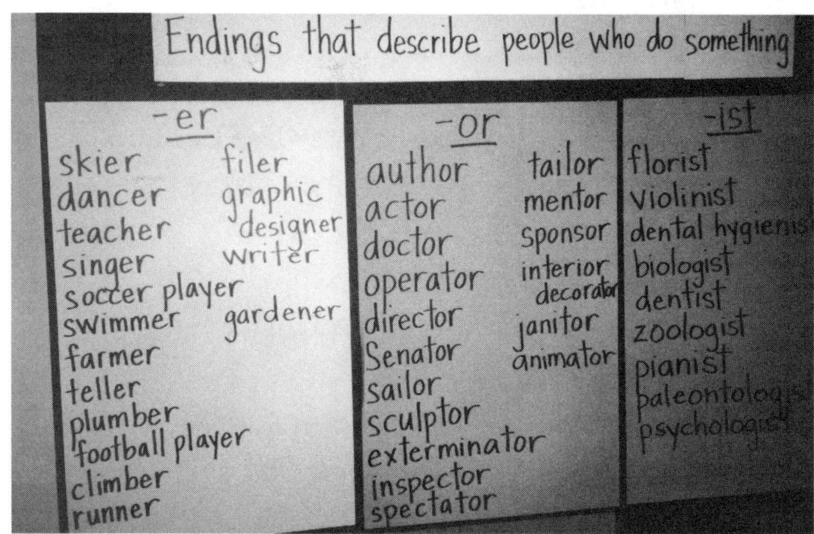

Phonics, Spelling, and Word Study

Selecting Goals **Behaviors and Understandings to Notice, Teach, and Support**

Word Meaning

Figurative Language

- Recognize and use words as metaphors and similes to make comparisons

Idioms

- Recognize and use metaphors that have become traditional sayings and in which the comparisons are not evident (*raining cats and dogs*)

Word Origins

- Understand many English words are derived from new inventions, technology, or current events

Words with Latin Roots

- Understand many English words have Latin roots–*ab, and, bene, cap, ce, cide, cor, cred, dic, duce, equa, fac, fer, form, grac, grad, hab, ject, lit, loc, man, mem, miss, mob, mimr, ped, pens, port, pos, prim, uer, scub, sep, sist, spec, train, tract, val, ven, vens, vid, voc*

Words with Greek Roots

- Understand many English words have Greek roots–*aer, arch, aster, bio, centr, chron, eye, dem, derm, geo, gram, graph, dydr, ology, meter, micro, phon, photo, phys, pol, scope, sphere, tel*

Word Structure

Syllables

- Recognize and use syllables: open syllable (*ho-tel*), closed syllable (*lem-on*), syllables with a vowel and silent *e* (*hope-ful*), syllables with vowel combinations (*poi-son, cray-on*), syllables with a vowel and *r* (*corn-er, cir-cus*), syllables in words with VV pattern (*ri-ot*), syllables with double consonants (*lad-der*), syllables with consonant and *le* (*ta-ble*)

Plurals

- Understand the concept of plurals and plural forms: adding *-s* (*dogs, cats, apples, cans, desks, faces, trees, monkeys*); adding *-es* (when words end in *x, ch, sh, s, ss, tch, zz*); changing *-y* to *-i* and adding *-es;* changing spelling (*foot/feet, goose/geese, man/men, mouse/mice, woman/women*); adding an unusual suffix (*ox/oxen, child/students*), keep the same spelling in singular and plural form (*deer, lamb, sheep, mouse*), add either *-s* or *-es* in words that end in a vowel and *o* or a consonant and *o* (*radios, rodeos, kangaroos, zeroes, heroes, potatoes, volcanoes*)

Verb Endings

- Recognize and form various tenses by adding endings (*-es, -e, -ing, -d, -ful*) to verbs

Endings for Adjectives

- Recognize and use endings for adjectives that add meaning or change the adjective to an adverb (*-ly, -ally*)
- Recognize and use endings for adjectives that add meaning or change the adjective to a noun (*-tion, -ible* for partial words; *-able* for whole words) and some exceptions

Nouns

- Recognize and use nouns that are formed by adding *-ic, -al, -ian, -ial, -cial;* add *-er* or *-ar* to a verb; *-ment*
- Recognize and use nouns that are formed by adding *-tion, -ion, -sion, -ment, -ant, -ity, -ence, -ance, -ure, -ture,* including words that end in silent *e* or *y*

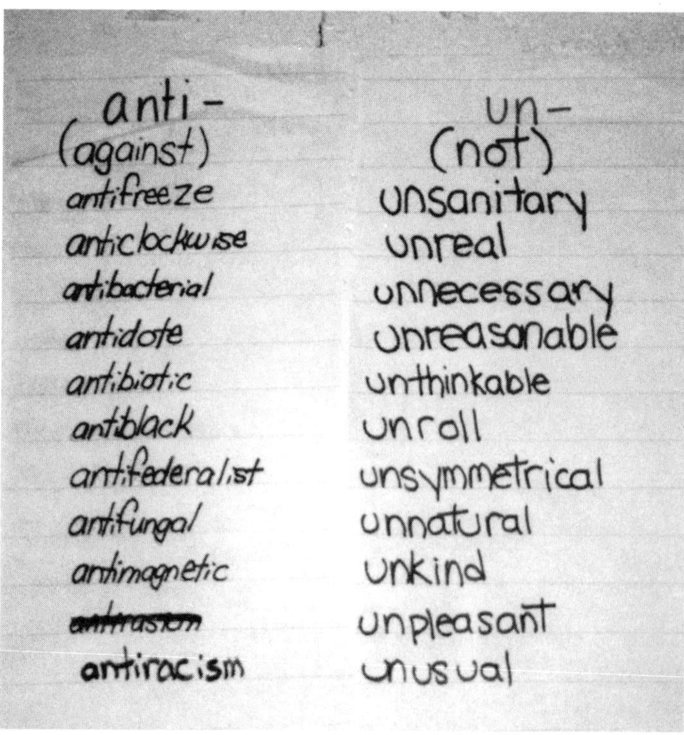

Phonics, Spelling, and Word Study

Selecting Goals Behaviors and Understandings to Notice, Teach, and Support

Adverbs

- Recognize and use adverbs that end in *e* (keep or drop the *e: truly, merely*), that end in *-ic* (*tragically, frantically*)

Suffixes

- Recognize and use suffixes that change verbs and nouns for different functions, such as adjectives and adverbs (*-er, -es, -r, -ing, -ily, -able, -ible, -ar, -less, -ness, -ous, -cious, -tious*)

Contractions

- Recognize and understand multiple contractions with *not* and *have* (*shouldn't've*)

Possessives

- Recognize and use possessives that add an apostrophe and an *s* to a singular noun (*dog/dog's, woman/woman's, girl/girl's, boy/boy's*), that *its* does not use an apostrophe, and that a plural possessive like *women* uses an apostrophe and an *s* (*students/children's; men/men's*)

Prefixes

- Recognize and use common prefixes (*re-, un-, im-, in-, il-, dis-, non-, mis-, trans-, pre-, en-, em-, inter-, intra-, con-, com-, sub-, super-, mal-, ex-, per-, circum-, in-, ad-, ob-, sujb-, com-, dis-, ex-*) as well as prefixes that refer to numbers (*uni-, bi-, tri-, cent-, dec-, mon-, multi-, cot-, pent-, poly-, quad-, semi-*)
- Recognize and use assimilated prefixes that change form to match the root word: *in-* (*immigrate, illegal, irregular*), *ad-* (*address, approach, aggressive*), *ob-* (*obstruct, opportunity*), *sub-* (*subtract, suppose, surround*), *com-* (*commit, collide, corrode*), *dis-* (*distinguish, difference*), *ex-* (*expand, expose, eccentric, efficicient*)

Abbreviations

- Recognize and use abbreviation (state names; weights; *Sr., Jr., Ph.D.*)

Word-Solving Actions

- Use word parts to derive the meaning of a word
- Use the context of the sentence, paragraph, or whole text to help determine the precise meaning of a word
- Use the pronunciation guide in a dictionary
- Connect words that are related to each other because they have the same base or root word (*direct, direction, directional*)
- Use the dictionary to discover word history
- Distinguish between multiple meanings of words when reading texts
- Recognize and use the different types of dictionaries: general, specialized (synonyms, abbreviations, theme or topic, foreign language, thesaurus, electronic)
- Understand the concept of *analogy* and its use in discovering relationships between and among words
- Use knowledge of Greek and Latin roots in deriving the meaning of words while reading texts
- Use knowledge of prefixes, root words, and suffixes to derive the meaning of words while reading texts

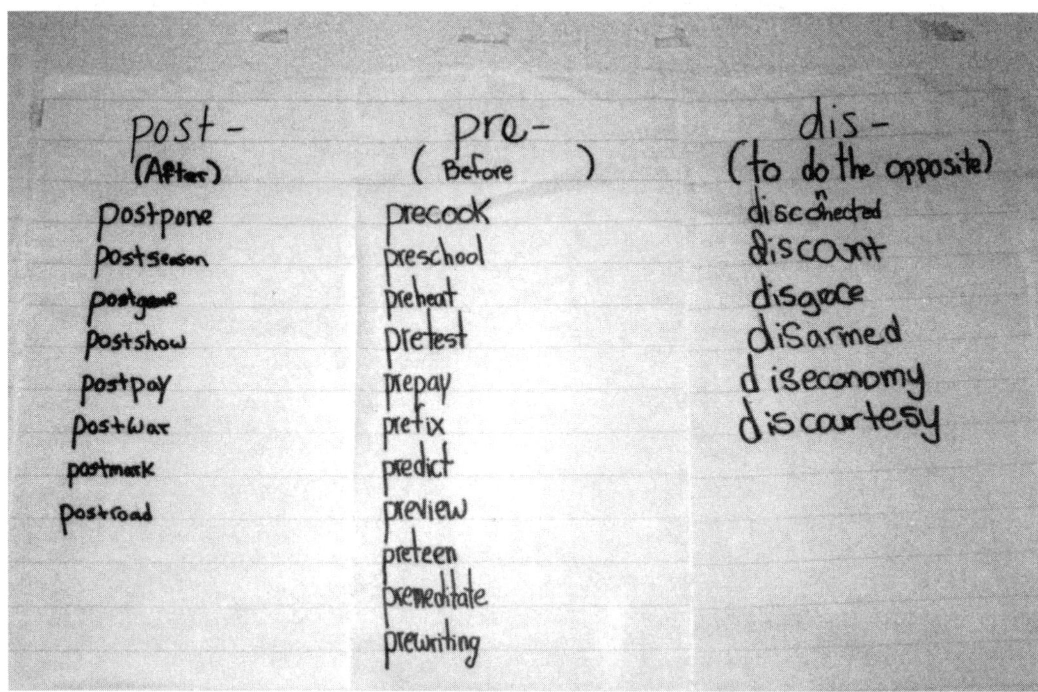

Phonics, Spelling, and Word Study

Selecting Goals Behaviors and Understandings to Notice, Teach, and Support

Word Meaning

Figurative Language

- Recognize and use words as metaphors and similes to make comparisons

Idioms

- Recognize and use metaphors that have become traditional sayings and in which the comparisons are not evident (*raining cats and dogs*)

Word Origins

- Understand many English words are derived from new inventions, technology, or current events

Words with Latin Roots

- Understand many English words have Latin roots–*ab, and, bene, cap, ce, cide, cor, cred, dic, duce, equa, fac, fer, form, grac, grad, hab, ject, lit, loc, man, mem, miss, mob, mimr, ped, pens, port, pos, prim, uer, scub, sep, sist, spec, train, tract, val, ven, vens, vid, voc*

Words with Greek Roots

- Understand many English words have Greek roots–*aer, arch, aster, bio, centr, chron, eye, dem, derm, geo, gram, graph, dydr, ology, meter, micro, phon, photo, phys, pol, scope, sphere, tel*

Word Structure

Syllables

- Recognize and use syllables: open syllable (*ho-tel*), closed syllable (*lem-on*), syllables with a vowel and silent *e* (*hope-ful*), syllables with vowel combinations (*poi-son, cray-on*), syllables with a vowel and *r* (*corn-er, cir-cus*), syllables in words with VV pattern (*ri-ot*), syllables with double consonants (*lad-der*), syllables with consonant and *le* (*ta-ble*)

Plurals

- Understand the concept of plurals and plural forms: adding *-s* (*dogs, cats, apples, cans, desks, faces, trees, monkeys*); adding *-es* (when words end in *x, ch, sh, s, ss, tch, zz*); changing *-y* to *-i* and adding *-es;* changing spelling (*foot/feet, goose/geese, man/men, mouse/mice, woman/women*); adding an unusual suffix (*ox/oxen, child/students*), keep the same spelling in singular and plural form (*deer, lamb, sheep, mouse*), add either *-s* or *-es* in words that end in a vowel and *o* or a consonant and *o* (*radios, rodeos, kangaroos, zeroes, heroes, potatoes, volcanoes*)

Verb Endings

- Recognize and form various tenses by adding endings (*-es, -e, -ing, -d, -ful*) to verbs

Endings for Adjectives

- Recognize and use endings for adjectives that add meaning or change the adjective to an adverb (*-ly, -ally*)
- Recognize and use endings for adjectives that add meaning or change the adjective to a noun (*-tion, -ible* for partial words; *-able* for whole words) and some exceptions

Nouns

- Recognize and use nouns that are formed by adding *-tion, -ion, -sion, -ment, -ant, -ity, -ence, -ance, -ure, -ture,* including words that end in silent *e* or *y*

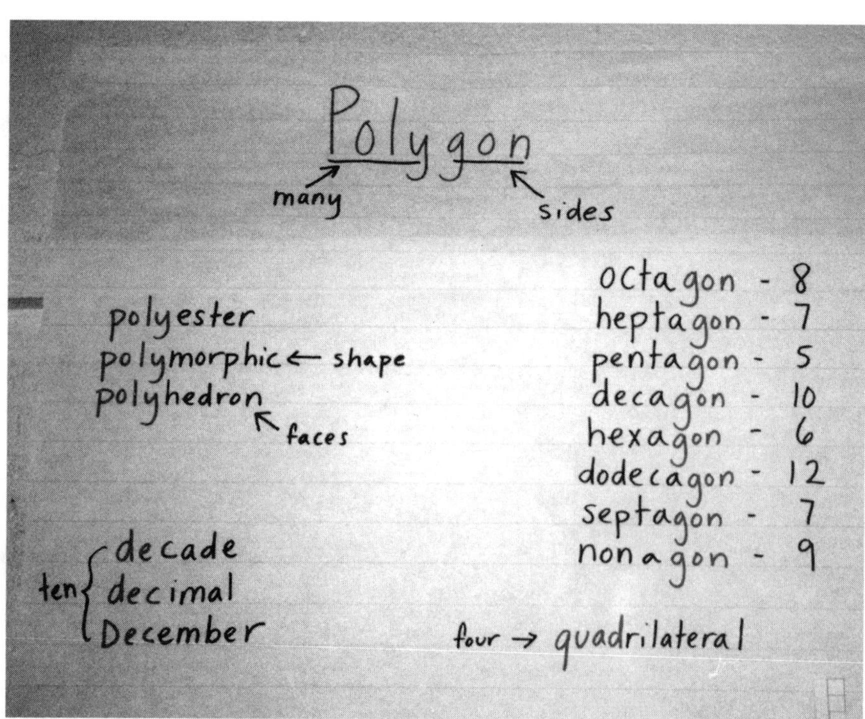

Phonics, Spelling, and Word Study

Selecting Goals Behaviors and Understandings to Notice, Teach, and Support

Adverbs

- Recognize and use adverbs that end in *e* (keep or drop the *e*: *truly, merely*), that end in *-ic* (*tragically, frantically*)

Suffixes

- Recognize and use suffixes that change verbs and nouns for different functions, such as adjectives and adverbs (*-er, -es, -r, -ing, -ily, -able, -ible, -ar, -less, -ness, -ous, -cious, -tious*)

Contractions

- Recognize and understand multiple contractions with *not* and *have* (*shouldn't've*)

Possessives

- Recognize and use possessives that add an apostrophe and an *s* to a singular noun (*dog/dog's, woman/woman's, girl/girl's, boy/boy's*), that *its* does not use an apostrophe, and that a plural possessive like *women* uses an apostrophe and an *s* (*students/children's; men/men's*)

Prefixes

- Recognize and use common prefixes (*re-, un-, im-, in-, il-, dis-, non-, mis, trans-, pre-, en-, em-, inter-, intra-, con-, com-, sub-, super-, mal-, ex-, per-, circum-, in-, ad-, ob-, sujb-, com-, dis-, ex-*) as well as prefixes that refer to numbers (*uni-, bi-, tri-, cent-, dec-, mon-, multi-, cot-, pent-, poly-, quad-, semi-*).
- Recognize and use assimilated prefixes that change form to match the root word: *in-* (*immigrate, illegal, irregular*), *ad-* (*address, approach, aggressive*), *ob-* (*obstruct, opportunity*), *sub-* (*subtract, suppose, surround*), *com-* (*commit, collide, corrode*), *dis-* (*distinguish, difference*), *ex-* (*expand, expose, eccentric, efficicient*)

Abbreviations

- Recognize and use abbreviation (state names; weights; *Sr., Jr., Ph.D.*)

Word-Solving Actions

- Use the context of the sentence, paragraph, or whole text to help determine the precise meaning of a word
- Connect words that are related to each other because they have the same base or root word (*direct, direction, directional*)
- Use the dictionary to discover word history
- Distinguish between multiple meanings of words when reading texts
- Recognize and use the different types of dictionaries: general, specialized (synonyms, abbreviations, theme or topic, foreign language, thesaurus, electronic)
- Understand the concept of *analogy* and its use in discovering relationships between and among words
- Use knowledge of Greek and Latin roots in deriving the meaning of words while reading texts
- Use knowledge of prefixes, root words, and suffixes to derive the meaning of words while reading texts

deci 10	cent 100	milli 1,000
decade	cent	• millennium
decimal	• centennial	• milliliter
decahedron	centigrade	millimeter
• decathlon	centimeter	million
• decasyllabic	• centiliter	millionth
• decennium	centipede	millionaire
December		• millionairess
		millipede
		millisecond

Guided Reading

Introduction to Guided Reading

The following level-by-level continuum contains detailed descriptions of ways readers are expected to think *within, beyond,* and *about* the texts they are processing. We have produced the A–Z continuum to assist teachers who are using a gradient of texts to teach guided reading lessons or other small-group lessons. It may also be helpful as you confer with individual students during independent reading.

Guided reading is a highly effective form of small-group instruction. Based on assessment, the teacher brings together a group of readers who are similar enough in their reading development that they can be taught together. They read independently at about the same level and can take on a new text selected by the teacher that is just a little more challenging. The teacher supports the reading in a way that enables students to read a more challenging text with effective processing, thus expanding their reading powers. The framework of a guided reading lesson is detailed in Figure I–3.

General Aspects of the Continuum

As you use the continuum, there are several important points to keep in mind.

1. ***The cognitive actions that readers employ while processing print are essentially the same across levels. Readers are simply applying them to successively more demanding levels of text.*** Beginning readers are sorting out the complex concepts related to using print (left-to-right directionality, word-by-word matching, the relationships between spoken and written language), so their processing is slower and their overt behaviors show us how they are working on print. They are reading texts with familiar topics and very simple, natural language, yet even these texts demand that they understand story lines, think about characters, and engage in more complex thinking such as making predictions.

For higher-level readers, most of the processing is unconscious. These readers automatically and effortlessly solve large numbers of words, tracking print across complex sentences that they process without explicit attention to the in-the-head actions that are happening. While reading, they focus on the meaning of the text and engage in complex thinking processes (for example, inferring what the writer is implying but not saying, critically examining the ideas in the text, or noticing aspects of the writer's craft). Yet at times, higher-level readers will need to closely

FIG. I–3. *Framework for Guided Reading*

STRUCTURE OF A GUIDED READING LESSON	
Element	**Potential Teaching Moves to Support Reading with Comprehension and Fluency**
Introduction to the Text	• Activate and/or provide needed background knowledge. • Invite students to share thinking. • Enable students to hear and sometimes say new language structures. • Have students say and sometimes locate specific words in the text. • Help students make connections to present knowledge of texts, content, and experiences. • Reveal the structure of the text. • Use new vocabulary words in conversation to reveal meaning. • Prompt students to make predictions based on the information revealed so far. • Draw attention to the writer's craft to support analysis. • Draw attention to accuracy or authenticity of the text—writer's credentials, references, or presentation of evidence as appropriate. • Draw attention to illustrations—pictures, charts, graphs, maps, cutaways—and the information they present.
Reading the Text	• Demonstrate, prompt for, or reinforce the effective use of systems of strategic actions (including word solving, searching for and using information, maintaining fluency, detecting and correcting errors, summarizing, and adjusting reading). • Prompt for fluency and phrasing.
Discussing the Meaning	• Gather evidence of comprehension by observing what students say about the text. • Invite students to pose questions and clarify their understanding. • Help students learn to discuss the meaning of the text together. • Extend students' expression of understandings through questioning, summarizing, restating, and adding to their comments.
Teaching for Processing Strategies	• Revisit the text to demonstrate or reinforce any aspect of reading, including all systems of strategic actions: • Solving words • Predicting • Monitoring and checking • Making connections • Searching for and using information • Inferring • Remembering information—(summarizing) • Synthesizing • Maintaining fluency • Analyzing • Adjusting reading—(purpose and genre) • Critiquing • Provide explicit demonstrations of strategic actions using any part of the text that has just been read.
Word Work (optional)	• Teach any aspect of word analysis—letter-sound relationships, using analogy, or breaking words apart. • Have students manipulate words using magnetic letters or use white boards or pencil and paper to make or take apart words.
Extending the Meaning (optional)	• Use writing, drawing, or extended talk to explore any aspect of understanding the text.

examine a word to solve it or reread it to tease out the meaning of especially complex sentence structures.

All readers are simultaneously employing a wide range of systems of strategic actions while processing print. These include:

- ***Solving the words using a flexible range of strategies.*** Early readers are just beginning to acquire ways of looking at words, and they work with a few signposts and word features (simple letter-sound relationships and word parts). High-level readers employ a broad and flexible range of word-solving strategies that are largely unconscious, freeing attention for deep thinking.

- ***Self-monitoring their reading for accuracy and understanding and self-correcting when necessary.*** Beginning readers will overtly display evidence of monitoring and self-correcting while higher-level readers keep this evidence "underground"; but readers are always monitoring, or checking on themselves as they read.
- ***Searching for and using information.*** Beginning readers will overtly search for information in the letters and words, the pictures, or the sentence structure; they also use their own background knowledge. Proficient readers pick up information quickly and "in the head" so it usually cannot be observed.
- ***Remembering information in summary form.*** Summary implies the selection and reorganization of important information. Readers constantly summarize information as they read a text, thus forming prior knowledge with which to understand the rest of the text; they also remember this summary information long after reading.
- ***Sustaining fluent, phrased reading.*** At early levels (A, B, C), readers will be working to match one spoken word to one written word and will usually be pointing crisply at each word to assist the eye and voice in this process; however, even at level C, when dialogue is first presented, they will begin to make their reading sound like talking. As the finger is withdrawn and the eyes take over the process at subsequent levels, children will read increasingly complex texts with appropriate rate, word stress, phrasing, and pausing in a smoothly operating system. In and of itself, fluency is not a stage or level of reading. Readers apply strategies in an integrated way to achieve fluent reading at every level after the early behaviors are in place. Fluency is an important aspect of effective reading at all levels after C.
- ***Adjusting reading in order to process a variety of texts.*** At all levels, readers may slow down to problem solve words or complex language and resume a normal pace, although at higher levels this process is mostly unobservable. Readers make adjustments as they search for information; they may reread, search graphics or illustrations, go back to specific references in the text, or use specific readers' tools. At all levels, readers also adjust expectations and ways of reading according to purpose, genre, and previous reading experiences. At early levels, readers have only beginning experiences to draw on, but at more advanced levels, they have rich resources in terms of the knowledge of genre (see Fountas and Pinnell 2006).
- ***Making predictions.*** At all levels, readers constantly make and confirm or disconfirm predictions. Usually, these predictions are implicit rather than

voiced, and they add not only to understanding but also to enjoyment of a text. All readers predict based on the information in the text and their own background knowledge, with more advanced readers bringing a rich foundation of knowledge, including how many varieties of texts work.

- ***Synthesizing new information.*** At all levels, readers gain new information from the texts they read, although beginning readers are processing texts on very familiar topics. As they move through successive levels of text, readers encounter much new information, which they incorporate into their own background knowledge.

- ***Making connections.*** At all levels, readers use their prior knowledge as well as their personal experiences and knowledge of other texts to interpret a text. As they expand knowledge through reading experience, they have more information to help them understand every text. At the most advanced levels, readers are required to understand mature and complex ideas and themes that are in most cases beyond their personal experience; yet they can empathize with the human condition, drawing from previous reading.

- ***Reading "between the lines" to infer what is not explicitly stated in the text.*** To some degree, all texts require inference. At very simple levels, readers may infer characters' feelings (surprised, happy, sad) or traits (lazy, greedy). But at high levels, readers need to infer constantly to understand both fiction and nonfiction texts.

- ***Thinking analytically about a text to notice how it is constructed or how the writer has crafted language.*** Thinking analytically about a text means reflecting on it, holding it up for examination, and drawing some conclusions about it. Readers at early levels may comment that the text was funny or exciting; they do not, however, engage in a great deal of analysis, which could be artificial and detract from enjoying the text. More advanced readers will notice more about how the writer (and illustrator when appropriate) has organized the text and crafted the language and this kind of analysis often enhances enjoyment.

- ***Thinking critically about a text.*** Thinking critically about a text involves complex ways of evaluating it. Beginning readers may simply say what they like or dislike about a text, sometimes being specific about why; but increasingly advanced readers engage in higher-level thinking as they evaluate the quality or authenticity of a text.

2. ***Readers are always meeting greater demands at every level because the texts are increasingly challenging.*** The categories for these demands may be similar, but the specific challenges are constantly increasing. For example, at many of the lower levels of text, readers are challenged to use phonogram patterns (or

consonant clusters and vowel patterns) to solve one-syllable words. At upper levels, they are challenged to use these same patterns in multisyllable words. In addition, at every level after E readers must use word endings as they take apart words. Word endings change words and add meaning. At lower levels, readers are attending to endings such as *-s*, *-ed*, and *–ing*, but as words become increasingly complex at successive levels, they will encounter endings such as *-ment*, *-ent*, *-ant*, *-ible*, and *-able*.

At all levels, readers must identify characters and follow plots; but at lower levels, characters are one-dimensional and plots are a simple series of events. Across the levels, however, readers encounter multiple characters that are highly complex and change over time. Plots have more episodes; subplots are full of complexity.

3. *Readers' knowledge of genres expands over time but also grows in depth within genres.* For some texts at very low levels, it is difficult to determine genre. For example, a simple repetitive text may focus on a single topic, such as fruit, with a child presenting an example on each page. The pages could be in just about any order, except that there is often some kind of conclusion at the end. Such a text is organized in a structure characteristic of nonfiction, which helps beginning readers understand information presented in categories, but it is technically fiction because the narrator is not real. At this level, however, it is not important for children to read pure genre categories, but simply to experience and learn about a variety of ways to organize texts.

Moving across the levels of the gradient, however, examples of genres become more precise and varied. At early levels, children read examples of fiction (usually realistic fiction, traditional literature, and simple fantasy) and simple informational texts on single topics. Across the levels, nonfiction texts become more and more complex, offering information on a variety of topics, as well as a range of underlying structures for presentation (description; comparison and contrast; cause and effect; temporal sequence; and problem and solution). These underlying structures appear at all levels after the very beginning ones, but they are combined in increasingly complex ways.

4. *At each level, the content load of texts becomes heavier, requiring an increased amount of background knowledge.* Content knowledge is a key factor in understanding texts; it includes vocabulary and concepts. Beginning texts are necessarily structured to take advantage of familiar content that most young children know; yet, even some very simple texts may require knowledge of some labels (for example, *zoo animals*) that are unfamiliar to the children. Effective reading at successively more difficult levels will depend not only on study in the content areas but on wide reading of texts that expand the individual's vocabulary and content knowledge.

5. *At each level, the themes and ideas are more mature, requiring readers to consider perspectives and understand cultures beyond their own.* Children can connect simple themes and ideas to their own lives, but even at beginning levels they find that their experiences are stretched by realistic stories, simple fantasy, and traditional tales. At levels of increasing complexity, readers are challenged to understand and empathize with characters (and the subjects of biography) who lived in past times or in distant places and who have very different perspectives from the readers' own. At higher levels, fantasy requires that readers understand completely imaginary worlds. As they meet greater demands across the levels, they must depend on previous reading, as well as on discussions of the themes and ideas.

6. *The specific descriptions of thinking within, beyond, and about text do not change dramatically from level to level.* As you look at the continuum of text features along the gradient A to Z, you will see only small changes level to level. The gradient represents a gradual increase in the demands of texts on readers. Similarly, the expectations for readers' thinking change gradually over time as they develop from kindergarten through grade eight. If you look at the demands across two or three levels you will notice only a few changes in expectations. But if you contrast levels like the following, you will find some very clear differences.

- Level A with Level D
- Level E with Level H
- Level I with Level N
- Level O with Level R
- Level S with Level U
- Level V with Level Z

The continuum represents progress over time, and if you examine the expectations in the ranges suggested, you get a picture of the remarkable growth our students make over kindergarten through grade eight.

Using the Continuum

The guided reading continuum is organized by level, A to Z. Each level has several sections.

Section 1: Characteristics of Readers

The first section provides a brief description of what you may find to be generally true of readers at the particular level. For a much more detailed description, see our *Leveled Books, K–8: Matching Texts to Readers for Effective Teaching* (2005). Remember that all readers are individuals and that individuals vary widely. It is impossible to create a description that is true of all readers for whom a level is appropriate for independent reading or instruction. In fact, it is inappropriate to refer to any individual as "a level ___ reader"! We level books, not readers. But it is helpful to keep in mind the general expectations of readers at a level so that books may be well selected and appropriate support may be given to individuals and groups.

Section 2: Selecting Texts

This section provides detailed descriptions of texts characteristic of each level. It is organized into ten categories:

1. *Genre/Form.* *Genre* is the type of text and refers to a system by which fiction and nonfiction texts are classified. *Form* is the format in which a genre may be presented. Forms and genres have characteristic features.

2. *Text Structure.* *Structure* is the way the text is organized and presented. The structure of most fiction and biographical texts is *narrative,* arranged primarily in chronological sequence. Factual texts are organized categorically or topically and may have sections with headings. Writers of factual texts use several underlying structural patterns to provide information to readers. The most important are *description; chronological sequence; comparison and contrast; cause and effect;* and *problem and solution.* The presence of these structures, especially in combination, can increase the challenge for readers.

3. *Content.* *Content* refers to the subject matter of the text—the concepts that are important to understand. In fiction, content may be related to the setting or to the kinds of problems characters have. In factual texts, content refers to the topic of focus. Content is considered in relation to the prior experience of readers.

4. *Themes and Ideas.* These are the big ideas that are communicated by the writer. Ideas may be concrete and accessible or complex and abstract. A text may have multiple themes or a main theme and several supporting themes.

5. *Language and Literary Features.* Written language is qualitatively different from spoken language. Fiction writers use dialogue, figurative language, and other kinds of literary structures such as character, setting, and plot. Factual writers use description and technical language. In hybrid texts you may find a wide range of literary language.

6. *Sentence Complexity.* Meaning is mapped onto the syntax of language. Texts with simpler, more natural sentences are easier to process. Sentences with embedded and conjoined clauses make a text more difficult.

7. *Vocabulary.* *Vocabulary* refers to words and their meanings. The more words in a text the reader understands, the easier the text will be. The individual's *reading and writing vocabularies* refer to words that he or she understands and can also read or write.

8. *Words.* This category refers to recognizing and solving the printed words in the text. The challenge in a text partly depends on the number and the difficulty of the words that the reader must solve by recognizing them or decoding them. Having a great many of the same high-frequency words makes a text more accessible to readers.

9. *Illustrations.* Drawings, paintings, or photographs accompany the text and add meaning and enjoyment. In factual texts, illustrations also include graphics that provide a great deal of information that readers must integrate with the text. Illustrations are an integral part of a high-quality text. Increasingly, fiction texts are including a range of graphics.

10. *Book and Print Features.* *Book and print features* are the physical aspects of the text—what readers cope with in terms of length, size, and layout. Book and print features also include tools like the table of contents, glossary, pronunciation guides, indexes, and sidebars.

Studying the text characteristics of books at a given level will provide a good inventory of the challenges readers will meet across that level. Remember that there are a great variety of texts within each level, and that these characteristics apply to what is *generally true* for texts at the level. For the individual text, some factors may be more important than others in making demands on the readers. Examining these text factors relative to the books you select for guided reading will help in planning introductions that help readers meet the demands of more challenging texts and process them effectively.

Section 3: Demands of the Text—Ways of Thinking

The heart of the guided reading continuum is a description of the expectations for thinking on the part of readers at the level. The descriptions are organized into three larger categories and twelve subcategories, as shown in Figure I–4 and inside the back cover of this book.

As teachers work with readers at each level, they examine the specific descriptions within categories. This analysis will be helpful with

- ***Planning introductions to texts.*** Teachers examine the categories to determine what might be challenging for readers and frame the introduction to help students engage in particular thinking processes.
- ***Guiding interactions with individual readers.*** Teachers observe reading behaviors and converse with students to determine what they are noticing and

FIG. I–4 Systems of Strategic Actions

WAYS OF THINKING	SYSTEMS OF STRATEGIC ACTIONS FOR PROCESSING WRITTEN TEXTS	
Thinking Within the Text	Solving Words	Using a range of strategies to take words apart and understand what words mean while reading continuous text.
	Monitoring and Correcting	Checking on whether reading sounds right, looks right, and makes sense.
	Searching for and Using Information	Searching for and using all kinds of information in a text.
	Summarizing	Putting together important information while reading and disregarding irrelevant information.
	Maintaining Fluency	Integrating sources of information in a smoothly operating process that results in expressive, phrased reading.
	Adjusting	Reading in different ways as appropriate to purpose for reading and type of text.
Thinking Beyond the Text	Predicting	Thinking about what will follow while reading continuous text.
	Making Connections • personal • world • text	Searching for and using connections to knowledge that readers have gained through their personal experiences, learning about the world, and reading other texts.
	Inferring	Going beyond the literal meaning of a text to think about what is not there but is implied by the writer.
	Synthesizing	Putting together information from the text and from the reader's own background knowledge in order to create new understandings.
Thinking About the Text	Analyzing	Examining elements of a text to know more about how it is constructed.
	Critiquing	Evaluating a text based on the reader's personal, world, or text knowledge.

thinking about. They draw students' attention to what they need to know through demonstrating, prompting, or reinforcing actions.

- ***Discussing the meaning of a text after reading the whole text or a part of it.*** Teachers invite readers to comment on various aspects of the text and to build on one another's points. They refer to the continuum while thinking about the evidence of understanding students are demonstrating through conversation. They guide the discussion when appropriate to help students engage in new ways of thinking.

- ***Making specific teaching points after reading.*** Based on observation of how the readers process the text, select and demonstrate effective ways of operating on a text in a way that will help readers learn how to do something as readers that they can apply to other texts.

- ***Planning ways to extend the understanding of the text.*** Plan writing, drawing, or deeper discussion that will support students in engaging in deeper ways of thinking about texts. (See the Writing About Reading continuum for examples.)

Section 4: Planning Word Work for Guided Reading

In thinking-within-the-text at each level, a separate section provides suggestions for phonics and word work. Guided reading is intended to be used as one component of an integrated literacy framework that includes specific lessons on phonics, spelling, and word study. The details of that curriculum—for lessons and independent activities—are presented in the Phonics, Spelling, and Word Study continuum (see pages 204–219) and expanded in *Phonics Lessons* (Pinnell and Fountas 2003) and *Word Study Lessons,* K–3 (Fountas and Pinnell 2004). These lessons are systematic, sequenced, and multilevel in the activities used to help children apply principles, usually as whole-class activities. The goals embedded in guided reading apply the principles during text reading where phonics and word study instruction is most effective.

As they read texts, individuals are always applying phonics principles, and across the gradient they do so on more and more complex words. Word solving includes not only decoding but deriving the meaning of words, as indicated in the Solving Words category in the second column of Figure I–4, Section 3.

In addition, an important component of a guided reading lesson is some brief but focused attention to letters, words, and how they work. This quick letter or word work should address the students' needs in visual processing. The goal is to build their fluency and flexibility in taking words apart. In this section, a list of suggestions helps teachers select word study activities to tailor instruction on words to the specific demands of the level of text. Teachers can make principles related to word solving visible to students through the following types of activities:

- Having students match or sort picture cards to illustrate letter-sound relationships.
- Having students match or sort letters.
- Demonstrating the principle using a white board (or chalkboard) that all students can see. Students read the examples from the white board. The teacher changes, takes away, or adds word parts to build students' flexibility and speed.
- Demonstrating the principle using magnetic letters on a vertical board. Magnetic letters are particularly helpful when demonstrating how to take words apart or change words to make new ones.
- Having students make words, change words, and take apart words using magnetic letters.
- Having students use individual small white boards (or chalkboards) to write and change words to demonstrate the principles. (Each student can have a small eraser or an old sock on one hand so that changes can be made quickly.)

- Giving students individual word cards for instant word recognition.
- Asking students to sort word cards into categories to illustrate a principle.
- Having students match word cards to illustrate a principle.
- Making word webs to illustrate the connections and relationships between words.

This continuum is intended to be a teaching tool for use during guided reading. Teachers can keep the description of expectations for thinking (within, beyond, and about the text) available when they are planning, teaching, and reflecting on guided reading lessons at that level. The continuum helps them realize the scope of strategies that students must use to independently read at the level; each one of the behaviors can be incorporated into the introduction, prompting during reading, and teaching points after reading. The word work section of the continuum can be used to preplan one or two minutes of word work at the end of the lesson. Finally, the Guided Reading continuum will be helpful to focus the conversation between colleagues for professional development.

Guided Reading

Readers at **Level A:**

At Level A, readers are just beginning to learn how print works and to construct the *alphabetic principle* (that there are relationships between sounds and letters). They are learning to look (aided by the finger) left to right across words and lines of print. They are learning to use information from pictures and to use simple language structures to help them learn about print. They differentiate print from pictures and begin to notice the distinctive features of letters, attaching names to them. They are learning to read texts with one line of print with simple words and on familiar topics. They are learning how to match one spoken word with one word in print. As they read, they begin to learn some easy, high-frequency words, to notice and use visual signposts of some words, and to notice mismatches. They use what they know (for example, a sound and related letter) to begin to self-monitor reading. Reading and rereading these very simple texts will help them gain gradual control of ways to work with print.

Selecting Texts **Characteristics of Texts at This Level**

Genre/Forms

Genre

- Some simple factual texts
- Simple animal fantasy
- Realistic fiction

Forms

- Picture books

Text Structure

Fiction

- Very simple narratives with stories carried by pictures

Nonfiction

- Focused on a single idea or one simple topic
- Underlying text structure (description)
- Present one simple category of information
- Some texts with sequential information

Content

- Familiar, easy content (family, play, pets, school)
- All concepts supported by picture information

Themes and Ideas

- Very familiar themes and ideas

Language and Literary Features

- Mostly nameless, flat characters
- Repeating language patterns (simple three to six words on each page)
- Texts with familiar settings close to children's experience
- A few simple elements of fantasy (for example, talking animals)

Sentence Complexity

- Short, predictable sentences that are close to oral language
- Simple sentences (no embedded phrases or clauses)
- Subject preceding verb in most sentences
- Simple sentences (subject and predicate)

Vocabulary

- Almost all vocabulary familiar to children and likely to be used in their oral language
- Word meanings illustrated by pictures

Words

- Mostly one-syllable words with very easy and predictable letter-sound relationships
- Nouns, verbs, pronouns
- Some simple plurals
- Repeated use of a few easy high-frequency words
- Some words with *-s* and *-ing*
- Many words with easy, predictable letter-sound relationships (decodable)
- Words with easy spelling patterns

Illustrations

General

- Illustrations that match print very closely
- Clear Illustrations that fully support meaning
- Illustrations that support each page of text
- Very simple illustrations with no distracting detail
- Consistent layout of illustrations and print

Book and Print Features

Length

- One line of text on each page
- Very short, usually eight pages of print and illustrations

Print and Layout

- Ample space between words and lines
- Print in large plain font
- Print clearly separated from pictures
- Consistent placement of print (layout)

Punctuation

- Period only punctuation in most texts

We like to slide.

10

Guided Reading

Selecting Goals

Behaviors and Understandings to Notice, Teach, and Support

Thinking *within* the Text

Solving Words
- Recognize most words quickly with the support of meaning and language structure
- Say a word and predict its first letter before locating it
- Say a word slowly to hear and identify the first sound and connect to a letter
- Recognize a few easy high-frequency words
- Locate familiar, easy high-frequency words by noticing anything about the word
- Locate easy high-frequency words in a text
- Slow down speech to assist in word-by-word matching

Monitoring and Correcting
- Reread the sentence to problem solve, self-correct, or confirm
- Reread to search for and use information
- Use prior knowledge to self-monitor and self-correct
- Self-monitor and self-correct using language structure
- Use word-by-word matching to self-monitor and self-correct
- Show evidence of close attention to print
- Use known words to self-monitor and self-correct

Searching for and Using Information
- Read left to right across a line of print
- Match one spoken work with one printed word
- Search for and use information in the print
- Use oral language in combination with pointing, matching voice with words on the page (indicated by crisp pointing)
- Search for and use information in pictures
- Reread to search for and use information
- Use the language structure to learn about the print

Summarizing
- Remember what the story is about during reading
- Remember information to help in understanding the end of a story
- Remember important information

Maintaining Fluency
- Point crisply and read at a steady rate slow enough to match but without long pauses
- Notice and use end punctuation and reflect it in voice

Adjusting
- Slow down to problem solve words and resume reading with momentum

Thinking *beyond* the Text

Predicting
- Use knowledge of language structure to anticipate the text
- Make predictions based on information in the pictures
- Predict the ending of a story based on reading the beginning and middle
- Make predictions based on personal experiences and knowledge

Making Connections
- Talk about own experiences in relation to the text
- Make connections between texts on the same topic or with the same content
- Identify recurring characters when applicable

Synthesizing
- Talk about what the reader already knows relative to information in the text
- Identify new information in text or pictures

Inferring
- Talk about characters' feelings
- Talk about the pictures, revealing interpretation of a problem or of characters' feelings

Thinking *about* the Text

Analyzing
- Understand how the ideas in a book are related to each other
- Understand how the ideas in a text are related to the title

Critiquing
- Share opinions about a text
- Share opinions about illustrations

Planning for Word Work during Guided Reading

One- to three-minute demonstrations and active student engagement using a chart or easel, white board, magnet letters, or pencil and paper can develop fluency and flexibility in visual processing. Plan for explicit work in specific visual processing areas that need support.

Examples:
- Recognize a few easy high-frequency words (for example, *the, a, I, and, is, can, in, it*) quickly
- Recognize a few easy CVC words (*can, get*) quickly
- Make a few easy CVC words (*cat, pin, sat, hot, can*)
- Make a few easy high-frequency words (*it, is, in, we, me, to, the*)
- Write a few easy CVC words (*can, I, run*)
- Write a few easy high-frequency words (*a, an, the, me, to*)
- Match or sort pictures by initial sounds
- Match or sort pictures by final sounds
- Match or sort letters by a variety of features (uppercase or lowercase; tall or short; with and without sticks, circles, tails, dots, tunnels)
- Match lowercase letters with speed
- Clap the syllables in one- and two-syllable words (from pictures)
- Search for and locate letters by name quickly
- Read the Alphabet Linking Chart by letter names, pictures and words, and in different ways (all vowels, all consonants, letters only, backward order, every other letter)

Guided Reading

Readers at **Level B:**

At Level B, readers are learning how print works, particularly developing the concepts of left-to-right directionality across words and across lines of print. They are firming up word-by-word matching while reading texts with two or more lines of print. Readers may recognize repeating language patterns in texts that have very simple stories and focus on a single idea, as well as learn more about the distinctive features of letters and the connections between sounds and letters. It is very important that they begin to self-monitor their reading and attempt to self-correct as they notice the mismatches and begin to check one source of information against another. They are beginning to notice and use visual signposts and are expanding their core of sample high-frequency words.

Selecting Texts — Characteristics of Texts at This Level

Genre/Forms

Genre

- Some simple factual texts
- Simple animal fantasy
- Realistic fiction

Forms

- Picture books

Text Structure

Fiction

- Simple narratives with stories carried by pictures

Nonfiction

- Focused on a single idea or one simple topic
- Underlying text structure (description)
- Present one simple category of information
- Some texts with sequential information

Content

- Familiar, easy content (family, play, pets, school)
- All concepts supported by picture information

Themes and Ideas

- Very familiar themes and ideas

Language and Literary Features

- Mostly nameless, flat characters
- Repeating language patterns (simple three to seven words on each page)
- Texts with familiar settings close to children's experience
- A few simple elements of fantasy (for example, talking animals)

Sentence Complexity

- Short, predictable sentences that are close to oral language
- Mostly simple sentences (no embedded phrases or clauses)
- Subject preceding verb in most sentences
- Simple sentences (subject and predicate)

Vocabulary

- Almost all vocabulary familiar to children and likely to be used in their oral language
- Word meanings illustrated by pictures

I like to play
with the ball.

6

Guided Reading

Words

- Mostly one-syllable words with very easy and predictable letter-sound relationships
- Nouns, verbs, pronouns, adjectives, prepositions
- Some simple plurals
- Repeated use of a few easy high-frequency words
- Some words with *-s* and *-ing*
- Many words with easy, predictable letter-sound relationships (decodable)
- Words with easy spelling patterns

Illustrations

General

- Illustrations that match print very closely
- Clear Illustrations that fully support meaning
- Illustrations that support each page of text
- Very simple illustrations with little distracting detail
- Consistent layout of illustrations and print

Book and Print Features

Length

- Very short, usually eight pages of print and illustrations
- Two lines of text on each page

Print and Layout

- Ample space between words and lines
- Print in large plain font
- Sentences turn over one or more lines
- Print clearly separated from pictures
- Consistent placement of print (layout)
- Line breaks match ends of phrases and sentences

Punctuation

- Period only punctuation in most texts

My little dog likes
to read with me.
14
15

Guided Reading

Selecting Goals

Behaviors and Understandings to Notice, Teach, and Support

Thinking *within* the Text

Solving Words

- Recognize most words quickly with the support of meaning and language studies
- Use the first letter of a word in connection with meaning or language syntax to solve it
- Locate unknown words by identifying the first letter
- Say a word slowly to hear and identify the first sound and connect to a letter
- Recognize a few easy high-frequency words
- Locate high-frequency words in a text
- Use knowledge of syllables to help in word-by-word matching
- Slow down speech to assist in word-by-word matching

Monitoring and Correcting

- Reread the sentence to problem solve, self-correct, or confirm
- Reread to search for and use information
- Use first letters of words (and related sounds) to monitor and self-correct
- Use prior knowledge to monitor and self-correct
- Self-monitor and self-correct using language structure
- Begin to cross-check one kind of information against another to monitor and self-correct reading (for example, meaning with visual information)
- Self-monitor and self-correct using meaning in text and pictures
- Use word-by-word matching to self-monitor and self-correct
- Show evidence of close attention to print
- Use known words to self-monitor and self-correct

Searching for and Using Information

- Read left to right across a line of print
- Return to the left to read the next line of print
- Match one spoken word with one printed word
- Search for and use information in print (letters and sounds, known words)
- Ask questions to clarify meaning or get information
- Search for and use information in pictures
- Reread to search for and use information
- Remember and use language patterns to help in reading a text

Summarizing

- Remember what the story is about during reading
- Remember details while reading
- Remember information to help in understanding the end of a story
- Discuss the text after reading, remembering important information or details of a story

Maintaining Fluency

- Point and read at a steady rate slow enough to match but without long pauses
- Notice and use ending punctuation and reflect it in the voice

Adjusting

- Slow down to problem solve words and resume reading with momentum

Planning for Word Work during Guided Reading

One- to three-minute demonstrations and active student engagement using a chart or easel, white board, magnet letters, or pencil and paper can develop fluency and flexibility in visual processing. Plan for explicit work in specific visual processing areas that need support.

Examples:

- Recognize a few easy high-frequency words (for example, *the, and, my, like, see, is, can, in, it*) quickly
- Recognize and make a few CVC words (*hit, cut, man, dog, pet*)
- Write a few CVC words (*run, can, pet*)
- Write a few easy high-freqeuncy words (for example, *can, like, the, me, we, is*)
- Match or sort pictures by initial sounds (*bear, bike, bone*)
- Match or sort pictures by ending sounds (*horse, glass, dress*)
- Match or sort letters by a variety of features quickly (uppercase or lowercase; tall or short; with and without sticks, circles, tails, dots, tunnels)
- Match or sort pictures with rhyming sounds (*pen, ten, hen*)
- Match or sort upper- and lowercase letters quickly (*Aa, Dd*)
- Clap the syllables in words with one, two, or three parts
- Recognize letters by name and locate them quickly in words
- Read Alphabet Linking Chart in different ways (sing, read consonants, read letter names, read pictures, backward order, every other letter)

Guided Reading

Selecting Goals Behaviors and Understandings to Notice, Teach, and Support

Thinking *beyond* the Text

Predicting
- Use knowledge of language structure to anticipate the text
- Make predictions using language structure
- Make predictions based on the information in pictures
- Predict the ending of a story based on reading the beginning and middle
- Make predictions based on personal experiences and knowledge

Making Connections
- Discuss personal experiences in relation to the text
- Make connections between texts on the same topic or with the same content
- Identify recurring characters when applicable

Synthesizing
- Identify what the reader already knows relative to information in the text, prior to reading
- Identify new information in text or pictures

Inferring
- Understand characters' feelings and reveal through talk or drawing
- Understand the pictures, reveal interpretation of a problem or of characters' feelings

Thinking *about* the Text

Analyzing
- Notice and appreciate humor (and show by verbal or nonverbal means)
- Realize stories have a beginning and an end
- Understand how the ideas in a book are related to each other
- Understand how the ideas in a text are related to the title

Critiquing
- Share opinions about books
- Share opinions about illustrations

Guided Reading

Readers at **Level C:**

At Level C, readers encounter simple stories and familiar topics in texts that have two to six lines of print on each page. They smoothly and automatically move left to right across words and across lines of print, sweeping back to the left margin for each new line and reading print on both left and right pages. Pointing is smooth, allowing for some phrasing, and the eyes are taking over the process of matching the spoken word to the printed word. Readers are moving away from needing to point and are showing phrased reading. Readers are noticing quotation marks and reflecting dialogue with the voice. They are developing a larger core of high-frequency words that they recognize quickly and easily. At this level, readers are consistently monitoring their reading and cross-checking one source of information against another. Overt self-correction reveals readers' growing control of the ability to process print.

Selecting Texts **Characteristics of Texts at This Level**

Genre/Forms

Genre

- Some simple factual texts
- Simple animal fantasy
- Realistic fiction

Forms

- Picture books

Text Structure

Fiction

- Simple narratives with several episodes (usually similar or repetitive)

Nonfiction

- Focused on a single idea or one simple topic
- Underlying text structure (description)
- Present one simple category of information
- Some texts with sequential information

Content

- Familiar, easy content (family, play, pets, school)
- All concepts supported by pictures

Themes and Ideas

- Familiar themes and ideas

Language and Literary Features

- Amusing one-dimensional characters
- Repeating natural language patterns
- Texts with familiar settings close to children's experience
- Simple dialogue (assigned by *said* in most texts)
- A few simple elements of fantasy (for example, talking animals)

Sentence Complexity

- Simple, predictable sentence structure but patterns vary
- Many sentences with prepositional phrases and adjectives
- Subject preceding verb in most sentences
- Simple sentences (subject and predicate)

Vocabulary

- Almost all vocabulary familiar to children and likely to be used in their oral language
- Word meanings illustrated by pictures
- Some variation in words used to assign dialogue (mostly *said*)

Words

- Mostly one- or two-syllable words
- Nouns, verbs, pronouns, adjectives, adverbs, prepositions
- Simple plurals
- Some simple contractions and possessives (words with apostrophes)
- Greater range of easy high-frequency words
- Some words with *-s* and *-ing*
- Many words with easy, predictable letter-sound relationships (decodable)
- Some words used in different language structures (*said Mom; Mom said*)
- Words with easy spelling patterns

Illustrations

General

- Illustrations that match print very closely
- More meaning carried in the text and less with picture support
- Illustrations on every page or every other page
- Very simple illustrations with little distracting detail
- Consistent layout of illustrations and print

Book and Print Features

Length

- Very short, usually eight pages of print
- One to five lines of text on each page

Print and Layout

- Ample space between words and lines
- Print in large plain font
- Some words in bold or larger font for emphasis
- Sentences turn over one line
- Print clearly separated from pictures
- Consistent placement of print (layout)
- Line breaks match ends of phrases and sentences

Punctuation

- Ellipses in some texts to create expectation
- Periods, commas, quotation marks, exclamation points, and question marks in most texts

Socks was sleeping
on my chair.
I said,
"Wake up, Socks!"

4

5

Guided Reading

Selecting Goals Behaviors and Understandings to Notice, Teach, and Support

Thinking *within* the Text

Solving Words
- Recognize easy high-fequency words and simple regular words easily with support of meaning and language structures
- Locate the first and last letters of words in continuous text
- Notice the beginning letter of a word, connect to a sound, and say the first sound of a word
- Use letter-sound information in coordination with meaning and language structure to solve words
- Say words slowly to identify first sound, connect to letter, and locate the word in a text
- Recognize ten or more high-frequency words within continuous text
- Make connections between words by letters, sounds, or spelling patterns
- Use known words to make connections and solve words

Monitoring and Correcting
- Reread the sentence to problem solve, self-correct, or confirm
- Reread to search for and use information
- Self-monitor and self-correct reading using initial letters and connections to sounds
- Self-monitor and self-correct using language structure
- Cross-check one kind of information against another to monitor and self-correct reading (for example, meaning with visual information)
- Self-monitor and self-correct using meaning in text and pictures
- Use known words to self-monitor and self-correct

Searching for and Using Information
- Read left to right across a line of print
- Return to the left to read the next line of print
- Search for and use information in print (letters, sounds, known words)
- Ask questions to clarify meaning or get information
- Search for and use information in pictures
- Process texts with simple dialogue, all assigned to speakers
- Reread to search for and use information
- Remember and use language patterns to help in reading a text

Summarizing
- Remember information to help in understanding the end of a story
- Remember and use details when discussing a story after reading
- Understand and identify a simple sequence of events in a story

Maintaining Fluency
- Reflect language syntax by putting words together in phrases
- Notice and use ending punctuation and reflect it in the voice
- Notice and use quotation marks and reflect dialogue with the voice
- Demonstrate appropriate stress on words in a sentence

Adjusting
- Slow down to problem solve words and resume reading with momentum

Thinking *beyond* the Text

Predicting
- Use knowledge of language structure to anticipate the text
- Make predictions using information from pictures
- Predict the ending of a story based on reading the beginning and middle
- Make predictions based on personal experiences and knowledge
- Make predictions based on information gained through reading

Making Connections
- Make and discuss connections between texts and reader's personal experiences
- Make connections between texts that are alike in some way (topic, ending, characters)
- Identify recurring characters when applicable

Synthesizing
- Identify what the reader already knows relative to information in the text
- Identify new information in text or pictures
- Remember new information for discussion
- Talk about what the reader already knows about a topic or character prior to reading
- Show evidence in the text of new ideas or information

Inferring
- Talk about characters' feelings and motives
- Show evidence in the print or pictures to support inference

Thinking *about* the Text

Analyzing
- Notice and point out connections between text and pictures
- Realize stories have a beginning and an end
- Understand how the ideas in a text are related to the title

Critiquing
- Share opinions about the text as a whole (beginning, characters, ending)
- Share opinions about illustrations

Planning for Word Work during Guided Reading

One- to three-minute demonstrations and active student engagement using a chart or easel, white board, magnet letters, or pencil and paper can develop fluency and flexibility in visual processing. Plan for explicit work in specific visual processing areas that need support.

Examples:
- Recognize a few easy high-frequency words (e.g., *the, and, like, here, look, see, is, can, in, it*)
- Make several CVC words (*cat, but, can, hot, get*)
- Recognize several CVC words (for example, *get, sun, man, not*)
- Write/make several easy high-frequency words
- Sort letters quickly by a variety of features (uppercase or lowercase; tall or short; with and without sticks, circles, tails, dots, tunnels)
- Match/sort words with rhymes (using pictures)
- Match pictures with letters using beginning sounds
- Say and clap syllables in one-, two-, and three-syllable words (from pictures)
- Locate words rapidly using first letter and related sounds
- Say words slowly and write letters related to sounds
- Read the Alphabet Linking Chart in a variety of ways (for example, all consonants, all vowels, every other letter)

Guided Reading

Readers at **Level D:**

At Level D, readers follow simple stories of fiction and fantasy and easy informational texts. They can track print with their eyes only over two to six lines per page and process texts with fewer repeating language patterns (and those patterns that exist are more complex). They notice and use a range of punctuation and read dialogue, reflecting the meaning through phrasing. Readers can solve many regular easy two-syllable words, usually those with inflectional endings (*-ing*) and simple compound words. Word-by-word matching is smooth and automatic, and pointing is rarely needed, only at difficulty. The core of known high-frequency words is expanding. They consistently monitor their reading and cross-check one source of information with another.

Selecting Texts Characteristics of Texts at This Level

Genre/Forms

Genre

- Some simple factual texts
- Simple animal fantasy
- Realistic fiction

Forms

- Picture books

Text Structure

Fiction

- Simple narratives with several episodes (usually similar or repetitive)

Nonfiction

- Focused on a single idea or one simple topic
- Underlying text structure (description)
- Present one simple category of information
- Some texts with sequential information

Content

- Familiar, easy content (family, play, pets, school)
- Most concepts supported by pictures

Themes and Ideas

- Familiar themes and ideas

Language and Literary Features

- Amusing or engaging one-dimensional characters
- More complex repeating language patterns
- Texts with familiar settings close to children's experience
- Simple dialogue and some split dialogue
- Simple dialogue assigned to speaker
- Variety in assignment to speaker (other than *said*)
- Simple sequence of events (often repeated)
- A few simple elements of fantasy (for example, talking animals)

Sentence Complexity

- Some longer sentences (some with more than six words)
- Some sentences that are questions
- Many sentences with prepositional phrases and adjectives
- A few sentences beginning with phrases
- Simple sentences (subject and predicate)

Vocabulary

- Almost all vocabulary familiar to children and likely to be used in their oral language
- Word meanings illustrated by pictures
- Variation in words used to assign dialogue

We like our school.
We like to read books.

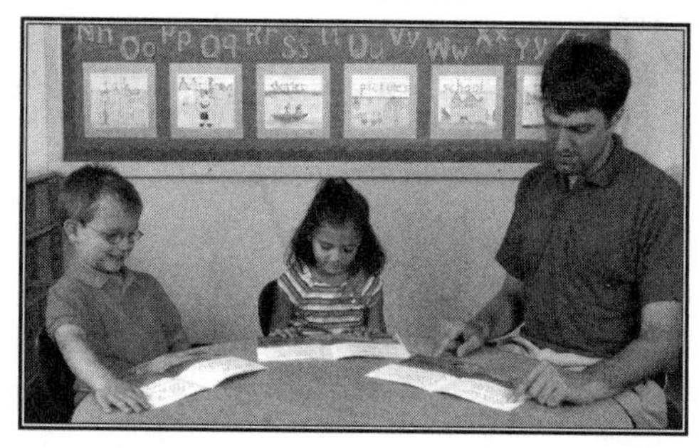

14

We like to write stories.
We like to play ball.

15

Guided Reading

Words

- Mostly one- to two-syllable words
- Nouns, verbs, pronouns, prepositions, adjectives, adverbs
- Simple plurals
- Many high-frequency words
- Some words with *-s* and *-ing*
- Some words with inflectional endings (*-ing*)
- Many words with easy, predictable letter-sound relationships (decodable)
- Some words used in different language structures (*said Mom; Mom said*)
- Mostly simple spelling patterns

Illustrations

General

- Highly supportive illustrations that generally match the text
- Illustrations on every page or every other page
- More details in the Illustrations

Book and Print Features

Length

- Very short, usually eight pages of print
- Mostly two to six lines of print per page (but variable)

Print and Layout

- Ample space between words and lines
- Print in large plain font
- Some words in bold or larger font for emphasis
- Some sentences turn over one line
- Sentences beginning on the left in most texts
- Print clearly separated from pictures
- Line breaks match ends of phrases and sentences

Punctuation

- Ellipses in some texts to create expectation
- Periods, commas, quotation marks, exclamation points, and question marks in most texts

The duck went
in the little house.
She said,
"What a nice
little house!"
10
11

Guided Reading

Selecting Goals — Behaviors and Understandings to Notice, Teach, and Support

Thinking *within* the Text

Solving Words

- Recognize a large number of regular words and easy high-frequency words quickly with the support of the meaning and language structure
- Locate the first and last letters of words in continuous text
- Say words slowly to identify first sound, connect to letter, and locate the word in a text
- Take apart words by using the sounds of individual letters in words with CVC patterns
- Recognize twenty or more high-frequency words within continuous text quickly
- Make connections between words by letters, sounds, or spelling patterns

Monitoring and Correcting

- Reread the sentences to problem solve, self-correct, or confirm
- Reread to search for information
- Self-monitor accuracy and self-correct using known words, letter-sound information, and word parts
- Cross-check one kind of information against another to monitor and self-correct reading (for example, meaning with visual information)
- Use two or more sources of information (meaning, language structure, visual information) to self-monitor and self-correct reading
- Use known words to self-monitor and self-correct

Searching for and Using Information

- Notice details in pictures and use information to understand the text
- Process texts with simple dialogue and some pronouns, all assigned to speakers
- Reread to search for and use information
- Notice, search for, remember, and discuss information that is important to understanding
- Use text meaning and language structure to solve new words

Summarizing

- Remember information to help in understanding the end of a story
- Recall and retell the important information in or events from the text
- Understand and talk about a simple sequence or events or steps

Maintaining Fluency

- Identify and read some phrases as word groups
- Reflect words in bold with use of voice
- Reflect punctuation through appropriate pausing and intonation while reading orally
- Demonstrate appropriate stress on words in a sentence

Adjusting

- Slow down to problem solve and resume good rate of reading
- Anticipate and use language patterns when available but do not depend on them

Planning for Word Work during Guided Reading

One- to three-minute demonstrations and active student engagement using a chart or easel, white board, magnet letters, or pencil and paper can develop fluency and flexibility in visual processing. Plan for explicit work in specific visual processing areas that need support.

Examples:

- Recognize a few easy high-frequency words quickly (for example, *at, an, am, do, go, he, in, like, me, my, no, see, so, to, up, we*)
- Review high-frequency words from previous levels
- Write or make several high-frequency words quickly
- Add -*s* to words to make a plural and read them (*cat/cats*)
- Recognize several CVC words easily and quickly (*hot, bug, pin*)
- Make several CVC words (*cat, but, can, hot, get*) quickly
- Write several CVC words quickly
- Sort letters quickly by a variety of features (uppercase or lowercase; tall or short; with and without sticks, circles, tails, dots, tunnels)
- Match pictures with letters using beginning sounds
- Change the beginning letter to make a one-syllable word (*man/can*)
- Change ending letters to make a new one-syllable word (*cat/can*)
- Say and clap the syllables in one-, two-, three-, and four-syllable words (from pictures)
- Read the Alphabet Linking Chart in a variety of ways (sing, read letter names, read words, read pictures, read every other letter)

Guided Reading

Selecting Goals

Behaviors and Understandings to Notice, Teach, and Support

Thinking *beyond* the Text

Predicting

- Use knowledge of language structure to anticipate the text
- Make predictions using picture information
- Predict the ending of a story based on reading the beginning and middle
- Make predictions based on personal experiences and knowledge
- Make predictions based on information gained through reading

Making Connections

- Make and discuss connections between texts and reader's personal experiences
- Make connections between texts that are alike in some way (topic, ending, characters)
- Recognize and apply attributes of recurring characters where relevant

Synthesizing

- Identify what reader already knows relative to information in the text
- Identify new information in text or pictures
- Acquire and report new information from text
- Talk about what the reader already knows about a topic or character prior to reading
- Show evidence in the text of new ideas or information

Inferring

- Infer and talk about characters' feelings, motives, and attributes
- Show evidence in the print or pictures to support inference

Thinking *about* the Text

Analyzing

- Notice how the writer has made a story funny or surprising
- Identify and appreciate humor in a text
- Notice and comment on the connections between the print and the pictures
- Understand that a story has a beginning, a series of events, and an end
- Understand and discuss how writers use interesting characters and situations

Critiquing

- Share opinions about the text as a whole (beginning, characters, ending)
- Share opinions about illustrations

Guided Reading

Readers at **Level E:**

At Level E, readers encounter texts with three to eight lines of print per page. They are flexible enough to process texts with varied placement of print and a full range of punctuation. Texts have more subtle ideas and complex stories and require more attention to understand, but other processes are becoming automatic for readers. They take apart longer words with inflectional endings and read some sentences that carry over two to three lines or even two pages. Readers are relying much more on the print as they encounter texts with less supportive pictures. Left-to-right directionality and word-by-word matching are automatic and effortless and oral reading demonstrates fluency and phrasing with appropriate stress on words. They read without pointing, bringing in the finger only at point of difficulty. They recognize a large number of high-frequency words and easily solve words with regular letter-sound relationships as well as a few irregular words.

Selecting Texts

Characteristics of Texts at This Level

Genre/Forms

Genre

- A variety of informational texts on easy topics
- Simple animal fantasy
- Realistic fiction
- Some very simple retellings of traditional tales

Forms

- Picture books
- Simple plays

Text Structure

Fiction

- Narrative texts with clear beginning, series of events, and ending

Nonfiction

- Focused on a single idea or one simple topic
- Underlying text structure (description)
- Present one simple category of information
- Some texts with sequential information

Content

- Familiar content that expands beyond home, neighborhood, and school
- Most concepts supported by pictures

Themes and Ideas

- Themes related to typical experiences of children
- Many light, humorous stories, typical of childhood experiences
- Concrete, easy-to-understand ideas

Language and Literary Features

- Amusing or engaging one-dimensional characters
- More literary stories and language
- Texts with familiar settings close to children's experience
- Both simple and split dialogue, speaker usually assigned
- Some longer stretches of dialogue
- Simple sequence of events (often repeated)
- A few simple elements of fantasy (for example, talking animals)

Sentence Complexity

- Some longer sentences (some with more than ten words)
- Some sentences that are questions
- Some complex sentences with variety in order of clauses
- Some sentences with prepositional phrases and adjectives
- Some sentences with verb preceding subject
- Use of commas to set words apart (addressee in dialogue, qualifiers, etc.)
- Simple sentences (subject and predicate)

Vocabulary

- Almost all vocabulary familiar to children and likely to be used in their oral language
- Word meanings illustrated by pictures
- Variation in use of words to assign dialogue in some texts (*said, cried, shouted*)

Kate played
with her tooth
at lunch.
She wiggled it
and wiggled it.
10
"Don't wiggle your tooth,"
said Ben.
"I want to eat my lunch."
11

Guided Reading

Words

- Mostly one- to two-syllable words
- Some three-syllable words
- Nouns, verbs, pronouns, prepositions, adjectives, adverbs
- Simple plurals and possessives
- Many high-frequency words
- Some words with inflectional endings (*-ing*)
- Mostly words with easy predictable letter-sound relationships and spelling patterns (decodable)
- Some words used in different language structures (*said Mom; Mom said*)
- Variety of easy spelling patterns
- Easy contractions

Illustrations

General

- Highly supportive illustrations that generally match the text
- Illustrations on every page or every other page
- More details in the Illustrations

Book and Print Features

Length

- Short, eight to sixteen pages of print
- Most texts two to eight lines per page

Print and Layout

- Ample space between words and lines
- Print in large plain font
- Some words in bold or larger font for emphasis
- Some sentences turn over one line
- Sentences beginning on the left in most texts
- Sentences carrying over two to three lines and some over two pages
- Print in most texts clearly separated from pictures
- Line breaks match ends of phrases and sentences
- Some limited variation in print placement

Punctuation

- Periods, commas, quotation marks, exclamation points, question marks, and ellipses

You can see brown bears
at the zoo.
The baby bears stay
with their mother.

4

5

Guided Reading

Selecting Goals Behaviors and Understandings to Notice, Teach, and Support

Thinking *within* the Text

Solving Words
- Recognize many regular words and high-frequency words quickly and easily
- Use beginning and ending parts of words to solve them
- Use sounds related to vowels to solve words
- Use sounds related to consonants and consonant clusters to solve words
- Recognize and use word parts (onsets and rimes) to solve words while reading
- Make connections between words by letters, sounds, or spelling patterns
- Use what is known about a word to solve an unknown word while reading
- Take apart many new words "on the run"
- Take apart compound words to solve them

Monitoring and Correcting
- Reread the sentence or beginning of a phrase to problem solve, self-correct, or confirm
- Reread the sentence to search for and use information
- Use sounds related to consonants and consonant clusters to monitor and correct reading
- Use meaning, language structure, and visual information to monitor and self-correct reading
- Use known words to self-monitor and self-correct

Searching for and Using Information
- Notice details in pictures and use information to understand the text
- Process texts with simple dialogue and some pronouns, all assigned to speakers
- Reread to search for and use information from language structures or meaning
- Use all sources of information together to solve new words while reading
- Notice, search for, remember, and discuss information that is important to understanding

Summarizing
- Remember information to help in understanding the end of a story
- Recall important details after reading a text
- Recall a series of events in order
- Understand a simple sequence or events or steps
- Provide an oral summary of a text with appropriate details

Maintaining Fluency
- Demonstrate phrased, fluent oral reading
- Reflect language syntax and meaning through phrasing and expression
- Reflect punctuation through appropriate pausing and intonation while reading orally
- Demonstrate appropriate stress on words in a sentence

Adjusting
- Slow down to problem solve and resume good rate of reading
- Have expectations for reading fiction and nonfiction texts
- Reread to solve words or think about ideas and resume good rate of reading

Planning for Word Work during Guided Reading

One- to three-minute demonstrations and active student engagement using a chart or easel, white board, magnet letters, or pencil and paper can develop fluency and flexibility in visual processing. Plan for explicit work in specific visual processing areas that need support.

Examples:
- Recognize many easy high-frequency words (for example, *at, an, am, do, go, he, in, like, me, my, no, see, so, to, up, we, look, hers, this*)
- Write or make many high-frequency words (for example, *this, here, look, like, but*)
- Review high-frequency words from previous levels
- Add -*s* or -*es* to a word to make it plural (*bike/bikes, glass/glasses*)
- Make words using VC (*is*), CVC (*cat*), and CVCe (*take*) patterns
- Use parts of known words to read new words (*today*)
- Read simple compound words (*into, airplane*)
- Using phonogram patterns, make new words by changing first and last letters to make new words (*pin/pit/hit*)
- Build words quickly with magnetic letters
- Change beginning, middle, or ending of a word to make a new word (*hop/stop, stop/stay, hot/hit*)
- Use what is known about words to read new words (*no, go; get, wet*)
- Say words slowly to write them letter by letter
- Read the Consonant Cluster Linking Chart in a variety of ways (all words, every other box, backward order)

Guided Reading

Selecting Goals Behaviors and Understandings to Notice, Teach, and Support

Thinking *beyond* the Text

Predicting
- Use knowledge of language structure to anticipate the text
- Predict the ending of a story based on reading the beginning and middle
- Make predictions based on personal experiences and knowledge
- Make predictions based on information gained through reading

Making Connections
- Make and discuss connections between texts and reader's personal experiences
- Make connections between the text and other texts that have been read or heard
- Recognize and apply attributes of recurring characters where relevant

Synthesizing
- Identify what the reader already knows relative to information in the text
- Identify new information in text or pictures
- Acquire new information while reading a text
- Talk about what the reader already knows about a topic or character prior to reading
- Show evidence in the text of new ideas or information

Inferring
- Infer and talk about characters' feelings, motives, and attributes
- Infer and talk about causes for feelings, motives, or actions
- See changes in characters across time and articulate possible reasons for development
- Show evidence in the print or pictures to support inference
- Infer causes and effects as implied in the text
- Show evidence in the print or pictures to support inferences

Thinking *about* the Text

Analyzing
- Recognize how the author or illustrator has created humor
- Recognize whether a text is fiction or nonfiction
- Discuss the difference between photographs and drawings
- Recognize and discuss how print layout or features are used to reflect meaning (such as large or bold words)
- Understand that a story has a beginning, a series of events, and an end
- Recognize when the writer is presenting a sequence of events or set of directions
- Understand how writers use interesting characters and situations

Critiquing
- Share opinions about the text as a whole (beginning, characters, ending)
- Express opinions about the quality of the illustrations
- Express opinions about the information in a text
- Make judgments about characters or events in a text

Guided Reading

Readers at **Level F:**

At Level F, readers are beginning to build knowledge of the characteristics of different genres of texts. They can read stretches of both simple and split dialogue. They quickly and automatically recognize a large number of high-frequency words and use letter-sound information to take apart simple, regular words as well as some multisyllable words while reading. They recognize and use inflectional endings, plurals, contractions, and possessives. They can also process and understand syntax that largely reflects patterns particular to written language, stories that have multiple episodes. In fiction, they are beginning to meet characters that are more developed, as well as some literary language. Left-to-right directionality and word-by-word matching are completely automatic, and they read without pointing and with appropriate rate, phrasing, intonation, and word stress.

Selecting Texts

Characteristics of Texts at This Level

Genre/Forms

Genre

- A variety of informational texts on easy topics
- Simple animal fantasy
- Realistic fiction
- Some very simple retellings of traditional tales

Forms

- Picture books
- Simple plays

Text Structure

Fiction

- Narrative texts with clear beginning, series of events, and ending

Nonfiction

- Focused on a single idea or one simple topic
- Underlying text structure (description, comparison and contrast)
- Present one simple category of information
- Some texts with sequential information

Content

- Familiar content that expands beyond home, neighborhood, and school
- Concepts accessible through text and illustrations

Themes and Ideas

- Themes related to typical experiences of children
- Many light, humorous stories, typical of childhood experiences
- Concrete, easy-to-understand ideas

Language and Literary Features

- Amusing or engaging one-dimensional characters
- More literary stories and language
- Texts with familiar settings close to children's experience
- Both simple and split dialogue, speaker usually assigned
- Some longer stretches of dialogue
- Simple sequence of events (often repeated)
- A few simple elements of fantasy (for example, talking animals)

Sentence Complexity

- Some long sentences (more than ten words) with prepositional phrases, adjectives, and clauses
- Some sentences that are questions in simple sentences and in dialogue
- Some complex sentences with variety in order of clauses
- Sentences with prepositional phrases and adjectives
- Variation in placement of subject, verb, adjectives, and adverbs
- Use of commas to set words apart (addressee in dialogue, qualifiers, etc.)
- Some compound sentences conjoined by *and*

Vocabulary

- Most vocabulary words familiar to children and likely to be used in their oral language
- Variation in use of words to assign dialogue in some texts (*said, cried, shouted*)

Anna and her mom walked to school.

Anna looked at her new teacher. She opened her backpack and put on her new glasses.

15

Guided Reading

Words

- Mostly one- to two-syllable words
- Some three-syllable words
- Nouns, verbs, prepositions, adjectives, adverbs, conjunctions
- Plurals, easy contractions, possessives, and pronouns
- Many high-frequency words
- Many words with inflectional endings
- Mostly words with easy predictable letter-sound relationships and spelling patterns (decodable)
- Some complex letter-sound relationships in words
- Some words used in different language structures (*said Mom; Mom said*)
- Variety of easy spelling patterns

Illustrations

General

- Highly supportive illustrations that generally match the text
- Illustrations that support the text but do not carry important aspects of meaning
- Illustrations on every page or every other page in most texts
- More details in the Illustrations

Book and Print Features

Length

- Short, eight to sixteen pages of print
- Most texts three to eight lines of print per page

Print and Layout

- Ample space between words and lines
- Print in large plain font
- Some words in bold or larger font for emphasis
- Some sentences turn over one line
- Sentences carrying over two to three lines and some over two pages
- Longer sentences starting on left margin
- Some short sentences, starting middle of a line
- Print in most texts clearly separated from pictures
- Many texts with layout supporting phrasing
- Some limited variation in print placement

Punctuation

- Periods, commas, quotation marks, exclamation points, question marks, and ellipses

Why does Mother Bird
need a nest?
Mother Bird needs a nest
for her eggs!
She lays eggs
in the nest.
The eggs are blue.
4
5

Guided Reading

Selecting Goals **Behaviors and Understandings to Notice, Teach, and Support**

Thinking *within* the Text

Solving Words
- Recognize most words quickly
- Remove the ending from base words to solve new words
- Use letter-sound analysis from left to right to read a new word
- Use sounds related to vowels to solve words
- Use sounds related to consonants and consonant clusters to solve words
- Recognize fifty or more high-frequency words within continuous text automatically
- Use word parts (onsets and rimes) to efficiently take words apart while reading for meaning
- Make connections between words by letters, sounds, or spelling patterns
- Use language structure, meaning, and visual information in a coordinated way to solve words
- Take apart compound words to solve them

Monitoring and Correcting
- Self-correct closer to the point of error
- Reread a phrase to problem solve, self-correct, or confirm
- Use letter-sound relationships and word parts to monitor and self-correct reading
- Use meaning, language structure, and visual information to self-monitor and self-correct reading
- Use known words to self-monitor and self-correct

Searching for and Using Information
- Reread to search for and use information or confirm reading
- Use all sources of information together to solve words while reading
- Use simple organizational features (titles and headings)
- Notice and use readers' tools, such as table of contents, where applicable
- Process texts with simple dialogue and some pronouns, all assigned to speakers
- Search for specific facts in informational text
- Notice, search for, remember, and discuss information that is important to understanding
- Reread to search for and use information
- Use all sources of information together to solve new words

Summarizing
- Remember information to help in understanding the end of a story
- Recall a series of events in order
- Understand a simple sequence of events or steps
- Provide an oral summary with appropriate details in sequence

Maintaining Fluency
- Demonstrate phrased, fluent oral reading
- Reflect language syntax and meaning through phrasing and expression
- Reflect punctuation through appropriate pausing and intonation while reading orally
- Demonstrate appropriate stress on words in a sentence

Adjusting
- Slow down or repeat to think about the meaning of the text and resume normal speed
- Have expectations for reading realistic fiction, simple animal fantasy, simple traditional tales, and easy informational books
- Reread to solve words or think about ideas and resume good rate of reading

Planning for Word Work during Guided Reading

One- to three-minute demonstrations and active student engagement using a chart or easel, white board, magnet letters, or pencil and paper can develop fluency and flexibility in visual processing. Plan for explicit work in specific visual processing areas that need support.

Examples:
- Recognize many easy high-frequency words (for example, *all, are, be, but, for, got, had, of, on, then, this, your*)
- Write many high-frequency words quickly
- Review high-frequency words from previous levels
- Change words to add simple inflectional endings (*-ed, -ing; stopped, stopping*)
- Change words to make plurals by adding *-es* (*box/boxes, glass/glasses*)
- Recognize words that have short (CVC: *pet*) and long (CVCe: *bike*) vowel patterns
- Recognize, make or write words using phonograms with CVCe patterns (*take*) and phonograms with double vowel letters (*moon, green*)
- Take apart compound words (*doghouse, butterfly*)
- Change beginning, middle, and ending letters—single consonants and vowels as well as blends and digraphs—to make new words (*call/ball, ball/bell, bell/best*)
- Use what is known about words to read or write new words (*we, me; on, in*)
- Recognize words that begin with consonant digraphs (*she, chin, what*)
- Take apart words that begin with initial consonants, consonant clusters, and consonant digraphs (*s-ell, sm-ell, sh-ell*)
- Read, write, or sort words with consonant clusters that blend two or three consonant sounds (*tree, stream*)
- Read words with double consonant letters in middle from white board (*better*)
- Take apart and make contractions with *am* (*I'm*) and *not* (*don't*)
- Read the Consonant Cluster Linking Chart a variety of ways

Guided Reading

Selecting Goals

Behaviors and Understandings to Notice, Teach, and Support

Thinking *beyond* the Text

Predicting

- Make predictions using language structure
- Predict the ending of a story based on reading the beginning and middle
- Make predictions based on personal experiences and knowledge
- Make predictions based on information gained through reading
- Make predictions based on knowledge of characters or type of story

Making Connections

- Make and discuss connections between texts and reader's personal experiences
- Make connections between the text and other texts that have been read or heard
- Recognize and apply attributes of recurring characters where relevant

Synthesizing

- Discuss prior knowledge of content prior to reading
- Identify new information in text or pictures
- Notice and acquire new information while reading a text
- Interpret and talk about characters' underlying motivations, attributes, and feelings

Inferring

- Infer characters' feelings, motives, and attributes
- Interpret causes for feelings, motives, or actions
- Show empathy for characters and infer their feelings and motivations
- Show evidence in the print or pictures to support inference
- Infer causes and effects as implied in the text
- Show evidence in the print or pictures to support inferences

Thinking *about* the Text

Analyzing

- Understand what the writer has done to make a text surprising, funny, or interesting
- Recognize whether a text is fiction or nonfiction
- Recognize whether a text is realistic fiction or fantasy
- Recognize an informational text by its features
- Recognize and discuss how print layout or features are used to reflect meaning (such as large or bold words)
- Understand that a story has a beginning, a series of events, and an end
- Identify chronological sequence were applicable
- Notice how the writer has selected interesting information for factual texts

Critiquing

- Share opinions about the text as a whole (beginning, characters, ending)
- Express opinions about a text and state reasons
- Express opinions about the quality of the illustrations
- Express opinions about the information in a text
- Make judgments about characters or events in a text

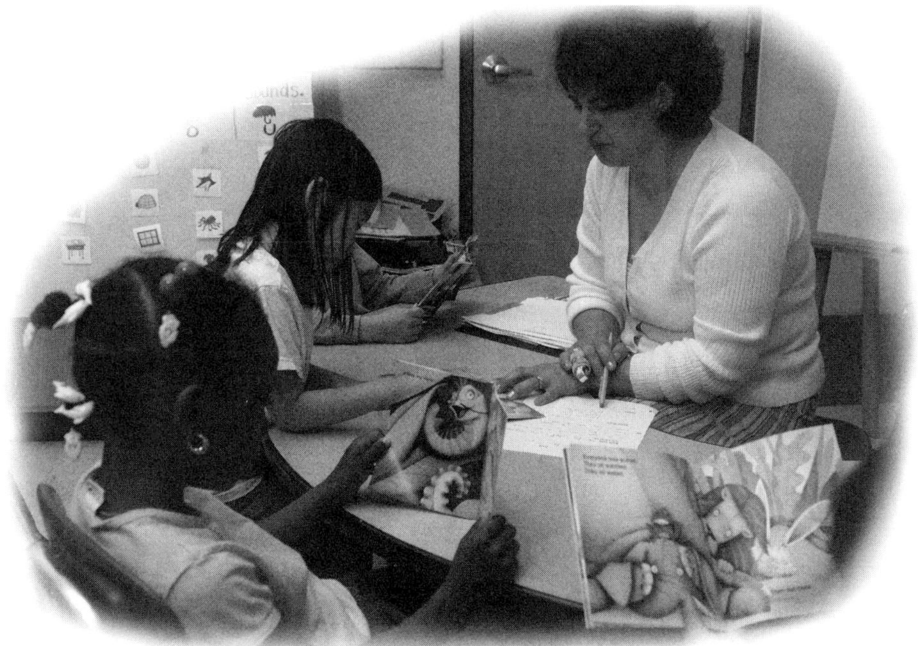

Guided Reading

Readers at **Level G:**

At Level G, readers encounter a wider range of texts and continue to internalize knowledge of different genres. They are still reading texts with three to eight lines of print per page, but print size is slightly smaller. With early reading behaviors completely automatic and quick and automatic recognition of a large number of high-frequency words, they have attention to give to slightly more complex story lines and ideas. They are able to use a range of word-solving strategies (letter-sound information, making connections between words, and using word parts) as they go while attending to meaning. They read texts with some content-specific words, but most texts have only a few challenging vocabulary words. In their oral reading they demonstrate (without pointing) appropriate rate, phrasing, intonation, and word stress.

Selecting Texts **Characteristics of Texts at This Level**

Genre/Forms

Genre

- A variety of informational texts on easy topics
- Simple animal fantasy
- Realistic fiction
- Traditional literature (mostly folktales)

Forms

- Picture books
- Simple plays

Text Structure

Fiction

- Narrative texts with straightforward structure (beginning, series of episodes, ending) but more episodes included

Nonfiction

- Focused on a single idea/topic or series of related ideas/topics
- Include underlying text structures (description, comparison and contrast)
- Largely focused on one category of information
- Some longer texts with repeating longer and more complex patterns
- Some unusual formats, such as letters or questions followed by answers

Content

- Accessible content that expands beyond home, neighborhood, and school
- Concepts accessible through text and illustrations

Themes and Ideas

- Themes related to typical experiences of children
- Many light, humorous stories, typical of childhood experiences
- Concrete, easy-to-understand ideas

Language and Literary Features

- Amusing or engaging one-dimensional characters
- More literary stories and language
- Some texts with settings that are not typical of many children's experience
- Variety in presentation of dialogue (simple with pronouns, split, direct, with some longer stretches of dialogue)
- Simple sequence of events (often repeated)
- A few simple elements of fantasy (for example, talking animals)

Sentence Complexity

- Some long sentences (more than ten words) with prepositional phrases, adjectives, and clauses
- Some sentences that are questions in simple sentences and in dialogue
- Sentences with clauses and embedded phrases, some introductory
- Some complex sentences with variety in order of clauses, phrases, subject, verb, and object

Vocabulary

- Most vocabulary words familiar to children and likely to be used in their oral language
- Some content-specific words introduced, explained, and illustrated in the text
- Variation in use of words to assign dialogue in some texts (*said, cried, shouted*)

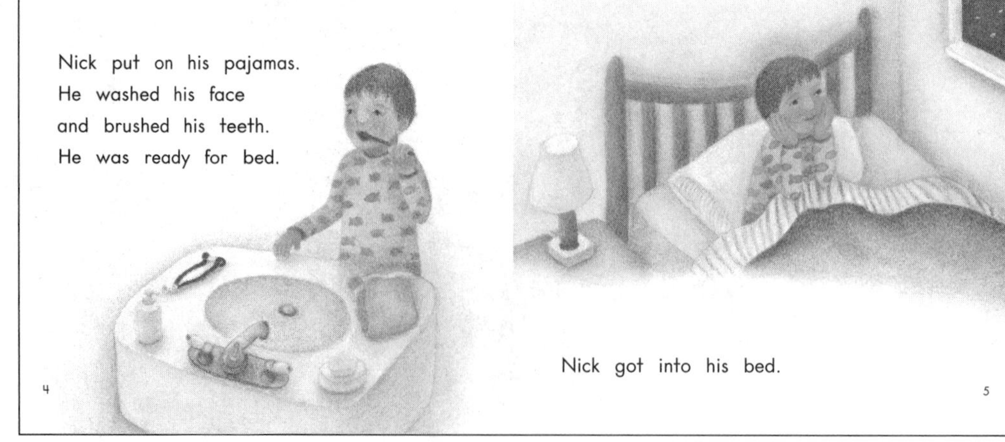

Nick put on his pajamas.
He washed his face
and brushed his teeth.
He was ready for bed.
4
Nick got into his bed.
5

Guided Reading

Words

- Mostly one- to two-syllable words
- Some three-syllable words
- Nouns, verbs, pronouns, adjectives, adverbs, prepositions, conjunctions
- Plurals, easy contractions, possessives, and pronouns
- Many high-frequency words
- Many words with inflectional endings
- Some complex letter-sound relationships in words
- Some words used in different language structures (*said Mom; Mom said*)
- Wide variety of easy spelling patterns

Illustrations

General

- Illustrations that support and extend meaning
- Illustrations on every page or every other page in most texts
- Complex illustrations depicting multiple ideas

Book and Print Features

Length

- Short, eight to sixteen pages of print
- Most texts three to eight lines of print per page

Print and Layout

- Ample space between words and lines
- Print in large plain font
- Some words in bold or larger font for emphasis
- Sentences carrying over two to three lines and some over two pages
- Longer sentences starting on left margin
- Some short sentences, starting middle of a line
- Print in most texts clearly separated from pictures
- Many texts with layout supporting phrasing
- Some limited variation in print placement

Punctuation

- Periods, commas, quotation marks, exclamation points, question marks, and ellipses

What is inside all the bubbles?
Bubbles are like little balloons.
They are filled with air.

6

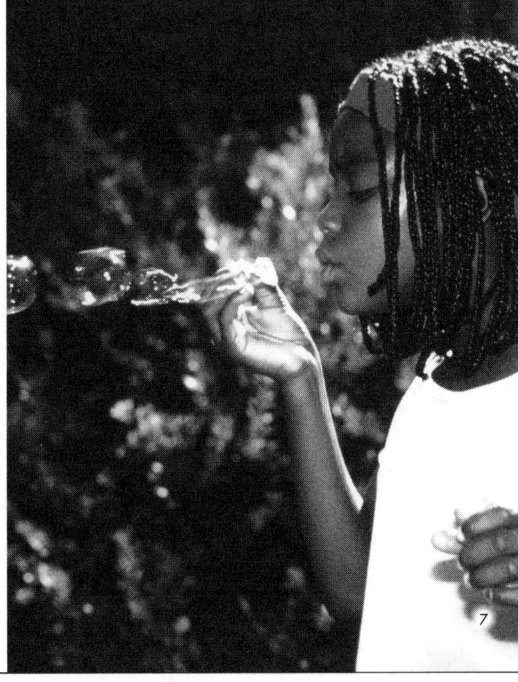

7

Guided Reading

Selecting Goals **Behaviors and Understandings to Notice, Teach, and Support**

Thinking *within* the Text

Solving Words

- Recognize most words quickly and easily
- Remove the ending from base words to solve new words
- Use letter clusters (blends and digraphs) to solve words
- Use left-to-right letter-sound analysis to read a word
- Use consonant and vowel sound-letter relationships to solve words
- Quickly and automatically recognize seventy-five or more high-frequency words within continuous text
- Use known words and word parts (including onsets and rimes) to solve unknown words
- Make connections between words by letters, sounds, or spelling patterns
- Connect words that mean the same or almost the same to derive meaning from the text
- Use context and pictures to derive the meaning of unfamiliar vocabulary
- Take apart compound words to solve them

Monitoring and Correcting

- Self-correct close to the point of error (reread a phrase or word)
- Reread to problem solve, self-correct, or confirm
- Use relationships between sounds and letters, letter clusters, and large parts of words to monitor accuracy of reading
- Use meaning, language structure, and visual information to monitor and self-correct reading
- Realize when more information is needed to understand a text
- Use known words to self-monitor and self-correct

Searching for and Using Information

- Search for and use all sources of information in the text
- Use all sources of information together to solve new words
- Notice and use labels for pictures
- Use simple organizational features (titles and headings)
- Notice and use readers' tools, such as table of contents, where applicable
- Process texts with some split dialogue, all assigned to speakers
- Search for specific facts in informational text
- Notice, search for, remember, and discuss information that is important to understanding

Summarizing

- Remember information to help in understanding the end of a story
- Remember the important information from a factual text
- Understand and talk about a simple sequence or events or steps
- Provide an oral summary with appropriate details in sequence after reading
- Follow and reflect in discussion the multiple events of a story

Maintaining Fluency

- Demonstrate phrased, fluent oral reading
- Reflect language syntax and meaning through phrasing and expression
- Reflect punctuation through appropriate pausing and intonation while reading orally
- Demonstrate appropriate stress on words to reflect the meaning

Adjusting

- Slow down or repeat to think about the meaning of the text and resume normal speed
- Have expectations for reading realistic fiction, simple animal fantasy, simple traditional tales, and easy informational books
- Reread to solve words or think about ideas and resume good rate of reading

Planning for Word Work during Guided Reading

One- to three-minute demonstrations and active student engagement using a chart or easel, white board, magnet letters, or pencil and paper can develop fluency and flexibility in visual processing. Plan for explicit work in specific visual processing areas that need support.

Examples:

- Recognize many easy high-frequency words (for example, *all, are, be, but, for, got, had, of, on, then, this, your*)
- Review high-frequency words from previous levels
- Change words to add simple inflectional endings (*-ed, -ing; stopped, stopping*)
- Change words to make plurals by adding *-es* (*churches, foxes, dishes*)
- Take apart and read words using phonograms with VCe (*tale*) patterns and phonograms with double vowel letters (*meet*)
- Read, write, or make words that have short (CVC: *let*) and long (CVCe: *make*) vowel patterns
- Take apart compound words (*door-bell*)
- Change beginning, middle, and ending letters—single consonants and vowels as well as blends and digraphs—to make new words (*can/than/thin/thick*)
- Use what is known about words to read new words (*not, got; and, hand*)
- Recognize words that begin with consonant digraphs (*thin, shell*)
- Solve words using letter-sound analysis from left to right (*st-e-p*)
- Take apart or make words that begin with initial consonants, consonant clusters, and consonant digraphs (*tr-uck*)
- Take apart or make words with consonant clusters that blend two or three consonant sounds (*spell, splash*)
- Take apart or make words with double consonant letters in middle from white board (*ladder, summer*)
- Read Consonant Cluster Linking Chart in a variety of ways

Guided Reading

Selecting Goals Behaviors and Understandings to Notice, Teach, and Support

Thinking *beyond* the Text

Predicting
- Make predictions using language structure
- Predict the ending of a story based on reading the beginning and middle
- Make predictions based on personal experiences and knowledge
- Make predictions based on information gained through reading
- Make predictions based on knowledge of characters or type of story
- Support predictions with evidence from the text or personal experience and knowledge

Making Connections
- Make and discuss connections between texts and reader's personal experiences
- Make connections between the text and other texts that have been read or heard
- Recognize and apply attributes of recurring characters where relevant

Synthesizing
- Relate the content of the text to what is already known
- Identify new information in text or pictures
- Identify new information from simple informational texts and incorporate into personal knowledge
- Interpret characters' underlying motivations, attributes, and feelings

Inferring
- Infer characters' feelings, motives, and attributes
- Infer causes for feelings, motives, or actions
- Show empathy for characters
- Use and interpret information from pictures without depending on them to construct meaning
- Infer causes and effects as implied in the text
- Justify inferences with evidence from the text

Thinking *about* the Text

Analyzing
- Identify what the writer has done to make a text surprising, funny, or interesting
- Recognize whether a text is fiction or nonfiction
- Identify characteristics of genres (simple animal fantasy, easy factual texts, realistic fiction, traditional literature, plays)
- Notice how writers or illustrators use layout and print features for emphasis
- Identify parts of a text (beginning, series of episodes, end)
- Notice writer's use of specific words to convey meaning (for example, *shouted, cried*)
- Identify a point in the story when the problem is resolved
- Discuss whether a story (fiction) could be true and tell why

Critiquing
- Share opinions about the text as a whole (beginning, characters, ending)
- Express opinions about the quality of a text
- Express opinions about the quality of the illustrations
- Agree or disagree with the ideas in a text
- Make judgments about characters or events in a text

Guided Reading

Readers at **Level H:**

At Level H, readers encounter challenges similar to Level G; but the language and vocabulary are even more complex, the stories longer and more literary, and there is less repetition in the episodic structure. They process a great deal of dialogue and reflect it through appropriate word stress and phrasing in oral reading. Readers will find that plots and characters are more elaborate but are still simple and straightforward. They solve a large number of multisyllable words (many words with inflectional endings), plurals, contractions, and possessives. Readers automatically read a large number of high-frequency words in order to meet the demands for more in-depth thinking and also to solve words with complex spelling patterns. In order to achieve efficient and smooth processing, readers will begin to read more new texts silently. In oral reading, they demonstrate (without pointing) appropriate rate, phrasing, intonation, and word stress.

Selecting Texts **Characteristics of Texts at This Level**

Genre/Forms

Genre

- Informational texts
- Simple animal fantasy
- Realistic fiction
- Traditional literature (mostly folktales)

Forms

- Picture books
- Simple plays

Text Structure

Fiction

- Narrative texts organized in predictable ways (beginning, series of repeated episodes, ending)
- Narratives with more episodes and less repetition

Nonfiction

- Focused on a single idea/topic or series of related ideas/topics
- Include underlying structures clearly (description, comparison and contrast, temporal sequence, problem and solution)
- Largely focused on one category of information
- Some longer texts with repeating longer and more complex patterns
- Some unusual formats, such as letters or questions followed by answers

Content

- Accessible content that expands beyond home, neighborhood, and school
- Concepts accessible through text and illustrations

Themes and Ideas

- Many light, humorous stories, typical of childhood experiences
- Greater variety in themes (going beyond everyday events)

Language and Literary Features

- Amusing or engaging one-dimensional characters
- Some stretches of descriptive language
- Some texts with settings that are not typical of many children's experience
- Almost all dialogue assigned to speaker
- Full variety in presentation of dialogue (simple, simple using pronouns, split, direct)
- Use of dialogue for drama
- Multiple episodes taking place across time
- Simple, traditional elements of fantasy

Sentence Complexity

- Some long sentences (more than ten words) with prepositional phrases, adjectives, and clauses
- Some sentences that are questions in simple sentences and in dialogue
- Some complex sentences with variety in order of clauses, phrases, subject, verb, and object
- Variation in placement of subject, verb, adjectives, and adverbs

Vocabulary

- Most vocabulary words known by children through oral language or reading
- Some content-specific words introduced, explained, and illustrated in the text
- Wide variety in words used to assign dialogue to speaker

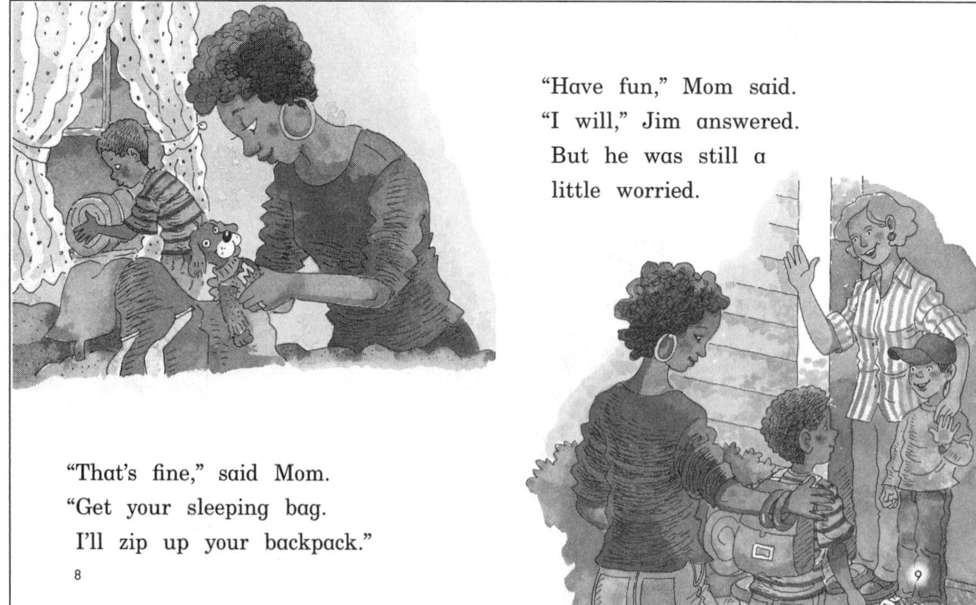

"That's fine," said Mom.
"Get your sleeping bag.
I'll zip up your backpack."
8
"Have fun," Mom said.
"I will," Jim answered.
But he was still a
little worried.
9

Guided Reading

Words

- Mostly one- to two-syllable words
- Some three-syllable words
- All parts of speech
- Plurals, contractions, possessives, and pronouns
- Wide range of high-frequency words
- Many words with inflectional endings
- Some complex letter-sound relationships in words
- Some complex spelling patterns
- Multisyllable words that are generally easy to take apart or decode
- Some easy compound words

Illustrations

General

- Complex illustrations depicting multiple ideas

Fiction

- Most texts with no or only minimal illustrations
- In illustrated texts, highly complex and artistic illustrations that communicate meaning to match or extend the text (mood, symbolism)
- Illustrations that support interpretation, enhance enjoyment, set mood but are not necessary for understanding

Nonfiction

- One kind of graphic on a page
- Some simple graphics (illustrations with labels)

Book and Print Features

Length

- Short, eight to sixteen pages of print
- Most texts three to eight lines of print per page

Print and Layout

- Ample space between words and lines
- Print in large plain font
- Italics indicating unspoken thought
- Some texts in smaller font size
- Words in bold and italics that are important to meaning and stress
- Sentences carrying over two to three lines and some over two pages
- Longer sentences starting on left margin
- Some short sentences, starting middle of a line
- Print in most texts clearly separated from pictures
- Many texts with layout supporting phrasing
- Some limited variation in print placement

Punctuation

- Periods, commas, quotation marks, exclamation points, question marks, dashes, and ellipses in some texts

This is a fire truck.
Fire trucks help put out fires.
This truck has a long hose
that shoots water on the fire.

4

Guided Reading

Selecting Goals — Behaviors and Understandings to Notice, Teach, and Support

Thinking *within* the Text

Solving Words

- Use letter-sound relationships in sequence to solve more complex words
- Use consonant and vowel sound-letter relationships to solve words
- Quickly and automatically recognize one hundred or more high-frequency words within continuous text
- Use known words and word parts (including onsets and rimes) to solve unknown words
- Make connections between words by letters, sounds, or spelling patterns
- Connect words that mean the same or almost the same to derive meaning from the text
- Demonstrate knowledge of flexible ways to solve words (taking it apart, using meaning, etc.)
- Break down a longer word into syllables in order to decode manageable units
- Use context and pictures to derive the meaning of unfamiliar vocabulary
- Use context to derive meaning of new words
- Take apart compound words to solve them
- Demonstrate competent, active word solving while reading at a good pace—less overt problem solving

Monitoring and Correcting

- Self-correct close to the point of error
- Reread to problem solve, self-correct, or confirm when needed but less frequently than in previous levels
- Use multiple sources of information to monitor and self-correct (language structure, meaning, and letter-sound information)
- Realize when more information is needed to understand a text
- Use known words to self-monitor and self-correct

Searching for and Using Information

- Use some simple graphics, labeled pictures, that add information to the text
- Use a table of contents to locate information in a text
- Process texts with some split dialogue, all assigned to speakers
- Notice, search for, remember, and discuss information that is important to understanding

Summarizing

- Remember information to help in understanding the end of a story
- Demonstrate understanding of sequence when summarizing a text
- Identify and understand a set of related ideas in a text
- After reading, provide an oral summary with appropriate details in sequence
- Summarize narratives with multiple episodes as part of the same simple plot

Maintaining Fluency

- Demonstrate phrased, fluent oral reading
- Reflect language syntax and meaning through phrasing and expression
- Demonstrate awareness of the function of the full range of punctuation
- Demonstrate appropriate stress on words to reflect the meaning
- Use multiple sources of information (language structure, meaning, fast word recognition) to support fluency and phrasing

Adjusting

- Slow down or repeat to think about the meaning of the text and resume normal speed
- Have expectations for reading realistic fiction, simple animal fantasy, simple traditional tales, and easy informational books
- Reread to solve words or think about ideas and resume good rate of reading

Planning for Word Work during Guided Reading

One- to three-minute demonstrations and active student engagement using a chart or easel, white board, magnet letters, or pencil and paper can develop fluency and flexibility in visual processing. Plan for explicit work in specific visual processing areas that need support.

Examples:

- Recognize and write many high-frequency words (for example, *come, came, from, her, him, his, one, out, said, saw, she, that, their, there, they, was, went, were, with*)
- Review high-frequency words from previous levels
- Change words to add simple inflectional endings (*-ed, -ing; stopped, stopping*)
- Change words to make plurals by adding *-es* (*dresses, crashes*)
- Make or take apart words using phonograms with VCe patterns (*sale, rule*) and phonograms with double vowel letters (*spoon, keep*)
- Write words with inflectional endings, plurals, VCe patters, etc.
- Read or make words that have short (CVC: *hat*) and long (CVCe: *game*) vowel patterns
- Take apart compound words (*every-one*)
- Change beginning, middle, and ending letters—single consonants and vowels as well as blends and digraphs—to make new words (*cot/cat/cash/trash*)
- Make possessives by adding an apostrophe and an *s* to a singular noun (*the dog's bone*)
- Solve words using letter-sound analysis from left to right (*s-t-r-ea-m*)
- Use what is known about words to read new words (*but, butter; in, spin*)
- Take apart words that begin with initial consonants, consonant clusters, and consonant digraphs (*ch-air*)
- Take apart words with consonant clusters that blend two or three consonant sounds (*spin, sprint*)
- Take apart words with consonant clusters at the beginning—both blends and digraphs (*crib, while*)
- Take apart words with double consonant letters in middle (*butter*)
- Read contractions with *is* (*he's, she's*) or not (*don't*)
- Read Consonant Cluster Chart in a variety of ways

Guided Reading

Selecting Goals

Behaviors and Understandings to Notice, Teach, and Support

Thinking *beyond* the Text

Predicting

- Make predictions using language structure
- Use understanding of text structure to make predictions about what will happen next
- Make predictions based on knowledge of characters or type of story
- Use background information, personal experience, and information from the text to make predictions
- Support predictions with evidence from the text or personal experience and knowledge

Making Connections

- Bring knowledge from personal experiences to the interpretation of characters and events
- Bring background knowledge to the understanding of a text before, during, and after reading
- Make connections between the text and other texts that have been read or heard
- Recognize and apply attributes of recurring characters where relevant

Synthesizing

- Differentiate between what is known and new information
- Identify new information and incorporate it into present understandings
- Demonstrate learning new content from reading

Inferring

- Show empathy for characters and infer their feelings and motivations
- Interpret and talk about causes for feelings, motives, or actions
- Use and interpret information from pictures without depending on them to construct the meaning derived from reading words
- Infer causes and effects as implied in the text
- Justify inferences with evidence from the text

Thinking *about* the Text

Analyzing

- Understand what the writer has done to make a text surprising, funny, or interesting
- Discuss characteristics of genres (simple animal fantasy, easy factual texts, realistic fiction, traditional literature, plays)
- Differentiate between informational and fiction texts
- Understand, talk about, write, or draw when a writer has used description or compare and contrast
- Notice and discuss how writers or illustrators use layout and print features for emphasis
- Identify parts of a text (beginning, series of episodes, end)
- Notice writer's use of specific words to convey meaning (for example, *shouted, cried*)
- Identify a point in the story when the problem is resolved
- Discuss whether a story (fiction) could be true and tell why

Critiquing

- Share opinions about the text as a whole (beginning, characters, ending)
- Express opinions about the quality of a text
- Express opinions about the quality of the illustrations
- Notice how the illustrations are consistent (or inconsistent) with meaning and extend the meaning
- Agree or disagree with the ideas in a text
- Make judgments about characters or events in a text

Guided Reading

Readers at **Level I:**

At Level I, readers will be processing texts that are mostly short (eight to sixteen pages), as well as some easy illustrated chapter books (forty to sixty pages) that require them to sustain attention and memory over time. They will meet some long sentences of more than ten words that contain prepositional phrases, adjectives, and clauses. They will also encounter compound sentences. They can effectively process complex sentences when required by a text. In addition to automatically recognizing a large number of words, they are using word-solving strategies for complex spelling patterns, multisyllable words, and many words with inflectional endings, plurals, contractions, and possessives. They read many texts silently, following the text with their eyes and without pointing. In oral reading, they reflect appropriate rate, word stress, intonation, phrasing, and pausing.

Selecting Texts **Characteristics of Texts at This Level**

Genre/Forms

Genre

- Informational texts
- Simple animal fantasy
- Realistic fiction
- Traditional literature (mostly folktales)

Forms

- Picture books
- Simple plays

Text Structure

Fiction

- Narratives with multiple episodes and little repetition of similar episodes
- Narratives with more elaborated episodes

Nonfiction

- Focused on a single idea/topic or series of related ideas/topics
- Underlying structures used and presented clearly (description, comparison and contrast, temporal sequence, problem and solution)
- Texts organized into a few simple categories
- Some longer texts that repeat longer and more complex patterns
- Some unusual formats, such as letters or questions followed by answers

Content

- Familiar content and some new content that typically children would not know
- Concepts accessible through text and illustrations

Themes and Ideas

- Many light, humorous stories, typical of childhood experiences
- Some ideas that are new to most children
- Themes accessible given typical experiences of children
- A few abstract ideas that are highly supported by text and illustrations

Language and Literary Features

- Amusing or engaging one-dimensional characters
- More elaborated description of character attributes
- Language characteristic of traditional literature in some texts
- Some texts with settings that are not typical of many children's experience
- Variety of dialogue (between more than two characters in many texts)
- Multiple episodes taking place across time
- Simple, traditional elements of fantasy
- Most texts told from a single point of view with some texts showing more than one

Sentence Complexity

- Some long sentences (more than ten words) with prepositional phrases, adjectives, and clauses
- Questions in dialogue (fiction) and questions and answers (nonfiction)
- Many sentences with embedded clauses and phrases
- Variation in placement of subject, verb, adjectives, and adverbs
- Use of commas to set words apart (addressee in dialogue, qualifiers, etc.)
- Sentences with nouns, verbs, adjectives, and adverbs in series, divided by commas
- Many compound sentences

Vocabulary

- Most vocabulary words known by children through oral language or reading
- Some content-specific words introduced, explained, and illustrated in the text
- Wide variety of words to assign dialogue (*said, cried, shouted, thought, whispered*) and adjectives describing the dialogue (*quietly, loudly*)

Spencer sat down
and looked around.
He was worried.
"There are so many cats.
But is there a cat for me?"
he asked.

14

Spencer heard a soft meow.
He looked down
and saw a tiny kitten
looking back at him.
The kitten put her paw
on Spencer's leg.
She purred and purred.

15

Guided Reading

Words

- Many two- to three-syllable words
- All parts of speech
- Plurals, contractions, possessives, and pronouns
- Wide range of high-frequency words
- Many words with inflectional endings
- Some complex letter-sound relationships in words
- Some complex spelling patterns
- Multisyllable words that are generally easy to take apart or decode
- Some easy compound words

Illustrations

General

- Two or more kinds of graphics on a page
- Some illustrations complex with many ideas

Fiction

- Most texts with no or only minimal illustrations
- In illustrated texts, highly complex and artistic illustrations that communicate meaning to match or extend the text (mood, symbolism)
- Illustrations that support interpretation, enhance enjoyment, set mood but are not necessary for understanding

Nonfiction

- One or two kinds of graphics on a page
- Some simple graphics (illustrations with labels)

Book and Print Features

Length

- Short, eight to sixteen pages of print
- Most texts three to eight lines of print per page
- Some easy illustrated chapter books of fifty to sixty pages

Print and Layout

- Ample space between words and lines
- Print in large plain font
- Italics indicating unspoken thought
- Some texts in smaller font size
- Words in bold and italics that are important to meaning and stress
- Sentences carrying over two to three lines and some over two pages
- Longer sentences starting on left margin
- Some short sentences, starting middle of a line
- Print in most texts clearly separated from pictures
- Some limited variation in print placement

Punctuation

- Periods, commas, quotation marks, exclamation points, question marks, dashes, and ellipses in some texts

Tools

- Some informational texts with a table of contents
- Some informational texts with a simple glossary

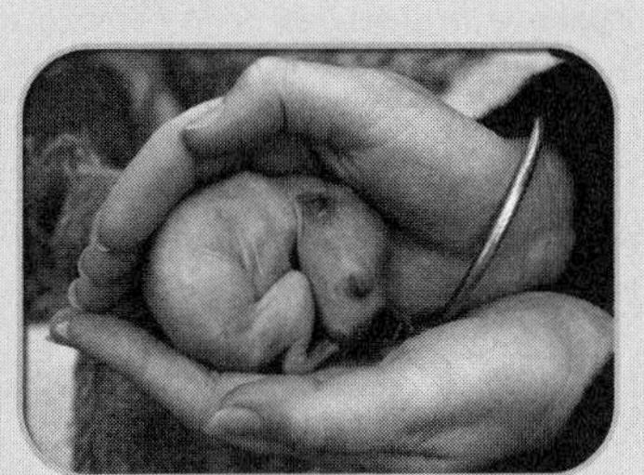

Koalas do not drink water.
There is water
in the leaves koalas eat.
They get food and water
at the same time.
8
This is a baby koala.
A young koala is called a joey,
just like a baby kangaroo.
When a joey is born,
it has no hair.
9

Guided Reading

Selecting Goals Behaviors and Understandings to Notice, Teach, and Support

Thinking *within* the Text

Solving Words

- Use letter-sound relationships in sequence to solve new words
- Use consonant and vowel sound-letter relationships to solve words
- Recognize one hundred to one hundred fifty high-frequency words within continuous text quickly and automatically
- Use known words and word parts (including onsets and rimes) to solve unknown words
- Make connections between words by letters, sounds, or spelling patterns
- Connect words that mean the same or almost the same to help in understanding a text and acquiring new vocabulary
- Demonstrate knowledge of flexible ways to solve words (taking it apart, using meaning, use letter sequence, etc.)
- Break down a longer word into syllables in order to decode manageable units
- Use context and pictures to derive the meaning of unfamiliar vocabulary
- Use context to derive meaning of new words
- Take apart compound words to solve them
- Use meaning, structure, and visual information to solve words
- Demonstrate competent, active word solving while reading at a good pace—less overt problem solving

Monitoring and Correcting

- Self-correct at point of error (or before overt error)
- Use multiple sources of information to monitor and self-correct (language structure, meaning, and letter-sound information)
- Realize when more information is needed to understand a text
- Reread to confirm word solving by checking other sources of information
- Use known words to self-monitor and self-correct

Searching for and Using Information

- Use multiple sources of information to solve words
- Notice and use graphics such as labels and captions for pictures and simple diagrams
- Use simple readers' tools (table of contents, index, glossary) to find information in texts
- Process texts with some split dialogue, all assigned to speakers
- Notice, search for, remember, and discuss information that is important to understanding

Summarizing

- Follow and remember a series of events over a longer text in order to understand the ending
- Report episodes in a text in the order they happened
- Identify and understand a set of related ideas in a text
- Summarize a longer narrative text with multiple episodes
- Identify important ideas in a text and report them in an organized way, either orally or in writing
- Understand the problem of a story and its solution

Maintaining Fluency

- Demonstrate phrased, fluent oral reading
- Read dialogue with phrasing and expression that reflects understanding of characters and events
- Demonstrate awareness of the function of the full range of punctuation
- Demonstrate appropriate stress on words to reflect the meaning
- Use multiple sources of information (language structure, meaning, fast word recognition) to support fluency and phrasing
- Quickly and automatically solve most words in the text in a way that supports fluency
- Read silently at a good rate

Planning for Word Work during Guided Reading

One- to three-minute demonstrations and active student engagement using a chart or easel, white board, magnet letters, or pencil and paper can develop fluency and flexibility in visual processing. Plan for explicit work in specific visual processing areas that need support.

Examples:

- Recognize a few easy high-frequency words (select from list of one hundred high-frequency words)
- Review high-frequency words from previous levels
- Change words to add simple inflectional endings (*-ed, -ing; stopped, stopping*)
- Change words to make plurals by adding *-es* (*buses*)
- Read plural and singular forms for words that change the spelling (*child/children, foot/feet*)
- Recognize homophones (same pronunciation, different spelling and meaning) (*write, right*)
- Take apart words with double vowel patterns (*feet, room*)
- Take apart compound words (*every-thing*)
- Take apart and make one-syllable words with a variety of phonogram patterns (*cl-ay, dr-ip*)
- Take apart two-syllable words (*drag-on*)
- Change beginning, middle and ending letters—single consonants and vowels as well as blends and digraphs—to make new words (*band/sand/send/sent*)
- Make possessives by adding an apostrophe and an *s* to a singular noun (*the girl's shoe*)
- Use what is known about words to read new words (*tree, top, treetop; ape, shape*)
- Take apart, make, or write words with initial consonant clusters and consonant digraphs (*pr-int, sh-ake*)
- Read words with double consonant letters in middle (*ladder*)
- Read, write, or make words with consonant clusters—both blends and digraphs (*drip, ring, crash, shape*)
- Read, write, or make words with consonant clusters that blend two or three consonant sounds (*steam, street*)
- Read contractions with *is* and *not* (*she's, can't*)

Guided Reading

Selecting Goals Behaviors and Understandings to Notice, Teach, and Support

Adjusting
- Slow down to search for information and resume normal pace of reading again
- Demonstrate different ways of reading fiction and nonfiction texts
- Reread to solve words or think about ideas and resume good rate of reading

Thinking *beyond* the Text

Predicting
- Make predictions using language structure
- Use text structure to predict the outcome of a narrative
- Make predictions based on knowledge of characters or type of story
- Make predictions about the solution to the problem of a story
- Make predictions based on personal experiences, content knowledge, and knowledge of similar texts
- Search for and use information to confirm or disconfirm predictions
- Justify predictions using evidence

Making Connections
- Bring knowledge from personal experiences to the interpretation of characters and events
- Bring background knowledge to the understanding of a text before, during, and after reading
- Make connections between the text and other texts that have been read or heard
- Recognize and apply attributes of recurring characters where relevant

Synthesizing
- Differentiate between what is known and new information
- Demonstrate learning new content from reading
- Express changes in ideas after reading a text

Inferring
- Infer characters' feelings and motivations through reading their dialogue
- Demonstrate understandings of characters, using evidence from text to support statements
- Infer cause and effect in influencing characters' feelings or underlying motives
- Infer causes of problems or of outcomes in fiction and nonfiction texts

Thinking *about* the Text

Analyzing
- Notice some characteristics of genre (for example, traditional language, literary language, descriptive language)
- Differentiate between informational and fiction texts
- Understand and talk about when a writer has used underlying structures (description, compare and contrast, temporal sequence, problem and solution)
- Notice the fit between pictures and text
- Notice how writers or illustrators use layout and print features for emphasis
- Notice and speculate why the writer has selected information to present in particular ways (photograph, caption, boxes, pictures)
- Identify a point in the story when the problem is resolved
- Discuss whether a story (fiction) *could* be true and tell why

Critiquing
- Express opinions about the quality of a text
- Notice how the illustrations are consistent (or inconsistent) with meaning and extend the meaning
- Discuss the quality of illustrations or graphics
- Agree or disagree with the ideas in a text and give reasons
- Hypothesize how characters could have behaved differently
- Judge the text as to whether it is interesting, humorous, or exciting, and specify why

Guided Reading

Readers at **Level J:**

At Level J, readers process a variety of texts, including short informational texts on familiar topics, short fiction texts, and longer illustrated narratives that have short chapters. They adjust their reading strategies to process not only realistic fiction and informational texts but to read very simple biographies. In fiction, characters generally do not change very much since the plots are relatively simple and texts are not long. Readers process an increased number of longer and more complex sentences (those with more than ten words containing prepositional phrases, adjectives, clauses, and many compound sentences). Readers are able to automatically recognize a large number of words, and can quickly apply word-solving strategies to multisyllable words with inflectional endings, suffixes, and prefixes. They can read a wide range of plurals, contractions, and possessives. In oral reading, they reflect appropriate rate, word stress, intonation, phrasing, and pausing (recognizing and using a range of punctuation). They read silently in independent reading.

Selecting Texts

Characteristics of Texts at This Level

Genre/Forms

Genre

- Informational texts
- Simple animal fantasy
- Realistic fiction
- Traditional literature (mostly folktales)
- Some simple biographies on familiar subjects

Forms

- Picture books
- Plays
- Beginning chapter books with illustrations

Text Structure

Fiction

- Narratives with little repetition of similar episodes
- Narratives with more elaborated episodes
- Some beginning chapter books with short chapters
- Chapters connected by character or broad theme
- Chapters usually connected to a longer plot

Nonfiction

- Focused on a single idea/topic or series of related ideas/topics
- Underlying structures used and presented clearly (description, comparison and contrast, temporal sequence, problem and solution)
- Texts organized into a few simple categories of information
- Some longer texts with repeating longer and more complex patterns
- Some unusual formats, such as letters or questions followed by answers

Content

- Familiar content and some new content that typically children would not know
- New content accessible through text and illustrations

Themes and Ideas

- Many light, humorous stories, typical of childhood experiences
- Some ideas new to most children
- Themes accessible given typical experiences of children
- A few abstract ideas that are highly supported by text and illustrations

Language and Literary Features

- Amusing or engaging characters, some of which have more than one dimension
- Elaborated description of character traits
- Language characteristic of traditional literature in some texts
- Some texts with settings that are not typical of many children's experience
- Variety of dialogue (may be between more than two characters in many texts)
- Multiple episodes taking place across time
- Simple, traditional elements of fantasy
- Most texts told from a single point of view, with some having several points of view

"Horses?" Everyone looked at one another.
"Horses on our street?" asked Dad.
"I hope they're ponies," said Ben. "When we have birthday parties, we can have pony rides."
"I hope they're big white horses," said Polly. "Maybe they'll give us a ride."
4
5

Guided Reading

Sentence Complexity

- Many longer (more than ten words), more complex sentences (prepositional phrases, introductory clauses, lists of nouns, verbs, or adjectives)
- Questions in dialogue (fiction) and questions and answers (nonfiction)
- Many sentences with embedded clauses and phrases
- Occasional use of parenthetical material embedded in sentences
- Variation in placement of subject, verb, adjectives, and adverbs
- Many compound sentences

Vocabulary

- Most vocabulary words known by children through oral language or reading
- Content words illustrated with pictures or other graphics
- Some new vocabulary and content-specific words introduced that are explained and illustrated in the text
- Wide variety of words to assign dialogue (*said, cried, shouted, thought, whispered*) and adjectives describing the dialogue (*quietly, loudly*)

Words

- Many two- to three-syllable words
- All parts of speech
- Plurals, contractions, and possessives
- Wide range of high-frequency words
- Many words with inflectional endings
- Many words with complex letter-sound relationships
- Some complex spelling patterns
- Multisyllable words that are generally easy to take apart or decode
- Some easy compound words

Illustrations

General

- Two or more kinds of graphics on a page
- Some illustrations complex with many ideas

Fiction

- Most texts with no or only minimal illustrations
- In illustrated texts, highly complex and artistic illustrations that communicate meaning to match or extend the text (mood, symbolism)
- Illustrations that support interpretation, enhance enjoyment, set mood but are not necessary for understanding

Nonfiction

- More than one kind of graphic on a page
- Some simple graphics (illustrations with labels)

Book and Print Features

Length

- Chapter books (most approximately forty to seventy-five pages)
- Many lines of print on a page (approximately three to twelve lines)
- Shorter (most approximately twenty-four to thirty-six pages of print) texts on single topics (usually nonfiction)

Print and Layout

- Ample space between lines
- Print in large plain font
- Italics indicating unspoken thought
- Some texts in smaller font size
- Words in bold and italics that are important to meaning and stress
- Sentences carrying over two to three lines and some over two pages
- Longer sentences starting on left margin in most texts
- Some sentences, starting middle of a line
- Print in most texts clearly separated from pictures
- Variety in layout, reflecting different genres

Punctuation

- Periods, commas, quotation marks, exclamation points, question marks, dashes, and ellipses in most texts

Tools

- Some texts with a table of contents
- Some texts with a simple glossary
- Chapter titles in some books
- Some texts with headings in bold to show sections

Guided Reading

Selecting Goals Behaviors and Understandings to Notice, Teach, and Support

Thinking *within* the Text

Solving Words

- Use letter-sound relationships in sequence to solve more complex words
- Recognize many high-frequency words within continuous text quickly and automatically
- Use known words and word parts (including onsets and rimes) to solve unknown words
- Make connections between words by letters, sounds, or spelling patterns
- Use multiple sources of information to solve words
- Connect words that mean the same or almost the same to help in understanding a text and acquiring new vocabulary
- Demonstrate knowledge of flexible ways to solve words (noticing word parts, noticing endings and prefixes)
- Break down a longer word into syllables in order to decode manageable units
- Solve words of two or three syllables, many words with inflectional endings and complex letter-sound relationships
- Use known words to solve new words
- Use context to derive meaning of new words
- Demonstrate competent, active word solving while reading at a good pace—less overt problem solving

Monitoring and Correcting

- Self-correct at point of error (or before overt error)
- When reading aloud, self-correct information when it does not reflect the meaning
- Use multiple sources of information to monitor and self-correct (language structure, meaning, and letter-sound information)
- Realize when more information is needed to understand a text
- Reread to confirm word solving by checking other sources of information
- Use known words to self-monitor and self-correct

Searching for and Using Information

- Use multiple sources of information to solve new words
- Notice and use graphics such as labels and captions for pictures and simple diagrams
- Use chapter titles as to foreshadow content
- Use readers' tools (table of contents, headings, and glossary) to find information
- Process long sentences (ten or more words) with many embedded phrases and clauses
- Process texts with a variety of dialogue, all assigned to speakers

Summarizing

- Follow and remember a series of events over a longer text in order to understand the ending
- Report episodes in a text in the order they happened
- Summarize ideas from a text and tell how they are related
- Summarize a longer narrative text with multiple episodes
- Identify important ideas in a text and report them in an organized way, either orally or in writing
- Understand the problem of a story and its solution

Maintaining Fluency

- Demonstrate phrased, fluent oral reading
- Read dialogue with phrasing and expression that reflects understanding of characters and events
- Demonstrate awareness of the function of the full range of punctuation
- Demonstrate appropriate stress on words, pausing and phrasing, intonation, and use of punctuation
- Use multiple sources of information (language structure, meaning, fast word recognition) to support fluency and phrasing
- Quickly and automatically solve most words in the text in a way that supports fluency
- Read silently at a good rate

Planning for Word Work during Guided Reading

One- to three-minute demonstrations and active student engagement using a chart or easel, white board, magnet letters, or pencil and paper can develop fluency and flexibility in visual processing. Plan for explicit work in specific visual processing areas that need support.

Examples:

- Recognize or write many high-frequency words (select from list of one hundred high-frequency words)
- Change words to add inflectional endings (*-ing, -ed; running, smiled*)
- Change words to make plurals by changing *y* to *i* and adding *-es* (*bunny, bunnies*)
- Write plural and singular forms for a wide range of plurals (*cars, boxes, pennies*)
- Change words by attaching simple prefixes and suffixes (*redo, runner*)
- Recognize and connect homophones (same pronunciation, different spelling and meaning) (*nose, knows*)
- Read or write words that have double vowel patterns (VVC: *keep, good*) as well as words with *y* as a vowel (*my*)
- Change words to create comparatives (*-er, -est*) (*dark/darker/darkest*)
- Take apart compound words (*some-thing*)
- Take apart and make words with two or three syllables (*um-brell-a*)
- Take apart one-syllable words with a variety of phonogram patterns (*sl-eep, dr-eam*)
- Read words using letter-sound analysis from left to right (*b-e-f-ore*)
- Use what is known about words to read new words (*and, candy; before, begin*)
- Read contractions with *am, is, not,* and *are* (*I'm, he's, can't, we're*)

Guided Reading

Selecting Goals Behaviors and Understandings to Notice, Teach, and Support

Adjusting

- Slow down to search for information and resume normal pace of reading again
- Demonstrate different ways of reading fiction and nonfiction texts
- Demonstrate adjustment of reading for simple biographies
- Reread to solve words or think about ideas and resume good rate of reading

Thinking *beyond* the Text

Predicting

- Use text structure to predict the outcome of a narrative
- Make predictions about the solution to the problem of a story
- Make predictions based on personal experiences, content knowledge, and knowledge of similar texts
- Search for and use information to confirm or disconfirm predictions
- Justify predictions using evidence
- Predict what characters will do based on the traits revealed by the writer

Making Connections

- Bring knowledge from personal experiences to the interpretation of characters and events
- Bring background knowledge to the understanding of a text before, during, and after reading
- Make connections between the text and other texts that have been read or heard
- Specify the nature of connections (topic, content, type of story, writer)

Synthesizing

- Differentiate between what is known and new information
- Demonstrate learning new content from reading
- Express changes in ideas after reading a text

Inferring

- Demonstrate understandings of characters, using evidence from text to support statements
- Infer characters' feelings and motivations through reading their dialogue
- Show understanding of characters and their traits
- Infer cause and effect in influencing characters' feelings or underlying motives
- Infer causes of problems or of outcomes in fiction and nonfiction texts

Thinking *about* the Text

Analyzing

- Notice aspects of genres (fiction, nonfiction, realistic stories, and fantasy)
- Understand when a writer has used underlying structures (description, compare and contrast, temporal sequence, problem and solution)
- Notice the way the writer assigns dialogue
- Notice aspects of a writer's style after reading several texts by him or her
- Notice specific writing techniques (for example, question and answer format)
- Notice and interpret figurative language and discuss how it adds to the meaning or enjoyment of a text
- Notice descriptive language and discuss how it adds to enjoyment or understanding
- Identify a point in the story when the problem is resolved

Critiquing

- Express opinions about the quality of a text
- Notice how the illustrations are consistent (or inconsistent) with meaning and extend the meaning
- Notice the quality of illustrations or graphics
- Agree or disagree with the ideas in a text
- Hypothesize how characters could have behaved differently
- Judge the text as to whether it is interesting, humorous, or exciting, and specify why

Guided Reading

Readers at **Level K:**

At Level K, readers process a wider range of genres (realistic fiction, animal fantasy, traditional literature, some simple biographies, and more informational texts). They read many illustrated chapter books (including some series books). Most fiction texts have multiple episodes related to a single plot but the demand on the reader's memory is higher than previous levels. They read about characters that change very little but are at the same time more complex; texts have multiple characters. Readers process a great deal of dialogue, some of it unassigned, and are challenged to read stories based on concepts that are distant in time and space and reflect diverse cultures. Readers solve many content-specific words and some technical words in informational texts. They automatically recognize a large number of words and quickly apply word-solving strategies to multisyllable words with inflectional endings, and to words with suffixes and prefixes. They can read a wide range of plurals, contractions, and possessives. They read silently in independent reading, but when reading orally they demonstrate all aspects of fluent reading.

Selecting Texts

Characteristics of Texts at This Level

Genre/Forms

Genre

- Informational texts
- Simple animal fantasy
- Realistic fiction
- Traditional literature (mostly folktales)
- Some simple biographies on familiar subjects

Forms

- Picture books
- Plays
- Beginning chapter books with illustrations
- Series books

Text Structure

Fiction

- Narratives with many episodes
- Some beginning chapter books with short chapters
- Chapters connected by character or broad theme
- Chapters usually connected to a longer plot
- Simple, straightforward plots

Nonfiction

- Presentation of multiple topics
- Underlying structures (description, comparison and contrast, temporal sequence, problem and solution, cause and effect)
- Texts organized into a few simple categories
- Variety in organization and topic
- Variety in nonfiction formats (question and answer, paragraphs, boxes, legends, and call-outs)

Content

- Familiar content and some new content that typically children would not know
- New content requiring prior knowledge to understand in some informational texts
- Some texts with plots and situations outside typical experience
- Some texts with settings outside children's typical experience
- New content accessible through text and illustrations

Themes and Ideas

- Many light, humorous stories, typical of childhood experiences
- Some ideas new to most children
- Themes accessible given typical experiences of children
- A few abstract ideas, supported by the text but with less illustration support
- Texts with universal themes illustrating important human issues and attributes (friendship, courage)

Language and Literary Features

- Some complex and memorable characters
- Some figurative language (metaphor, simile)
- Some texts with settings that are not typical of many children's experience
- Setting important to understanding the plot in some texts
- Complex plots with numerous episodes and time passing
- Simple, traditional elements of fantasy
- Most texts told from a single point of view
- May have more than one point of view within one text

Sentence Complexity

- Variety in sentence length and complexity
- Longer (more than fifteen words), more complex sentences (prepositional phrases, introductory clauses, lists of nouns, verbs, or adjectives)
- Questions in dialogue (fiction) and questions and answers (nonfiction)
- Many complex sentences with embedded phrases and clauses
- Variation in placement of subject, verb, adjectives, and adverbs
- Wide variety of words to assign dialogue, with verbs and adverbs essential to meaning

Vocabulary

- Content words illustrated with pictures or other graphics
- Some new vocabulary and content-specific words introduced, explained, and illustrated in the text
- Wide variety of words to assign dialogue, with verbs and adverbs essential to meaning

Guided Reading

Words

- Many two- to three-syllable words
- All parts of speech
- Plurals, contractions, and possessives
- Many words with inflectional endings
- Many words with complex letter-sound relationships
- Some complex spelling patterns
- Multisyllable words that are challenging to take apart or decode
- Some easy compound words

Illustrations

General

- Two or more kinds of graphics on a page
- Some long stretches of text with no illustrations or graphics

Fiction

- Most texts with no or only minimal illustrations
- In illustrated texts, highly complex and artistic illustrations that communicate meaning to match or extend the text (mood, symbolism)
- Some texts with illustrations that are essential to interpretation
- Some illustrations that support interpretation, enhance enjoyment, set mood but are not necessary for understanding

Nonfiction

- More than one kind of graphic on a page
- Combination of graphics providing information that matches and extends the text
- In most texts, graphics that are clearly explained (simple diagrams, illustrations with labels, maps, charts)
- Variety in the layout of print in nonfiction texts (question and answer, paragraphs, boxes, legends, call-outs)

"Now the other side is too long," Mom complained. "Let's see if I can fix it."

Snip! Snip!

"It's still not right," said Dad. "Let me take a bit more off this side."

6

Edwin's mom and dad took turns snipping and trimming, but the more they snipped, the worse things got. Edwin's hair got more and more crooked.

"We'd better quit," said Mom.

Dad agreed. "If we don't, he's not going to have any hair left!" he said. ■

7

Book and Print Features

Length

- Many lines of print on a page (three to fifteen lines; more for fiction)
- Chapter books (sixty to one hundred pages of print)

Print and Layout

- Ample space between lines
- Print and font size vary with some longer texts in small fonts
- Use of words in italics, bold, or all capitals to indicate emphasis, level of importance, or signal other meaning
- Variety in print and background color
- Sentences carrying over two to three lines and some over two pages
- Print and illustrations integrated in many texts
- Variety in layout, reflecting different genres
- Usually friendly layout in chapter books, with sentences starting on the left

Punctuation

- Periods, commas, quotation marks, exclamation points, question marks, dashes, and ellipses in most texts

Tools

- Readers' tools (table of contents, a few headings, glossary, chapter titles, author's notes)

Guided Reading

Selecting Goals

Behaviors and Understandings to Notice, Teach, and Support

Thinking *within* the Text

Solving Words

- Use multiple sources of information in solving new words consistently
- Connect words that mean the same or almost the same to help in understanding a text and acquiring new vocabulary
- Demonstrate knowledge of flexible ways to solve words (noticing word parts, noticing endings and prefixes)
- Break down a longer word into syllables in order to decode manageable units
- Solve words of two or three syllables, many words with inflectional endings and complex letter-sound relationships
- Solve content-specific words, using graphics and definitions embedded in the text
- Use context to derive meaning of new words
- Understand longer descriptive words
- Demonstrate competent, active word solving while reading at a good pace—less overt problem solving

Monitoring and Correcting

- Self-correct at point of error (or before overt error)
- Self-correct when errors detract from the meaning of the text
- When reading aloud, self-correct information when it does not reflect the meaning
- Use multiple sources of information to monitor and self-correct (language structure, meaning, and letter-sound information)
- Realize when more information is needed to understand a text

Searching for and Using Information

- Search for information in illustrations to support text interpretation
- Search for information in graphics (simple diagrams, illustrations with labels, maps, charts, captions under pictures)
- Use chapter titles as to foreshadow content
- Use readers' tools (table of contents, headings, glossary, chapter titles, and author's notes) to gather information
- Process long sentences (fifteen or more words) with embedded clauses (prepositional phrases, introductory clauses, series of nouns, verbs, or adverbs)
- Process a wide range of dialogue, some unassigned

Summarizing

- Follow and remember a series of events over a longer text in order to understand the ending
- Report episodes in a text in the order they happened
- Summarize ideas from a text and tell how they are related
- Summarize a longer narrative text with multiple episodes
- Identify important ideas in a text and report them in an organized way, either orally or in writing
- Understand the problem of a story and its solution

Maintaining Fluency

- Demonstrate phrased, fluent oral reading
- Read dialogue with phrasing and expression that reflects understanding of characters and events
- Demonstrate awareness of the function of the full range of punctuation
- Demonstrate appropriate stress on words, pausing and phrasing, intonation, and use of punctuation
- Use multiple sources of information (language structure, meaning, fast word recognition) to support fluency and phrasing
- Quickly and automatically solve most words in the text in a way that supports fluency
- Read silently at a good rate

Planning for Word Work during Guided Reading

One- to three-minute demonstrations and active student engagement using a chart or easel, white board, magnet letters, or pencil and paper can develop fluency and flexibility in visual processing. Plan for explicit work in specific visual processing areas that need support.

Examples:

- Recognize, write, or make many high-frequency words
- Review high-frequency words from previous levels
- Change words to add inflectional endings (*-ed, -ing; finished, writing*)
- Change words to make a full range of plurals by adding -*s* or -*es* (*faces, dishes, boys, babies, heroes*)
- Read, make, or write plural and singular forms for a wide range of plurals (*duck/ducks, dish/dishes, fly/flies*)
- Change words by attaching simple prefixes and suffixes (*untie, hiker*)
- Recognize and connect homophones (same pronunciation, different spellings and meanings) (*their, they're*)
- Read and connect homographs (same spelling, different meanings and sometimes different pronunciations) (*read, read; present, present*)
- Recognize and pronounce vowel sounds in open (CV: *ho-tel*) and closed (CVC: *lem-on*) syllables
- Read words that have double vowel patterns (VVC: *seem*)
- Read words that have vowel sounds with *r* (*corn*)
- Take apart, make, and write words with letter combinations representing long vowel sounds (*same, say, pail*)
- Change words to create comparatives (*-er, -est*) (*long/longer/longest*)
- Take apart compound words and discuss how the parts are related to meaning (*play-ground*)
- Take apart two- and three-syllable words (*lit-tle, com-pu-ter*)
- Read words using letter-sound analysis from left to right (*gl-ance*)
- Use what is known about words to read new words (*soon, moon; art, party*)
- Take apart words with consonant blends and digraphs at the ends of words (*help, path*)
- Take apart and read words with silent consonants (*lamb, light*)
- Recognize and take apart the full range of contractions (*I'm, that's, he'll, won't, they're, you've*)

Guided Reading

Selecting Goals

Behaviors and Understandings to Notice, Teach, and Support

Adjusting

- Slow down to search for information and resume normal pace of reading again
- Demonstrate different ways of reading fiction and nonfiction texts
- Demonstrate adjustment of reading for simple biographies
- Reread to solve words or think about ideas and resume good rate of reading

Thinking *beyond* the Text

Predicting

- Use text structure to predict the outcome of a narrative
- Make predictions about the solution to the problem of a story
- Make predictions based on personal experiences, content knowledge, and knowledge of similar texts
- Search for and use information to confirm or disconfirm predictions
- Justify predictions using evidence
- Predict what characters will do based on the traits revealed by the writer

Making Connections

- Bring knowledge from personal experiences to the interpretation of characters and events
- Bring background knowledge to the understanding of a text before, during, and after reading
- Make connections between the text and other texts that have been read or heard
- Specify the nature of connections (topic, content, type of story, writer)

Synthesizing

- Differentiate between what is known and new information
- Demonstrate learning new content from reading
- Express changes in ideas after reading a text

Inferring

- Demonstrate through talk or writing understandings of characters, using evidence from text to support statements
- Infer characters' feelings and motivations through reading their dialogue
- Show understanding of characters and their traits
- Infer cause and effect in influencing characters' feelings or underlying motives
- Infer the big ideas or message (theme) of a text
- Infer causes of problems or of outcomes in fiction and nonfiction texts

Thinking *about* the Text

Analyzing

- Notice and discuss aspects of genres (fiction, nonfiction, realistic stories, and fantasy)
- Understand when a writer has used underlying organizational structures (description, compare/contrast, temporal sequence, problem/solution, cause/effect)
- Notice variety in layout (words in bold or larger font, or italics, variety in layout)
- Notice and discuss the way the writer assigns dialogue
- Notice aspects of a writer's style after reading several texts by the author
- Notice specific writing techniques (for example, question and answer format)
- Notice and interpret figurative language and discuss how it adds to the meaning or enjoyment of a text
- Notice descriptive language and discuss how it adds to enjoyment or understanding
- Understand the relationship between the setting and the plot of a story
- Identify a point in the story when the problem is resolved

Critiquing

- Express opinions about the quality of a text
- Discuss the quality of illustrations or graphics
- Agree or disagree with the ideas in a text
- Hypothesize how characters could have behaved differently
- Judge the text as to whether it is interesting, humorous, or exciting, and specify why

Guided Reading

Readers at **Level L:**

At Level L, readers process easy chapter books including some series books, with more sophisticated plots and few illustrations, as well as shorter informational and fiction books. They adjust their reading to process a range of genres (realistic fiction, simple fantasy, informational texts, traditional literature, and biography, as well as some special types of texts, for example, mysteries). They understand that chapters have multiple episodes related to a single plot. They learn some new content through reading and are required to bring more prior knowledge to the process; but the content is usually accessible through the text and illustrations. At this level, readers are beginning to recognize themes across texts (friendship, courage), and they understand some abstract ideas. They see multiple perspectives of characters as revealed through description, what they say, think, or do, and what others say about them. They process complex sentences with embedded clauses and figurative language. They recognize and/or flexibly solve a large number of words, including plurals, contractions, possessives, many multisyllable words, many content-specific words, and some technical words. They read silently in independent reading; in oral reading, they demonstrate all aspects of smooth, fluent processing.

Selecting Texts

Characteristics of Texts at This Level

Genre/Forms

Genre

- Informational texts
- Simple fantasy
- Realistic fiction
- Traditional literature
- Biography, mostly on well-known subjects
- Simple mysteries

Forms

- Picture books
- Plays
- Beginning chapter books with illustrations
- Series books

Text Structure

Fiction

- Narrative structure including chapters with multiple episodes related to a single plot
- Simple, straightforward plots

Nonfiction

- Presentation of multiple topics
- Underlying structures (description, comparison and contrast, temporal sequence, problem and solution, cause and effect)
- Texts organized into a few simple categories
- Variety in organization and topic
- Variety in nonfiction formats (question and answer, paragraphs, boxes, legends, and call-outs)

Content

- New content requiring prior knowledge to understand
- Some texts with plots, settings, and situations outside typical experience
- Some technical content that is challenging and not typically known
- New content accessible through text and illustrations

Themes and Ideas

- Many light, humorous stories, typical of childhood experiences
- Some ideas that are new to most students
- Themes accessible given typical experiences of students
- Texts with universal themes illustrating important human issues and attributes (friendship, courage)

Language and Literary Features

- Some complex and memorable characters
- Multiple characters to understand and follow development
- Various ways of showing characters' attributes (description, dialogue, thoughts, others' perspectives)
- Figurative language and descriptive language
- Setting important to understanding the plot in some texts
- Wide variety in showing dialogue, both assigned and unassigned
- Complex plots with numerous episodes and time passing
- Plots with numerous episodes, building toward problem resolution
- Simple, traditional elements of fantasy
- Texts with multiple points of view revealed through characters' behaviors and dialogue

The baby grabs the fur on his mother's belly and begins to feed. The baby is snug against his mother's warm body. Later, the baby curls his long tail, arms, and legs around his mother.

The First Weeks

For a few weeks, the baby rides on his mother's back. The mother carries, feeds, and grooms her baby. She keeps the baby safe from snakes, hawks, and big cats.

Sometimes, the baby monkey loses his grip and falls to the rain forest floor. A monkey from the troop climbs down the tree and

2

A baby capuchin clings to his mother's back.

picks up the baby. Back with his mother, the baby hangs on again.

After a month, the baby begins to learn about the world. He moves away from his mother. But he only goes as far as his tail will let him! The baby holds on to his mother using his long tail.

Caring for the baby is hard work! Other monkeys in the troop

3

Guided Reading

Sentence Complexity

- Variety in sentence length and complexity
- Longer (more than fifteen words), more complex sentences (prepositional phrases, introductory clauses, lists of nouns, verbs, or adjectives)
- Questions in dialogue (fiction) and questions and answers (nonfiction)
- Sentences with nouns, verbs, or adjectives in series, divided by commas

Vocabulary

- Some new vocabulary and content-specific words introduced, explained, and illustrated in the text
- Wide variety of words to assign dialogue, with verbs and adverbs essential to meaning
- New vocabulary in fiction texts (largely unexplained)

Words

- Many two- to three-syllable words
- Some words with more than three syllables
- All parts of speech
- Words with suffixes and prefixes
- Words with a wide variety of very complex spelling patterns
- Multisyllable words that are challenging to take apart or decode
- Many plurals, contractions, and compound words

Illustrations

General

- A variety of compex graphics, often more than one on a page
- Some long stretches of text with no illustrations or graphics

Fiction

- Most texts with no or only minimal illustrations
- In illustrated texts, highly complex and artistic illustrations that communicate meaning to match or extend the text (mood, symbolism)
- Some texts with illustrations that are essential to interpretation
- Some illustrations that support interpretation, enhance enjoyment, and set mood but are not necessary for understanding

Nonfiction

- More than one kind of graphic on a page
- Combination of graphics providing information that matches and extends the text
- Graphics that are clearly explained in most texts
- Variety in the layout of print in nonfiction texts (question and answer, paragraphs, boxes, maps, charts, call-outs, illustrations with labels and legends)

Book and Print Features

Length

- Chapter books (sixty to one hundred pages of print)
- Shorter texts (most approximately twenty-four to forty-eight pages of print) on single topics (usually nonfiction)
- Many lines of print on a page (five to twenty-four lines; more for fiction)

Print and Layout

- Ample space between lines
- Print and font size varying with some longer texts in small fonts
- Use of words in italics, bold, or all capitals to indicate emphasis, level of importance, or signal other meaning
- Variety in print and background color
- Some sentences continuing over several lines or to the next page
- Print and illustrations integrated in many texts
- Variety in layout, reflecting different genres
- Usually friendly layout in chapter books, with sentences starting on the left
- Variety in layout of nonfiction formats (question and answer, paragraphs, boxes, legends, call-outs)

Punctuation

- Periods, commas, quotation marks, exclamation points, question marks, dashes, and ellipses in most texts

Tools

- Readers' tools (table of contents, a few headings, glossary, chapter titles, author's notes)

Guided Reading

Selecting Goals

Behaviors and Understandings to Notice, Teach, and Support

Thinking *within* the Text

Solving Words

- Notice new and interesting words, and actively add them to speaking or writing vocabulary
- Connect words that mean the same or almost the same to help in understanding a text and acquiring new vocabulary
- Demonstrate knowledge of flexible ways to solve words (noticing word parts, noticing endings and prefixes)
- Solve words of two or three syllables, many words with inflectional endings and complex letter-sound relationships
- Solve content-specific words, using graphics and definitions embedded in the text
- Use context to derive meaning of new words
- Understand longer descriptive words
- Demonstrate competent, active word solving while reading at a good pace

Monitoring and Correcting

- Self-correct when errors detract from the meaning of the text
- Self-correct intonation when it does not reflect the meaning when reading aloud
- Use multiple sources of information to monitor and self-correct (language structure, meaning, and letter-sound information)
- Realize when more information is needed to understand a text

Searching for and Using Information

- Use multiple sources of information to solve new words
- Search for information in illustrations to support text interpretation
- Search for information in graphics (simple diagrams, illustrations with labels, maps, charts, captions under pictures)
- Use chapter titles to foreshadow content
- Use readers' tools (table of contents, headings, glossary, chapter titles, and author's notes) to gather information
- Process long sentences (fifteen or more words) with embedded clauses (prepositional phrases, introductory clauses)
- Process sentences with a series of nouns, verbs, or adverbs
- Process a wide range of dialogue, some unassigned

Summarizing

- Follow and remember a series of events over a longer text in order to understand the ending
- Summarize ideas from a text and tell how they are related
- Summarize a longer narrative text with multiple episodes, reporting events in the order they happened
- Identify important ideas in a text and report them in an organized way, either orally or in writing
- Understand the problem of a story and its solution

Planning for Word Work during Guided Reading

One- to three-minute demonstrations with active student engagement using a chart or easel, white board, or pencil and paper can develop fluency and flexibility in visual processing. Plan for explicit work in specific visual processing areas that need support.

Examples:

- Recognize and take apart words with inflectional endings (*painting, skated*)
- Make and change words to add inflectional endings (*-ing, -ed; cry-crying-cried*)
- Change words to make a full range of plurals by adding *-s* and *-es* (*stoves, axes, toys, hobbies, echoes*)
- Work flexibly with base words, taking apart and making new words by changing letters and adding prefixes and suffixes (*tie/tied/untie*)
- Recognize word patterns that look the same but sound different (*dear, bear*) and that sound the same but look different (*said, bed*)
- Recognize and connect homophones (same pronunciation, different spellings and meanings) (*dear, deer*)
- Read homographs (same spelling, different meanings, and sometimes different pronunciations) (*bear, bear; bass, bass*)
- Recognize and pronounce vowel sounds in open (CV: *ho-tel*) and closed (CVC: *lem-on*) syllables
- Read words that have double vowel patterns (VVC: *feel*) as well as words that have vowel sounds with *r* (*march*)
- Take apart and make words using more complex phonograms and long vowel patterns (VVC (*paint*), VVCe (*raise*), VCCe (*large*), VCCC (*lunch*), VVCCC (*health*))
- Make and change words to create comparatives (*-er, -est*) (*light/lighter/lightest*)
- Take apart words with comparatives (*short-er, short-est*)
- Take apart compound words and discuss how the parts are related to meaning (*cook-book*)
- Take apart two- and three-syllable words (*sal-ad, cu-cum-ber*)
- Read words using letter-sound analysis from left to right (*s-l-i-pp-er*)
- Use what is known about words to read new words (*fan, fancy; ate, later*)
- Read words with silent consonants (*sight, knife*)
- Read, take apart, or write words with consonant blends and digraphs at the ends (*spend, splash*)
- Recognize and take apart the full range of contractions (*I'm, that's, he'll, won't, they're, you've*)
- Take apart words with open and closed syllables (*fe-ver, ped-al*)

Guided Reading

Selecting Goals

Behaviors and Understandings to Notice, Teach, and Support

Maintaining Fluency

- Demonstrate phrased, fluent oral reading
- Read dialogue with phrasing and expression that reflects understanding of characters and events
- Demonstrate awareness of the function of the full range of punctuation
- Demonstrate appropriate stress on words, pausing and phrasing, intonation, and use of punctuation
- Use multiple sources of information (language structure, meaning, fast word recognition) to support fluency and phrasing
- Quickly and automatically solve most words in the text in a way that supports fluency
- Use multiple sources of information in a way that supports fluency
- Read silently and orally at an appropriate rate, not too fast and not too slow

Adjusting

- Slow down to search for information or think about ideas and resume normal pace of reading again
- Demonstrate different ways of reading fiction and nonfiction texts
- Demonstrate adjustment to process simple biographies
- Reread to solve words and resume normal rate of reading

Thinking *beyond* the Text

Predicting

- Use text structure to predict the outcome of a narrative
- Make predictions about the solution to the problem in a story
- Make a wide range of predictions based on personal experiences, content knowledge, and knowledge of similar texts
- Search for and use information to confirm or disconfirm predictions
- Justify predictions using evidence
- Predict what characters will do based on the traits revealed by the writer

Making Connections

- Bring knowledge from personal experiences to the interpretation of characters and events
- Before, during, and after reading, bring background knowledge to the understanding of a text
- Make connections between the text and other texts that have been read or heard
- Specify the nature of connections (topic, content, type of story, writer)

Synthesizing

- Differentiate between what is known and new information
- Demonstrate learning new content from reading
- Expresses changes in ideas after reading a text

Inferring

- Demonstrate understandings of characters, using evidence from text to support statements
- Infer characters' feelings and motivations through reading their dialogue
- Show understanding of characters and their traits
- Infer cause and effect in influencing characters' feelings or underlying motives
- Infer the big ideas or message (theme) of a text
- Infer causes of problems or of outcomes in fiction and nonfiction texts

Thinking *about* the Text

Analyzing

- Notice and discuss aspects of genres (fiction, nonfiction, realistic stories, and fantasy)
- Understand a writer's use of underlying organizational structures (description, compare/contrast, temporal sequence, problem/solution, cause/effect)
- Demonstrate the ability to identify how a text is organized (diagram or talk)
- Identify important aspects of illustrations (design related to the meaning of the text)
- Notice variety in layout (words in bold or larger font, or italics, variety in layout)
- Notice the way the writer assigns dialogue
- Notice aspects of a writer's style after reading several texts by the same author
- Notice specific writing techniques (for example, question and answer format)
- Notice and interpret figurative language and discuss how it adds to the meaning or enjoyment of a text
- Notice descriptive language and discuss how it adds to enjoyment or understanding
- Understand the relationship between the setting and the plot of a story
- Identify a point in the story when the problem is resolved

Critiquing

- State opinions about a text and provide evidence to support them
- Discuss the quality of illustrations or graphics
- Hypothesize how characters could have behaved differently
- Judge the text as to whether it is interesting, humorous, or exciting, and specify why

Guided Reading

Readers at **Level M:**

At Level M, readers know the characteristics of a range of genres (realistic fiction, simple fantasy, informational texts, traditional literature, and biography). Many fiction texts are chapter books and readers are becoming interested in special forms, such as series books and mysteries. Fiction narratives are straightforward but have elaborate plots and multiple characters that develop and show some change over time. They read shorter nonfiction texts, mostly on single topics, and are able to identify and use underlying structures (description, comparison and contrast, temporal sequence, problem and solution, cause and effect). They can process sentences that are complex, contain prepositional phrases, introductory clauses, lists of nouns, verbs, or adjectives. Word solving is smooth and automatic in both silent and oral reading. They can read and understand descriptive words, some complex content-specific words, and some technical words. They read silently and independently. In oral reading, they demonstrate all aspects of smooth, fluent processing.

Selecting Texts **Characteristics of Texts at This Level**

Genre/Forms

Genre

- Informational texts
- Simple fantasy
- Realistic fiction
- Traditional literature
- Biography, mostly on well-known subjects
- Simple mysteries

Forms

- Picture books
- Plays
- Beginning chapter books with illustrations
- Series books

Text Structure

Fiction

- Narrative structure including chapters with multiple episodes related to a single plot
- Simple, straightforward plots

Nonfiction

- Presentation of multiple topics
- Underlying structures (description, comparison and contrast, temporal sequence, problem and solution, cause and effect)
- Texts organized into a few simple categories
- Variety in organization and topic
- Variety in nonfiction formats (question and answer, paragraphs, boxes, legends, and call-outs)

Content

- Some technical content that is challenging and not typically known
- Most of content carried by the print rather than pictures
- Content supported or extended by illustrations in most informational texts

Themes and Ideas

- Many light, humorous stories, typical of childhood experiences
- Most ideas supported by the text but with less illustration support
- Texts with universal themes illustrating important human issues and attributes (friendship, courage)
- Some abstract themes requiring inferential thinking to derive

Language and Literary Features

- Some complex and memorable characters
- Various ways of showing characters' attributes (description, dialogue, thoughts, others' perspectives)
- Multiple characters to understand and notice how they develop and change over time
- Figurative and descriptive language
- Setting important to understanding the plot in some texts
- Various perspectives revealed through dialogue
- Wide variety in showing dialogue, both assigned and unassigned
- Complex plots with numerous episodes and time passing
- Plots with numerous episodes, building toward problem resolution
- Simple, traditional elements of fantasy
- Texts with multiple points of view revealed through characters' behaviors

was responsible enough to get a dog.

"Great! How can I prove I'm responsible? I'll do anything!"

"First, you should call the animal shelter and ask them how much it costs to get a dog. Then you'll have to save the money."

"I can certainly do that!" I said.

I called the shelter. I found out it costs one hundred and forty dollars to get a puppy and seventy dollars to get a dog. I decided to get a grown dog!

How long would it take me to save seventy dollars? I started to do the math.

My allowance was seven dollars a

2

week, if I did all my chores. I never used to save any of it. Now I'd have to save a whole lot. ■

With seven dollars a week, I'd have seventy dollars in ten weeks. But that was too long to wait!

I asked Mom about doing some extra jobs for her. She agreed to pay me three dollars for each one. She said I could clean the garage, vacuum the car, paint the kitchen door, brush all the cobwebs out of the basement (yuck!) . . .

"Okay, Mom, I think that's enough for now!" I said.

The next few weeks were really hard. I did all my chores, even

3

Guided Reading

Sentence Complexity

- Some longer (more than fifteen words), more complex sentences (prepositional phrases, introductory clauses, lists of nouns, verbs, or adjectives)
- Variety in sentence length, with some long and complex sentences
- Questions in dialogue (fiction) and questions and answers (nonfiction)
- Sentences with parenthetical material
- Sentences with nouns, verbs, or adjectives in series, divided by commas

Vocabulary

- Some new vocabulary and content-specific words introduced, explained, and illustrated in the text
- New vocabulary in fiction texts largely unexplained

Words

- Many two- to three-syllable words
- Some words with more than three syllables
- All parts of speech
- Words with suffixes
- Words with a wide variety of very complex spelling patterns
- Multisyllable words that are challenging to take apart or decode
- Many plurals, contractions, and compound words

Illustrations

General

- A variety of compex graphics, often more than one on a page
- Some long stretches of text with no illustrations or graphics

Fiction

- Most texts with no or only minimal illustrations
- In illustrated texts, highly complex and artistic illustrations that communicate meaning to match or extend the text (mood, symbolism)
- Black and white illustrations in most texts

Nonfiction

- More than one kind of graphic on a page
- Combination of graphics providing information that matches and extends the text
- Variety of graphics (diagrams, labels, cutaways, maps, scales with legends, illustrations with labels, charts)
- In most texts, graphics that are clearly explained
- Variety in the layout of print in nonfiction texts (question and answer, paragraphs, boxes, legends, call-outs)

Book and Print Features

Length

- Chapter books (sixty to one hundred pages of print)

Print and Layout

- Ample space between lines
- Print and font size varying with some longer texts in small fonts
- Use of words in italics, bold, or all capitals to indicate emphasis, level of importance, or signal other meaning
- Variety in print and background color
- Many sentences continuing over several lines or to the next page
- Print and illustrations integrated in many texts
- Captions under pictures that provide important information
- Usually friendly layout in chapter books, with sentences starting on the left
- Variety in layout of nonfiction formats (question and answer, paragraphs, boxes, legends, call-outs)

Punctuation

- Full range of punctuation, including dashes and ellipses

Tools

- Readers' tools (table of contents, a few headings, glossary, chapter titles, author's notes)

Guided Reading

Selecting Goals Behaviors and Understandings to Notice, Teach, and Support

Thinking *within* the Text

Solving Words

- Begin to notice new and interesting words, record them, and actively add them to speaking or writing vocabulary
- Connect words that mean the same or almost the same to help in understanding a text and acquiring new vocabulary
- Demonstrate knowledge of flexible ways to solve words (noticing word parts, noticing endings and prefixes)
- Solve words of two or three syllables, many words with inflectional endings and complex letter-sound relationships
- Solve content-specific words, using graphics and definitions embedded in the text
- Use the context of a sentence, paragraph, or whole text to determine the meaning of a word
- Understand longer descriptive words
- Demonstrate competent, active word solving while reading at a good pace–less overt problem solving

Monitoring and Correcting

- Self-correct when errors detract from the meaning of the text
- When reading aloud, self-correct intonation when it does not reflect the meaning
- Use multiple sources of information to monitor and self-correct (language structure, meaning, and letter-sound information)
- Consistently check on understanding and search for information when meaning breaks down

Searching for and Using Information

- Use multiple sources of information to solve new words
- Search for information in illustrations to support text interpretation
- Search for information in graphics (simple diagrams, illustrations with labels, maps, charts, captions under pictures)
- Use chapter titles to foreshadow content
- Use readers' tools (table of contents, headings, glossary, chapter titles, and author's notes) to gather information
- Process long sentences (fifteen or more words) with embedded clauses (prepositional phrases, introductory clauses)
- Process sentences with a series of nouns, verbs, or adverbs
- Process a wide range of dialogue, some unassigned

Summarizing

- Follow and remember a series of events over a longer text in order to understand the ending
- Report episodes in a text in the order they happened
- Summarize ideas from a text and tell how they are related
- Summarize a longer narrative text with multiple episodes
- Identify important ideas in a text and report them in an organized way, either orally or in writing
- Understand the problem of a story and its solution

Planning for Word Work during Guided Reading

One- to three-minute demonstrations with active student engagement using a chart or easel, white board, or pencil and paper can develop fluency and flexibility in visual processing. Plan for explicit work in specific visual processing areas that need support.

Examples:

- Take apart words with a variety of endings (*box-ful, caring*)
- Add a variety of endings to words (*-ing, -es, -ed, -er; walking, bushes, climbed, hiker*)
- Change words to make a full range of plurals by adding *-s* and *-es* (*pens, fairies, mixes*)
- Take apart words with common prefixes (*un-true, re-play*)
- Remove letters or letter clusters from the beginning of a word to recognize a base word (*un-friend-ly*)
- Work flexibly with base words taking apart and making new words by changing letters and adding prefixes and suffixes (*write/writing/rewrite*)
- Recognize words that have multiple meanings (a form of homograph: *spell, spell*), homographs (look the same, sound different: *present, present*), and homophones (sound the same, look different: *ate, eight*)
- Recognize and pronounce vowel sounds in open (CV: *mo-tel*) and closed (CVC: *rel-ish*) syllables
- Take apart and make words using more complex phonograms and long vowel patterns (VVC (*paint*), VVCe (*raise*), VCCe (*large*), VCCC (*lunch*), VVCCC (*health*))
- Take apart compound words and discuss how the parts are related to meaning (*bath-tub*)
- Take apart multisyllable words to decode manageable units (*sand-wich-es, hap-pi-ly*)
- Read words using letter-sound analysis from left to right (*g-ar-d-en*)
- Use what is known about words to read new words (*mean, clean; van, vanish*)
- Take apart and read the full range of contractions (*I'm, that's, he'll, won't, they're, you've*)

Guided Reading

Selecting Goals

Behaviors and Understandings to Notice, Teach, and Support

Maintaining Fluency

- Demonstrate phrased, fluent oral reading
- Read dialogue with phrasing and expression that reflects understanding of characters and events
- Demonstrate awareness of the function of the full range of punctuation
- Demonstrate appropriate stress on words, pausing and phrasing, intonation, and use of punctuation
- Use multiple sources of information (language structure, meaning, fast word recognition) to support fluency and phrasing
- Quickly and automatically solve most words in the text in a way that supports fluency
- Read silently and orally at an appropriate rate, not too fast and not too slow

Adjusting

- Slow down to search for information and resume normal pace of reading again
- Demonstrate different ways of reading fiction and nonfiction texts
- Demonstrate adjustment of reading for simple biographies
- Reread to solve words or think about ideas and resume good rate of reading

Thinking *beyond* the Text

Predicting

- Use text structure to predict the outcome of a narrative
- Make predictions about the solution to the problem of a story
- Make a wide range of predictions based on personal experiences, content knowledge, and knowledge of similar texts
- Search for and use information to confirm or disconfirm predictions
- Justify predictions using evidence
- Predict what characters will do based on the traits revealed by the writer

Making Connections

- Bring knowledge from personal experiences to the interpretation of characters and events
- Bring background content knowledge to the understanding of a text before, during, and after reading
- Make connections between the text and other texts that have been read or heard
- Specify the nature of connections (topic, content, type of story, writer)

Synthesizing

- Differentiate between what is known and new information
- Demonstrate learning new content from reading
- Expresses changes in ideas after reading a text

Inferring

- Demonstrate understandings of characters, using evidence from text to support statements
- Infer characters' feelings and motivations through reading their dialogue
- Infer cause and effect in influencing characters' feelings or underlying motives
- Infer the big ideas or message (theme) of a text
- Generate or react to alternative understandings of a text
- Infer causes of problems or outcomes in fiction and nonfiction texts
- Identify significant events and tell how they are related to the problem of the story or the solution

Thinking *about* the Text

Analyzing

- Notice aspects of genres (fiction, nonfiction, realistic stories, and fantasy)
- Understand when a writer has used underlying organizational structures (description, compare/contrast, temporal sequence, problem/solution, cause/effect)
- Demonstrate the ability to identify how a text is organized (diagram or talk)
- Identify important aspects of illustrations (design related to the meaning of the text)
- Notice variety in layout (words in bold or larger font, or italics, variety in layout)
- Notice the way the writer assigns dialogue
- Notice aspects of a writer's style after reading several texts by the same author
- Notice specific writing techniques (for example, question and answer format)
- Notice and interpret figurative language and discuss how it adds to the meaning or enjoyment of a text
- Notice descriptive language and discuss how it adds to enjoyment or understanding
- Understand the relationship between the setting and the plot of a story
- Identify a point in the story when the problem is resolved

Critiquing

- State opinions about a text and show evidence to support them
- Discuss the quality of illustrations or graphics
- Hypothesize how characters could have behaved differently
- Judge the text as to whether it is interesting, humorous, or exciting, and specify why

Guided Reading

Readers at **Level N:**

At Level N, readers will process the full range of genres, short fiction stories, chapter books, and shorter informational texts; also, they read special forms such as mysteries and series books. Fiction narratives are straightforward but have elaborate plots and multiple characters who develop and change over time. Some nonfiction texts provide information in categories on several related topics, and readers can identify and use underlying structures (description, compare and contrast, temporal sequence, problem and solution, cause and effect). They continue to read silently at a good rate and automatically use a wide range of word-solving strategies while focusing on meaning. In oral reading, they will continue to read with phrasing, fluency, and appropriate word stress in a way that reflects meaning and recognizes punctuation. Readers will slow down to problem solve or search for information and then resume normal pace; there is little overt problem solving. They can process sentences that are complex, with prepositional phrases, introductory clauses, lists of nouns, verbs, or adjectives. They can read and understand descriptive words, some complex content-specific words, and some technical words. Word solving is smooth and automatic in both silent and oral reading.

Selecting Texts — Characteristics of Texts at This Level

Genre/Forms

GENRE

- Informational texts
- Simple fantasy
- Realistic fiction
- Traditional literature
- Biography, mostly on well-known subjects
- Historical fiction
- Simple mysteries

FORMS

- Picture books
- Plays
- Beginning chapter books with illustrations
- Series books

Text Structure

FICTION

- Narrative structure including chapters with multiple episodes related to a single plot
- Plots with detailed episodes

NONFICTION

- Texts organized into categories and subcategories
- Presentation of multiple topics that represent subtopics of a larger content area or theme
- Underlying structures (description, comparison and contrast, temporal sequence, problem and solution, cause and effect)
- Variety in organization and topic
- Variety in nonfiction formats (question and answer, paragraphs, boxes, legends, and call-outs)

Content

- Content requiring prior knowledge to understand in many informational texts
- Most of content carried by the print rather than pictures
- Content supported or extended by illustrations and other graphics in most informational texts
- Content requiring the reader to take on perspectives from diverse cultures and bring cultural knowledge to understanding

Themes and Ideas

- Many light, humorous stories, typical of childhood experiences
- A few abstract ideas, supported by the text but with less illustration support
- Some abstract themes requiring inferential thinking to derive
- Texts with deeper meanings applicable to important human problems and social issues

Language and Literary Features

- Multiple characters to understand
- Characters and perspectives revealed by what they say, think, and do and what others say or think about them
- Memorable characters who change and develop over time
- Factors related to character change explicit and obvious
- Descriptive and figurative language that is important to understanding the plot
- Setting important to understanding the plot in some texts
- Wide variety in showing dialogue, both assigned and unassigned
- Complex plots with numerous episodes and time passing
- Plots with numerous episodes, building toward problem resolution
- Building suspense through events of the plot
- Simple, traditional elements of fantasy
- Texts with multiple points of view revealed through characters' behaviors

What Are Guide Dogs?

Guide dogs help blind people get from place to place and lead independent lives. With a guide dog, blind people can go to the grocery store, ride the bus, or take a trip on a plane. Guide dogs are allowed in places where most other dogs are not.

Not just any dog can be a guide dog. A guide dog needs many months of training at a special school.

At school they learn to behave quietly, especially in public. Guide dogs have to focus on helping their owners. They are taught to ignore other things, such as interesting smells and other animals.

2

Guide dogs help their owners cross streets safely.

They also learn to keep still and quiet in busy places, such as shopping malls or offices. Most dogs would have a very hard time doing that!

Dogs At Work

If you see a guide dog doing its job, remember not to pet or talk to it. Guiding is very hard to do. It requires a dog's full attention. ■

A guide dog wears a special harness, called a lead harness.

3

Guided Reading

Sentence Complexity

- Variety in sentence length, with some longer (more than fifteen words), more complex sentences (prepositional phrases, introductory clauses, lists of nouns, verbs, or adjectives)
- Questions in dialogue (fiction) and questions and answers (nonfiction)
- Sentences with parenthetical material
- Sentences with nouns, verbs, or adjectives in series, divided by commas

Vocabulary

- Many complex content-specific words in nonfiction, mostly defined in text, illustrations, or glossary
- New vocabulary in fiction texts largely unexplained
- Some words used figuratively
- Some words with connotative meanings that are essential to understanding the text
- Some longer descriptive words (adjectives and adverbs)

Words

- Many words with three or more syllables
- All parts of speech
- Words with suffixes and prefixes
- Words with a wide variety of very complex spelling patterns
- Multisyllable words that are challenging to take apart or decode
- Some multisyllable proper nouns that are difficult to decode
- Many plurals, contractions, and compound words
- Some words divided (hyphenated) across lines

Illustrations

General

- A variety of compex graphics, often more than one on a page
- Some long stretches of text with no illustrations or graphics

Fiction

- Most texts with no or only minimal illustrations
- Black and white illustrations in most texts
- In illustrated texts, highly complex and artistic illustrations that communicate meaning to match or extend the text (mood, symbolism)

Nonfiction

- Combination of graphics providing information that matches and extends the text
- Variety of graphics (diagrams, labels, cutaways, maps, scales with legends, illustrations with labels, charts)
- In most texts, graphics that are clearly explained
- Variety in the layout of print in nonfiction texts (question and answer, paragraphs, boxes, legends, call-outs)

Book and Print Features

Print and Layout

- Ample space between lines
- Print and font size varying with some longer texts in small fonts
- Use of words in italics, bold, or all capitals to indicate emphasis, level of importance, or signal other meaning
- Variety in print and background color
- Sentences continuing over several lines or to the next page
- Print and illustrations integrated in many texts
- Captions under pictures that provide important information
- Variety in layout, reflecting different genres
- Usually friendly layout in chapter books, with sentences starting on the left
- Variety in layout of nonfiction formats (question and answer, paragraphs, boxes, legends, call-outs)

Punctuation

- Full range of punctuation, including dashes and ellipses

Tools

- Readers' tools (table of contents, a few headings, glossary, chapter titles, author's notes)

Guided Reading

Selecting Goals Behaviors and Understandings to Notice, Teach, and Support

Thinking *within* the Text

Solving Words

- Begin to notice new and interesting words, and add them to speaking or writing vocabulary
- Connect words that mean the same or almost the same to help in understanding a text and acquiring new vocabulary
- Demonstrate knowledge of flexible ways to solve words (noticing word parts, noticing endings and prefixes)
- Solve words of two or three syllables, many words with inflectional endings and complex letter-sound relationships
- Solve content-specific words, using graphics and definitions embedded in the text
- Use the context of a sentence, paragraph, or whole text to determine the meaning of a word
- Understand longer descriptive words
- Apply problem-solving strategies to technical words or proper nouns that are challenging

Monitoring and Correcting

- Continue to monitor accuracy and understanding, self-correcting when errors detract from meaning

Searching for and Using Information

- Search for information in graphics (simple diagrams, illustrations with labels, maps, charts, captions under pictures)
- Use readers' tools (table of contents, headings, glossary, chapter titles, and author's notes) to gather information
- Process long sentences (fifteen or more words) with embedded clauses (prepositional phrases, introductory clauses, series of nouns, verbs, or adverbs)
- Process a wide range of dialogue, some unassigned
- Respond to plot tension or suspense by reading on to seek resolutions to problems

Summarizing

- Follow and remember a series of events and the story problem and solution over a longer text in order to understand the ending
- Identify and understand sets of related ideas organized into categories
- Summarize a text at intervals during the reading of a longer text
- Summarize longer narrative texts with multiple episodes either orally or in writing
- Identify important ideas in a text and report them in an organized way, either orally or in writing

Maintaining Fluency

- Demonstrate phrased, fluent oral reading
- Read dialogue with phrasing and expression that reflects understanding of characters and events
- Demonstrate appropriate stress on words, pausing and phrasing, intonation, and use of punctuation
- Use multiple sources of information (language structure, meaning, fast word recognition) to support fluency and phrasing

Adjusting

- Demonstrate different ways of reading related to genre, including simple biographies, fantasy, and historical fiction
- Adjust reading to process texts with difficult and complex layout
- Reread to solve words or think about ideas and resume good rate of reading

Planning for Word Work during Guided Reading

One- to three-minute demonstrations with active student engagement using a chart or easel, white board, or pencil and paper can develop fluency and flexibility in visual processing. Plan for explicit work in specific visual processing areas that need support.

Examples:

- Take apart and make words with a variety of endings (*-ing, -es, -ed,-er*) and discuss changes in spelling and meaning
- Take apart and make a full range of plurals, including irregular plurals and plurals that require spelling changes (*child/students, diary/diaries*)
- Work flexibly with base words, making new words by changing letters and adding prefixes and suffixes (*tip/tie/untie, grew/grow/growing*)
- Recognize words that have multiple meanings (a form of homograph: *train, train*), homographs (look the same, sound different: *lead, lead*), and homophones (sound the same, look different: *meet, meat*)
- Take apart and make words using more complex phonograms and long vowel patterns (VVCC (*east*), VVCe (*tease*), VCCe (*waste*), VCCC (*branch*), VVCCC (*wealth*))
- Take apart compound words (*mail-box*)
- Take apart multisyllable words to decode manageable units (*free-dom*)
- Solve words using letter-sound analysis from left to right (*r-e-m-e-m-b-er*)
- Use what is known about words to read new words (*reason, unreasonable*)
- Take apart and read the full range of contractions (*I'm, that's, he'll, won't, they're, you've*)
- Take apart words with open (ending in a vowel: *ri-ot*) and closed (ending in a consonant: *riv-er*) syllables

Guided Reading

Selecting Goals Behaviors and Understandings to Notice, Teach, and Support

Thinking *beyond* the Text

Predicting

- Use text structure to predict the outcome of a narrative
- Make a wide range of predictions based on personal experiences, content knowledge, and knowledge of similar texts
- Search for and use information to confirm or disconfirm predictions
- Justify predictions using evidence
- Continue to support predictions with evidence from the text what characters will do based on the traits revealed by the writer

Making Connections

- Bring knowledge from personal experiences to the interpretation of characters and events
- Bring background knowledge to the understanding of a text before, during, and after reading
- Make connections between the text and other texts that have been read or heard and demonstrate in writing
- Specify the nature of connections (topic, content, type of story, writer)

Synthesizing

- Differentiate between what is known and new information
- Through talk or writing, demonstrate learning new content from reading
- Demonstrate changing perspective as events in a story unfold
- Synthesize information across a longer text
- Expresses changes in ideas after reading a text

Inferring

- Demonstrate understandings of characters, using evidence from text to support statements
- Infer characters' feelings and motivations through reading their dialogue
- Infer cause and effect in influencing characters' feelings or underlying motives
- See changes in characters across time and articulate possible reasons for development
- Generate or react to alternative understandings of a text
- Infer causes of problems or of outcomes in fiction and nonfiction texts
- Identify significant events and tell how they are related to the problem of the story or the solution
- Infer the big ideas or message (theme) of a text

Thinking *about* the Text

Analyzing

- Notice aspects of genres (realistic and historical fiction, biography and other nonfiction, fantasy)
- Understand when a writer has used underlying organizational structures (description, compare/contrast, temporal sequence, problem/solution, cause/effect)
- Demonstrate the ability to identify how a text is organized
- Identify important aspects of illustrations (design related to the meaning of the text)
- Notice variety in layout (words in bold or larger font, or italics, variety in layout)
- Notice the way the writer assigns dialogue
- Notice aspects of a writer's style after reading several texts by him or her
- Notice specific writing techniques (for example, question and answer format)
- Notice and interpret figurative language and discuss how it adds to the meaning or enjoyment of a text
- Notice descriptive language and discuss how it adds to enjoyment or understanding
- Understand the relationship between the setting and the plot of a story

Critiquing

- State opinions about a text and show evidence to support them
- Discuss the quality of illustrations or graphics
- Hypothesize how characters could have behaved differently
- Evaluate aspects of a text that add to enjoyment (for example, humorous characters or situations)

Guided Reading

Readers at **Level O:**

At Level O, readers can identify the characteristics of a full range of genres. They read both chapter books and shorter fiction and informational texts. Also, they read special forms such as mysteries, series books, books with sequels, and short stories. Fiction narratives are straightforward but have elaborate plots and multiple characters who develop and change over time. Some nonfiction texts provide information in categories on several related topics, and readers can identify and use underlying structures (description, compare and contrast, temporal sequence, problem and solution, cause and effect). They can process sentences that are complex, contain prepositional phrases, introductory clauses, and lists of nouns, verbs, or adjectives. They solve new vocabulary words, some defined in the text and others unexplained. Word solving is smooth and automatic in both silent and oral reading. They can read and understand descriptive words, some complex content-specific words, and some technical words. They read silently with little overt problem solving; in oral reading, they demonstrate all aspects of smooth, fluent processing.

Selecting Texts **Characteristics of Texts at This Level**

Genre/Forms

Genre

- Informational texts
- Simple fantasy
- Realistic fiction
- Traditional literature
- Biography, mostly on well-known subjects
- Historical fiction
- Mysteries

Forms

- Picture books
- Plays
- Beginning chapter books with illustrations
- Chapter books
- Chapter books with sequels
- Series books
- Short stories

Text Structure

Fiction

- Narrative structure including chapters with multiple episodes related to a single plot
- Plots with detailed episodes

Nonfiction

- Presentation of multiple topics that represent subtopic of a larger topic or theme
- Underlying structures (description, comparison and contrast, temporal sequence, problem and solution, cause and effect)
- Texts organized into a few simple categories
- Variety in organization and topic
- Variety in nonfiction formats (question and answer, paragraphs, boxes, legends, and call-outs)

Content

- Prior knowledge needed to understand content in many informational texts
- Most of content carried by the print rather than pictures
- Content supported or extended by illustrations in most informational texts
- Content requiring the reader to take on perspectives from diverse cultures and bring cultural knowledge to understanding

Themes and Ideas

- Many light, humorous stories
- Some texts with deeper meaning—still familiar to most readers
- Some abstract themes requiring inferential thinking to derive
- Texts with deeper meanings applicable to important human problems and social issues
- Some more challenging themes (e.g., war, the environment)

Language and Literary Features

- Multiple characters to understand
- Characters revealed by what they say, think, and do and what others say or think about them
- Memorable characters, with both good and bad traits, who change and develop over time
- Factors related to character change explicit and obvious
- Descriptive and figurative language that is important to understanding the plot
- Setting important to understanding the plot in some texts
- Wide variety in showing dialogue, both assigned and unassigned
- Complex plots with numerous episodes and time passing
- Plots with numerous episodes, building toward problem resolution
- Building suspense through events of the plot
- Simple, traditional elements of fantasy
- Texts with multiple points of view revealed through characters' behaviors

Snakes' eyes are protected by a layer of clear scales.

Myth 2

Snakes' tongues are not dangerous.

That's another misunderstanding. In fact, only a snake's fangs are harmful. A snake flicks its tongue to smell the air. It can use smells to figure out which way its prey is moving or whether an enemy is near. If a snake flicks its tongue at you, it's just trying to figure out if you're something good to eat. (Don't worry—snakes rarely eat people!)

2

Poisonous snakes have two large fangs in the upper front part of the mouth.

Myth 3

Some people think that snakes feel wet and slimy. But a snake's skin is really very dry and smooth. This smoothness makes a snake's skin look shiny and wet. The way a snake's scales move, sliding along the ground, may also make them look slimy. ■

Myth 4

Snakes can bend and twist and slither and slide this way and that. Many people think they have no bones. But snakes do

3

Guided Reading

Sentence Complexity

- Many longer (more than fifteen words), more complex sentences (prepositional phrases, introductory clauses, lists of nouns, verbs, or adjectives)
- Variety in sentence length, with some long and complex sentences
- Questions in dialogue (fiction) and questions and answers (nonfiction)
- Sentences with parenthetical material
- Sentences with nouns, verbs, or adjectives in series, divided by commas

Vocabulary

- Many complex content-specific words in nonfiction, mostly defined in text, illustrations, or glossary
- New vocabulary in fiction texts largely unexplained
- Some words used figuratively
- Some words with connotative meanings that are essential to understanding the text

Words

- Many words with three or more syllables
- All parts of speech
- Words with suffixes and prefixes
- Words with a wide variety of very complex spelling patterns
- Multisyllable words that are challenging to take apart or decode
- Some multisyllable proper nouns that are difficult to decode
- Many plurals, contractions, and compound words
- Words divided (hyphenated) across lines and across pages

Illustrations

General

- A variety of compex graphics, often more than one on a page
- Some long stretches of text with no illustrations or graphics

Fiction

- Most texts with no or only minimal illustrations
- In illustrated texts, highly complex and artistic illustrations that communicate meaning to match or extend the text (mood, symbolism)
- Most illustrations are black and white

Nonfiction

- Combination of graphics providing information that matches and extends the text
- In most texts, graphics that are clearly explained (simple diagrams, illustrations with labels, maps, charts)
- Variety in the layout of print in nonfiction texts (question and answer, paragraphs, boxes, legends, call-outs)
- Variety of graphics (diagrams, labels, cutaways, maps, scales with legends, charts, photographs with legends)

Book and Print Features

Print and Layout

- Ample space between lines
- Varying print and font size with some longer texts in small fonts
- Use of words in italics, bold, or all capitals to indicate emphasis, level of importance, or signal other meaning
- Variety in print and background color
- Sentences continuing over several lines or to the next page
- Print and illustrations integrated in many texts
- Captions under pictures that provide important information
- Usually friendly layout in chapter books, with sentences starting on the left
- Variety in layout of nonfiction formats (question and answer, paragraphs, boxes, legends, call-outs)

Punctuation

- Full range of punctuation, including dashes and ellipses

Tools

- Readers' tools (table of contents, a few headings, glossary, pronunciation guides, chapter titles, author's notes, simple index)

A month later, Nora walked into her new school. Her sneakers squeaked on the shiny, polished floors. She was not surprised that the other kids turned, stared, and whispered, but didn't say hello. "No one ever talks to the new girl," she told herself.

At lunch, Nora looked around the crowded cafeteria. At every table kids were eating lunch with their special friends, talking and laughing. No kids invited Nora to sit with them. Only one girl smiled at Nora. She was sitting by herself looking lonely and nervous. "She's probably new, too," Nora thought, so she just ignored her. Nora dreamed of being in a group of friends, just as she was in her old school.

2

That night she told her mother about her terrible day. "Did you talk to anyone?" her mother asked. Nora shook her head. "All the kids ignored me." ■

"I'm sorry, honey," Mom said. "But remember, to get you have to give." She was always coming up with sayings that sounded like they belonged on bumper stickers. "There must be one other kid at your school who could use a friend," Mom added. "Maybe you should try making the first move."

The next day Nora saw the girl who had smiled at her the day before. This time Nora smiled back, and before long they were talking. The girl's name was Liz, and this was her seventh school in five years. She was an Army kid, too!

3

Guided Reading

Selecting Goals Behaviors and Understandings to Notice, Teach, and Support

Thinking *within* the Text

Solving Words

- Understand connotative meaning of words
- Understand figurative use of words
- Notice new and interesting words, and add them to speaking or writing vocabulary
- Demonstrate knowledge of flexible ways to solve words (noticing word parts, noticing endings and prefixes)
- Solve words of two or three syllables, many words with inflectional endings and complex letter-sound relationships
- Solve content-specific words, using graphics and definitions embedded in the text
- Solve some undefined words using background knowledge
- Use the context of a sentence, paragraph, or whole text to determine the meaning of a word
- Identify words with multiple meanings, discuss alternative meanings, and select the precise meaning within the text
- Read words that are hyphenated across lines and across pages
- Understand longer descriptive words
- Apply problem-solving strategies to technical words or proper nouns that are challenging

Monitoring and Correcting

- Continue to monitor accuracy and understanding, self-correcting when errors detract from meaning

Searching for and Using Information

- Search for information in graphics (simple diagrams, illustrations with labels, maps, charts, captions under pictures)
- Use a full range of readers' tools to search for information (table of contents, glossary, headings and subheadings, call-outs, pronunciation guides, index, references)
- Process many long sentences (fifteen or more words) with embedded clauses (parenthetical material, prepositional phrases, introductory clauses, series of nouns, verbs, or adverbs)
- Process a wide range of complex dialogue, some unassigned
- Process texts that have many lines of print on a page
- Form implicit questions and search for answers while reading
- Respond to plot tension or suspense by reading on to seek resolutions to problems
- Sustain attention to a text read over several days, remembering details and revising interpretations as new events are encountered

Summarizing

- Follow and remember a series of events and the story problem and solution over a longer text in order to understand the ending
- Identify and understand sets of related ideas organized into categories
- Summarize longer narrative texts with multiple episodes either orally or in writing
- Identify important ideas in a text and report them in an organized way, either orally or in writing
- Summarize a text at intervals during the reading of a longer text

Maintaining Fluency

- Demonstrate phrased, fluent oral reading
- Read dialogue with phrasing and expression that reflects understanding of characters and events
- Demonstrate appropriate stress on words, pausing, phrasing and intonation, using size of font, bold, and italics as appropriate
- Use multiple sources of information (language structure, meaning, fast word recognition) to support fluency and phrasing

Planning for Word Work during Guided Reading

One- to three-minute demonstrations with active student engagement using a chart or easel, white board, or pencil and paper can develop fluency and flexibility in visual processing. Plan for explicit work in specific visual processing areas that need support.

Examples:

- Take apart and add a variety of endings to words (*-ing, -es, -ed, -er; puzzle, puzzling, puzzled, puzzler*)
- Take apart and make a full range of plurals, including irregular plurals and plurals that require spelling changes (*foot/feet, shelf/shelves, berry/berries*)
- Take apart and recognize words with prefixes and suffixes (*pre-view, weari-ly*)
- Use base words, prefixes, and suffixes in the process of deriving word meaning
- Work flexibly with base words, making new words by changing letters (*grin/groan*) and adding prefixes (*do/undo*) and suffixes (*do/doable*)
- Recognize words that have multiple meanings (a form of homograph: *train, train*), homographs (look the same, sound different: *does, does*), and homophones (sound the same, look different: *flea, flee*)
- Take apart and make words with complex phonograms and long vowel patterns, including vowel patterns with *r* (VVCC (*board*), VVCe (*peace*), VCCe (*waste*), VCCC (*night*), VVCCC (*straight*))
- Take apart and recognize words with vowel sounds controlled by *r* (*far, board*)
- Take apart and make compound words (*note-book*)
- Take apart and recognize multisyllable words quickly (*fab-u-lous*)
- Take apart multisyllable words to decode manageable units (*cam-er-a*)
- Use what is known about words to read new words (*part, partner, partnership*)
- Take apart and recognize words with contractions (*I'm, that's, he'll, won't, they're, you've*)
- Take apart and read words using open (ending in a vowel: *se-cret*) and closed (ending in a consonant: *sec-ond*) syllables

Guided Reading

Selecting Goals

Behaviors and Understandings to Notice, Teach, and Support

Adjusting

- Demonstrate different ways of reading related to genre, including simple biographies, fantasy, and historical fiction
- Adjust reading to process texts with difficult and complex layout
- Slow down or reread to solve words or think about ideas and resume good rate of reading

Thinking *beyond* the Text

Predicting

- Make a wide range of predictions based on personal experiences, content knowledge, and knowledge of similar texts
- Search for and use information to confirm or disconfirm predictions
- Justify predictions using evidence
- Predict what characters will do based on the traits revealed by the writer as well as inferred characteristics

Making Connections

- Bring knowledge from personal experiences to the interpretation of characters and events that are not within the reader's experience
- Bring background knowledge to the understanding of a text before, during, and after reading
- Make connections between the text and other texts that have been read or heard and demonstrate in writing
- Use knowledge from one text to help in understanding diverse cultures and settings encountered in new texts
- Specify the nature of connections (topic, content, type of story, writer)

Synthesizing

- Differentiate between what is known and new information
- Mentally form categories of related information and revise them as new information is acquired across the text
- Demonstrate learning new content from reading
- Express changes in ideas or knowledge after reading a text
- Demonstrate changing perspective as events in a story unfold
- Synthesize information across a longer text

Inferring

- Follow multiple characters in different episodes, inferring their feelings about each other
- Demonstrate understandings of characters (their traits, how and why they change), using evidence to support statements
- Infer the big ideas or themes of a text and discuss how they are applicable to people's lives today
- Generate or react to alternative understandings of a text
- Infer causes of problems or of outcomes in fiction and nonfiction texts
- Identify significant events and tell how they are related to the problem of the story or the solution

Thinking *about* the Text

Analyzing

- Notice aspects of genres (realistic and historical fiction, biography and other nonfiction, fantasy)
- Understand when a writer has used underlying organizational structures (description, compare/contrast, temporal sequence, problem/solution, cause/effect)
- Demonstrate the ability to identify how a text is organized (diagram or talk)
- Notice how the author or illustrator has used illustrations and other graphics to convey meaning
- Notice variety in layout (words in bold or larger font, or italics, variety in layout)
- Notice the way the writer assigns dialogue
- Notice aspects of a writer's style after reading several texts by the same author
- Notice specific writing techniques (for example, question and answer format)
- Notice and interpret figurative language and discuss how it adds to the meaning or enjoyment of a text
- Notice descriptive language and discuss how it adds to enjoyment or understanding
- Notice how the setting is important in a story

Critiquing

- State opinions about a text and show evidence to support them
- Evaluate the quality of illustrations or graphics
- Hypothesize how characters could have behaved differently
- Evaluate aspects of a text that add to enjoyment (for example, humorous characters or situations)
- Assess whether a text is authentic and consistent with life experience or prior knowledge (for example, in historical fiction)

Guided Reading

Readers at **Level P:**

At Level P, readers can identify the characteristics of a full range of genres, including biographies on less well-known subjects and hybrid genres. They read both chapter books and shorter informational texts; also, they read special forms such as mysteries, series books, books with sequels, or short stories. Fiction narratives are straightforward but have elaborate plots and multiple characters who develop and change over time. Readers are able to understand abstract and mature themes and take on diverse perspectives and issues related to race, language, culture. Some nonfiction texts provide information in categories on several related topics, many of which are well beyond readers' typical experience. Readers can identify and use underlying structures (description, compare and contrast, temporal sequence, problem and solution, cause and effect). They can process sentences that are complex and contain prepositional phrases, introductory clauses, lists of nouns, verbs, or adjectives. They solve new vocabulary words, some defined in the text and others unexplained. Word solving is smooth and automatic in both silent and oral reading. They can read and understand descriptive words, some complex content-specific words, and some technical words. They read silently; in oral reading, they demonstrate all aspects of smooth, fluent processing with little overt problem solving.

Selecting Texts

Characteristics of Texts at This Level

Genre/Forms

Genre

- Informational texts
- Simple fantasy
- Realistic fiction
- Traditional literature
- Biography, many on less well-known subjects
- Historical fiction
- Mysteries
- Genre combination (hybrids)

Forms

- Picture books
- Plays
- Chapter books
- Chapter books with sequels
- Series books
- Short stories

Text Structure

Fiction

- Narrative structure including chapters with multiple episodes related to a single plot
- Plots with detailed episodes

Nonfiction

- Presentation of multiple topics that represent subtopic of a larger topic or theme
- Underlying structures (description, comparison and contrast, temporal sequence, problem and solution, cause and effect)
- Texts with multiple topics and categories within them
- Variety in organization and topic
- Variety in nonfiction formats (question and answer, paragraphs, boxes, legends, and call-outs)

Content

- Topics that go well beyond readers' personal experiences and content knowledge
- Most of content carried by the print rather than pictures
- Content supported or extended by illustrations in most informational texts
- Content requiring the reader to take on diverse perspectives (race, language, culture)

Themes and Ideas

- Some texts with deeper meaning—still familiar to most readers
- Ideas and themes requiring taking a perspective not familiar to the reader
- Many abstract themes requiring inferential thinking to derive
- Texts with deeper meanings applicable to important human problems and social issues
- Some more challenging themes (e.g., war, the environment)
- Many ideas and themes requiring understanding of cultural diversity

Language and Literary Features

- Multiple characters to understand
- Characters revealed by what they say, think, and do and what others say or think about them
- Memorable characters, with both good and bad traits, who change and develop over time
- Texts with multiple points of view revealed through characters' behaviors
- Descriptive language providing details important to understanding the plot
- Extensive use of figurative language that is important to understanding the plot
- Specific descriptions of settings that provide important information for understanding the plot
- Settings distant in time and space from students' experiences
- Wide variety in showing dialogue, both assigned and unassigned
- Complex plots with numerous episodes and time passing
- Building suspense through events of the plot
- Some more complex fantasy elements

The bell rang, and Nate grabbed his backpack and headed home in a downpour. His neighbor, Mrs. Gonzalez, pulled up beside him in her minivan. "Hop in," she said. "It's a deluge out there!" Even before the door closed, Nate's nose started to tickle.

"Achoo!" he sneezed loudly. "Achoo! Achoo!" Rubbing his red, itchy eyes, Nate croaked, "Is there an animal in here?"

"Just Daisy!" Mrs. Gonzalez said sheepishly, as a pudgy bulldog poked its head over the front seat. Nate walked home.

A sniffling Nate woke up Saturday morning feeling sorry for himself. "Why do I have to be allergic to everything?" he fretted as he trudged downstairs.

His mom smiled. "I have exciting

2

news!" she exclaimed. "My friend Dr. Hung, who works at the aquarium, could use your help with the animals on Saturdays. How about it?" ■

"Thanks, Mom, but the idea of sneezing all day doesn't appeal to me," said Nate.

"You're allergic to animals that have fur or feathers," Mom pointed out, "not to marine animals that live in the water."

Nate felt nervous as they drove to the aquarium, but after he met Dr. Hung, his anxiety melted away. Within minutes, they were standing next to a huge saltwater pool. "Meet our Pacific white-sided dolphins, Nate," said Dr. Hung. "They're ready for their lunch!"

Dr. Hung handed Nate a pair of floppy rubber gloves and a heavy pail

3

Guided Reading

Sentence Complexity

- Longer (some with more than fifteen words) complex sentence structures
- Questions in dialogue (fiction) and questions and answers (nonfiction)
- Sentences with parenthetical material
- Sentences with nouns, verbs, or adjectives in series, divided by commas
- Many complex content-specific words in nonfiction, mostly defined in text, illustrations, or glossary

Vocabulary

- Many new vocabulary words that depend on readers' tools (such as glossaries)
- Many new vocabulary words that readers must derive meaning from context
- Some words with connotative meanings that are essential to understanding the text
- Some words used figuratively (metaphor, simile, idiom)

Words

- All parts of speech
- Words with suffixes and prefixes
- Some words with simple prefixes
- Words with a wide variety of very complex spelling patterns
- Multisyllable proper nouns that are difficult to decode
- Many complex multisyllable words that are challenging to take apart
- Many plurals, contractions, and compound words

Illustrations

General

- A variety of compex graphics, often more than one on a page

Fiction

- Most texts with no or only minimal illustrations
- In illustrated texts, highly complex and artistic illustrations that communicate meaning to match or extend the text (mood, symbolism)
- Most illustrations are black and white

Nonfiction

- Full range of graphics providing information that matches and extends the text
- Variety in the layout of print in nonfiction texts (question and answer, paragraphs, boxes, legends, call-outs)
- Variety of graphics (diagrams, labels, cutaways, maps, scales with legends)
- Some texts with graphics that have scales or legends that require understanding and interpretation

Book and Print Features

Print and Layout

- Varied space between lines, with some texts having dense print
- Use of words in italics, bold, or all capitals to indicate emphasis, level of importance, or signal other meaning
- Variety in print and background color
- Large variation among print styles and font size (related to genre)
- Sentences continuing over several lines or to the next page
- Captions under pictures that provide important information
- Print and illustrations integrated in most texts, with print wrapping around pictures
- Variety in layout of nonfiction formats (question and answer, paragraphs, boxes, legends, call-outs)
- More difficult layout of informational text, and some fiction texts, with denser format

Punctuation

- Full range of punctuation as needed for complex sentences

Tools

- Full range of readers' tools (table of contents, glossary, headings and subheadings, call-outs, pronunciation guides, index, references)

Guided Reading

Selecting Goals Behaviors and Understandings to Notice, Teach, and Support

Thinking *within* the Text

Solving Words

- Understand connotative meaning of words
- Understand figurative use of words
- Notice new and interesting words, record them, and actively add them to speaking or writing vocabulary
- Demonstrate knowledge of flexible ways to solve words (noticing word parts, noticing endings and prefixes)
- Solve words of three or more syllables, many words with inflectional endings and complex letter-sound relationships
- Solve content-specific words, using graphics and definitions embedded in the text as well as background knowledge
- Solve some undefined words using background knowledge
- Use the context of a sentence, paragraph, or whole text to determine the meaning of a word
- Develop deeper understanding of words that have been encountered before but are not familiar
- Identify words with multiple meanings, discuss alternative meanings, and select the precise meaning within the text
- Read words that are hyphenated across lines and across pages
- Understand longer descriptive words
- Apply problem-solving strategies to technical words or proper nouns that are challenging

Monitoring and Correcting

- Continue to monitor accuracy and understanding, self-correcting when errors detract from meaning

Searching for and Using Information

- Search for information in graphics (simple diagrams, illustrations with labels, maps, charts, captions under pictures)
- Use a full range of readers' tools to search for information (table of contents, glossary, headings and subheadings, call-outs, pronunciation guides, index, references)
- Process long sentences (fifteen or more words) with embedded clauses (parenthetical material, prepositional phrases, introductory clauses, series of nouns, verbs, or adverbs)
- Process a wide range of complex dialogue, some unassigned
- Process texts that have many lines of print on a page
- Form implicit questions and search for answers while reading
- Respond to plot tension or suspense by reading on to seek resolutions to problems
- Sustain attention to a text read over several days, remembering details in order to revise interpretations as new events are encountered

Summarizing

- Follow and remember a series of events and the story problem and solution over a longer text in order to understand the ending
- Summarize a text at intervals during the reading of a longer text
- Identify and understand sets of related ideas organized into categories
- Summarize longer narrative texts with multiple episodes
- Identify important ideas in a text and report them in an organized way

Maintaining Fluency

- Demonstrate phrased, fluent oral reading
- Read dialogue with phrasing and expression that reflects understanding of characters and events
- Demonstrate appropriate stress on words, pausing, phrasing and intonation, using size of font, bold, and italics as appropriate
- Use multiple sources of information (language structure, meaning, fast word recognition) to support fluency and phrasing

Planning for Word Work during Guided Reading

One- to three-minute demonstrations with active student engagement using a chart or easel, white board, or pencil and paper can develop fluency and flexibility in visual processing. Plan for explicit work in specific visual processing areas that need support.

Examples:

- Take apart and recognize multisyllable words to decode manageable units
- Take apart and read words with a full range of plurals, including irregular plurals and plurals that require spelling changes (*man/men, life/lives*)
- Work flexibly with base words, making new words by changing letters (*part/port*) and adding prefixes (*trans-port*) and suffixes (*port-able*)
- Recognize words that have multiple meanings (a form of homograph: *play, play*), homographs (look the same, sound different: *use, use*), and homophones (sound the same, look different: *hair, hare*)
- Read words using complex phonograms and long vowel patterns, including vowel patterns with *r* (VVCC *(faith)*, VVCe (*release*), VCCe (*barge*), VCCC (*crunch*), VVCCC (*wealth*))
- Take apart and make compound words (*super-market*)
- Use what is known about words to read new words (*part, partner, partnership*)
- Take apart and read the full range of contractions (*I'm, that's, he'll, won't, they're, you've*)
- Recognize and solve words in which several different letters or clusters represent a single sound (/k/ = *ck* in *pick*, *c* in *picnic*, *k* in *kite*)
- Take apart and read words using open (ending in a vowel: *mo-ment*) and closed (ending in a consonant: *mod-el*) syllables

Guided Reading

Selecting Goals

Behaviors and Understandings to Notice, Teach, and Support

Adjusting

- Demonstrate different ways of reading related to genre, including simple biographies, fantasy, and historical fiction
- Sometimes adjust reading within texts to accommodate hybrid texts that combine genres
- Adjust reading to process texts with difficult and complex layout
- Slow down or reread to solve words, search for information, or think about meaning and resume good rate of reading

Thinking *beyond* the Text

Predicting

- Make a wide range of predictions based on personal experiences, content knowledge, and knowledge of similar texts
- Search for and use information to confirm or disconfirm predictions
- Justify predictions using evidence
- Predict what characters will do based on the traits revealed by the writer as well as inferred characteristics

Making Connections

- Bring background knowledge to the understanding of a text before, during, and after reading
- Make connections between the reader's real-life experiences or feelings and people who live in diverse cultures, distant places, and different times
- Interpret characters and events that are not within the reader's experience
- Make connections between the text and other texts that have been read or heard and demonstrate in writing
- Use knowledge from one text to help in understanding diverse cultures and settings encountered in new texts
- Specify the nature of connections (topic, content, type of story, writer)

Synthesizing

- Differentiate between what is known and new information
- Mentally form categories of related information and revise them as new information is acquired across the text
- Demonstrate learning new content from reading
- Expresses changes in ideas or opinions after reading a text and say why
- Demonstrate changing perspective as events in a story unfold, particularly applied to people and cultures different from the reader's own
- Synthesize information across longer texts

Inferring

- Infer cause and effect in influencing characters' feelings or underlying motives
- Infer characters' feelings and motivations through reading their dialogue and what other characters say about them
- Follow multiple characters in different episodes, inferring their feelings about each other
- Demonstrate understandings of characters (their traits, how and why they change), using evidence to support statements
- Take perspectives that may be unfamiliar in interpreting characters' motives, causes for action, or themes
- Infer the big ideas or themes of a text and discuss how they are applicable to people's lives today
- Generate or react to alternative understandings of a text
- Infer causes of problems or of outcomes in fiction and nonfiction texts
- Identify significant events and tell how they are related to the problem of the story or the solution

Thinking *about* the Text

Analyzing

- Notice combined genres in hybrid texts
- Understand when a writer has used underlying organizational structures (description, compare/contrast, temporal sequence, problem/solution, cause/effect)
- Demonstrate the ability to identify how a text is organized (talk or diagram)
- Notice how the author or illustrator has used pictures and other graphics to convey meaning
- Notice variety in layout (words in bold or larger font, or italics, variety in layout)
- Notice the way the writer assigns dialogue
- Notice aspects of a writer's style after reading several texts by the author
- Notice specific writing techniques (for example, question and answer format)
- Notice and interpret figurative language and discuss how it adds to the meaning or enjoyment of a text
- Notice descriptive language and discuss how it adds to enjoyment or understanding
- Notice how the setting is important in a story
- Understand how the writer built interest and suspense across a story
- Notice elements of fantasy (motifs, symbolism, magic)

Critiquing

- State opinions about a text and show evidence to support them
- Evaluate the quality of illustrations or graphics
- Assess how graphics add to the quality of the text or provide additional information
- Notice the author's qualifications to write an informational text
- Hypothesize how characters could have behaved differently
- Evaluate aspects of a text that add to enjoyment (for example, a humorous character) or interest (plot or information)
- Assess whether a text is authentic and consistent with life experience or prior knowledge (for example, in historical fiction)

Guided Reading

Readers at **Level Q:**

At Level Q, readers automatically read and understand a full range of genres, including biographies on less well-known subjects and hybrid genres. They read both chapter books and shorter informational texts; also, they read special forms such as mysteries, series books, books with sequels, and short stories. Fiction narratives are straightforward but have elaborate plots and many complex characters who develop and change over time. As readers, they understand perspectives different from their own as well as settings and people far distant in time and space. They can process sentences that are complex, contain prepositional phrases, introductory clauses, lists of nouns, verbs, or adjectives, and they solve new vocabulary words, some defined in the text and others unexplained. Most reading is silent, but fluency and phrasing in oral reading are well established. Readers are challenged by many longer descriptive words and by content-specific and technical words that require using embedded definitions, background knowledge, and readers' tools, such as glossaries. They can take apart multisyllable words and use a full range of word-solving skills. They read and understand texts in a variety of layouts as well as fonts and print characteristics and consistently search for information in illustrations and increasingly complex graphics.

Selecting Texts

Characteristics of Texts at This Level

Genre/Forms

Genre

- Informational texts
- More complex fantasy
- Realistic fiction
- Traditional literature
- Biography, memoir, and autobiography
- Historical fiction
- Mysteries
- Genre combination (hybrids)

Forms

- Picture books
- Plays
- Chapter books
- Chapter books with sequels
- Series books
- Short stories
- Diaries and logs

Text Structure

Fiction

- Narrative structure including chapters with multiple episodes related to a single plot
- Plots with detailed episodes

Nonfiction

- Presentation of multiple topics that represent subtopic of a larger topic or theme
- Underlying structures (description, comparison and contrast, temporal sequence, problem and solution, cause and effect)
- Texts with multiple topics and categories within them
- Variety in organization and topic
- Variety in nonfiction formats (question and answer, paragraphs, boxes, legends, and call-outs)

Content

- Topics that go well beyond readers' personal experiences and content knowledge
- Fiction–settings requiring knowledge of content (history, geography, etc.)
- Most of content carried by the print rather than pictures
- Content supported or extended by illustrations in most informational texts
- Content requiring the reader to take on diverse perspectives (race, language, culture)

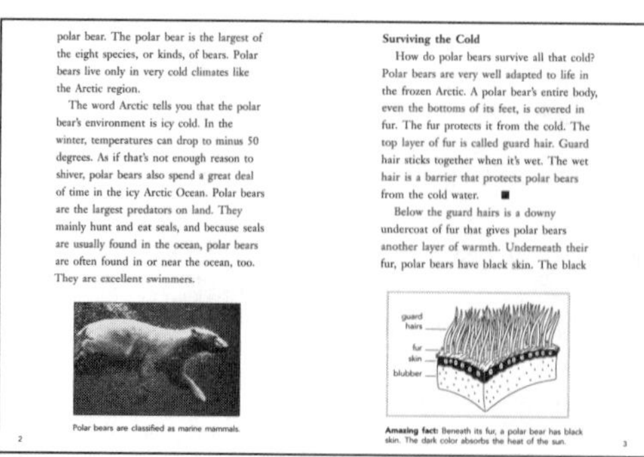

polar bear. The polar bear is the largest of the eight species, or kinds, of bears. Polar bears live only in very cold climates like the Arctic region.

The word Arctic tells you that the polar bear's environment is icy cold. In the winter, temperatures can drop to minus 50 degrees. As if that's not enough reason to shiver, polar bears also spend a great deal of time in the icy Arctic Ocean. Polar bears are the largest predators on land. They mainly hunt and eat seals, and because seals are usually found in the ocean, polar bears are often found in or near the ocean, too. They are excellent swimmers.

Polar bears are classified as marine mammals.

2

Surviving the Cold

How do polar bears survive all that cold? Polar bears are very well adapted to life in the frozen Arctic. A polar bear's entire body, even the bottoms of its feet, is covered in fur. The fur protects it from the cold. The top layer of fur is called guard hair. Guard hair sticks together when it's wet. The wet hair is a barrier that protects polar bears from the cold water. ■

Below the guard hairs is a downy undercoat of fur that gives polar bears another layer of warmth. Underneath their fur, polar bears have black skin. The black

Amazing fact: Beneath its fur, a polar bear has black skin. The dark color absorbs the heat of the sun.

3

Themes and Ideas

- Complex ideas on many different topics requiring real or vicarious experiences (through reading)
- Many abstract themes requiring inferential thinking to derive
- Texts with deeper meanings applicable to important human problems and social issues
- Some more challenging themes (e.g., war, the environment)
- Many ideas and themes requiring understanding of cultural diversity

Language and Literary Features

- Explicit and obvious reasons for character change
- Memorable characters, with both good and bad traits, who change and develop over time
- Multiple characters revealed by what they say, think, and do and what others say or think about them
- Descriptive language providing details important to understanding the plot
- Extensive use of figurative language that is important to understanding the plot
- Specific descriptions of settings that provide important information for understanding the plot
- Settings distant in time and space from students' typical experiences
- Wide variety in showing dialogue, both assigned and unassigned
- Complex plots with numerous episodes and time passing
- Suspense that builds through the events of the plot
- Some more complex fantasy elements
- Texts with multiple points of view revealed through characters' behaviors

Guided Reading

Sentence Complexity

- Longer and more complex sentence structures (some with more than fifteen words)
- Questions in dialogue (fiction) and questions and answers (nonfiction)
- Sentences with parenthetical material
- Sentences with nouns, verbs, or adjectives in series, divided by commas

Vocabulary

- Many complex content-specific words in nonfiction, mostly defined in text, illustrations, or glossary
- Many new vocabulary words that depend on readers' tools (such as glossaries)
- Many new vocabulary words for readers to derive meaning from context
- Many words used figuratively (use of common idioms, metaphor, simile)
- Words with connotative meanings essential to understanding the text

Words

- All parts of speech
- Many words with three or more syllables
- Many words with affixes (prefixes and suffixes, multisyllable proper nouns that are difficult to decode)
- Words with a wide variety of very complex spelling patterns
- Many multisyllable proper nouns that are difficult to decode
- Many technical words that are difficult to decode
- Words that are seldom used in oral language and are difficult to decode
- Many plurals, contractions, and compound words

Illustrations

General

- A variety of compex graphics, often more than one on a page

Fiction

- Most texts with no or only minimal illustrations
- In illustrated texts, highly complex and artistic illustrations that communicate meaning to match or extend the text (mood, symbolism)
- Black and white illustrations in most fiction texts

Nonfiction

- Full range of graphics providing information that matches and extends the text
- Variety of graphics (diagrams, labels, cutaways, maps, scales with legends)
- Some texts with graphics that have scales or legends that require understanding and interpretation

Book and Print Features

Print and Layout

- Varied space between lines, with some texts having dense print
- Use of words in italics, bold, or all capitals to indicate emphasis, level of importance, or signal other meaning
- Variety in print and background color
- Large variation among print styles and font size (related to genre)
- Some sentences continuing over several lines or to the next page
- Captions under pictures that provide important information
- Print and illustrations integrated in most texts, with print wrapping around pictures
- Variety in layout of nonfiction formats (question and answer, paragraphs, boxes, legends, call-outs)
- More difficult layout in informational text
- Some fiction texts, with denser format

Punctuation

- Full range of punctuation as needed for complex sentences

Tools

- Full range of readers' tools (table of contents, glossary, headings and subheadings, call-outs, pronunciation guides, index, references)

Guided Reading

Selecting Goals Behaviors and Understandings to Notice, Teach, and Support

Thinking *within* the Text

Solving Words

- Notice new and interesting words, record them, and actively add them to speaking or writing vocabulary
- Demonstrate knowledge of flexible ways to solve words (noticing word parts, noticing endings and prefixes)
- Solve multisyllable words (many with three or more syllables) using vowel patterns, phonogram patterns, affixes (prefixes and suffixes), and other word parts
- Solve content-specific words and technical words using graphics and definitions embedded in the text as well as background knowledge
- Solve some undefined words using background knowledge
- Use readers' tools such as glossaries, dictionaries, and pronunciation guides to solve words, including difficult proper nouns and technical words
- Understand connotative meaning of words
- Understand figurative use of words
- Use the context of a sentence, paragraph, or whole text to determine the meaning of a word
- Develop deeper understanding of words that have been encountered before but are not familiar
- Identify words with multiple meanings, discuss alternative meanings, and select the precise meaning within the text
- Apply problem-solving strategies to technical words or proper nouns that are challenging

Monitoring and Correcting

- Continue to monitor accuracy and understanding, self-correcting when errors detract from meaning

Searching for and Using Information

- Search for information in graphics (simple diagrams, illustrations with labels, maps, charts, captions under pictures)
- Use a full range of readers' tools to search for information (table of contents, glossary, headings and subheadings, call-outs, pronunciation guides, index, references)
- Process long sentences (fifteen or more words) that are carried over several lines or to the next page
- Process sentences with embedded clauses (parenthetical material, prepositional phrases, introductory clauses, series of nouns, verbs, or adverbs)
- Process a wide range of complex dialogue, some unassigned
- Process some texts with dense print
- Process texts with a variety of complex layouts
- Form implicit questions and search for answers while reading
- Respond to plot tension or suspense by reading on to seek resolutions to problems
- Sustain attention to a text read over several days, remembering details and revising interpretations as new events are encountered

Summarizing

- Summarize longer narrative texts with multiple episodes either orally or in writing
- Identify important ideas in a text and report them in an organized way, either orally or in writing
- Summarize a text at intervals during the reading of a longer text
- Remember the story problem or plot, as well as important information, over a longer text in order to continue to construct meaning

Planning for Word Work during Guided Reading

One- to three-minute demonstrations with active student engagement using a chart or easel, white board, or pencil and paper can develop fluency and flexibility in visual processing. Plan for explicit work in specific visual processing areas that need support.

Examples:

- Read words with a full range of plurals, including irregular plurals and plurals that require spelling changes (*mouse/mice, city/cities*)
- Add, delete, change letters or letter clusters to make words (*read, lead, leader, leaden, laden*)
- Use base words, prefixes, and suffixes in the process of deriving word meaning
- Work flexibly with base words, making new words by changing letters (*found/sound*) and adding and removing prefixes (*un-sound*) and suffixes (*sound-ly*)
- Recognize words that have multiple meanings (a form of homograph: *bank, bank*), homographs (look the same, sound different: *excuse, excuse*), and homophones (sound the same, look different: *one, won*)
- Take apart and read words with a vowel and *r* (*hairy, poor, dare*)
- Take apart and read words with complex phonograms and long vowel patterns, including vowel patterns with *r* (VVCC (*faith*), VVCe (*release*), VCCe (*barge*), VCCC (*crunch*), VVCCC (*health*))
- Use known words and word parts to take apart new words (*triangular/tri-angle*)
- Take apart more complex compound words and discuss how the parts are related to meaning (*out-line, tail-gate*)
- Take apart words with frequently appearing syllable patterns in multisyllable words (*humble*)
- Use what is known about words to read new words (*part, partner, partnership*)
- Recognize words in which several different letters or clusters represent a single sound (/f/ = *gh* in *rough, ff* in *fluff, f* in *finish*)
- Take apart and read words using open (ending in a vowel: *cli-mate*) and closed (ending in a consonant: *lev-el*) syllables

Guided Reading

Selecting Goals Behaviors and Understandings to Notice, Teach, and Support

Maintaining Fluency
- Demonstrate phrased, fluent oral reading
- Read dialogue with phrasing and expression that reflects understanding of characters and events
- Demonstrate appropriate stress on words, pausing and phrasing, intonation, and use of punctuation while reading in a way that reflects understanding

Adjusting
- Change style and pace of reading to reflect purpose
- Adjust reading to process texts with difficult and complex layout
- Slow down or reread to solve words or think about ideas and resume good rate of reading

Thinking *beyond* the Text

Predicting
- Make a wide range of predictions based on personal experiences, content knowledge, and knowledge of similar texts
- Search for and use information to confirm or disconfirm predictions
- Justify predictions using evidence

Making Connections
- Make connections between the reader's real-life experiences and people who live in diverse cultures, distant places, and different times
- Bring background (content) knowledge to understanding a wide variety of fiction and nonfiction texts
- Make connections between the text and other texts that have been read or heard
- Use knowledge from one text to help in understanding diverse cultures and settings encountered in new texts
- Specify the nature of connections (topic, content, type of story, writer)

Synthesizing
- Mentally form categories of related information and revise them as new information is acquired across the text
- Demonstrate learning new content from reading
- Demonstrate changing perspective as events in a story unfold, particularly applied to people and cultures different from the reader's own
- Through reading both fiction and nonfiction texts about diverse cultures, times, and places, acquire new content and perspectives

Inferring
- Infer cause and effect in influencing characters' feelings or underlying motives
- Infer characters' feelings and motivations through reading their dialogue and what other characters say about them
- Follow multiple characters in different episodes, inferring their feelings about each other
- Demonstrate understandings of characters (their traits, how and why they change), using evidence to support statements
- Take perspectives that may be unfamiliar in interpreting characters' motives, causes for action, or themes
- Infer the big ideas or themes of a text (some texts with mature themes and issues) and discuss how they are applicable to people's lives today
- Speculate on alternative meanings that the text may have
- Infer causes of problems or of outcomes in fiction and nonfiction texts
- Identify significant events and tell how they are related to the problem of the story or the solution

Thinking *about* the Text

Analyzing
- Notice aspects of genres (realistic and historical fiction, fantasy, biography, autobiography, memoir and diaries, and other nonfiction)
- Notice combined genres in hybrid texts
- Understand, talk about, and/or write or draw when a writer has used underlying organizational structures (description, compare/contrast, temporal sequence, problem/solution, cause/effect)
- Demonstrate the ability to identify how a text is organized (talk, diagram)
- Notice how the author or illustrator has used pictures and other graphics to convey meaning or create mood
- Notice and interpret figurative language and discuss how it adds to the meaning or enjoyment of a text
- Notice descriptive language and discuss how it adds to enjoyment or understanding
- Recognize the use of figurative or descriptive language (or special types of language such as irony) and talk about how it adds to the quality (enjoyment and understanding) of a text
- Understand and talk about the role of the setting in realistic and historical fiction as well as fantasy
- Talk about how the writer built interest and suspense across a story
- Notice aspects of a writer's craft (style, language, perspective, themes) after reading several texts by the same author

Critiquing
- State opinions about a text and show evidence to support them
- Evaluate the quality of illustrations or graphics
- Assess how graphics add to the quality of the text or provide additional information
- Notice and talk about the author's qualifications to write an informational text
- Hypothesize how characters could have behaved differently
- Evaluate aspects of a text that add to enjoyment (for example, a humorous character) or interest (plot or information)
- Assess whether a text is authentic and consistent with life experience or prior knowledge (for example, in historical fiction)
- Express tastes and preferences in reading and support choices with specific descriptions of text features (plots, use of language, kinds of characters, genres)

Guided Reading

Readers at **Level R:**

At Level R, readers automatically read and understand a full range of genres, including biographies on less well-known subjects, more complex fantasy, and hybrid genres. They read both chapter books and shorter informational texts. Also, they read special forms such as mysteries, series books, books with sequels, short stories, diaries, and logs. Fiction narratives are straightforward but have elaborate plots and many complex characters who develop and change over time. As readers, they understand perspectives different from their own as well as settings and people far distant in time and space. They can process sentences (some with more than fifteen words) that are complex, contain prepositional phrases, introductory clauses, lists of nouns, verbs, or adjectives, and they solve new vocabulary words, some defined in the text and others unexplained. Most reading is silent, but fluency and phrasing in oral reading are well established. Readers are challenged by many longer descriptive words and by content-specific and technical words that require using embedded definitions, background knowledge, and readers' tools, such as glossaries. They can take apart multisyllable words and use a full range of word-solving skills. They read and understand texts in a variety of layouts as well as fonts and print characteristics and consistently search for information in illustrations and increasingly complex graphics.

Selecting Texts **Characteristics of Texts at This Level**

Genre/Forms

Genre

- Informational texts
- More complex fantasy
- Realistic fiction
- Traditional literature
- Biography, memoir, and autobiography
- Historical fiction
- Mysteries
- Genre combination (hybrids)

Forms

- Picture books
- Plays
- Chapter books
- Chapter books with sequels
- Series books
- Short stories
- Diaries and logs

Text Structure

Fiction

- Narrative structure including chapters with multiple episodes related to a single plot
- Plots with detailed episodes
- Some collections of short stories that have interrelated themes or build a single plot across the book

Nonfiction

- Presentation of multiple topics that represent subtopic of a larger topic or theme
- Underlying structures (description, comparison and contrast, temporal sequence, problem and solution, cause and effect)
- Texts with multiple topics and categories within them
- Variety in organization and topic
- Variety in nonfiction formats (question and answer, paragraphs, boxes, legends, and call-outs)

Content

- Topics that go well beyond readers' personal experiences and content knowledge
- Fiction–settings requiring knowledge of content (history, geography, etc.)
- Most of content carried by the print rather than pictures
- Content supported or extended by illustrations in most informational texts
- Content requiring the reader to take on diverse perspectives (race, language, culture)

Themes and Ideas

- Complex ideas on many different topics requiring real or vicarious experiences (through reading)
- Many abstract themes requiring inferential thinking to derive
- Texts with deeper meanings applicable to important human problems and social issues
- Some more challenging themes (e.g., war, the environment)
- Many ideas and themes requiring understanding of cultural diversity

Language and Literary Features

- Memorable characters, with both good and bad traits, who change and develop over time
- Multiple characters revealed by what they say, think, and do and what others say or think about them
- Figurative language that is important to understanding the plot
- Long stretches of descriptive language that are important to understanding setting and characters
- Specific descriptions of settings that provide important information for understanding the plot
- Settings distant in time and space from students' experiences
- Some long strings of unassigned dialogue from which story action must be inferred
- Complex plots with numerous episodes and time passing
- Building suspense through events of the plot
- Some more complex fantasy elements
- Texts with multiple points of view revealed through characters' behaviors

Guided Reading

Sentence Complexity

- Many longer (some with more than fifteen words) complex sentence structures
- Questions in dialogue (fiction) and questions and answers (nonfiction)
- Sentences with parenthetical material
- Sentences with nouns, verbs, or adjectives in series, divided by commas

Vocabulary

- Many complex content-specific words in nonfiction, mostly defined in text, illustrations, or glossary
- Many new vocabulary words that readers must derive meaning from context or use glossaries or dictionaries
- Words with connotative meanings essential to understanding the text
- Many words used figuratively (metaphor, simile, idiom)

Words

- All parts of speech
- Many words with three or more syllables
- Many words with affixes (prefixes and suffixes that are difficult to decode)
- Words with a wide variety of very complex spelling patterns
- Many multisyllable proper nouns that are difficult to decode
- Many technical words that are difficult to decode
- Some words that are seldom used in oral language and are difficult to decode
- Many plurals, contractions, and compound words

Illustrations

General

- A variety of compex graphics, often more than one on a page

Fiction

- Most texts with no or only minimal illustrations
- In illustrated texts, highly complex and artistic illustrations that communicate meaning to match or extend the text (mood, symbolism)
- Black and white illustrations in fiction texts

Nonfiction

- Full range of graphics (diagrams, labels, cutaways, maps, scales with legends) providing information that extends the text
- Some texts with graphics that have scales or legends that require understanding and interpretation

Jill bolted upright in bed, feeling dazed.

Jill nodded slowly. "I'm okay," she said in an unconvincing voice. "What time is it?"

"Time to get ready to deliver your speech for class president," her mother said, smiling.

As the memory of her dream came flooding back, Jill felt a fresh wave of panic. "Mom, I don't know if I can do it. The thought of standing in front of all those people makes me feel sick!"

Jill's mother sat down next to her and smiled. "You know, Jill, sometimes I have to give speeches at big meetings." Jill's mother was a heart surgeon, an expert in her field. "I used to feel as frightened as you are now."

Jill asked, "How did you get over your fears?" ■

2

"Well," her mother began, "when I have to get up in front of hundreds of strangers, I focus on one friendly face I know. Then I imagine that the two of us are sitting across a table from each other and talking about work."

"And do you stop being scared?"

"Well, not completely. It's normal to feel nervous about something that's new to you. But if you can find the courage to do it anyway, it won't feel so scary the next time. You can do it—I'm sure of it."

Later that morning, Jill walked slowly across the auditorium stage and stood behind the podium. She took a deep breath and scanned the faces in the crowd. There, in the second row, was her friend Eduardo. He smiled at her encouragingly. Jill imagined herself talking directly to Eduardo, exactly as her mother had suggested.

3

Book and Print Features

Print and Layout

- Varied space between lines, with some texts having dense print
- Use of words in italics, bold, or all capitals to indicate emphasis, level of importance, or signal other meaning
- Variety in print and background color
- Large variation among print styles and font size (related to genre)
- Some sentences continuing over several lines or to the next page
- Captions under pictures that provide important information
- Print and illustrations integrated in most texts, with print wrapping around pictures
- Variety in layout of nonfiction formats (question and answer, paragraphs, boxes, legends, call-outs)
- More difficult layout in informational text, and some fiction texts, with denser format

Punctuation

- Full range of punctuation as needed for complex sentences

Tools

- Full range of readers' tools (table of contents, glossary, headings and subheadings, call-outs, pronunciation guides, index, references)

Guided Reading

Selecting Goals **Behaviors and Understandings to Notice, Teach, and Support**

Thinking *within* the Text

Solving Words

- Notice new and interesting words, record them, and actively add them to speaking or writing vocabulary
- Demonstrate knowledge of flexible ways to solve words (noticing word parts, noticing endings and prefixes)
- Solve multisyllable words (many with three or more syllables) using vowel patterns, phonogram patterns, affixes (prefixes and suffixes), and other word parts
- Solve content-specific words and technical words using graphics and definitions embedded in the text as well as background knowledge
- Solve some undefined words using background knowledge
- Use readers' tools such as glossaries, dictionaries, and pronunciation guides to solve words, including difficult proper nouns and technical words
- Understand connotative meaning of words
- Understand figurative use of words
- Use the context of a sentence, paragraph, or whole text to determine the meaning of a word
- Develop deeper understanding of words that have been encountered before but are not familiar
- Identify words with multiple meanings, discuss alternative meanings, and select the precise meaning within the text
- Apply problem-solving strategies to technical words or proper nouns that are challenging

Monitoring and Correcting

- Continue to monitor accuracy and understanding, self-correcting when errors detract from meaning

Searching for and Using Information

- Search for information in graphics (simple diagrams, illustrations with labels, maps, charts, captions under pictures)
- Use a full range of readers' tools to search for information (table of contents, glossary, headings and subheadings, call-outs, pronunciation guides, index, references)
- Process long sentences (fifteen or more words) that are carried over several lines or to the next page
- Process sentences with embedded clauses (parenthetical material, prepositional phrases, introductory clauses, series of nouns, verbs, or adverbs)
- Process a wide range of complex dialogue, some unassigned
- Process texts with a variety of complex layouts and with some pages of dense print
- Remember the details of complex plots with many episodes
- Form implicit questions and search for answers while reading
- Process long stretches of descriptive language and remember pertinent information
- Respond to plot tension or suspense by reading on to seek resolutions to problems
- Sustain attention to a text read over several days, remembering details and revising interpretations as new events are encountered

Summarizing

- Remember information in summary form over chapters, a series of short stories, or sequels in order to understand larger themes
- Summarize longer narrative texts with multiple episodes either orally or in writing
- Identify important ideas in a text (including some longer and more complex narratives) and report them in an organized way, either orally or in writing
- Summarize a text at intervals during the reading of a longer text
- Remember the story problem and significant details over the reading of a longer text in order to continue constructing meaning

Maintaining Fluency

- Demonstrate phrased, fluent oral reading
- Read dialogue with phrasing and expression that reflects understanding of characters and events
- Demonstrate appropriate stress on words, pausing and phrasing, intonation, and use of punctuation while reading in a way that reflects understanding

Planning for Word Work during Guided Reading

One- to three-minute demonstrations with active student engagement using a chart or easel, white board, or pencil and paper can develop fluency and flexibility in visual processing. Plan for explicit work in specific visual processing areas that need support.

Examples:

- Change words to make a full range of plurals, including irregular plurals and plurals that require spelling changes (*quilt/quilts, quiz/quizzes, octopus/octopi, self/selves*)
- Add, delete, change letter clusters to make or take apart words (*appear, disappear, disappearance, appearance*)
- Work flexibly with base words, making new words by changing letters and adding prefixes and removing suffixes (*merry/marry/marrying/remarry*)
- Recognize words that have multiple meanings (a form of homograph: *temple, temple*) homographs (look the same, sound different: *desert, desert*), and homophones (sound the same, look different: *presence, presents*)
- Take apart and read words with complex phonograms and long vowel patterns, including vowel patterns with *r* (VVCC *(faith)*, VVCe (*release*), VCCe (*barge*), VCCC (*crunch*), VVCCC (*stealth*))
- Take apart words with frequently appearing syllable patterns in multisyllable words (*-en-* in *enter, adventure; -o-* in *ago, omen*)
- Use what is known about words to read new words (*path, sympathy*)
- Recognize words in which several different letters or clusters represent a single sound (/k/ = *ck* in *pick, c* in *country, que* in *clique*)
- Take apart and read words using open (ending in a vowel: *po-lice*) and closed (ending in a consonant: *pol-ish*) syllables

Guided Reading

Selecting Goals Behaviors and Understandings to Notice, Teach, and Support

Adjusting
- Change style and pace of reading to reflect purpose
- Adjust reading to process texts with difficult and complex layout
- Reread to solve words or think about ideas and resume good rate of reading

Thinking *beyond* the Text

Predicting
- Make a wide range of predictions based on personal experiences, content knowledge, and knowledge of similar texts
- Search for and use information to confirm or disconfirm predictions
- Justify predictions using evidence
- Change predictions as new information is gathered from a text

Making Connections
- Make connections between the reader's real-life experiences and people who live in diverse cultures, distant places, and different times
- Bring background (content) knowledge to understanding a wide variety of fiction and nonfiction texts
- Make connections between the text and other texts that have been read or heard (particularly texts with diverse settings)
- Use knowledge from one text to help in understanding diverse cultures and settings encountered in new texts
- Make connections between characters in different texts (similar setting, type of problem, type of person)
- Specify the nature of connections (topic, content, type of story, writer)

Synthesizing
- Mentally form categories of related information and revise them as new information is acquired across the text
- Demonstrate learning new content from reading
- Demonstrate changing perspective as events in a story unfold, particularly applied to people and cultures different from the reader's own
- Through reading both fiction and nonfiction texts about diverse cultures, times, and places, acquire new content and perspectives
- When reading chapters, connected short stories, or sequels, incorporate new knowledge to better understand characters and plots from material previously read

Inferring
- Infer characters' feelings and motivations through reading their dialogue and what other characters say about them
- Demonstrate understanding of characters (their traits, how and why they change), using evidence to support statements
- Take perspectives that may be unfamiliar in interpreting characters' motives, causes for action, or themes
- Apply inferring to multiple characters and complex plots, with some subplots
- Infer the big ideas or themes of a text (some texts with mature themes and issues) and discuss how they are applicable to people's lives today
- Speculate on alternative meanings that the text may have
- Infer causes of problems or of outcomes in fiction and nonfiction texts
- Identify significant events and tell how they are related to the problem of the story or the solution

Thinking *about* the Text

Analyzing
- Notice aspects of genres (realistic and historical fiction, fantasy, biography, autobiography, memoir and diaries, and other nonfiction)
- Notice combined genres in hybrid texts
- Understand when a writer has used underlying organizational structures (description, compare/contrast, temporal sequence, problem/solution, cause/effect)
- Demonstrate the ability to identify the plot or how a text is organized (talk or diagram)
- Notice and discuss how the author or illustrator has used illustrations and other graphics to convey meaning or create mood
- Notice and interpret figurative language and discuss how it adds to the meaning or enjoyment of a text
- Notice descriptive language and discuss how it adds to enjoyment or understanding
- Recognize the use of figurative or descriptive language (or special types of language such as irony) and talk about how it adds to the quality (enjoyment and understanding) of a text
- Understand and talk about the role of the setting in realistic and historical fiction as well as fantasy
- Talk about how the writer built interest and suspense across a story
- Notice aspects of a writer's craft (style, language, perspective, themes) after reading several texts by the same author

Critiquing
- State opinions about a text and show evidence to support them
- Evaluate the quality of illustrations or graphics
- Assess how graphics add to the quality of the text or provide additional information
- Notice the author's qualifications to write an informational text
- Hypothesize how characters could have behaved differently
- Evaluate aspects of a text that add to enjoyment (for example, a humorous character) or interest (plot or information)
- Assess whether a text is authentic and consistent with life experience or prior knowledge (for example, in historical fiction)
- Express tastes and preferences in reading and support choices with specific descriptions of text features (plots, use of language, kinds of characters, genres)

Guided Reading

Readers at **Level S:**

At Level S, readers automatically read and understand a full range of genres, including biographies on less well-known subjects, more complex fantasy, and hybrid genres. They read both chapter books and shorter informational texts; also, they read special forms such as mysteries, series books, books with sequels, short stories, diaries, and logs. Fiction narratives are straightforward but have elaborate plots and many complex characters who develop and change over time. As readers, they understand perspectives different from their own as well as settings and people far distant in time and space. They can process sentences (some with more than fifteen words) that are complex, contain prepositional phrases, introductory clauses, lists of nouns, verbs, or adjectives, and they solve new vocabulary words, some defined in the text and others unexplained. Most reading is silent; fluency and phrasing in oral reading are well established. Readers are challenged by many longer descriptive words and by content-specific and technical words that require using embedded definitions, background knowledge, and readers' tools, such as glossaries. They can take apart multisyllable words and use a full range of word-solving skills. They read and understand texts in a variety of layouts as well as fonts and print characteristics and consistently search for information in illustrations and increasingly complex graphics.

Selecting Texts

Characteristics of Texts at This Level

Genre/Forms

Genre

- Informational texts
- More complex fantasy
- Realistic fiction
- Traditional literature
- Biography, memoir, and autobiography
- Historical fiction
- Mysteries
- Genre combination (hybrids)

Forms

- Picture books
- Plays
- Chapter books
- Chapter books with sequels
- Series books
- Short stories
- Diaries and logs

Text Structure

Fiction

- Narrative structure including chapters with multiple episodes related to a single plot
- Plots with detailed episodes
- Plots with subplots
- Some complex plots with multiple story lines
- Some collections of short stories that have interrelated themes or build a single plot across the book

Nonfiction

- Presentation of multiple topics that represent subtopic of a larger topic or theme
- Underlying structures (description, comparison and contrast, temporal sequence, problem and solution, cause and effect)
- Texts with multiple topics and categories within them
- Variety in organization and topic
- Variety in nonfiction formats (question and answer, paragraphs, boxes, legends, and call-outs)

Content

- Topics that go well beyond readers' personal experiences and content knowledge
- Fiction—settings requiring knowledge of content (history, geography, etc.)
- Most of content carried by the print rather than pictures
- Content supported or extended by illustrations in most informational texts
- Content requiring the reader to take on diverse perspectives (race, language, culture)
- Content particularly appealing to preadolescents

Themes and Ideas

- Complex ideas on many different topics requiring real or vicarious experiences (through reading)
- Texts with deeper meanings applicable to important human problems and social issues
- Some more challenging themes (e.g., war, the environment)
- Many ideas and themes requiring understanding of cultural diversity

Language and Literary Features

- Memorable characters, with both good and bad traits, who change and develop over time
- Multiple characters revealed by what they say, think, and do and what others say or think about them
- Long stretches of descriptive language that is important to understanding setting and characters
- Specific descriptions of settings that provide important information for understanding the plot
- Settings distant in time and space from students' experiences
- Some long strings of unassigned dialogue from which story action must be inferred
- Building suspense through events of the plot
- Some more complex fantasy elements
- Texts with multiple points of view revealed through characters' behaviors

Sentence Complexity

- Longer (some with more than fifteen words) complex sentence structures
- Questions in dialogue (fiction) and questions and answers (nonfiction)
- Sentences with parenthetical material
- Sentences with nouns, verbs, or adjectives in series, divided by commas

Vocabulary

- Many new vocabulary words that readers must derive meaning from context or use glossaries or dictionaries
- Words with connotative meanings essential to understanding the text
- Many words used figuratively (use of common idioms, metaphor, simile)
- Many highly technical words, mostly defined in text, illustrations, or glossary

Words

- Many words with affixes (prefixes and suffixes, multisyllable proper nouns that are difficult to decode)
- Words with a wide variety of very complex spelling patterns
- Many multisyllable words, including proper nouns that are difficult to decode
- Many technical words that are difficult to decode
- Words that are seldom used in oral language and are difficult to decode
- Many complex plurals, contractions, and compound words

Illustrations

General

- A variety of compex graphics, often more than one on a page

Fiction

- Most texts with no or only minimal illustrations
- In illustrated texts, highly complex and artistic illustrations that communicate meaning to match or extend the text (mood, symbolism)
- Black and white illustrations in most fiction texts

Nonfiction

- Full range of graphics providing information that extends the text
- Some texts with graphics that are complex and not fully explained
- Some texts with graphics that have scales or legends that require understanding and interpretation

Book and Print Features

Print and Layout

- Varied space between lines, with some texts having dense print
- Use of words in italics, bold, or all capitals to indicate emphasis, level of importance, or signal other meaning
- Variety in print and background color
- Large variation among print styles and font size (related to genre)
- Many sentences continuing over several lines or to the next page
- Captions under pictures that provide important information
- Print and illustrations integrated in most texts, with print wrapping around pictures
- Variety in layout of nonfiction formats (question and answer, paragraphs, boxes, legends, call-outs)
- More difficult layout of informational text, and some fiction texts, with denser format

Punctuation

- Full range of punctuation as needed for complex sentences
- Occasional use of less common punctuation (colon, semicolon)

Tools

- Full range of readers' tools (table of contents, glossary, headings and subheadings, call-outs, pronunciation guides, index, references)

"How 'bout you?" I casually asked.

"Already ate," he answered, just as casually.

He lied to me, and I lied to him. Ever since Dad lost his job and the money dried up, we lied and kept secrets. The façade helps us make it easier for each other.

Effortlessly, I told another one. "Dad? Anthony asked me to stay over again. OK?"

"An opportunity to sleep in a bed? Go for it." ■

Not to mention a home-cooked supper and breakfast. It was easier for Dad, too. Then he didn't have to feed me.

"Heads up!" said Dad. He lobbed over a brown bag. In the bag was my standard lunch: a peanut-butter sandwich and an apple.

"Thanks," I said as I hopped on my bike.

Dad told me where he'd be job-hunting that day, in case I needed him. "Come here right after school tomorrow," he said. "It's moving day." To be as inconspicuous as possible, we moved the van a lot.

2

I had an unauthorized stop to make on the way to school—one of those secrets I mentioned earlier. Dad didn't know that every Tuesday morning I earned a couple of bucks unloading produce behind Cardozo's Market. I used the money for school supplies that I couldn't bear to ask my dad to buy.

I worked for twenty minutes before I got up the nerve to ask, "Mr. Cardozo . . . I was wondering. Any chance you could hire me permanently?"

"I wish I could, Ray, but what I really need is a full-time produce manager. If you were older and out of school . . . " He shook his head sympathetically.

I got things settled with Anthony. Then all through math I thought about that job at Cardozo's. So during lunch period, I hand-lettered a flyer:

HELP WANTED
PRODUCE MANAGER
CARDOZO'S MARKET
THIRD AND CENTRAL PARKWAY

3

Guided Reading

Selecting Goals Behaviors and Understandings to Notice, Teach, and Support

Thinking *within* the Text

Solving Words

- Notice new and interesting words, record them, and actively add them to speaking or writing vocabulary
- Demonstrate knowledge of flexible ways to solve words (noticing word parts, noticing endings and prefixes)
- Solve multisyllable words (many with three or more syllables) using vowel patterns, phonogram patterns, affixes (prefixes and suffixes), and other word parts
- Solve content-specific words and technical words using graphics and definitions embedded in the text as well as background knowledge
- Solve some undefined words using background knowledge
- Use readers' tools such as glossaries, dictionaries, and pronunciation guides to solve words, including difficult proper nouns and technical words
- Understand connotative meaning of words
- Understand figurative use of words
- Use the context of a sentence, paragraph, or whole text to determine the meaning of a word
- Develop deeper understanding of words that have been encountered before but are not familiar
- Identify words with multiple meanings, discuss alternative meanings, and select the precise meaning within the text
- Apply problem-solving strategies to technical words or proper nouns that are challenging

Monitoring and Correcting

- Continue to monitor accuracy and understanding, self-correcting when errors detract from meaning

Searching for and Using Information

- Search for information in graphics (simple diagrams, illustrations with labels, maps, charts, captions under pictures)
- Use a full range of readers' tools to search for information (table of contents, glossary, headings and subheadings, call-outs, pronunciation guides, index, references)
- Process long sentences (fifteen or more words) that are carried over several lines or to the next page
- Process sentences with embedded clauses (parenthetical material, prepositional phrases, introductory clauses, series of nouns, verbs, or adverbs)
- Process a wide range of complex dialogue, some unassigned
- Process texts with a variety of complex layouts and with some pages of dense print
- Remember the details of complex plots with many episodes
- Form implicit questions and search for answers while reading
- Process long stretches of descriptive language and remember pertinent information
- Respond to plot tension or suspense by reading on to seek resolutions to problems
- Sustain attention to a text read over several days, remembering details and revising interpretations as new events are encountered

Summarizing

- Follow and remember a series of events and the story problem and solution over a longer text in order to understand the ending
- Remember information in summary form over chapters, a series of short stories, or sequels in order to understand larger themes
- Summarize longer narrative texts with multiple episodes
- Identify important ideas in a text (including some longer and more complex narratives) and report them in an organized way, either orally or in writing
- Remember important information about the plot and character over the reading of a larger text in order to continuously construct meaning
- Summarize a text at intervals during the reading of a longer text

Maintaining Fluency

- Demonstrate phrased, fluent oral reading
- Read dialogue with phrasing and expression that reflects understanding of characters and events
- Demonstrate appropriate stress on words, pausing and phrasing, intonation, and use of punctuation while reading in a way that reflects understanding

Adjusting

- Change style and pace of reading to reflect purpose
- Adjust reading to process texts with difficult and complex layout

Planning for Word Work during Guided Reading

One- to three-minute demonstrations with active student engagement using a chart or easel, white board, or pencil and paper can develop fluency and flexibility in visual processing. Plan for explicit work in specific visual processing areas that need support.

Examples:

- Add, delete, change letter clusters to make or take apart words (*giver/shiver/shivered/shivery/livery*)
- Read words with a full range of plurals, including irregular plurals (*cactus/cacti*) and plurals that require spelling changes (*spy/spies*)
- Work flexibly with base words, making new words by changing letters and adding prefixes and suffixes (*ordinary/ordinarily/extraordinary*)
- Recognize and understand words that have multiple meanings (a form of homograph: *story, story*), homographs (look the same, sound different: *address, address*), and homophones (sound the same, look different: *wade, weighed*)
- Take apart words with complex phonograms and long vowel patterns, including vowel patterns with *r* (VVCC (*faint*), VVCe (*praise*), VCCe (*lunge*), VCCC (*crunch*), VVCCC (*straight*))
- Take apart and understand words with several syllables (*mis-rep-re-sen-ta-tion*)
- Read frequently appearing syllable patterns in multisyllable words (*-er-* in *other, service; -at-* in *flatter, satisfy*)
- Use what is known about words to read new words (*path, sympathy*)
- Recognize words in which several different letters or clusters represent a single sound (/k/ = *ck* in *duck, que* in *unique, k* in *kayak, ch* in *choir*)
- Read words using open (ending in a vowel: *ri-val*) and closed (ending in a consonant: *riv-et*) syllables

Guided Reading

Selecting Goals

Behaviors and Understandings to Notice, Teach, and Support

- Reread to solve words or think about ideas and resume good rate of reading
- Change purpose and aspects of processing to reflect understanding of genre

Thinking *beyond* the Text

Predicting

- Make a wide range of predictions based on personal experiences, content knowledge, and knowledge of similar texts
- Search for and use information to confirm or disconfirm predictions
- Justify predictions using evidence
- Change predictions as new information is gathered from a text

Making Connections

- Make connections between the reader's real-life experiences and people who live in diverse cultures, distant places, and different times
- Bring background knowledge to the understanding of a text before, during, and after reading
- Bring knowledge from personal experiences to the interpretation of characters and events, particularly content and situations related to preadolescents
- Make connections between the text and other texts that have been read or heard (particularly texts with diverse settings) and demonstrate in writing
- Use knowledge from one text to help in understanding diverse cultures and settings encountered in new texts
- Make connections between characters in different texts (similar setting, type of problem, type of person)
- Specify the nature of connections (topic, content, type of story, writer)

Synthesizing

- Mentally form categories of related information and revise them as new information is acquired across the text
- Demonstrate learning new content from reading
- Express changes in ideas or perspective across the reading (as events unfold) after reading a text
- Acquire new content and perspectives through reading both fiction and nonfiction texts about diverse cultures, times, and places
- When reading chapters, connected short stories, or sequels, incorporate new knowledge to better understand characters and plots from material previously read

Inferring

- Infer cause and effect in influencing characters' feelings or underlying motives
- Infer characters' feelings and motivations through reading their dialogue and what other characters say about them
- Follow multiple characters in different episodes, inferring their feelings about each other
- Demonstrate through talk or writing understandings of characters (their traits, how and why they change), using evidence to support statements
- Take perspectives that may be unfamiliar in interpreting characters' motives, causes for action, or themes
- Apply inferring to multiple characters and complex plots, with some subplots
- Infer the big ideas or themes of a text (some texts with mature themes and issues) and discuss how they are applicable to people's lives today
- Speculate on alternative meanings that the text may have
- Infer the meaning of symbols that the writer is using
- Infer causes of problems or of outcomes in fiction and nonfiction texts
- Identify significant events and tell how they are related to the problem of the story or the solution

Thinking *about* the Text

Analyzing

- Notice and discuss aspects of genres (realistic and historical fiction, fantasy, biography, autobiography, memoir and diaries, and other nonfiction)
- Notice combined genres in hybrid texts
- Understand, talk about, and/or write or draw when a writer has used underlying organizational structures (description, compare/contrast, temporal sequence, problem/solution, cause/effect)
- Demonstrate the ability to identify how an informational text is organized (categories, sequence, etc.)
- Notice how the author or illustrator has used pictures and other graphics to convey meaning or create mood
- Notice and interpret figurative language and discuss how it adds to the meaning or enjoyment of a text
- Notice descriptive language and how it adds to enjoyment or understanding
- Recognize the use of figurative or descriptive language (or special types of language such as irony) and talk about how it adds to the quality (enjoyment and understanding) of a text
- Understand the role of the setting in realistic and historical fiction as well as fantasy
- Notice how the writer built interest and suspense across a story
- Analyze complex plots and sometimes represent in diagrams or drawings
- Notice aspects of a writer's craft (style, language, perspective, themes) after reading several texts by him/her
- Notice writer's use of symbolism

Critiquing

- Evaluate the text in terms of readers' own experience as preadolescents
- Assess how graphics add to the quality of the text or provide additional information
- Notice and talk about the author's qualifications to write an informational text
- Hypothesize how characters could have behaved differently
- Evaluate aspects of a text that add to enjoyment (for example, a humorous character) or interest (plot or information)
- Assess whether a text is authentic and consistent with life experience or prior knowledge (for example, in historical fiction)
- Express tastes and preferences in reading and support choices with specific descriptions of text features (plots, use of language, kinds of characters, genres)

Guided Reading

Readers at **Level T:**

At Level T, readers will process the full range of genres, and texts will be longer with many lines of print on each page, requiring readers to remember information and connect ideas over a long period of time (as much as a week or two). Complex fantasy, myths, and legends offer added challenge and an increased use of symbolism. Readers understand perspectives different from their own, and understand settings and people far distance in time or space. Most reading is silent; fluency and phrasing in oral reading is well established. Readers are challenged by many longer descriptive words and by content-specific and technical words that require using embedded definitions, background knowledge, and readers' tools, such as glossaries. They can take apart multisyllable words and use a full range of word-solving strategies. They search for and use information in an integrated way, using complex graphics and texts that present content requiring background knowledge.

Selecting Texts

Characteristics of Texts at This Level

Genre/Forms

Genre

- Informational texts
- Fantasy
- Realistic fiction
- Traditional literature, including myths and legends
- Biography, memoir, and autobiography
- Historical fiction
- Mysteries
- Genre combination (hybrids)

Forms

- Picture books
- Plays
- Chapter books
- Chapter books with sequels
- Series books
- Short stories
- Diaries and logs

Text Structure

Fiction

- Narrative structure including chapters with multiple episodes related to a single plot
- Plots with detailed episodes
- Plots with subplots
- Some complex plots with multiple story lines
- Some collections of short stories that have interrelated themes or build a single plot across the book

Nonfiction

- Presentation of multiple topics that represent subtopic of a larger topic or theme
- Underlying structures (description, comparison and contrast, temporal sequence, problem and solution, cause and effect)
- Texts with multiple topics and categories and subcategories within them
- Variety in organization and topic
- Variety in nonfiction formats (question and answer, paragraphs, boxes, legends, and call-outs)

Content

- Topics that go well beyond readers' personal experiences and content knowledge
- Fiction–settings requiring knowledge of content (history, geography, etc.)
- Most of content carried by the print rather than pictures
- Content supported or extended by illustrations in most informational texts
- Content requiring the reader to take on diverse perspectives (race, language, culture)
- Content particularly appealing to preadolescents

Themes and Ideas

- Themes focusing on the problems of preadolescents
- Texts with deeper meanings applicable to important human problems and social issues
- Many ideas and themes requiring understanding of cultural diversity
- Some themes presenting mature issues and the problems of society (e.g., racism)
- Many texts focusing on human problems (war, hardship, or economic issues)
- Themes that evoke alternative interpretations

Language and Literary Features

- Memorable characters, with both good and bad traits, who change and develop over time
- Multiple characters revealed by what they say, think, and do and what others say or think about them
- Long stretches of descriptive language that is important to understanding setting and characters
- Specific descriptions of settings that provide important information for understanding the plot
- Settings distant in time and space from students' experiences
- Some long strings of unassigned dialogue from which story action must be inferred
- Building suspense through events of the plot
- Many complex narratives that are highly literary
- Some more complex fantasy elements, some showing conflict between good and evil
- Some obvious symbolism
- Texts with multiple points of view revealed through characters' behaviors

Guided Reading

Sentence Complexity

- Longer (some with more than twenty words) complex sentence structures
- Sentences with parenthetical material
- Many complex sentences including dialogue and many embedded phrases and clauses
- Sentences with nouns, verbs, or adjectives in series, divided by commas
- Wide range of declarative, imperative, or interrogative sentences

Vocabulary

- Many new vocabulary words that readers must derive meaning from context or use glossaries or dictionaries
- Words with connotative meanings essential to understanding the text
- Many words used figuratively (metaphor, simile, idiom)
- Many highly technical words, mostly defined in text, illustrations, or glossary
- Words used in regional or historical dialects
- Some words from languages other than English

Words

- All parts of speech
- Many words with a large number of syllables
- Many words with affixes (prefixes and suffixes, multisyllable proper nouns that are difficult to decode)
- Words with a wide variety of very complex spelling patterns
- Many multisyllable proper nouns that are difficult to decode
- Many technical words that are difficult to decode
- Words that are seldom used in oral language and are difficult to decode
- Many complex plurals, contractions, and compound words

Illustrations

General

- A variety of compex graphics, often more than one on a page

Fiction

- Most texts with no or only minimal illustrations
- In illustrated texts, highly complex and artistic illustrations that communicate meaning to match or extend the text (mood, symbolism)
- Black and white illustrations in some fiction texts

Nonfiction

- Full range of graphics providing information that matches and extends the text
- Some texts with graphics that are complex and not fully explained
- Some texts with graphics that have scales or legends that require understanding and interpretation

Book and Print Features

Print and Layout

- Varied space between lines, with some texts having dense print
- Use of words in italics, bold, or all capitals to indicate emphasis, level of importance, or signal other meaning
- Variety in print and background color
- Large variation among print styles and font size (related to genre)
- Many sentences continuing over several lines or to the next page
- Captions under pictures that provide important information
- Print and illustrations integrated in most texts, with print wrapping around pictures
- Variety in layout of nonfiction formats (question and answer, paragraphs, boxes, legends, call-outs)
- More difficult layout in informational text, and some fiction texts, with denser format

Punctuation

- Full range of punctuation as needed for complex sentences
- Occasional use of less common punctuation (colon, semicolon)

Tools

- Full range of readers' tools (table of contents, glossary, headings and subheadings, call-outs, pronunciation guides, index, references)

coat, gloves, a leather cap, and a pair of goggles for protection.

The year was 1904, and everybody in Detroit had been talking about the horseless carriage that Henry Ford had invented. Ford called it the automobile, because it moved on its own. No horse was required. Ford said that the automobile was going to replace the horse and carriage, but most people didn't believe it. People had been riding in horse-drawn carriages and wagons for hundreds of years, and it was a great way to get around. ■

The automobile pulled up in front of the house enveloped in a cloud of dust. As the driver removed his cap and goggles, Ethan thought, "Oh no!" Seeing that the driver was his father, Ethan wanted to sink down into his shoes in embarrassment.

The crowd was chanting, "Get a horse! Get a horse!"

But Ethan's dad seemed unconcerned; in fact, he looked very pleased with himself. "What do you think, Ethan? I thought I'd surprise you and your mother. Want to go for a spin in our new Model A?" His father helped him clamber onto the seat next to him.

2

The motor wheezed, rattled, and roared into action. They whizzed down the street in a cloud of dust while barking dogs and laughing children chased them. The chickens in front of Mr. Grant's house flapped, squawked, and scurried out of the way.

Ethan's hair blew into his eyes as the Model A roared down the winding dirt road.

Ethan was slightly frightened to be riding in an automobile, but he was having a lot of fun, too. He was even a little disappointed when Father shouted that it was time to go home.

That night, Ethan's mother said, "Tom, everybody in town thinks you're crazy!"

"Not everybody," replied Ethan's father. "I predict that before long everyone will be driving an automobile."

Ethan had to admit that riding with his father had been exciting. He never thought he'd ever go as fast as 20 miles an hour! But he was worried about one thing.

"Dad," he said, "what's going to happen to Chester?" Chester was the aging horse they'd had for as long as Ethan could remember. "Are we still going

3

Guided Reading

Selecting Goals — Behaviors and Understandings to Notice, Teach, and Support

Thinking *within* the Text

Solving Words

- Notice new and useful words and intentionally record and remember them to expand oral and written vocabulary
- Demonstrate ability to use automatically and flexibly a wide range of word-solving strategies (for example, dividing words into syllables, using phonograms within multisyllable words, using word parts, using prefixes and affixes, and connecting words to known words)
- Solve some undefined words using background knowledge
- Use readers' tools such as glossaries, dictionaries, and pronunciation guides to solve words, including difficult proper nouns and technical words
- Understand connotative meaning of words
- Understand figurative use of words
- Use the context of a sentence, paragraph, or whole text to determine the meaning of a word
- Develop deeper understanding of words that have been encountered before but are not familiar
- Derive the meaning of words that reflect regional or historical dialects as well as words from languages other than English

Monitoring and Correcting

- Continue to monitor accuracy and understanding, self-correcting when errors detract from meaning

Searching for and Using Information

- Search for and use information in a wide range of graphics and integrate with information from print (for example, pictures, captions, diagrams, illustrations with labels, maps, charts)
- Use a full range of readers' tools to search for information (table of contents, glossary, headings and subheadings, call-outs, pronunciation guides, index, references)
- Process long sentences (twenty or more words) with embedded clauses (prepositional phrases, introductory clauses, series of nouns, verbs, or adverbs)
- Process texts with a variety of complex layouts and with some pages of dense print
- Form implicit questions and search for answers while reading
- Gain important information from longer texts with complex plots, multiple characters and episodes, and long stretches of descriptive language and dialogue

Summarizing

- Identify important ideas and information (longer texts with chapters and sometimes multiple texts)
- Organize important information in summary form in order to remember and use them as background knowledge in reading or for discussion and writing

Maintaining Fluency

- Demonstrate phrased, fluent oral reading
- Read dialogue with phrasing and expression that reflects understanding of characters and events
- Demonstrate appropriate stress on words, pausing and phrasing, intonation, and use of punctuation while reading in a way that reflects understanding

Adjusting

- Change style and pace of reading to reflect purpose
- Slow down or reread to solve words or think about ideas and resume good rate of reading
- Change purpose and aspects of processing to reflect understanding of genre

Thinking *beyond* the Text

Predicting

- Make a wide range of predictions based on personal experiences, content knowledge, and knowledge of similar texts
- Support predictions with evidence from the text or from knowledge of genre
- Change predictions as new information is gathered from a text

Planning for Word Work during Guided Reading

One- to three-minute demonstrations with active student engagement using a chart or easel, white board, or pencil and paper can develop fluency and flexibility in visual processing. Plan for explicit work in specific visual processing areas that need support.

Examples:

- Take apart and read a full range of plurals, including irregular plurals and plurals that require spelling changes (*goose/geese, life/lives*)
- Work flexibly with base words, making new words by changing letters and adding prefixes and suffixes
- Recognize words that have multiple meanings (a form of homograph: *major, major*), homographs (look the same, sound different: *contest, contest*), and homophones (sound the same, look different: *peel, peal*)
- Notice and use word roots (Greek and Latin) to take apart and understand words (*aqua-: aquarium, aquatic, aquaduct*)
- Solve words using all consonant clusters and long and short vowel patterns, including vowel patterns with *r*, that appear in multisyllable words
- Take apart a wide range of multisyllable words with ease (*mi-cro-or-gan-ism*) and use the parts to assist pronunciation and derive meaning
- Read and derive the meaning of words that are related to each other because they have the same base or root word (*direct, directs, directed, direction, misdirect, directional*)
- Notice and use frequently appearing vowel and syllable patterns in multisyllable words (*-is(s)-* in *whisper, missing; -un-* in *sunny, munch*)
- Use what is known about words to read new words (*path, sympathy*)
- Quickly recognize and solve a large number of words, including multisyllable words

Guided Reading

Selecting Goals — Behaviors and Understandings to Notice, Teach, and Support

Making Connections

- Bring background knowledge to the understanding of a text before, during, and after reading
- Bring knowledge from personal experiences to the interpretation of characters and events, particularly content and situations related to preadolescents
- Make connections between the text and other texts that have been read or heard (particularly texts with diverse settings) and demonstrate in writing
- Use knowledge from one text to help in understanding diverse cultures and settings encountered in new texts
- Make connections between characters in different texts (similar setting, type of problem, type of person)
- Specify the nature of connections (topic, content, type of story, writer)

Synthesizing

- Mentally form categories of related information and revise them as new information is acquired across the text
- Integrate existing content knowledge with new information from a text to consciously create new understandings
- Express changes in ideas or perspective across the reading (as events unfold) after reading a text
- Acquire new content and perspectives through reading both fiction and nonfiction texts about diverse cultures, times, and places
- Use situations that focus on the problems of preadolescents to develop new perspectives on readers' own lives
- When reading chapters, connected short stories, or sequels, incorporate new knowledge to better understand characters and plots from material previously read

Inferring

- In texts with multiple complex characters, infer traits, motivations, and changes through examining how the writer describes them, what they do, what they say and think, and what other characters say about them
- Infer characters' or subjects' thinking processes and struggles at key decision points in their lives in fiction or biography
- Infer the big ideas or themes of a text (some texts with mature themes and issues) and discuss how they are applicable to people's lives today
- Infer the meaning of symbols (objects, events, motifs, characters) that the writer uses to convey and enhance meaning
- Infer causes of problems or of outcomes in fiction and nonfiction texts
- Identify significant events and tell how they are related to the problem of the story or the solution

Thinking *about* the Text

Analyzing

- Notice aspects of genres (realistic and historical fiction, fantasy, myths and legends, biography, autobiography, memoir and diaries, and other nonfiction)
- Notice combined genres in hybrid texts
- Understand when a writer has used underlying organizational structures (description, compare/contrast, temporal sequence, problem/solution, cause/effect)
- Notice how the author or illustrator has used illustrations and other graphics to convey meaning or create mood
- Notice descriptive language and discuss how it adds to enjoyment or understanding
- Recognize the use of figurative or descriptive language (or special types of language such as irony) and talk about how it adds to the quality (enjoyment and understanding) of a text
- Understand the role of the setting in realistic and historical fiction as well as fantasy
- Understand how the writer built interest and suspense across a story, providing examples
- Understand the structure of complex plots in fiction and the organization of the text in nonfiction, sometimes using graphic organizers or diagrams
- Notice aspects of a writer's craft (style, language, perspective, themes) after reading several texts by the same author
- Notice as well as discuss writer's use of symbolism
- Understand alternative interpretations of symbolism
- Understand the meaning of symbolism when used by a writer to create texts, including complex fantasy where the writer is representing good and evil
- Notice the writer's choice of words that are not English and reflect on the reasons for these choices and how those words add to the meaning of a text
- Notice the way writers use regional dialect and discuss how it adds to the authenticity of the text or characters

Critiquing

- Evaluate the text in terms of readers' own experience as preadolescents
- Critique a text as an example of a genre
- Evaluate the author's qualifications to write an informational text
- Evaluate the author's use of characterization and plot (for example, believability or depth)
- Evaluate aspects of a text that add to enjoyment (for example, a humorous character) or interest (plot or information)
- Assess whether a text is authentic and consistent with life experience or prior knowledge, including how the text reflects the lives of preadolescents or adolescents
- Use other sources of information to check the authenticity of a text (fiction, historical fiction, nonfiction) when questions arise
- Assess whether social issues and different cultural groups are accurately represented in a fiction or nonfiction text
- Express tastes and preferences in reading and support choices with specific descriptions of text features (plots, use of language, kinds of characters, genres)

Guided Reading

Readers at **Level U:**

At Level U, readers will process the full range of genres, and texts will be longer, requiring readers to remember information and connect ideas over many days of reading. Complex fantasy, myths, and legends offer added challenge and an increased use of symbolism. Readers understand perspectives different from their own, and understand settings and people far distance in time or space. Most reading is silent; fluency and phrasing in oral reading is well established. Readers are challenged by many longer descriptive words and by content-specific and technical words that require using embedded definitions, background knowledge, and readers' tools, such as glossaries. They can take apart long multisyllable words and use a full range of word-solving strategies. They search for and use information in an integrated way, using complex graphics and texts that present content requiring background knowledge.

Selecting Texts **Characteristics of Texts at This Level**

Genre/Forms

Genre

- Informational texts
- Fantasy
- Realistic fiction
- Traditional literature, including myths and legends
- Biography, memoir, and autobiography
- Historical fiction, many with settings different from students' own cultural histories
- Mysteries
- Genre combination (hybrids)

Forms

- Picture books
- Plays
- Chapter books
- Chapter books with sequels
- Series books
- Short stories
- Diaries and logs

Text Structure

Fiction

- Narrative structure including chapters with multiple episodes related to a single plot
- Plots with detailed episodes
- Plots with subplots
- Some complex plots with multiple story lines
- Some collections of short stories that have interrelated themes or build a single plot across the book

Nonfiction

- Presentation of multiple topics that represent subcategories of a larger topic or theme
- Variety of underlying structures often combined in complex ways (description, comparison and contrast, temporal sequence, problem and solution, cause and effect)
- Texts with multiple topics and categories within them
- Variety in nonfiction formats (question and answer, paragraphs, boxes, legends, and call-outs)

Content

- Topics that go well beyond readers' personal experiences and content knowledge
- Fiction–settings requiring knowledge of content (history, geography, etc.)
- Most of content carried by the print rather than pictures
- Content supported or extended by illustrations in most informational texts
- Content requiring the reader to take on diverse perspectives (race, language, culture)
- Content particularly appealing to preadolescents

Themes and Ideas

- Themes focusing on the problems of preadolescents
- Many ideas and themes requiring understanding of cultural diversity
- Many themes presenting mature issues and the problems of society (e.g., racism, war)
- Many texts focusing on human problems (war, hardship, or economic issues)
- Themes that evoke alternative interpretations

Language and Literary Features

- Multiple characters revealed by what they say, think, and do and what others say or think about them
- Texts requiring inference to understand characters and why they change
- Multidimensional characters that develop over time
- Long stretches of descriptive language that are important to understanding setting and characters
- Specific descriptions of settings that provide important information for understanding the plot and character development
- Settings distant in time and space from students' experiences
- Some long strings of unassigned dialogue from which story action must be inferred
- Many complex narratives that are highly literary
- Fantasy and science fiction showing struggle of good and evil
- Some obvious symbolism
- Some literary devices (for example, stories within stories, symbolism, and figurative language)
- Texts with multiple points of view revealed through characters' behaviors

Guided Reading

Sentence Complexity

- Longer (some with more than twenty words) complex sentence structures
- Sentences with parenthetical material
- Many complex sentences including dialogue and many embedded phrases and clauses
- Sentences with nouns, verbs, or adjectives in a series, divided by commas
- Wide range of declarative, imperative, or interrogative sentences

Vocabulary

- Many new vocabulary words that readers must derive meaning from context or use glossaries or dictionaries
- Words with connotative meanings essential to understanding the text
- Many words used figuratively (common idioms, metaphor, simile)
- Many highly technical words that require background knowledge and are not defined in the text
- Words used in regional or historical dialects
- Some words from languages other than English

Words

- All parts of speech
- Many words with affixes (prefixes and suffixes, multisyllable proper nouns that are difficult to decode)
- Words with a wide variety of very complex spelling patterns
- Many multisyllable proper nouns that are difficult to decode
- Many technical words that are difficult to decode
- Words that are seldom used in oral language and are difficult to decode
- Long, multisyllable words requiring attention to roots to read and understand
- Many complex plurals, contractions, and compound words

Illustrations

Fiction

- Most texts with no illustrations other than cover jacket or symbolic decoration on margins or at chapter headings
- Black and white illustrations in some texts

Nonfiction

- Full range of graphics providing information that matches and extends the text
- Some texts with graphics that are dense and challenging
- Many texts that have scales or legends that require understanding and interpretation
- A wide variety of complex graphics that require interpretation (photos with legends, diagrams, labels, cutaways, graphs, maps)

Book and Print Features

Print and Layout

- Varied space between lines, with some texts having dense print
- Use of words in italics, bold, or all capitals to indicate emphasis, level of importance, or signal other meaning
- Large variation among print styles, font size, and color
- Many texts with very small font
- Many sentences continuing over several lines or to the next page
- Print and illustrations integrated in most texts, with print wrapping around pictures
- More difficult layout of informational text, and some fiction texts, with denser format
- Variety in layout of nonfiction formats (question and answer, paragraphs, boxes, legends, call-outs) often occurring across a two-page spread

Punctuation

- Full range of punctuation as needed for complex sentences
- Occasional use of less common punctuation (colon, semicolon)

Tools

- Full range of readers' tools (table of contents, glossary, headings and subheadings, call-outs, pronunciation guides, index, references)

Scientists describe the seismograph's measurements with numbers. Since the 1930s, they have used a system called the Richter [RIK-ter] scale. If an earthquake measures below 3.0 on the Richter, people usually can't feel it. Earthquakes over 5.0 on the scale can cause damage, while a measurement of 7.0 is evidence of a major earthquake.

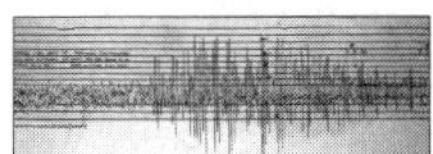

A pen attached to a seismograph draws an image that shows the magnitude of an earthquake.

What Causes Earthquakes?

How and why do all these earthquakes occur? Earth has many different layers. Its outermost layer is called the crust and is made up of huge sections called tectonic plates. Below the crust is another layer, called the mantle, which is made up of softer rock. When tectonic plates push against each other, a huge amount of force or pressure builds up. ■

Eventually, the force causes the plates to shift on top of the mantle in different ways: they can push toward each other, pull away from each other, or simply slide past each other. These movements are

2

usually so small that people aren't aware of them, but when tectonic plates collide, there's no mistaking what has occurred—an earthquake!

Plate movements can cause Earth's crust to crack, causing a break called a fault. Along the Pacific Coast of the United States lies a 700-mile-long fault. The rocks below the earth's surface frequently shift or break along this fault, making the state of California vulnerable to many earthquakes.

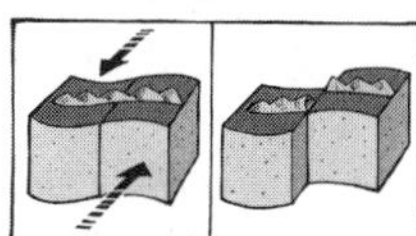

Rocks below the earth's surface can shift along a fault.

Some Famous Earthquakes

A major earthquake jolted San Francisco on April 18, 1906. It caused a huge fire and the destruction of 28,000 buildings. Many people were killed or injured in this terrible quake. Scientists believe this earthquake may have registered as high as 8.3 on the Richter scale.

3

Guided Reading

Selecting Goals Behaviors and Understandings to Notice, Teach, and Support

Thinking *within* the Text

Solving Words

- Notice new and useful words and intentionally record and remember them to expand oral and written vocabulary
- Demonstrate ability to use automatically and flexibly a wide range of word-solving strategies (for example, dividing words into syllables, using phonograms within multisyllable words, using word parts, using prefixes and affixes, and connecting words to known words)
- Using word-solving strategies, background knowledge, graphics, text context, and readers' tools (glossaries, dictionaries) to solve words, including content-specific and technical words
- Derive the meaning of words that reflect regional or historical dialects as well as words from languages other than English

Monitoring and Correcting

- Continue to monitor accuracy and understanding, self-correcting when errors detract from meaning

Searching for and Using Information

- Search for and use information in a wide range of graphics and integrate with information from print (for example, pictures, captions, diagrams, illustrations with labels, maps, charts)
- Use a full range of readers' tools to search for information (table of contents, glossary, headings and subheadings, call-outs, pronunciation guides, index, references)
- Process long sentences (twenty or more words) with embedded clauses (prepositional phrases, introductory clauses, series of nouns, verbs, or adverbs)
- Process texts with a variety of complex layouts and with some pages of dense print
- Follow complex plots, including texts with literary devices (for example, flashbacks and stories within stories)
- Form implicit questions and search for answers while reading
- Gain important information from longer texts with complex plots, multiple characters and episodes, long stretches of descriptive language and dialogue, and no illustrations
- Search for and use information from texts (both fiction and nonfiction) that have many new and unfamiliar concepts and ideas within a single chapter or section (dense concepts)

Summarizing

- Identify important ideas and information (longer texts with chapters and sometimes multiple texts) and organize them in summary form in order to remember and use them as background knowledge in reading or for discussion and writing
- Exercise selectivity in summarizing the information in a text (most important information or ideas and facts focused by the reader's purpose)
- Construct summaries that are concise and reflect the important and overarching ideas and information in texts

Maintaining Fluency

- Read dialogue with phrasing and expression that reflects understanding of characters and events
- Demonstrate appropriate stress on words, pausing and phrasing, intonation, and use of punctuation while reading in a way that reflects understanding

Adjusting

- Change style and pace of reading to reflect purpose
- Slow down and reread to solve words or think about ideas and resume good rate of reading
- Change purpose and aspects of processing to reflect understanding of genre

Thinking *beyond* the Text

Predicting

- Support predictions with evidence from the text or from knowledge of genre
- Use characteristics of genre as a source of information to make predictions before and during reading
- Change predictions as new information is gathered from a text
- Make and continually revise a wide range of predictions (what characters will do, what will happen to solve the problem) based on personal experiences, content knowledge, and knowledge of similar texts

Planning for Word Work during Guided Reading

One- to three-minute demonstrations with active student engagement using a chart or easel, white board, or pencil and paper can develop fluency and flexibility in visual processing. Plan for explicit work in specific visual processing areas that need support.

Examples:

- Read words with a full range of plurals, including irregular plurals and plurals that require spelling changes (*marigold/marigolds, volcano/volcanoes, louse/lice, loaf/loaves*)
- Use base words, prefixes, and suffixes in the process of deriving word meaning
- Work flexibly with base words, making new words by changing letters and adding prefixes and suffixes
- Read words that have multiple meanings (a form of homograph: *scale, scale*), homographs (look the same, sound different: *content, content*), and homophones (sound the same, look different: *capital, capitol*)
- Notice and use word roots (Greek and Latin) to take apart and understand words (*class-: classical, classify, classification*)
- Read words using all consonant clusters and long and short vowel patterns, including vowel patterns with *r,* that appear in multisyllable words
- Take apart long multisyllable words with ease (*un-ex-cep-tion-able*)
- Read and determine the meaning of words that are related to each other because they have the same base or root word (*porter, portable, transport, import, export*)
- Notice and use frequently appearing vowel and syllable patterns in multisyllable words (*-or-* in *border, ordinary; -a-* in *bacon, station*)

Guided Reading

Selecting Goals

Behaviors and Understandings to Notice, Teach, and Support

Making Connections

- Before, during, and after reading, bring background knowledge to the understanding of a text
- Bring knowledge from personal experiences to the interpretation of characters and events, particularly content and situations related to preadolescents
- Make connections between the text and other texts that have been read or heard (particularly texts with diverse settings) and demonstrate in writing
- Connect and compare texts within genres and across genres
- Use knowledge from one text to help in understanding diverse cultures and settings encountered in new texts
- Connect characters across texts and genres by circumstances, traits, or actions
- Specify the nature of connections (topic, content, type of story, writer)

Synthesizing

- Mentally form categories of related information and revise them as new information is acquired across the text
- Integrate existing content knowledge with new information from a text to consciously create new understandings
- Express changes in ideas or perspective across the reading (as events unfold) after reading a text
- Acquire new perspectives and content through reading both fiction and nonfiction texts about diverse cultures, times, and places
- Use situations focusing on the problems of preadolescents to develop new perspectives on readers' own lives
- When reading chapters, connected short stories, or sequels, incorporate new knowledge to better understand characters and plots from material previously read

Inferring

- In texts with multiple complex characters, infer traits, motivations, and changes through examining how the writer describes them, what they do, what they say and think, and what other characters say about them
- Infer characters' or subjects' thinking processes and struggles at key decision points in their lives in fiction or biography
- Infer the big ideas or themes of a text (some texts with mature themes and issues) and discuss how they are applicable to people's lives today
- Infer the meaning of symbols (objects, events, motifs, characters) that the writer uses to convey and enhance meaning
- Infer causes of problems or of outcomes in fiction and nonfiction texts
- Identify significant events and tell how they are related to the problem of the story or the solution

Thinking *about* the Text

Analyzing

- Notice aspects of genres (realistic and historical fiction, fantasy, myths and legends, biography, autobiography, memoir and diaries, and other nonfiction, hybrid texts)
- Identify the selection of genre in relation to inferred writer's purpose for a range of texts
- Understand when a writer has combined underlying organizational structures (description, compare and contrast, temporal sequence, problem and solution, cause and effect)
- Notice and discuss how the author or illustrator has used illustrations and other graphics to convey meaning or create mood
- Notice and interpret figurative language and discuss how it adds to the meaning or enjoyment of a text
- Notice descriptive language and discuss how it adds to enjoyment or understanding
- Notice how an author uses words in a connotative way (to imply something beyond the literal meaning)
- Understand and talk about the role of the setting in realistic and historical fiction as well as fantasy
- Understand how the writer built interest and suspense across a story, providing examples
- Notice the structure of complex plots in fiction and the organization of the text in nonfiction and sometimes show in a graphic organizer or diagram
- Notice aspects of a writer's craft (style, language, perspective, themes) after reading several texts by him/her
- Notice and understand the meaning of symbolism when used by a writer to create texts, including complex fantasy where the writer is representing good and evil
- Notice the writers choice of words that are not English and reflect on the reasons for these choices and how those words add to the meaning of a text
- Notice the way writers use regional dialect and discuss how it adds to the authenticity of the text or characters
- Examine character traits in a complex way, recognizing that they are multidimensional and change over time

Critiquing

- Evaluate the text in terms of readers' own experience as preadolescents
- Critique a text as an example of a genre
- Assess the author's qualifications to write an informational text
- Evaluate the author's use of characterization and plot (for example, believability or depth)
- Evaluate aspects of a text that add to enjoyment (for example, a humorous character) or interest (plot or information)
- Assess whether a text is authentic and consistent with life experience or prior knowledge, including how the text reflects the lives of preadolescents or adolescents
- Use other sources of information to check the authenticity of a text (fiction, historical fiction, nonfiction) when questions arise
- For historical fiction, evaluate the authenticity of the details of the setting and reporting of events against knowledge from other sources
- Discuss whether social issues and different cultural groups are accurately represented in a fiction or nonfiction text
- Express tastes and preferences in reading and support choices with specific descriptions of text features (plots, use of language, kinds of characters, genres)

Guided Reading

Readers at **Level V:**

At Level V, readers will process the full range of genres, and texts will be longer, requiring readers to remember information and connect ideas over many days of reading. Complex fantasy, myths, and legends offer added challenge and an increased use of symbolism. In addition, readers will encounter some abstract special forms of literature, such as satire. Readers understand perspectives different from their own, and understand settings and people far distance in time or space. Most reading is silent; fluency and phrasing in oral reading is well established. In addition, readers can be very expressive when they present poetry or readers' theater. Readers are challenged by many longer descriptive words and by content-specific and technical words that require using embedded definitions, background knowledge, and readers' tools, such as glossaries. They can take apart multisyllable words and use a full range of word-solving strategies. They search for and use information in an integrated way, using complex graphics and texts that present content requiring background knowledge.

Selecting Texts **Characteristics of Texts at This Level**

Genre/Forms

Genre

- Informational texts
- Fantasy
- Realistic fiction
- Traditional literature, including myths and legends
- Biography, memoir, and autobiography
- Historical fiction, many with settings different from students' own cultural histories
- Mysteries
- Genre combination (hybrids)
- Satire

Forms

- Picture books
- Plays
- Chapter books
- Chapter books with sequels
- Series books
- Short stories
- Diaries and logs

Text Structure

Fiction

- Narrative structure including chapters with multiple episodes related to a single plot
- Plots with detailed episodes
- Plots with subplots
- Some complex plots with multiple story lines
- Some collections of short stories that have interrelated themes or build a single plot across the book

Nonfiction

- Presentation of multiple topics that represent subtopic of a larger topic or theme
- Variety of underlying structures often combined in complex ways (description, comparison and contrast, temporal sequence, problem and solution, cause and effect)
- Texts with multiple topics, categories, and subcategories
- Variety in organization and topic
- Variety in nonfiction formats (question and answer, paragraphs, boxes, legends, and call-outs)

Content

- Many texts requiring knowledge of history
- Content supported or extended by illustrations in most informational texts
- Content requiring the reader to take on diverse perspectives (race, language, culture)
- Content particularly appealing to preadolescents and adolescents
- Critical thinking required to judge authenticity of informational texts, historical fiction, and biography
- Heavy content load in many texts, both fiction and nonfiction, requiring study

Themes and Ideas

- Themes focusing on the problems of preadolescents and adolescents
- Many ideas and themes requiring understanding of cultural diversity
- Some themes presenting mature issues and the problems of society (e.g., racism, war)
- Many texts focusing on human problems (hardship, or economic issues)
- Themes that evoke alternative interpretations

Language and Literary Features

- Multiple characters revealed by what they say, think, and do and what others say or think about them
- Interpretation of characters essential to understanding the theme
- Multidimensional characters that develop over time, requiring inference to understand how and why they change
- Long stretches of descriptive language that are important to understanding setting and characters
- Specific descriptions of settings that provide important information for understanding the plot
- Settings distant in time and space from students' experiences
- Some long strings of unassigned dialogue from which story action must be inferred
- Some switching from setting to setting, including time change (often unsignaled or signaled only by dialogue)
- Many complex narratives that are highly literary
- Full range of literary devices (for example, flashback, stories within stories, symbolism, and figurative language)
- Texts with multiple points of view revealed through characters' behaviors

Guided Reading

Sentence Complexity

- Longer (some with more than twenty words) complex sentence structures
- Sentences with parenthetical material
- Many complex sentences including dialogue and many embedded phrases and clauses
- Sentences with nouns, verbs, or adjectives in series, divided by commas
- Wide range of declarative, imperative, and interrogative sentences

Vocabulary

- Many new vocabulary words that readers must derive meaning from context or use glossaries or dictionaries
- Words used figuratively or with unusual or hard-to-understand connotations
- Many highly technical words that require background knowledge and are not defined in the text
- Words used in regional or historical dialects
- Some words from languages other than English

Words

- All parts of speech
- Many words with three or more syllables
- Many words with affixes (prefixes and suffixes, multisyllable proper nouns that are difficult to decode)
- Words with a wide variety of very complex spelling patterns
- Many multisyllable words and proper nouns that are difficult to decode
- Many technical words that are difficult to decode
- Words that are seldom used in oral language and are difficult to decode
- Long, multisyllable words requiring attention to roots to read and understand
- Many complex plurals, contractions, and compound words
- Archaic words or words from languages other than English that do not follow conventional pronunciation patterns

Illustrations

Fiction

- Most texts with no illustrations other than cover jacket or symbolic decoration on margins or at chapter headings
- Black and white illustrations in some fiction texts

Nonfiction

- Some texts with graphics that are complex, dense, and challenging
- Many texts that have scales or legends that require understanding and interpretation
- A wide variety of complex graphics that require interpretation (photos with legends, diagrams, labels, cutaways, graphs, maps)

Book and Print Features

Print and Layout

- Varied space between lines, with some texts having dense print
- Use of words in italics, bold, or all capitals to indicate emphasis, level of importance, or signal other meaning
- Large variation among print styles, color, and font size
- Many texts with very small font
- Many sentences continuing over several lines or to the next page
- Print and illustrations integrated in most texts, with print wrapping around pictures
- More difficult layout of informational text, and some fiction texts, with denser format
- Variety in layout of nonfiction formats (question and answer, paragraphs, boxes, legends, call-outs) often occurring across a two-page spread

Punctuation

- Full range of punctuation as needed for complex sentences
- Occasional use of less common punctuation (colon, semicolon)

Tools

- Full range of readers' tools (table of contents, glossary, headings and subheadings, call-outs, pronunciation guides, index, references)

With no food or water, Ari clung to a piece of wood for five days. When he spotted an abandoned fishing raft, Ari mustered what little strength he had left and climbed on. Once on the raft, he discovered a few bottles of fresh water. Later, he spotted some coconuts drifting in the ocean, snatched them up, and, because he had no tools, cracked them open with his teeth! Miraculously, Ari was able to survive for two more weeks on nothing but coconuts and water. As each day passed, Ari began to doubt that he would survive.

He could see many ships sailing along the horizon, but none of them could see him. Finally, a ship caught sight of Ari, rescued him, and delivered him home safely. He was dehydrated but lucky to be alive. ■

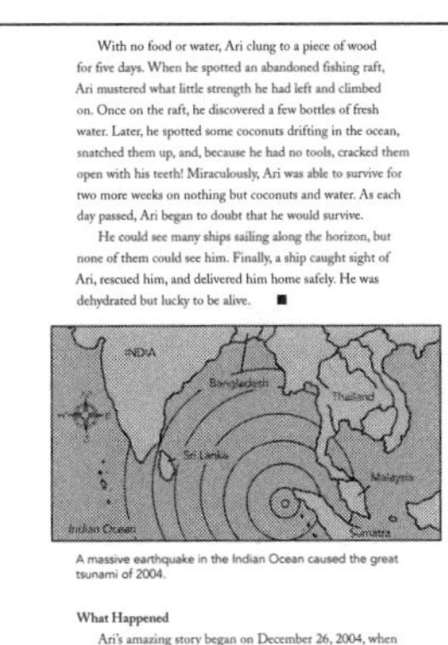

A massive earthquake in the Indian Ocean caused the great tsunami of 2004.

What Happened

Ari's amazing story began on December 26, 2004, when an earthquake off the coast of Sumatra in the Indian Ocean

2

produced a series of powerful waves called a tsunami. *Tsunami* is a Japanese word meaning "harbor wave." The 2004 tsunami pulsed across the ocean and slammed violently against the coastlines of more than a dozen countries, leaving hundreds of thousands of people dead and more than a million homeless.

What Are Tsunamis?

Tsunamis are incredibly powerful, and their waves become even more treacherous when they enter harbors or bays. They can travel at the speed of a jet airliner, cross the Pacific Ocean in a single day, and attain heights of over 100 feet.

What Causes Tsunamis?

Earthquakes that are just below the ocean floor cause the floor to rise and fall; when that happens, they have the potential to trigger tsunamis. Like ripples in a pond, tsunamis reverberate from the earthquake zone. The waves continually pile up behind each other; as they reach shallow water, their speed decreases, while their height increases. Their maximum height depends partly on the characteristics of the shoreline they are moving toward.

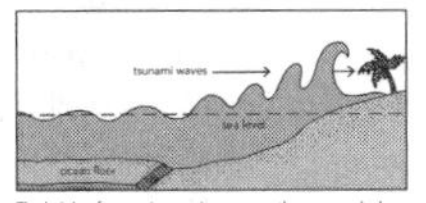

The height of tsunami waves increases as they approach shore.

3

Guided Reading

Selecting Goals Behaviors and Understandings to Notice, Teach, and Support

Thinking *within* the Text

Solving Words

- Notice new and useful words and intentionally record and remember them to expand oral and written vocabulary
- Demonstrate ability to use automatically and flexibly a wide range of word-solving strategies (for example, dividing words into syllables, using phonograms within multisyllable words, using word parts, using prefixes and affixes, and connecting words to known words)
- Using word-solving strategies, background knowledge, graphics, text context, and readers' tools (glossaries, dictionaries) to solve words, including content-specific and technical words
- Derive the meaning of words that reflect regional or historical dialects as well as words from languages other than English

Monitoring and Correcting

- Continue to monitor accuracy and understanding, self-correcting when errors detract from meaning

Searching for and Using Information

- Search for and use information in a wide range of graphics and integrate with information from print (for example, pictures, captions, diagrams, illustrations with labels, maps, charts)
- Use a full range of readers' tools to search for information (table of contents, glossary, headings and subheadings, call-outs, pronunciation guides, index, references)
- Process long sentences (twenty or more words) with embedded clauses (prepositional phrases, introductory clauses, series of nouns, verbs, or adverbs)
- Process texts with a variety of complex layouts and with some pages of dense print
- Follow complex plots, including texts with literary devices (for example, flashbacks and stories within stories)
- Form implicit questions and search for answers while reading
- Gain important information from longer texts with complex plots, multiple characters and episodes, and long stretches of descriptive language and dialogue
- Gain important information from much longer texts, most with no illustrations (fiction)
- Search for and use information from texts (both fiction and nonfiction) that have many new and unfamiliar concepts and ideas within a single chapter or section (dense concepts)

Summarizing

- Identify important ideas and information (longer texts with chapters and sometimes multiple texts) and organize them in summary form in order to remember and use them as background knowledge in reading or for discussion and writing
- Exercise selectivity in summarizing the information in a text (most important information or ideas and facts focused by the reader's purpose)
- Construct summaries that are concise and reflect the important and overarching ideas and information in texts

Maintaining Fluency

- Read dialogue with phrasing and expression that reflects understanding of characters and events
- Practice some texts in order to read them aloud with expression or dramatic performance
- Demonstrate appropriate stress on words, pausing and phrasing, intonation, and use of punctuation while reading in a way that reflects understanding

Planning for Word Work during Guided Reading

One- to three-minute demonstrations with active student engagement using a chart or easel, white board, or pencil and paper can develop fluency and flexibility in visual processing. Plan for explicit work in specific visual processing areas that need support.

Examples:

- Add a variety of endings to words (*-able, -ible, -ent, -ant*) and discuss changes in spelling and meaning
- Work flexibly with base words, making new words by changing letters and adding prefixes and suffixes
- Recognize words that have multiple meanings (a form of homograph: *bay, bay*) homographs (look the same, sound different: *contract, contract*), and homophones (sound the same, look different: *flair, flare*)
- Notice and use word roots (Greek and Latin) to take apart words (*commun-: community, communicate, communism*)
- Read and derive meaning of words that are related to each other because they have the same base or root word (*monarch, monarchs, monarchy, oligarchy, patriarch, matriarch*)
- Recognize words with frequently appearing vowel and syllable patterns (*ic(k)* in *dicker, organic; -ble* in *implausible, stable*)
- Read words with consonant clusters and long and short vowel patterns, including vowel patterns with *r,* that appear in multisyllable words

Guided Reading

Selecting Goals Behaviors and Understandings to Notice, Teach, and Support

Adjusting

- Change style and pace of reading to reflect purpose
- Adjust the reader's stance to better understand genres, such as complex fantasy, and special forms, such as satire
- Reread to solve words or think about ideas and resume good rate of reading
- Change purpose and aspects of processing to reflect understanding of genre

Thinking *beyond* the Text

Predicting

- Support predictions with evidence from the text or from knowledge of genre
- Use characteristics of genre as a source of information to make predictions before and during reading
- Change predictions as new information is gathered from a text
- Make and continually revise a wide range of predictions (what characters will do, what will happen to solve the problem) based on personal experiences, content knowledge, and knowledge of similar texts

Making Connections

- Before, during, and after reading, bring background knowledge to the understanding of a text
- Bring knowledge from personal experiences to the interpretation of characters and events, particularly content and situations related to preadolescents and adolescents
- Make connections between the text and other texts that have been read or heard (particularly texts with diverse settings) and demonstrate in writing
- Connect and compare texts within genres and across genres
- Use knowledge from one text to help in understanding diverse cultures and settings encountered in new texts
- Connect characters across texts and genres by circumstances, traits, or actions
- Specify the nature of connections (topic, content, type of story, writer)

Synthesizing

- Mentally form categories of related information and revise them as new information is acquired across the text
- Integrate existing content knowledge with new information from a text to consciously create new understandings
- Express changes in ideas or perspective across the reading (as events unfold) after reading a text
- Acquire new content and perspectives through reading both fiction and nonfiction texts about diverse cultures, times, and places
- Use situations focusing on the problems of preadolescents and adolescents to develop new perspectives on readers' own lives
- When reading chapters, connected short stories, or sequels, incorporate new knowledge to better understand characters and plots from material previously read

Guided Reading

Selecting Goals

Inferring

- In texts with multiple complex characters, infer traits, motivations, and changes through examining how the writer describes them, what they do, what they say and think, and what other characters say about them
- In fiction or biography, infer characters' or subjects' thinking processes and struggles at key decision points in their lives
- Infer the big ideas or themes of a text (some texts with mature themes and issues) and discuss how they are applicable to people's lives today
- Infer the meaning of symbols (objects, events, motifs, characters) that the writer uses to convey and enhance meaning
- Infer causes of problems or of outcomes in fiction and nonfiction texts
- Identify significant events and tell how they are related to the problem of the story or the solution

Thinking *about* the Text

Analyzing

- Begin to recognize and understand satire and its purposes and characteristics
- Notice aspects of genres (realistic and historical fiction, fantasy, myths and legends, biography, autobiography, memoir and diaries, and other nonfiction, hybrid texts)
- Discuss the selection of genre in relation to inferred writer's purpose for a range of texts
- Understand when a writer has combined underlying organizational structures (description, compare and contrast, temporal sequence, problem and solution, cause and effect)
- Notice how the author or illustrator has used illustrations and other graphics to convey meaning or create mood
- Notice and understand figurative and descriptive language and the role it plays in enhancing a text (providing examples)
- Notice and reflect on a writer's use of idiom

Guided Reading

Selecting Goals

Behaviors and Understandings to Notice, Teach, and Support

- Notice and understand a writer's use of language to convey irony or to satirize a person or event (providing examples)
- Notice how an author uses words in a connotative way (to imply something beyond the literal meaning)
- Understand and talk about the role of the setting in realistic and historical fiction as well as fantasy
- Talk about how the writer built interest and suspense across a story
- Understand the structure of complex plots in fiction and the organization of the text in nonfiction (sometimes represented by a graphic organizer or diagram)
- Notice aspects of a writer's craft (style, language, perspective, themes) after reading several texts by the same author
- Notice and discuss the meaning of symbolism when used by a writer to create texts, including complex fantasy where the writer is representing good and evil
- Notice the writer's choice of words that are not English and reflect on the reasons for these choices and how those words add to the meaning of a text
- Notice the way writers use regional dialect and discuss how it adds to the authenticity of the text or characters
- Examine character traits in a complex way, recognizing that they are multidimensional and change over time

Critiquing

- Evaluate the text in terms of readers' own experience as preadolescents
- Critique a text as an example of a genre
- Assess the author's qualifications to write an informational text
- Evaluate the author's use of characterization and plot (for example, believability or depth)
- Assess whether a text is authentic and consistent with life experience or prior knowledge, including how the text reflects the lives of preadolescents or adolescents
- Use other sources of information to check the authenticity of a text (fiction, historical fiction, nonfiction) when questions arise
- For historical fiction, evaluate the authenticity of the details of the setting and reporting of events against knowledge from other sources
- Discuss whether social issues and different cultural groups are accurately represented in a fiction or nonfiction text
- Express tastes and preferences in reading and support choices with specific descriptions of text features (plots, use of language, kinds of characters, genres)

Guided Reading

Readers at **Level W:**

At Level W, readers will process the full range of genres, and texts will be longer, requiring readers to remember information and connect ideas over many days of reading. Complex fantasy, myths, and legends offer added challenge and require readers to identify classical motifs such as "the quest." Biographies offer a range of individuals who may not be previously known to readers and may not be admirable. Readers will encounter mature themes that expand their knowledge of social issues. In addition, readers will encounter abstract special forms of literature, such as satire, and literary devices, such as irony. Themes are multidimensional and may be understood on several levels. Most reading is silent; fluency and phrasing in oral reading is well established. In addition, students are able to read aloud with expressiveness after practice (for example, readers' theater). Readers are challenged by heavy load of content-specific and technical words that require using embedded definitions, background knowledge, and readers' tools, such as glossaries. They search for and use information in an integrated way, using complex graphics and texts that present content requiring background knowledge. Many texts require knowledge of historical events and may contain language that is archaic or from regional dialects or languages other than English.

Selecting Texts **Characteristics of Texts at This Level**

Genre/Forms

GENRE

- Informational texts
- High fantasy and science fiction
- Realistic fiction
- Traditional literature, including myths and legends
- Biography, memoir, and autobiography
- Historical fiction, many with settings different from students' own cultural histories
- Mysteries
- Genre combination (hybrids)
- Satire

FORMS

- Picture books
- Plays
- Chapter books
- Chapter books with sequels
- Series books
- Short stories
- Diaries and logs
- Photo essays

Text Structure

FICTION

- Unusual text organizations (e.g., flashbacks)
- Plots with detailed episodes
- Plots with subplots
- Some complex plots with multiple story lines
- Some collections of short stories that have interrelated themes or build a single plot across the book

NONFICTION

- Presentation of multiple topics that represent subcategories of a larger topic or theme
- Variety of underlying structures often combined in complex ways (description, comparison and contrast, temporal sequence, problem and solution, cause and effect)
- Variety in nonfiction formats (question and answer, paragraphs, boxes, legends, and call-outs)

Content

- Many texts requiring knowledge of history and current world events
- Content requiring the reader to take on diverse perspectives (race, language, culture)
- Content particularly appealing to adolescents
- Critical thinking required to judge authenticity of informational texts, historical fiction, and biography
- Heavy content load in many texts, both fiction and nonfiction, requiring study

Themes and Ideas

- Many ideas and themes requiring understanding of cultural diversity
- Many texts with complex themes focusing on human problems (war, hardship, social class barriers, or racism)
- Many texts presenting mature societal issues, especially those important to adolescents (family issues, growing up, sexuality)
- Many texts presenting multiple themes that may be understood in many layers
- Wide range of challenging themes that build social awareness and reveal insights into the human condition

Language and Literary Features

- Multiple characters revealed by what they say, think, and do and what others say or think about them
- Multidimensional characters that develop over time
- Character interpretation essential to understand the theme
- Some texts with heroic or larger-than-life characters who represent the symbolic struggle of good and evil
- Long stretches of descriptive language that are important to understanding setting and characters
- Some texts with archaic language, included for authenticity
- Specific descriptions of settings that provide important information for understanding the plot
- Many texts with settings distant in time and space from students' experiences
- Some long strings of unassigned dialogue from which story action must be inferred
- Some switching from setting to setting, including time change (often unsignaled or signaled only by dialogue)
- Many complex narratives that are highly literary
- Fantasy incorporating classical motifs (such as "the quest")
- Use of symbolism to convey meaning
- Full range of literary devices (for example, flashback, stories within stories, symbolism, and figurative language)

Guided Reading

Sentence Complexity

- Longer (some with more than twenty words) complex sentence structures
- Many complex sentences including dialogue and many embedded phrases and clauses, as well as parenthetical material
- Sentences with nouns, verbs, or adjectives in series, divided by commas
- Wide range of declarative, imperative, and interrogative sentences

Vocabulary

- Many new vocabulary words that readers must derive meaning from context or use glossaries or dictionaries
- Words used figuratively or with unusual or hard-to-understand connotations
- Many technical words requiring background knowledge or use of glossary or dictionary
- Words used in regional or historical dialects
- Some words from languages other than English
- Some archaic words

Words

- Many words with three or more syllables
- All parts of speech
- Many words with affixes (prefixes and suffixes, multisyllable proper nouns that are difficult to decode)
- Words with a wide variety of very complex spelling patterns
- Many multisyllable proper nouns that are difficult to decode
- Many technical words that are difficult to decode
- Words that are seldom used in oral language and are difficult to decode
- Long, multisyllable words requiring attention to roots to read and understand
- Words that offer decoding challenges because they are archaic, come from regional dialect, or from languages other than English
- Many complex plurals, contractions, and compound words

Illustrations

Fiction

- Most texts with no illustrations other than cover jacket or symbolic decoration on margins or at chapter headings

Nonfiction

- Some texts with graphics that are complex, dense, and challenging
- Many texts that have scales or legends that require understanding and interpretation
- A wide variety of complex graphics that require interpretation (photos with legends, diagrams, labels, cutaways, graphs, maps)

Book and Print Features

Print and Layout

- Varied space between lines, with some texts having dense print
- Use of words in italics, bold, or all capitals to indicate emphasis, level of importance, or signal other meaning
- Large variation among print styles, color, and font size
- Many texts with very small font
- Print and illustrations integrated in most texts, with print wrapping around pictures
- More difficult layout of informational text, and some fiction texts, with denser format
- Variety in layout of nonfiction formats (question and answer, paragraphs, boxes, legends, call-outs) often occurring across a two-page spread
- Some text layouts in columns

Punctuation

- Full range of punctuation as needed for complex sentences
- Occasional use of less common punctuation (colon, semicolon)

Tools

- Full range of readers' tools (table of contents, glossary, headings and subheadings, call-outs, pronunciation guides, index, references)

After nearly two days of seemingly endless travel, we finally arrived at our assigned village. There we were greeted by our hosts, seventeen-year-old Daw and her older brother Aran.

Aran took Dad to the site of the school he'd be helping rebuild, while Daw showed Mom and me the temporary school. Mom would instruct the children—mostly orphans—in English. I felt absolutely useless: I couldn't teach or build. Had I traveled so far to do nothing? ■

But Daw had plans for me. "We're going to the beach, Kim," Daw said to me the next morning, and I thought, "Great—I love the beach."

"Twice a day the tide comes in and leaves what it took in December," she said, as she handed me a pair of gloves. "Our job is to clean it up." Of course. I felt like an idiot.

At the beach, Daw gave me a plastic bag and began walking along the high tide line. The last high tide had deposited its debris: chunks of metal, wood, and plastic; cups, cans, and ropes. I knew that thousands of bodies had never been recovered, and I prayed that none had washed ashore last night. It was difficult work: bending, stooping, filling the bags, and hauling them up on the beach where the tide couldn't pull them back.

In the following days, we spent the majority of our time collecting garbage. When we'd rest on the sand, gazing out to sea, I tried to imagine what it felt like to watch a looming, 33-foot wall of water crashing towards me, what it felt like to be swallowed up by the wave, and what it would be like never to see my family again.

2

When Daw talked, she admitted that she got weary from the backbreaking work. But she kept at it in honor of those who were lost. After that, so did I.

One morning I found a shoe. It was a child's shoe—tiny and worn. I collapsed and cried. I cried for the thousands who lost their lives in Thailand on that horrifying day. And I cried because I knew then how profoundly lucky I was to be able to help the survivors. Daw put her arms around me and held on.

I don't know how many bags of garbage we collected, but I do know that Daw and I talked and laughed as we worked and that the two weeks flew by. When we said goodbye, it was Daw's turn to cry. I took off my locket and fastened it around her neck. It was a symbol of survival. It testified to life going on, even after disaster strikes.

I touched my neck often as we made our way home and thought about the great-grandmother I barely knew. Even without her locket, we were linked in some way, heart to heart. So were Daw and I now.

I don't know if I accomplished anything meaningful, but I do know that I learned something about myself; maybe someday I'll be able to put a name to it. Meanwhile, I'm going to ask Dad if we can go back next year.

3

Guided Reading

Selecting Goals Behaviors and Understandings to Notice, Teach, and Support

Thinking *within* the Text

Solving Words

- Notice new and useful words and intentionally record and remember them to expand oral and written vocabulary
- Demonstrate ability to use automatically and flexibly a wide range of word-solving strategies (for example, dividing words into syllables, using phonograms within multisyllable words, using word parts, using prefixes and affixes, and connecting words to known words)
- Using word-solving strategies, background knowledge, graphics, text context, and readers' tools (glossaries, dictionaries) to solve words, including content-specific and technical words
- Begin to use word roots and origins to understand meaning of words
- Derive the meaning of words that reflect regional or historical dialects as well as words from languages other than English

Monitoring and Correcting

- Continue to monitor accuracy and understanding, self-correcting when errors detract from meaning
- Monitor understanding closely, searching for information within and outside the text when needed

Searching for and Using Information

- Search for and use information in a wide range of graphics and integrate with information from print (for example, pictures, captions, diagrams, illustrations with labels, maps, charts)
- Use a full range of readers' tools to search for information (table of contents, glossary, headings and subheadings, call-outs, pronunciation guides, index, references)
- Process long sentences (twenty or more words) with embedded clauses (prepositional phrases, introductory clauses, series of nouns, verbs, or adverbs)
- Process texts with a variety of complex layouts and with some pages of dense print and some printed in columns
- Follow complex plots, including texts with literary devices (for example, flashbacks and stories within stories)
- Gain important information from longer texts with complex plots, multiple characters and episodes, and long stretches of descriptive language and dialogue
- Gain important information from much longer texts, most with no illustrations (fiction)
- Search for and use information from texts (both fiction and nonfiction) that have many new and unfamiliar concepts and ideas within a single chapter or section (dense concepts)
- Process sentences with the syntax of archaic or regional dialects

Summarizing

- Identify important ideas and information (longer texts with chapters and sometimes multiple texts) and organize them in summary form in order to remember and use them as background knowledge in reading or for discussion and writing
- Exercise selectivity in summarizing the information in a text (most important information or ideas and facts focused by the reader's purpose)
- Construct summaries that are concise and reflect the important and overarching ideas and information in texts

Maintaining Fluency

- Read dialogue with phrasing and expression that reflects understanding of characters and events
- Demonstrate appropriate stress on words, pausing and phrasing, intonation, and use of punctuation while reading in a way that reflects understanding
- With rehearsal, read texts orally with dramatic expression that reflects interpretation of the deeper meaning of a text

Adjusting

- Change style and pace of reading to reflect purpose
- Adjust the reader's stance to better understand genres, such as complex fantasy, and special forms, such as satire
- Change style, pace, and processing to reflect understanding of genre

Guided Reading

Selecting Goals Behaviors and Understandings to Notice, Teach, and Support

Thinking *beyond* the Text

Predicting

- Support predictions with evidence from the text or from knowledge of genre
- Use characteristics of genre as a source of information to make predictions before and during reading
- Change predictions as new information is gathered from a text
- Make and continually revise a wide range of predictions (what characters will do, what will happen to solve the problem) based on personal experiences, content knowledge, and knowledge of similar texts

Making Connections

- Bring knowledge from personal experiences to the interpretation of characters and events, particularly content and situations related to adolescents
- Make connections between the text and other texts that have been read or heard (particularly texts with diverse settings) and demonstrate in writing
- Connect characters within and across texts and genres by circumstances, traits, or actions
- Specify the nature of connections (topic, content, type of story, writer)
- Make connections between the social and moral issues of today and those presented in realistic and historical fiction, in biography, and in the imaginary worlds of high fantasy
- Make connections between satirical literature and the social issues they represent

Synthesizing

- Mentally form categories of related information and revise them as new information is acquired across the text
- Integrate existing content knowledge with new information from a text to consciously create new understandings
- Express changes in ideas or perspective across the reading (as events unfold) after reading a text
- Acquire new content and perspectives through reading both fiction and nonfiction texts about diverse cultures, times, and places
- Use situations focusing on the problems of adolescents to develop new perspectives on readers' own lives
- When reading chapters, connected short stories, or sequels, incorporate new knowledge to better understand characters and plots from material previously read

Inferring

- In texts with multiple complex characters, infer traits, motivations, and changes through examining how the writer describes them, what they do, what they say and think, and what other characters say about them
- Infer characters' or subjects' thinking processes and struggles at key decision points in their lives in fiction or biography
- Infer the big ideas or themes of a text (some texts with mature themes and issues) and discuss how they are applicable to people's lives today
- Infer the meaning of symbols (objects, events, motifs, characters) that the writer uses to convey and enhance meaning
- Infer causes of problems or of outcomes in fiction and nonfiction texts
- Identify significant events and tell how they are related to the problem of the story or the solution

Guided Reading

Selecting Goals

Thinking *about* the Text

Analyzing

- Begin to recognize and understand satire and its purposes and characteristics
- Notice and understand aspects of genres (realistic and historical fiction, fantasy, myths and legends, biography, autobiography, memoir and diaries, and other nonfiction, hybrid texts)
- Identify the selection of genre in relation to inferred writer's purpose for a range of texts
- Understand when a writer has combined underlying organizational structures (description, compare and contrast, temporal sequence, problem and solution, cause and effect) and be able to represent in diagrams or graphic organizers
- Notice how the author or illustrator has used illustrations and other graphics to convey meaning or create mood
- Recognize the use of figurative or descriptive language (or special types of language such as irony) and talk about how it adds to the quality (enjoyment and understanding) of a text
- Notice how an author uses words in a connotative way (to imply something beyond the literal meaning)
- Understand the role of the setting in realistic and historical fiction as well as fantasy
- Represent the structure of complex plots in fiction and the organization of the text in nonfiction in diagrams or graphic organizers
- Analyze works of fantasy to notice classical motifs such as "the quest," "the hero," and symbolism representing good and evil
- Notice aspects of a writer's craft (style, language, perspective, themes) after reading several texts by the same author
- Notice and discuss the meaning of symbolism when used by a writer to create texts, including complex fantasy where the writer is representing good and evil
- Notice the writer's choice of words that are not English and reflect on the reasons for these choices and how those words add to the meaning of a text
- Notice the way writers use regional dialect and discuss how it adds to the authenticity of the text or characters
- Examine character traits in a complex way, recognizing that they are multidimensional and change over time

Guided Reading

Selecting Goals Behaviors and Understandings to Notice, Teach, and Support

Critiquing

- Evaluate the text in terms of readers' own experience as adolescents
- Critique a text as an example of a genre
- Assess the author's qualifications to write an informational text
- Evaluate the author's use of characterization and plot (for example, believability or depth)
- Assess whether a text is authentic and consistent with life experience or prior knowledge, including how the text reflects the lives of preadolescents or adolescents
- Use other sources of information to check the authenticity of a text (fiction, historical fiction, nonfiction) when questions arise
- Evaluate the authenticity of the details of the setting and reporting of events against knowledge from other sources for historical fiction
- Discuss whether social issues and different cultural groups are accurately represented in a fiction or nonfiction text
- Express tastes and preferences in reading and support choices with specific descriptions of text features (plots, use of language, kinds of characters, genres)
- Become critical of the subjects of biography (decisions, motivations, accomplishments)
- Critique the biographers presentation of a subject, noticing bias

Guided Reading

Readers at **Level X:**

At Levels X, Y, and Z, readers are able to process and understand a wide range of texts, including all genres. Although many texts are long and have complex sentences and paragraphs as well as many multisyllable words, they vary greatly because readers are expected to understand and respond to mature themes such as sexuality, abuse, poverty, and war. Complex fantasy, myths, and legends offer added challenge and require readers to identify classical motifs such as "the quest" and to identify moral issues. Biographies offer a range of individuals who may not be previously known to readers and may not be admirable, requiring critical thinking on the part of readers. In addition, readers will encounter abstract special forms of literature, such as satire, and literary language to convey irony. Themes and characters are multidimensional, may be understood on several levels, and are developed in complex ways. Most reading is silent; fluency and phrasing in oral reading is well established. Readers are challenged by a heavy load of content-specific and technical words that require using embedded definitions, background knowledge, and readers' tools, such as glossaries. Texts include archaic language or regional dialect. Readers search for and use information in an integrated way, using complex graphics and texts that present content requiring background knowledge. They have developed knowledge of content, including scientific information and historical events and apply prior understandings in a critical way when reading fiction and nonfiction texts.

Selecting Texts — Characteristics of Texts at This Level

Genre/Forms

Genre

- Informational texts
- High fantasy and science fiction
- Realistic fiction
- Traditional literature, including myths and legends
- Biography, memoir, and autobiography
- Historical fiction, many with settings different from students' own cultural histories
- Mysteries
- Genre combination (hybrids)
- Satire

Forms

- Picture books
- Plays
- Chapter books
- Chapter books with sequels
- Series books
- Short stories
- Diaries and logs
- Photo essays

Text Structure

Fiction

- Unusual text organizations (e.g., flashbacks)
- Plots with detailed episodes
- Plots with subplots
- Some complex plots with multiple story lines
- Some collections of short stories that have interrelated themes or build a single plot across the book

Nonfiction

- Presentation of multiple topics that represent subtopic of a larger topic or theme
- Underlying structures (description, comparison and contrast, temporal sequence, problem and solution, cause and effect)
- Variety of underlying structures often combined in complex ways (description, comparison and contrast, temporal sequence, problem and solution, cause and effect)
- Texts with multiple topics and categories within them
- Variety in organization and topic
- Variety in nonfiction formats (question and answer, paragraphs, boxes, legends, and call-outs)

Content

- Many texts requiring knowledge of history or current world events
- Content requiring the reader to take on diverse perspectives (race, language, culture)
- Content particularly appealing to adolescents
- Critical thinking required to judge authenticity of informational texts, historical fiction, and biography
- Heavy content load in many texts, both fiction and nonfiction, requiring study

Themes and Ideas

- Many ideas and themes requiring understanding of cultural diversity
- Many texts with complex themes focusing on human problems (war, hardship, social class barriers, or racism)
- Many texts presenting mature societal issues, especially those important to adolescents
- Many texts presenting multiple themes that may be understood in many layers
- Wide range of challenging themes that build social awareness and reveal insights into the human condition

Language and Literary Features

- Multiple characters revealed by what they say, think, and do and what others say or think about them
- Multidimensional characters that develop over time
- Character interpretation necessary for comprehending theme
- Some texts with heroic or larger-than-life characters who represent the symbolic struggle of good and evil
- Long stretches of descriptive language that are important to understanding setting and characters
- Many texts with archaic language to create authenticity
- Specific descriptions of settings that provide important information for understanding the plot
- Many texts with settings distant in time and space from students' experiences
- Some long strings of unassigned dialogue from which story action must be inferred
- Some switching from setting to setting, including time change (often unsignaled or signaled only by dialogue)
- Many complex narratives that are highly literary
- Fantasy incorporating classical motifs (such as "the quest")
- Full range of literary devices (for example, flashback, stories within stories, symbolism, and figurative language)

Guided Reading

Sentence Complexity

- Some very long sentences (some with more than thirty words)
- Sentences with parenthetical material
- Many complex sentences including dialogue, many embedded phrases and clauses, and parenthetical material
- Sentences with nouns, verbs, or adjectives in series, divided by commas
- Wide range of declarative, imperative, and interrogative sentences

Vocabulary

- Many new vocabulary words that readers must derive meaning from context or use glossaries or dictionaries
- Words used figuratively or with unusual or hard-to-understand connotations
- Many technical words requiring background knowledge or use of glossary or dictionary
- Words used in regional or historical dialects
- Some words from languages other than English
- Many archaic words

Words

- All parts of speech
- Many words with affixes (prefixes and suffixes, multisyllable proper nouns that are difficult to decode)
- Many multisyllable proper nouns that are difficult to decode
- Many technical words that are difficult to decode
- Words that are seldom used in oral language and are difficult to decode
- Long, multisyllable words requiring attention to roots to read and understand
- Words that offer decoding challenges because they are archaic, come from regional dialect, or from languages other than English
- Many complex plurals, contractions, and compound words

Illustrations

Fiction

- Most texts with no illustrations other than cover jacket or symbolic decoration on margins or at chapter headings

Nonfiction

- A wide variety of complex graphics that require interpretation (photos with legends, diagrams, labels, cutaways, graphs, maps)
- Some texts with graphics that are dense and challenging
- Many texts with graphics that are complex, dense, and challenging
- Many texts that have scales or legends that require understanding and interpretation

Book and Print Features

Print and Layout

- Varied space between lines, with some texts having dense print
- Use of words in italics, bold, or all capitals to indicate emphasis, level of importance, or signal other meaning
- Variety in print and background color
- Large variation among print styles and font size (related to genre)
- Many texts with very small font
- Many sentences continuing over several lines or to the next page
- Print and illustrations integrated in most texts, with print wrapping around pictures
- More difficult layout of informational text, and some fiction texts, with denser format
- Variety in layout of nonfiction formats (question and answer, paragraphs, boxes, legends, call-outs) often occurring across a two-page spread
- Some text layouts in columns

Punctuation

- Full range of punctuation as needed for complex sentences
- Occasional use of less common punctuation (colon, semicolon)

Tools

- Full range of readers' tools (table of contents, glossary, headings and subheadings, call-outs, pronunciation guides, index, references)

Guided Reading

Selecting Goals **Behaviors and Understandings to Notice, Teach, and Support**

Thinking *within* the Text

Solving Words

- Notice new and useful words and intentionally record and remember them to expand oral and written vocabulary
- Demonstrate ability to use automatically and flexibly a wide range of word-solving strategies (for example, dividing words into syllables, using phonograms within multisyllable words, using word parts, using prefixes and affixes, and connecting words to known words)
- Using word-solving strategies, background knowledge, graphics, text context, and readers' tools (glossaries, dictionaries) to solve words, including content-specific and technical words
- Use word roots and origins to understand their meaning
- Derive the meaning of words that reflect regional or historical dialects as well as words from languages other than English

Monitoring and Correcting

- Continue to monitor accuracy and understanding, self-correcting when errors detract from meaning
- Monitor understanding closely, searching for information within and outside the text when needed

Searching for and Using Information

- Search for and use information in a wide range of graphics and integrate with information from print (for example, pictures, captions, diagrams, illustrations with labels, maps, charts)
- Use a full range of readers' tools to search for information (table of contents, glossary, headings and subheadings, call-outs, pronunciation guides, index, references)
- Process long sentences (thirty or more words) with embedded clauses (prepositional phrases, introductory clauses, series of nouns, verbs, or adverbs)
- Process texts with a variety of complex layouts and with some pages of dense print and some printed in columns
- Follow complex plots, including texts with literary devices (for example, flashbacks and stories within stories)
- Gain important information from much longer texts, most with no illustrations (fiction)
- Search for and use information from texts (both fiction and nonfiction) that have many new and unfamiliar concepts and ideas within a single chapter or section (dense concepts)
- Gain important information from texts with complex plots (often with subplots), multiple characters and episodes, and long stretches of descriptive language and dialogue
- Process sentences with the syntax of archaic or regional dialects

Summarizing

- Identify important ideas and information (longer texts with chapters and sometimes multiple texts) and organize them in summary form in order to remember and use them as background knowledge in reading or for discussion and writing
- Exercise selectivity in summarizing the information in a text (most important information or ideas and facts focused by the reader's purpose)
- Construct summaries that are concise and reflect the important and overarching ideas and information in texts

Maintaining Fluency

- Demonstrate appropriate stress on words, pausing and phrasing, intonation, and use of punctuation while reading in a way that reflects understanding
- Demonstrate all aspects of phrased, fluent, and expressive reading
- After rehearsal, present expressive oral reading that reflects interpretation of the theme, characters, or message of a text

Guided Reading

Selecting Goals Behaviors and Understandings to Notice, Teach, and Support

Adjusting

- Change style and pace of reading to reflect purpose
- Adjust the reader's stance to better understand genres, such as complex fantasy, and special forms, such as satire

Thinking *beyond* the Text

Predicting

- Support predictions with evidence from the text or from knowledge of genre
- Use characteristics of genre as a source of information to make predictions before and during reading
- Make and continually revise a wide range of predictions (what characters will do, what will happen to solve the problem) based on personal experiences, content knowledge, and knowledge of similar texts

Making Connections

- Bring knowledge from personal experiences to the interpretation of characters and events, particularly content and situations related to adolescents
- Make connections between the text and other texts that have been read or heard (particularly texts with diverse settings) and demonstrate in writing
- Connect characters within and across texts and genres by circumstances, traits, or actions
- Specify the nature of connections (topic, content, type of story, writer)
- Make connections between the social and moral issues of today and those presented in realistic and historical fiction, in biography, and in the imaginary worlds of high fantasy
- Make connections between satirical literature and the social issues they represent

Synthesizing

- Mentally form categories of related information and revise them as new information is acquired across the text
- Integrate existing content knowledge with new information from a text to consciously create new understandings
- Express changes in ideas or perspective across the reading (as events unfold) after reading a text
- Acquire new content and perspectives through reading both fiction and nonfiction texts about diverse cultures, times, and places
- Use situations focusing on the problems of adolescents to develop new perspectives on readers' own lives
- When reading chapters, connected short stories, or sequels, incorporate new knowledge to better understand characters and plots from material previously read

E-Mail

When computer users send an e-mail they are initiating a series of electronic pulses. For these digital signals to be transmitted and received, they must first be broken down into very small packets by the sender's Internet Service Provider (ISP). Each packet of data contains information about its origin and destination. A set of instructions called the Transmission Control Protocol (TCP) performs the function of creating data packets. ■

The Internet Protocol (IP) makes sure the packets are sent to the right place via the router, a network device that determines the next point to which a data packet should be forwarded. When the packets reach their destination, the TCP reassembles them into the original message.

History of the Internet

You may think that the Internet is a recent phenomenon, but according to some historians, it was developed by the U.S. Department of Defense in the 1960s as a civil defense tool during the Cold War. The prospect of a nuclear war created a perceived need for an efficient communications network that would be less vulnerable than existing systems. A network like the Internet might survive the devastation of a nuclear holocaust or similar disaster.

The Internet Today

Today's Internet consists of several different kinds of information systems, each of which was developed independently. Probably the most widely used and most influential of these multiple systems are e-mail and the World Wide Web.

2

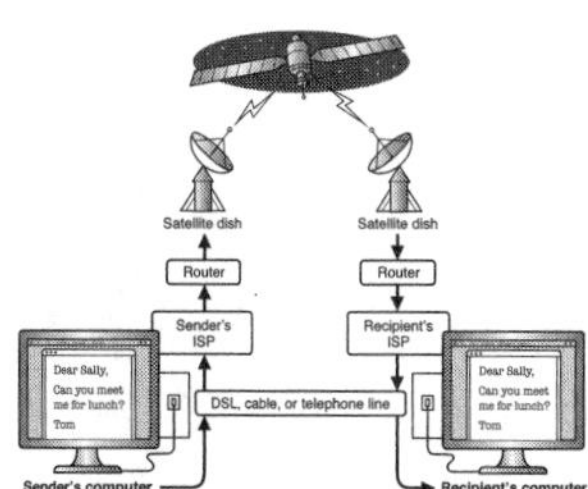

Billions of e-mail messages are exchanged every day.

For several decades, the Internet was viewed as unappealing in appearance and impractical for use by the general public; then, however, computer scientists began integrating leading technological developments like URLs (Uniform Resource Locators) and hypertext. By 1990, it was possible for the Internet to display not only words but also a whole range of multimedia. By the mid-nineties, inventions like Web browsers and search engines had turned the Web into an easy-to-use and exciting feature of the whole Internet experience. A visually uninspiring tool before the World Wide Web came into use, the Internet came alive with color, graphics, live pictures, as well as audio and video streaming. Users have "virtually" at their fingertips, virtually every kind of information they might want to seek. Public consumption has exploded, and this dynamic tool continues to evolve.

3

Guided Reading

Selecting Goals

Inferring

- In texts with multiple complex characters, infer traits, motivations, and changes through examining how the writer describes them, what they do, what they say and think, and what other characters say about them
- In fiction or biography, infer characters' or subjects' thinking processes and struggles at key decision points in their lives
- Infer the big ideas or themes of a text (some texts with mature themes and issues) and discuss how they are applicable to people's lives today
- Infer the meaning of symbols (objects, events, motifs, characters) that the writer uses to convey and enhance meaning
- Infer causes of problems or of outcomes in fiction and nonfiction texts
- Identify significant events and tell how they are related to the problem of the story or the solution

Thinking *about* the Text

Analyzing

- Recognize and understand satire and its purposes and characteristics
- Notice aspects of genres (realistic and historical fiction, fantasy, myths and legends, biography, autobiography, memoir and diaries, and other nonfiction, hybrid texts)
- Analyze the selection of genre in relation to inferred writer's purpose for a range of texts
- Understand when a writer has combined underlying organizational structures (description, compare and contrast, temporal sequence, problem and solution, cause and effect)
- Analyze how language, illustrations, and layout work together as a unified whole to set mood and convey meaning
- Recognize the use of figurative or descriptive language (or special types of language such as irony) and talk about how it adds to the quality of a text
- Notice how an author uses words in a connotative way (to imply something beyond the literal meaning)
- Understand and talk about the role of the setting in realistic and historical fiction as well as fantasy
- Understand the structure of complex plots in fiction and the organization of the text in nonfiction and represent it in diagrams or graphic organizers
- Analyze works of fantasy to notice classical motifs such as "the quest," "the hero," and symbolism representing good and evil
- Notice aspects of a writer's craft (style, language, perspective, themes) after reading several texts by him/her
- Discuss alternative interpretations of symbolism

Guided Reading

Selecting Goals

Behaviors and Understandings to Notice, Teach, and Support

- Notice and discuss the meaning of symbolism when used by a writer to create texts, including complex fantasy where the writer is representing good and evil
- Notice the writer's choice of words that are not English and reflect on the reasons for these choices and how those words add to the meaning of a text
- Notice the way writers use regional dialect and how it adds to the authenticity of the text or characters
- Analyze texts to determine the writer's point of view or bias, identifying specific language that reveals bias or qualifies as propaganda
- Notice and compare the traits and development of characters within and across genres (well-developed characters vs. flat characters; heroic, multidimensional, etc.)

Critiquing

- Evaluate the text in terms of readers' own experience as adolescents
- Critique a text as an example of a genre
- Assess the author's qualifications to write an informational text
- Evaluate the author's use of characterization and plot (for example, believability or depth)
- Assess whether a text is authentic and consistent with life experience or prior knowledge, including how the text reflects the lives of adolescents
- Use other sources of information to check the authenticity of a text (fiction, historical fiction, nonfiction) when questions arise
- For historical fiction, evaluate the authenticity of the details of the setting and reporting of events against knowledge from other sources
- Discuss whether social issues and different cultural groups are accurately represented in a fiction or nonfiction text
- Express tastes and preferences in reading and support choices with specific descriptions of text features (plots, use of language, kinds of characters, genres)
- Become critical of the subjects of biography (decisions, motivations, accomplishments)
- Critique the biographer's presentation of a subject, noticing bias
- Critique texts in terms of the writer's bias or the use of exaggeration and subtle misinformation (as in propaganda)

Guided Reading

Readers at **Level Y:**

At Levels X, Y, and Z, readers are able to process and understand a wide range of texts, including all genres. Although many texts are long and have complex sentences and paragraphs as well as many multisyllable words, they vary greatly because readers are expected to understand and respond to mature themes such as sexuality, abuse, poverty, and war. Complex fantasy, myths, and legends offer added challenge and require readers to identify classical motifs such as "the quest" and to identify moral issues. Biographies offer a range of individuals who may not be previously known to readers and may not be admirable, requiring critical thinking on the part of readers. In addition, readers will encounter abstract special forms of literature, such as satire, and literary language to convey irony. Themes and characters are multidimensional, may be understood on several levels, and are developed in complex ways. Most reading is silent; fluency and phrasing in oral reading is well established. Readers are challenged by a heavy load of content-specific and technical words that require using embedded definitions, background knowledge, and readers' tools, such as glossaries. Texts include archaic language or regional dialect. Readers search for and use information in an integrated way, using complex graphics and texts that present content requiring background knowledge. They have developed knowledge of content, including scientific information and historical events and apply prior understandings in a critical way when reading fiction and nonfiction texts.

Selecting Texts **Characteristics of Texts at This Level**

Genre/Forms

Genre

- Informational texts
- High fantasy and science fiction
- Realistic fiction
- Traditional literature, including myths and legends
- Biography, memoir, and autobiography
- Historical fiction, many with settings different from students' own cultural histories
- Mysteries
- Genre combination (hybrids)
- Satire

Forms

- Picture books
- Plays
- Chapter books
- Chapter books with sequels
- Series books
- Short stories
- Diaries and logs
- Photo essays

Text Structure

Fiction

- Unusual text organizations (e.g., flashback, flashforward, time lapses)
- Texts with unusual structures for presenting information (combination of different genres)
- Many texts with the complex structure of adult-level reading
- Complex plots, many with multiple story lines and subplots
- Some collections of short stories that have interrelated themes or build a single plot across the book

Nonfiction

- Presentation of multiple topics that represent subtopic of a larger topic or theme
- Variety of underlying structures often combined in complex ways (description, comparison and contrast, temporal sequence, problem and solution, cause and effect)
- Variety in nonfiction formats (question and answer, paragraphs, boxes, legends, and call-outs)

Content

- Many texts requiring knowledge of history or current world events
- Content requiring the reader to take on diverse perspectives (race, language, culture)
- Content particularly appealing to adolescents
- Critical thinking required to judge authenticity of informational texts, historical fiction, and biography
- Heavy content load in many texts, both fiction and nonfiction, requiring study

Themes and Ideas

- Many ideas and themes requiring understanding of cultural diversity
- Many texts with complex themes focusing on human problems (war, hardship, social class barriers, or racism)
- Many texts presenting mature societal issues, especially those important to adolescents
- Many texts presenting multiple themes that may be understood in many layers
- Wide range of challenging themes that build social awareness and reveal insights into the human condition

Language and Literary Features

- Multiple characters revealed by what they say, think, and do and what others say or think about them
- Character interpretation necessary for comprehending theme
- Some texts with heroic or larger-than-life characters who represent the symbolic struggle of good and evil
- Long stretches of descriptive language that are important to understanding setting and characters
- Many texts with archaic language to create authenticity
- Specific descriptions of settings that provide important information for understanding the plot
- Many texts with settings distant in time and space from students' experiences
- Some long strings of unassigned dialogue from which story action must be inferred
- Some switching through dialogue from setting to setting, including time change (often unsignaled)
- Fantasy incorporating classical motifs (such as "the quest")
- Full range of literary devices (for example, flashback, stories within stories, symbolism, and figurative language)

Guided Reading

Sentence Complexity

- Some very long sentences (some with more than thirty words)
- Many complex sentences including dialogue and many embedded phrases and clauses
- Sentences with nouns, verbs, or adjectives in series, divided by commas
- Complex sentences with compound sentences joined by semicolons or colons
- Wide range of declarative, imperative, and interrogative sentences

Vocabulary

- Many new vocabulary words that readers must derive meaning from context or use glossaries or dictionaries
- Words used figuratively or with unusual or hard-to-understand connotations
- Many technical words requiring background knowledge or use of glossary or dictionary
- Words used in regional or historical dialects
- Some words from languages other than English
- Many archaic words

Words

- All parts of speech
- Many words with affixes (prefixes and suffixes, multisyllable proper nouns that are difficult to decode)
- Many multisyllable proper nouns that are difficult to decode
- Many technical words that are difficult to decode
- Words that are seldom used in oral language and are difficult to decode
- Long, multisyllable words requiring attention to roots to read and understand
- Words that offer decoding challenges because they are archaic, come from regional dialect, or from languages other than English
- Many complex plurals, contractions, and compound words

Illustrations

Fiction

- Most texts with no illustrations other than cover jacket or symbolic decoration on margins or at chapter headings

Nonfiction

- A wide variety of complex graphics that require interpretation (photos with legends, diagrams, labels, cutaways, graphs, maps)
- Many texts with graphics that are complex, dense, and challenging
- Many texts that have scales or legends that require understanding and interpretation

Book and Print Features

Print and Layout

- Varied space between lines, with some texts having dense print
- Use of words in italics, bold, or all capitals to indicate emphasis, level of importance, or signal other meaning
- Variety in print and background color
- Large variation among print styles and font size (related to genre)
- Many texts with very small font
- Many sentences continuing over several lines or to the next page
- Print and illustrations integrated in most texts, with print wrapping around pictures
- More difficult layout of informational text, and some fiction texts, with denser format
- Variety in layout of nonfiction formats (question and answer, paragraphs, boxes, legends, call-outs) often occurring across a two-page spread
- Some text layouts in columns

Punctuation

- Full range of punctuation as needed for complex sentences
- Occasional use of less common punctuation (colon, semicolon)

Tools

- Full range of readers' tools (table of contents, glossary, headings and subheadings, call-outs, pronunciation guides, index, references)

"Don't worry about tomorrow," he'd say. "Like my *abuelo* told me, Luis, 'just do the best that you can, and then let it go. *Qué será, será*—what will be, will be.'" And then we'd go for a long hike in sweltering Penitente Canyon or run punishing laps on the track.

One minute he was here, alive and breathing. The next he was gone. Gerald Delgado, exceptional student, brilliant athlete, an icon in that little town of Monte and my best buddy since third grade, was dead.

How could this happen? The black cloud engulfed me. I quit the soccer team. I just couldn't stand to be on the field without my *hermano*. My days revolved around after-school visits to the cemetery with Carlos, Patricia, and Shawanna. We, the walking wounded, reminisced about Gerald—things he said, things we had done with him, and things we remembered about him. Eventually, though, Shawanna said she wouldn't be able to come to the cemetery any more for our extended wake.

"I landed the lead in the school play," she said, "and I have rehearsal every day."

Then Carlos said softly, "Yeah, and I'm going to look for an after-school job."

When I looked over at Patricia, she just shrugged. Light dawned, and I realized that my friends had been showing up for my sake, not for Gerald at all; they'd abandoned his memory, and now they were reluctantly abandoning me, too. Apparently, I'd used up all the time I'd been allotted for grieving. Some part of my brain understood, but my heart screamed that they were betraying me, and Gerald's memory, by moving on.

2

When I got home from the cemetery that afternoon, exhausted and feeling like broken shards of glass, I opened my e-mail and searched for old messages from Gerald. I was looking for a Sign from Beyond the Grave, I guess. There were five or six messages from him, mostly appallingly juvenile jokes, nothing the least bit comforting. Then an unexpected e-mail arrived from Celine, who hadn't been around much since the accident. She said she wasn't sleeping, wasn't eating much, and was contemplating dropping out of school. She seemed to be convinced that what happened to Gerald was her fault.

I reread the message, thinking, that is so wrong-headed! What happened was not Celine's responsibility. Gerald would be the first to tell her that she needed to let go of useless self-blame. Then I heard myself and laughed, a shaky laugh, maybe, but the first since the accident. I'd received my sign after all.

So here I am six months later. Celine and I talk a lot. I'm playing soccer again, and I still go for runs in Penitente Canyon. And when the sky gets dark and it looks like rain, I hear a voice whispering in my ear, "Hey buddy, *qué será, será*, stop worrying. Come on, Luis, it'll all work out." I smile and pick up the pace.

3

Guided Reading

Selecting Goals **Behaviors and Understandings to Notice, Teach, and Support**

Thinking *within* the Text

Solving Words

- Notice new and useful words and intentionally record and remember them to expand oral and written vocabulary
- Demonstrate ability to use automatically and flexibly a wide range of word-solving strategies (for example, dividing words into syllables, using phonograms within multisyllable words, using word parts, using prefixes and affixes, and connecting words to known words).
- Using word-solving strategies, background knowledge, graphics, text context, and readers' tools (glossaries, dictionaries) to solve words, including content-specific and technical words
- Begin to use word roots and origins to understand their meaning
- Derive the meaning of words that reflect regional or historical dialects as well as words from languages other than English

Monitoring and Correcting

- Continue to monitor accuracy and understanding, self-correcting when errors detract from meaning
- Monitor understanding closely, searching for information within and outside the text when needed

Searching for and Using Information

- Search for and use information in a wide range of graphics and integrate with information from print (for example, pictures, captions, diagrams, illustrations with labels, maps, charts)
- Use a full range of readers' tools to search for information (table of contents, glossary, headings and subheadings, call-outs, pronunciation guides, index, references)
- Process long sentences (thirty or more words) with embedded clauses (prepositional phrases, introductory clauses, series of nouns, verbs, or adverbs)
- Process texts with a variety of complex layouts and with some pages of dense print and some printed in columns
- Follow complex plots, including texts with literary devices (for example, flashbacks and stories within stories)
- Gain important information from much longer texts, most with no illustrations (fiction)
- Search for and use information from texts (both fiction and nonfiction) that have many new and unfamiliar concepts and ideas within a single chapter or section (dense concepts)
- Gain important information from texts with complex plots (often with subplots), multiple characters and episodes, and long stretches of descriptive language and dialogue
- Process sentences with the syntax of archaic or regional dialects

Summarizing

- Identify important ideas and information (longer texts with chapters and sometimes multiple texts) and organize them in summary form in order to remember and use them as background knowledge in reading or for discussion and writing
- Exercise selectivity in summarizing the information in a text (most important information or ideas and facts focused by the reader's purpose)
- Construct summaries that are concise and reflect the important and overarching ideas and information in texts

Maintaining Fluency

- Demonstrate phrased, fluent oral reading
- Demonstrate appropriate stress on words, pausing and phrasing, intonation, and use of punctuation while reading in a way that reflects understanding
- After rehearsal, perform oral reading in an expressive way that reflects interpretation of the text

Guided Reading

Selecting Goals Behaviors and Understandings to Notice, Teach, and Support

Adjusting
- Change style and pace of reading to reflect purpose
- Adjust the reader's stance to better understand genres, such as complex fantasy, and special forms, such as satire

Thinking *beyond* the Text

Predicting
- Support predictions with evidence from the text or from knowledge of genre
- Use characteristics of genre as a source of information to make predictions before and during reading
- Make and continually revise a wide range of predictions (what characters will do, what will happen to solve the problem) based on personal experiences, content knowledge, and knowledge of similar texts

Making Connections
- Bring knowledge from personal experiences to the interpretation of characters and events, particularly content and situations related to adolescents
- Make connections between the text and other texts that have been read or heard (particularly texts with diverse settings) and demonstrate in writing
- Connect characters within and across texts and genres by circumstances, traits, or actions
- Specify the nature of connections (topic, content, type of story, writer)
- Make connections between the social and moral issues of today and those presented in realistic and historical fiction, in biography, and in the imaginary worlds of high fantasy
- Make connections between satirical literature and the social issues they represent

Synthesizing
- Mentally form categories of related information and revise them as new information is acquired across the text
- Integrate existing content knowledge with new information from a text to consciously create new understandings
- Express changes in ideas or perspective across the reading (as events unfold) after reading a text
- Acquire new content and perspectives through reading both fiction and nonfiction texts about diverse cultures, times, and places
- Use situations focusing on the problems of adolescents to develop new perspectives on readers' own lives
- When reading chapters, connected short stories, or sequels, incorporate new knowledge to better understand characters and plots from material previously read

Inferring
- Infer traits, motivations, and changes through examining how the writer describes them, what they do, what they say and think, and what other characters say about them in texts with multiple complex characters
- Infer characters' or subjects' thinking processes and struggles at key decision points in their lives in fiction or biography
- Infer the big ideas or themes of a text (some texts with mature themes and issues) and discuss how they are applicable to people's lives today
- Infer the meaning of symbols (objects, events, motifs, characters) that the writer uses to convey and enhance meaning
- Infer causes of problems or of outcomes in fiction and nonfiction texts
- Identify significant events and tell how they are related to the problem of the story or the solution

Guided Reading

Selecting Goals

Thinking *about* the Text

Analyzing

- Recognize and understand satire and its purposes and characteristics
- Recognize and interpret a writer's use of language to convey irony
- Notice aspects of genres (realistic and historical fiction, fantasy, myths and legends, biography, autobiography, memoir and diaries, and other nonfiction, hybrid texts)
- Analyze the selection of genre in relation to inferred writer's purpose for a range of texts
- Understand when a writer has combined underlying organizational structures (description, compare and contrast, temporal sequence, problem and solution, cause and effect)
- Recognize the use of figurative or descriptive language and talk about how it adds to the quality of a text
- Notice how an author uses words in a connotative way (to imply something beyond the literal meaning)
- Understand the role of the setting in realistic and historical fiction as well as fantasy
- Understand the structure of complex plots in fiction and the organization of the text in nonfiction and represent in a diagram or graphic organizer
- Analyze works of fantasy to notice classical motifs such as "the quest," "the hero," and symbolism representing good and evil
- Notice aspects of a writer's craft (style, language, perspective, themes) after reading several texts by the same author
- Engage in critical thinking across a writer's body of work or across works on the same content and discuss findings or produce a literary essay
- Understand the meaning of symbolism when used by a writer to create texts, including complex fantasy where the writer is representing good and evil
- Notice the writer's choice of words that are not English and reflect on the reasons for these choices and how those words add to the meaning of a text
- Notice the way writers use regional dialect and how it adds to the authenticity of the text or characters
- Analyze texts to determine the writer's point of view or bias, identifying specific language that reveals bias or qualifies as propaganda
- Notice and compare the traits and development of characters within and across genres (well-developed characters vs. flat characters; heroic, multidimensional, etc.)
- Analyze how language, illustrations, and layout work together as a unified whole to set mood and convey meaning

Guided Reading

Selecting Goals Behaviors and Understandings to Notice, Teach, and Support

Critiquing

- Evaluate the text in terms of readers' own experience as adolescents
- Critique a text as an example of a genre
- Assess the author's qualifications to write an informational text
- Evaluate the author's use of characterization and plot (for example, believability or depth)
- Assess whether a text is authentic and consistent with life experience or prior knowledge, including how the text reflects the lives of preadolescents or adolescents
- Use other sources of information to check the authenticity of a text (fiction, historical fiction, nonfiction) when questions arise
- Evaluate the authenticity of the details of the setting and reporting of events against knowledge from other sources for historical fiction
- Assess whether a text is authentic and consistent with life experience or prior knowledge, including how the text reflects the lives of adolescents
- Evaluate whether social issues and different cultural groups are accurately represented in a fiction or nonfiction text
- Express tastes and preferences in reading and support choices with specific descriptions of text features (plots, use of language, kinds of characters, genres)
- Become critical of the subjects of biography (decisions, motivations, accomplishments)
- Critique the biographer's presentation of a subject, noticing bias
- Critique texts in terms of the writer's bias or the use of exaggeration and subtle misinformation (as in propaganda)

Guided Reading

Readers at **Level Z:**

At Levels X, Y, and Z, readers are able to process and understand a wide range of texts, including all genres. Although many texts are long and have complex sentences and paragraphs as well as many multisyllable words, they vary greatly because readers are expected to understand and respond to mature themes such as sexuality, abuse, poverty, and war. Complex fantasy, myths, and legends offer added challenge and require readers to identify classical motifs such as "the quest" and to identify moral issues. Biographies offer a range of individuals who may not be previously known to readers and may not be admirable, requiring critical thinking on the part of readers. In addition, readers will encounter abstract special forms of literature, such as satire, and literary language to convey irony. Themes and characters are multidimensional, may be understood on several levels, and are developed in complex ways. Most reading is silent; fluency and phrasing in oral reading is well established. Readers are challenged by a heavy load of content-specific and technical words that require using embedded definitions, background knowledge, and readers' tools, such as glossaries. Texts include archaic language or regional dialect. Readers search for and use information in an integrated way, using complex graphics and texts that present content requiring background knowledge. They have developed knowledge of content, including scientific information and historical events and apply prior understandings in a critical way when reading fiction and nonfiction texts.

Selecting Texts **Characteristics of Texts at This Level**

Genre/Forms

Genre

- Informational texts
- High fantasy and science fiction
- Realistic fiction
- Traditional literature, including myths and legends
- Biography, memoir, and autobiography
- Historical fiction, many with settings different from students' own cultural histories
- Mysteries
- Genre combination (hybrids)
- Satire

Forms

- Picture books
- Plays
- Chapter books
- Chapter books with sequels
- Series books
- Short stories
- Diaries and logs
- Photo essays

Text Structure

Fiction

- Unusual text organizations (e.g., flashback, flashforward, shifts in time, embedded diverse stories)
- Texts with unusual structures for presenting information (combination of different genres)
- Many texts with the complex structure of adult-level reading
- Complex plots, many with multiple story lines and subplots
- Some collections of short stories that have interrelated themes or build a single plot across the book

Nonfiction

- Presentation of multiple topics that represent subtopic of a larger topic or theme
- Variety of underlying structures often combined in complex ways (description, comparison and contrast, temporal sequence, problem and solution, cause and effect)
- Variety in nonfiction formats (question and answer, paragraphs, boxes, legends, and call-outs)

Content

- Many texts requiring knowledge of history
- Content supported or extended by illustrations in most informational texts or current world events
- Content requiring the reader to take on diverse perspectives (race, language, culture)
- Content particularly appealing to adolescents
- Critical thinking required to judge authenticity of informational texts, historical fiction, and biography
- Heavy content load in many texts, both fiction and nonfiction, requiring study

Themes and Ideas

- Many ideas and themes requiring understanding of cultural diversity
- Many texts with complex themes focusing on human problems (war, hardship, social class barriers, or racism)
- Many texts presenting mature societal issues, especially those important to adolescents
- Many texts presenting multiple themes that may be understood in many layers
- Wide range of challenging themes that build social awareness and reveal insights into the human condition
- Texts that explicitly present mature issues such as sexuality, murder, abuse, nuclear war

Language and Literary Features

- Multiple characters revealed by what they say, think, and do and what others say or think about them
- Character interpretation and why they change
- Multidimensional characters that develop over time
- Understanding of multiple characters necessary for comprehending theme
- Some texts with heroic or larger-than-life characters who represent the symbolic struggle of good and evil
- Long stretches of descriptive language that are important to understanding setting and characters
- Many texts with archaic language to create authenticity
- Specific descriptions of settings that provide important information for understanding the plot
- Many texts with settings distant in time and space from students' experiences
- Some long strings of unassigned dialogue from which story action must be inferred
- Texts switching from setting to setting, including time change (often unsignaled)
- Fantasy incorporating classical motifs (such as "the quest")
- Full range of literary devices (for example, flashback, stories within stories, symbolism, and figurative language)

Guided Reading

Sentence Complexity

- Some very long sentences (some with more than thirty words)
- Many complex sentences including dialogue, many embedded phrases and clauses, and parenthetical material
- Sentences with nouns, verbs, or adjectives in series, divided by commas
- Complex sentences with compound sentences joined by semicolons or colons
- Wide range of declarative, imperative, and interrogative sentences

Vocabulary

- Many new vocabulary words that readers must derive meaning from context or use glossaries or dictionaries
- Words used figuratively or with unusual or hard-to-understand connotations
- Many technical words requiring background knowledge or use of glossary or dictionary
- Many archaic words

Words

- Many words with affixes (prefixes and suffixes, multisyllable proper nouns that are difficult to decode)
- Many multisyllable proper nouns that are difficult to decode
- Many technical words that are difficult to decode
- Words that are seldom used in oral language and are difficult to decode
- Long, multisyllable words requiring attention to roots to read and understand
- Words that offer decoding challenges because they are archaic, come from regional dialect, or from languages other than English
- Many complex plurals, contractions, and compound words

Illustrations

Fiction

- Most texts with no illustrations other than cover jacket or symbolic decoration on margins or at chapter headings

Nonfiction

- A wide variety of complex graphics that require interpretation (photos with legends, diagrams, labels, cutaways, graphs, maps)
- Some texts with graphics that are dense and challenging
- Many texts with graphics that are complex, dense, and challenging
- Many texts that have scales or legends that require understanding and interpretation

Book and Print Features

Print and Layout

- Varied space between lines, with some texts having dense print
- Use of words in italics, bold, or all capitals to indicate emphasis, level of importance, or signal other meaning
- Variety in print and background color
- Large variation among print styles and font size (related to genre)
- Many texts with very small font
- Many sentences continuing over several lines or to the next page
- Print and illustrations integrated in most texts, with print wrapping around pictures
- More difficult layout of informational text, and some fiction texts, with denser format
- Variety in layout of nonfiction formats (question and answer, paragraphs, boxes, legends, call-outs) often occurring across a two-page spread
- Some text layouts in columns

Punctuation

- Full range of punctuation as needed for complex sentences
- Occasional use of less common punctuation (colon, semicolon)

Tools

- Full range of readers' tools (table of contents, glossary, headings and subheadings, call-outs, pronunciation guides, index, references)

necessary to blast tunnels through mountains of solid granite had to be brought up to one of the highest and most remote regions of the planet. The challenge of building a railroad across these elevations was met with an extensive network of tunnels, bridges, and platforms of concrete and steel that could be riveted to the mountainsides. ■

Another major stumbling block was the permafrost (a layer of ice that melts and refreezes each day with the rising and setting of the sun) on which the last third of the railway is built. The heat generated by the fast-moving train would normally turn the top layer of the permafrost to mud, making it unstable and dangerous.

To protect the permafrost and the stability of the railroad, engineers designed sunshades, cooling pipes, and gravel beds to take heat away from the ground, thus ensuring that the rail bed itself would stay frozen and stable. In some places, elevated tracks allow the trains to ride above the permafrost.

Health Risks

The terrain was not the only concern during the construction of the railroad. Performing hard manual labor at such high altitudes was extremely risky for the huge number of workers who participated in the project. The shortage of oxygen at high

The cooling pipes look like big metal golf tees and act like tiny refrigerators or air conditioners to cool the ground.

2

altitudes can result in a number of uncomfortable symptoms like headaches, nausea, and shortness of breath, as well as dangerous conditions like potentially fatal swelling of the brain. More than 14,500 workers and engineers had to be hospitalized with altitude sickness, 3,500 of them in critical condition, but none died.

The railroad's passengers also assume some risk. To alleviate the effects of high altitude, all the trains are outfitted with oxygen-supplying equipment, and every passenger is provided with an oxygen mask. On early trips, a medical team checked on passengers and attended to people who were feeling ill. But the trip is worth some discomfort.

Acute Mountain Sickness		
Mild 4,000–9,000 feet	Moderate 10,000–13,000 feet	Severe 14,000–18,000 feet
headache fatigue loss of appetite nausea and dizziness vomiting disturbed sleep shortness of breath	profound lethargy confusion lack of coordination severe headache weakness	increased breathlessness inability to walk decreased mental state fluid in lungs death

The scenes that roll past the windows (specially tinted to protect passengers' eyes from strong ultra-violet rays) are spectacular. In some spots, snow-capped mountain peaks rise out of a landscape where the sky looks like it was painted bright blue. At lower elevations, herds of antelopes, wild donkeys, yaks, and sheep run away from the train, or just stare at it curiously from the spongy, green ground of the tundra.

3

Guided Reading

Selecting Goals   Behaviors and Understandings to Notice, Teach, and Support

Thinking *within* the Text

Solving Words

- Notice new and useful words and intentionally record and remember them to expand oral and written vocabulary
- Demonstrate ability to use automatically and flexibly a wide range of word-solving strategies (for example, dividing words into syllables, using phonograms within multisyllable words, using word parts, using prefixes and affixes, and connecting words to known words)
- Using word-solving strategies, background knowledge, graphics, text context, and readers' tools (glossaries, dictionaries) to solve words, including content-specific and technical words
- Begin to use word roots and origins to understand their meaning
- Derive the meaning of words that reflect regional or historical dialects as well as words from languages other than English

Monitoring and Correcting

- Continue to monitor accuracy and understanding, self-correcting when errors detract from meaning
- Monitor understanding closely, searching for information within and outside the text when needed

Searching for and Using Information

- Search for and use information in a wide range of graphics and integrate with information from print (for example, pictures, captions, diagrams, illustrations with labels, maps, charts)
- Use a full range of readers' tools to search for information (table of contents, glossary, headings and subheadings, call-outs, pronunciation guides, index, references)
- Process long sentences (thirty or more words) with embedded clauses (prepositional phrases, introductory clauses, series of nouns, verbs, or adverbs)
- Process texts with a variety of complex layouts and with some pages of dense print and some printed in columns
- Follow complex plots, including texts with literary devices (for example, flashbacks and stories within stories)
- Gain important information from much longer texts, most with no illustrations (fiction)
- Search for and use information from texts (both fiction and nonfiction) that have many new and unfamiliar concepts and ideas within a single chapter or section (dense concepts)
- Gain important information from texts with complex plots (often with subplots), multiple characters and episodes, and long stretches of descriptive language and dialogue
- Process sentences with the syntax of archaic or regional dialects

Summarizing

- Identify important ideas and information (longer texts with chapters and sometimes multiple texts) and organize them in summary form in order to remember and use them as background knowledge in reading or for discussion and writing
- Exercise selectivity in summarizing the information in a text (most important information or ideas and facts focused by the reader's purpose)
- Construct summaries that are concise and reflect the important and overarching ideas and information in texts

Maintaining Fluency

- Demonstrate phrased, fluent oral reading
- Demonstrate appropriate stress on words, pausing and phrasing, intonation, and use of punctuation while reading in a way that reflects understanding
- After rehearsal, perform oral reading in an expressive way that reflects interpretation of a text

Adjusting

- Change style and pace of reading to reflect purpose
- Adjust the reader's stance to better understand genres, such as complex fantasy, and special forms, such as satire

Guided Reading

Selecting Goals Behaviors and Understandings to Notice, Teach, and Support

Thinking *beyond* the Text

Predicting

- Support predictions with evidence from the text or from knowledge of genre
- Use characteristics of genre as a source of information to make predictions before and during reading
- Make and continually revise a wide range of predictions (what characters will do, what will happen to solve the problem) based on personal experiences, content knowledge, and knowledge of similar texts

Making Connections

- Bring knowledge from personal experiences to the interpretation of characters and events, particularly content and situations related to adolescents
- Make connections between the text and other texts that have been read or heard (particularly texts with diverse settings) and demonstrate in writing
- Connect and compare all aspects of texts within and across genres
- Specify the nature of connections (topic, content, type of story, writer)
- Make connections between the social and moral issues of today and those presented in realistic and historical fiction, in biography, and in the imaginary worlds of high fantasy
- Make connections between satirical literature and the social issues they represent

Synthesizing

- Mentally form categories of related information and revise them as new information is acquired across the text
- Integrate existing content knowledge with new information from a text to consciously create new understandings
- Express changes in ideas or perspective across the reading (as events unfold) after reading a text
- Acquire new content and perspective through reading both fiction and nonfiction texts about diverse cultures, times, and places
- Use situations focusing on the problems of adolescents to develop new perspectives on readers' own lives
- When reading chapters, connected short stories, or sequels, incorporate new knowledge to better understand characters and plots from material previously read

Guided Reading

Selecting Goals

Inferring

- In texts with multiple complex characters, infer traits, motivations, and changes through examining how the writer describes them, what they do, what they say and think, and what other characters say about them
- In fiction or biography, infer characters' or subjects' thinking processes and struggles at key decision points in their lives
- Infer the feelings of characters who have severe problems, with some texts explicitly presenting mature issues (sexuality, murder, abuse, war, addiction)
- Infer the big ideas or themes of a text (some texts with mature themes and issues) and assess how they are applicable to people's lives today
- Infer the meaning of symbols (objects, events, motifs, characters) that the writer uses to convey and enhance meaning
- Infer causes of problems or of outcomes in fiction and nonfiction texts
- Identify significant events and tell how they are related to the problem of the story or the solution

Thinking *about* the Text

Analyzing

- Recognize and understand satire and its purposes and characteristics
- Recognize and interpret a writer's use of language to convey irony
- Notice aspects of genres (realistic and historical fiction, fantasy, myths and legends, biography, autobiography, memoir and diaries, and other nonfiction, hybrid texts)
- Analyze the selection of genre in relation to inferred writer's purpose for a range of texts
- Understand when a writer has combined underlying organizational structures (description, compare and contrast, temporal sequence, problem and solution, cause and effect)
- Notice how the author or illustrator has used illustrations and other graphics to convey meaning or create mood
- Recognize the use of figurative or descriptive language (or special types of language such as irony) and talk about how it adds to the quality (enjoyment and understanding) of a text
- Notice how an author uses words in a connotative way (to imply something beyond the literal meaning)
- Analyze the role of the setting in realistic and historical fiction as well as fantasy
- Analyze the structure of complex plots in fiction and the organization of the text in nonfiction
- Analyze works of fantasy to notice classical motifs such as "the quest," "the hero," and symbolism representing good and evil
- Analyze aspects of a writer's craft (style, language, perspective, themes) after reading several texts by the same author
- Engage in critical thinking across a writer's body of work or across works on the same content and discuss findings or produce a literary essay
- Notice and discuss the meaning of symbolism when used by a writer to create texts, including complex fantasy where the writer is representing good and evil
- Notice the writer's choice of words that are not English and reflect on the reasons for these choices and how those words add to the meaning of a text
- Analyze how the writer has combined language, illustrations, and layout as a unified whole to set mood and convey meaning
- Notice the way writers use regional dialect and analyze how it adds to the authenticity of the text or characters
- Analyze texts to determine the writer's point of view or bias, identifying specific language that reveals bias or qualifies as propaganda
- Notice and compare the traits and development of characters within and across genres (well-developed characters vs. flat characters; heroic, multidimensional, etc.)

Guided Reading

Selecting Goals Behaviors and Understandings to Notice, Teach, and Support

Critiquing

- Evaluate the text in terms of readers' own experience as adolescents
- Critique a text as an example of a genre
- Assess the author's qualifications to write an informational text
- Evaluate the author's use of characterization and plot (for example, believability or depth)
- Assess whether a text is authentic and consistent with life experience or prior knowledge, including how the text reflects the lives of preadolescents or adolescents
- Use other sources of information to check the authenticity of a text (fiction, historical fiction, nonfiction) when questions arise
- For historical fiction, evaluate the authenticity of the details of the setting and reporting of events against knowledge from other sources
- Assess whether a text is authentic and consistent with life experience or prior knowledge, including how the text reflects the lives of adolescents
- Assess whether social issues and different cultural groups are accurately represented in a fiction or nonfiction text
- Express tastes and preferences in reading and support choices with specific descriptions of text features (plots, use of language, kinds of characters, genres)
- Become critical of the subjects of biography (decisions, motivations, accomplishments)
- Critique the biographer's presentation of a subject, noticing bias
- Critique texts in terms of the writer's bias or the use of exaggeration and subtle misinformation (as in propaganda)

Glossary

Glossary

abbreviation Shortened form of a word that has come to be used in place of the whole word *(Mr., etc., NY).*

acronym A word formed from the initial letters of related words or word parts (*radar* = *ra*dio *d*etecting *a*nd *r*anging).

adjust (as a strategic action) To read in different ways as appropriate to the purpose for reading and type of text.

adventure book A text in which the plot depends on the main character's overcoming danger and risk.

affix A part added to the beginning or ending of a base or root word to change its meaning or function (a *prefix* or a *suffix*).

alliteration The repetition of the same initial consonant sounds of neighboring words or syllables.

alphabet book (ABC book) A book that helps children develop the concept and sequence of the alphabet by pairing alphabet letters with pictures of people, animals, or objects with labels related to the letters.

alphabet linking chart A chart containing upper- and lowercase letters of the alphabet paired with pictures representing words beginning with each letter (*a, apple*).

alphabetic principle The concept that there is a relationship between the spoken sounds in oral language and the graphic forms in written language.

analogy The resemblance of a known word to an unknown word that helps you solve the unknown word's meaning.

analyze (as a strategic action) To examine the elements of a text in order to know more about how it is constructed, and to notice aspects of the writer's craft.

animal fantasy A make-believe story in which personified animals are the main characters.

antonym A word that has the opposite meaning from another word *(cold* versus *hot).*

archaic words Words that are part of the language of the past and have specialized uses in language today.

assessment A means for gathering information or data that reveals what learners control, partially control, or do not yet control consistently.

autobiography The biography of a person written and narrated by himself or herself. See also *personal narrative.*

automaticity Rapid, accurate, fluent word decoding without conscious effort or attention.

base word A whole word to which you can add affixes, creating new word forms (*wash* and *–ing; washing*).

behaviors Observable actions.

biography A written history about a person's life or part of his or her life.

blend To combine sounds or word parts.

bold (boldface) Type that is heavier and darker than usual, often used for emphasis.

book and print features (as text characteristics) The physical attributes of a text (for example, font, layout, and length).

callout A nonfiction text feature, such as a definition, a quote, or an important concept, that is highlighted by being set to one side of a text or enlarged within the body of the text.

capitalization The use of capital letters, usually the first letter in a word, as a convention of written language (for example, for proper names and to begin sentences).

chapter book An early reading text that is divided into chapters, each of which narrates an episode in the whole.

choral reading To read aloud in unison with a group.

circular story A type of story in which a sense of completeness or closure originates in the way the end of a piece returns to subject matter, wording, or phrasing found at the beginning of the story.

closed syllable A syllable that ends in one or more consonants (*lemon*).

comparative form A word that describes a person or thing in relation to another person or thing (*more, less; taller, shorter*).

compound word A word made up of two or more other words or morphemes (*play ground*). The meaning of a compound word can be a combination of the meanings of the words it is made of or can be unrelated to the meanings of the combined units.

concept book A book organized to develop an understanding of an abstract or generic idea or categorization.

concept words Words that represent abstract ideas or names. Categories of concept words include colors, numbers, months, days of the week, position words, and so on.

connecting strategies Ways of solving words that use connections or analogies with similar known words (knowing *she* and *out* helps with *shout*).

connotation The emotional meaning or association each word carries beyond the strict definition found in a dictionary.

consonant A speech sound made by partial or complete closure of the airflow that causes friction at one or more points in the breath channel. The consonant sounds are represented by the letters *b, c, d, f, g, h, j, k, l, m, n, p, q, r, s, t, v, w* (in most of their uses), *x, y* (in most of their uses), and *z*.

consonant blend Two or more consonant letters that often appear together in words and represent sounds that are smoothly joined, although each of the sounds can be heard in the word (*tr*im).

consonant cluster A sequence of two or three consonant letters that appears together in words (*tr*im, *ch*air).

consonant cluster linking chart A chart of common consonant clusters paired with pictures representing words beginning with each (*bl, block*).

consonant digraph Two consonant letters that appear together and represent a single sound that is different from the sound of either letter (she*ll*).

consonant-vowel-consonant (CVC) A common sequence of sounds in a single syllable (*hat*).

contraction A shortening of a syllable, word, or word groups usually by the omission of a sound or letters (*didn't*).

content (as a text characteristic) The subject matter of a text.

conventions (in writing) Formal usage that has become customary in written language. Grammar, capitalization, and punctuation are three categories of writing conventions.

counting book A book in which the structure depends on a numerical progression.

critique (as a strategic action) To evaluate a text based on the reader's personal, world, or text knowledge, and to think critically about the ideas in the text.

cumulative tale A story with many details repeated until the climax.

cursive A form of handwriting in which letters are connected.

decoding Using letter-sound relationships to translate a word from a series of symbols to a unit of meaning.

dialect A regional variety of a language. In most languages, including English and Spanish, dialects are mutually intelligible; the differences are actually minor.

dialogue Spoken words, usually set off with quotation marks in text.

diary A form of personal narrative written in the first person and usually consisting of sequential, dated entries.

diction Clear pronunciation and enunciation in speech.

dimension (of a character) Traits, characteristics, or attributes that a character in fiction might have (brave, funny, selfish, friendly).

directionality The orientation of print (in the English language, from left to right).

distinctive letter features Visual features that make every letter of the alphabet different from every other letter.

draft (in writing) An early version of a writer's composition.

drafting and revising (in writing) The process of getting ideas down on paper and shaping them to convey the writer's message.

early literacy concepts Very early understandings related to how written language or print is organized and used—how it works.

editing and proofreading (in writing) The process of polishing the final draft of a written composition to prepare it for publication.

editorial See *opinion editorial.*

endpaper The sheets of heavy paper at the front and back of a hardback book that join the book block to the hardback binding; sometimes printed with text, maps, or design.

English language learners People whose native language is not English and who are acquiring English as an additional language.

essay An analytic or interpretive piece of writing with a focused point of view.

expository text A composition that explains a concept, using information and description.

fable A fictitious story designed to teach a lesson, often with personified animal characters.

factual text See *informational text.*

fantasy An imaginative, fictional text containing elements that are highly unreal.

feature article A nonfiction text that focuses on one aspect of a topic.

fiction An invented story, usually narrative.

figurative language Language that is filled with word images and metaphorical language to express more than a literal meaning.

fluency in reading To read continuous text with good momentum, phrasing, appropriate pausing, intonation, and stress.

fluency in word solving Speed, accuracy, and flexibility in solving words.

folktale A traditional story, originally passed down orally.

font In printed text, the collection of type (letters) in a particular style.

form (as a text characteristic) A kind of text that is characterized by particular elements. Mystery, for example, is a form of writing within the narrative fiction genre.

formal letter A written communication, usually to a stranger, in which the form follows specific conventions (for example, a business letter).

free verse A poem whose rhythm (meter) is not regular.

friendly letter A written communication, usually to friends and family (for example, notes, invitations, emails).

functional genres A category of text in which the purpose is to accomplish a practical task. Friendly and business letters and directions are kinds of functional text.

gathering seeds (in writing) Collecting ideas, snippets of language, descriptions, and sketches for potential use in written composition.

genre A category of written text that is characterized by a particular style, form, or content.

grammar Complex rules by which people can generate an unlimited number of phrases, sentences, and longer texts in that language. Conventional grammar refers to the accepted conventions in a society.

grapheme A letter or cluster of letters representing a single sound, or phoneme (*a, eigh, ay*).

graphophonic relationship The relationship between the oral sounds of the language and the written letters or clusters of letters.

guide words The words at the top of a dictionary page to indicate the first and last word on the page.

have a try To write a word, notice that it doesn't look quite right, try it two or three other ways, and decide which construction looks right; to make an attempt and self-check.

high-frequency words Words that occur often in the spoken and written language (*the*).

historical fiction An imagined story set in the realistically (and often factually) portrayed setting of a past era.

homograph One of two or more words spelled alike but different in meaning, derivation, or pronunciation (the *bat* flew away, he swung the *bat;* take a *bow, bow* and arrow).

homonym (a type of homograph) One of two or more words spelled and pronounced alike but different in meaning (we had *quail* for dinner; I would *quail* in fear).

homophone One of two or more words pronounced alike but different in spelling and meaning (*meat, meet; bear, bare*).

hybrid texts A text containing multiple genres within one piece.

idea development (in writing) The craft of presenting and elaborating the ideas and themes of a text.

idiom A phrase with meaning that cannot be derived from the conjoined meanings of its elements (for example, *raining cats and dogs*).

illustrations (as a text characteristic) Graphic representations of important content (for example, art, photos, maps, graphs, charts).

infer (as a strategic action) To go beyond the literal meaning of a text and to think about what is not stated but is implied by the writer.

inflectional ending A suffix added to a base word to show tense, plurality, possession, or comparison (dark-*er*).

informational genres A category of texts in which the purpose is to inform or to give facts about a topic. Nonfiction feature articles and essays are examples of informational text.

interactive read-aloud A teaching context in which students are actively listening and responding to an oral reading of a text.

interactive writing A teaching context in which the teacher and students cooperatively plan, compose, and write a group text; both teacher and students act as scribes (in turn).

intonation The rise and fall in pitch of the voice in speech to convey meaning.

italic (italics) A type style that is characterized by slanting letters.

label (in writing) Written word or phrase that names the content of an illustration.

label book A picture book consisting of illustrations with brief identifying text.

language and literary features (as text characteristics) Qualities particular to written language are qualitatively different from spoken language (for example, dialogue, figurative language, and literary structures such as character, setting, and plot in fiction or description and technical language in nonfiction).

language use (in writing) The craft of using sentences, phrases, and expressions to describe events, actions, or information.

layout The way the print is arranged on a page.

legend (as genre) A tale, usually from the past, that tells about a noteworthy person or event.

legend (as text feature) A key on a map or chart that explains what symbols stand for.

letter knowledge The ability to recognize and label the graphic symbols of language.

letters Graphic symbols representing the sounds in a language. Each letter has particular distinctive features and may be identified by letter name or sound.

letter (as genre) See *friendly letter* and *formal letter.*

letter-sound correspondence Recognizing the corresponding sound of a specific letter when that letter is seen or heard.

letter-sound relationships See *letter-sound correspondence.*

lexicon Words that make up language.

lists and procedures (in writing) Functional genres that include simple lists and how-to texts.

literary devices Techniques used by a writer to convey or enhance the story, such as figures of speech, imagery, symbolism, and point of view.

literary nonfiction Engaging factual texts that present information on a topic in interesting ways.

log (as genre) A chronological, written record, usually of a journey.

long vowel The elongated vowel sound that is the same as the name of the vowel. It is sometimes represented by two or more letters (c*a*k*e*, *ei*ght, m*ai*l).

lowercase letter A small letter form that is usually different from its corresponding capital or uppercase form.

maintain fluency (as a strategic action) To integrate sources of information in a smoothly operating process that results in expressive, phrased reading.

make connections (as a strategic action) To search for and use connections to knowledge gained through personal experiences, learning about the world, and reading other texts.

media Channels of communication for information or entertainment. Newspapers and books are print media; television and the Internet are electronic media.

memoir An account of something important, usually part of a person's life. A memoir is a kind of biography, autobiography, or personal narrative.

mentor texts Books or other texts that serve as examples of excellent writing. Mentor texts are read and reread to provide models for literature discussion and student writing.

metaphor A figure of speech that makes a comparison of two unlike things without using the words *like* or *as*.

modeled writing An instructional technique in which a teacher demonstrates the process of composing a particular genre, making the process explicit for students.

monitor and correct (as a strategic action) To check whether the reading sounds right, looks, right, and makes sense, and to solve problems when it doesn't.

mood The emotional atmosphere or tone communicated by an author in his or her work; usually established by details, imagery, figurative language, and setting.

morpheme The smallest unit of meaning in a language. Morphemes may be free or bound. For example, *run* is a unit of meaning that can stand alone (a free morpheme). In *runs* and *running*, the added *-s* and *-ing* are also units of meaning. They cannot stand alone but add meaning to the free morpheme. The *-s* and *-ing* are examples of bound morphemes.

morphemic strategies Ways of solving words by discovering meaning through the combination of significant word parts or morphemes (*happy, happiest; run, runner, running*).

morphological system Rules by which morphemes (building blocks of vocabulary) fit together into meaningful words, phrases, and sentences.

morphology The combination of morphemes (building blocks of meaning) to form words; the rules by which words are formed from free and bound morphemes—for example, root words, prefixes, and suffixes.

multisyllable word A word that contains more than one syllable.

multiple-meaning word A words that means something different depending on the way it is used (*run—home run, run* in your stocking, *run* down the street, a *run* of bad luck).

mystery A form of writing in which the plot hinges on a puzzling situation or event that is resolved by the end.

myth A traditional story originally created to explain natural phenomena or events.

narrative genres A category of texts in which the purpose is to tell a story. Stories and biographies are kinds of narrative.

nonfiction A text based on fact.

nursery rhyme A short rhyme for children, usually telling a story.

onomatopoetic words Words for which the pronunciations suggests the words' meaning.

onset In a syllable, the part (consonant, consonant cluster, or consonant digraph) that comes before the vowel (*cr*-eam).

onset-rime segmentation The identification and separation of onsets (first part) and rimes (last part, containing the vowel) in words (*dr-ip*).

open syllable A syllable that ends in a vowel sound (*ho*-tel).

opinion editorial A type of text in which the purpose is to state and defend an opinion, usually by an editor of a magazine, newspaper, or TV news show.

organization (in writing) The craft of arranging ideas in a written text according to a logical structure.

orthographic awareness The knowledge of the visual features of written language, including distinctive features of letters as well as spelling patterns in words.

orthography The representation of the sounds of a language with the proper letters according to standard usage (spelling).

performance reading An instructional context in which the students read orally to perform for others; they may read in unison or take parts. Shared reading, choral reading, and readers' theater are kinds of performance reading.

personal narrative A brief text, usually autobiographical and written in the first person, that tells about one event in the writer's life.

phoneme The smallest unit of sound in spoken language. There are approximately forty-four units of speech sounds in English.

phoneme addition To add a beginning or ending sound to a word (h + and, an + t).

phoneme blending To identify individual sounds and then to put them together smoothly to make a word (c-a-t = cat).

phoneme deletion To omit a beginning, middle, or ending sound of a word (cart – c = art).

phoneme-grapheme correspondence The relationship between the sounds (phonemes) and letters (graphemes) of a language.

phoneme isolation The identification of an individual sound—beginning, middle, or end—in a word.

phoneme manipulation The movement of sounds from one place in a word to another.

phoneme reversal The exchange of the first and last sounds of a word to make a different word.

phoneme substitution The replacement of the beginning, middle, or ending sound of a word with a new sound.

phonemic (or phoneme) awareness The ability to hear individual sounds in words and to identify particular sounds.

phonemic strategies Ways of solving words that use how words sound and relationships between letters and letter clusters and phonemes in those words (*cat, make*).

phonetics The scientific study of speech sounds—how the sounds are made vocally and the relation of speech sounds to the total language process.

phonics The knowledge of letter-sound relationships and how they are used in reading and writing. Teaching phonics refers to helping children acquire this body of knowledge about the oral and written language systems; additionally, teaching phonics helps children use phonics knowledge as part of a reading and writing process. Phonics instruction uses a small portion of the body of knowledge that makes up phonetics.

phonogram A phonetic element represented by graphic characters or symbols. In word recognition, a graphic sequence composed of a vowel grapheme and an ending consonant grapheme (such as *an* or *it*) is sometimes called a word family.

phonological awareness The awareness of words, rhyming words, onsets and rimes, syllables, and individual sounds (phonemes).

phonological system The sounds of the language and how they work together in ways that are meaningful to the speakers of the language.

photo essay An informational text that uses captioned photographs to convey its message.

picture book A highly illustrated fiction or nonfiction text in which pictures work with the text to tell a story or provide information.

plural Of, relating to, or constituting more than one.

poetic genres A category of texts in which the purpose is to use poetic form to explain feelings, sensory images, ideas, or stories. Free verse, traditional rhymes, and limericks are kinds of poetic genre.

point of view The way an author chooses to tell or narrate a story, such as through characters, events, or ideas.

portmanteau word A word made from combining two other words and meanings *(smoke + fog = smog).*

possessive Grammatical constructions used to show ownership *(John's, his)* .

pourquoi tale A legend told to explain why certain events happened (originally French).

predict (as a strategic action) To use what is known to think about what will follow while reading continuous text.

prefix A group of letters that can be placed in front of a base word to change its meaning (*pre*plan).

principle In phonics, a generalization or a sound-spelling relationship that is predictable.

propaganda One-sided speaking or writing deliberately used to influence the thoughts and actions of someone in alignment with specific ideas or views.

publishing (in writing) The process of making the final draft of a written composition public.

punctuation Marks used in written text to clarify meaning and separate structural units. The comma and the period are common punctuation marks.

purpose (in writing) The writer's overall intention in creating a text. To tell a story and to inform or explain are two standard purposes for writing.

r-controlled vowel sound The modified or *r*-influenced sound of a vowel when it is followed by *r* in a syllable (*hurt*).

reader's notebook A notebook or folder of bound pages in which students write about their reading. The reader's notebook is used to keep a record of texts read and to express thinking. It may have several different sections to serve a variety of purposes.

readers' theater A performance of literature, as a story, play, or poetry, read aloud expressively by one or more persons, rather than acted.

realistic fiction An invented story that could happen.

rehearsing and planning (in writing) The process of collecting, working with, and selecting ideas for a written composition.

report A text written to provide facts about a specific topic.

rhyme The ending part (rime) of a word that sounds like the ending part (rime) of another word (*mail, tale*).

rhythm The regular or ordered repetition of stressed and unstressed syllables in speech or writing.

rime The ending part of a word containing the vowel; the letters that represent the vowel sound and the consonant letters that follow it in a syllable (dr-*eam*).

root The part of a word that contains the main meaning component.

satire A literary narrative in which human failures are portrayed and ridiculed.

schwa The sound of the middle vowel in an unstressed syllable (the *o* in *done* and the sound between the *k* and l in *freckle*).

science fiction A form of fictional narrative in which real or imagined scientific phenomena influence the plot.

search for and use information (as a strategic action) To look for and to think about all kinds of content in order to make sense of text while reading.

segment To divide into parts (*to-ma-to*).

semantic system The system by which speakers of a language communicate meaning through language.

sentence complexity (as a text characteristic) The complexity of the structure or syntax of a sentence. Addition of phrases and clauses to simple sentences increases complexity.

series book One of a collection of books about the same character or characters and the different events or situations encountered.

shared reading An instructional technique in which the teacher involves a group of students in the reading of a particular big book in order to introduce aspects of literacy (such as print conventions), develop reading strategies (such as decoding or predicting), and teach vocabulary.

shared writing An instructional technique in which the teacher involves a group of students in the composing of a coherent text together. The teacher writes while scaffolding children's language and ideas.

short vowel A brief-duration sound represented by a vowel letter (*cat*).

silent e The final *e* in a spelling pattern that usually signals a long vowel sound in the word and does not represent a sound itself (*make*).

simile A comparison of two unlike things in which a word of comparison (often *like* or *as*) is used.

sketching and drawing (in writing) To create a rough (sketch) or finished (drawing) image of a person, a place, a thing, or an idea to capture, work with, and render the writer's ideas.

solve words (as a strategic action) To use a range of strategies to take words apart and understand their meaning.

sources of information The various cues in a written text that combine to make meaning (for example, syntax, meaning, and the physical shape and arrangement of type).

spelling patterns Beginning letters (onsets) and common phonograms (rimes) form the basis for the English syllable; knowing these patterns, a student can build countless words.

split dialogue Written dialogue in which a "said phrase" divides the speaker's words: "Come on," said Mom. "Let's go home."

strategic action Any one of many simultaneous, coordinated thinking activities that go on in a reader's head. See *thinking within, beyond, and about the text.*

stress The emphasis given to some syllables or words.

suffix An affix or group of letters added at the end of a base or root word to change its function or meaning (hand*ful*, hope*less*).

summarize (as a strategic action) Put together and remember important information, disregarding irrelevant information, while reading

survival story A form of adventure story in which

syllabication The division of words into syllables (*pen-cil*).

syllable A minimal unit of sequential speech sounds composed of a vowel sound or a consonant-vowel combination. A syllable always contains a vowel or vowel-like speech sound (*to-ma-to*).

synonym One of two or more words that have different sounds but the same meaning *(chair, seat).*

syntactic awareness The knowledge of grammatical patterns or structures.

syntactic system Rules that govern the ways in which morphemes and words work together in sentence patterns. Not the same as proper grammar, which refers to the accepted grammatical conventions.

syntax The study of how sentences are formed and of the grammatical rules that govern their formation.

synthesize (as a strategic action) To combine new information or ideas from reading text with existing knowledge to create new understandings.

tall tale A fictional narrative characterized by exaggeration.

text structure The overall architecture or organization of a piece of writing. Chronology (sequence) and description are two common text structures.

test writing A functional genre required in schools.

theme The central idea or concept in a story or the message that the author is conveying.

thinking within, beyond, and about the text Three ways of thinking about a text while reading. Thinking within the text involves efficiently and effectively understanding what's on the page, the author's literal message. Thinking beyond the text requires making inferences and putting text ideas together in different ways to construct the text's meaning. In thinking about the text, readers analyze and critique the author's craft.

tone An expression of the author's attitude or feelings toward a subject reflected in the style of writing.

tools (as text characteristics) Parts of a text designed to help the reader access or better understand it (table of contents, glossary, photo captions, headings).

tools (in writing) References that support the writing process (dictionary, thesaurus).

topic The subject of a piece of writing.

understandings Basic concepts that are critical to comprehending a particular area.

viewing self as writer Attitudes and practices that support a student's becoming a lifelong writer.

visual strategies Ways of solving words that use knowledge of how words look, including the clusters and patterns of the letters in words (*bear, light*).

vocabulary (as a text characteristic) Words and their meanings.

voice (in writing) The craft of creating a unique style.

vowel A speech sound or phoneme made without stoppage of or friction in the airflow. The vowel sounds are represented by *a, e, i, o, u,* and sometimes *y* and *w.*

vowel combinations Two vowels that appear together in words (m*ea*t).

vowel digraph Two successive vowel letters that represent a single vowel sound (b*oa*t), a vowel combination.

word A unit of meaning in language.

word analysis To break apart words into parts or individual sounds in order to parse them.

word boundaries The white space that defines a word; the white space before the first letter and after the last letter of a word. It is important for young readers to learn to recognize word boundaries.

word-by-word matching Usually applied to a beginning reader's ability to match one spoken word with one printed word while reading and pointing. In older readers, the eyes take over the process.

word choice (in writing) The craft of choosing words to convey precise meaning.

word family A term often used to designate words that are connected by phonograms or rimes (*hot, not, pot, shot*). A word family can also be a series of words connected by meaning (affixes added to a base word; for example: *base, baseball, basement, baseman, basal, basis, baseless, baseline, baseboard, abase, abasement, off base, home base; precise, précis, precisely, precision).*

wordless picture book A story told exclusively with pictures.

words (as a text characteristic) Decodability of words in a text; phonetic and structural features of words.

word-solving actions See *solve words.*

writer's notebook A written log of potential writing topics or ideas that a writer would like to explore; a place to keep the writer's experimentations with writing styles.

References

Fountas, Irene C., and Gay Su Pinnell. 2007. *Fountas and Pinnell Benchmark Assessment System.* Portsmouth, NH: Heinemann.

Use this system to determine reading levels, gain specific information about reader's strengths and needs, and document progress over time.

———. 2006. *Teaching for Comprehending and Fluency: Thinking, Talking, and Writing About Reading K–8.* Portsmouth, NH: Heinemann.

Use this book in your studies of the interactive read-aloud and literature discussions, shared and performance reading, and guided reading continua to skillfully teach meaning making and fluency within any instructional context.

——. 2005. *Leveled Books, K–8: Matching Texts to Readers for Effective Teaching.* Portsmouth, NH: Heinemann.

Use this book and the leveled books website, www.FountasandPinnellLeveledBooks.com, with your studies of the guided reading continuum to analyze the characteristics of texts and select just-the-right book to use for guided reading.

——. 2004. *Word Study Lessons: Phonics, Spelling, and Vocabulary (Grade 3).* Portsmouth, NH: *first*hand.

Use these books with your studies of the guided reading continuum to choose the lessons that align with your students' needs.

——. 2001a. *Guided Reading: Essential Elements, The Skillful Teacher* (videotapes). Portsmouth, NH: Heinemann.

Use these videotapes with your studies in the interactive read-aloud and literature discussion and guided reading continua to see Guided Reading *in action. In the first part,* Essential Elements, *watch guided reading lessons as they unfold to see how teachers introduce a text, support children as they read orally and silently, discuss text meaning, use "teaching points" to reinforce effective reading strategies, revisit the text to extend meaning, and conduct word work as needed.*

In part two, The Skillful Teacher, *observe the planning and organizing behind guided reading and learn how to meet the needs of individual readers. You'll discover how to group children, select books, plan book introductions, support word solving, teach comprehension strategies, develop fluency, and take running records.*

———. 2001b. *Guiding Readers and Writers: Teaching Comprehension, Genre, and Content Literacy.* Portsmouth, NH: Heinemann.

Engage, inform, and inspire early readers and writers with this book that explores the essential components of a quality upper elementary literacy program.

———. 1996. *Guided Reading: Good First Teaching for All Children.* Portsmouth, NH: Heinemann.

Use this book for help with teaching guided reading lessons. Learn how to select and introduce texts, teach during and after reading, and assess student progress.

McCarrier, Andrea, Irene C. Fountas, and Gay Su Pinnell. 2000. *Interactive Writing: How Language & Literacy Come Together, K–2.* Portsmouth, NH: Heinemann.

Use this book to assist with early writing—modeled, shared, or interactive. It will help you teach children how to write in many genres and forms for varied purposes.

Pinnell, Gay Su, and Irene C. Fountas. 2003. *Phonics Lessons: Letters, Words, and How They Work (Grades K, 1, and 2).* Portsmouth, NH: *first*hand.

Use these books with your studies of the phonics and word study and guided reading continua to choose the lessons that align with your students' needs.

———. 1998. *Word Matters: Teaching Phonics and Spelling in the Reading-Writing Classroom.* Portsmouth, NH: Heinemann.

This book will help you design and teach for effective word-solving strategies.

Appendix

Early Literacy Concepts

Learning about literacy begins long before children enter school. Many children hear stories read aloud and try out writing for themselves; through such experiences, they learn some basic concepts about written language. Nearly all children begin to notice print in the environment and develop ideas about the purposes of print. The child's name, for example, is a very important word. Kindergartners and first graders are still acquiring some of these basic concepts, and they need to generalize and systematize their knowledge. In the classroom, they learn a great deal through experiences such as shared and modeled reading and shared and interactive writing. Explicit teaching can help children learn much more about these early concepts, understand their importance, and develop ways of using them in reading and writing.

Early Literacy Concepts

P-K | GRADE K (E M L) | GRADE 1 (E M L) | GRADE 2 (E M L) | GRADE 3 (E M L) | GRADE 4 (E M L) | GRADE 5 (E M L) | GRADES 6–8

Principle	Explanation of Principle
Distinguishing between print and pictures	**"We read the print to find out what the words say."**
Understanding the purpose of print in reading	**"We look at the print to read the words in stories and other messages."**
Understanding the purpose of print in writing	**"We write letters and words so readers will understand what we mean."**
Recognizing one's name	**"Your name has letters in it."**
	"Your name starts with a letter that is always the same."
	"Your name starts with a capital letter. The other letters are lowercase."
	"Your name is always written the same way."
	"You can find your name by looking for the first letter."
Using letters in one's own name to represent it or "write" a message	**"You can write the letters in your name."**
	"You can use the letters in your name along with other letters to write messages."
Understanding the concept of "letter"	**"A letter has a name and a shape."**
Understanding the concept of "word"	**"A word is a group of sounds that mean something."**
	"A word in writing is a group of letters with space on either side."
Using left-to-right directionality of print	**"We read and write from left to right."**
Understanding the concepts of *first* and *last* in written language	**"The first word in a sentence is on the left."**
	"The last word in a sentence is before the period or question mark."
	"The first letter in a word is on the left."
	"The last letter in a word is before the space."
	"The first part of a page is at the top."
	"The last part of a page is at the bottom."

P-K | GRADE K (E M L) | GRADE 1 (E M L) | GRADE 2 (E M L) | GRADE 3 (E M L) | GRADE 4 (E M L) | GRADE 5 (E M L) | GRADES 6–8

Key: E = Early in school year, M = Mid-year, L = Late in school year

Early Literacy Concepts, continued

Principle	Explanation of Principle
Understanding that one spoken word matches one group of letters	**"We say one word for each word we see in writing."**
Using one's name to learn about words and make connections to words	**"Your name is a word."** **"You can connect your name with other words."**
Locating the first and last letters of words in continuous text	**"You can find a word by noticing how it looks."** **"You can find a word by looking for the first letter."** **"You can check a word by looking at the first and last letters."**
Understanding the concept of a sentence	**"A sentence is a group of words that makes sense."**

P-K | GRADE K (E M L) | GRADE 1 (E M L) | GRADE 2 (E M L) | GRADE 3 (E M L) | GRADE 4 (E M L) | GRADE 5 (E M L) | GRADES 6–8

Phonological Awareness

Phonological awareness is a broad term that refers to both explicit and implicit knowledge of the sounds in language. It includes the ability to hear and identify words (word awareness), rhymes (rhyme awareness), syllables (syllable awareness), onsets and rimes (onset and rime awareness), and individual sounds (sound awareness).

Phonemic awareness is one kind of phonological awareness. Phonemic awareness refers to the ability to identify, isolate, and manipulate the individual sounds (*phonemes*) in words. Principles categorized as phonemic awareness are labeled Phonemes [PA] in this continuum.

Phonological awareness (and phonemic awareness) is taught orally or in connection with letters, when it is called *phonics.* Phonics instruction refers to teaching children to connect letters and sounds in words. While very early experiences focus on hearing and saying sounds in the absence of letters, most of the time you will want to teach children to hear sounds in connection with letters. Many of the lessons related to this section begin with oral activity but move toward connecting the sounds to letters. You will not want to teach all of the PA principles in this continuum. It is more effective to teach children only two or three ways to manipulate phonemes in words so that they learn how words work.

Principles related to letter/sound relationships, or phonics, are included in the Letter/Sound Relationships category of this continuum.

Phonological Awareness

Principle	Explanation of Principle (P-K · GRADE K E M L · GRADE 1 E M L · GRADE 2 E M L · GRADE 3 E M L · GRADE 4 E M L · GRADE 5 E M L · GRADES 6–8)
Words	
Hearing and recognizing word boundaries	**"You say words when you talk."**
	"You can hear words in a sentence if you stop after each one. [*I - have - a - dog.*]"
Segmenting sentences into words	**"You can say each word in a sentence. [*I - like - to - go - shopping.*]"**
Rhyming Words	
Hearing and saying rhyming words	**"Some words have end parts that sound alike. They *rhyme* [*new, blue*]."**
	"You can hear the rhymes in poems and songs."
	"You can say words and hear how they rhyme."
Hearing and connecting rhyming words	**"You can hear and connect words that rhyme [*fly, high, buy, sky*]."**
Hearing and generating rhyming words	**"You can make rhymes by thinking of words that end the same. [*I can fly in the* ___.]"**
Syllables	
Hearing and saying syllables	**"You can hear and say the syllables in a word [*to-ma-to, tomato*]."**
	"Some words have one syllable [*cat*]."
	"Some words have two syllables [*can-dy, candy*]."
	"Some words have three or more syllables [*um-brel-la, umbrella*]."
Blending syllables	**"You can blend syllables together [*pen-cil, pencil*]."**

P-K · GRADE K E M L · GRADE 1 E M L · GRADE 2 E M L · GRADE 3 E M L · GRADE 4 E M L · GRADE 5 E M L · GRADES 6–8

Key: E = Early in school year, M = Mid-year, L = Late in school year

Phonological Awareness, continued

Principle	Explanation of Principle
	P-K · GRADE K (E M L) · GRADE 1 (E M L) · GRADE 2 (E M L) · GRADE 3 (E M L) · GRADE 4 (E M L) · GRADE 5 (E M L) · GRADES 6–8
Onsets and Rimes	
Hearing and segmenting onsets and rimes	**"You can hear and say the first and last parts of a word [*c-ar, car; pl-ay, play*]."**
Blending onsets with rimes	**"You can blend word parts together [*d-og, dog*]."**
Phonemes [PA]	
Hearing and saying individual phonemes (sounds) in words	**"You can say a word slowly."**
	"You can hear the sounds in a word [*m-a-k, make*]."
Segmenting words into phonemes	**"You can say each sound in a word [*b-a-t*]."**
Hearing and saying two or three phonemes in a word	**"You can say a word slowly to hear all the sounds [*r-u-n*]."**
Hearing and saying beginning phonemes in words	**"You can hear the first sound in a word [*s-u-n*]."**
	"You can say a word to hear the first sound."
Hearing and saying ending phonemes in words	**"You can hear the last sound in a word [*r-u-n*]."**
	"You can say a word to hear the last sound."
Hearing similar beginning phonemes in words	**"Some words sound the same at the beginning [*run, race*]."**
	"You can connect words that sound the same at the beginning [*mother, mom, make*]."
Hearing similar ending phonemes in words	**"Some words sound the same at the end [*win, fun*]."**
	"You can connect words that sound the same at the end [*get, sit, Matt*]."
Blending two or three phonemes in words	**"You can blend sounds together to say a word [*d-o-g* = *dog*]."**
Adding phonemes to the beginning of words	**"You can add sounds to a word [*it* + *s* = *sit*]."**
	"You can add sounds to the beginning of a word [*rate* + *c* = *crate*]."
Manipulating phonemes at the beginning of words	**"You can change the first sound in a word to make a new word [*not, hot*]."**
Manipulating phonemes at the ending of words	**"You can change the last sound in a word to make a new word [*his, him*]."**
Hearing and saying middle phonemes in words	**"You can hear and say the sound in the middle of a word [*s-u-n*]."**
Hearing similar middle phonemes in words	**"Some words sound the same in the middle [*cat, ran*]."**
	"You can match words that sound the same in the middle [*stop, hot, John*]."
Hearing four or more phonemes in a word	**"You can say a word slowly to hear all the sounds [*s-p-e-n-d*]."**
Hearing and identifying phonemes in a word in sequence	**"You can say a word slowly to hear all the sounds, from first to last [/r/ (*first*), /u/ (*next*), /n/ (*last*) = *run*]."**
	"You can write the letter or letters for each sound."
Blending three or four phonemes in words	**"You can blend sounds together to say a word [*n-e-s-t* = *nest*]."**
Deleting phonemes in words	**"You can say words without some of the sounds [*can* – *c* = *an; sand* – *s* = *and*]."**
	"You can say a word without the first sound [*ch* – *air* = *air*]."
	"You can say a word without the last sound [*ant* – *t* = *an*]."
Adding phonemes to the end of words	**"You can add sounds to the end of a word [*an* + *d* = *and; and* + *y* = *Andy*]."**
Manipulating phonemes in the middle of words	**"You can change the sounds in the middle of a word to make a new word [*hit, hot*]."**
	P-K · GRADE K (E M L) · GRADE 1 (E M L) · GRADE 2 (E M L) · GRADE 3 (E M L) · GRADE 4 (E M L) · GRADE 5 (E M L) · GRADES 6–8

Letter Knowledge

Letter knowledge refers to what children need to learn about the graphic characters that correspond with the sounds of language. A finite set of twenty-six letters, two forms of each, is related to all of the sounds of the English language (approximately forty-four phonemes). The sounds in the language change as dialect, articulation, and other speech factors vary. Children will also encounter alternative forms of some letters—for example, g, g; a, a; y, y—and will eventually learn to recognize letters in cursive writing. Children need to learn the names and purposes of letters, as well as the particular features of each. When children can identify letters by noticing the very small differences that make them unique, they can then associate letters and letter clusters with phonemes and parts of words. Knowing the letter names is useful information that helps children talk about letters and understand what others say about them. As writers, children need to be able to use efficient directional movements when making letters.

Letter Knowledge

Principle	Explanation of Principle
	P-K · GRADE K (E M L) · GRADE 1 (E M L) · GRADE 2 (E M L) · GRADE 3 (E M L) · GRADE 4 (E M L) · GRADE 5 (E M L) · GRADE 6–8
Identifying Letters	
Understanding the concept of a letter	**"The alphabet has twenty-six letters."**
	"A letter has a name and a shape."
Distinguishing letter forms	**"Letters are different from each other."**
	"You can notice the parts of letters."
	"Some letters have long sticks. Some letters have short sticks."
	"Some letters have curves, circles, tunnels, tails, crosses, dots, slants."
Producing letter names	**"You can look at the shape of a letter and say its name."**
Categorizing letters by features	**"You can find parts of letters that look the same."**
	"You can find the letters that have long sticks [short sticks, curves, circles, tunnels, tails, crosses, dots, slants]."
Understanding alphabetical order	**"The letters in the alphabet are in a special order."**
Recognizing uppercase and lowercase letters	**"A letter has two forms. One form is uppercase (or capital) and the other is lowercase (or small) [*B, b*]."**
	"Your name starts with an uppercase letter."
	"The other letters in your name are lowercase letters."
	"Some lowercase forms look like the uppercase forms [*W, w*] and some look different [*R, r*]."
Recognizing consonants and vowels	**"Some letters are consonants [*b, c, d, f, g, h, j, k, l, m, n, p, q, r, s, t, v, w, x, y, z*]."**
	"Some letters are vowels [*a, e, i, o, u,* and sometimes *y* and *w*]."
	"Every word has a vowel."
Understanding special uses of letters	**"Your initials are the first letters of your first name and your last name."**
	"You use capital letters to write your initials."
	P-K · GRADE K (E M L) · GRADE 1 (E M L) · GRADE 2 (E M L) · GRADE 3 (E M L) · GRADE 4 (E M L) · GRADE 5 (E M L) · GRADES 6–8

Key: E = Early in school year, M = Mid-year, L = Late in school year

Letter Knowledge, continued

Principle	Explanation of Principle
Recognizing Letters in Words and Sentences	
Understanding that words are made up of letters	**"Words have letters in them."** **"Your name has letters in it."** **"You can say the first letter of your name."**
Making connections between words by recognizing letters	**"You can find words that have the same letters in them."**
Recognizing the sequence of letters in words	**"Letters in a word are always in the same order."** **"The first letter is on the left."** **"You can find the first letter in a word."**
Recognizing letters in words	**"You can find letters in words."** **"You can say the names of letters in words."**
Recognizing letters in continuous text	**"You can find letters in sentences and stories."**
Making connections between words by recognizing letter placement	**"You can find words that begin with the same letter."** **"You can find words that end with the same letter."** **"You can find words that have the same letter in the middle."**
Forming Letters	
Using efficient and consistent motions to form letters	**"You can make the shape of a letter."** **"You can say words that help you learn how to make a letter."** **"You can check to see if your letter looks right."**

P-K GRADE K (E M L) GRADE 1 (E M L) GRADE 2 (E M L) GRADE 3 (E M L) GRADE 4 (E M L) GRADE 5 (E M L) GRADES 6–8

Letter/Sound Relationships

The sounds of oral language are related in both simple and complex ways to the twenty-six letters of the alphabet. Learning the connections between letters and sounds is basic to understanding written language. Children first learn simple relationships that are regular in that one phoneme is connected to one grapheme, or letter. But sounds are also connected to letter clusters, which are groups of letters that appear often together (for example, *cr, str, st, bl, fr*), in which you hear each of the associated sounds of the letters; and consonant digraphs (*sh, ch*), in which you hear only one sound. Vowels may also appear in combinations (*ea, oa*) in which you usually hear the first vowel (ai) or you hear a completely different sound (*ou*). Children learn to look for and recognize these letter combinations as units, which makes their word solving more efficient. It is important to remember that children will be able to hear and connect the easy-to-identify consonants and vowels early and progress to the harder-to-identify and more difficult letter/sound relationships—for example, letter clusters with two and three letters and those that have more than one sound. You will want to connect initial consonant cluster sounds to the Consonant Cluster Linking Chart. It is not necessary to teach every cluster as a separate lesson. We also provide lessons for cursive writing and keyboarding for the computer.

Letter/Sound Relationships

Principle	Explanation of Principle (P-K; GRADE K E M L; GRADE 1 E M L; GRADE 2 E M L; GRADE 3 E M L; GRADE 4 E M L; GRADE 5 E M L; GRADES 6–8)
Consonants	
Recognizing that letters represent consonant sounds	**"You can match letters and sounds in words. For example: *b* is the letter that stands for the first sound in *bear.*"**
Recognizing and using beginning consonant sounds and the letters that represent them: *s, m, t, b, f, r, n, p, d, h, c, g, j, l, k, v, w, z, qu, y, x*	**"You can hear the sound at the beginning of a word."** **"You can match letters and sounds at the beginning of a word."** **"When you see a letter at the beginning of a word, you can make its sound."** **"When you know the sound, you can find the letter."** **"You can find a word by saying it and thinking about the first sound."**
Recognizing similar beginning consonant sounds and the letters that represent them	**"Words can start with the same sound and letter [*b*ox, *b*ig]."**
Recognizing and using ending consonant sounds and the letters that represent them: *b, m, t, d, g, n, p, f, l, r, s, z, ff, ss, ll, tt, ck*	**"You can hear sounds at the end of a word."** **"You can match letters and sounds at the end of a word."** **"When you see the letter at the end of a word, you can make the sound."** **"When you know the sound, you can find the letter."** **"You can find a word by saying it and thinking about the ending sound."**
Recognizing similar ending consonant sounds and the letters that represent them	**"Words can end with the same sound and letter [*duck*, *book*]."**

E M L E M L E M L E M L E M L E M L
P-K GRADE K GRADE 1 GRADE 2 GRADE 3 GRADE 4 GRADE 5 GRADES 6–8

Key: E = Early in school year, M = Mid-year, L = Late in school year

Letter/Sound Relationships, continued

Principle	Explanation of Principle
	P-K · GRADE K (E M L) · GRADE 1 (E M L) · GRADE 2 (E M L) · GRADE 3 (E M L) · GRADE 4 (E M L) · GRADE 5 (E M L) · GRADES 6–8
Consonants continued	
Recognizing and using letters that represent two or more consonant sounds at the beginning of a word: *c, g, th, ch* (*car, city; get, gym; think, they; chair, chorus, chateau*)	**"Some consonants or consonant clusters stand for two or more different sounds."**
Recognizing and using consonant clusters that blend two or three consonant sounds [onsets]: *bl, cl, fl, pl, pr, br, dr, gr, tr, cr, fr, gl, sl, sn, sp, st, sw, sc, sk, sm, scr, squ, str, thr, spr, spl, shr, sch, tw*	**"A group of two or three consonants is a consonant cluster."** **"You can usually hear each sound in a consonant cluster."**
Recognizing and using consonant sounds represented by consonant digraphs: *sh, ch, th, wh*	**"Some clusters of consonants stand for one sound that is different from either of the letters. They are called *consonant digraphs*."** **"You can hear the sound of a consonant digraph at the beginning or ending of a word."**
Recognizing and using middle consonant sounds sometimes represented by double letters: *bb, cc, dd, ff, ll, mm, nn, pp, rr, ss, tt, zz*	**"Sometimes double consonant letters stand for a consonant sound in the middle of a word [*rubber, arrive, coffee, lesson*]."**
Recognizing and using letters that represent consonant clusters [blends] at the end of a word: *ct, ft, ld, lp, lt, mp, nd, nk, pt, rd, rk, sk, sp, st, lf, nt*	**"Some words have consonant clusters at the end."** **"You can hear each sound in a consonant cluster at the end of a word."**
Recognizing and using consonant letters that represent no sound: *lamb, know, pick, wrap, gnome, scene, sign, rhyme, khaki, calm, island, listen, light*	**"Some words have consonant letters that are silent [*wrap, gnome, know, climb, honor, who*]."**
Recognizing and using letters that represent consonant digraphs at the end of a word (making one sound): *sh, th, ch, ck, tch, dge, ng, ph, gh*	**"Some words have consonant clusters at the end that make only one sound."**
Recognizing and using letters that represent less frequent consonant digraph at the beginning or ending of a word (making one sound): *gh, ph,* (*rough, phone, graph*)	**"Consonant digraphs stand for one sound that is different from either of the letters."** **"You can hear the sound of a consonant digraph at the beginning or end of a word."**
Understanding that some consonant sounds can be represented by several different letters or letter clusters: final *k* sound: *picnic, unique, make, kayak, duck;* final *f* sound: *stiff, cough*	**"Some consonant sounds are represented by several different letters or letter clusters."**
Understanding that some consonant letters represent several different sounds: *ch: cheese, school, machine, choir, yacht*	**"Some consonant letters represent more than one sound."**
	P-K · GRADE K (E M L) · GRADE 1 (E M L) · GRADE 2 (E M L) · GRADE 3 (E M L) · GRADE 4 (E M L) · GRADE 5 (E M L) · GRADES 6–8

Letter/Sound Relationships, continued

Principle	Explanation of Principle
	P-K · GRADE K (E M L) · GRADE 1 (E M L) · GRADE 2 (E M L) · GRADE 3 (E M L) · GRADE 4 (E M L) · GRADE 5 (E M L) · GRADES 6–8
Vowels	
Understanding letters that represent consonant sounds or vowel sounds	**"Some letters are consonants and some letters are vowels."** **"Every word has a vowel sound."** **"*A, e, i, o,* and *u* are vowels (and sometimes *y* and *w*)."**
Hearing and identifying short vowel sounds in words and the letters that represent them	**"In some words, *a* sounds like the *a* in *apple* and *can*."** **"In some words, *e* sounds like the *e* in *egg* and *net*."** **"In some words, *i* sounds like the *i* in *igloo* and *sit*."** **"In some words, *o* sounds like the *o* in *octopus* and *hot*."** **"In some words, *u* sounds like the *u* in *umbrella* and *cup*."**
Recognizing and using short vowel sounds at the beginning of words: *at, apple, Andrew*	**"Some words have one vowel at the beginning [*apple, at, Andrew*]."** **"The sound of the vowel is *short*."**
Recognizing and using short vowels in the middle of words [CVC]: *hat, bed*	**"Some words have one vowel between two consonants [*hat, bed*] and the sound of the vowel is *short*."**
Hearing and identifying long vowel sounds in words and the letters that represent them	**"In some words, *a* sounds like the *a* in *name* and *came*."** **"In some words, *e* sounds like the *e* in *eat* and *seat*."** **"In some words, *i* sounds like the *i* in *ice* and *kite*."** **"In some words, *o* sounds like the *o* in *go* and *boat*."** **"In some words, *u* sounds like the *u* in *use* and *cute*."**
Recognizing and using long vowel sounds in words	**"You can hear and say the vowel in words like *make, pail, day*."** **"You can hear and say the vowel in words like *eat, meat, see*."** **"You can hear and say the vowel in words like *I, ice, ride*."** **"You can hear and say the vowel in words like *go, grow, boat*."** **"You can hear and say the vowel in words like *use, cute, huge*."**
Recognizing and using vowels in words with silent e (CVCe): *make, take, home* A: *make, ate, take, came, same, base* [Exceptions: *are, dance*] E: *Pete, breeze* [Exception: *edge*] I: *bite, bike, five, ice, slime, shine* [Exceptions: *mince, fringe,* which have a CVCCe pattern] O: *rode, hole, joke* [Exceptions: *come, some, goose*] U: *use, cube, cute, fume* [Exceptions: *judge, nurse*]	**"Some words end in an *e* that is silent and the vowel usually has a long sound (sounds like its name)."**
Contrasting long and short vowel sounds in words	**"A vowel can have a sound like its name [*a* as in *make*] and it is called a long vowel sound."** **"A vowel can have a sound that is different from its name [*a* as in *apple*] and it is called a short vowel sound."**
	P-K · GRADE K (E M L) · GRADE 1 (E M L) · GRADE 2 (E M L) · GRADE 3 (E M L) · GRADE 4 (E M L) · GRADE 5 (E M L) · GRADES 6–8

Key: E = Early in school year, M = Mid-year, L = Late in school year

Letter/Sound Relationships, continued

Principle	Explanation of Principle
	P-K · GRADE K (E M L) · GRADE 1 (E M L) · GRADE 2 (E M L) · GRADE 3 (E M L) · GRADE 4 (E M L) · GRADE 5 (E M L) · GRADES 6–8
Vowels continued	
Recognizing and using *y* as a vowel sound: *happy, family, my, sky, monkey, key*	**"*Y* is a letter that sometimes makes a vowel sound."** **"*Y* sounds like /e/ on the end of words like *happy, funny, family, monkey, key*."** **"*Y* sounds like /i/ in words like *my, sky, by*."**
Recognizing and using letter combinations that represent long vowel sounds: *ai, ay, ee, ea, oa, oe, ow, ue, ui, ew: chair, play, meet, near, roar, toe, blow, blue, suit, new*	**"Some vowels go together in words and make one sound."** **"When there are two vowels [*ai, ay, ee, ea, oe, oa, ow, ui, ue, ew*], they usually make the sound of the name of the first vowel or a long vowel sound [*rain, day, feet, meat, toe, boat, snow, suit, new*]."**
Recognizing and using letter combinations that represent other vowel sounds: *oo* as in *moon, look; oi* as in *oil; oy* as in *boy; ou* as in *house; ow* as in *cow; aw* as in *paw; ay* as in *always; au* as in *autumn*	**"Some letters go together and make other vowel sounds [*autumn, moon, look, boy, oil, cow, house, paw*]."**
Recognizing that letter combinations may represent two different vowel sounds: *oo–moon, look; ow–snow, cow; ea–bear, meat, break*	**"Two letters that go together can stand for different sounds in different words [*moon, look, snow, cow, meat, break.*]"**
Recognizing and using vowel sounds in open syllables: [CV]: *ho-tel*	**"Some syllables have a consonant followed by a vowel."** **"The sound of the vowel is long [*ho-tel, Pe-ter, lo-cal*]."** **"The first or second syllable can be stressed."**
Recognizing and using vowel sounds in closed syllables: [CVC]: *lem-on*	**"Some syllables have one vowel that is between two consonants."** **"The sound of the vowel is short [*lem-on; cab-in*]."** **"The first syllable is stressed."**
Recognizing and using vowel sounds with *r: car, first, hurt, her, corn, floor, world, near*	**"When vowels are with *r* in words, you blend the vowel sound with *r* [*car, her, fir, corn, hurt, nerve, door, world, near*]."**
Letter/Sound Representations	
Learning about words with capital letters	**"You use capital letters at the beginning of some words to show the beginning of a sentence or to show a proper noun."**
Forming cursive letters correctly, efficiently, and fluently	**"You can write letters smoothly and efficiently in cursive form."**
Using the computer keyboard	**"You can use efficient finger movements to type words on the computer."**
	P-K · GRADE K (E M L) · GRADE 1 (E M L) · GRADE 2 (E M L) · GRADE 3 (E M L) · GRADE 4 (E M L) · GRADE 5 (E M L) · GRADES 6–8

Spelling Patterns

One way to look at spelling patterns is to examine the way simple words and syllables are put together. Here we include the consonant-vowel-consonant (CVC) pattern in which the vowel often has a short, or terse, sound; the consonant-vowel-consonant-silent *e* (CVC*e*) pattern in which the vowel usually has a long, or lax, sound; and the consonant-vowel-vowel-consonant (CVVC) pattern in which the vowel combination may have either one or two sounds.

Phonograms are spelling patterns that represent the sounds of *rimes* (last parts of words). They are sometimes called *word families*. You will not need to teach children the technical word *phonogram*, although you may want to use *pattern* or *word part*. A phonogram is the same as a rime, or vowel-bearing part of a word or syllable. We have included a large list of phonograms that will be useful to children in reading or writing, but you will not need to teach every phonogram separately. Once children understand that there are patterns and learn how to look for patterns, they will quickly discover more for themselves.

Knowing spelling patterns helps children notice and use larger parts of words, thus making word solving faster and more efficient. Patterns are also helpful to children in writing words because they will quickly write down the patterns rather than laboriously work with individual sounds and letters. Finally, knowing to look for patterns and remembering them help children make the connections between words that make word solving easier. In column one we list a wide range of phonograms. The thirty-seven most common phonograms are marked with an asterisk.

Spelling Patterns

Principle	Explanation of Principle P-K · GRADE K (E M L) · GRADE 1 (E M L) · GRADE 2 (E M L) · GRADE 3 (E M L) · GRADE 4 (E M L) · GRADE 5 (E M L) · GRADE 6–8
Phonogram Patterns	
Recognizing that words have letter patterns that are connected to sounds (phonograms are spelling patterns)	**"Some words have parts (patterns) that are the same."** **"You can find patterns (parts) that are the same in many words."**
Recognizing and using the consonant-vowel-consonant (CVC) pattern	**"Some words have a consonant, a vowel, and then another consonant. The vowel sounds like the *a* in *apple* [e in *egg*, *i* in *igloo*, o in *octopus*, *u* in *umbrella*]."**
Recognizing and using simple phonograms with a VC pattern (easiest): *-ad, -ag, -an*, -am, -at*, -ed, -en, -et, -ig, -in*, -it*, -og, -op*, -ot, -ut*	**"You can look at the pattern (part) you know to help you read a word."** **"You can use the pattern (part) you know to help you write a word."** **"You can make new words by putting a letter or letter cluster before the word part or pattern."**
Recognizing and using more difficult phonograms with a VC pattern: *-ab, -ap*, - ar, -aw*, -ay*, -ed, -eg, -em, -en, -ib, -ip*, -ix, -ob, -od, -ow* (*blow*), *-ow* (*cow*), *-ug*, -um, -un*	**"You can look at the pattern (part) you know to help you read a word."** **"You can use the pattern (part) you know to help you write a word."** **"You can make new words by putting a letter or letter cluster before the word part or pattern."**
Recognizing and using phonograms that end with double letters (VCC): *-all*, -ell*, -ill*, -oll, -uff*	**"Some words have double consonants at the end. The sound of the vowel is usually short."**

*Indicates most common phonograms

P-K · GRADE K (E M L) · GRADE 1 (E M L) · GRADE 2 (E M L) · GRADE 3 (E M L) · GRADE 4 (E M L) · GRADE 5 (E M L) · GRADES 6–8

Key: E = Early in school year, M = Mid-year, L = Late in school year

Spelling Patterns, continued

P-K | GRADE K (E M L) | GRADE 1 (E M L) | GRADE 2 (E M L) | GRADE 3 (E M L) | GRADE 4 (E M L) | GRADE 5 (E M L) | GRADES 6–8

Principle	Explanation of Principle
Phonogram Patterns continued	
Recognizing and using phonograms with double vowels (VVC): *-eed, -eek, -eel, -een, -eem, -eep, -eer, -eet, -ood, -ook, -ool, -oom, -oon*	**"Some words have double vowels followed by a consonant."** **"Sometimes vowels sound like their name (long sound)."** **"Sometimes vowels stand for other sounds."**
Recognizing and using phonograms with a vowel-consonant-silent e (VCe) pattern: *-ade, -ace, -age, -ake*, -ale*, -ame*, -ane, -ape, -ate*, -ice*, -ide*, -ike, -ile, -ime, -ine*, -ite, -ive, -obe, oke*, -ope, -ore*	**"Some words have a vowel, a consonant, and a silent *e*. The vowel sound is usually the name of the vowel [*a* in *make*, *e* in *Pete*, *i* in *ride*, *o* in *rode*, *u* in *cute*]."**
Recognizing and using phonograms with ending consonant clusters (VCC): *ack*, -act, -alk, -amp, -and, -ank*, -ant, -ard, -art, -ark, -arm, -ash*, -ask, -ath, -eck, -elt, -elp, -end, -ent, -esh, -est*, -ick*, -igh, -ift, -ing*, -ink*, -ish, -ock*, -old, -ong, -uck*, -ump*, -ung, -unk*, -ush*	**"Some words have patterns that end with consonant clusters [*mask, lump*]."**
Recognizing and using phonograms with vowel combinations (VVC): *-aid, -ail*, -ain*, -air, -ait, -ay*, -aw, -ea, -ead, -eak, -eam, -ean, -eap, -ear, -eat*, -oad, -oak*	**"Some words have two vowels together (vowel combinations). The vowel sound is usually the name of the first vowel [*stream, road*]."**
Sound to Letter Patterns in Single-Syllable Words	
Recognizing and using phonogram patterns with a short vowel sound in single-syllable words: *-at, -an, -am, -ad, -ag, -ap, -ack, -ed, -ell, -en, -et, -end, -ent, -est; -it, -in, -ill, -id, -ig, -ing, -ip, -ick, -ish, -op, -ot, -ock, -ug, -un, -ut, -up, -ub, -ump, -unk, -us(s), -ust, -uck*	**"Some words have a short vowel pattern. You can hear the short vowel sound [*man, best, pick, not, rust*]."**
Recognizing and using phonogram patterns with a long vowel sound in single-syllable words: *-ake, -ame, -ate, -ave, -ade, -ace, -age, -ale, -ain, -ane, -ay, -e, -ee, -ea, -ey, -eep, -een, -eet, -eal, -ead, -eam, -ew, -ie, -igh, -ight, -ike, -ide, -ime, -yme, -ine, -ice, -ile, -ite, -ire, -y, -o, -oe, -ow, -oat, -oad, -ole, -old, -oak, -ose, -one, -ule, -use, -uge, -ute*	**"Some words have a long vowel pattern. You can hear the long vowel sound [*make, green, pie, coat, few*]."**
Recognizing and using phonogram patterns with vowels and *r* in single-syllable words: *-ar, -ark, -air, -are, -arm, -art, -ear, -eart, -er, -ear, -erd, -earn, -eard, -ird, -ir, -or, -ore, -ord, -oor, -our, -orn, -ur, -urse, -urn*	**"Some words have a vowel pattern with one or two vowels and *r*."** **"When vowels are with *r* in words, you usually blend the sound with *r* [*nurse, third*]."**
Recognizing and using phonogram patterns with the */aw/* sound (as in *saw*) in single-syllable words: *-all, -aw, -alk, -aught, -ought, -ost, -ong*	**"Some words have patterns with vowels that make the /aw/ sound as in *saw*."** **"Several patterns of letters can stand for the sound [*wall, paw, taught, cost*]."**
Recognizing and using phonogram patterns with the */ū/* sound (as in *moon*) in single-syllable words: *-oo, -oon, -une, -ew, -ue, -oot, -uit, -ool, -ule, -oom, -oup*	**"Some words have patterns with vowels that make the /oo/ sound as in *moon*."** **"Several patterns of letters can stand for the long /u/ sound [*tune, suit, soup*]."**

P-K | GRADE K (E M L) | GRADE 1 (E M L) | GRADE 2 (E M L) | GRADE 3 (E M L) | GRADE 4 (E M L) | GRADE 5 (E M L) | GRADES 6–8

Spelling Patterns, continued

Principle	Explanation of Principle
Sound to Letter Patterns in Single-Syllable Words continued	
Recognizing and using phonogram patterns with the /oo/ sound (as in *book*) in single-syllable words: *-ook, -ood, -ould, -ull, ush*	**"Some words have patterns with vowels that make the /oo/ sound as in *book.*"** **"Several patterns of letters can stand for the sound [*book, could*]."**
Recognizing and using phonogram patterns with the /ow/ sound (as in *cow*) in single-syllable words: *-ow; -own; -ound; -ow, -owd; -out, -outh, -our, -ouse*	**"Some words have patterns with vowels that make the /ow/ sound as in *cow.*"** **"Several patterns of letters can stand for the sound [*clown, crowd, hour, mouth*]."**
Recognizing and using phonogram patterns with the /oy/ sound in single-syllable words: *-oy, -oil, -oin, -oice, -oise*	**"Some words have patterns with vowels that make the /oy/ sound as in *boy.*"** **"Several patterns of letters can stand for the sound [*coin, voice, noise*]."**
Recognizing and using more difficult phonogram patterns in single-syllable words (VVCC, VVCe, VCCe, VCCC, VVCCC): *-aint, -aise, -ance, -anch, -arge, -aste, -atch, -each, -ealth, -east, -eath, eave, -edge, -eech, -eeze, -ench, -ight*, -itch, -ooth, -ouch, -ound, -udge, -unch, -aight, -eight*	**"Some words have parts (patterns) that are the same."** **"You can find patterns (parts) that are the same in many words."** **"You can use the pattern you know to help you read (or write) a word."**
Sound to Letter Patterns in Multisyllable Words	
Understanding that some words have double consonants in the pattern: *coffee, address, success, accident, mattress, occasion*	**"Some words have double consonant letters in the patterns."**
Noticing and using a frequently appearing syllable pattern in multisyllable words: */a/ alone*	**"You see some patterns often in multisyllable words."** **"You see *a* at the beginning of some words and it sounds like the *a* in *alone.*"**
Noticing and using frequently appearing syllable patterns in multisyllable words: *-en – enter; o – ago; -er – other; -ar – partner; -at – batter; -it – bitten; -in – winter; -is(s) – whisper; -un – sunny; -be – begin; re – repeat; -or – border; -a – bacon; -y – candy; -ey – monkey; -ble – trouble; -i – pilot; -ur – burden; -um – humble; -ic(k) – chicken; -et – better; -im – simple*	**"You see some patterns often in multisyllable words."** **"You can look for the pattern you know to help you read a word."** **"You can think about the pattern you know to help you spell a word."**

P-K | GRADE K (E M L) | GRADE 1 (E M L) | GRADE 2 (E M L) | GRADE 3 (E M L) | GRADE 4 (E M L) | GRADE 5 (E M L) | GRADES 6–8

Key: E = Early in school year, M = Mid-year, L = Late in school year

Principle	Explanation of Principle
Sound to Letter Patterns in Multisyllable Words continued	
Noticing and using short vowel patterns that appear in multisyllable words (other than most frequent): *-ab – absent; -ad – address; -ag – magnet; -age – garbage; -ang – anger; -am – hammer; -an – handle; -ant – gigantic; -ap – happen; -ent – center; -el(l) – yellow; -ep – pepper; -es – estimate; -ev – seven; -id – middle; -ig – figure; -il(l) – familiar; -ob – hobby or robot; -oc(k) – October; -od – body; -ol – follow; -om – complete; -on – honest; -op – opportunity; -ot – bottom; -ub – rubber; -uc(k) – lucky; -ud – puddle; -uf – muffin; -ug – ugly; -up – puppy; -um – humble; -us – customer; -ut – butter; -uz – puzzle*	**"You see short vowel patterns in multisyllable words."** **"Looking for the pattern you know helps you read the word."** **"Thinking about the pattern you know helps you spell the word."**
Noticing and using long vowel patterns that appear in multisyllable words: *-e – beginning; -ee – agree; -ea – reason; -ide – decide; -ire – entirely; -ise – revise; -ive – survive; -ize – realize; -ade – lemonade; -aid – braided; -ail – railroad; -ale – female; -ain – painter; -ate – crater; -ope – antelope; -one – telephone; -oke – spoken; -u – tutor; -ture – future*	**"You can see long vowel patterns in multisyllable words."** **"Looking for the pattern you know helps you read and spell the word."**
Noticing and using other vowel patterns that appear in multisyllable words (easier): *-al – always; -au – author; -aw – awfully; -ea – weather; -i – sillier*	**"You can see many vowel patterns in multisyllable words."** **"Looking for the pattern you know helps you read and spell the word."**
Noticing and using other vowel patterns that appear in multisyllable words (harder): *-i-e – police; -tion – attention; -sion – tension; -y – reply; -oi – noisy; -oy – enjoy; -ou – about; -ow – power; -oo – booster; -ove – remove; -u – tuna; -ook – looking; -oot – football; -ood – woodpile; -ul(l) – grateful*	**"You can see many vowel patterns in multisyllable words."** **"Looking for the pattern you know helps you read and spell the word."**

P-K | GRADE K E M L | GRADE 1 E M L | GRADE 2 E M L | GRADE 3 E M L | GRADE 4 E M L | GRADE 5 E M L | GRADES 6–8

High-Frequency Words

A core of known high-frequency words is a valuable resource as students build processing strategies for reading and writing. Young children notice words that appear frequently in the simple texts they read; eventually, their recognition of these words becomes automatic. In this way, their reading becomes more efficient, enabling them to decode words using phonics as well as the meaning in the text. These words are powerful examples that help them grasp that a word is always written the same way. They can use known high-frequency words to check on the accuracy of their reading and as resources for solving other words (for example, *this* starts like *the*). In general, students learn the simpler words earlier and in the process develop efficient systems for learning words. They continuously add to the core of high-frequency words they know as they move to late primary and early intermediate grades. Lessons on high-frequency words help them look more carefully at words and develop more efficient systems for word recognition.

High-Frequency Words

P-K | GRADE K (E M L) | GRADE 1 (E M L) | GRADE 2 (E M L) | GRADE 3 (E M L) | GRADE 4 (E M L) | GRADE 5 (E M L) | GRADE 6–8

Principle	Explanation of Principle
Recognizing and using high-frequency words with one or two letters	**"You see some words many times when you read: *I, is, in, at, my, we, to, me, am, an.*"**
	"Some have only one letter: *I* and *a*."
	"Some have two letters: *am, an, as, at, be, by, do, go, he, in, is, it, me, my, of, on, or, so, to, up, us, we.*"
	"Words you see a lot are important because they help you read and write."
Locating and reading high-frequency words in continuous text	**"When you know a word, you can read it every time you see it."**
	"You can find a word by knowing how it looks."
Recognizing and using high-frequency words with three or more letters	**"You see some words many times when you read."**
	"Some have three or more letters [*the, and, but, she, like, come, this*]."
	"Words you see a lot are important because they help you read and write."
Recognizing and using high-frequency words with five or more letters	**"You see some words many times when you read."**
	"Some have five or more letters [*would, could, where, there, which*]."
	"Words you see a lot are important because they help you read and write."
Noticing patterns and categorizing high-frequency words to assist in learning them quickly	**"You can notice patterns in high-frequency words."**
	"You can make connections among high-frequency words to help you learn them."
Developing self-monitoring strategies for acquiring a large core of high-frequency words	**"You can add to the number of high-frequency words you can write."**
	"You can write high-frequency words quickly."
	"You can check to see how many words you know."

P-K | GRADE K (E M L) | GRADE 1 (E M L) | GRADE 2 (E M L) | GRADE 3 (E M L) | GRADE 4 (E M L) | GRADE 5 (E M L) | GRADES 6–8

Key: E = Early in school year, M = Mid-year, L = Late in school year

Word Meaning/Vocabulary

Students need to know the meaning of the words they are learning to read and write. It is important for them constantly to expand their vocabularies as well as to develop a more complex understanding of words they already know. And they need to have multiple encounters with those words. Word meaning is related to the development of vocabulary—labels, concept words, synonyms, antonyms, and homonyms. The meaning of a word often varies with the specific context and can be related to its spelling.

Accuracy in spelling often requires knowing the meaning of the word you want to write. Comprehension and accurate pronunciation are also related to knowing word meanings. In this section, we include synonyms, antonyms, and homonyms, which may be homographs (same spelling, different meaning and sometimes different pronunciation) or homophones (same sound, different spelling). Knowing synonyms and antonyms will help students build more powerful systems for connecting and categorizing words; it will also help them comprehend texts better and write in a more interesting way. Though students may understand the category, words in the category can be simple or complex. Being able to distinguish between homographs and homophones assists in comprehension and helps spellers to avoid mistakes. We also include work with categorization of words and their relationships as well as figurative language. We introduce basic dictionary skills.

Word Meaning/Vocabulary

Principle	Explanation of Principle P-K · GRADE K (E M L) · GRADE 1 (E M L) · GRADE 2 (E M L) · GRADE 3 (E M L) · GRADE 4 (E M L) · GRADE 5 (E M L) · GRADE 6–8
Concept Words	
Recognizing and learning concept words: color names, number words, days of the week, months of the year, seasons	**"A color (number, day, month) has a name."** **"Days of the week have names and are always in the same order."** **"Months of the year have names and are always in the same order."** **"You can read and write the names of colors (numbers, days, months)."** **"You can find the names of colors (numbers, days, months)."**
Recognizing and using concept words that imply sets and subsets: *countries-states-counties-cities and towns; fruit-apples, pears; liquids-water, milk; president, vice-president*	**"Some words represent big ideas or items. You can find words that represent smaller ideas or items related to the big ideas."**
Related Words	
Recognizing and using words that are related in many ways: sound, spelling, meaning	**"Some words go together because of how they sound: *sleep/slip; sore/soar.*"** **"Some words go together because of how they look: *read/read.*"** **"Some words go together because of what they mean: family (*mother-father; sister-brother*); clothing; animals; food; swim, swimmer; hot, cold."**
Recognizing and using synonyms (words that mean about the same)	**"Some words mean about the same and are called synonyms: *begin/start, close/shut, fix/mend, earth/world, happy/glad, high/tall, jump/leap, keep/save, large/big.*"**
Recognizing and using antonyms (words that mean the opposite)	**"Some words mean about the opposite and are called antonyms: *hot/cold, all/none, break/fix, little/big, long/short, sad/glad, stop/start.*"**
	P-K · GRADE K (E M L) · GRADE 1 (E M L) · GRADE 2 (E M L) · GRADE 3 (E M L) · GRADE 4 (E M L) · GRADE 5 (E M L) · GRADES 6–8

Word Meaning/Vocabulary, continued

Principle	Explanation of Principle (P-K, GRADE K, GRADE 1, GRADE 2, GRADE 3, GRADE 4, GRADE 5, GRADES 6–8; E M L)
Related Words continued	
Recognizing and using homophones (same sound, different spelling and meaning) (It is not necessary to teach children the technical term *homophone*.)	**"Some words sound the same but look different and have different meanings: *to/too/two; there/their/they're; hare/hair; blue/blew.*"**
Related Words and Word Functions	
Recognizing and using homographs (same spelling, different meaning and they may have different pronunciation–heteronym) (It is not necessary to teach children the technical terms *homograph* or *heteronym*.)	**"Some words look the same, have a different meaning, and may sound different: *bat/bat, well/well; read/read; wind/wind.*"**
Recognizing and using words with the multiple meanings (a form of homograph): *can, beat*	**"Some words are spelled the same but have more than one meaning."**
Recognizing nouns (words that represent a person, place, or thing)	**"Some words stand for a person, a place, or a thing. They are called *nouns.*"**
Recognizing and using action words (verbs)	**"Some words tell what a person, object, or animal does. They are called *action words* or *verbs.*"**
Recognizing adjectives (words that describe)	**"Some words describe a person, place, or thing. They are called *adjectives.*"**
Combined and Created Words	
Recognizing and using simple compound words: *into, something*	**"Some words are made up of two words that are combined. They are *compound* words."**
Recognizing and using compound words with frequently used components: *where, thing, one, every, air,* family names (*grandmother*), *home, walk, some, sun, when, under, body, head, cycle*	**"You see some words in many compound words."**
Recognizing and using hyphenated compound words: *jack-in-the-box*	**"Some compound words are joined by a hyphen."**
Recognizing and using words that are blended together (portmanteau words): *brunch, horrific, smog, clash, smash, squiggle, o'clock, skylab*	**"Some words are made by blending together two words. The meaning of the blended word is related to both parts."**
Recognizing and using words that are made by combining initials: *NATO, UNICEF*	**"You can take the first letter from each word in a group of words and put them together to make an *acronym.*"**
Recognizing palindromes (words that can be spelled frontward or in reverse) as interesting aspects of language: *mom, noon, radar, madam, Hannah, did, pop*	**"Some words can be spelled the same frontward or backward."**
Poetic Uses of Words	
Recognizing and using words that are "mixed up" for humorous effect: *spoonerisms* like *dop tog* for *top dog*	**"You can mix of the starting letters of words to make up *spoonerisms.*"**
Recognizing and using onomatopoetic words: *crash, slush, bang, zoom, whir*	**"Some words mimic the sounds they represent. You often see these words in books and poetry."**
Recognizing and using words as metaphors and similes to make a comparison: *light as air, dogged, stormed out*	**"You can use words to compare things to make your writing more interesting."**

E M L E M L E M L E M L E M L E M L
P-K GRADE K GRADE 1 GRADE 2 GRADE 3 GRADE 4 GRADE 5 GRADES 6–8

Key: E = Early in school year, M = Mid-year, L = Late in school year

Word Meaning/Vocabulary, continued

Principle	Explanation of Principle
Poetic Uses of Words continued	
Recognizing and using idioms or expressions (metaphors that have become traditional sayings and the comparisons are not evident): *raining cats and dogs, sweating bullets*	**"Some phrases have a meaning that is different from the words because of tradition."**
Word Origins	
Making connections to understand words	**"You can make connections to help you to understand a word better."**
Understanding that English words come from many different sources: other languages, technology, place names	**"Over many years, English words have been added from many different sources."**
Understanding that some English words come from names: *hamburger, sandwich*	**"Some English words come from the name of a person or a place."**
Understanding that many English words come from other languages	**"Many English words come from other languages."**
Understanding the concept of Greek and Latin "roots" and their use in learning to pronounce and think about the meaning of a word	**"A *root* is a word part from another language that can be found in English words."** **"A root can help you pronounce the word and understand its meaning. You can notice the way a word is used to help you think about what it means or how it is pronounced."**
Understanding that many English words and word parts have Latin roots: *and, bene, cap, ce, cide, cor, cred, dic, duce, equa, fac, fer, form, grac, grad, hab, ject, lit, loc, man, mem, miss, mob, mimr, ped, pens, port, pos, prim, quer, scub, setn, sist, spec, train, tract, val, ven vens, vid, voc*	**"Many English words come from Latin. They have Latin 'roots.'"**
Many English words and word parts have Greek roots: *aer, arch, aster, bio, centr, chron, eyel, dem, derm, geo, gram, graph, dydr, ology, meter, micro, phon, photo, phys, pol, scope, sphere, tel*	**"Many English words come from Greek. They have Greek 'roots.'"**

P-K | GRADE K E M L | GRADE 1 E M L | GRADE 2 E M L | GRADE 3 E M L | GRADE 4 E M L | GRADE 5 E M L | GRADES 6–8

Word Structure

Looking at the structure of words will help students learn how words are related to each other and how they can be changed by adding letters, letter clusters, and larger word parts. Being able to recognize syllables, for example, helps readers and writers break down words into smaller units that are easier to analyze.

Words often have affixes, parts added before or after a word to change its meaning. An affix can be a prefix or a suffix. The word to which affixes are added can be a *base* word or a *root* word. A base word is a complete word; a root word is a part that may have Greek or Latin origins (such as *phon* in *telephone*). It will not be necessary for young children to make this distinction when they are beginning to learn about simple affixes, but working with suffixes and prefixes will help children read and understand words that use them as well as use affixes accurately in writing.

Endings or word parts that are added to base words signal meaning. For example, they may signal relationships (*prettier, prettiest*) or time (*running, planted*). Principles related to word structure include understanding the meaning and structure of compound words, contractions, plurals, and possessives as well as knowing how to make and use them accurately. We have also included the simple abbreviations that students often see in the books they read and want to use in their writing.

Word Structure

Principle	Explanation of Principle
Syllables	
Understanding the concept of syllable	**"A syllable is a word part you can hear."**
Hearing and identifying syllables	**"You can hear the syllables in words."**
	"You can look at the syllables to read a word."
Recognizing and using one or two syllables in words	**"You can look at the syllables in a word to read it [*horse, a-way, farm-er, morn-ing*]."**
Understanding how vowels appear in syllables	**"Every syllable of a word has a vowel."**
Recognizing and using syllables in words with double consonants	**"Divide the syllables between the consonants when a word has two similar consonants in the middle [*run-ning, bet-ter*]."**
Recognizing and using syllables ending in a vowel (open syllable)	**"When a syllable ends with a vowel, the vowel is usually long [*ho-tel*]."**
Recognizing and using syllables ending in a vowel and at least one consonant (closed syllable)	**"When a syllable ends with a vowel and at least one consonant, the vowel sound is usually short [*lem-on*]."**
Recognizing and using syllables with a vowel and a silent *e*	**"When a vowel and a silent *e* are in a word, the pattern makes one syllable with a long vowel sound [*hope-ful*]."**
Recognizing and using syllables with vowel combinations	**"When vowel combinations are in words, they usually go together in the same syllable [*poi-son, cray-on*]."**
Recognizing and using syllables with vowel and *r*	**"When a vowel is followed by an *r*, the *r* and the vowel form a syllable [*cor-ner, cir-cus*]."**

Grade scale: P-K | GRADE K (E M L) | GRADE 1 (E M L) | GRADE 2 (E M L) | GRADE 3 (E M L) | GRADE 4 (E M L) | GRADE 5 (E M L) | GRADES 6–8

Key: E = Early in school year, M = Mid-year, L = Late in school year

Word Structure, continued

Principle	Explanation of Principle
	P-K · GRADE K (E M L) · GRADE 1 (E M L) · GRADE 2 (E M L) · GRADE 3 (E M L) · GRADE 4 (E M L) · GRADE 5 (E M L) · GRADES 6–8
Syllables continued	
Recognizing and using syllables in words with the the VCC pattern (syllable juncture)	**"Divide the word after the first consonant in a consonant blend that joins two syllables in a word [*plas-tic*]."** **"Divide the word after the consonant digraph that joins two syllables in a word [*wish-ful*]."**
Recognizing and using syllables with consonant and *le*	**"When a consonant and *le* appear at the end of a word, the consonant and *le* form the final syllable [*ta-ble, ket-tle*]."**
Recognizing and using three or more syllables in words	**"You can look at the syllables in a word to read it [*bi-cy-cle, to-geth-er, ev-er-y, won-der-ful, li-brar-y, com-put-er, au-to-mo-bile, a-quar-i-um, un-der-wat-er*]."**
Recognizing and using syllables in words with the VV pattern: *ri-ot; di-et.*	**"Divide the word after the long vowel sound in words with two vowels that each contribute a sound."**
Compound Words	
Recognizing and understanding simple compound words: *into, itself, myself, cannot, inside, maybe, nobody, outside, sunshine, today, together, upset, yourself, without, sometimes, something*	**"Some words are made of two whole words and are called compound words."**
Noticing words as patterns that appear frequently in compound words: *some, thing, side, every, any, one, under, ever, where*	**"You see some words often in compound words."** **"You can make connections among compound words that have the same word parts."**
Recognizing and understanding more complex compound words: *airplane, airport, another, anyone, homesick, indoor, jellyfish, skyscraper, toothbrush*	**"The word parts in compound words often help you think about the meaning."**
Contractions	
Understanding the concept of contractions	**"A contraction is one word made from two words [*can* + *not* = *can't*]. A letter or letters are left out and an apostrophe is put in."** **"A contraction is a short form of the two words."**
Recognizing and understanding contractions with am: *I'm*	**"To make a contraction, put two words together and leave out a letter or letters. Write an apostrophe where letter(s) are left out. Here is a contraction made with *I* + *am: I'm*."**
Recognizing and understanding contractions with is: *here's, he's, it's, she's, that's, there's, what's, where's, who's*	**"To make a contraction, put two words together and leave out a letter or letters. Write an apostrophe where the letter(s) are left out."** **"Many contractions are made with *is: here* + *is* = *here's*."**
Recognizing and understanding contractions using *has: he's, it's, she's, that's, there's, what's, where's, who's*	**"To make a contraction, put two words together and leave out a letter or letters. Write an apostrophe where the letter(s) are left out."** **"Many contractions are made with *is* and/or *has: he* + *is* = *he's [He's going to the zoo.]; he* + *has* = *he's [He's finished his work.]*"**
Recognizing and understanding contractions using *will: I'll, it'll, he'll, she'll, that'll, they'll, we'll, you'll*	**"To make a contraction, put two words together and leave out a letter or letters. Write an apostrophe where the letter(s) are left out."** **"Many contractions are made with *will: I* + *will* = *I'll*."**
Recognizing and understanding contractions using *are: they're, we're, you're*	**"To make a contraction, put two words together and leave out a letter or letters. Write an apostrophe where the letter(s) are left out."** **"Many contractions are made with *are: they* + *are* = *they're*."**
	P-K · GRADE K (E M L) · GRADE 1 (E M L) · GRADE 2 (E M L) · GRADE 3 (E M L) · GRADE 4 (E M L) · GRADE 5 (E M L) · GRADES 6–8

Word Structure, continued

Principle	Explanation of Principle
Contractions continued	
Recognizing and understanding contractions using *not: aren't, can't, couldn't, didn't, doesn't, don't, hadn't, hasn't, haven't, isn't, mustn't, needn't, shouldn't, wouldn't*	**"To make a contraction, put two words together and leave out a letter. Write an apostrophe where the letter(s) are left out."** **"Many contractions are made with *not: can* + *not* = *can't.*"**
Recognizing and understanding contractions using *have: could've, I've, might've, should've, they've, we've, would've, you've*	**"To make a contraction, put two words together and leave out a letter or letters. Write an apostrophe where the letter(s) are left out."** **"Many contractions are made with *have: should* + *have* = *should've.*"**
Recognizing and understanding contractions using *us: let's*	**"To make a contraction, put two words together and leave out a letter or letter(s). Write an apostrophe where the letters are left out."** **"Many contractions are made with *us: let* + *us* = *let's* [*Let's go.*]"**
Recognizing and understanding contractions using *would* or *had: I'd, it'd, she'd, there'd, they'd, we'd, you'd*	**"To make a contraction, put two words together and leave out a letter or letters. Write an apostrophe where the letter(s) are left out."** **"Many contractions are made with *would* or *had: she* + *would* =*she'd; they* + *would* = *they'd.*"**
Recognizing and understanding multiple contractions using *not* and *have: shouldn't've; mustn't've; wouldn't've*	**"Some contractions put together three words and leave out letters."** **"You write an apostrophe every time a letter is left out."** **"These contractions are usually made with *not* and *have.*"**
Plurals	
Understanding the concept of plural	**"Plural means more than one."**
Recognizing and using plurals that add s: *dogs, cats, apples, cans, desks, faces, trees, monkeys*	**"Add *s* to some words to make them plural."** **"You can hear the *s* at the end."**
Recognizing and using plurals that add *es* when words end with *x, ch, sh, s, ss, tch, zz: buzzes, branches, buses, boxes, dishes, foxes, kisses, patches, peaches*	**"Add *es* to words that end with *x, ch, sh, s, ss, tch, zz* to make them plural."** **"The *s* at the end sounds like /z/."**
Recognizing and using plurals that add *s* to words that end in vowel and *y: boys, days, keys, plays, says, valleys*	**"Add *s* to words that end in a vowel and *y* to make them plural."**
Recognizing and using plurals that add *es* to words that end in consonant and *y: babies, candies, cities, countries, flies, families, ladies, ponies, skies, stories*	**"Change the *y* to *i* and add *es* to words that end in consonant and *y* to make them plural."**
Recognizing and using plurals that change *f* to *v* and add *es* for words that end with *f, fe, lf: wolves, hooves, lives, scarves, selves, shelves, wives*	**"Change *f* to *v* and add *es* to words that end with *f, fe, or lf* to make them plural."**
Recognizing and using plurals for words that end in a vowel and *o* by adding *s: radios, rodeos, kangaroos*	**"Add *s* to words that end in a vowel and *o* to make them plural."**
Recognizing and using plurals for words that end in a consonant and *o* by adding *es: zeroes, heroes, potatoes, volcanoes*	**"Add *es* to words that end in a consonant and *o* to make them plural."**

P-K | GRADE K (E M L) | GRADE 1 (E M L) | GRADE 2 (E M L) | GRADE 3 (E M L) | GRADE 4 (E M L) | GRADE 5 (E M L) | GRADES 6–8

Key: E = Early in school year, M = Mid-year, L = Late in school year

Word Structure, continued

Principle	Explanation of Principle
	P-K · GRADE K (E M L) · GRADE 1 (E M L) · GRADE 2 (E M L) · GRADE 3 (E M L) · GRADE 4 (E M L) · GRADE 5 (E M L) · GRADES 6–8
Plurals continued	
Recognizing and using plurals that change the spelling of the word: *child/children, foot/feet, goose/geese, man/men, mouse/mice, ox/oxen, woman/women*	**"Change the spelling of some words to make them plural."**
Recognizing and using plurals that are the same word for singular and plural: *deer, lamb, sheep, moose, salmon*	**"Some words are spelled the same in both the singular and plural forms."**
Recognizing and using plurals that are formed by changing some of the letters of the base word or by adding an unusual suffix: one *ox* – herd of *oxen;* a *medium* – different *media; tooth – teeth; goose – geese*	**"You form some plurals by changing some of the letters of the base word or by adding an unusual suffix."**
Suffixes	
Understanding the concept of a suffix	**"A suffix is a word part that is added at the end of a word to change its meaning or function in a sentence."**
Understanding that adding a suffix to a word may change the spelling	**"Sometimes when you add a suffix to the word, you add or drop letters."**
Understanding that the final *e* is usually dropped when adding suffixes that begin with a vowel or when adding *y* to words: *raced, racing, noisy*	**"Drop the *e* before adding a suffix that begins with a vowel when *y* is added."**
Understanding that the final *e* is kept when adding suffixes that begin with a consonant to words: *rarely, careful, careless, likeness, wholesome*	**"Keep the final *e* when adding a suffix that begins with a consonant."**
Understanding that the *y* is changed to *i* when adding a suffix that begins with a consonant: *happily*	**"Change the *y* to *i* before adding a suffix that begins with a consonant."**
Understanding that when the word part before the suffix ends in *ns,* you add the suffix *-ible: sensible, responsible*	**"Add the suffix *-ible* when the part before the suffix ends in *–ns.*"**
Understanding that the final *e* is kept when adding the suffix *-able* to words ending in *-ce* or *-ge* ("soft" sound of *c* or *g*): *manageable, traceable*	**"Do not drop the final *e* when adding *-able* to words ending in the soft sound of *c* or *g.*"**
Understanding that *-able* is added to base words and *-ible* is added to root words: *washable, credible*	**"Add *-able* to a base word. Add *-ible* to a root word."**
Suffixes [Verb Endings]	
Recognizing and using endings that add *s* to a verb to make it agree with the subject: *skate/skates; run/runs*	**"Add *s* to the end of a word to make it sound right in a sentence."** **"She can run."** **"She runs."** **"She can skate."** **"She skates."**
	P-K · GRADE K (E M L) · GRADE 1 (E M L) · GRADE 2 (E M L) · GRADE 3 (E M L) · GRADE 4 (E M L) · GRADE 5 (E M L) · GRADES 6–8

Principle	Explanation of Principle
Suffixes [Verb Endings] continued	
Recognizing and using endings that add *ing* to denote the present participle: *play/playing; send/sending*	**"Add *ing* to a word to show you are doing something now."** **"I can *read.*"** **"I am *reading.*"** **"She can *jump.*"** **"She is *jumping.*"**
Recognizing and using endings that add *ed* to a verb to make it past tense: *walk/walked; play/played; want/wanted*	**"Add *ed* to the end of a word to show that you did something in the past."** **"I can *play* a game today."** **"I *played* a game yesterday."** **"I *want* to play."** **"I *wanted* to play."**
Recognizing and using endings that add *d* to a verb ending in silent *e* to make it past tense: *like/liked*	**"Add *d* to words ending in silent *e* to make the *ed* ending and show it was in the past."** **"I *like* vanilla ice cream."** **"I *liked* vanilla ice cream but I don't anymore."**
Recognizing and using endings that add *ing* to words that end in *y* to denote the present participle: *carry/carrying; marry/marrying*	**"Add *ing* to words that end in *y.*"** **"I can *carry* the flag."** **"I am *carrying* the flag."**
Recognizing and using endings that add *-ing* to words of one syllable ending in *y: lying, crying, dying, flying, trying*	**"Add *-ing* to one-syllable words that end in *y.*"** **"I *cry.*"** **"I am *crying.*"**
Recognizing and using endings that add *ing* to words that end in a single vowel and consonant to denote the present participle: *run/running, bat/batting, sit/sitting*	**"Double the consonant and add *ing* to words ending in a single vowel and consonant."** **"I can *run.*"** **"I am *running.*"**
Recognizing and using endings that add *ing* to a word ending in silent *e* to denote the present participle: *come/coming; write/writing; bite/biting*	**"Drop the e and add *ing* to most words that end with silent *e.*** **"Will she *come?*"** **"She is *coming.*"** **"I can *write.*"** **"I am *writing.*"**
Recognizing that *ed* added to a word to make it past tense can sound several different ways	**"When you add *ed* to a word, sometimes it sounds like /d/: *grabbed, played, yelled.*"** **"Sometimes you change the *y* to *i* and add *ed* and the ending sounds like /d/: *cried, fried, carried.*"** **"When you add *ed* to a word, sometimes it sounds like /ed/ (short *e* plus the /d/ sound): *added, landed, melted.*"** **"When you add *ed* to a word, it may sound like /t/: *dressed, liked, talked, laughed, walked.*"**

P-K | GRADE K (E M L) | GRADE 1 (E M L) | GRADE 2 (E M L) | GRADE 3 (E M L) | GRADE 4 (E M L) | GRADE 5 (E M L) | GRADES 6–8

Key: E = Early in school year, M = Mid-year, L = Late in school year

Word Structure, continued

Principle	Explanation of Principle (P-K, Grade K–Grades 6–8: E M L)
Suffixes [Verb Endings] continued	
Recognizing and using endings that that add *es* or *ed* to verbs ending in a consonant and *y* to form the present or past tense: *cry/cries/cried; try/tries/tried*	**"You can add word parts to the end of a word to show when you did something in the present or in the past."** **"Change the *y* to *i* and add *es* or *ed* to words that end in a consonant and *y*."** **"I can *try* to run fast."** **"He *tries* to run fast."** **"We *tried* to run fast in the race yesterday."**
Recognizing and using endings that add *ed* to verbs ending in a single short vowel and consonant or a vowel and double consonant to make it past tense: *grab/grabbed; grill/grilled; yell/yelled*	**"You add word parts to the endings of words to show when you did something in the past."** **"Double the consonant before adding *ed* to words ending in a short vowel and one consonant."** **"*Grab* the end of the rope."** **"She *grabbed* the end of the rope."** **"Add *ed* if the word ends with a vowel and a double consonant."** **"She can *yell* loud."** **"She *yelled*, 'Run!'"** **"Mom can *grill* the hot dogs."** **"Mom *grilled* the hot dogs."**
Recognizing and using endings add *-er* to a verb to make it a noun: *read/reader; play/player; jump/jumper*	**"Add *-er* to a word to tell about a person who can do something."** **"John can read."** **"John is a reader."**
Recognizing and using endings that add *-er* to a verb that ends with a short vowel and a consonant: *dig/digger; run/runner*	**"Double the consonant and add *-er* when words end in a short vowel and a consonant."** **"Sarah can run."** **"Sarah is a runner."**
Recognizing and using endings that add *r* to a verb that ends in silent *e: bake/baker; hike/hiker*	**"Add *r* to words that end in silent *e* to make the *-er* ending."** **"I like to hike."** **"I am a hiker."**
Recognizing and using endings that add *-er* to a verb that ends in *y: carry/carrier*	**"Change the *y* to *i* and add *-er* to words that end in *y*."** **"He can *carry* the mail."** **"He is a mail *carrier*."**
Recognizing and using words that change spelling to show past tense: *write/wrote; catch/caught; teach/taught*	**"You can change the spelling of some words to show something happened in the past."**
Recognizing and using endings that add *-ing* to a word that ends in *-oe: hoe/hoeing*	**"Add *ing* to a word that ends in *oe*."**

P-K | GRADE K (E M L) | GRADE 1 (E M L) | GRADE 2 (E M L) | GRADE 3 (E M L) | GRADE 4 (E M L) | GRADE 5 (E M L) | GRADES 6–8

Word Structure, continued

Principle	Explanation of Principle
	P-K · GRADE K (E M L) · GRADE 1 (E M L) · GRADE 2 (E M L) · GRADE 3 (E M L) · GRADE 4 (E M L) · GRADE 5 (E M L) · GRADES 6–8
Suffixes [Verb Endings] continued	
Recognizing and using endings that add an ending that begins with a vowel to a word that ends in *c*: *picnic–picnicking; traffic–trafficking*	**"When you are adding an ending that starts with a vowel to a word that ends in *c*, put a *k* after the *c*."**
Suffixes [Adjectives]	
Recognizing and using endings that show comparison (*-er, -est*): *cold/colder; hard/harder; dark/darker; fast/faster; tall/taller; rich/richest; thin/thinner/thinnest*	**"Add *-er* or *-est* to show how one thing compares with another."** **"John can run *fast* but Monica can run *faster*."** **"Carrie is the *fastest* runner in the class."**
Recognizing and using endings that show comparison for words ending in *e*: *pale/paler/palest; ripe/riper/ripest, cute/cuter/cutest*	**"Add *r* or *st* to words that end in silent e to make the *-er* or *-est* ending."** **"Jolisa has a *cute* puppy."** **"Matthew has a *cuter* puppy."** **"Jaqual has the *cutest* puppy."**
Recognizing and using endings that show comparison for words ending in a short vowel and a consonant: *red, redder, reddest*	**"Double the consonant and add *-er* or *-est* to words that end in a short vowel and one consonant."** **"The red box is *big*."** **"The blue box is *bigger*."** **"The green box is *biggest*."**
Recognizing and using endings that show comparison for words ending in *y*: *scary/scarier/scariest; funny/funnier/funniest*	**"Change *y* to *i* and add *-er* or *-est* to words that end in *y*."** **"Ciera told a *funny* story."** **"Kyle's story was *funnier* than Ciera's."** **"Amanda told the *funniest* story of all."**
Recognizing and using endings for adjectives that add *-ible* (added to partial words) and *-able* (added to whole words): *acceptable, doable, breakable, dependable; horrible, visible.* [Exceptions: *portable, capable, distractible, incomprehensible*]	**"Add *-ible* to partial words or root words."** **"Add *-able* to whole words or base words."** **"This is a *horrible* situation."** **"He is a *dependable* friend."**
Understanding that when you add *-able* to a verb you may change the spelling: *apply–applicable; vary–variable*	**"When you add *-able* to a verb, change the spelling."**
Understanding that when you add *-able* to base words ending in *e*, you delete the *e* before adding the suffix: *love–lovable*	**"Delete the final e before adding the suffix *-able* to base words ending in e."**
Understanding that when a base word ends in *y*, you change the *y* to *i* before adding the suffix *-able*: *rely–reliable*	**"Change the *y* to *i* before adding the suffix *-able* to a base word ending in *y*."**
Recognizing and using word endings that add *-ful* (meaning "full of" or "like"): *grateful, graceful, peaceful, handful*	**"Add *-ful* to words to show they are 'full of something.'"**
	P-K · GRADE K (E M L) · GRADE 1 (E M L) · GRADE 2 (E M L) · GRADE 3 (E M L) · GRADE 4 (E M L) · GRADE 5 (E M L) · GRADES 6–8

Key: E = Early in school year, M = Mid-year, L = Late in school year

Word Structure, continued

Principle	Explanation of Principle
Suffixes [Adjectives] continued	
Recognizing and using word endings that add *less* (meaning without) and *ness* (meaning condition): add the ending to most words: *sleepless, tireless, joyless; kindness.* Change *y* to *i* and add the ending for words that end in vowel + *y: penniless; happiness*	**"Add *-less* or *-ness* to words to mean a condition. If the word ends in a vowel and *y* change the *y* to *i* before adding *-less* or *-ness.*"**
Recognizing and using adjectives that are formed by adding *-ous, -cious,* or *-tious* (full of; characterized by): *joyous, beautious, capatious, spacious, cautious, rambunctious, gracious*	**"Add *-ous* , *-cious,* or *-tious* to words (adjectives) to show they are full of or characterized by something."**
Recognizing and using nouns that are formed by adding *-ic, -al, -ian, -ial, -cial* (like, of the nature of, suitable for): *stoic, hectic, volcanic; hysterical, theatrical; reptilian, artificial*	**"Add *-ic, -al, -ian, -ial,* or *-cial* to words (nouns) to show they are like, suitable for, or of the nature of something."**
Suffixes [Adverbs]	
Understanding the concept that an adjective (describing word) can become an adverb to tell how something is done: *happy–happily*	**"You can change a describing word to a word that tells how something is done."**
Recognizing and using adverbs that add *-ly* (meaning *like*) to a base word: *sadly, really, carefully, quickly*	**"To show how something is done, you can add *-ly* to words."** **"Words like *quickly* are called adverbs."**
Understanding that for most words, you add *-ly* or *-ally* to change an adjective to an adverb: *beautiful–beautifully, automatic–automatically*	**"Add *-ly* or *-ally* to change a describing word to a word that tells how."**
Recognizing and using adverbs that end in *y* and change *y* to *i* and add *-ly: happy–happily, noisy–noisily*	**"For words that in *y* change the *y* to *i* and add *-ly* to make an adverb."**
Recognizing and using adverbs that end in *ic* and add *al* before adding *-ly: tragic–tragically; magic–magically; automatic–automatically; frantic–frantically*	**"For words that end in *-ic,* add *-al* before adding *-ly* to make an adverb."**
Recognizing and using adverbs that end in *e* and either keep the *e* (*sincerely, merely, extremely*) or drop the *e* (*truly, duly*)	**"Keep the *e* before adding *-ly* for some words that end in *e.*"** **"Drop the *e* before adding *-ly* for some words that end in *e.*"**
Suffixes [Nouns]	
Recognizing and using nouns that are formed by adding *-teen,* used to form the suffixes for the cardinal numbers (13 to 19)	**"Add *-teen* to the number word to show ten plus the number."**
Recognizing and using nouns that are formed by adding *-er* to a verb to indicate "one who" does something: *fighter*	**"You can add *-er* to a verb to show someone who does something."**

P-K GRADE K GRADE 1 GRADE 2 GRADE 3 GRADE 4 GRADE 5 GRADES 6–8

Word Structure, continued

Principle	Explanation of Principle
	P-K · GRADE K (E M L) · GRADE 1 (E M L) · GRADE 2 (E M L) · GRADE 3 (E M L) · GRADE 4 (E M L) · GRADE 5 (E M L) · GRADES 6–8
Suffixes [Nouns] continued	
Understanding that you add *-ar* or *-or* to some verbs to indicate "one who does something": *actor, elevator*	**"Add *-ar* or *-or* to some verbs to show one who does something."**
Understanding that when making a noun by adding *-er* to a verb that has a short vowel and one consonant, double the final consonant: *robber, swimmer, runner, beggar*	**"Double the consonant on words ending with a short vowel and one consonant before adding the suffix *–er* to show someone who does something."**
Understanding that when making a noun by adding *-er* or *-ar* to a verb that ends in silent *e*, you drop the *e* before adding the suffix: *writer, rider, liar, burglar*	**"Delete the *e* before adding the suffix *-er* or *-ar* to words ending in *e* to show someone who does something."**
Understanding that when making a noun by adding *–er* to a verb that ends in *y*, you change the *y* to *i* before adding the suffix: *worrier, carrier*	**"Change the *y* to *i* for words ending in *y* before adding the suffix *-er* to show someone who does something."**
Understanding that when making a noun by adding *-er* to a verb that ends in hard *c*, you add a *k* before the suffix: *picnicker, frolicker*	**"Add *k* to words ending with hard *c* before adding the suffix *-er* to show one who does something."**
Recognizing and using nouns that are formed from adjectives or verbs by adding *-tion* or *-ion: perfect–perfection, contract–contraction, infect–infection*	**"You can make some verbs into nouns by addition *-tion* or *-ion.*"**
Recognizing and using nouns that are formed from verbs with silent *e* by dropping the *e* and adding *-tion: vacate–vacation, define–definition, prepare–preparation, regulate–regulation*	**"You can make some verbs into nouns with silent *e* by dropping the *e* and adding *-tion.*"**
Recognizing and using nouns that are formed from verbs by adding *-sion: persuade–persuasion, decide–decision, provide–provision, revise–revision.* The silent *e* and sometimes more of the base word are omitted.	**"You can make some verbs into nouns by adding *-sion.*"** **"Omit the silent *e* and sometimes more of the base word."**
Recognizing and using nouns that are formed by adding *-ment* (a result or product): *basement, easement, enchantment*	**"Add *-ment* to nouns to mean a result or product."**
Recognizing and using nouns that are formed by adding *-ent* or *-ant* (shows or does): *superintendent, solvent, accountant*	**"Add *-ent* or *-ant* to nouns to mean *one who shows or does.*"**
Recognizing and using adjectives that are formed by adding *-ent* or *-ant* to indicate "characterized by": *insistent, defiant, radiant*	**"Add *-ent* or *-ant* to verbs to describe something or someone."**
Recognizing and using nouns that are formed by adding *-ity* (state or condition of being): *chastity, possibility, entity*	**"Add *-ity* to nouns to show the state or condition of being."**
Recognizing and using nouns that are formed by adding *-ence* and *-ance* (act, fact, quality, state, result, or degree): *excellence, conference, hindrance, utterance, remittance*	**"To add the suffixes *-ance, -ence, -ant, -ent* to a base word, double the final consonant and add the ending."**
	P-K · GRADE K (E M L) · GRADE 1 (E M L) · GRADE 2 (E M L) · GRADE 3 (E M L) · GRADE 4 (E M L) · GRADE 5 (E M L) · GRADES 6–8

Key: E = Early in school year, M = Mid-year, L = Late in school year

Word Structure, continued

Principle	Explanation of Principle
	P-K · GRADE K (E M L) · GRADE 1 (E M L) · GRADE 2 (E M L) · GRADE 3 (E M L) · GRADE 4 (E M L) · GRADE 5 (E M L) · GRADES 6–8
Suffixes [Nouns] continued	
Understanding that when you form a noun by adding *-ance, -ence, -ant,* or *-ent* to a base word ending in *e,* you remove the final *e* from the base word: *observe, observance*	**"To add the suffixes *–ance, -ence, -ant,* or *–ent* to a base word ending in *e,* remove the final *e* and the add the suffix."**
Understanding that when you form a noun by adding *-ance, -ence, -ant,* or *-ent* to words ending in *y,* change the *y* to *i* and add the ending: *rely, reliance*	**"When you add *-ance, -ence, -ant,* or *-ent* to words ending in *y,* change the *y* to *i* and add the ending."**
Recognizing and using nouns that are formed by adding *-ure* or *-ture* (act, process, or state of being): *legislature, exposure, composure, literature*	**"Add *-ure* or *-ture* to nouns to mean 'act, process, or state of being.'"**
Prefixes	
Recognizing and using common prefixes (*re-* meaning *again*): *make–remake, do–redo, live–relive*	**"Add a word part or prefix to the beginning of a word to change its meaning."** **"Add *re-* to the beginning of a word to mean *do again.*"** **"I *made* the bed and took a nap. I had to *remake* the bed."**
Recognizing and using common prefixes (*un-* meaning *not* or *the opposite of*): *do–undo, tie–untie, known–unknown, believable–unbelievable*	**"Add a word part or prefix to the beginning of a word to change the meaning."** **"Add *un-* to the beginning of a word to mean *not* or *the opposite of.*"** **"I don't *believe* it. That is *unbelievable.*"** **"I *tied* my shoes and then they came *untied.*"**
Recognizing and using more complex prefixes (*im-, in-, il-, dis-, non-* [meaning *not*]): *possible–impossible, valid–invalid, like–dislike, literate–illiterate, legal–illegal*	**"Add a word part or prefix to the beginning of a word to change the meaning."** **"Add *im-, in-, il-,* or *dis-* to the beginning of words to mean *not.*"** **"That is not *possible.* It is *impossible.*"** **"We cannot *cure* the disease. It is *incurable.*"** **"It is not *legal.* It is *illegal.*"** **"I do not *like* broccoli. I *dislike* broccoli."**
Recognizing and using more prefixes that mean *wrong* (*mis*): *misinform, misinformation, mistake, mishandle, mispronounce*	**"Add *mis* before a word to change the meaning."** **"He *pronounced* the word wrong. He *mispronounced* the word."**
Recognizing and using prefixes that refer to numbers (*uni-, bi-, tri-, cent-, dec-, mon-, mult-, cot-, pent-, poly-, quad-, semi-*): *uniform, unicycle, unicorn; bicycle, biweekly, biannual; tricycle, triceratops; tricolor*	**"You can add some prefixes to words to refer to numbers."** **"We are all wearing the same uniform."** **"My bicycle has two wheels."** **"My mother has trifocals that have three different lens strengths."**
Recognizing and using prefixes that mean *before* (*pre-*): *preface, preamble, preapprove, prearrange, precaution, pregame, prefigure, preplan*	**"Add a prefix to a word to show something happening before."** **"Let's go to the *pregame* ceremony."**
Recognizing and using prefixes that mean *make* (*en-, em-*): *enable, entrap, empower, embed, embody*	**"Add the prefix to a word to show making something happen."** **"This money will *enable* me to buy a ticket."** **"The king *empowered* the people to vote."**
	P-K · GRADE K (E M L) · GRADE 1 (E M L) · GRADE 2 (E M L) · GRADE 3 (E M L) · GRADE 4 (E M L) · GRADE 5 (E M L) · GRADES 6–8

Word Structure, continued

Principle	Explanation of Principle
Prefixes continued	
Recognizing and using prefixes that mean across (*transportation; translate; transaction*)	**"Add the prefix *trans-* to a word to mean 'across.'"**
Recognizing and using prefixes that mean *between* or *together* (*interaction; interfaith, interfere, intermediate*)	**"Add the prefix *inter-* to a word to mean *between* or *together*."**
Recognizing and using prefixes that mean within or inside (*intra-*): *intramural, intrapersonal, intravenous*	**"Add the prefix *intra-* to words to mean 'within' or 'under.'"**
Recognizing and using prefixes that mean *with* or *together* (*con-, com-*): *compose, composition, confer, conference, conceal, concern, compound, compare*	**"Add the prefix *con-* or *com-* to words to mean 'with' or 'together.'"**
Recognizing and using prefixes that mean *under* (*sub-*): *submarine, subcategory, subdivision, sublethal, subzero, subculture, subway*	**"Add a prefix to show that something is below or under."** **"I traveled below the streets on the *subway*."**
Recognizing and using prefixes that mean *above* (*super-*); *supermarket, superordinate, supervisor, superintendent*	**"Add the prefix *super-* to mean 'above.'"**
Recognizing and using prefixes that mean *bad* (*mal-*): *malpractice, malcontent, malnourished, malformation, malediction*	**"Add a prefix *mal-* to show that something is bad."** **"The patient died and they suspected *malpractice* by the doctor at the hospital."**
Recognizing and using prefixes that mean *out* (*ex-*): *exit, extend, expand, exotic*	**"Add the prefix *ex-* to words to mean 'out.'"**
Recognizing and using prefixes that mean *going beyond or through* (*per-*): *perform, perhaps, perforate, perceive*	**"Add the prefix *per-* to words to mean 'going beyond or through.'"**
Recognizing and using prefixes that mean *around* (*circum-*); *circumnavigate, circumvent, circumference*	**"Add the prefix *circum-* to words to mean 'around.'"**
Recognizing and using prefixes that change form to match the root word (assimilated prefixes): *in-* (*immigrate, illegal, irregular*); *ad-* (*address, approach, aggressive*); *ob-* (*obstruct, opportunity*); *sub-* (*subtract, suppose, surround*); *com-* (*commit, collide, corrode*); *dis-* (*distinguish; difference*); *ex-* (*expand, expose, eccentric, efficient*)	**"When you add some prefixes to change word meaning, you change the spelling of the word."** **"The prefix may become a part of the root word."**
Possessives	
Recognizing and using possessives that add an apostrophe and an *s* to a singular noun: *dog–dog's, woman–woman's, girl–girl's, boy–boy's*	**"A person, animal, place, or thing can own something. To show ownership, you add *'s* to a word."** **"The collar belongs to the *dog*. It is the *dog's* collar."** **"The ball belongs to the *girl*. It is the *girl's* ball."** **"The *book* has a cover. It is the *book's* cover."**

P-K | GRADE K (E M L) | GRADE 1 (E M L) | GRADE 2 (E M L) | GRADE 3 (E M L) | GRADE 4 (E M L) | GRADE 5 (E M L) | GRADES 6–8

Key: E = Early in school year, M = Mid-year, L = Late in school year

Word Structure, continued

Principle	Explanation of Principle
Possessives continued	
Recognizing and using possessives for names that end in *s* and singular words that end in *s*—add an apostrophe: *Marcus' papers, Charles' lunch box; the octopus' ink*	**"If a name or other object already ends in *s*, just add an apostrophe to show ownership."** **"Here is *Marcus'* lunch box. It belongs to *Marcus*."**
Recognizing and using plural possessives to show that the item belongs to a group—add apostrophe after the *s: boys' game, girls' dresses, dogs' dishes, pigs' houses*	**"For a plural noun that ends in *s*, show possession by adding an apostrophe only."** **"The *girls* are getting the jump ropes. The ropes belong to the *girls*. They are the *girls'* jump ropes."** **"Those balls belong to the *boys*. They are the *boys'* balls."**
Understanding that when you make the word *it* show possession, you do not use an apostrophe	**"No apostrophe is needed when you use *its* to show possession."**
Recognizing and using plural possessives that do not end in *s*—add apostrophe + *s: women's room, children's party*	**"For a plural noun that does not end in *s*, show possession by adding apostrophe + *s*."**
Abbreviations	
Recognizing and using common abbreviations: *Mrs., Ms., Mr., Dr., St., Ave., Rd.,* months of the year, days of the week	**"Some words are made shorter by using some of the letters and a period. They are called *abbreviations*."**
Recognizing and using more complex abbreviations: state names, weights, *Sr., Jr, Ph.D.*	**"Some words are made shorter by using some of the letters and a period. They are called *abbreviations*."**
Root Words	
Understanding that many English words are derived from other languages: *charade, bouquet*	**"Many words and parts of words come from ancient languages called Greek and Latin. You can use Greek and Latin word roots to help you learn the meaning of a word."**
Recognizing and using word roots from Greek or Latin: *aero, bio, chron, geo, meter, photo, ject, struct, dict, mit, flex, cred, duc, pend, pel, fac, vert*	**"Many words and parts of words come from ancient languages called Greek and Latin. You can use Greek and Latin word roots to help you learn the meaning of a word."**
Combining roots from Greek and taking words apart into morphemes: *micro, scope, photo, graph, tele, phon, geo, -meter, -ology, -itis*	**"Word roots are sometimes combined to make words. You can notice Greek word roots to understand the meaning of words."**
Understanding that many English words are derived from new inventions, technology, or current events	**"The origin of a word can help you learn its meaning."**

Grade scale (header and footer): P-K | GRADE K (E M L) | GRADE 1 (E M L) | GRADE 2 (E M L) | GRADE 3 (E M L) | GRADE 4 (E M L) | GRADE 5 (E M L) | GRADES 6–8

Word-Solving Actions

Word-solving actions are the strategic moves readers and writers make when they use their knowledge of the language system to solve words. These strategies are "in-the-head" actions that are invisible, although we can often infer them from overt behaviors. The principles listed in this section represent children's ability to *use* the principles in all previous sections of the continuum.

All lessons related to the continuum provide opportunities for children to apply principles in active ways; for example, through sorting, building, locating, reading, or writing. Lessons related to word-solving actions demonstrate to children how they can problem-solve by working on words in isolation or while reading or writing continuous text. The more children can integrate these strategies into their reading and writing systems, the more flexible they will become in solving words. The reader/writer may use knowledge of letter/sound relationships, for example, either to solve an unfamiliar word or to check that the reading is accurate. Rapid, automatic word solving is a basic component of fluency and important for comprehension because it frees children's attention to focus on the meaning and language of the text.

Word-Solving Actions

Principle	Explanation of Principle (P-K; GRADE K; GRADE 1; GRADE 2; GRADE 3; GRADE 4; GRADE 5; GRADE 6–8 — E M L)
Using What Is Known to Solve Words	
Recognizing and locating words (names)	**"You can find your name by looking for the letters in it."**
Making connections between names and other words	**"You can find the letters that are in your name in other words."** **"You can connect your name with other names [*Mark, Maria*]."** **"You can connect your name with other words [*Mark, make*]."**
Using the letters in names to read and write words: *Chuck, chair*	**"You can connect your name with the words you want to spell or read."**
Using known words to monitor reading and spelling	**"You can use words you know to check on your reading."**
Using first and last names to read and write words	**"You can think of the first and last names you know to help you read and spell words [*Angela, Andy*]."**
Recognizing and spelling known words quickly	**"You can read or write a word quickly when you know how it looks [*the*]."** **"When you know how to read some words quickly, it helps you read fast."** **"When you know how to write some words quickly, it helps you write fast."**
Using letter/sound knowledge to monitor reading and spelling accuracy	**"You can use what you know about letters and sounds to check on your reading (and writing)."**
Using parts of known words that are like other words: *my, sky; tree, try; she, shut*	**"You can use parts of words you know to read or write new words."**
Using what you know about a word to solve an unknown word: *her, mother*	**"You can use what you know about words to read new words."**

E M L E M L E M L E M L E M L E M L
P-K GRADE K GRADE 1 GRADE 2 GRADE 3 GRADE 4 GRADE 5 GRADES 6–8

Key: E = Early in school year, M = Mid-year, L = Late in school year

Principle	Explanation of Principle P-K · GRADE K (E M L) · GRADE 1 (E M L) · GRADE 2 (E M L) · GRADE 3 (E M L) · GRADE 4 (E M L) · GRADE 5 (E M L) · GRADES 6–8
Taking Words Apart to Solve Them	
Saying words slowly to hear sounds in sequence	**"You can say words slowly to hear the sounds."** **"You can hear the sounds at the beginning, middle, or end of a word."** **"You can write the letters for the sounds you can hear."** **"You can say words slowly to hear the sounds from left to right."**
Solving words by thinking about the order of the sounds and letters	**"You can figure out how to spell new words by thinking about the order of the sounds and letters."**
Changing beginning letters to make new words: *sit, hit; day, play*	**"You can change the first letter or letters of a word to make a new word."**
Listening for sounds to write letters in words	**"You can say words slowly to hear the sounds."** **"Hearing and saying the sounds helps you write words."**
Changing ending letters to make new words: *car, can, cat*	**"You can change the last letter or letters of a word to make a new word."**
Changing middle letters to make new words: *hit, hot; sheet, shirt*	**"You can change the middle letter or letters of a word to make a new word."**
Using letter/sound analysis from left to right to read a word	**"You can read words by looking at the letters and thinking about the sounds from left to right."**
Noticing and using word parts (onsets and rimes) to read a word: *br-ing*	**"You can use word parts to solve a word."** **"You can look at the first and last parts of a word to read it."**
Changing the onset and rime to make a new word: *bring, thing; bring, brown*	**"You can change the first part or the last part to make a new word."**
Adding letters to the beginning or end of a word to make a new word: *in, win; bat, bats; the, then*	**"You can add letters to the beginning of a word to make a new word."** **"You can add letters to the end of a word to make a new word."**
Adding letter clusters to beginning or end of a word to make a new word: *an, plan; cat, catch*	**"You can add letter clusters to the beginning or end of a word to make a new word."**
Removing letters or letter clusters from the beginning of words: *sit, it; stand, and; his, is*	**"You can take away letters at the beginning of a word to make a new word."**
Removing letters from the end of a word to make a new word: *and, an; Andy, and; kite, kit*	**"You can take away letters at the end of a word to make a new word."**
Recognizing and using word parts (onsets, rimes) to read a word: *br-ing; cl-ap*	**"You can notice and use word parts to read (or write) a new word."** **"You can look at the first part and last part to read a word."**
Taking apart compound words or joining words to make compound words: *into, sidewalk, sideways*	**"You can read compound words by finding the two smaller words."** **"You can write compound words by joining two smaller words."**
Removing letter clusters from the end of a word to make a new word: *catch, cat*	**"You can take away letter clusters from the end of a word to make a new word."**
Removing the ending from a base word to make a new word: *sit, sits, sitting; big, bigger, biggest*	**"You can take off the ending to help you read a word."**

E M L E M L E M L E M L E M L E M L
P-K GRADE K GRADE 1 GRADE 2 GRADE 3 GRADE 4 GRADE 5 GRADES 6–8

Word-Solving Actions, continued

Principle	Explanation of Principle
	P-K · GRADE K (E M L) · GRADE 1 (E M L) · GRADE 2 (E M L) · GRADE 3 (E M L) · GRADE 4 (E M L) · GRADE 5 (E M L) · GRADES 6–8
Taking Words Apart to Solve Them continued	
Learning to notice the letter sequence to spell a word accurately	**"You can make a word several times to learn the sequence of letters."**
Studying features of words to remember the spelling	**"You can look at a word, say it, cover it, write it, and check it to help you learn to spell it correctly."**
Noticing and correcting spelling errors	**"You can write a word, look at it, and try again to make it 'look right.'"** **"You can notice and think about the parts of words that are tricky for you."** **"You can write words to see if you know them."**
Breaking down a longer word into syllables in order to decode manageable units: *for-got-ten*	**"You can divide a word into syllables to read it."**
Making Connections Between and Among Words to Solve Them	
Connecting words that start the same: *tree, tray*	**"You can connect the beginning of the word with a word you know."**
Connecting words that end the same: *candy, happy*	**"You can connect the ending of the word with a word you know."**
Connecting words that mean the same or almost the same: *wet, damp*	**"You think about the words that mean almost the same."**
Connecting words that have the same pattern: *light, night; running, sitting*	**"You can connect words that have the same letter patterns."**
Connecting words that sound the same but look different and have different meanings: *blew, blue*	**"You can read words by noticing that they sound the same but look different and have different meanings."**
Connecting words that rhyme: *fair, chair*	**"You can think about words that rhyme."**
Connecting words that look the same but sometimes sound different, and have different meanings: *read, read*	**"You can read words by remembering that some words look the same but sometimes sound different and have different meanings."**
Connecting and comparing word patterns that look the same but sound different: *dear, bear*	**"You can read words by remembering that some words have parts or patterns that look the same but sound different."**
Connecting and comparing word patterns that sound the same but look different: *said, bed*	**"You can read words by remembering that some words have parts or patterns that sound the same but look different."**
Using dictionary entries	**"Dictionary entries have many different kinds of information about a word."**
Connecting words that are related to each other because they have the same base or root word: *direct, directs, directed, direction, misdirect, directional*	**"You can make lists of words that have the same base or root word but different suffixes or prefixes. The words have different but related meanings."**
Using Word Roots to Determine Meaning and Pronunciation	
Understanding the concept of analogy and its use in discovering relationships between and among words	**"Some words are related to other words in specific ways."** **"You can think about how words are related and think of other words that are related in the same way."**
Understanding that common Greek roots are related to the meaning of words	**"You can use the meaning of some common Greek roots to help you think about the meaning of English words."**
Using Latin roots to understand the meaning of words	**"You can use the meaning of some Latin roots to help you think about the meaning of some English words."**
Using word history to learn about words	**"You can learn about the spelling of a word by knowing its history. The history of words is called *etymology* (e.g. *boc* is Old English for *book*)."**
	P-K · GRADE K (E M L) · GRADE 1 (E M L) · GRADE 2 (E M L) · GRADE 3 (E M L) · GRADE 4 (E M L) · GRADE 5 (E M L) · GRADES 6–8

Key: E = Early in school year, M = Mid-year, L = Late in school year

Word-Solving Actions, continued

Principle	Explanation of Principle
Using Strategies to Determine the Meaning of a Word	
Understanding that the context of the sentence, paragraph, or whole text helps determine the meaning of a word	**"When you read a word but don't know what it means, you can think about the meaning of the sentence to figure it out."**
Understanding that word parts help you learn what a word means	**"You can think about the meaning of parts of words to help you understand a new word."**
Spelling Strategies–Ways of Studying and Remembering the Spelling of Words	
Using syllables to remember the spelling of a word	**"You can notice the syllables in a word to help you remember its spelling."**
Using the whole words within compound words to remember the spelling	**"You can notice the two whole words in a compound word to help you remember the spelling and think about the meaning."**
Using letter/sound order to help in spelling a word	**"You can use the order of sounds and letters in a word to spell a word or check on your spelling."**
Using the letter patterns in words to help you remember the spelling	**"You can notice the letter patterns in words to help you remember their spelling."**
Using "hard parts" of a word to help you remember its spelling	**"You can concentrate on the "hard" part of a word to help you remember how it spelled."**
Using "look, say, cover, write, and check" to help you remember how a word is spelled	**"You can look at a word, say it, cover it, write it, and then check it to help you remember how it is spelled."**
Using special devices to help in remember the spelling of a word: *friends to the end; a bear bit my ear*	**"You can make up a phrase or rhyme to remind you (or help you remember how to spell) how to spell tricky words. Memory helpers are called *mnemonic devices*."**
Making a first attempt in the process of spelling a word	**"When you are not sure how to write a word, try it first and see if it looks right."**
Using the dictionary to learn how to spell a word	**"You can use the dictionary to learn how to spell a word or to check on your spelling."**
Remembering and applying principles to solve words	**"You can figure out how to spell new words by thinking about principles you know."**
Using an acronym to help in remembering a phrase or sentence: *pin–personal identification number*	**"You can take the first letter from each word in a group and put them together to form an *acronym*."**
Using word history to assist in spelling a word	**"You can figure out how to spell a word by thinking about the history of the word or its meaning."**
Using "spell-check" to check and correct your spelling	**"You can use spell-check to check and correct your spelling."**
Asking for help when you have used all the strategies you know	**"When you have used all your strategies, ask for help in spelling a word."**
Using References and Resources to Learn About Words	
Using resources to learn about word meanings	**"You can use a dictionary, glossary, or thesaurus to help you think about the meaning of a word."**
Understanding when to use a dictionary to assist in spelling and make writing efficient	**"You can tell when you need to use a dictionary to learn how to spell a word: When it doesn't 'look right' the way you have spelled it. When you are not sure exactly what it means. When you want a more interesting synonym."**

P-K | GRADE K (E M L) | GRADE 1 (E M L) | GRADE 2 (E M L) | GRADE 3 (E M L) | GRADE 4 (E M L) | GRADE 5 (E M L) | GRADES 6–8

Word-Solving Actions, continued

Principle	Explanation of Principle P-K · GRADE K (E M L) · GRADE 1 (E M L) · GRADE 2 (E M L) · GRADE 3 (E M L) · GRADE 4 (E M L) · GRADE 5 (E M L) · GRADES 6–8
Using References and Resources to Learn About Words continued	
Understanding alphabetical order and how to use it in references and resources	**"You can use alphabetical order to locate words in a dictionary, glossary, or thesaurus."** **"You can use alphabetical order to find or organize information."**
Distinguishing between the multiple meanings of words	**"When you look up a word in the dictionary, you will need to choose which meaning is right for the word you have used."**
Noticing and using syllable divisions in a dictionary	**"You can find syllable divisions in a dictionary entry."**
Becoming a collector of interesting words (developing the Word Study Notebook)	**"You can collect interesting words."**
Noticing and using accent marks to help in pronouncing a word	**"You can use accent marks in a dictionary entry to help you pronounce a word."**
Noticing and using guide words to locate words in a dictionary	**"You can use guide words to help you find words quickly in a dictionary."**
Using the pronunciation guide in a dictionary	**"The pronunciation guide in the dictionary helps you know how to say a word."**
Using the dictionary to discover word history	**"You can find a word's history in the dictionary entry."**
Recognizing and using the different types of dictionaries: general, specialized (synonyms, abbreviations, theme or topic, foreign language, thesaurus, electronic dictionaries)	**"There are different kinds of dictionaries and you use them for different purposes."**
	P-K · GRADE K (E M L) · GRADE 1 (E M L) · GRADE 2 (E M L) · GRADE 3 (E M L) · GRADE 4 (E M L) · GRADE 5 (E M L) · GRADES 6–8

Key: E = Early in school year, M = Mid-year, L = Late in school year